FAMILY IN TRANSITION

8/25   Chap 1   SS —
9/1   2 + 3   1 + 5
9/8   4   29 + 30
9/15   5 + 6   33 + 34

9/22   TEST

9/29   7   7-28-29

10/6   NO School
10/13   8 + 9   —
10/20   10 + 11   12
10/27   12   14

11/3   TEST

11/10   13 + 14   21-25-26
11/17   15   15
11/22   16   16-28-31
12/1   17   17-18-19-20
12/8   18   2
12/15   FINAL 6'-8'⁵ pm

FAMILIES IN TRANSITION

FAMILY IN TRANSITION

EIGHTH EDITION

ARLENE S. SKOLNICK
University of California, Berkeley

JEROME H. SKOLNICK
University of California, Berkeley

■ HarperCollins*CollegePublishers*

Acquisitions Editor: Alan McClare
Production Coordination, Text, and Cover Design: York Production Services
Photo Researcher: Kelly Mountain
Compositor: ATLIS Graphics & Design, Inc.
Printer and Binder: R.R. Donnelley & Sons Company
Cover Printer: The Lehigh Press, Inc.
Cover Photos: Front cover: Top left, Ken Fisher/Tony Stone Worldwide; top right,
Myrleen Ferguson/PhotoEdit; center left, Ken Fisher/Tony Stone Worldwide; center
right, Dale Durfee/Tony Stone Worldwide; bottom, Andy Sacks/Tony Stone Worldwide.
Back cover: Skolnick family portrait, Lenore Weitzman; lower left, © Julie O'Neil/THE
PICTURE CUBE.

Family in Transition, Eighth Edition
Copyright © 1994 by HarperCollins College Publishers

Library of Congress Cataloging-in-Publication Data

Family in transition / [edited by] Arlene S. Skolnick, Jerome H.
  Skolnick. — 8th ed.
      p.   cm.
    Includes bibliographical references.
    ISBN 0-673-52324-1
    1. Family.   I. Skolnick, Arlene S.   II. Skolnick,
  Jerome H.
  HQ518.F336   1993
  306.85—dc20   93-27285
                                                        CIP

    94 95 96 9 8 7 6 5 4 3 2

Contents

v

Preface

*T*his is our eighth edition. Since we began work on the first edition more than two decades ago, the family—a term which should be taken to mean "family life"— has been in transition. Not only has the family changed, but the climate of opinion surrounding family issues has also shifted. New problems have arisen and new approaches to earlier problems have emerged.

Most strikingly, the state of the family has developed into a major public issue. "Family values" became a battle cry in the presidential election of 1992. Opposing views over such family related matters as abortion, homosexuality, gay families, and sex education have begun to constitute one of the major fault lines in American society.

We have had three aims in this edition: First, we have tried to capture and accurately portray the remarkable changes and diversity of family life, and locate them in historical context.

Second, we have always tried to include articles representing the cutting edge of family scholarship. We have never found it difficult to locate new articles, since scholarship continues to grow in quantity and quality. As editors, our task has been to retain and balance excellent older articles while adding significant new ones.

Third, we have always tried to select articles that, while scholarly, are understandable to an audience largely of undergraduate students. Most of the writers we include are leading researchers whose writing, however complex in ideas and analysis, is clear and readable.

In this edition nearly half of the articles are new. There is a greater emphasis on men's roles in the family than in previous editions. We are happy to welcome a revision of William J. Goode's article on men's resistance to change. The reading by Tamara Hareven is also an updated version of one we've included in earlier editions.

We have finally retired Alice Rossi's classic article on the transition to parent-hood. It has been replaced with a selection by Carolyn and Philip Cowan, describing the findings of their research on the process of becoming a parent for the first time. Some of the newer readings also deal with nostalgia and its effects on perceptions of the family, past and present; how family law is grappling with changes in the traditional family; and the cultural war over how to define the family. We have also included an article on characteristics of long, satisfying marriages.

By now we have had so many useful conversations with friends and colleagues about family matters in general and this book in particular that it's hard to list them all; let us just say "thank you." Thanks also to Jennifer Biserto whose literature searches and general helpfulness made this edition possible and to Rod Watanabe and the staff of the Center for the Study of Law and Society who supported the project in many ways. Finally, we are grateful to the many reviewers whose useful suggestions we have tried to incorporate in this edition. These include:

Keith E. Davis, University of South Carolina
Gregory E. Kennedy, Central Missouri State University
Mary Jo Neitz, University of Missouri
Cherylon Robinson, University of Texas at San Antonio
Richard Seibert, Buffalo State College
Don Swenson, Mount Royal College
J. Gipson Wells, Mississippi State University

Arlene S. Skolnick
Jerome H. Skolnick

Introduction:
Family in Transition

*I*n the election campaign of 1992, then Vice President Dan Quayle set off a firestorm of debate with a remark denouncing a fictional television character for choosing to give birth out of wedlock. The "Murphy Brown" show, according to Quayle, was "mocking the importance of fathers." It reflected the "poverty of values" that was responsible for the nation's ills. From the talk shows to the front pages of newspapers to dinner tables across the nation, arguments broke out about the meaning of the Vice President's remarks.

Comedians found Quayle's battle with a TV character good for laughs. But others saw serious issues being raised. Many people saw Quayle's comments as a stab at single mothers and working women. Some saw them as an important statement about the decline of family values and the importance of the two parent family. In the opening show of the Fall season, "Murphy Brown" fought back by poking fun at Quayle and telling the audience that families come in many different shapes and sizes. After the election, the debate seemed to fade away. It flared up again the Spring of 1993, after the *Atlantic Monthly* featured a cover story entitled "Dan Quayle was Right."

Why did a brief remark in a political speech set off such a heated and long lasting debate? The Dan Quayle–Murphy Brown affair struck a nerve because Americans have not yet come to terms with almost three decades of turbulent change. Contrary to the widespread notion that some flaw in American character or culture is to blame for these trends, comparable shifts are found throughout the industrialized world. All advanced modern countries have experienced shifts in women's roles, rising divorce rates, lower marriage and birth rates, and an increase in single parent families. In no other country, however, has family change been so traumatic and divisive as ours (Skolnick, 1993).

The transformation of family life has been so dramatic that to many Americans it has seemed as if "an earthquake had shuddered through the American family" (Preston, 1984). Divorce rates first skyrocketed, then stabilized at historically high levels. Women have surged into the workplace. Birth rates have declined. The women's movement has changed the way men and women think and act toward one another, both inside the home and in the world at large. Furthermore, social and sexual rules that once seemed carved in stone have crumbled away: Unmarried couples can live together openly; unmarried mothers can keep their babies. Abortion has become legal. Remaining single and remaining childless, thought to be highly deviant once (though not illegal) have both become acceptable lifestyle options.

Today most people live in ways that do not conform to the cultural ideal that prevailed in the '50s. The traditional breadwinner/housewife family with minor children today represents only a small minority of families. The "typical" American family in the last two decades of the twentieth century is likely to be one of four other kinds: the two-earner family, the single-parent family, the "blended" family of remarriage, or the "empty nest" couple whose children have grown up and moved out. Indeed, in 1984 fully half of American families had no children under age 18 (Norton & Glick, 1986, p. 9). Apart from these variations, large numbers of people will spend part of their lives living apart from their families—as single young adults, as divorced singles, as older people who have lost a spouse.

The changes of recent decades have affected more than the forms of family life; they have been psychological as well. A major study of American attitudes over two decades revealed a profound shift in how people think about family life, work, and themselves (Veroff, Douvan, & Kulka, 1981). In 1957 four fifths of the respondents thought that a man or woman who did not want to marry was sick, immoral, and selfish. By 1976 only one fourth of the respondents thought that choice was bad. Two thirds were neutral, and one seventh viewed the choice as good. Summing up many complex findings, the authors conclude that America underwent a "psychological revolution" in the two decades between surveys. Twenty years earlier, people defined their satisfaction and problems—and indeed themselves—in terms of how well they lived up to traditional work and family roles. More recently, people have become more introspective, more attentive to inner experience. Fulfillment now means finding intimacy, meaning, and self-definition, rather than satisfactory performance of traditional roles.

A DYING INSTITUTION?

All of these changes, occurring as they did in a relatively short period of time, gave rise to fears about the decline of the family. By the early 1970s anyone watching television or reading newspapers and magazines would hear again and again that the family is breaking down, falling apart, disintegrating, and even becoming "an endangered species." There also began a great nostalgia for the "good old days" when Mom was in the kitchen, families were strong and stable, and life was uncomplicated. This mood of nostalgia mixed with anxiety contributed to the rise of the conservative New Right and helped to propel Ronald Reagan into the White House.

In the early '80s, heady with victory, the conservative movement hoped that by dismantling the welfare state and overturning the Supreme Court's abortion decision, the clock could be turned back and the "traditional" family restored. As the Reagan presidency ended, it became clear that such hopes had failed. Women had not returned to full-time homemaking; divorce rates had not returned to the levels of the 1950s. The "liberated" sexuality of the '60s and '70s had given way to greater restraint, largely due to fear of AIDS, although the norms of the '50s did not return.

Despite all the changes, however, the family in America is "here to stay" (Bane, 1976). The vast majority of Americans—at least 90 percent—marry and have children, and surveys repeatedly show that family is central to the lives of most Americans. They find family ties their deepest source of satisfaction and meaning, as well as the source of their greatest worries (Mellman et al., 1990). In sum, family life in America is a complex mixture of both continuity and change.

While the transformations of the past three decades do not mean the end of family life, they have brought a number of new difficulties. For example, most families now depend on the earnings of wives and mothers, but the rest of society has not caught up to the new realities. There is still an earnings gap between men and women. Employed wives and mothers still bear the major workload in the home. For both men and women, the demands of the job are often at odds with family needs. Debates about whether or not the family is "in decline" do little to solve these dilemmas.

During the same years in which the family was becoming the object of public anxiety and political debate, a torrent of new research on the family was pouring forth. The study of the family had come to excite the interest of scholars in a range of disciplines—history, demography, economics, law, psychology. As a result of this research, we now have much more information available about the family than ever before. Ironically, much of the new scholarship is at odds with the widespread assumption that family had a long, stable history until hit by the social "earthquake" of the '60s and '70s. We have learned from historians that the "lost" golden age of family happiness and stability we yearn for never actually existed.

Because of the continuing stream of new family scholarship, as well as shifts in public attitudes toward the family, each edition of *Family in Transition* has been different from the one before it. When we put together the first edition of this book in the early 1970s, the first rumblings of change were beginning to be felt. The youth movements of the 1960s and the emerging women's movement were challenging many of the assumptions on which conventional marriage and family patterns had been based. The mass media were regularly presenting stories that also challenged in one way or another traditional views on sex, marriage, and family. There was talk, for example, of "the population explosion" and of the desirability of "zero population growth." There was a growing perception that the ideal three-, four-, or five-child family of the '50s was not necessarily good for the country as a whole, or for every couple.

Meanwhile, Hollywood movies were presenting a new and cynical view of marriage. It was almost taken for granted that marriages were unhappy, particularly if the spouses were middle class, middle aged, or affluent. Many people were openly defying conventional standards of behavior: College girls were beginning to live openly with young men, unwed movie actresses were publicizing rather than hiding their pregnancies, and homosexuals were beginning openly to protest persecution and discrimination.

It seemed as if something was happening to family life in America, even if there were no sharp changes in the major statistical indicators. People seemed to be looking at sex, marriage, parenthood, and family life in new ways, even if behavior on a mass scale was not changing very noticeably. Thus, we argued that significant social and cultural change could happen even without massive changes in overt behavior patterns. John Gagnon and William Simon (1970) had observed that the moment of change may be when new forms of behavior seem "plausible." For example, even though there was no evidence that the homosexual population had grown, homosexuality had become a more plausible form of behavior. Knowing someone was a homosexual did not automatically mean that he or she was to be defined as a moral pariah.

In putting together the readings for that first edition of *Family in Transition,* we found that the professional literature of the time seemed to deny that change was possible in family structure, the relations between the sexes, and parenthood. An extreme version of this view was the statement by an anthropologist that the nuclear family (mother, father, and children) "is a biological phenomenon . . . as rooted in organs and physiological structures as insect societies" (LaBarre, 1954, p. 104). Any changes in the basic structure of the family roles or in childrearing were assumed to be unworkable, if not unthinkable.

The family in modern society was portrayed as a streamlined, more highly evolved version of a universal family. According to the sociological theorist Talcott Parsons and his followers (1951, 1954), the modern family had become more specialized. It transferred work and educational roles to other agencies and specialized in childrearing and emotional support. No less important for having relinquished certain tasks, the modern family was now the only part of society to carry out such functions.

The family theories of the postwar era were descriptively correct insofar as they portrayed the ideal middle-class family patterns of a particular society at a particular historical period. But they went astray in elevating the status quo to the level of a timeless necessity. In addition, the theories in did not acknowledge the great diversity among families that has always existed in America. For example, the working mother or the single-parent family could be seen only as deviant. Ethnic differences also received very little attention, or were considered undesirable variations from the mainstream, middle class norm.

Still another flaw in the dominant view was its neglect of internal strains within the family, even when it was presumably functioning as it was supposed to. Paradoxically, these strains were vividly described by the very theorists who idealized the role of the family in modern society. Parsons, for example, observed that when home no longer functioned as an economic unit, women, children, and old people were placed in an ambiguous position. They became dependent on the male breadwinner and were cut off from society's major source of achievement and status.

Parsons saw women's roles as particularly difficult: Being a housewife was not a real occupation; it was vaguely defined, highly demanding, yet not considered real work in a society that measures achievement by the size of one's paycheck. The combination of existing strains and the demystifying effects of the challenges to the family status quo seems to have provided, as Judith Blake (1978, p. 11) points out, a classic set of conditions for social change.

A TIME OF TROUBLES

Major changes in the family would have been unsettling even if other social conditions had remained stable. But everything else was also changing quickly. Despite assassinations and turmoil in the streets, the '60s was an optimistic period. Both dissidents and the establishment agreed that progress was possible, that problems could be solved, and that today's children would live in a better world. Both sides believed in limitless economic growth.

No one foresaw that the late 1970s would dramatically reverse this optimism and the social and economic conditions that had sustained it. Rather than hearing of an end to scarcity and poverty, we began to hear of lowered expectations, survival, and lifeboat ethics. For the first time in history, Americans had to confront the possibility that their children and their children's children might not lead better lives. A popular country and western song expressed the national mood when it asked, "Are the good times really over for good?" (Haggard, 1982).

The "malaise" of the late 1970s, followed by the conservative renewal of the 1980s, once again changed the terms in which family issues were discussed and debated. There was a general withdrawal from political activity among all Americans, most surprisingly, perhaps, on the part of the young people who had been active in the 1960s and 1970s. The large baby boom generation, which had begun to enter college in the 1960s, was moving on to marriage and parenthood by the end of the 1970s.

Among family scholars and other social commentators, the terms of the debate about the family were also changed by shifts in feminist thinking. Some of the most vocal feminists of the 1960s had criticized the family as the major source of the oppression of women. By the 1970s, many feminists had articulated a new emphasis on nurturance, care, and intimacy. In fact, one of the surprising themes to emerge in that era was the celebration of family in the name of social criticism.

Some radical attacks on the modern world and its ways seem consonant with traditional conservative arguments. Historian Christopher Lasch (1978) argued that while the family once provided a haven of love and decency in a heartless world, it no longer does so. The family has been "invaded" by outside forces—advertising, the media, experts, and family professionals—and stripped of its functions and authority. Corporate capitalism, with its need for limitless consumption, has created a "culture of narcissism," in which nobody cares about anybody else. Other scholars, as we noted earlier, insist that the family remains a vital and resilient institution.

THE STATE OF THE CONTEMPORARY FAMILY

What sense *can* be made of changes in family life over the past three decades? The various statistics we quoted earlier can be and are being interpreted to show that the family is either thriving or falling apart. Falling birthrates can be taken to mean that people are too selfish to want to have any or many children. Or they can mean that people are no longer having children by accident, or because of social pressure, but because they truly want children. High divorce rates can signify that marriage either is an institution on the rocks or is considered so important that people will no longer put up with the kinds of dissatisfactions and empty-shell marriages previous generations tolerated. Is the rise in unmarried motherhood a sign of moral breakdown? Or does it simply reflect a different, more enlightened set of moral norms, a society no longer eager to punish unmarried mothers or to damage a child's life chances because of the circumstances of its birth?

Part of the confusion surrounding the current status of the family arises from the fact that the family is a surprisingly problematic area of study; there are few if any self-evident facts, even statistical ones. Researchers have found, for example, that when the statistics of family life are plotted for the entire twentieth century, or back into the nineteenth century, a surprising finding emerges: today's young people—with their low marriage, high divorce, and low fertility rates—appear to be behaving in ways consistent with long-term historical trends (Cherlin, 1981; Masnick & Bane, 1980). The recent changes in family life only appear deviant when compared to what people were doing in the 1940s and 1950s. But it was the postwar generation that married young, moved to the suburbs, and had three, four, or more children that departed from twentieth-century trends. As one study put it, "Had the 1940s and 1950s not happened, today's young adults would appear to be behaving normally" (Masnick & Bane, 1980, p. 2).

Thus, the meaning of change in a particular indicator of family life depends on the time frame in which it is placed. If we look at trends over too short a period of time—say ten or twenty years—we may think we are seeing a marked change, when, in fact, an older pattern may be reemerging. For some issues, even discerning what the trends are can be a problem. Whether or not we conclude that there is an "epidemic" of teenage pregnancy depends on how we define adolescence and what measure of illegitimacy we use. Contrary to the popular notion of skyrocketing teenage pregnancy, teenaged childbearing has actually been on the decline during the past two decades (Luker, this volume). It is possible for the *ratio* of illegitimate births to all births to go up at the same time as there are declines in the *absolute* number of such births and in the likelihood that an individual will bear an illegitimate child. This is not to say that concern about teenage pregnancy is unwarranted; but the reality is much more complex than the simple and scary notion of an "epidemic" implies.

Given the complexities of interpreting data on the family, it is little wonder that, as Joseph Featherstone observes (1979, p. 37), the family is a "great intellectual Rorschach blot." One's conclusions about the current state of the family often derive from deeper values and assumptions one holds in the first place about the definition and role of the family in society. We noted earlier that the family theories of the postwar era were largely discredited within sociology itself (Blake, 1978; Elder, 1978). Yet many of the assumptions of those theories continue to influence discussions of the family in both popular and scholarly writings. Let us look in more detail at these persistent assumptions.

1. The Assumption of the Universal Nuclear Family

To say that the family is the same everywhere is in some sense true. Yet families vary in organization, membership, life cycles, emotional environments, ideologies, social and kin networks, and economic and other functions. Although anthropologists have tried to come up with a single definition of family that would hold across time and place, they generally have concluded that doing so is not useful (Geertz, 1965; Stephens, 1963).

Biologically, of course, a woman and a man must unite sexually to produce a child—even if only sperm and egg meet in a test tube. But no social kinship ties or living arrangements flow inevitably from biological union. Indeed, the definition of marriage is not the same across cultures. Although some cultures have weddings and notions of monogamy and permanence, many cultures lack one or more of these attributes. In some cultures, the majority of people mate and have children without legal marriage and often without living together. In other societies, husbands, wives, and children do not live together under the same roof.

In our own society, the assumption of universality has usually defined what is normal and natural both for research and therapy and has subtly influenced our thinking to regard deviations from the nuclear family as sick or perverse or immoral. As Suzanne Keller (1971) points out:

> The fallacy of universality has done students of behavior a great disservice. By leading us to seek and hence to find a single pattern, it has blinded us to historical precedents for multiple legitimate family arrangements.

An example of this disservice is the treatment of illegitimacy. For decades the so-called principle of legitimacy, set forth by Malinowski (1930), was taken as evidence for the universality of the nuclear family. The principle stated that in every society a child must have a socially recognized father to give the child a status in the community. Malinowski's principle naturally leads to the assumption that illegitimacy is a sign of social breakdown.

Although the principle usually has been treated by social scientists as if it were a natural law, in fact it is based on certain prior assumptions about society (Goode, 1960; Blake, 1978). Chiefly, it assumes that children inherit their status from their father or from family origin rather than achieving it themselves. The traditional societies that anthropologists study are, of course, societies that do ascribe status in this way. In modern, democratic societies, such as the United States, a child's future is not supposed to be determined solely by who its father happens to be. The Malinowski principle, however compelling in understanding traditional societies, has decreasing relevance for modern ones. Current legal changes that blur the distinction between legitimate and illegitimate births may be seen as a way of bringing social practice in line with national ideals.

2. The Assumption of Family Harmony

Every marriage, as Jessie Bernard (1982) points out, contains two marriages: the husband's and the wife's. Similarly, every family contains as many families as family members. Family members with differing perspectives may find themselves in conflict, occasionally in bitter conflict. Outside intervention is sometimes necessary to protect the weaker from the stronger.

To question the idea of the happy family is not to say that love and joy are not found in family life or that many people do not find their deepest satisfactions in their families. Rather, the happy family assumption omits important, if unpleasant, aspects of family life. Western society has not always assumed such a sentimental model of the family. From the Bible to the fairy tale, from Sophocles to Shakespeare, from Eugene O'Neill to the soap opera, there is a tragic tradition portraying the family as a high-voltage emotional setting, charged with love and hate, tenderness and spite, even incest and murder.

There is also a low-comedy tradition. George Orwell once pointed out that the world of henpecked husbands and tyrannical mothers-in-law is as much a part of the Western cultural heritage as is Greek drama. Although the comic tradition tends to portray men's discontents rather than women's, it scarcely views the family as a setting for ideal happiness.

Social theorists have not always portrayed the family as harmoniously fulfilling the needs of its members and society. Around the turn of the century, the founders of sociology took for granted that conflict was a basic part of social life and that individuals, classes, and social institutions would struggle to promote their own interests and values. Freud and Simmel were among the leading conflict theorists of the family. They argued that intimate relations inevitably involve antagonism as well as love. This mixture of strong positive and negative feelings sets close relationships apart from less intimate ones.

In recent years, family scholars have been studying such family violence as child abuse and wife beating to understand better the realistic strains of family life. Long-known facts about family violence have recently been incorporated into a general analysis of the family. More police officers are killed and injured dealing with family fights than in dealing with any other kind of situation; of all the relationships between murderers and their victims, the family relationship is most common (Steinmetz & Straus, 1974). Studies of family violence reveal that it is much more widespread than had been assumed, cannot easily be attributed to mental illness, and is not confined to the lower classes. Family violence seems to be a product of psychological tensions and external stresses that can affect all families at all social levels.

The study of family interaction has also undermined the traditional image of the happy, harmonious family. About two decades ago, researchers and therapists began to bring mental patients and their families together to watch how they behaved with one another. Oddly, whole family groups had not been systematically studied before.

At first the family interactions were interpreted as pathogenic: a parent expressing affection in words but showing nonverbal hostility, alliances being made between different family members, families having secrets, one family member being singled out as a scapegoat to be blamed for the family's troubles. As more and more families were studied, such patterns were found in many families, not just in those families with a schizophrenic child. Although this line of research did not uncover the cause of schizophrenia, it made an important discovery about family life: so-called normal families can often be, in the words of one study, "difficult environments for interaction."

3. The Assumption of Parental Determinism

Throughout American history, the family has been seen as the basis of social order and stability. Through reproduction and socialization, the family presumably guarantees the continuation of society through time. Traditionally, theories of socialization have taken either of two perspectives. In the first—social molding—the child is likened to a blank slate or lump of clay, waiting to be written on or shaped by the environment. In the second the infant is thought to be something like a wild animal whose antisocial instincts need to be tamed by the parents.

Despite their differences, both views of socialization have much in common. Both consider children as passive objects and assign an all-powerful, Pygmalionlike role to parents. Both view the child's later life as a reenactment of early experience. Both view conformity to social norms as the outcome of successful socialization. Both tend to blame deviance of any kind (mental illness, crime, drug use) on the family.

Although early family experience is certainly a powerful influence in a child's life, there are two serious flaws in the notion that early relations with parents determine the course of the child's future: the assumption of the passive child and the assumption that parents independently exert influence in a virtual vacuum.

The model of the passive child is no longer tenable. Recent empirical work in human development shows that children come into the world with unique temperamental and other characteristics, so that children shape parents while parents shape children. Further, we also know that the child's mind is not an empty vessel or a blank slate to be filled with parental instruction. Children are active agents in the construction of knowledge about the world.

Children also learn from the world around them. The parental-determinism model has encouraged the peculiar belief that children know nothing about the world except what parents teach. Poor black children therefore are said to do badly in school because their parents fail to use the right teaching techniques. It is easier to blame the parents than to change the neighborhood, the school, or the economy or to assume that ghetto children's correct perception of their life chances has something to do with school performance. Finally, other kinds of research show that early experience is not the all-powerful, irreversible kind of influence it has been thought to be. An unfortunate childhood does not necessarily lead to a despairing adulthood. Nor does a happy childhood guarantee a similarly sunny adulthood (Macfarlane, 1964; Emde & Harmon, 1984).

4. The Assumption of a Stable, Harmonious Past

Laments about the current decay of the family imply some earlier era when the family was more stable and harmonious than it is now. But unless we can agree what earlier time should be chosen as a baseline and what characteristics of the family should be selected for, it makes little sense to speak of family decline. Historians have not, in fact, located a golden age of the family gleaming at us from the depths of history (Demos, 1975).

Recent historical studies of family life also cast doubt on the reality of family tranquility. Historians have found that premarital sexuality, illegitimacy, generational conflict, and even infanticide can best be studied as a part of family life itself rather than as separate categories of deviation. For example, William Kessen (1965), in his history of the field of child study, observes:

> Perhaps the most persistent single note in the history of the child is the reluctance of mothers to suckle their babies. The running war between the mother, who does not want to nurse, and the philosopher-psychologists, who insist she must, stretches over two thousand years (pp. 1–2).

The most shocking finding of the recent wave of historical studies is the prevalence of infanticide throughout European history. Infanticide has long been attributed to primitive peoples or assumed to be the desperate act of an unwed mother. It now appears that infanticide provided a major means of population control in all societies lacking reliable contraception, Europe included, and that it was practiced by families on legitimate children. Historians now believe that rises and falls in recorded birthrates may actually reflect variations in infanticide rates.

Rather than being an instinctive trait, having tender feelings toward infants— baby as a precious individual—seems to emerge only when infants have a decent chance of surviving and adults experience enough security to avoid feeling that children are competing with them in a struggle for survival. Throughout many centuries of European history, both of these conditions were lacking. In the allocation of scarce resources, European society, as one historian put it, preferred adults to children (Trexler, 1973, p. 110).

It is hard to comprehend how profoundly family life has been affected by the reduction in mortality and spread of contraception in the twentieth century. Although infant and child mortality rates had begun to decline a century earlier, the average family could not assume it would see all its infants survive to middle or old age. Death struck most often at children. But adults with an average life expectancy of about fifty years (Ridley, 1972) would often die in the prime of their productive years. The widow and widower with young children were more familiar figures on the social landscape than the divorced person is today.

To put it another way, it has been only during the twentieth century that a majority of people would expect to live out a normal family cycle: leaving home, marrying, having children, and surviving to age fifty with one's spouse still alive. Before 1900 only 40 percent of the female population experienced this life cycle. The majority either died before they got married, never married, died before childbirth, or were widowed while their children were still young (Uhlenberg, 1974).

Contrary to the myth of the three-generation family in past time, grandparents can almost be said to be a twentieth-century phenomenon (Hareven, 1978). In the past, when people lived shorter lives, they married later. The lives of parents and children thus had fewer years in which to overlap. As a result of these trends, there is for the first time in history a significant number of families with four generations alive at the same time.

A HERITAGE OF FAMILY CRISIS

Our ancestors not only experienced chronic uncertainty in their personal family lives, but they also worried about the shakiness of the family as an institution. In fact, if we use a deep enough historical perspective, we see that the postwar era with its optimistic view of family life was the exception rather than the rule in American life. It was part of what one historian calls "the long amnesia" (Filene, 1986): the decades between the 1920s and the 1960s, during which concerns were muted about family crises, women's roles, childrearing, and declining morals, which had so agitated earlier generations. Anxiety about the family is an American tradition. Some historians trace it to the 1820s when America first began to be urban and industrial. Others would date the sense of crisis even earlier, from the time the first settlers set foot on American soil. Immigration, the frontier, geographic and social mobility—the basic ingredients of the American experience—were all disruptive of parental authority and familial bonds.

Although concern about the family may have begun earlier, anxiety increased during the second quarter of the nineteenth century, and discussions took on an entirely new tone. There began to be a widespread sense of alarm about the decline of the family and of parental authority. A new self-consciousness about family life emerged; writings about the family dealt anxiously with the proper methods of childrearing and with women's special roles.

In contrast to earlier periods, people began to experience a split between public and private life: The world outside the home came to be seen as cold, ugly, and threatening, while the home became a cozy retreat. The home was idealized as a place of perfect love and harmony, while at the same time it was blamed as the cause of juvenile delinquency, crime, and mental illness. These conflicting themes have a decidedly contemporary ring.

THE RISE OF THE MODERN FAMILY

These anxieties about the family that began in the 1820s were in response to the changed circumstances brought about by "modernization." Although this is a much-debated term, it is useful as a shorthand way of referring to social changes that accompanied the growth of urban industrial society in the nineteenth century. Modernization implies not merely economic or technological change but also profound social and psychological change. It affects all aspects of life: the physical environment, the types of communities people live in, the way they view the world, the way they organize their daily lives, the meaning of work, the emotional quality of family relationships, plus the most private aspects of individual experience.

It is, of course, a great oversimplification to talk about the effects of modernization on family life. Living in an industrial economy has had a different impact on people in different social classes and ethnic groups. Poor and working-class families were, and still are, confronted with survival issues: the need for steady incomes, decent housing, and health care, the tensions that result from not being sure basic needs will be met. In order to ensure survival and because their values tend to be familistic rather than individualistic, working-class, immigrant, and poor families have usually depended on strong networks of kin and kinlike friendships. Middle-class, affluent families, freed from worries about basic subsistence, confront in more acute ways the social and psychological dilemmas brought on by modernization. They more often fit the model of the inwardly turned, emotionally intense, relatively isolated nuclear family.

Since the nineteenth century, when the effects of industrialism and urbanization really began to be felt, scholars have debated the impact of industrialization on the family. Many scholars and laypeople were convinced that the family had outlived its usefulness. For the first time in history, men and women could find work and satisfy basic needs outside the bonds of blood or marriage. They felt, therefore, that the family would disintegrate.

The functional sociologists of the postwar era scoffed at predictions of family disintegration. As we saw earlier, they judged it to be more important than ever. The family nurtured and raised children and provided refuge for adults from the impersonality and competition of public and industrial life.

It now appears that both views were both right and wrong. Those who thought that life in a modern society would undermine family life were correct. But they were wrong in assuming that most people would want to spend their lives as isolated individuals. Those who argued that the conditions of urban-industrial society create exceptional needs for nurturant, intimate relationships were also correct. But they never understood that those same conditions would make it hard for the family to fulfill such needs. Family ties have become more intense than they were in the past, and yet at the same time they have become more fragile.

Although most western Europeans never lived in large extended-family households (Laslett & Wall, 1972), kinship ties extended much stronger constraints over the individual before the modern era. A person's economic and marital destinies were determined by hereditary status, tradition, and economic necessity. Continuity of marriages and conformity to prescribed behavior, both within the family and outside it, were enforced by severe economic, familial, and community sanctions.

Another extremely important aspect of family life in past times was its embeddedness in the community. The home was not set off as a private place, a refuge to make up for deprivations in the world of work. There was no world of work outside the home; family members were fellow workers. Nor did the world outside one's front door consist of strangers or half-strangers, as neighbors often are today. Rather, most people lived in a community of people known since childhood and with whom one would expect to have dealings for the rest of one's life. These outsiders could enter the household freely and were entitled, and even obligated, to intervene if relations between parents and children and husbands and wives were not as they should be. The most vivid example of community control over family life in preindustrial times was the practice known as *charivari:* community festivals in which people who violated family norms would be mocked and shamed (Shorter, 1975).

Modernization involves political as well as economic and social change. In English and American history, striking parallels exist between political ideals and the family, with the family being seen as a small version of the state—a little commonwealth. When the divine right of kings prevailed, the family ideal was likewise hierarchy and authority, with children and wives owing unquestioning obedience. When ideas about democracy and individual rights challenged the rule of kings, family ideologies also became more democratic (Stone, 1977). An ideology of liberation still accompanies replacement of the traditional pattern of work and family by the modern one. Modernization promises freedom of opportunity to find work that suits one's talents, freedom to marry for love and dissolve the marriage if it fails to provide happiness, and greater equality in the family between husband and wife and between parents and children (Goode, 1963).

In addition to promoting an ideology of individualism, modern technological societies change the inner experience of the self. The person living in an unchanging, traditional social world does not have to construct an identity to discover who he or she really is. "I am the son of this man, I came from that village, I work at that trade" would be enough to tell a man who he was.

There is still another source of the modern preoccupation with self. Much of daily life in modern society is spent in such roles as student, worker, customer, client. People begin to experience themselves as replaceable role players (Berger, Berger, & Kellner, 1973; Davis, 1973). As we become aware of a discrepancy between the role we are playing and our real and whole selves, we come to have a need for a private world, a set of relationships in which we can express those aspects of ourselves that must be repressed in role demands of work and public behavior. Individualization and intimacy are, as Howard Gadlin (1977) puts it, "the Siamese twins of modernization."

Although the need for intimacy increases, the very conditions creating that need make it more difficult to satisfy. For example, affluence may buy privacy, but, like King Midas's touch, family privacy is a drama that turns up unexpected costs when fulfilled. The family's "major burden," writes Napier (1972), "is its rootlessness, its aloneness with its tasks. Parents are somewhere else; the business you can't trust; the neighbors you never see; and friends are a help, when you see them, but never enough. Sometimes, late at night, the parent wakes up and on a sea of silence hears the ship creak, feels it drift, fragile and solitary, with its cargo of lives" (p. 540).

Family privacy needs illustrate only one example of how contradictory cultural instructions clash in the modern family. There is also the contradiction between a newer morality of enjoyment and self-fulfillment and an older morality of duty, responsibility, work, and self-denial. Fun morality is expressed by the advertising industry, credit cards, the buy-now-pay-later philosophy. The new morality can reunite families in activities that everyone can enjoy, but it also pulls family members apart in its emphasis on individual pursuit of enjoyment. Also, fun morality imposes a paradoxical demand: In the past, one could live up to demands of marriage and parenthood by doing one's duty. Today duty is not enough; we are also obliged to enjoy family life (Wolfenstein, 1954).

Ironically, then, many of the difficulties besetting family life today are the consequences of some very positive changes: the decline of infant mortality and death rates in general, the fact that people are living longer, the use of birth control, the spread of mass education, and the increasing control of the individual over basic life decisions (whether to marry, when to marry, whom to marry, whether or not to have children, and how many children to have).

This very voluntariness can be disturbing. Freedom in modern family life is bought at the price of fragility and instability. Now the whole structure of family life comes to rest on a tenuous basis: the mutual feelings of two individuals. As George Simmel (1950) has shown, the couple or dyad is not only the most intimate of social relationships, it is also the most unstable. In traditional family systems, the inevitable tensions of marriage are contained by kin and community pressures, as well as by low expectations concerning the romance or happiness to be found in marriage.

Demographic and economic change has had a profound effect on women's roles. When death rates fall, as they do with modernization, women no longer have to have five or seven or nine children to make sure that two or three will survive to adulthood. Women today are living longer and having fewer children. After rearing children, the average woman can look forward to three or four decades without maternal responsibilities. Since traditional assumptions about women are based on the notion that women are constantly involved with pregnancy, childrearing, and related domestic concerns, the current ferment about women's roles may be seen as a way of bringing cultural attitudes in line with existing social realities.

As people live longer, they can stay married longer. Actually, the biggest change in twentieth-century marriage is not the proportion of marriages disrupted through divorce, but the potential length of marriage and the number of years spent without children in the home. Census data suggest that the statistically average couple marrying now will spend only 18 percent of their married lives raising young children, compared with 54 percent a century ago (Bane, 1976). As a result, marriage is becoming less of a union between parents raising a brood of children and more of a personal relationship between two people.

To sum it up then, a knowledge of family history reveals that the solution to contemporary problems will not be found in some lost golden age. Families have always struggled with outside circumstances and inner conflict. Our current troubles inside and outside the family are genuine, but we should never forget that many of the most vexing issues confronting us as men and women, parents and children, derive from the very benefits of modernization—benefits too easily taken for granted or forgotten in the lately fashionable denunciation of modern times. There was no problem of the aged in the past, because most people never aged; they died before they got old. Nor was adolescence a difficult stage of the life cycle when children worked, education was a privilege of the rich, and a person's place in society was determined by heredity rather than choice. And when most people were hungry illiterates, only aristocrats could worry about sexual satisfaction and self-fulfillment.

In short, there is no point in giving in to the lure of nostalgia. There is no golden age of the family to long for, nor even some past pattern of behavior and belief that would guarantee us harmony and stability if only we had the will to return to it. Family life is bound up with the social, economic, and ideological circumstances of particular times and places. We are no longer peasants, Puritans, pioneers, or even suburbanites circa 1955. We face conditions unknown to our ancestors, and we must find new ways to cope with them.

A Note on "the Family"

Some family scholars have suggested that we drop the term "the family" and re-place it with "families" or "family life." The problem with "the family" is that it calls to mind the stereotyped image of the Ozzie and Harriet kind of family—two parents and their two or three minor children. But those other terms don't always work. In our own writing we use the term "the family" in much the same way we use "the economy"—as an abstract term that refers to a mosaic of forms and prac-tices in the real world.

REFERENCES

Bane, M. J. 1976. *Here to Stay*. New York: Basic Books.

Berger, P., Berger, B., and Kellner, H. 1973. *The Homeless Mind: Modernization and Con-sciousness*. New York: Random House.

Bernard, J. 1982. *The Future of Marriage*. New York: Bantam.

Bernard, J. 1975. "Adolescence and Socialization for Motherhood." In Dragastin, S. E., and G. H. Elder. *Adolescence in the Life Cycle*. New York: Wiley, pp. 227–252.

Blake, J. 1978. "Structural Differentiation and the Family: A Quiet Revolution." Presenta-tion at American Sociology Association, San Francisco.

Cherlin, A. J. 1981. *Marriage, Divorce, Remarriage*. Cambridge, Mass: Harvard University Press.

Davis, M. S. 1973. *Intimate Relations*. New York: The Free Press.

Demos, J. 1975. "Myths and Realities in the History of American Family Life," In H. Grunebaum and J. Christ (eds.). *Contemporary Marriage: Structure, Dynamics and Therapy*. Boston: Little, Brown and Company.

Elstain, J. B. "Feminists Against the Family." *The Nation*, November 17, 1979, pp. 482ff.

Emde, R. N. and Harmon, R. J. (eds.). 1984. *Continuities and Discontinuities in Develop-ment*. New York: Plenum Press.

Featherstone, J. 1979. Family Matters, *Harvard Educational Review*, 49, No. 1, pp. 20–52.

Filene, P. 1986. *Him, Her, Self: Sex Roles in Modern America*. Baltimore: Johns Hopkins University Press.

Furstenberg, F. F., Jr., Lincoln, R., and Menken, J. 1981. *Teenage Sexuality, Pregnancy and Childbearing.* Philadelphia: University of Pennsylvania Press.

Gadlin, H. 1977. "Private Lives and Public Order." In *Close Relationships: Perspectives in the Meaning of Intimacy.* Amherst: University of Massachusetts Press, pp. 73–86.

Gagnon, J. H. and Simon, W. 1970. *The Sexual Scene.* Chicago: Transaction.

Geertz, G. 1965. "The Impact of the Concept of Culture on the Concept of Man." In *New Views of the Nature of Man,* edited by J. R. Platt, pp. 93–118. Chicago: University of Chicago Press.

Goode, W. J. 1960. "A Deviant Case: Illegitimacy in the Caribbean." *American Sociological Review,* vol. 25, pp. 21–30.

Goode, W. J. 1963. *World Revolution and Family Patterns.* New York: The Free Press.

Haggard, M. 1982. "Are the Good Times Really Over for Good?" Song copyright 1982.

Hareven, T. K. 1978. "Family Time and Historical Time." In *The Family,* edited by A. S. Rassi, J. Kagan, and T. K. Hareven. New York: W. W. Norton and Company, pp. 57–70. (Reprint of *Daedalus,* Spring 1977.)

ISR Newsletter. 1979. Institute for Social Research. The University of Michigan. Winter.

Keller, S. 1971. "Does the Family Have a Future?" *Journal of Comparative Studies,* Spring, 1971.

Keniston, K. 1977. *All Our Children: The American Family Under Pressure.* New York: Harcourt Brace Jovanovich.

Kessen, E. W. 1965. *The Child.* New York: John Wiley.

LaBarre, W. 1954. *The Human Animal.* Chicago: University of Chicago Press.

Lasch, C. 1978. *Haven in a Heartless World.* New York: Basic Books.

Laslett, P. and Wall, R. (eds.). 1972. *Household and Family in Past Time.* Cambridge, England: Cambridge University Press.

Macfarlane, J. W. 1964. "Perspectives on Personality Consistency and Change from the Guidance Study." *Vita Humana,* vol 7, pp. 115–126.

Malinowski, B. 1930. "Parenthood, the Basis of the Social Order." In *The New Generation,* Calverton and Schmalhousen, New York: Macauley Company, pp. 113–168.

Masnick, G. and Bane, M. J. 1980. *The Nation's Families: 1960–1990.* Boston: Auburn House.

Mason, K. O., Czajka, J., and Aiker, S. 1976. "Change in U.S. Women's Sex Role Attitudes, 1964–1974." *American Sociological Review,* 41, pp. 573–596.

Mellman, A., Lazarus, E., and Rivlin, A. 1990. "Family Time, Family Values." In *Rebuilding the Nest,* edited by D. Blankenhorn, S. Bayme, and J. Elshtain. Milwaukee: Family Service America.

Napier, A. 1972. Introduction to section four in *The Book of Family Therapy,* edited by A. Farber, M. Mendelsohn, and A. Napier. New York: Science House.

Norton, A. J. and Glick, P. C. 1986. "One-Parent Families: A Social and Economic Profile." *Family Relations,* 35, pp. 9–17.

Parsons, T. 1951. *The Social System.* Glencoe, Ill.: Free Press.

Parsons, T. 1954. The Kinship System of the Contemporary United States. In *Essays in Sociological Theory.* Glencoe, Ill.: Free Press.

Preston, S. H. 1984. Presidential address to the Population Association of America. Quoted in *Family and Nation* by D. P. Moynihan (1986). San Diego: Harcourt Brace Jovanovich.

Ridley, J. C. 1972. "The Effects of Population Change on the Roles and Status of Women." In *Toward a Sociology of Women,* edited by S. Safilios-Rothschild, Lexington, Mass.: Xerox College Publishing, pp. 372–386.

Rossi, A. S. 1978. "A Biosocial Perspective on Parenting." In *The Family,* edited by A. S. Rossi, J. Kagan, and T. K. Hareven. New York: W. W. Norton and Company. (Reprint of Daedalus, Spring 1977.)

Shorter, E. 1973. "Infanticide in the Past." *History of Childhood Quarterly,* Summer, pp. 178–180.

Shorter, E. 1975. *The Making of the Modern Family.* New York: Basic Books.

Simmel, G. 1950. *The Sociology of George Simmel,* edited by K. Wolff. New York: Free Press.

Steinmetz, D. and Straus, M. A. (eds.) 1974. *Violence in the Family.* New York: Dodd, Mead Co.

Stephens, W. N. 1963. *The Family in Cross-Cultural Perspective.* New York: World.

Stone, L. 1977. *The Family, Sex and Marriage in England, 1500–1800.* New York: Harper and Row.

Strober, M. 1988. "Two-earner families." In *Feminism, Children, and the New Families,* edited by S. M. Dornbusch and M. H. Strober. New York: Guilford Press.

Trexler, R. C. 1973. "Infanticide in Florence: New Sources and First Results." *History of Childhood Quarterly,* Summer, pp. 98–116.

Trost, J. 1979. *Unmarried Cohabitation.* Vasteros, Sweden: International Library.

Uhlenberg, P. 1974. "Cohort Variations in Family Life Cycle Experiences of U.S. Females." *Journal of Marriage and the Family,* pp. 284–292.

Veroff, J., Douvan, E., and Kulka, R. A. 1981. *The Inner American: A Self-Portrait from 1957 to 1976* New York: Basic Books.

Weed, J. A. 1981. *Status of Families.* Unpublished manuscript. Bureau of the Census, Population Division, September.

Wolfenstein, M. 1954. "Fun Morality: An Analysis of Recent American Child Training Literature." In *Childhood in Contemporary Cultures,* edited by M. Mead and M. Wolfenstein. Chicago: University of Chicago Press, pp. 168–178.

One

THE CHANGING FAMILY

INTRODUCTION

*T*he study of the family does not fit neatly within the boundaries of any single scholarly field; genetics, physiology, archeology, history, anthropology, sociology, psychology, and economics all touch upon it. Religious and ethical authorities claim a stake in the family, and troubled individuals and families generate therapeutic demands on family scholarship. In short, the study of the family is interdisciplinary, controversial, and necessary for the formulation of social policy and practices. Interdisciplinary subjects demand competence in more than one field. At a time when competent scholars find it difficult to master even one corner of a field, intellectual demands on students of the family become vast. Although writers on the family confront many issues, their professional competence is usually limited. Thus a biologist may cite articles in psychology to support a position, without comprehending the tentativeness with which psychologists regard the researcher and his work. Similarly, a psychologist or sociologist may draw upon controversial biological studies. Professional competence means more than the ability to read technical journals; it includes informal knowledge—being "tuned in" to verbal understandings and evaluations of research validity. Usually a major theory or line of research is viewed more critically in its own field than outsiders realize.

Interdisciplinary subjects present other characteristic problems. Each discipline has its own assumptions and views of the world, which may not directly transfer into another field. Some biologists and physically oriented anthropologists, for example, analyze human affairs in terms of individual motives and instincts; for them, society is a shadowy presence, serving mainly as the setting for biologically motivated individual action. Many sociologists and cultural anthropologists, in contrast, perceive the individual as an actor playing a role written by culture and society; according to this view, the individual has no wholly autonomous thoughts and impulses. An important school of psychologists sees people neither as passive recipients of social pressures nor as creatures driven by powerful lusts, but as information processors trying to make sense of their environment. There is no easy way to reconcile such perspectives. Scientific paradigms—characteristic ways of looking at the world—determine not only what answers will be found but what questions will be asked. This fact has perhaps created special confusion in the study of the family.

"We speak of families," R. D. Laing has observed, "as though we know what families are. We identify, as families, networks of people who live together over time, who have ties of marriage or kinship to one another" (Laing 1971, p. 3). Yet as Laing observes further, the more one studies the emotional dynamics of groups called "families," the less clear it becomes how these differ from groups not designated "families." Further, today's family patterns and emotional dynamics may not appear in other places and times.

As an object of study, the family is thus plagued with a unique set of problems. There is the assumption that family life, so familiar a part of everyday experience, is easily understood. But familiarity may breed a sense of destiny—what we experience is transformed into the "natural":

> One difficulty in the psychological sciences lies in the familiarity of the phenomena with which they deal. A certain intellectual effort is required to see how such phenomena can pose serious problems or call for intricate explanatory theories. One is inclined to take them for granted as necessary or somehow "natural." (Chomsky 1968, p. 21)

The selections in Part I discuss both the concept of the family and the development of the family from prehistoric times through the contemporary United States.

The selections in Part I take nothing for granted or as given. Kathleen Gough's classic article examines families across time and culture and concludes, most importantly, that the family is a *human* institution and that its forms and gender roles are not programmed into the genes. Family forms are adaptable, and help us to survive our present circumstances. Therefore, the family of past times and places does not limit how the family of the future should be considered or limited.

Tamara Hareven's historical examination of the American family enlarges on Gough's insights. Hareven shows how family forms and relations are linked to industrial opportunity and economic necessity. Hareven is, moreover, exceedingly skeptical of those who believe that the families of earlier times were somehow freer of problems and dilemmas than today's families.

This point is clearly demonstrated in Linda Gordon's historical study of family violence. Gordon finds that family violence was certainly present in times past, and indeed may have been more pitiless and brutal. It came to light only when a powerful women's movement emerged in the late nineteenth century and continues to be perceived as a problem depending on the strength of feminist influence.

Today we talk about divorce, broken homes, and their baleful influence on children. We imagine a lost time when marriages were more stable, homes united. But we tend to forget about the effect of death on every aspect of family life from economic stability to emotional bonding. Arlene Skolnick's article reveals the profound and disturbing impact death used to have on family life and how some of our new problems arise from the extension of the lifespan over the course of the twentieth century.

Stephanie Coontz' article points to futher flaws in nostalgic assumptions about the family in past times. What comes to mind when you think of "the traditional family?" Many people conjure up a mix of characteristics that never existed at any one time. Nostalgia, she argues, not only distorts the past but also leads to mistaken ideas about the present.

The articles in Chapter 1 deal mainly with the past. Chapter 2 focuses more on the present. Changes in family life have been vast and significant over the century, even over the past twenty years. Paul Glick, who has studied family demography for decades, shows how sharply family statistics have shifted as, for example, in the much larger number of unmarried couples who cohabit today. Glick argues that there is no perfect pattern for organizing families and that every family fashion has benefits and limitations.

As we have seen, in earlier times death took family members at relatively younger ages. In "the good old days" grandparents used to be a rare family species. But since World War II, modern medicine has increased longevity and made grandparenthood an expectable part of the average life cycle. As Cherlin and Furstenberg observe in their selection, grandparenthood should not be taken for granted; it is having a significant effect on family relations.

In her selection here, Juliet Schor focuses an economic lens on the problem of household work. Why is it that a woman who puts in 40 hours on the job still does anywhere from 25 to 45 hours in the home? Part of the answer is that so-called labor-saving devices such as washers and dryers actually increased the amount of time devoted to doing laundry. We have gotten locked into ways of doing things that are inefficient and burdensome, and that take time away from the most important work of the home, the care of the people who live there.

As one reads the selections, one observes the enormous variation that is possible in family structure and family organization through time and its accompanying economic and social conditions. Moreover, a careful examination of every family system reveals deeply embedded notions of propriety, health, legality, sex, and age role assignments. Only one thing seems constant through time and place with respect to relations among men, women, and children— everyone feels strongly about these. Moreover, prevailing family forms and norms tend to be idealized as the right and proper ones. Perhaps that is because, although the family is scarcely the building block of society claimed by early functional sociologists, it is without doubt the institution possessing the most emotional significance in society. If you believe in a woman's right to medical abortion, or if you don't, and if you have an egalitarian or subordinate vision of the roles of men, women, and children, you probably feel strongly about these. The family grabs us where we live. Not only do we become excited about it, but it seems more than any other institution to generate controversy and moral indignation.

REFERENCES

Chomsky, N. 1968. *Language and Mind*. New York: Harcourt, Brace and World.

Laing, R. D. 1971. *The Politics of the Family*. New York: Random House.

Chapter
1

Family Origins and History

Reading 1   9/1/94

The Origin of the Family

Kathleen Gough

The trouble with the origin of the family is that no one really knows. Since Engels wrote *The Origin of the Family, Private Property and the State* in 1884, a great deal of new evidence has come in. Yet the gaps are still enormous. It is not known *when* the family originated, although it was probably between 2 million and 100,000 years ago. It is not known whether some kind of embryonic family came before, with, or after the origin of language. Since language is the accepted criterion of humanness, this means that we do not even know whether our ancestors acquired the basics of family life before or after they were human. The chances are that language and the family developed together over a long period, but the evidence is sketchy.

Although the origin of the family is speculative, it is better to speculate with than without evidence. The evidence comes from three sources. One is the social and physical lives of nonhuman primates—especially the New and Old World

From *Journal of Marriage and the Family*, November 1971, pp. 760–770. © 1971 National Council on Family Relations, 1910 West County Road B, Suite 147, St. Paul, MN 55113. Reprinted by permission. Portions of the original have been deleted and several references have been added.

monkeys and, still more, the great apes, humanity's closest relatives. The second source is the tools and homesites of prehistoric humans and proto-humans. The third is the family lives of hunters and gatherers of wild provender who have been studied in modern times.

Each of these sources is imperfect: monkeys and apes, because they are *not* prehuman ancestors, although they are our cousins; fossil hominids, because they left so little vestige of social life; hunters and gatherers, because none of them has, in historic times, possessed a technology and society as primitive as those of early humans. All show the results of long endeavor in specialized marginal environments. But together, these sources give valuable clues.

DEFINING THE FAMILY

To discuss the origin of something we must first decide what it is. I shall define the family as "a married couple or other group of adult kinsfolk who cooperate economically and in the upbringing of children, and all or most of whom share a common dwelling."

This includes all forms of kin-based household. Some are extended families containing three generations of married brothers and sisters. Some are "grandfamilies" descended from a single pair of grandparents. Some are matrilineage households, in which brothers and sisters share a house with the sisters' children, and men merely visit their wives in other homes. Some are compound families, in which one man has several wives, or one woman, several husbands. Others are nuclear families composed of a father, mother, and children.

Some kind of family exists in all known human societies, although it is not found in every segment or class of all stratified, state societies. Greek and American slaves, for example, were prevented from forming legal families, and their social families were often disrupted by sale, forced labor, or sexual exploitation. Even so, the family was an ideal which all classes and most people attained when they could.

The family implies several other universals. (1) Rules forbid sexual relations and marriage between close relatives. Which relatives are forbidden varies, but all societies forbid mother-son mating, and most, father-daughter and brother-sister. Some societies allow sex relations but forbid marriage between certain degrees of kin. (2) The men and women of a family cooperate through a division of labor based on gender. Again, the sexual division of labor varies in rigidity and in the tasks performed. But in no human society to date is it wholly absent. Child care, household tasks, and crafts closely connected with the household tend to be done by women; war, hunting, and government, by men. (3) Marriage exists as a socially recognized, durable, although not necessarily lifelong relationship between individual men and women. From it springs social fatherhood, some kind of special bond between a man and the child of his wife, whether or not they are his own children physiologically. Even in polyandrous societies, where women have several husbands, or in matrilineal societies, where group membership and property pass through women, each child has one or more designated "fathers" with whom he has a special social, and often religious, relationship. This bond of *social* fatherhood is recognized among people who do not know about the male role in procreation or where, for various reasons, it is not clear who the physiological father of a particular infant is. Social fatherhood seems to come from the division and interdependence of male and female tasks, especially in relation to children, rather than directly from physiological fatherhood, although in most societies, the social father of a child is usually presumed to be its physiological father as well. Contrary to the beliefs of some feminists, however, I think that in no human society do men, as a whole category, have *only* the role of insemination and *no* other social or economic role in relation to women and children. (4) Men in general have higher status and authority over the women of their families, although older women may have influence, even some authority, over junior men. The omnipresence of male authority, too, goes contrary to the belief of some feminists that in "matriarchal" societies, women were either completely equal to or had paramount authority over men, either in the home or in society at large.

It is true that in some matrilineal societies, such as the Hopi of Arizona or the Ashanti of Ghana, men exert little authority over their wives. In some, such as the Nayars of South India or the Minangkabau of Sumatra, men may even live separately from their wives and children, that is, in different families. In such societies, however, the fact is that women and children fall under greater or lesser authority from the women's kinsmen—their eldest brothers, mothers' brothers, or even their grown-up sons.

In matrilineal societies, where property, rank, office, and group membership are inherited through the female line, it is true that women tend to have greater independence than in patrilineal societies. This is especially so in matrilineal tribal societies where residence is matrilocal—that is, men come to live in the homes or villages of their wives. Even so, in all matrilineal societies for which adequate descriptions are available, the ultimate headship of households, lineages, and local groups is usually with men. (See Schneider and Gough, 1961, for common and variant features of matrilineal systems.)

There is in fact no true "matriarchal," as distinct from "matrilineal," society in existence or known for literature, and the chances are there never has been.° This does not mean that women and men have never had relations that were dignified and creative for both sexes, appropriate to the knowledge, skills, and technology of their times. Nor does it mean that the sexes cannot be equal in the future or that the sexual division of labor cannot be abolished. I believe that it can and must be. But it is not necessary to believe myths of a feminist Golden Age in order to plan for parity in the future.

°The Iroquois are often quoted as a "matriarchal" society, but in fact Morgan himself refers to the "absence of equality between the sexes" and notes that women were subordinate to men, ate after men, and that women (not men) were publicly whipped as punishment for adultery. Warleaders, tribal chiefs, and *sachems* (heads of matrilineal lineages) were men. Women did, however, have a large say in the government of the long-house or home of the matrilocal extended family, and women figured as tribal counselors and religious officials, as well as in arranging marriages. (Lewis H. Morgan: The League of the *Ho-de-ne Sau-nee or Iroquois*, Human Relations Area Files, 1954)

PRIMATE SOCIETIES

Within the primate order, humans are most closely related to the anthropoid apes (the African chimpanzee and gorilla and the Southeast Asian orang-utan and gibbon), and of these, to the chimpanzee and the gorilla. More distantly related are the Old, and then the New, World monkeys, and finally, the lemurs, tarsiers, and tree shrews.

All primates share characteristics without which the family could not have developed. The young are born relatively helpless. They suckle for several months or years and need prolonged care afterwards. Childhood is longer, the closer the species is to humans. Most monkeys reach puberty at about 4 to 5 and mature socially between 5 and 10. Chimpanzees, by contrast, suckle for up to 3 years. Females reach puberty at 7 to 10; males enter mature social and sexual relations as late as 13. The long childhood and maternal care produce close relations between children of the same mother who play together and help tend their juniors until they grow up.

Monkeys and apes, like humans, mate in all months of the year instead of in a rutting season. Unlike humans, however, female apes experience unusually strong sexual desire for a few days shortly before and during ovulation (the oestrus period) and have intensive sexual relations at that time. The males are attracted to the females by their scent or by brightly colored swellings in the sexual region. Oestrus mating appears to be especially pronounced in primate species more remote from humans. The apes and some monkeys carry on less intensive, month-round sexuality in addition to oestrus mating, approaching human patterns more closely. In humans, sexual desires and relations are regulated less by hormonal changes and more by mental images, emotions, cultural rules, and individual preferences.

Year-round (if not always month-round) sexuality means that males and females socialize more continuously among primates than among most other mammals. All primates form bands or troops composed of both sexes plus children. The numbers and proportions of the sexes vary, and in some species an individual, a mother with her young, or a subsidiary troop of male juveniles may travel temporarily alone. But in general, males and females socialize continually through mutual grooming° and playing as well as through frequent sex relations. Keeping close to the females, primate males play with their children and tend to protect both females and young from predators. A "division of labor" based on gender is thus already found in primate society between a female role of prolonged child care and a male role of defense. Mates may also carry or take care of children briefly, and nonnursing females may fight. But a kind of generalized "fatherliness" appears in the protective role of adult males toward young, even in species where the sexes do not form long-term individual attachments.

°Combing the hair and removing parasites with hands or teeth.

SEXUAL BONDS AMONG PRIMATES

Some nonhuman primates do have enduring sexual bonds and restrictions, super-ficially similar to those in some human societies. Among gibbons a single male and female live together with their young. The male drives off other males and the female, other females. When a juvenile reaches puberty it is thought to leave or be expelled by the parent of the same sex, and he eventually finds a mate elsewhere. Similar *de facto,* rudimentary "incest prohibitions" may have been passed on to humans from their prehuman ancestors and later codified and elaborated through language, moral custom, and law. Whether this is so may become clearer when we know more about the mating patterns of the other great apes, especially of our closest relatives, the chimpanzees. Present evidence suggests that male chimpan-zees do not mate with their mothers.

Orang-utans live in small, tree-dwelling groups like gibbons, but their forms are less regular. One or two mothers may wander alone with their young, mating at intervals with a male; or a male-female pair or several juvenile males may travel together.

Among mountain gorillas of Uganda, South Indian langurs, and hamadryas baboons of Ethiopia, a single, fully mature male mates with several females, espe-cially in their oestrus periods. If younger adult males are present, the females may have occasional relations with them if the leader is tired or not looking.

Among East and South African baboons, rhesus macaques, and South Ameri-can woolly monkeys, the troop is bigger, numbering up to 200. It contains a num-ber of adult males and a much larger number of females. The males are strictly ranked in terms of dominance based on both physical strength and intelligence. The more dominant males copulate intensively with the females during the latter's oestrus periods. Toward the end of the oestrus a female may briefly attach herself to a single dominant male. At other times she may have relations with any male of higher or lower rank provided that those of higher rank permit it.

Among some baboons and macaques the young males travel on the outskirts of the group and have little access to females. Some macaques expel from the troop a proportion of the young males, who then form "bachelor troops." Bachelors may later form new troops with young females.

Other primates are more thoroughly promiscuous, or rather indiscriminate, in mating. Chimpanzees and also South American howler monkeys live in loosely structured groups, again (as in most monkey and ape societies) with a preponder-ance of females. The mother-child unit is the only stable group. The sexes copulate almost at random and most intensively and indiscriminately during oestrus.

A number of well-known anthropologists have argued that various attitudes and customs often found in human societies are instinctual rather than culturally learned and come from our primate heritage. They include hierarchies of ranking among men, male political power over women, and the greater tendency of men to form friendships with one another, as opposed to women's tendencies to cling to a man. (See, for example, Morris, 1967; Fox, 1967.)

I cannot accept these conclusions and think that they stem from the male chauvinism of our own society. A "scientific" argument which states that all such features of female inferiority are instinctive is obviously a powerful weapon in maintaining the traditional family with male dominance. But in fact, these features are *not* universal among nonhuman primates, including some of those most closely related to humans. Chimpanzees have a low degree of male dominance and male hierarchy and are sexually virtually indiscriminate. Gibbons have a kind of fidelity for both sexes and almost no male dominance or hierarchy. Howler monkeys are sexually indiscriminate and lack male hierarchies or dominance.

The fact is that among nonhuman primates male dominance and male hierarchies seem to be adaptations to particular environments, some of which did become genetically established through natural selection. Among humans, however, these features are present in variable degrees and are almost certainly learned, not inherited at all. Among nonhuman primates there are fairly general differences between those that live mainly in trees and those that live largely on the ground. The tree dwellers (for example gibbons, orang-utans, South American howler, and woolly monkeys) tend to have to defend themselves less against predators than do the ground dwellers (such as baboons, macaques, or gorillas). Where defense is important, males are much larger and stronger than females, exert dominance over females, and are strictly hierarchized and organized in relation to one another. Where defense is less important there is much less sexual dimorphism (difference in size between male and female), less or no male dominance, a less pronounced male hierarchy, and greater sexual indiscriminacy.

Comparatively speaking, humans have a rather small degree of sexual dimorphism, similar to chimpanzees. Chimpanzees live much in trees but also partly on the ground, in forest or semiforest habitats. They build individual nests to sleep in, sometimes on the ground but usually in trees. They flee into trees from danger. Chimpanzees go mainly on all fours, but sometimes on two feet, and can use and make simple tools. Males are dominant, but not very dominant, over females. The rank hierarchy among males is unstable, and males often move between groups, which vary in size from two to fifty individuals. Food is vegetarian, supplemented with worms, grubs, or occasional small animals. A mother and her young form the only stable unit. Sexual relations are largely indiscriminate, but nearby males defend young animals from danger. The chances are that our prehuman ancestors had a similar social life. Morgan and Engels were probably right in concluding that we came from a state of "original promiscuity" before we were fully human.

HUMAN EVOLUTION

Judging from the fossil record, apes ancestral to humans, gorillas, and chimpanzees roamed widely in Asia, Europe and Africa some 12 to 28 million years ago. Toward the end of that period (the Miocene) one appears in North India and East Africa, Ramapithecus, who may be ancestral both to later hominids and to modern humans. His species were small like gibbons, walked upright on two feet, had human rather than ape cornerteeth, and therefore probably used hands rather than teeth to tear their food. From that time evolution toward humanness must have proceeded through various phases until the emergence of modern homo sapiens, about 70,000 years ago.

In the Miocene period before Ramapithecus appeared, there were several time spans in which, over large areas, the climate became dryer and subtropical forests dwindled or disappeared. A standard reconstruction of events, which I accept, is that groups of apes, probably in Africa, had to come down from the trees and adapt to terrestrial life. Through natural selection, probably over millions of years, they developed specialized feet for walking. Thus freed, the hands came to be used not only (as among apes) for grasping and tearing, but for regular carrying of objects such as weapons (which had hitherto been sporadic) or of infants (which had hitherto clung to their mothers' body hair).

The spread of indigestible grasses on the open savannahs may have encouraged, if it did not compel, the early ground dwellers to become active hunters rather than simply to forage for small, sick, or dead animals that came their way. Collective hunting and tool use involved group cooperation and helped foster the growth of language out of the call systems of apes. Language meant the use of symbols to refer to events not present. It allowed greatly increased foresight, memory, planning, and division of tasks—in short, the capacity for human thought.

With the change to hunting, group territories became much larger. Apes range only a few thousand feet daily; hunters, several miles. But because their infants were helpless, nursing women could hunt only small game close to home. This then produced the sexual division of labor on which the human family has since been founded. Women elaborated upon ape methods of child care and greatly expanded foraging, which in most areas remained the primary and most stable source of food. Men improved upon ape methods of fighting off other animals and of group protection in general. They adapted these methods to hunting, using weapons which for millennia remained the same for the chase as for human warfare.

Out of the sexual division of labor came, for the first time, home life as well as group cooperation. Female apes nest with and provide foraged food for their infants. But adult apes do not cooperate in food getting or nest building. They build new nests each night wherever they may happen to be. With the development of a hunting-gathering complex, it became necessary to have a G.H.Q., or home. Men could bring meat to this place for several days' supply. Women and children could meet men there after the day's hunting and could bring their vegetable produce for general consumption. Men, women, and children could build joint shelters, butcher meat, and treat skins for clothing.

Later, fire came into use for protection against wild animals, for lighting, and eventually for cooking. The hearth then provided the focus and symbol of home. With the development of cookery, some humans—chiefly women and perhaps some children and old men—came to spend more time preparing nutrition so that all people need spend less time in chewing and tearing their food. Meals—already less frequent because of the change to a carnivorous diet—now became brief, periodic events instead of the long feeding sessions of apes.

The change to humanness brought two bodily changes that affected birth and child care. These were head size and width of the pelvis. Walking upright produced a narrower pelvis to hold the guts in position. Yet as language developed, brains and hence heads grew much bigger relative to body size. To compensate, humans are born at an earlier stage of growth than apes. They are helpless longer and require longer and more total care. This in turn caused early women to concentrate more on child care and less on defense than do female apes.

Language made possible not only a division and cooperation in labor but also all forms of tradition, rules, morality, and cultural learning. Rules banning sex relations among close kinfolk must have come very early. Precisely how or why they developed is unknown, but they had at least two useful functions. They helped to preserve order in the family as a cooperative unit by outlawing competition for mates. They also created bonds *between* families, or even between separate bands, and so provided a basis for wider cooperation in the struggle for livelihood and the expansion of knowledge.

It is not clear when all these changes took place. Climatic change with increased drought began regionally up to 28 million years ago. The divergence between prehuman and gorilla-chimpanzee stems had occurred in both Africa and India at least 12 million years ago. The prehuman stem led to the Australopithecenes of East and South Africa, about 1,750,000 years ago. These were pygmy-like, two-footed, upright hominids with larger than ape brains, who made tools and probably hunted in savannah regions. It is unlikely that they knew the use of fire.

The first known use of fire is that of cave-dwelling hominids (Sinanthropus, a branch of the Pithecanthropines) at Choukoutien near Peking, some half a million years ago during the second ice age. Fire was used regularly in hearths, suggesting cookery, by the time of the Acheulean and Mousterian cultures of Neanderthal man in Europe, Africa, and Asia before, during, and after the third ice age, some 150,000 to 100,000 years ago. These people, too, were often cave dwellers and buried their dead ceremonially in caves. Cave dwelling by night as well as by day was probably, in fact, not safe for humans until fire came into use to drive away predators.

Most anthropologists conclude that home life, the family, and language had developed by the time of Neanderthal man, who was closely similar and may have been ancestral to modern homo sapiens. At least two anthropologists, however, believe that the Australopithecenes already had language nearly 2 million years ago, while another thinks that language and incest prohibitions did not evolve until the time of homo sapiens some 70,000 to 50,000 years ago. (For the former view, see Hockett and Ascher, 1968; for the latter, Livingstone, 1969.) I am myself inclined to think that family life built around tool use, the use of language, cookery, and a sexual division of labor must have been established sometime between about 500,000 and 200,000 years ago.

HUNTERS AND GATHERERS

Most of the hunting and gathering societies studied in the eighteenth to twentieth centuries had technologies similar to those that were widespread in the Mesolithic period, which occurred about 15,000 to 10,000 years ago, after the ice ages ended but before cultivation was invented and animals domesticated.

Modern hunters live in marginal forest, mountain, arctic, or desert environments where cultivation is impracticable. Although by no means "primeval," the
hunters of recent times do offer clues to the types of family found during that 99
percent of human history before the agricultural revolution. They include the Eskimo, many Canadian and South American Indian groups, the forest BaMbuti
(Pygmies) and the desert Bushmen of Southern Africa, the Kadar of South India,
the Veddah of Ceylon, and the Andaman Islanders of the Indian Ocean. About 175
hunting and gathering cultures in Oceania, Asia, Africa, and America have been
described in fair detail.

In spite of their varied environments, hunters share certain features of social
life. They live in bands of about 20 to 200 people, the majority of bands having
fewer than 50. Bands are divided into families, which may forage alone in some
seasons. Hunters have simple but ingenious technologies. Bows and arrows,
spears, needles, skin clothing, and temporary leaf or wood shelters are common.
Most hunters do some fishing. The band forages and hunts in a large territory and
usually moves camp often.

Social life is egalitarian. There is of course no state or organized government.
Apart from religious shamans or magicians, the division of labor is based only on
sex and age. Resources are owned communally; tools and personal possessions are
freely exchanged. Everyone works who can. Band leadership goes to whichever
man has the intelligence, courage, and foresight to command the respect of his
fellows. Intelligent older women are also looked up to.

The household is the main unit of economic cooperation, with the men,
women, and children dividing the labor and pooling their produce. In 97 percent
of the 175 societies classified by G. P. Murdock, hunting is confined to men; in the
other 3 percent it is chiefly a male pursuit. Gathering of wild plants, fruits, and nuts
is women's work. In 60 percent of societies, only women gather, while in another
32 percent gathering is mainly feminine. Fishing is solely or mainly men's work in
93 percent of the hunting societies where it occurs.

For the rest, men monopolize fighting, although interband warfare is rare.
Women tend children and shelters and usually do most of the cooking, processing,
and storage of food. Women tend, also, to be foremost in the early household crafts
such as basketry, leather work, the making of skin or bark clothing, and, in the
more advanced hunting societies, pottery. (Considering that women probably invented all of these crafts, in addition to cookery, food storage and preservation,
agriculture, spinning, weaving, and perhaps even house construction, it is clear
that women played quite as important roles as men in early cultural development.)
Building dwellings and making tools and ornaments are variously divided between
the sexes, while boat building is largely done by men. Girls help the women, and
boys play in hunting or hunt small game until they reach puberty, when both take
on the roles of adults. Where the environment makes it desirable, the men of a
whole band or of some smaller cluster of households cooperate in hunting or fishing and divide their spoils. Women of nearby families often go gathering together.

Family composition varies among hunters as it does in other kinds of societies.
About half or more of known hunting societies have nuclear families (father,
mother, and children) with polygynous households (a man, two or more wives, and

children) as occasional variants. Clearly, nuclear families are the most common among hunters, although hunters have a slightly higher proportion of polygynous families than do nonhunting societies.

About a third of hunting societies contain some stem-family households—that is, older parents live together with one married child and grandchildren, while the other married children live in independent dwellings. A still smaller proportion live in large extended families containing several married brothers (or several married sisters), their spouses, and children. (For exact figures, see Murdock, 1957; Coult, 1965; and Murdock, 1967. In the last named survey, out of 175 hunting societies, 47 percent had nuclear family households, 38 percent had stem families, and 14 percent had extended families.) Hunters have fewer extended and stem families than do nonhunting societies. These larger households become common with the rise of agriculture. They are especially found in large, preindustrial agrarian states such as ancient Greece, Rome, India, the Islamic empires, and China.

Hunting societies also have few households composed of a widow or divorcee and her children. This is understandable, for neither men nor women can survive long without the work and produce of the other sex, and marriage is the way to obtain them. That is why so often young men must show proof of hunting prowess and girls of cooking before they are allowed to marry.

The family, together with territorial grouping, provides the framework of society among hunters. Indeed, as Morgan and Engels clearly saw, kinship and territory are the foundations of all societies before the rise of the state. Not only hunting and gathering bands, but the larger and more complex tribes and chiefdoms of primitive cultivators and herders organize people through descent from common ancestors or through marriage ties between groups. Among hunters, things are simple. There is only the family, and beyond it the band. With the domestication of plants and animals, the economy becomes more productive. More people can live together. Tribes form, containing several thousand people loosely organized into large kin groups such as clans and lineages, each composed of a number of related families. With still further development of the productive forces the society throws up a central political leadership, together with craft specialization and trade, and so the chiefdom emerges. But this, too, is structured through ranked allegiances and marriage ties between kin groups.

Only with the rise of the state does class, independently of kinship, provide the basis for relations of production, distribution, and power. Even then, kin groups remain large in the agrarian state and kinship persists as the prime organizing principle within each class until the rise of capitalism. The reduction in significance of the family that we see today is the outgrowth of a decline in the importance of "familism" relative to our institutions, that began with the rise of the state but became speeded up with the development of capitalism and machine industry. In most modern socialist societies, the family is even less significant as an organizing principle. It is reasonable to suppose that in the future it will become minimal or may disappear, at least as a legally constituted unit for exclusive forms of sexual and economic cooperation and of child care. [Some nineteenth century theorists, for example, Lloyd Morgan (1877) and Frederick Engels (1955)] thought that from a state of original promiscuity, early humans at first banned sex relations between parents and children but continued to allow them between brothers, sisters, and all kinds of cousins within the band. They thought that later, all mating within the family or some larger kin group became forbidden, but that there was a stage in which a group of sisters or other close kinsmen from one band were married jointly to a group of brothers or other close kinsmen from another. Only later [according to this view] did the "pairing family" develop in which each man was married to one (or two) women individually.

These writers drew their conclusions not from evidence of actual group-marriage among primitive peoples but from the kinship terms found today in certain tribal and chiefly societies. Some of these equate all kin of the same sex in the parents' generation, suggesting brother-sister marriage. Others equate the father's brothers with the father and the mother's sisters with the mother, suggesting the marriage of a group of brothers with a group of sisters.

Modern evidence does not bear out these conclusions about early society. All known hunters and gatherers live in families, not in communal sexual arrangements. Most hunters even live in nuclear families rather than in large extended kin groups. Mating is individualized, although one man may occasionally have two wives, or (very rarely) a woman may have two husbands. Economic life is built primarily around the division of labor and partnership between individual men and women. The hearths, caves, and other remains of Upper Paleolithic hunters suggest that this was probably an early arrangement. We cannot say that Engel's sequences are completely ruled out for very early hominids—the evidence is simply not available. But it is hard to see what economic arrangements among hunters would give rise to group, rather than individual or pairing marriage arrangements, and this Engels does not explain.

Soviet anthropologists continued to believe in Morgan and Engel's early "stages" longer than did anthropologists in the West. Today, most Russian anthropologists admit the lack of evidence for "consanguineal" and "punaluan" arrangements, but some still believe that a different kind of group marriage intervened between indiscriminate mating and the pairing family. Semyonov, for example, argues that in the stage of group marriage, mating was forbidden within the hunting band, but that the men of two neighboring bands had multiple, visiting sex relations with women of the opposite band (Semyonov, 1967).

While such an arrangement cannot be ruled out, it seems unlikely because many of the customs which Semyonov regards as "survivals" of such group marriage (for example, visiting husbands, matrilineage dwelling groups, widespread clans, multiple sources for both sexes, men's and women's communal houses, and prohibitions of sexual intercourse inside the huts of the village) are actually found not so much among hunters as among horticultural tribes and even quite complex agricultural states. Whether or not such a stage of group marriage occurred in the earliest societies, there seems little doubt that pairing marriage (involving family households) came about with the development of elaborate methods of hunting, cooking, and the preparation of clothing and shelters—that is, with a fully fledged division of labor.

Even so, there *are* some senses in which mating among hunters has more of a group character than in archaic agrarian states or in capitalist society. Murdock's sample shows that sex relations before marriage are strictly prohibited in only 26 percent of hunting societies. In the rest, marriage is either arranged so early that premarital sex is unlikely, or (more usually) sex relations are permitted more or less freely before marriage.

With marriage, monogamy is the normal *practice* at any given time for most hunters, but it is not the normal *rule*. Only 19 percent in Murdock's survey prohibit plural unions. Where polygyny is found (79 percent) the most common type is for a man to marry two sisters or other closely related women of the same kin group— for example, the daughters of two sisters or of two brothers. When a woman dies it is common for a sister to replace her in the marriage, and when a man dies, for a brother to replace him.

Similarly, many hunting societies hold that the wives of brothers or other close kinsmen are in some sense wives of the group. They can be called on in emergencies or if one of them is ill. Again, many hunting societies have special times for sexual license between men and women of a local group who are not married to each other, such as the "lights out" games of Eskimo sharing a communal snow house. In other situations, an Eskimo wife will spend the night with a chance guest of her husband's. All parties expect this as normal hospitality. Finally, adultery, although often punished, tends to be common in hunting societies, and few if any of them forbid divorce or the remarriage of divorcees and widows.

The reason for all this seems to be that marriage and sexual restrictions are practical arrangements among hunters designed mainly to serve economic and survival needs. In these societies, some kind of rather stable pairing best accomplishes the division of labor and cooperation of men and women and the care of children. Beyond the immediate family, either a larger family group or the whole band has other, less intensive but important kinds of cooperative activities. Therefore, the husbands and wives of individuals within that group can be summoned to stand in for each other if need arises. In the case of Eskimo wife lending, the extreme climate and the need for lone wandering in search for game dictate high standards of hospitality. This evidently becomes extended to sexual sharing.

In the case of sororal polygny or marriage to the dead wife's sister, it is natural that when two women fill the same role—either together or in sequence—they should be sisters, for sisters are more alike than other women. They are likely to care more for each other's children. The replacement of a dead spouse by a sister or a brother also preserves existing intergroup relations. For the rest, where the economic and survival bonds of marriage are not at stake, people can afford to be freely companionate and tolerant. Hence, premarital sexual freedom, seasonal group license, and a pragmatic approach to adultery.

Marriages among hunters are usually arranged by elders when a young couple are ready for adult responsibilities. But the couple know each other and usually have some choice. If the first marriage does not work, the second mate will almost certainly be self-selected. Both sexual and companionate love between individual men and women are known and are deeply experienced. With comparative freedom of mating, love is less often separated from or opposed to marriage than in archaic states or even than in some modern nations.

THE POSITION OF WOMEN

Even in hunting societies it seems that women are always in some sense the "second sex," with greater or less subordination to men. This varies. Eskimo and Australian aboriginal women are far more subordinate than women among the Kadar, the Andamanese, or the Congo Pygmies—all forest people.

I suggest that women have greater power and independence among hunters when they are important food obtainers than when they are mainly processors of meat or other supplies provided by men. The former situation is likelier to exist in societies where hunting is small-scale and intensive than where it is extensive over a large terrain, and in societies where gathering is important by comparison with hunting.

In general in hunting societies, women are less subordinated in certain crucial respects than they are in most, if not all, of the archaic states, or even in some capitalist nations. These respects include men's ability to deny women sexuality or to force it upon them, to command or exploit their labor or to control their produce, to control or rob them of their children, to confine them physically and prevent their movement, to use them as objects in male transactions, to cramp their creativeness, or to withhold from them large areas of the society's knowledge and cultural attainments.

Especially lacking in hunting societies is the kind of male possessiveness and exclusiveness regarding women that leads to such situations as savage punishments or death for female adultery, the jealous guarding of female chastity and virginity, the denial of divorce to women, or the ban on a woman's remarriage after her husband's death.

For these reasons, I do not think we can speak, as some writers do, of a class division between men and women in hunting societies. True, men are more mobile than women and they lead in public affairs. But class society requires that one class control the means of production, dictate its use by the other classes, and expropriate the surplus. These conditions do not exist among hunters. Land and other resources are held communally, although women may monopolize certain gathering areas, and men, their hunting grounds. There is rank difference, role difference, and some difference respecting degrees of authority between the sexes, but there is reciprocity rather than domination or exploitation.

As Engels saw, the power of men to exploit women systematically springs from the existence of surplus wealth and, more directly, from the state, social stratification, and the control of property by men. With the rise of the state, because of their monopoly over weapons, and because freedom from child care allows them to enter specialized economic and political roles, some men—especially ruling-class men—acquire power over other men and over women. Almost all men acquire it over women of their own or lower classes, especially within their own kinship groups. These kinds of male power are shadowy among hunters.

To the extent that men *have* power over women in hunting societies, this seems to spring from the male monopoly of heavy weapons, from the particular division of labor between the sexes, or from both. Although men seldom use weapons against women, they *possess* them (or possess superior weapons) in addition to their physical strength. This does give men an ultimate control of force. When old people or babies must be killed to ensure band or family survival, it is usually men who kill them. Infanticide—rather common among hunters, who must limit the mouths to feed—is more often female infanticide than male.

The hunting of men seems more often to require them to organize in groups than does the work of women. Perhaps because of this, 60 percent of hunting societies have predominantly virilocal residence. That is, men choose which band to live in (often, their fathers'), and women move with their husbands. This gives a man advantages over his wife in terms of familiarity and loyalties, for the wife is often a stranger. Sixteen to 17 percent of hunting societies are, however, uxorilocal, with men moving to the households of their wives, while 15 to 17 percent are bilocal—that is, either sex may move in with the other on marriage.

Probably because of male cooperation in defense and hunting, men are more prominent in band councils and leadership, in medicine and magic, and in public rituals designed to increase game, to ward off sickness, or to initiate boys into manhood. Women do, however, often take part in band councils; they are not excluded from law and government as in many agrarian states. Some women are respected as wise leaders, story tellers, doctors, or magicians or are feared as witches. Women have their own ceremonies of fertility, birth, and healing, from which men are often excluded.

In some societies, although men control the most sacred objects, women are believed to have discovered them. Among the Congo Pygmies, religion centers about a beneficent spirit, the Animal of the Forest. It is represented by wooden trumpets that are owned and played by men. Their possession and use are hidden from the women and they are played at night when hunting is bad, someone falls ill, or death occurs. During the playing men dance in the public campfire, which is sacred and is associated with the forest. Yet the men believe that women originally owned the trumpet and that it was a woman who stole fire from the chimpanzees or from the forest spirit. When a woman has failed to bear children for several years, a special ceremony is held. Women lead in the songs that usually accompany the trumpets, and an old woman kicks apart the campfire. Temporary female dominance seems to be thought necessary to restore fertility.

In some hunting societies women are exchanged between local groups, which are thus knit together through marriages. Sometimes, men of different bands directly exchange their sisters. More often there is a generalized exchange of women between two or more groups or a one-way movement of women within a circle of groups. Sometimes the husband's family pays weapons, tools, or ornaments to the wife's in return for the wife's services and, later, her children.

In such societies, although they may be well treated and their consent sought, women are clearly the movable partners in an arrangement controlled by men. Male anthropologists have seized on this as evidence of original male dominance and patrilocal residence. Fox and others, for example, have argued that until recently, *all* hunting societies formed outmarrying patrilocal bands, linked together politically by the exchange of women. The fact that fewer than two-thirds of hunting societies are patrilocal today and only 41 percent have band-exogamy is explained in terms of modern conquest, economic change, and depopulation.

I cannot accept this formula. It is true that modern hunting societies have been severely changed, deculturated, and often depopulated by capitalist imperialism. I can see little evidence, however, that the ones that are patrilocal today have undergone less change than those that are not. It is hard to believe that in spite of enormous environmental diversity and the passage of thousands, perhaps millions, of years, hunting societies all had band exogamy with patrilocal residence until they were disturbed by western imperialism. It is more likely that early band societies, like later agricultural tribes, developed variety in family life and the status of women as they spread over the earth.

There is also some likelihood that the earliest hunters had matrilocal rather than patrilocal families. Among apes and monkey, it is almost always males who leave the troop or are driven out. Females stay closer to their mothers and their original site; males move about, attaching themselves to females where availability and competition permit. Removal of the wife to the husband's home or band may have been a relatively late development in societies where male cooperation in hunting assumed overwhelming importance.° Conversely, after the development of horticulture (which was probably invented and is mainly carried out by women), those tribes in which horticulture predominated over stock raising were most likely to be or to remain matrilocal and to develop matrilineal descent groups with a relatively high status of women. But where extensive hunting of large animals or, later, the herding of large domesticates, predominated, patrilocal residence flourished and women were used to form alliances between male-centered groups. With the invention of metallurgy and of agriculture as distinct from horticulture after 4000 B.C., men came to control agriculture and many crafts, and most of the great agrarian states had patrilocal residence with patriarchal, male-dominant families.

CONCLUSIONS

The family is a human institution, not found in its totality in any prehuman species. It required language, planning, cooperation, self-control, foresight, and cultural learning and probably developed along with these.

The family was made desirable by the early human combination of prolonged child care with the need for hunting with weapons over large terrains. The sexual division of labor on which it was based grew out of a rudimentary prehuman division between male defense and female child care. But among humans this sexual

---

°Upper Palaeolithic hunters produced female figurines that were obvious emblems of fertility. The cult continued through the Mesolithic and into the Neolithic period. Goddesses and spirits of fertility are found in some patrilineal as well as matrilineal societies, but they tend to be more prominent in the latter. It is thus possible that in many areas even late Stone Age hunters had matrilocal residence and perhaps matrilineal descent, and that in some regions this pattern continued through the age of horticulture and even—as in the case of the Nayars of Kerala and the Minangkabau of Sumatra—into the age of plow agriculture, or writing, and of the small-scale state.

division of functions for the first time became crucial for food production and so laid the basis for future economic specialization and cooperation.

Morgan and Engels were probably right in thinking that the human family was preceded by sexual indiscriminacy. They were also right in seeing an egalitarian group quality about early economic and marriage arrangements. They were without evidence, however, in believing that the earliest mating and economic patterns were entirely group relations.

Together with tool use and language, the family was no doubt the most significant invention of the human revolution. All three required reflective thought, which above all accounts for the vast superiority in consciousness that separates humans from apes.

The family provided the framework for all prestate society and the fount of its creativeness. In groping for survival and for knowledge, human beings learned to control their sexual desires and to suppress their individual selfishness, aggression, and competition. The other side of this self-control was increased capacity for love—not only love of a mother for her child, which is seen among apes, but of male for female in enduring relationships and of each sex for ever-widening groups of humans. Civilization would have been impossible without this initial self-control, seen in incest prohibitions and in the generosity and moral orderliness of primitive family life.

From the start, women have been subordinate to men in certain key areas of status, mobility, and public leadership. But before the agricultural revolution, and even for several thousands of years thereafter, the inequality was based chiefly on the unalterable fact of long child care combined with the exigencies of primitive technology. The extent of inequality varied according to the ecology and the resulting sexual division of tasks. But in any case it was largely a matter of survival rather than of man-made cultural impositions. Hence the impressions we receive of dignity, freedom, and mutual respect between men and women in primitive hunting and horticultural societies. This is true whether these societies are patrilocal, bilocal, or matrilocal, although matrilocal societies, with matrilineal inheritance, offer greater freedom to women than do patrilocal and patrilineal societies of the same level of productivity and political development.

A distinct change occurred with the growth of individual and family property in herds, in durable craft objects and trade objects, and in stable, irrigated farm-sites or other forms of heritable wealth. This crystallized in the rise of the state, about 4000 B.C. With the growth of class society and of male dominance in the ruling class of the state, women's subordination increased and eventually reached its depths in the patriarchal families of the great agrarian states. Knowledge of how the family arose is interesting to women because it tells us how we differ from prehumans, what our past has been, and what have been the biological and cultural limitations from which we are emerging. It shows us how generations of male scholars have distorted or overinterpreted the evidence to bolster beliefs in the inferiority of women's mental processes—for which there is no foundation in fact. Knowing about early families is also important to correct a reverse bias among some feminist writers, who hold that in "matriarchal" societies women were completely equal with or were even dominant over men. For this, too, there seems to be no basis in evidence.

The past of the family does not limit its future. Although the family probably emerged with humanity, neither the family itself nor particular family forms are genetically determined. The sexual division of labor—until recently, universal—need not, and in my opinion should not, survive in industrial society. Prolonged child care ceases to be a basis for female subordination when artificial birth control, spaced births, small families, patent feeding, and communal nurseries allow it to be shared by men. Automation and cybernation remove most of the heavy work for which women are less equipped than men. The exploitation of women that came with the rise of the state and of class society will presumably disappear in poststate classless society—for which the technological and scientific basis already exists.

The family was essential to the dawn of civilization, allowing a vast qualitative leap forward in cooperation, purposive knowledge, love, and creativeness. But today, rather than enhancing them, the confinement of women in homes and small families—like their subordination in work—artificially limits these human capacities. It may be that the human gift for personal love will make some form of voluntary, long-term mating and of individual devotion between parents and children continue indefinitely, side by side with public responsibility for domestic tasks and for the care and upbringing of children. There is no need to legislate personal relations out of existence. But neither need we fear a social life in which the family is no more.

REFERENCES

Coult, Allen D. *Cross Tabulations of Murdock's World Ethnographic Sample.* Columbia: University of Missouri Press. 1965.

Engels, F. *The Origin of the Family, Private Property and the State.* Moscow: Foreign Language Publishing House. 1955.

Fox, Robin. *Kinship and Marriage.* London: Pelican Books. 1967.

Hockett, Charles F., and Robert Ascher. "The Human Revolution." In *Man in Adaptation: The Biosocial Background,* edited by Yehudi A. Cohen. Chicago: Aldine. 1968.

Livingstone, Frank B. "Genetics, Ecology and the Origin of Incest and Exogamy." *Current Anthropology.* February 1969.

Morgan, L. F. *Ancient Society* (1877). New York: Holt, reprinted 1963.

Morris, Desmond. *The Naked Ape.* Jonathan Cape. 1967.

Murdock, G. P. "World Ethnographic Sample." *American Anthropologist.* 1957.

Murdock, G. P. *Ethnographic Atlas.* Pittsburgh: University of Pittsburgh. 1967.

Schneider, David M., and Kathleen Gough. *Matrilineal Kinship.* Berkeley and Los Angeles: University of California Press. 1961.

Semyonov, Y. I. "Group Marriage, Its Nature and Role in the Evolution of Marriage and Family Relations." In *Seventh International Congress of Anthropological and Ethnological Sciences.* Vol. IV. Moscow. 1967.

Reading 2

Continuity and Change in American Family Life

Tamara K. Hareven

. . . Recent research on the family in colonial American society has dispelled the myths about the existence of ideal three-generational families in the American past. The historical evidence now shows that there never has been in American society an era when coresidence of three generations in the same household was the dominant pattern. The "great extended families" that became part of the folklore of modern industrial society were rarely in existence. Early American households and families were simple in their structure and not drastically different in their organization from contemporary families. The most typical residential family unit was nuclear—consisting of parents and their children, not extended kin. Three generations seldom lived together in the same household. Given the high mortality rate in preindustrial societies, most parents could not have expected to overlap with their grandchildren. It would thus be futile to argue that industrialization destroyed the great extended family of the past. In reality, such a family type rarely existed.

Family arrangements in the colonial period differed, however, from those in our times. Even though they did not contain extended kin, these households did include unrelated individuals, boarders, lodgers, apprentices, or servants. In this respect the composition of the household in the colonial period was significantly different from that in contemporary society. The tendency of families to include nonrelatives in the household was connected with an entirely different concept of family life. In contrast to the current emphasis on the family home as a private retreat, the household of the past was the site of a broad array of functions and activities that transcended the more restricted circle of the nuclear family. The household was a place of production and served as an abode for servants, apprentices, and dependent members of the community, such as orphaned children and old men or women without relatives.

A considerable number of urban families continued to take in nonrelatives as boarders as late as the 1920s. The practice of young people boarding with other

From Leudtke, L.S. (editor). 1992. *Making America: The Society and Culture of the U.S.* Chapel Hill and London: The University of North Carolina Press.

families thus continued even after the practice of masters having apprentices reside in their households had disappeared. Through the nineteenth and into the early twentieth century about one-fourth to one-third of the population either had lived in someone's household as a boarder or had taken boarders or lodgers at some point in their lives. Boarding or lodging with urban families was an important form of exchange between generations. It enabled young men and women in their late teens and twenties who had left their parents' households or who had migrated from other communities to live as boarders in the households of older people whose own children had left home. This practice enabled young people to stay in surrogate family arrangements; at the same time it provided old people with the opportunity to continue heading their own households without being isolated. Boarding and lodging also fulfilled a critical function in providing continuity in urban life and helping new migrants and immigrants adapt to urban living. Its existence suggests great flexibility in families and households, a flexibility that has been lost over the past half century.

Increasing availability of housing since the 1920s and the rise of values of privacy in family life have led to the phasing out of borading and lodging, except among black families. The practice has virtually disappeared from the larger society. With its disappearance the family has lost some of its major sources of resilience in adapting to urban living. Thus, the most important change in American family life has not been the breakdown of a three-generational family but rather the retreat of the family into its private household and the withdrawal of nonrelatives from the family's abode. Since the beginning of this century the home has become identified as a retreat from the outside world, and the presence of nonrelatives has been considered threatening to the privacy of the family.

Because of the decline in boarding and lodging, the number of households containing only one member has been increasing steadily since the 1920s. While in the nineteenth century solitary residence was almost unheard of, now a major portion of the population resides alone. The disquieting aspect of this pattern is the high percentage of aging widows living by themselves. For a large part of the population, living alone is not a matter of free choice but rather an unavoidable and often painful arrangement. What has been lost over the past two centuries is not the great extended family, but the flexibility of the family that enabled households to expand when necessary and to take people in to live in surrogate family settings rather than in isolation.

KIN RELATIONS

Another pervasive myth about family life in the past has been the assumption that industrialization broke up traditional kinship ties and destroyed the organic interdependence between the family and the community. Once again historical research has shown that industrialization, rather than breaking up traditional family structures, has led to the redefinition of family functions. In industrial communities the family continued to function as a work unit. Relatives acted as recruitment, migration, and housing agents for industrial laborers, helping each other to shift from rural to industrial life and work patterns. Families migrated in groups to industrial centers, and relatives were active in the recruitment of workers into the factory system. Often several family members, even distant kin, continued to work in the same place and fulfilled valuable functions in providing mutual assistance and support in the workplace. Migration to industrial communities did not break up traditional kinship ties; rather, families used these ties to facilitate their own transitions into industrial life and to adapt to new living conditions and life-styles.

During the periods of adjustment to migration, to settlement in new places, and to industrial work, reliance on kin persisted as the most basic resource for assistance. Following the early period of industrialization, kin in rural and urban areas continued to engage in mutual assistance and in reciprocal services. Kin performed a crucial role in initiating and organizing migration from rural areas to factory towns locally, and from rural communities abroad to industrial communities in the United States. Thus, although the majority of families lived in nuclear household arrangements, they were still enmeshed in kinship networks outside the household and depended heavily on mutual assistance.

Even in the late nineteenth and early twentieth centuries, workers who migrated from rural areas to the cities in most industrializing communities carried parts of their kinship ties and family traditions into new settings. Young unmarried sons and daughters of working age, or young married couples without their children, tended to migrate first. After they found jobs and housing, they sent for their relatives. Chain migration thus helped maintain ties and continuities between family members in their new communities of settlement.

In factories and other places of employment, newly arrived workers utilized the connections established by relatives who were already working there to facilitate their hiring and adaptation to work. Hiring and placement through kin often continued even in large-scale modern factories. Kinship networks infiltrated formal, bureaucratized industrial organizations and clustered within them. Even when they worked in different locales, kin made collective decisions about each other's work careers.

Kinship networks also formed an important part of the fiber of urban neighborhoods. Relatives tended to settle in proximity to each other, and as immigrants arrived in American cities, they preferred to live close to their kin whenever possible. So kinship ties brought both coherence and mutual support to the urban neighborhood. This pattern has persisted to some extent among ethnic groups but has gradually weakened in the remainder of the population. While major portions of the American population are still in close contact with their kin, the interdependence that was typical of earlier times has eroded considerably as a result of the continuing redefinition of individualism, as well as patterns of migration and the development of mass transportation. Kin have ceased to be the major source of social security, and some of the functions of mutual assistance formerly found among kin have been replaced by public programs.

Even if industrialization did not bring about major changes in the structure of the family, it did produce changes in the functions of the family and in the values governing family life. Since the early nineteenth century the family gradually has surrendered to other social institutions functions previously concentrated within it.

CHANGING FAMILY FUNCTIONS AND VALUES

During the preindustrial period the family not only reared children but also served as a workshop, a school, a church, and a welfare agency. Preindustrial families meshed closely with the community and carried a variety of public responsibilities within the larger society. "Family and community," John Demos writes, "private and public life, formed part of the same moral equation. The one supported the other and they became in a sense indistinguishable." In preindustrial society most of the work took place in the household. Roles of parenting were therefore congruent with social and economic roles. Children were considered members of the work force and were seen as economic assets. Childhood was treated as a brief preparatory period terminated by apprenticeship and the commencement of work, generally before puberty. Adolescence was virtually unknown as a distinct stage of life. Family members were integrated into common economic activities. The segregation of roles in the family along gender and age lines that characterizes middle-class family life in modern society had not yet appeared. As long as the household functioned as a workshop as well as a family home, family life was not clearly separated from work life.

Even though preindustrial families contained large numbers of children, women invested relatively less time in motherhood than their successors in the nineteenth century and in our time did still do. Child care was part of a general effort of household production rather than a woman's exclusive preoccupation; children were viewed not merely as objects of nature but as productive members of the family from an early age on. The tasks of child rearing did not fall exclusively on mothers; other relatives living nearby also participated in this function.

The integration of family and work in preindustrial society allowed for an intensive sharing of labor between husbands and wives and between parents and children that was later diminished in industrial society. Housework was inseparable from domestic industries or agricultural work, and it was valued, therefore, as an economic asset. Since children constituted part of the labor force, motherhood, too, was valued for its economic contributions and not only for its nurturing tasks.

Under the impact of industrialization many of these functions were transferred to agencies and institutions outside the family. The workplace was separated from the home, and functions of social welfare were transferred from the family to asylums and reformatories. "The family has become *a more specialized agency than before*," wrote Talcott Parsons, "probably more specialized than it has been in any previously known society . . . but not in any general sense less important, because the society is dependent *more* exclusively on it for the performance of *certain* of its vital functions." These vital functions include childbearing, child rearing, and socialization. The family has ceased to be a work unit and has limited its economic activities primarily to consumption and child care.

The transformation of the household from a busy workplace and social center to a private family abode involved the withdrawal of strangers, such as business associates, partners, journeymen, apprentices, and boarders and lodgers, from the household; it also involved a more rigorous separation of husbands from wives and fathers from children in the course of the workday. Specialization in work schedules significantly altered the daily lives of family members in urban society, since the majority of men worked outside the home while women stayed at home and children went to school. In working-class families this specialization was even more far-reaching, since women also worked outside the home, but often on different schedules than the men in their households.

Under the impact of industrialization, in middle-class families housework lost its economic and productive value. Since it was not paid for, and since it no longer led to the production of visible goods, it lost its place in the occupational hierarchy. Housework continued to be governed by nonstandardized time schedules, thus remaining through the nineteenth century a nonindustrial occupation. This is another reason (in addition to economic ones) why housework has been devalued in modern society—where achievement is measured not only by products but also by systematic time and production schedules.

These changes brought about in family life by industrialization were gradual and varied significantly from class to class as well as among different ethnic groups. While scholars have sometimes generalized for an entire society on the basis of the middle-class experience, it is now becoming clear that preindustrial family patterns persisted over longer time periods in rural and in urban working-class families. Since the process of industrialization was gradual, domestic industries and a variety of small family enterprises were carried over into the industrial system. In most working-class families work was still considered a family enterprise, even when their members were employed in different enterprises and the work did not take place in the home. In such families the work of wives, sons, and daughters was carefully regulated by the collective strategies of the family unit. Much of what we perceive today as individual vocational activity was actually considered in earlier times part of a collective family effort.

With the growth of industrial child labor in the nineteenth century, working-class families continued to recognize the economic value of motherhood, as they had in rural society. Segregation along age groups within working-class families was almost nonexistent. Children were socialized for industrial work from an early age and began to contribute to the family's work effort at a younger age than specified by law. They were considered assets, both for their contribution to the family's economy during their youth and for the prospect of their support during their parents' old age. Parents viewed their efforts in child rearing as investments in future social security.

In working-class families, even though the process of industrialization offered women opportunities for independent work outside their homes, women continued to function as an integral part of the family's productive effort. Even when they worked in factories, single working women were bound by family obligations and contributed most of their earnings to their parents. A woman's work was considered part of the family's economic effort, not an independent career. During periods of large-scale industrial development families continued to function as collective economic units in which husbands, wives, and children were all responsible for the well-being of the family.

THE ROLE OF WOMEN

This continuity in the function of the family as a collaborative economic unit is significant for understanding the changes in the roles of women that industrialization introduced into working-class life. By introducing changes in the modes of production as well as in the nature and pace of work, industrialization offered women the opportunity to become wage earners outside the household. Industrialization did not, however, bring about immediate changes in the family's corporate identity in the working class—at least not during the early stages of industrialization. Among middle-class families, on the other hand, industrialization had a more dramatic impact on gender roles: the separation between the home and the workplace that followed in the wake of industrialization led to the glorification of the home as a domestic retreat from the outside world. The new ideology of domesticity that developed in the first half of the nineteenth century relegated women to the home and glorified their role as homemakers and mothers.

The emergence of the ideology of domesticity and of full-time motherhood was closely connected with the decline in the average number of children a woman had and with the new attitudes toward childhood that were emerging in the nineteenth century. One of these major changes was the recognition of childhood as a distinct stage of life among urban middle-class families. Children began to be treated as objects of nurture rather than as working members of the family. Stripped of the multiplicity of functions that had been previously concentrated in the family, urban middle-class families developed into private, domestic, and child-centered retreats from the world of work and politics. Children were no longer expected to join the work force until their late teens, a major indication of the growing recognition of childhood as a distinct stage of development. Instead of considering children as potential working members of the family group, parents began to view them as dependent objects of tender nurture and protection.

This marked the emergence of the domestic middle-class family as we know it today. The glorification of motherhood as a full-time career served both to enshrine the family as a domestic retreat from the world of work and to make families child centered. The gradual separation of the home from the workplace that had started with industrialization reached its peak in the designation of the home as a therapeutic refuge from the outside world. As custodians of this retreat, women were expected to concentrate on making the home a perfect place and on child rearing, rather than on being economic partners in the family. Tenderness, gentleness, affection, sweetness, and a comforting demeanor began to emerge as a central value at the base of family relationships.

The ideology of domesticity and the new view of childhood combined to revise expectations of parenthood. The roles of husbands and wives became gradually more separate; a clear division of labor replaced the old economic cooperation, and the wife's efforts concentrated on homemaking and child rearing. With men leaving the home to work elsewhere, time invested in fatherhood was concentrated primarily on leisure hours. Thus the separation of husbands from wives and parents from children for major parts of the day came about. These patterns, which emerged in the early nineteenth century, formed the base of relations characteristic of the contemporary American family. Some of these patterns persist to the present day and are the root of problems and crises in the family.

The cult of domesticity that emerged in the nineteenth century as a major part of the ideology of family life in America has dominated perceptions of women's roles until very recently and has shaped prevailing assumptions governing family life. One of its consequences was the insistence that confinement of women's main activities to the domestic sphere and the misguided assumption that mothers' work in the labor market would be harmful to the family and to society. Only over the past few decades have these values been criticized and partly rejected. Since the prejudices against mothers' labor force participation persevered as long as they did in American society, and have handicapped women's pursuit of occupations outside the home, it is important to understand their origin in the nineteenth-century cult of domesticity.

Although the ideology of domesticity originated in urban middle-class families, it was gradually adopted as the dominant model for family life in the entire society. Second- and third-generation immigrant families, who originally held a more integrated view of the family as a corporate unit, and who had earlier accepted the wife's work outside the home, began to embrace the ideology of domesticity as part of their "Americanization" process. The ideals of urban middle-class life subsequently handicapped the role of women as workers outside the home. As immigrants became "Americanized" in the early part of the twentieth century, they internalized the values of domesticity and began to view women's labor force participation as demeaning, as carrying low status, or as compromising for the husband and dangerous for the children. Consequently, married women entered the labor force only when driven by economic necessity.

Despite the impact of the ideal of domesticity in American culture, working-class and ethnic families to a significant degree continued to adhere to the earlier ways of life and maintained a collective view of the family and its economy. In contrast to the values of individualism that govern much of family life today, traditional values of family collectivity have persisted among various ethnic groups and, to some extent, among black families. In working-class and ethnic families the relationships between husbands and wives, parents and children, and other kin were based upon reciprocal assistance and support. Such relations, often defined as "instrumental," drew their strength from the assumption that family members were all engaged in mutual obligations and in reciprocity. Although obligations were not specifically defined by contract, they rested on the accepted social values as to what family members owed to each other. In the period preceding the welfare state instrumental relationships among family members and more distant kin provided important supports to individuals and families, particularly during critical life situations.

A collective view of familial obligations was the very basis of survival in earlier time periods. From such a perspective marriage and parenthood were not merely love relationships but partnerships governed by family economic and social needs. In this respect the experience of working-class families in the nineteenth century and of ethnic families in the more recent past was drastically different from that of middle-class families, in which sentimentality emerged as the dominant base of family relationships. Among traditional families sentiment was secondary to family needs and survival strategies. Under such conditions childbearing and work were not governed by individual decisions. Mate selection and the timing of marriage were regulated in accordance with collective family considerations rather than directed by strictly individual whim. The transfer of property and work were not regulated strictly according to individual decisions. At times collective family "plans" took priority over individual preferences. For example, parents often tried to delay the marriage of the last child in the household, commonly a daughter, in order to secure continued economic support, especially in later life when they were withdrawing from the labor force.

Thus, the major historical change in family values has been one from a collective view of the family to one of individualization and sentiment. Over the past several decades American families have been experiencing an increasing emphasis on individual priorities and preferences over collective family needs. This individualization of family relations has also led to an exaggerated emphasis on emotional nurture, intimacy, and privacy as the major base of family relations. It has contributed considerably to the liberation of individuals, but it has also eroded the resilience of the family and its ability to withstand crises. Moreover, it has contributed to a greater separation among family members and especially to the isolation of older people. . . .

Reading 3

The Politics and History of Family Violence

Linda Gordon

In the past twenty-five years, family violence has appeared as a substantial social problem in the United States. Starting with a wave of concern about child abuse in the 1960s, the concern widened to include wife-beating, incest (the sexual abuse of children in the family), and marital rape, as the women's liberation movement of the 1970s drew those crimes to public attention. The actual extent of family violence is controversial; estimates of child abuse vary, for example, from 50,000 to 1.5 million cases a year in the United States. Whatever the real figure, the general awareness of the problem has increased substantially.

For most of these two and one half decades, I was not a family-violence scholar. My responses were probably typical: First, I wondered how anyone could be so bestial as to beat or mutilate their children (beating and mutilation were at first the dominant media representations of child abuse); then, as I gathered how widespread the problem was, I wondered that so many could have so little self-control; then, as I began to meet former victims and perpetrators, I began to suspect that the boundary separating me from those experiences was by no means invulnerable. Finally, the issue provoked my historian's curiosity. I noticed that family violence had had virtually no history; that most who discussed it—experts, journalists, friends—assumed they were discussing a *new* problem. As my preliminary forays into libraries revealed, it was an old problem. I began to notice the distortions created in the public discussion by the lack of a history.

One example is the tendency of the media to cover only the most cruel cases, creating the impression that these were typical. I learned that, a century ago, the problem had also gained public attention through sensational cases, while the majority of cases were ambiguous, not life-threatening, more often crimes of neglect than of assault. Another example is that many diagnoses of the *causes* of family violence—e.g., the increasing permissiveness of recent family and sexual life—assume that the problem is unprecedented, which is not the case. By contrast, the ebb-and-flow pattern of concern about family violence over the last century suggests that its incidence has not changed as much as its visibility.

The changing visibility of family violence is, in my opinion, the leading indicator of the necessity of an historical approach to understanding it. Concern with family violence has been a weathervane identifying the prevailing winds of anxiety about family life in general. The periods of silence about family violence are as significant as periods of concern. Both reveal the longing for peaceful family life, the strength of the cultural image of home life as a harmonious, loving, and supportive environment. One response to this longing has been a tendency to deny, even suppress, the evidence that families are not always like that. Denying the problem serves to punish the victims of family violence doubly by forcing them to hide their problems and to blame themselves. Even the aggressors in family violence suffer from denial, since isolation and the feeling that they are unique make it difficult to ask for the help they want.

About 110 years ago there arose for the first time a different response—an attempt to confront the facts of family violence and to stop or at least control it. The first social agencies devoted to family-violence problems arose in the 1870s, called Societies for the Prevention of Cruelty to Children. They originally focused only on child abuse, but were soon drawn into other forms of family violence as well. It is important to learn and evaluate this history for its contemporary value as well as its historical interest.

The central argument of this article is that family violence has been historically and politically constructed. I make this claim in a double sense. First, the very definition of what constitutes unacceptable domestic violence, and appropriate responses to it, developed and then varied according to political moods and the force of certain political movements. Second, violence among family members arises from family conflicts which are not only historically influenced but political in themselves, in the sense of that word as having to do with power relations. Family violence usually arises out of power struggles in which individuals are contesting real resources and benefits. These contests arise not only from personal aspirations but also from changing social norms and conditions.

The historical developments that influenced family violence—through the behavior of family members and the responses of social-control agencies—include, prominently, changes in the situation of women and children. Another major argument of this article, therefore, is that family violence cannot be understood outside the context of the overall politics of the family. Today's anxiety about family issues—divorce, sexual permissiveness, abortion, teenage pregnancy, single mothers, runaway or allegedly stolen children, gay rights—is not unprecedented. For at least 150 years there have been periods of fear that "the family"—meaning a popular image of what families were supposed to be like, by no means a correct recollection of any actual "traditional family"—was in decline; and these fears have tended to escalate in periods of social stress. Anxieties about family life, furthermore, have usually expressed socially conservative fears about the increasing power and autonomy of women and children, and the corresponding decline in male, sometimes rendered as fatherly, control of family members. For much of the history of the family-violence concern, moreover, these anxieties have been particularly projected onto lower-class families. Thus an historical analysis of family violence must include a view of the changing power relations among classes, sexes, and generations.

Yet family-violence policy is mainly discussed today without an historical dimension, and with its political implications hidden. The result has been a depoliticization of family-violence scholarship, as if this were a social problem above politics, upon which "objective" scientific expertise could be brought to bear. The questions raised by proposed remedies cannot be answered by "neutral" experts, but only by public decisions about the extent and limits of public responsibility.

A few examples may offer an introductory sense of what it means to call family violence a political problem. For over a century there has been a consensus that there must be some limits placed on the treatment family "heads" can mete out to their dependents. But setting and enforcing those limits encounters a fundamental tension between civil liberties and social control. In policing private behavior, one person's right may be established only by invading another person's privacy. Moreover, social control of family violence is made difficult by our dominant social norm that families ought to be economically independent. There is a consensus that children ought to have some minimal guarantees of health and welfare, no matter how poor their parents. Yet there is a consistent tendency to insist that social welfare be a temporary expedient, made uncomfortable, and its recipients stigmatized. These dilemmas must be confronted by political choices; they cannot be ironed out by expert rationalization.

The political nature of family violence is also revealed in the source of the campaign against it. For most of the 110 years of this history, it was the women's-rights movement that was most influential in confronting, publicizing, and demanding action against family violence. Concern with family violence usually grew when feminism was strong and ebbed when feminism was weak. Women's movements have consistently been concerned with violence not only against women but also against children. But this does not mean that anti-family-violence agencies, once established, represented feminist views about the problem. On the contrary, anti-feminism often dominated not only among those who would deny or ignore the problem but also among those who defined and treated it. In some periods the experts confronted wife-beating and sexual assault, male crimes, while in others they avoided or soft-pedaled these crimes and emphasized child neglect, which they made by definition a female crime. In some periods they identified class and in others gender inequalities as relevant, and in still others ignored connections between family violence and the larger social structure.

Political attitudes have also affected research "findings" about family violence. For example, in the last two decades, experts on the problem have tended to divide into two camps. A psychological interpretation explains the problem in terms of personality disorders and childhood experience. A sociological explanatory model attributes the problem primarily to social stress factors such as poverty, unemployment, drinking, and isolation. In fact, these alternatives have been debated for a century, and the weight of opinion has shifted according to the dominant political mood. More conservative times bring psychological explanations to the foreground, while social explanations dominate when progressive attitudes and social reform movements are stronger. The debate is intense because it is not mainly about diagnoses but about their implications for policy. Social diagnoses imply social action and demand resources; psychological diagnoses may point to the need for psychotherapy but also justify criminal penalties and remove family violence from the range of problems called upon to justify welfare spending. When caseworkers lack the resources to help clients materially, they may focus on psychological problems—which are usually present—because at least something can be done about them. Those opposed to the commitment of resources on social spending are more likely to focus on individual psychological deviance as the problem. But both sides have often ignored the gender politics of family-violence issues, and the gender implications of policy recommendations, not only when women or girls were the victims of men, but also when women were the abusers.

Political attitudes have determined the very *meanings* of family violence. Family violence is not a fixed social illness which, like tuberculosis, can have its causal microorganism identified and then killed. Rather, its definitions have changed substantially since it first appeared as a social problem. Most of the discussion of family violence today assumes that what makes it problematic and requires social action is self-evident. Yet what was considered spanking a century ago might be considered abusive today, and the standards for what constitutes child neglect have changed greatly.

To insist that family violence is a political issue is not to deny its material reality as a problem for individuals—a painful, often terrifying reality. If there were any doubt, the victims', and often aggressors', pleas for help would erase it. But to discuss the violence itself without attention to the conflicts that give rise to it is to avoid the roots of the problem.

It is equally important to look at the history of attempts to control family violence. These efforts illustrate many of the general problems of "social control," a phrase often used to describe processes by which deviant and, presumably, dangerous behavior is disciplined by the larger society. Agencies devoted to the problem of family violence are in many ways typical of the entire welfare state. They have faced great difficulties in maintaining a balance between social order and privacy, between protecting the rights of some individuals and preserving the autonomy of others, and they have often been the means of imposing dominant values on subordinate groups. As with other activities of the state, social control of family violence could hardly be expected to be administered fairly in a society of such great inequalities of power. Yet it is precisely those inequalities that create such desperate need for the intervention of a welfare state.

Thus the example of family violence also produces a more complex view of social control than has been customary among social theorists. One of the most striking findings of this study is how often the objects of social control themselves asked for intervention from child-protection agencies. Clients were troubled by their inability to raise children according to their own standards, or to escape domestic violence themselves, and were eager for outside help. Moreover, once becoming clients, they attempted aggressively to influence agency policy and the definitions of the problems themselves, sometimes successfully.

TYPES OF FAMILY VIOLENCE

Four major types of family violence predominated in the eighty years covered by this study. The original one was cruelty to children, a notion which evolved into the modern category: child abuse. In 1880, as today, child-saving propaganda emphasized violent assault as the archetypical problem. In fact, child abuse is (and was) less common than child neglect, but it is more dramatic, less ambiguous, and—above all—it stimulates more outrage and financial generosity. Social workers in the nineteenth century, as those today, were aware that for effective fund-raising, they had to offer a distorted image of the nature of their work.

Child neglect soon became the most common form of family "violence" met by agencies. Its definition is of course extremely variable and relative to economic class, cultural standards, and family structure. What child-neglect cases have in common is that they must by definition project an inverse standard, a norm of proper child-raising.

Sexual abuse of children in the family—incest—figured prominently in family-violence case records. The "discovery" of child sexual abuse in the last decade has been only a rediscovery of a problem well known to social workers in the nineteenth century and the Progressive era.

Finally, wife-beating was also common in the case records. Logically, this should not have been the case, since the agencies studied here were exclusively devoted to child welfare. But women frequently and energetically attempted to force child-welfare agencies to defend their own interests as well as their children's. Included in their complaints were accusations of what we would today call marital rape, usually seen along with beatings as part of a generic male violence.

These themes are addressed through a case study: how Boston-area social-work agencies approached family-violence problems, from 1880 to 1960. These dates cover the period since the "discovery" of family violence in the late 1870s, stopping just before the latest wave of alarm about child abuse. Although the data in this [work] come exclusively from the Boston metropolitan area, which had certain demographic and social peculiarities, there is reason to consider the findings of this study typical of the urban United States. The largest environmental factors affecting family violence (e.g., poverty, unemployment, illness, alcoholism) were common to many areas. Moreover, the "discovery" of this social problem occurred simultaneously throughout the United States and in much of Europe, in the course of a single decade, suggesting similar patterns. The agencies whose records formed the source material for this study were local, but they were part of a national social-work profession—indeed, for most of this period the Boston groups were a leading influence in national family-violence policy.

THE CLIENTS

The protagonists of this story are the victims and assailants in family-violence cases: unusual heroes and heroines, to be sure, for they were almost always quite wretched, innocent and guilty alike. Nevertheless they were people with aspirations and complex emotions as well as ill luck and, often, self-destructive impulses.

These clients of children's protective agencies were mainly poor immigrants of non-elite ethnic and racial backgrounds. These groups were the most numerous, not because they are the only ones involved in family violence, but because they were more likely to be "caught."

Because I mean to describe these people as individuals rather than statistical generalizations, it will be useful here to offer a general profile of these clients. This profile cannot be construed to tell us anything about the characteristics that promote family violence, however, because this was not a controlled study. For example, the clients I studied were mostly poor and uneducated; but I have no way of knowing how many other poor and uneducated people did not have family-violence problems, or how many prosperous and educated people did. My guesses about the characteristics that contribute to family violence will rely on qualitative, not quantitative, evidence. But the reader will be able to know these people better, to understand their problems more readily, with a general description of the social and economic outlines of their lives.

The clients' most pronounced characteristic was their poverty. Twenty-one percent were lacking basic necessities, such as food and fuel, and an additional 48 percent lived in constant insecurity as to whether they could maintain bare subsistence. Relatively more clients were extremely poor in the last century, confirming what is known about the disastrous living conditions in poor urban neighborhoods in the nineteenth century. While there was a decline in the poorest categories after 1910, the number of prosperous or even middle-class clients did not increase greatly.

The clients' poverty was reflected in how they supported themselves. Once federal welfare aid developed in the 1930s, 42 percent relied on it chronically and only one-quarter had never received welfare. The proportion of fathers who were main supporters of their families went down over time, not because women were increasingly employed, but because welfare contributed more. Very few of the client families contained regularly employed women. Employed women were probably less likely to need the help of, or to come to the attention of, child-protection agencies, because their families were better off and because they themselves had more independence and self-esteem. The extreme poverty of the clients was also indicated by the fact that for 40 percent of families, children were vital contributors to the family budget. After World War II, when child labor had become virtually negligible in the urban population, 31 percent of these clients still needed their children's wages to survive.

The clients were extremely transient. Forty-one percent had lived at their present address less than two years, and only 18 percent more than five years. The clients also appeared rather isolated, judging from the few social contacts they seemed to have. These characteristics do not necessarily distinguish family-violence clients, since poor people are often more isolated than the prosperous, but they illustrate one of the indirect ways in which poverty, through the lack of community rootedness it creates, reduced their social resources of coping with family conflict.

There is a common view that large households promote family violence, either directly or through the correlation of large families with poverty and overcrowding. On the contrary, neither the families nor the households of the clients were consistently larger than average, and in the first four decades of this study, they were a little smaller than Boston's average. This was probably because of the tendency to family disorganization associated with poverty and family violence: children tended to leave home earlier, marital separation and illegitimacy were frequent, and living arrangements with boarders were unstable.

The clients were mainly immigrants or children of immigrants. Until World War II, the foreign-born were overrepresented in proportion to their numbers in Boston's population, but not in proportion to their numbers among the poor. The leading foreign ethnic groups among the family-violence clients were the Irish, the Italians, and the Canadians. In later years, Afro-Americans and West Indian blacks became another large ethnic group in this study. No ethnic group was significantly overrepresented in any of the four major types of family violence (child abuse, child neglect, wife-beating, and sexual abuse). The proportion of foreign-born clients shifted from 70 percent in the first decades of this study to just under 20 percent at the end, a decline consistent with the slowing of immigration.

However, there were behavioral differences among ethnic groups which affected family-violence problems. Perhaps the most notorious of them was the heavy drinking of the Irish. Although there is no reason to share the caseworkers' (many of whom were abstainers) moralistic condemnations, the case records provide evidence that the Irish were heavier drinkers than any other nationality. The Irish stood out even more in the amount of women's drinking. With respect to family violence, Irish alcoholism contributed to unusually high rates of desertion, poverty, dependency, infant mortality, and fighting. In the case records of this study, while the Irish were not disproportionately represented in cases of wife-beating, they did more often engage in mutual marital combat. But there is no reason to focus on liquor as the cause of this: the combativeness of Irish women may result from other factors in Irish and Irish-American history which accustomed Irish women to unusual independence.

The Italians were the poorest of Boston's ethnic groups at the turn of the century. Yet unlike the Irish, they were underrepresented in the city's almshouses. This contradiction may be explained by the strong family cohesion among Italian-Americans, as evidenced, for example, in their low desertion rates. Moreover, heavy drinking was rare among Italians. There was less street brawling and marital fighting than among the Irish, yet plenty of wife-beating. The Italian-American families in these case records included many of the most patriarchal, in terms of fathers' control over wives, authority over sons, and sequestering of daughters. (These patterns were shared by other southern-European and Mediterranean immigrants, such as the Lebanese, Syrians, and Greeks, of whom there were many fewer in Boston.)

The Canadian immigrants were of French, Scotch, and English origin, and had no single ethnic identity. Many had lived long in Canada, particularly Nova Scotia, before coming to the United States; others, particularly French Canadians, had lived in northern New England before migrating to Boston. Thus many Boston clients of Canadian origin had relatives with farms in New England or Canada to whom they turned for help, a substantial advantage in coping with family stress which European immigrants did not have. According to studies of Massachusetts as a whole, the French Canadians resembled the Irish in their extreme poverty and concentration in unskilled jobs, but resembled more the Italians in their low rates of female employment; like all the rural immigrants, they had high rates of child labor.

There were few Afro-Americans in the first decades of this study, and even by 1960 Boston had a much smaller black population than most other large eastern cities. Like all the other "ethnic" groups, they were overrepresented in family-violence case records in proportion to their numbers in the population, but not in proportion to their numbers among the poor. As with other ethnic groups, the increase of the black population came mainly from migration, and in many ways they shared with other immigrants the stresses of being alien. Contrary to what contemporary expectations might suggest, blacks were not overrepresented in any characteristic relevant to family violence: not poverty, or single-mother families, or drinking.

Overall these ethnic cultural differences were of minimal importance in constructing family-violence problems in comparison to the general influence of being poor, migratory, or alien. The single ethnic patterns that can be identified as influential were Irish drinking-and-fighting behavior and Italian fathers' patriarchal control over family members. Even these fade in comparison to experiences that were common to all ethnic groups in this study. Yet that commonness was not perceived by the clients themselves. Ethnic stereotyping was practiced, of course, not only by agency workers but also among clients. They experienced themselves as ethnically unique and frequently attempted to interpret their behavior to case-workers in terms of ethnic traditions. Among the clients themselves a kind of "plu-ralistic ignorance" is visible: Irish women, for example, were convinced that deser-tion was unique to their men; Italian women that wife-beating was an Italian problem. They were wrong in these analyses. Yet their frequent references to their cultural origins and traditions were attempts to assert to social workers something important about their identities, vital for caseworkers to understand if they were to help.

The "clients" in this study were as varied as any collection of several thousand people, perhaps more so, since many of them had recently come from separate foreign cultures. Yet they also had a great deal in common: their poverty, above all, and their experience of helplessness in the context of radical social and economic change, the more acute for those who had recently immigrated from agrarian soci-eties into the metropolis of Boston. Most of them were inadequately housed; many of their children had serious medical problems; many of the men were frequently and sometimes chronically unemployed or underemployed. For the purposes of this study, what united them most was their common experience as "clients" of an agency of social control, devoted to protecting their children—from themselves. The very definition of their problems arose through their interactions with individ-ual caseworkers and the developing child-welfare establishment.

THE CHILD PROTECTORS AND THEIR RECORDS

In tracking the history of family violence, I turned to a source relatively new to historians: case records of social work agencies devoted to child protection. Case records are rich in detail about daily life and personal relations. They are not, however, universally reliable, understandable, or easy to use. Since the nature of these records affects so much how I know what I assert in this article, it is impor-tant to discuss briefly here the nature of the records and their limitations.

This study is based on the work of three Boston agencies, each exemplary of a certain type of child welfare agency, and each involved in family violence in a different way. The major source, and the dominant type of agency in this field, was the Massachusetts Society of the Prevention of Cruelty to Children (MSPCC, or the Society). Societies for the Prevention of Cruelty to Children (SPCCs), or child-protection agencies, as they were later called, arose throughout the United States and Europe in the 1870s; nearly every state in the United States had such an agency, and the Massachusetts SPCC was one of the most influential. The MSPCC investigated and prosecuted parents for child abuse and neglect and, in coopera-tion with other governmental and private agencies, arranged the placements of children ordered removed from their parents.

A second agency active in child-saving, the Boston Children's Service Associ-ation (BCSA), developed from alms-giving and asylum-providing groups. While the BCSA always conceded to the MSPCC primary jurisdiction over protective work, the MSPCC in turn referred to the BCSA much of the arrangement and supervision of placements.

A third major type of child-saving agency, which came into existence toward the end of the Progressive era, were clinics offering psychological diagnosis and treatment for disturbed or delinquent children. The example used in this study, one of the leading such clinics in the United States, is the Judge Baker Guidance Center (JBGC), established in Boston in 1917. This clinic was the major place of referral by the courts and by other social work agencies, including the MSPCC and BCSA, when children were thought to need professional mental health services. A substantial proportion of JBGC clients had backgrounds of family violence, making its records a rich source of data for the second half of this period of study.

The keeping of case records was a basis for the professionalization of social work. In the nineteenth century, when the agencies studied here were charities, using volunteer and/or untrained labor, their record-keeping was skimpy and inconsistent. They used ledger books in which handwritten notes were entered about cases as they came in. If a "case" continued for more than one day, the worker might or might not remember to write on the bottom of the first entry, say, "cont'd volume IX p. 396." After five or six further entries, it was very easy to lose the trail. Since a worker had to pull down many heavy volumes to trace the history of a case, it seems reasonable to surmise that many did not bother to do this. The Progressive-era transformation of social work in the early twentieth century brought modern record-keeping: card files and a "loose-leaf" system, generally a folder and a case number for each case, so that new material could be added continually. Thus, from the point of view of the historian, the quality of records took a great advance around 1910, and that is reflected (here) in the disproportion of quotations from case histories after 1910.

Despite improvements, case records continued uneven in the information they contained. There were many reasons for this: sometimes the clients were so reluctant to cooperate at all that the workers did not want to struggle to get information beyond the absolutely necessary; sometimes the workers simply deemed some information irrelevant; sometimes the client interviewed did not know what the worker wanted; sometimes the workers were hurried. Case records varied also in length: from one paragraph to several hundred pages. All, however, consisted primarily of notes written by the caseworker(s), summarizing contacts with and information from or about clients. There were many interagency memoranda and, infrequently, notes from the clients themselves. With few exceptions, the case records represent the caseworkers' opinions, even when they were trying to represent the clients' point of view.

Thus agency workers, "child protectors," are also protagonists in this story, but only collectively. I have not attempted to individualize them here (indeed, I would have had no basis on which to do so, for *their* foibles and problems were not laid out in agency records). In that neglect, I am simplifying an already extremely complicated tale; I do not wish to distract attention too far from the central position of the clients. In avoiding distinctions among social workers, I am doing some of them an injustice; the limitations of the agencies as a whole did not pertain to each of the workers. But some might benefit from my generalizations, too, since some were even more limited in what they offered than the norm.

The bias, not to mention outright prejudice, of these caseworkers was often substantial. For the first twenty-five years of this study the workers were almost always male, while the clients were virtually all female. For the first fifty years of this study, the workers were almost always white, native-born Protestants, dealing with clients who were in the majority Catholic immigrants. Lack of adequate translators was a chronic problem. The most common result was the conclusion that clients were stupid or ignorant because of their inadequacy in answering questions or following instructions. Sometimes the caseworkers could not gather basic family information accurately because of their lack of language skills. Often case records were duplicated because, due to mistakes in spelling foreign names, workers did not find a previously existing record.

Social workers often disdained many aspects of the ethnic and religious cultures of their clients; for most of the period of this study, the child protectors were overwhelmingly native-born white Protestants, while the clients were immigrant or second-generation Catholics. Most caseworkers, reflecting the cultures in which they had been raised, assumed subnormal intelligence among their poorer clients. The agents' comments and expectations about immigrants in this early period were similar to views of black clients in the mid-twentieth century. The records abound with derogatory references, even when made with kind intent. One girl making an incest allegation against her father in 1910, and being accused of lying, was called "a romancer but not more so than the average foreign born child." Black women were described as "primitive," "limited," "not nearly as talkative as many of her race, but apparently truthful," "fairly good for a colored woman." White immigrants came in for similar abuse: e.g., "a typical low-grade Italian woman." The characterizations of clients were also saturated with class arrogance. "A young girlish appearing woman with dark bobbed curly hair, ignorant, brassy, indifferent . . . coarse, had very poor standards. . . . Seemed to lack feeling, sympathy and understanding, decidedly hard." Some social workers disdained their clients partly because they *were* clients: "typical Puerto Ricans who loved fun, little work and were dependent people," a caseworker wrote in 1960.

After about 1920 these informal judgments were supposed to be replaced by scientific intelligence tests. It has been well documented that these tests were biased against immigrant, non-English-speaking, and poor people, and the case records provide direct evidence for that conclusion. In the Judge Baker records, the children's actual tests, in their own handwriting, are included, and one can imagine the experience of immigrant children in trying to answer them. Some 1930 examples: Make as many words as you can from the letters AEIRLP; Fill in the blanks: "The poor baby_____as if it were_____sick"; Answer: "Why did the Pilgrims come to this country?" Moreover, the testing merely supplemented, but did not replace, arbitrary race and class labeling of clients. I compared the epithets used by MSPCC caseworkers, the least professionalized of the agencies in this study, to those used by Judge Baker professionally trained psychiatric social workers, for the same years (1910–17). The MSPCC records called clients shiftless, coarse, low type, uncouth, immoral, feebleminded, lazy, and worthless (or occasionally, positively, good or sober); Judge Baker workers characterized their clients as low-grade, of weak character, ignorant type, degenerate, of low mentality (or once, positively, as refined)—hardly a more scientific set of categories. Yet the caseworkers were often so in thrall to the objectivity of such testing that they credited it above the evidence of their own observation: "The psychological testing brought forth the fact very plainly that the child [Italian-born, fifteen years old] has a very distinct language handicap that is not evident when one is talking with her."

Equally questionable was the use of testing to evaluate parents, almost always mothers. Test results might decide whether girls were placed in institutions; they might decide whether mothers could keep their children. For example:

> . . . she graded at a median mental age of 7³⁄₁₂ years, which is 6⁹⁄₁₂ years below the average. As she could speak no English, test had to be given through an interpreter. . . . Although initial performance on Healy A was total failure, she showed good learning ability after demonstration. She did surprisingly well on problems of simple change from Stanford scale though she failed to count backwards from 20 to 1. . . . Her method on tests was a combination of chance, trial and error, and some elements of planning. . . . Although this woman . . . can neither read nor write Italian, speaks only a few words of English, is unable to spell her own name, does not know the year or the month, she does, however, know the date . . . that every child was born, is able to make change and manifests fairly good practical ability. She will probably be capable of caring for two or more of her children. Her responsibilities, however, should be carefully guarded and it should be kept constantly before her that the return of the children is to be the reward for the effort she makes to care for them. [This woman, deserted by her husband and left with four children, had come herself to a family service agency seeking help. . . .]

In the face of such discriminatory attitudes and procedures, and of such power to disrupt clients' lives, it is to be expected that clients would not be frank with caseworkers. Even caseworkers trying to avoid arrogance and to help clients achieve their own goals met uncooperativeness and lack of understanding. From the clients' point of view, even well-meaning caseworkers could do a good deal of damage through misunderstandings and the structural inflexibilities of the system. What caseworkers saw as professional standards and procedures had entirely different meanings to clients. When the former asked personal questions, clients did not understand their relevance, considered them nosy, and did not trust the confidentiality of their responses. Most child-protection workers had no material aid to offer clients, but had to rely primarily on moral exhortation, counseling, or threats of punitive measures, even with clients who had themselves asked for help with violence problems. Clients interpreted this emphasis on talk instead of action as meaning that the caseworkers did not really want to help. Clients so often had something to hide—who among us would agree to allow caseworkers free entry to their homes at any time? Boyfriends, liquor, boarders and guests, children not at school, luxuries that might provide evidence against needed relief, baby and child care that did not conform to expert recommendations, food that did not conform to American tastes—all these and many other infractions that clients might not even notice could convince a caseworker that the client was an unfit parent.

These mutually distrustful relationships were by no means the fault of individual caseworkers. Many caseworkers managed despite these limitations to offer sympathy and help to clients. These useful services were of many types: sometimes what clients wanted was exactly what agencies could provide, as in cases of prosecution of child abusers or wife-beaters; sometimes caseworkers provided referrals to other agencies that did have material aid to offer; sometimes the child protectors themselves provided encouragement, advice, confirmation of a client's own good judgment, or a brake on bad judgment; sometimes they offered informal support quite beyond the bounds of the professional minimum, ranging from small gifts to trips to the country to an ongoing, steady relationship.

The caseworker in her turn faced pressures that militated against scrupulously honest case records. These records were often the basis of the worker's evaluation by her superior and she needed, therefore, to note what she ought to have done, not what she did do. Furthermore, she needed to justify her actions by showing that they were appropriate to her clients—evidence that would mainly be taken from the record she prepared. She sometimes had to disguise both her inadequacies and her excellence; the case record could be allowed to show neither too little nor too much action for clients. I tried, where possible, to check caseworkers' characterizations against more reliable, objective data. Where caseworkers said that clients were mainly drunkards, I tried to look myself for clear evidence of alcohol abuse, for example. But since the evidence was usually presented or suppressed by the caseworker, these efforts were limited.

The interpretation of such records involves the historian's creativity, even imagination—although not necessarily more so than with other sorts of historical sources. Their status as historical documents does not make them infallible; their truth must be gathered from among the varied and often conflicting stories they contain, and from the complex relationships that they expressed—between agency representatives, clients, and family members. In trying to grasp the will of the clients, I weighed what they did more heavily than what they said (i.e., what caseworkers said clients said). I tried to identify the actions taken by agency workers, not their promises and waverings.

I argued above that individual outcomes were not determined, that the collectively greater power of the social workers and the social order they represented could not predict any individual case. The interactions between client and worker which are central to my argument, central to the whole historical construction of family violence, can only be revealed in actual case histories. Throughout . . . I have chosen to tell, as much as possible, whole stories rather than excerpts from stories, so that the peculiarities of every situation are inescapable, and so that my generalizations are seen for what they are: abstractions, not "typical cases." I also tell whole stories in order to maximize the readers' opportunity to "see" my interpretation and to argue with it, conscious that readers do not immediately have access to these confidential case records as they might to other forms of historical documents.

As we turn now to examine the historical construction and reconstruction of definitions of family violence, one such case history will serve as an example of the interaction of client and social worker. The "Amatos" were clients of MSPCC from

1910 to 1916. They had five young children from the current marriage and Mrs. Amato had three from a previous marriage, two of them still in Italy and one daughter in Boston. Mrs. Amato kept that daughter at home to do housework and look after the younger children while she earned money doing home piece-rate sewing. This got the family in trouble with a truant officer, and they were also accused, in court, of lying, saying that the father had deserted when he was in fact at home. Furthermore, once while left alone, probably in charge of a sibling, one of the younger children fell out of a window and had to be hospitalized, making the mother suspect of negligence.

Despite her awareness of these suspicions against her, Mrs. Amato went to many different agencies, starting with those of the Italian immigrant community and then reaching out to elite (Protestant) social work agencies, seeking help, reporting that her husband was a drunkard, a gambler, a non-supporter, and a wife-beater. The Massachusetts Society for the Prevention of Cruelty to Children agents at first doubted her claims because Mr. Amato impressed them as a "good and sober man," and blamed the neglect of the children on his wife's incompetence in managing the wages he gave her. The Society ultimately became convinced of her story because of her repeated appearance with severe bruises and the corroboration by the husband's father. Mr. Amato, Sr., was intimately involved in the family troubles, and took responsibility for attempting to control his son. Once, he came to the house and gave the son "a warning and a couple of slaps," after which the son improved for a while. Another time he extracted from his son a pledge not to beat his wife for two years.

Mrs. Amato did not trust this method of controlling her husband. She begged the MSPCC agent to help her get a divorce; then she withdrew this request; later she claimed that she had not dared take this step because his relatives threatened to beat her if she tried it. Finally Mrs. Amato's daughter (from her previous marriage) took action, coming independently to the MSPCC to bring an agent to the house to help her mother. As a result of this complaint Mr. Amato was convicted of assault once and sentenced to six months. During that time Mrs. Amato survived by "a little work" and help from "Italian friends," according to her caseworker. Her husband returned more violent than before: he went at her with an ax, beat the children so much on the head that their "eyes wabbled" [sic], and supported his family so poorly that the children went out begging. This case closed, like so many, without a resolution.

The Amatos, it must be remembered, exist only as they were interpreted for us by social workers in a particular historical period—the Progressive era. I want to press the Amatos into service to help illustrate the historicity and political construction of family violence, by imagining how social workers might have responded to the Amatos differently in different periods. A summary of these changes produces a rough periodization of the history of family violence:

1. The late nineteenth century, approximately 1875–1910, when family violence agencies were part of the general charity organization and moral reform movement, influenced by feminism.

2. The Progressive era and its aftermath, approximately 1910–1930, when family violence work was incorporated into professional social work and a reform program relying heavily on state regulation.
3. The Depression, when intrafamily violence was radically deemphasized in favor of amelioration of economic hardship.
4. The 1940s and 1950s, when psychiatric categories and intensely "pro-family" values dominated the social work approach to family problems.
5. The 1960s and 1970s, when feminist and youth movements began a critique of the family which forced open the doors of closets that hid family problems.

This chronology is schematic, not only because the transitions between different periods were gradual and the boundaries blurred, but also because the histories of the four types of family violence with which this [work] is concerned were different. . . .

[M]y premise is that family violence is a problem inseparable from the family norms of a whole society or from the overall political conflicts in that society. It is a changing historical and cultural issue, not a biological or sociobiological universal. As a public issue, family violence has been a virtual lightning rod for different social and political perspectives. Born as a social problem in an era of a powerful women's rights movement, the 1870s, campaigns against child abuse and wife-beating have tended to lose momentum and support, even to disappear altogether, when feminist influence is in decline. In such periods family togetherness is often sought at the expense of individual rights and by ignoring intrafamily problems, rather than by exposing and attacking them. Alternatively, in periods without much feminist influence family-violence problems are redefined in ways less threatening to myths of the harmony of the normative family.

Reading 4

The Life Course Revolution

Arlene Skolnick

Many of us, in moments of nostalgia, imagine the past as a kind of Disneyland—a quaint setting we might step back into with our sense of ourselves intact, yet free of the stresses of modern life. But in yearning for the golden past we imagine we have lost, we are unaware of what we have escaped.

In our time, for example, dying before reaching old age has become a rare event; about three-quarters of all people die after their sixty-fifth birthday. It is hard for us to appreciate what a novelty this is in human experience. In 1850, only 2 percent of the population lived past sixty-five. "We place dying in what we take to be its logical position," observes the social historian Ronald Blythe, "which is at the close of a long life, whereas our ancestors accepted the futility of placing it in any position at all. In the midst of life we are in death, they said, and they meant it. To them it was a fact; to us it is a metaphor.

This longevity revolution is largely a twentieth-century phenomenon. Astonishingly, two-thirds of the total increase in human longevity since prehistoric times has taken place since 1900—and a good deal of that increase has occurred in recent decades. Mortality rates in previous centuries were several times higher than today, and death commonly struck at any age. Infancy was particularly hazardous; "it took two babies to make one adult," as one demographer put it. A white baby girl today has a greater chance of living to be sixty than her counterpart born in 1870 would have had of reaching her first birthday. And after infancy, death still hovered as an ever-present possibility. It was not unusual for young and middle-aged adults to die of tuberculosis, pneumonia, or other infectious diseases. (Keats died at twenty-five, Schubert at thirty-one, Mozart at thirty-five.)

These simple changes in mortality have had profound, yet little-appreciated effects on family life; they have encouraged stronger emotional bonds between parents and children, lengthened the duration of marriage and parent-child rela-

---

tionships, made grandparenthood an expectable stage of the life course, and increased the number of grandparents whom children actually know. More and more families have four or even five generations alive at the same time. And for the first time in history, the average couple has more parents living than it has children. It is also the first era when most of the parent-child relationship takes place after the child becomes an adult.

In a paper entitled "Death and the Family," the demographer Peter Uhlenberg has examined some of these repercussions by contrasting conditions in 1900 with those in 1976. In 1900, for example, half of all parents would have experienced the death of a child; by 1976 only 6 percent would. And more than half of all children who lived to the age of fifteen in 1900 would have experienced the death of a parent or sibling, compared with less than 9 percent in 1976. Another outcome of the lower death rates was a decline in the number of orphans and orphanages. Current discussions of divorce rarely take into account the almost constant family disruption children experienced in "the good old days." In 1900, 1 out of 4 children under the age of fifteen lost a parent; 1 out of 62 lost both. The corresponding figures for 1976 are, respectively, 1 out of 20 and 1 out of 1,800.

Because being orphaned used to be so common, the chances of a child's not living with either parent was much greater at the turn of the centruy than it is now. Indeed, some of the current growth in single-parent families is offset by a decline in the number of children raised in institutions, in foster homes, or by relatives. This fact does not diminish the stresses of divorce and other serious family problems of today, but it does help correct the tendency to contrast the terrible Present with an idealized Past.

Today's children rarely experience the death of a close relative, except for elderly grandparents. And it is possible to grow into adulthood without experiencing even that loss. "We never had any deaths in my family," a friend recently told me, explaining that none of her relatives had died until she was in her twenties. In earlier times, children were made aware of the constant possibility of death, attended deathbed scenes, and were even encouraged to examine the decaying corpses of family members.

One psychological result of our escape from the daily presence of death is that we are ill prepared for it when it comes. For most of us, the first time we feel a heightened concern with our own mortality is in our thirties and forties when we realize that the years we have already lived outnumber those we have left.

Another result is that the death of a child is no longer a sad but normal hazard of parenthood. Rather, it has become a devastating, life-shattering loss from which a parent may never fully recover. The intense emotional bonding between parents and infants that we see as a sociobiological given did not become the norm until the eighteenth and nineteenth centuries. The privileged classes created the concept of the "emotionally priceless" child, a powerful ideal that gradually filtered down through the rest of society.

The high infant mortality rates of premodern times was partly due to neglect, and often to lethal child-rearing practices such as sending infants off to a wet nurse° or, worse, infanticide. It now appears that in all societies lacking reliable contraception, the careless treatment and neglect of unwanted children acted as a major form of birth control. This does not necessarily imply that parents were uncaring toward all their children; rather, they seem to have practiced "selective neglect" of sickly infants in favor of sturdy ones, or of later children in favor of earlier ones.† In 1801 a writer observed of Bavarian peasants:

> The peasant has joy when his wife brings forth the first fruit of their love, he has joy with the second and third as well, but not with the fourth. . . . He sees all children coming thereafter as hostile creatures, which take the bread from his mouth and the mouths of his family. Even the heart of the most gentle mother becomes cold with the birth of the fifth child, and the sixth, she unashamedly wishes death, that the child should pass to heaven.

Declining fertility rates are another major result of falling death rates. Until the baby boom of the 1940s and 1950s, fertility rates had been dropping continuously since the eighteenth century. By taking away parents' fear that some of their children would not survive to adulthood, lowered early-childhood mortality rates encouraged careful planning of births and smaller families. The combination of longer lives and fewer, more closely spaced children created a still-lengthening empty-nest stage in the family. This in turn has encouraged the companionate style of marriage, since husband and wife can expect to live together for many years after their children have moved out.

Many demographers have suggested that falling mortality rates are directly linked to rising divorce rates. In 1891 W.F. Willcox of Cornell University made one of the most accurate social science predictions ever. Looking at the high and steadily rising divorce rates of the time, along with falling mortality rates, he predicted that around 1980, the two curves would cross and the number of marriages ended by divorce would equal those ended by death. In the late 1970s, it all happened as Willcox had predicted. Then divorce rates continued to increase before leveling off in the 1980s, while mortality rates continued to decline. As a result, a

---

°Wet-nursing—the breastfeeding of an infant by a woman other than the mother—was widely practiced in premodern Europe and colonial America. Writing of a two-thousand-year-old "war of the breast," the developmental psychologist Willliam Kessen notes that the most persistent theme in the history of childhood is the reluctance of mothers to suckle their babies, and the urgings of philosophers and physicians that they do so. Infants were typically sent away from home for a year and a half or two years to be raised by poor country women, in squalid conditions. When they took in more babies than they had milk enough to suckle, the babies would die of malnutrition.

The reluctance to breast-feed may not have reflected maternal indifference so much as other demands in premodern, precontraceptive times—the need to take part in the family economy, the unwillingness of husbands to abstain from sex for a year and a half or two. (Her milk would dry up if a mother became pregnant.) Although in France and elsewhere the custom persisted into the twentieth century, large-scale wet-nursing symbolizes the gulf between modern and premodern sensibilities about infants and their care.

†The anthropoligist Nancy Scheper-Hughes describes how impoverished mothers in northeastern Brazil select which infants to nurture.

couple marrying today is more likely to celebrate a fortieth wedding anniversary than were couples around the turn of the century.

In statistical terms, then, it looks as if divorce has restored a level of instability to marriage that had existed earlier due to the high mortality rate. But as Lawrence Stone observes, "it would be rash to claim that the psychological effects of the termination of marriage by divorce, that is by an act of will, bear a close resemblance to its termination by the inexorable accident of death."

THE NEW STAGES OF LIFE

In recent years it has become clear that the stages of life we usually think of as built into human development are, to a large degree, social and cultural inventions. Although people everywhere may pass through infancy, childhood, adulthood, and old age, the facts of nature are "doctored," as Ruth Benedict once put it, in different ways by different cultures.

The Favorite Age

In 1962 Phillipe Ariès made the startling claim that "in medieval society, the idea of childhood did not exist." Ariès argued not that parents then neglected their children, but that they did not think of children as having a special nature that required special treatment; after the age of around five to seven, children simply joined the adult world of work and play. This "small adult" conception of childhood has been observed by many anthropologists in preindustrial societies. In Europe, according to Ariès and others, childhood was discovered, or invented, in the seventeenth and nineteenth centuries, with the emergence of the private, domestic, companionate family and formal schooling. These institutions created distinct roles for children, enabling childhood to emerge as a distinct stage of life.

Despite challenges to Ariès's work, the bulk of historical and cross-cultural evidence supports the contention that childhood as we know it today is a relatively recent cultural invention; our ideas about children, child-rearing practices, and the conditions of children's lives are dramatically different from those of earlier centuries. The same is true of adolescence. Teenagers, such a conspicuous and noisy presence in modern life, and their stage of life, known for its turmoil and soul searching, are not universal features of life in other times and places.

Of course, the physical changes of puberty—sexual maturation and spurt in growth—happen to everyone everywhere. Yet, even here, there is cultural and historical variation. In the past hundred years, the age of first menstruation has declined from the mid-teens to twelve, and the age young men reach their full height has declined from twenty-five to under twenty. Both changes are believed to be due to improvements in nutrition and health care, and these average ages are not expected to continue dropping.

Some societies have puberty rites, but they bring about a transition from childhood not to adolescence but to adulthood. Other societies take no note at all of the changes, and the transition from childhood to adulthood takes place simply and without social recognition. Adolescence as we know it today appears to have evolved late in the nineteenth century; there is virtual consensus among social scientists that it is "a creature of the industrial revolution and it continues to be shaped by the forces which defined that revolution: industrialization, specialization, urbanization . . . and bureaucratization of human organizations and institutions, and continuing technological development."

In America before the second half of the nineteenth century, youth was an ill-defined category. Puberty did not mark any new status or life experience. For the majority of young people who lived on farms, work life began early, at seven or eight years old or even younger. As they grew older, their responsibility would increase, and they would gradually move toward maturity. Adults were not ignorant of the differences between children and adults, but distinctions of age meant relatively little. As had been the practice in Europe, young people could be sent away to become apprentices or servants in other households. As late as the early years of this century, working-class children went to work at the age of ten or twelve.

A second condition leading to a distinct stage of adolescence was the founding of mass education systems, particularly the large public high school. Compulsory education helped define adolescence by setting a precise age for it; high schools brought large numbers of teenagers together to create their own society for a good part of their daily lives. So the complete set of conditions for adolescence on a mass scale did not exist until the end of the nineteenth century.

The changed family situations of late-nineteenth- and early-twentieth-century youth also helped make this life stage more psychologically problematic. Along with the increasing array of options to choose from, rapid social change was making one generation's experience increasingly different from that of the next. Among the immigrants who were flooding into the country at around the time adolescence was emerging, the generation gap was particularly acute. But no parents were immune to the rapid shifts in society and culture that were transforming America in the decades around the turn of the century.

Further, the structure and emotional atmosphere of middle-class family life was changing also, creating a more intimate and emotionally intense family life. Contrary to the view that industrialization had weakened parent-child relations, the evidence is that family ties between parents and adolescents intensified at this time: adolsecents lived at home until they married, and depended more completely, and for a longer time, on their parents than in the past. Demographic change had cut family size in half over the course of the century. Mothers were encouraged to devote themselves to the careful nurturing of fewer children.

This more intensive family life seems likely to have increased the emotional strain of adolescence. Smaller households and a more nurturing style of child rearing, combined with the increased contact between parents, especially mothers, and adolescent children, may have created a kind of " 'Oedipal family' in middle class America."

The young person's awakening sexuality, particularly the young male's is likely to have been more disturbing to both himself and his parents than during the era when young men commonly lived away from home. . . . There is evidence that during the Victorian era, fears of adolescent male sexuality, and of masturbation in particular, were remarkably intense and widespread.

Family conflict in general may have been intensified by the peculiar combination of teenagers' increased dependence on parents and increased autonomy in making their own life choices. Despite its tensions, the new emotionally intense middle-class home made it more difficult than ever for adolescents to leave home for the heartless, indifferent world outside.

By the end of the nineteenth century, conceptions of adolescence took on modern form, and by the first decades of the twentieth century, *adolescence* had become a household word. As articulated forcefully by the psychologist G. Stanley Hall in his 1904 treatise, adolescence was a biological process—not simply the onset of sexual maturity but a turbulent, transitional stage in the evolution of the human species: "some ancient period of storm and stress when old moorings were broken and a higher level attained."

Hall seemed to provide the answers to questions people were asking about the troublesome young. His public influence eventually faded, but his conception of adolescence as a time of storm and stress lived on. Adolescence continued to be seen as a period of both great promise and great peril: "every step of the upward way is strewn with the wreckage of body, mind and morals." The youth problem— whether the lower-class problem of delinquency, or the identity crises and other psychological problems of middle-class youth—has continued to haunt America, and other modern societies, ever since.

Ironically, then, the institutions that had developed to organize and control a problematic age ended by heightening adolescent self-awareness, isolating youth from the rest of society, and creating a youth culture, making the transition to adulthood still more problematic and risky. Institutional recognition in turn made adolescents a more distinct part of the population, and being adolescent a more distinct and self-conscious experience. As it became part of the social structure of modern society, adolescence also became an important stage of the individual's biography—an indeterminate period of being neither child nor adult that created its own problems. Any society that excludes youth from adult work, and offers them what Erikson calls a "moratorium"—time and space to try out identities and lifestyles—and at the same time demands extended schooling as the route to success is likely to turn adolescence into a "struggle for self." It is also likely to run the risk of increasing numbers of mixed-up, rebellious youth.

But, in fact, the classic picture of adolescent storm and stress is not universal. Studies of adolescents in America and other industrialized societies suggest that extreme rebellion and rejection of parents, flamboyant behavior, and psychological turmoil do not describe most adolescents, even today. Media images of the youth of the 1980s and 1990s as a deeply troubled, lost generation beset by crime, drug abuse, and teenage pregnancy are also largely mistaken.

Although sexual activity and experimenting with drugs and alcohol have become common among middle-class young people, drug use has actually declined in recent years. Disturbing as these practices are for parents and other adults, they apparently do not interfere with normal development for most adolescents. Nevertheless, for a significant minority, sex and drugs add complications to a period of development during which a young person's life can easily go awry—temporarily or for good.

More typically, for most young people, the teen years are marked by mild rebelliousness and moodiness—enough to make it a difficult period for parents, but not one of a profound parent-child generation gap or of deep alienation from conventional values. These ordinary tensions of family living through adolescence are exacerbated in times of rapid social change, when the world adolescents confront is vastly different from the one in which their parents came of age. Always at the forefront of social change, adolescents in industrial societies inevitably bring discomfort to their elders, who "wish to see their children's adolescence as an enactment of the retrospectively distorted memory of their own. . . . But such intergenerational continuity can occur only in the rapidly disappearing isolation of the desert or the rain forest.

If adolescence is a creation of modern culture, that culture has also been shaped by adolescence. Adolescents, with their music, fads, fashions, and conflicts, not only are conspicuous, but reflect a state of mind that often extends beyond the years designated for them. The adolescent mode of experience—accessible to people of any age—is marked by "exploration, becoming, growth, and pain."

Since the nineteenth century, for example, the coming-of-age novel has become a familiar literary genre. Patricia Spacks observes that while Victorian authors looked back at adolescence from the perspective of adulthood, twentieth-century novelists since James Joyce and D.H. Lawrence have become more intensely identified with their young heroes, writing not from a distance but from "deep inside the adolescence experience." The novelist's use of the adolescent to symbolize the artist as romantic outsider mirrors a more general cultural tendency. As Phillipe Ariès observes, "Our society has passed from a period which was ignorant of adolescence to a period in which adolescence is the favorite age. We now want to come to it early and linger in it as long as possible."

The Discovery of Adulthood

Middle age is the latest life stage to be discovered, and the notion of mid-life crisis recapitulates the storm-and-stress conception of adolescence. Over the course of the twentieth century, especially during the years after World War II, a developmental conception of childhood became institutionalized in public thought. Parents took it for granted that children passed through ages, stages, and phases: the terrible twos, the teenage rebel. In recent years the idea of development has been increasingly applied to adults, as new stages of adult life are discovered. Indeed, much of the psychological revolution of recent years—the tendency to look at life through psychological lenses—can be understood in part as the extension of the developmental approach to adulthood.

In 1976 Gail Sheehy's best-selling *Passages* popularized the concept of mid-life crisis. Sheehy argued that every individual must pass through such a watershed, a time when we reevaluate our sense of self, undergo a crisis, and emerge with a new identity. Failure to do so, she warned, can have dire consequences. The book was the most influential popular attempt to apply to adults the ages-and-stages approach to development that had long been applied to children. Ironically, this came about just as historians were raising questions about the universality of those stages.

Despite its popularity, Sheehy's book, and the research she reported in it, have come under increasing criticism. "Is the mid-life crisis, if it exists, more than a warmed-over identity crisis?" asked one review of the research literature on mid-life. In fact, there is little or no evidence for the notion that adults pass through a series of sharply defined stages, or a series of crises that must be resolved before passing from one stage to the next.

Nevertheless, the notion of a mid-life crisis caught on because it reflected shifts in adult experience across the life course. Most people's decisions about marriage and work are no longer irrevocably made at one fateful turning point on the brink of adulthood. The choices made at twenty-one may no longer fit at forty or fifty—the world has changed; parents, children, and spouses have changed; working life has changed. The kind of issue that makes adolescence problematic— the array of choices and the need to fashion a coherent, continuous sense of self in the midst of all this change—recurs throughout adulthood. As a Jules Feiffer cartoon concludes, "Maturity is a phase, but adolescence is forever."

Like the identity crisis of adolescence, the concept of mid-life crisis appears to reflect the experience of the more educated and advantaged. Those with more options in life are more likely to engage in the kind of introspection and reappraisal of previous choices that make up the core of the mid-life crisis. Such people realize that they will never fulfill their earlier dreams, or that they have gotten what they wanted and find they are still not happy. But as the Berkeley longitudinal data show, even in that segment of the population, mid-life crisis is far from the norm. People who have experienced fewer choices in the past, and have fewer options for charting new directions in the future, are less likely to encounter a mid-life crisis. Among middle Americans, life is dominated by making ends meet, coping with everyday events, and managing unexpected crises.

While there may be no fixed series of stages or crises adults must pass through, middle age or mid-life in our time does have some unique features that make it an unsettled time, different from other periods in the life course as well as from mid-life in earlier eras. First, as we saw earlier, middle age is the first period in which most people today confront death, illness, and physical decline. It is also an uneasy age because of the increased importance of sexuality in modern life. Sexuality has come to be seen as the core of our sense of self, and sexual fulfillment as the center of the couple relationship. In mid-life, people confront the decline of their physical attractiveness, if not of their sexuality.

There is more than a passing resemblance between the identity problems of adolescence and the issues that fall under the rubric of "mid-life crisis." In a list of themes recurring in the literature on the experience of identity crisis, particularly in adolescence, the psychologist Roy Baumeister includes: feelings of emptiness, feelings of vagueness, generalized malaise, anxiety, self-consciousness. These symptoms describe not only adolescent and mid-life crises but what Erikson has labeled identity problems—or what has, of late, been considered narcissism.

Consider, for example, Heinz Kohut's description of patients suffering from what he calls narcissistic personality disorders. They come to the analyst with vague symptoms, but eventually focus on feelings about the self—emptiness, vague depression, being drained of energy, having no "zest" for work or anything else, shifts in self-esteem, heightened sensitivity to the opinions and reactions of others, feeling unfulfilled, a sense of uncertainty and purposelessness. "It seems on the face of it," observes the literary critic Steven Marcus, "as if these people are actually suffering from what was once called unhappiness."

The New Aging

Because of the extraordinary revolution in longevity, the proportion of elderly people in modern industrial societies is higher than it has ever been. This little-noticed but profound transformation affects not just the old but families, an individual's life course, and society as a whole. We have no cultural precedents for the mass of the population reaching old age. Further, the meaning of *old age* has changed—indeed, it is a life stage still in process, its boundaries unclear. When he came into office at the age of sixty-four, George Bush did not seem like an old man. Yet when Franklin Roosevelt died at the same age, he did seem to be "old."

President Bush illustrates why gerontologists in recent years have had to revise the meaning of "old." He is a good example of what they have termed the "young old" or the "new elders"; the social historian Peter Laslett uses the term "the third age." Whatever it is called, it represents a new stage of life created by the extension of the life course in industrialized countries. Recent decades have witnessed the first generations of people who live past sixty-five and remain healthy, vigorous, alert, and, mostly due to retirement plans, financially independent. These people are "pioneers on the frontier of age," observed the journalist Frances Fitzgerald, in her study of Sun City, a retirement community near Tampa, Florida, "people for whom society had as yet no set of expectations and no vision."

The meaning of the later stages of life remains unsettled. Just after gerontologists had marked off the "young old"—people who seemed more middle-aged than old—they had to devise a third category, the "oldest old," to describe the fastest-growing group in the population, people over eighty-five. Many if not most of these people are like Tithonus, the mythical figure who asked the gods for eternal life but forgot to ask for eternal youth as well. For them, the gift of long life has come at the cost of chronic disease and disability.

The psychological impact of this unheralded longevity revolution has largely been ignored, except when misconstrued. The fear of age, according to Christopher Lasch, is one of the chief symptoms of this culture's alleged narcissism. But when people expected to die in their forties or fifties, they didn't have to face the problem of aging. Alzheimer's disease, for example, now approaching epidemic proportions, is an ironic by-product of the extension of the average life span. When living to seventy or eighty is a realistic prospect, it makes sense to diet and exercise, to eat healthy foods, and to make other "narcissistic" investments in the self.

Further "the gift of mass longevity," the anthropologist David Plath argues, has been so recent, dramatic, and rapid that it has become profoundly unsettling in all postindustrial societies: "If the essential cultural nightmare of the nineteenth century was to be in poverty, perhaps ours is to be old and alone or afflicted with terminal disease."

Many people thus find themselves in life stages for which cultural scripts have not yet been written; family members face one another in relationships for which tradition provides little guidance. "We are stuck with awkward-sounding terms like 'adult children' and . . . 'grandson-in-law.' " And when cultural rules are ambiguous, emotional relationships can become tense or at least ambivalent.

A study of five-generation families in Germany reveals the confusion and strain that result when children and parents are both in advanced old age—for example, a great-great-grandmother and her daughter, who is herself a great-grandmother. Who has the right to be old? Who should take care of whom? Similarly, Plath, who has studied the problems of mass longevity in Japan, finds that even in that familistic society the traditional meaning of family roles has been put into question by the stretching out of the life span. In the United States, some observers note that people moving into retirement communities sometimes bring their parents to live with them. Said one disappointed retiree: "I want to enjoy my grandchildren; I never expected that when I was a grandparent I'd have to look after my parents."

Reading 5   9\1

The Way We Wish We Were
Stephanie Coontz

When I begin teaching a course on family history, I often ask my students to write down ideas that spring to mind when they think of the "traditional family." Their lists always include several images. One is of extended families in which all members worked together, grandparents were an integral part of family life, children learned responsibility and the work ethic from their elders, and there were clear lines of authority based on respect for age. Another is of nuclear families in which

---

nurturing mothers sheltered children from premature exposure to sex, financial worries, or other adult concerns, while fathers taught adolescents not to sacrifice their education by going to work too early. Still another image gives pride of place to the couple relationship. In traditional families, my students write—half derisively, half wistfully—men and women remained chaste until marriage, at which time they extricated themselves from competing obligations to kin and neighbors and committed themselves wholly to the marital relationship, experiencing an all-encompassing intimacy that our more crowded modern life seems to preclude. As one freshman wrote: "They truly respected the marriage vowels"; I assume she meant I-O-U.

Such visions of past family life exert a powerful emotional pull on most Americans, and with good reason, given the fragility of many modern commitments. The problem is not only that these visions bear a suspicious resemblance to reruns of old television series, but also that the scripts of different shows have been mixed up: June Cleaver suddenly has a Grandpa Walton dispensing advice in her kitchen; Donna Stone, vacuuming the living room in her inevitable pearls and high heels, is no longer married to a busy modern pediatrician but to a small-town sheriff who, like Andy Taylor of "The Andy Griffith Show," solves community problems through informal, old-fashioned common sense.

Like most visions of a "golden age," the "traditional family" my students describe evaporates on closer examination. It is an ahistorical amalgam of structures, values, and behaviors that never coexisted in the same time and place. The notion that traditional families fostered intense intimacy between husbands and wives while creating mothers who were totally available to their children, for example, is an idea that combines some characteristics of the white, middle-class family in the mid-nineteenth century and some of a rival family ideal first articulated in the 1920s. The first family revolved emotionally around the mother-child axis, leaving the husband-wife relationship stilted and formal. The second focused on an eroticized couple relationship, demanding that mothers curb emotional "overinvestment" in their children. The hybrid idea that a woman can be fully absorbed with her youngsters while simultaneously maintaining passionate sexual excitement with her husband was a 1950s invention that drove thousands of women to therapists, tranquilizers, or alcohol when they actually tried to live up to it.

Similarly, an extended family in which all members work together under the top-down authority of the household elder operates very differently from a nuclear family in which husband and wife are envisioned as friends who patiently devise ways to let the children learn by trial and error. Children who worked in family enterprises seldom had time for the extracurricular activities that Wally and the Beaver recounted to their parents over the dinner table; often, they did not even go to school full-time. Mothers who did home production generally relegated child care to older children or servants; they did not suspend work to savor a baby's first steps or discuss with their husband how to facilitate a grade-schooler's "self-esteem." Such families emphasized formality, obedience to authority, and "the way it's always been" in their childrearing.

Nuclear families, by contrast, have tended to pride themselves on the "modernity" of parent-child relations, diluting the authority of grandparents, denigrating "old-fashioned" ideas about childraising, and resisting the "interference" of relatives. It is difficult to imagine the Cleavers or the college-educated title figure of "Father Knows Best" letting grandparents, maiden aunts, or in-laws have a major voice in childrearing decisions. Indeed, the kind of family exemplified by the Cleavers . . . represented a conscious *rejection* of the Waltons' model.

THE ELUSIVE TRADITIONAL FAMILY

Whenever people propose that we go back to the traditional family, I always suggest that they pick a ballpark date for the family they have in mind. Once pinned down, they are invariably unwilling to accept the package deal that comes with their chosen model. Some people, for example, admire the discipline of colonial families, which were certainly not much troubled by divorce or fragmenting individualism. But colonial families were hardly stable: High mortality rates meant that the average length of marriage was less than a dozen years. One-third to one-half of all children lost at least one parent before the age of twenty-one; in the South, more than half of all children aged thirteen or under had lost at least one parent.

While there are a few modern Americans who would like to return to the strict patriarchal authority of colonial days, in which disobedience by women and children was considered a small form of treason, these individuals would doubtless be horrified by other aspects of colonial families, such as their failure to protect children from knowledge of sexuality. Eighteenth-century spelling and grammar books routinely used *fornication* as an example of a four-syllable word, and preachers detailed sexual offenses in astonishingly explicit terms. Sexual conversations between men and women, even in front of children, were remarkably frank. It is worth contrasting this colonial candor to the climate in 1991, when the Department of Health and Human Services was forced to cancel a proposed survey of teenagers' sexual practices after some groups charged that such knowledge might "inadvertently" encourage more sex.

Other people searching for an ideal traditional family might pick the more sentimental and gentle Victorian family, which arose in the 1830s and 1840s as household production gave way to wage work and professional occupations outside the home. A new division of labor by age and sex emerged among the middle class. Women's roles were redefined in terms of domesticity rather than production, men were labeled "breadwinners" (a masculine identity unheard of in colonial days), children were said to need time to play, and gentle maternal guidance supplanted the patriarchal authoritarianism of the past.

But the middle-class Victorian family depended for its existence on the multiplication of other families who were too poor and powerless to retreat into their own little oases and who therefore had to provision the oases of others. Childhood was prolonged for the nineteenth-century middle class only because it was drastically foreshortened for other sectors of the population. The spread of textile mills, for example, freed middleclass women from the most time-consuming of their former chores, making cloth. But the raw materials for these mills were produced by slave labor. Slave children were not exempt from field labor unless they were infants, and even then their mothers were not allowed time off to nurture them. Frederick Douglass could not remember seeing his mother until he was seven.

Domesticity was also not an option for the white families who worked twelve hours a day in Northern factories and workshops transforming slave-picked cotton into ready-made clothing. By 1820, "half the workers in many factories were boys and girls who had not reached their eleventh birthday." Rhode Island investigators found "little half-clothed children" making their way to the textile mills before dawn. In 1845, shoemaking families and makers of artificial flowers worked fifteen to eighteen hours a day, according to the New York *Daily Tribune.*

Within the home, prior to the diffusion of household technology at the end of the century, house cleaning and food preparation remained mammoth tasks. Middle-class women were able to shift more time into childbearing in this period only by hiring domestic help. Between 1800 and 1850, the proportion of servants to white households doubled, to about one in nine. Some servants were poverty-stricken mothers who had to board or bind out their own children. Employers found such workers tended to be "distracted," however; they usually preferred young girls. In his study of Buffalo, New York, in the 1850s, historian Lawrence Glasco found that Irish and German girls often went into service at the age of eleven or twelve.

For every nineteenth-century middle-class family that protected its wife and child within the family circle, then, there was an Irish or a German girl scrubbing floors in that middle-class home, a Welsh boy mining coal to keep the home-baked goodies warm, a black girl doing the family laundry, a black mother and child picking cotton to be made into clothes for the family, and a Jewish or an Italian daughter in a sweatshop making "ladies" dresses or artificial flowers for the family to purchase.

Furthermore, people who lived in these periods were seldom as enamored of their family arrangements as modern nostalgia might suggest. Colonial Americans lamented "the great neglect in many parents and masters in training up their children" and expressed the "greatest trouble and grief about the rising generation." No sooner did Victorian middle-class families begin to withdraw their children from the work world than observers began to worry that children were becoming *too* sheltered. By 1851, the Reverend Horace Bushnell spoke for many in bemoaning the passing of the traditional days of household production, when the whole family was "harnessed, all together, into the producing process, young and old, male and females, from the boy who rode the plough-horse to the grandmother knitting under her spectacles."

The late nineteenth century saw a modest but significant growth of extended families and a substantial increase in the number of families who were "harnessed" together in household production. Extended families have never been the norm in America; the highest figure for extended-family household ever recorded in American history is 20 percent. Contrary to the popular myth that industrialization destroyed "traditional" extended families, this high point occurred between 1850 and 1885, during the most intensive period of early industrialization. Many of these extended families, and most "producing" families of the time, depended on the labor of children; they were held together by dire necessity and sometimes by brute force.

There was a significant increase in child labor during the last third of the nineteenth century. Some children worked at home in crowded tenement sweatshops that produced cigars or women's clothing. Reformer Helen Campbell found one house where "nearly thirty children of all ages and sizes, babies predominating, rolled in the tobacco which covered the floor and was piled in every direction." Many producing households resembled the one described by Mary Van Kleeck of the Russell Sage Foundation in 1913:

> In a tenement on MacDougal Street lives a family of seven—grandmother, father, mother and four children aged four years, three years, two years and one month respectively. All excepting the father and the two babies make violets. The three year old girl picks apart the petals; her sister, aged four years, separates the stems, dipping an end of each into paste spread on a piece of board on the kitchen table; and the mother and grandmother slip the petals up the stems.

Where children worked outside the home, conditions were no better. In 1900, 120,000 children worked in Pennsylvania mines and factories; most of them had started work by age eleven. In Scranton, a third of the girls between the ages of thirteen and sixteen worked in the silk mills in 1904. In New York, Boston, and Chicago, teenagers worked long hours in textile factories and frequently died in fires or industrial accidents. Children made up 23.7 percent of the 36,415 workers in southern textile mills around the turn of the century. When reformer Marie VanVorse took a job at one in 1903, she found children as young as six or seven working twelve-hour shifts. At the end of the day, she reported: "They are usually beyond speech. They fall asleep at the tables, on the stairs; they are carried to bed and there laid down as they are, unwashed, undressed; and the inanimate bundles of rags so lie until the mill summons them with its imperious cry before sunrise."

By the end of the nineteenth century, shocked by the conditions in urban tenements and by the sight of young children working full-time at home or earning money out on the streets, middle-class reformers put aside nostalgia for "harnessed" family production and elevated the antebellum model once more, blaming immigrants for introducing such "un-American" family values as child labor. Reformers advocated adoption of a "true American" family—a restricted, exclusive nuclear unit in which women and children were divorced from the world of work.

In the late 1920s and early 1930s, however, the wheel turned yet again, as social theorists noted the independence and isolation of the nuclear family with renewed anxiety. The influential Chicago School of sociology believed that immigration and urbanization had weakened the traditional family by destroying kinship and community networks. Although sociologists welcomed the increased democracy of "companionate marriage," they worried about the rootless of nuclear families and the breakdown of older solidarities. By the time of the Great Depression, some observers even saw a silver lining in economic hardship, since it revived the economic functions and social importance of kin and family ties. With housing starts down by more than 90 percent, approximately one-sixth of urban families had to "double up" in apartments. The incidence of three-generation households increased, while recreational interactions outside the home were cut back or confined to the kinship network. One newspaper opined: "Many a family that has lost its car has found its soul."

Depression families evoke nostalgia in some contemporary observers, because they tended to create "dependability and domestic inclination" among girls and "maturity in the management of money" among boys. But, in many cases, such responsibility was inseparable from "a corrosive and disabling poverty that shattered the hopes and dreams of . . . young parents and twisted the lives of those who were 'stuck together' in it." Men withdrew from family life or turned violent; women exhausted themselves trying to "take up the slack" both financially and emotionally, or they belittled their husbands as failures; and children gave up their dreams of education to work at dead-end jobs.

From the hardships of the Great Depression and the Second World War and the euphoria of the postwar economic recovery came a new kind of family ideal that still enters our homes in "Leave It to Beaver" and "Donna Reed" reruns. . . . [T]he 1950s were no more a "golden age" of the family than any other period in American history. . . . [O]ur recurring search for a traditional family model denies the diversity of family life, both past and present, and leads to false generalizations about the past as well as wildly exaggerated claims about the present and the future.

THE COMPLEXITIES OF ASSESSING FAMILY TRENDS

If it is hard to find a satisfactory model of the traditional family, it is also hard to make global judgments about how families have changed and whether they are getting better or worse. Some generalizations about the past are pure myth. Whatever the merit of recurring complaints about the "rootlessness" of modern life, for instance, families are *not* more mobile and transient than they used to be. In most nineteenth-century cities, both large and small, more than 50 percent—and often up to 75 percent—of the residents in any given year were no longer there ten years later. People born in the twentieth century are much more likely to live near their birthplace than were people born in the nineteenth century.

This is not to say, of course, that mobility did not have different effects then than it does now. In the nineteenth century, claims historian Thomas Bender, people moved from community to community, taking advantage . . . of nonfamilial networks and institutions that integrated them into new work and social relations. In the late twentieth century, people move from job to job, following a career path that shuffles them from one single-family home to another and does not link them to neighborly networks beyond the family. But this change is in our community ties, not in our family ones.

A related myth is that modern Americans have lost touch with extended-kinship networks or have let parent-child bonds lapse. In fact, more Americans than ever before have grandparents alive, and there is good evidence that ties between grandparents and grandchildren have become stronger over the past fifty years. In the late 1970s, researchers returned to the "Middletown" studied by sociologists Robert and Helen Lynd in the 1920s and found that most people there maintained closer extended-family networks than in earlier times. There had been some decline in the family's control over the daily lives of youth, especially females, but "the expressive/emotional function of the family" was "more important for Middletown students of 1977 than it was in 1924." More recent research shows that visits with relatives did *not* decline between the 1950s and the late 1980s.

Today 54 percent of adults see a parent, and 68 percent talk on the phone with a parent, at least once a week. Fully 90 percent of Americans describe their relationship with their mother as close, and 78 percent say their relationship with their grandparents is close. And for all the family disruption of divorce, most modern children live with at least *one* parent. As late as 1940, 10 percent of American children did not live with either parent, compared to only one in twenty-five today.

What about the supposed eclipse of marriage? Neither the rising age of those who marry nor the frequency of divorce necessarily means that marriage is becoming a less prominent institution than it was in earlier days. Ninety percent of men and women eventually marry, more than 70 percent of divorced men and women remarry, and fewer people remain single for their entire lives today than at the turn of the century. One author even suggests that the availability of divorce in the second half of the twentieth century has allowed some women to try marriage who would formerly have remained single all their lives. Others argue that the rate of hidden marital separation in the late nineteenth century was not much less than the rate of visible separation today.

Studies of marital satisfaction reveal that more couples reported their marriages to be happy in the late 1970s than did so in 1957, while couples in their second marriages believe them to be much happier than their first ones. Some commentators conclude that marriage is becoming less permanent but more satisfying. Others wonder, however, whether there is a vicious circle in our country, where no one even tries to sustain a relationship. Between the late 1970s and late 1980s, moreoever, reported marital happiness did decline slightly in the United States. Some authors see this as reflecting our decreasing appreciation of marriage, although others suggest that it reflects unrealistically high expectations of love in a culture that denies people safe, culturally approved ways of getting used to marriage or cultivating other relationships to meet some of the needs that we currently load onto the couple alone.

Part of the problem in making simple generalizations about what is happening to marriage is that there has been a polarization of experiences. Marriages are much more likely to be ended by divorce today, but marriages that do last are described by their participants as happier than those in the past and are far more likely to confer such happiness over many years. It is important to remember that the 50 percent divorce rate estimates are calculates in terms of a forty-year period and that many marriages in the past were terminated well before that date by the death of one partner. Historian Lawrence Stone suggests that divorce has become "a functional substitute for death" in the modern world. At the end of the 1970s, the rise in divorce rates seemed to overtake the fall in death rates, but the slight decline in divorce rates since then means that "a couple marrying today is more likely to celebrate a fortieth wedding anniversary than were couples around the turn of the century."

A similar polarization allows some observers to argue that fathers are deserting their children, while others celebrate the new commitment of fathers to childrearing. Both viewpoints are right. Sociologist Frank Furstenberg comments on the emergence of a "good dad–bad dad complex": Many fathers spend more time with their children than ever before and feel more free to be affectionate with them; others, however, feel more free simply to walk out on their families. According to 1981 statistics, 42 percent of the children whose father had left the marriage had not seen him in the past year. Yet studies show steadily increasing involvement of fathers with their children as long as they are in the home.

These kinds of ambiguities should make us leery of hard-and-fast pronouncements about what's happening to the American family. In many cases, we simply don't know precisely what our figures actually mean. For example, the proportion of youngsters receiving psychological assistance rose by 80 percent between 1981 and 1988. Does that mean they are getting more sick or receiving more help, or is it some complex combination of the two? Child abuse reports increased by 225 percent between 1976 and 1987. Does this represent an actual increase in rates of abuse or a heightened consciousness about the problem? During the same period, parents' self-reports about very severe violence toward their children declined 47 percent. Does this represent a real improvement in their behavior or a decreasing willingness to admit to such acts?

Assessing the direction of family change is further complicated because many contemporary trends represent a reversal of developments that were themselves rather recent. The expectation that the family should be the main source of personal fulfillment, for example, was not traditional in the eighteenth and nineteenth centuries. . . . Prior to the 1900s, the family festivities that now fill us with such nostalgia for "the good old days" (and cause such heartbreak when they go poorly) were "relatively undeveloped." Civic festivals and Fourth of July parades were more important occasions for celebration and strong emotion than family holidays, such as Thanksgiving. Christmas "seems to have been more a time for attending parties and dances than for celebrating family solidarity." Only in the twentieth century did the family come to be the center of festive attention and emotional intensity.

Today, such emotional investment in the family may be waning again. This could be interpreted as a reestablishment of balance between family life and other social ties; on the other hand, such a trend may have different results today than in earlier times, because in many cases the extrafamilial institutions and customs that used to socialize individuals and provide them with a range of emotional alternatives to family life no longer exist.

In other cases, analysis of statistics showing a deterioration in family well-being supposedly caused by abandonment of tradition suggests a more complicated train of events. Children's health, for example, improved dramatically in the 1960s and 1970s, a period of extensive family transformation. It ceased to improve, and even slid backward, in the 1980s, when innovative social programs designed to relieve families of some "traditional" responsibilities were repealed. While infant mortality rates fell by 4.7 percent a year during the 1970s, the rate of decline decreased in the 1980s, and in both 1988 and 1989, infant mortality rates did not show a statistically significant decline. Similarly, the proportion of low-birth-weight babies fell during the 1970s but stayed steady during the 1980s and had even increased slightly as of 1988. Child poverty is lower today than it was in the "traditional" 1950s but much higher than it was in the nontraditional late 1960s.

WILD CLAIMS AND PHONY FORECASTS

Lack of perspective on where families have come from and how their evolution connects to other social trends tends to encourage contradictory claims and wild exaggerations about where families are going. One category of generalizations seems to be a product of wishful thinking. As of 1988, nearly half of all families with children had both parents in the work force. The two-parent family in which only the father worked for wages represented just 25 percent of all families with children, down from 44 percent in 1975. For people overwhelmed by the difficulties of adjusting work and schools to the realities of working moms, it has been tempting to discern a "return to tradition" and hope the problems will go away. Thus in 1991, we saw a flurry of media reports that the number of women in the work force was headed down: "More Choose to Stay Home with Children" proclaimed the headlines; "More Women Opting for Chance to Watch Their Children Grow."

The cause of all this commotion? The percentage of women aged twenty-five to thirty-four who were employed dropped from 74 percent to 72.8 percent between January 1990 and January 1991. However, there was an exactly equal decline in the percentage of men in the work force during the same period, and for both genders the explanation was the same. "The dip is the recession," explained Judy Waldrop, research editor at *American Demographics* magazine, to anyone who bothered to listen. In fact, the proportion of *mothers* who worked increased slightly during the same period.

This is not to say that parents, especially mothers, are happy with the pressures of balancing work and family life. Poll after poll reveals that both men and women feel starved for time. The percentage of women who say they would prefer to stay home with their children if they could afford to do so rose from 33 percent in 1986 to 56 percent in 1990. Other polls show that even larger majorities of women would trade a day's pay for an extra day off. But, above all, what these polls reveal is women's growing dissatisfaction with the failure of employers, schools, and government to pioneer arrangements that make it possible to combine work and family life. They do not suggest that women are actually going to stop working, or that this would be women's preferred solution to their stresses. The polls did not ask, for example, how *long* women would like to take off work, and failed to take account of the large majority of mothers who report that they would miss their work if they did manage to take time off. Working mothers are here to stay, and we will not meet the challenge this poses for family life by inventing an imaginary trend to define the problem out of existence.

At another extreme is the kind of generalization that taps into our worst fears. One example of this is found in the almost daily reporting of cases of child moles-tation or kidnapping by sexual predators. The highlighting of such cases, drawn from every corner of the country, helps disguise how rare these cases actually are when compared to crimes committed within the family.

A well-publicized instance of the cataclysmic predictions that get made when family trends are taken out of historical context is the famous *Newsweek* contention that a single woman of forty has a better chance of being killed by a terrorist than of finding a husband. It is true that the proportion of never-married women under age forty has increased substantially since the 1950s, but it is also true that the proportion has *decreased* dramatically among women over that age. A woman over thirty-five has a *better* change to marry today than she did in the 1950s. In the past twelve years, first-time marriages have increased almost 40 percent for women aged thirty-five to thirty-nine. A single woman aged forty to forty-four still has a 24 percent probability of marriage, while 15 percent of women in their late forties will marry. These figures would undoubtedly be higher if many women over forty did not simply pass up opportunities that a more desperate generation might have snatched.

Yet another example of the exaggeration that pervades many analyses of modern families is the widely quoted contention that "parents today spend 40 percent less time with their children than did parents in 1965." Again, of course, part of the problem is where researchers are measuring from. A comparative study of Muncie, Indiana, for example, found that parents spent much more time with their children in the mid-1970s than did parents in the mid-1920s. But another problem is keeping the categories consistent. Trying to track down the source of the 40 percent decline figure, I called demographer John P. Robinson, whose studies on time formed the basis of this claim. Robinson's data, however, show that parents today spend about the same amount of time caring for children as they did in 1965. If the total amount of time devoted to children is less, he suggested, I might want to check how many fewer children there are today. In 1970, the average family had 1.34 children under the age of eighteen; in 1990, the average family had only .96 children under age eighteen—a decrease of 28.4 percent. In other words, most of the decline in the total amount of time parents spend with children is because of the decline in the number of children they have to spend time with!

Now I am not trying to say that the residual amount of decrease is not serious, or that it may not become worse, given the trends in women's employment. Robinson's data show that working mothers spend substantially less time in primary child-care activities than do nonemployed mothers (though they also tend to have fewer children); more than 40 percent of working mothers report feeling "trapped" by their daily routines; many routinely sacrifice sleep in order to meet the demands of work and family. Even so, a majority believe they are *not* giving enough time to their children. It is also true that children may benefit merely from having their parents available, even though the parents may not be spending time with them.

But there is no reason to assume the worst. Americans have actually gained free time since 1965, despite an increase in work hours, largely as a result of a decline in housework and an increasing tendency to fit some personal requirements and errands into the work day. And according to a recent Gallup poll, most modern mothers think they are doing a better job of communicating with their children (though a worse job of house cleaning) than did their own mothers and that they put a higher value on spending time with their family than did their mothers. . . .

NEGOTIATING THROUGH THE EXTREMES

Most people react to these conflicting claims and contradictory trends with understandable confusion. They know that family ties remain central to their own lives, but they are constantly hearing about people who seem to have *no* family feeling. Thus, at the same time as Americans report high levels of satisfaction with their *own* families, they express a pervasive fear that other people's families are falling apart.

In a typical recent poll, for example, 71 percent of respondents said they were "very satisfied" with their own family life, but more than half rated the overall quality of family life as negative: "I'm okay; you're not."

This seemingly schizophrenic approach does not reflect an essentially intolerant attitude. People worry about families, and to the extent that they associate modern social ills with changes in family life, they are ambivalent about innovations. Voters often defeat measures to grant unmarried couples, whether heterosexual or homosexual, the same rights as married ones. In polls, however, most Americans support tolerance for gay and lesbian relationships. Although two-thirds of respondents to one national poll said they wanted "more traditional standards of family life," the same percentage rejected the idea that "women should return to their traditional role." Still larger majorities support women's right to work, including their right to use child care, even when they worry about relying on day-care centers too much. In a 1990 *Newsweek* poll, 42 percent predicted that the family would be worse in ten years and exactly the same percentage predicted that it would be better. Although 87 percent of people polled in 1987 said they had "old-fashioned ideas about family and marriage," only 22 percent of the people polled in 1989 defined a family solely in terms of blood, marriage, or adoption. Seventy-four percent declared, instead, that family is any group whose members love and care for one another.

These conflicted responses do not mean that people are hopelessly confused. Instead, they reflect people's gut-level understanding that the "crisis of the family" is more complex than is often asserted by political demagogues or others with an ax to grind. In popular commentary the received wisdom is to "keep it simple." I know one television reporter who refuses to air an interview with anyone who uses the phrase "on the other hand." But my experience in discussing these issues with both the general public and specialists in the field is that people are hungry to get beyond oversimplifications. They don't want to be told that everything is fine in families or that if the economy improved and the government mandated parental leave, everything would be fine. But they don't believe that every hard-won victory for women's rights and personal liberty has been destructive of social bonds and that the only way to find a sense of community is to go back to some sketchily defined "traditional" family that clearly involves denying the validity of any alternative familial and personal choices.

Americans understand that along with welcome changes have come difficult new problems; uneasy with simplistic answers, they are willing to consider more nuanced analyses of family gains and losses during the past few decades. Indeed, argues political reporter E. J. Dionne, they are *desperate* to engage in such analyses. Few Americans are satisfied with liberal and feminist accounts that blame all modern family dilemmas on structural inequalities, ignoring the moral crisis of commitment and obligation in our society. Yet neither are they convinced that "in the final analysis," as David Blankenhorn of the Institute for American Values puts it, "the problem is not the system. The problem is us."

Despite humane intentions, an overemphasis on personal responsibility for strengthening family values encourages a way of thinking that leads to moralizing rather than mobilizing for concrete reforms. While values are important to Americans, most do not support the sort of scapegoating that occurs when all family problems are blamed on "bad values." Most of us are painfully aware that there is no clear way of separating "family values" from "the system." Our values may make a difference in the way we respond to the challenges posed by economic and political institutions, but those institutions also reinforce certain values and extinguish others. The problem is not to berate people for abandoning past family values, nor to exhort them to adopt better values in the future—the problem is to build the institutions and social support networks that allow people to act on their best values rather than on their worst ones. We need to get past abstract nostalgia for traditional family values and develop a clearer sense of how past families actually worked and what the different consequences of various family behaviors and values have been. Good history and responsible social policy should help people incorporate the full complexity and the tradeoffs of family change into their analyses and thus into action. Mythmaking does not accomplish this end.

Chapter
2

Contemporary Trends

Reading 6

Overwork in the Household

Juliet Schor

As a society we have been loathe to acknowledge the chronic overwork that plagues the American household, preferring to romanticize the role of housewife and mother. Yet the shortage of time is not merely a problem of our paying jobs—we spend just as much time working in the home as we do outside of it. Houses, yards, and children devour our time, seemingly without limit. For many with two jobs—so-called working mothers—the burden is enormous. In addition to the forty-plus hours of work a week a full-time woman employee puts in on the job, different studies estimate that she does anywhere from twenty-five to forty-five hours in the home.

All this household work often seems unavoidable, like death and taxes. Children have to be cared for, and food needs to be cooked. When attention is directed to the time squeeze, it is rarely suggested that we should curtail household work. The message is that we need time so we can do *more* at home. And perhaps we do—at least with existing methods for taking care of home and family. But we need to consider the possibility that we have gotten locked into a household technology and a culture of domestic work that are more inefficient, time consuming, and onerous than they need to be.

The long hours of the housewife have a variety of causes. One is the continual upgrading of standards of performance. A second is that commerical alternatives to private provision were stymied at an early stage of development. A third is that since housework was never professionalized, it has not benefited from specialization. Underlying each of these was a common economic factor: the low cost of the housewife's labor. Because married women were largely excluded from the labor force, the incentives to conserve their labor were blunted. Instead, a powerful bias toward using up their time developed. This led, quite naturally, to higher expectations regarding household services and to an artificial inflation of the costs of commercial alternatives and professionalization, in comparison with the do-it-at-home solution. Although in recent years household hours have begun to fall, progress has been hampered by a culture and a technology of domestic labor that is far more difficult, labor-intensive, and inefficient than it needs to be.

By looking at domestic labor in economic terms—such as the "cost" of a housewife and the "efficiency" of home technologies—we can better see the economic structures that have determined how we feed ourselves, clean our houses, and even raise our children. Yet the household has traditionally been out of the purview of economics, being rather the domain of sociology and anthropology. We have preferred to think of our private lives as exempt from those factors that rule the market. We have also avoided putting into the same category what we do in our jobs and what we do at home. Domestic activity has been excluded from the realm of labor. As any woman can attest, the query, "Do you work?" is meant to distinguish between those who are employed in the market economy, and those whose labors are confined to the home. The expected answer of the housewife to this question would typically be "No"—at least until recently, when the feminist movement has attempted to overcome her economic invisibility.

This was not always so. In the colonial period, women's household activities were not devalued by being denied the status of work. Economist Nancy Folbre notes: "In 1800, women whose work consisted largely in caring for their families without pay were widely considered productive workers. By 1900, however, they had been formally relegated to the census category of 'dependents' that included infants, young children, the sick, and elderly." The dominant discourse characterized women as "supported" by their husbands.

The official statistics measuring the yearly flow of production and income embody this sexist bias as well. As virtually every introductory economics textbook points out in its opening chapter, if a man marries his housekeeper, the gross national product will fall. The paid labor of the housekeeper is replaced by the unmarketed services of the wife, and the country looks to be poorer as a result. The reality is that the actual work being performed may well be identical, and the reduction in GNP is a statistical artifact. At this point, the textbook writer moves on and never looks back. So, too, have most economists, who have chosen the trivial method of identifying work with income-generating activity and shunned the household as "uneconomic."

If we care to look, we can see that the American household really is an economic institution. Food preparation, child rearing, laundry services, house cleaning, the transportation of people, care of the sick and elderly, the acquisition of

goods and services (shopping), gardening and lawn care, home and car maintenance and repair, and financial accounting are all services typically produced in
American homes. Perhaps the most convincing argument that these are economic
activities—real and valuable work—is the fact that as the paid employment of
women grows, and with it family income, more and more of these services are
purchased in the market. Children are placed in day-care centers. Meals are eaten
in restaurants. Shirts are sent to the laundry. Those who can afford it hire cleaning
help, accountants, car mechanics, gardeners, and people to paint their houses.

Of course, there are big differences between household labor and the experience of being "on the job." The two do not share the same structures of pay, ac-
countability, control, or technology. Many people will (and have) protested that
taking care of children is not work, but a meaningful and pleasurable part of life. So
it is. But the fact that we can enjoy our labor or find it satisfying does not mean that
it is not work. If we consider the differences between a corporate executive and an
orchestra conductor (highly satisfied occupational groups) and the lowly counter-
person in a fast-food establishment, it is obvious that the world of "real work"
is characterized by differences equally profound as those separating home and
market.

THE CONSTANCY OF HOUSEWIVES' HOURS

The twentieth century radically transformed America. We went from the horse
and buggy to the Concorde, from farm to city and then to suburb, from silent
movies to VCRs. Throughout all these changes, one thing stayed constant: the
amount of work done by the American housewife. In the 1910s, she was doing
about fifty-two hours a week. Fifty or sixty years later, the figure wasn't much
different.

This conclusion comes from a set of studies recording the daily activities of
full-time housewives. The first was carried out in 1912–14 by a Ph.D. candidate at
Columbia University named John Leeds. Leeds surveyed a group of sixty middle-
class families, with employed husbands, full-time homemakers, and an average of
2.75 children. After watching the routine of the housewives in this group, Leeds
found that they spent an average of fifty-six hours each week at their work. This
number is actually slightly higher than most subsequent findings, but the difference appears not to be meaningful and is attributable to some peculiarities of
Leeds's families.

Over the next few decades, many more housewives were surveyed under the
auspices of the U.S. Bureau of Home Economics. Another Ph.D. candidate, Joann
Vanek from the University of Michigan, compiled the results of these surveys, all
of which followed a common set of guidelines. Vanek found that in 1926–27, and
again in 1929, housewives were putting in about fifty-two hours. The strange thing
is that in 1936, 1943, and 1953, years of additional studies, the findings were un-
changed. The housewife was still logging in fifty-two hours. In the 1960s and
1970s, more surveys were undertaken. A large one in Syracuse, New York, in 1967
and 1968 found that housewives averaged fifty-six hours per week. And according

to my own estimates, from 1973, a married, middle-class housewife with three children did an average of fifty-three hours of domestic work each week (see Figure 1).

The odd thing about the constancy of hours is that it coincided with a technological revolution in the household. When the early studies were done, American homes had little sophisticated equipment. Many were not yet wired for gas and electricity. They did not have automatic washers and dryers or refrigerators. Some homes even lacked indoor plumbing, so that every drop of water that entered the house had to be carried in by hand and then carried out again.

By 1950, the amount of capital equipment in the home had risen dramatically. Major technological systems, such as indoor plumbing, electricity, and gas, had been installed virtually everywhere. At the same time, many labor-saving appliances also came into vogue—automatic washing machines and dryers, electric irons, vacuum cleaners, refrigerators and freezers, garbage disposals. By the 1990s, we had added dishwashers, microwaves, and trash compacters. Each of these innovations had the potential to save countless hours of labor. Yet none of them did. In terms of reducing time spent on domestic work, all this expensive labor-saving technology was an abject failure.

Researchers have documented this failure. After conducting a large, twelve-country study, in which conditions ranged from the most modern to rather primi-

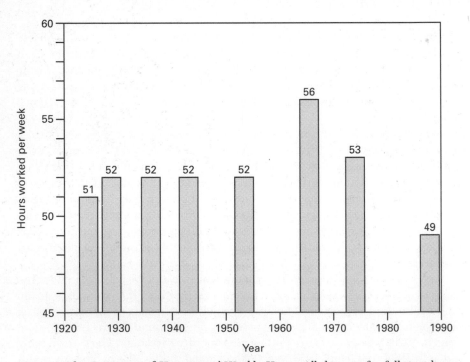

Figure 1 The Constancy of Housewives' Weekly Hours. All data are for full-time housewives. Source: Estimates from 1926–27 through 1965–66 are from Joann Vanek. "Time Spent in Housework," *Scientific American*, 231 (5 November 1974): 116–20. 1973 and 1987 are author's calculations.)

tive (lack of indoor plumbing, appliances, and so forth), the authors tentatively suggested the opposite: technical sophistication may *increase* the amount of time given over to household work. Studies of U.S. women also found that those with more durable equipment in their homes work no fewer hours than those with less. Only one major appliance has been shown to save significant amounts of time (the microwave oven). Some actually increase housework (freezers and washing machines).

Of course, technology was not without its effects. Some activities became less time consuming and others more. Between the 1920s and the 1960s, food preparation fell amost ten hours a week, but was offset by a rise in shopping, managerial tasks, and child care. Certain innovations were labor saving on their own, but led to new tasks. The refrigerator eliminated the need for daily shopping and storing ice at home, but helped drive the door-to-door vendor out of business, thereby contributing to the rise of the supermarket, with its self-service and greater travel time.

THE UPGRADING OF STANDARDS AND THE EXPANSION OF SERVICES

Laundry provides the best example of how technology failed to reduce labor time. During the period from 1925 to 1965, automatic washers and dryers were introduced. The new machines did cut the time needed to wash and dry a load of clothes. Yet laundry time rose. The reason was that housewives were doing more loads—in part, because investment in household-level capital undermined commercial establishments. Laundry that had previously been sent out began to stay at home. At the same time, standards of cleanliness went up.

The escalation of standards for laundering has been a long process, stretching back to colonial times. In those days, washing would be done once a month at most and, in many families, much less—perhaps four times per year. Nearly everyone wore dirty clothes nearly all the time. Slowly the frequency of washing rose. When the electric washer was introduced (1925), many Americans enjoyed a clean set of clothes (or at least a fresh shirt or blouse) every Saturday night. By the 1950s and 1960s, we washed after one wearing.

Standards have crept up for nearly everything housewives do—laundry, cooking, care of children, shopping, care of the sick, cleaning. Estimates from a mid-1970s survey show that the housewife spent an average of 10.3 hours a week getting the floors "spic and span," cleaning toilets, dusting, and waxing. In recent decades, homes have received "deep cleaning," with concerted attacks on "germs" and an "eat-off-the-floor" standard. Americans have taken seriously the dictum that "cleanliness is next to godliness." One 1920s housewife realized:

> Because we housewives of today have the tools to reach it, we dig every day after dust that grandmother left to a spring cataclysm. If few of us have nine children for a weekly bath, we have two or three for a daily immersion. If our consciences don't prick over vacant pie shelves or empty cookie jars, they do over meals in which a vitamin may be omitted or a calorie lacking.

But we were not always like this. Contemporary standards of housecleaning are a modern invention, like the vacuum cleaners and furniture polishes that make them possible. Europeans (and Americans) joined the cleanliness bandwagon quite recently. It was not until the late eighteenth century that people in England even began to wash themselves systematically. And it was only the rich who did so. Body odors and excretions offended no one. For example, menstrual blood just dripped onto the floor. In terms of personal hygiene, a crust of dirt was thought to foster a good complexion underneath. Noses would be blown onto clothing; feces were often left lying around the house, even among the genteel classes.

In other parts of the world, higher standards of hygiene prevailed. Medieval and early modern European travelers in Asia, for example, were considered to be extremely uncouth. In matters of housekeeping, filth and neglect were the order of the day. Anything more was considered "a waste of time." These habits were transported to America with the first European settlers, whose bodies and homes reproduced European-style filth. The culture of cleanliness was at least a century away.

It was delayed because it was expensive. The labor of colonial women was far too valuable to be spent creating spic-and-span. For most colonists, survival entailed the labor of both adults (and their children and perhaps someone else's children as well). Women were busy making yarn, cloth, candles, and soap. They were butchering animals, baking bread, churning butter, and brewing beer. They tended gardens and animals, concocted medicines, and cared for the sick. They sewed and mended garments, and typically had time to clean their houses only once a year. According to historian Mary Beth Norton, "it seems clear either that cleanliness was not highly valued or that farm wives, fully occupied with other tasks, simply had no time to worry about sweeping floors, airing bedding, or putting things away." Undoubtedly, some colonial women did take great pains with their homes, but sanitation could be infeasible. Rural dwellings were rudimentary, with dirt floors and few pieces of furniture or other possessions. Open-hearth fires spewed out soot. Hauling and heating water was arduous and expensive; it was used sparingly for luxuries such as washing dishes.

The less well-off segments of U.S. society, who were by no means a minority, faced similar living conditions, throughout the nineteenth century. Slaves, and then sharecroppers, lived in primitive cabins, which were "extremely difficult to keep clean and tidy." In urban tenements, housekeeping was hard even to recognize:

> There was no furniture to speak of, few clothes to wash, little food to prepare. . . . Washing and cleaning were difficult since all water had to be carried up the stairs. People tracked in dirt from the muddy streets; plaster crumbled; chimneys clogged and stoves smoked. . . . Cleaning was only a small part of complicated and arduous family economies. The major effort went into acquiring necessities—food, fuel and water.

As the nation grew richer, it got cleaner. Prosperity freed many married women from the burdens of earning money and producing necessities and gave them time to devote to housekeeping. As they did, higher standards emerged. The shift began among the middle classes and eventually filtered down to the less well-to-do. By the last quarter of the nineteenth century, America was well into its longstanding affair with the immaculate. Victorian-era homes were subjected to strenuous cleaning exercises, which were further complicated by the clutter and bric-a-brac that was the fashion of the day. In households with servants, requirements would be even more exacting. By the turn of the century, the once-yearly cleaning had given way to a daily routine. Each and every morning, women would be sweeping, dusting, cleaning, washing, and straightening up. And those were just the daily tasks. Bigger jobs (washing clothes, ironing clothes, baking, canning, washing walls, and so on) were done on a weekly, monthly, and seasonal basis. The rituals had become endless.

The trend to more and better was not confined to housecleaning and laundry but included activities such as cooking and baking. To some extent, what occurred was a shift from the production of the food itself (gardening, raising animmals, making butter or beer) to more elaborate preparation. In earlier days, "the simplest and least exerting forms of cooking had to be utilized most frequently; hence the ubiquity and centrality of those classic 'one-pot' dishes, soup and stew." Now women learned the art and craft of cooking, as soup and stew gave way to fried chicken and angel food cake. Nutrition and esthetics became preoccupations. All these changes in the standards of housekeeping helped keep the housewife's hours long even as progress made it possible to save her labor. But the area where the upgrading was most dramatic was in the care of children.

Being a mother—and increasingly, being a father as well—is a highly labor-intensive and demanding job. It is an article of faith that infants and small children need constant attention, supervision, and love. As they grow older, they also require education and moral training. All these needs translate into countless hours. One might have thought that mothering was always like this. Newborn babies in the fifteenth century were just as helpless as those in the twentieth. But three hundred years ago, parents acted very differently. Children were hardly "raised" in today's sense of the term. Historians of the family and "private life" have discovered that we cannot project contemporary child-rearing practices backward in time. Like housecleaning, laundering, cooking, and many other domestic labors, the standards and norms of mothering have been dramatically upgraded.

Part of the transformation has been psychological. In the past (before about the sixteenth century in England and later in other parts of Europe), parent-child relationships appear to have been much less emotional. What is seen today as a deep biological bond between parent and child, particularly mother and child, is very much a social construction. For the most part, children were not "cared for" by their parents. The rich had little to do with their offspring until they were grown. Infants were given to wetnurses, despite widespread evidence of neglect and markedly lower chances of survival. Older children were sent off to school. Those in less economically fortunate families fared no better. They would be sent as servants or into apprenticeships, often in the homes of strangers. In all social classes, infants and children were routinely left unattended for long periods of time. To make them less of a nuisance, babies were wrapped in swaddling clothes, their limbs completely immobilized, for the first months of their lives. Another custom was the violent rocking of infants "which puts the babe into a dazed condition, in order that he may not trouble those that have the care of him." However harmful these practices may have been for children, they were convenient for their elders.

Among the poor and laboring classes, economic stress made proper care virtually impossible. In the worst cases, there was not sufficient income to feed children, and infanticide and abandonment were not unusual. When families did keep (and feed) their offspring, they could rarely spare even the ill-paid labor of women. Time for mothering was an unaffordable luxury. Women had to work for pay, and the children were frequently left alone:

> The children are then in many cases left without any person in charge of them, a sufficient quantity [of opium] being given by the parents to keep them in a state of stupor until they return home. . . . When under the influence of this mixture, the children lie in a perfectly torpid state for hours together. "The young 'uns all lay about on the floor," said one woman to me who was in the habit of dosing her children with it, "like dead 'uns, and there's no bother with 'em. When they cry we gives 'em a little of it—p'raps half a spoonful and that quiets 'em."

The relative lack of parental love and attention can partly be explained by the high probability that children might not survive. The ephemerality of life until at least the mid-eighteenth century is revealed by the practice of giving two children the same name, in the expectation that only one would live. Under these circumstances, the absence of deep emotional ties to children is understandable. But the picture is actually more complicated. Parental indifference was not merely a result of infant mortality. It was also a cause. Historians now realize that one reason many children died is that their parents did not, or could not, take sufficient pains to keep them alive. Neglect and abuse were dangerous, in both rich and poor families.

More caring attitudes began to emerge in the eighteenth century, in both Europe and the United States. Eventually some of the more odious child-rearing practices started to fade away, such as swaddling; and by the end of the century, wetnursing was in decline. Parental affection became more common, and the individuality of the child was recognized. Middle-class families, often religious reformers, began to devote considerable attention to the education of their children. The biggest changes came in the nineteenth century. The idealization of mother love, vigilant attention to the needs of children, and recognition of the unique potential of each individual came to dominate child-rearing ideology. These beliefs may appear natural; but, as a leading historian of the family has noted, "motherhood as we know it today is a surprisingly new institution."

By the last quarter of the nineteenth century, what historians have called "conscious motherhood" and a bona-fide mothers' movement emerged. As the "century of the child" opened, mothers were providing their children with all manner of new services. They breast-fed. They began to toilet-train, schedule, and educate. They learned to worry about germs, nutrition, and the quality of the air. They practiced "scientific nursing" on sick children. The long legacy of child neglect gave way, particularly in America, to the most labor-intensive mothering process in human history.

Children benefited from all this attention. "But the burden that it placed upon the new American housewife was immense. Children had to be kept in bed for weeks at a time; bedpans had to be provided and warmed . . . utensils had to be boiled, alcohol baths administered, hands scrupulously washed, mouths carefully masked." And all these practical duties were embedded in a new cultural icon: the selfless mother. She was a romantic ideal, but eventually became a reality. Mothers actually did become altruistic—and unsparing with their time.

In all these ways, then, was the American household and the labor of its mistress transformed. The old tasks of animal husbandry, sewing, and candlemaking disappeared, and women took on new ones. They made their family's beds and breast-fed their own babies. The motto was more and better. Looking back on this history, some observers have noted the operation of a Parkinson's Law of housework, in which "work expands to fill the time available for its completion." And there is a certain amount of truth in this characterization: the housewife's work *did* expand to fill her customary schedule. As the market economy produced low-cost versions of what women had made at home, they transferred their labor to other tasks. Housewifery remained a full-time job irrespective of the appliances or the technological systems at the housewife's disposal. The 1950s and 1960s were particularly labor-intensive. Middle-class women were trapped in a stultifying domesticity, following "Hints from Heloise" on how to prepare homemade dog food or turn Clorox bottles into birdfeeders.

Reading 7

American Families: As They Are and Were

Paul C. Glick

The average American family of today is not the same as the average family a generation ago because social conditions have changed, and family life has adapted

From *Sociology and Social Research*, Volume 74, No. 3, April 1990, pp. 139–145. Copyright © 1990 by *Sociology and Social Research*. Reprinted by permission.

to the new conditions. As recently as 1920, one-third of the population in the United States lived on farms, as contrasted with 2 percent today. One could venture a guess that half of the grandparents or great-grandparents of adults in 1990 grew up on a farm or heard about farm life from their parents. In those earlier days, farm life was close to nature, families were large, and the thought of growing up with several brothers and sisters tends to produce some nostalgia.

Today, fully 60 percent of the young married couples will have only one or two children. This means that only about one-third of the children in these one-or-two-child families will experience a brother-and-sister relationship. And research demonstrates that the marriages of couples who have sons are significantly more likely to remain intact than marriages of couples who have daughters but no sons (Spanier and Glick, 1981; Morgan, Lye, and Contran, 1988). This is one hard demographic factor among the many factors that determine whether marriages will hold together or not.

FAMILY LIFE CYCLES HAVE BEEN UNDERGOING CHANGE

Most of my studies have dealt with family demography. These studies have focused on trends and variations in marriage, fertility, and living arrangements of the U.S. population. One specialty has been making analyses of the family life cycle, meaning by that the timing of pivotal events in family life, including when young adults are most likely to marry, when they have their first and last children, when the children leave home, and when the marriage ends with the death of one of the spouses.

My first article on the subject was published over 40 years ago (Glick, 1947). It started with information about the situation 50 years earlier than that. In brief, it showed that in 1890 the median age of the wife at marriage was 22 years and that the median age of the wife when she or her husband died was only 53 years. A century ago families were so large, and the mortality rate was so high that the chances were 50-50 that the marriage would actually end two years before the last child was expected to leave home. But because of the much longer length of life today, the corresponding age of the wife at the dissolution of the marriage is now 68 years. This means, among other things, that the average age length of married life back in 1890 was a little over 30 years but now is nearly 45 years. For simplicity this assumes that the marriage is not meanwhile dissolved by divorce, whereas that happens to about one-half of the marriages at the present time. But more about that later.

SOME MARRIAGE-LIKE BEHAVIOR OCCURS BEFORE MARRIAGE

A few years ago I was asked to speak to a group of statisticians who compiled information about religious affiliation. The topic they gave me was "Fertility and

Marriage." Perhaps the topic should have been "Marriage and Fertility" because the events usually happen in that order, but of course, they do not always do so. For the record, only 5 percent of births in 1960 occurred to unmarried women (two percent of white births and 22 percent of black births), but currently (in 1987) fully 24 percent of births occur to women out of wedlock (17 percent of white births and 62 percent of black births). In addition, one in every eight women is pregnant at the time of first marriage (about the same for white and black women). Therefore, one-third of all current first births result from premarital pregnancies. This is one of the more serious aspects of the changing family situation because of its impact on the health and welfare of those involved.

Ever since the mid-1950s, marriages have been increasingly delayed while more young adults were attending school or college longer, more women were entering the labor force, and more young couples were living together before marriage. Specifically, in 1960, less than one-half million heterosexual unmarried couples were sharing their living quarters, and at that time, the typical situation was that an older woman was renting a room to a young single man. But by 1988, over five times that many (2.6 million) unrelated couples of the opposite sex were living together, and 56 percent of the women involved had never been married. Now the typical situation is an unmarried man under 35 sharing his home with an unrelated young woman "for economic and other benefits." Close to one of every three of these cohabiting couples has young children living with them, about three-fourths of whom are the women's children, and the rest are his children or their children.

These facts about cohabitation refer to given points in time. But the lifetime experience of young adults with cohabitation is far greater. Some have never had the experience but will do so later on, and others who have experienced it have become married. A conservative estimate is that one-tenth of all married plus unmarried couples under 35 of opposite sex are unmarried cohabitors at the present time. Research also suggests that one-third of the young unmarried adults (18 to 35) will eventually cohabit while they are unmarried (Thornton, 1988).

OTHER SIGNS THAT MARRIAGE IS BECOMING LESS POPULAR

During the 1940s and 1950s when Evelyn Duvall and others of us were writing about stages of the family life cycle, we generally started with a discussion of marriage, on the assumption that nearly all adults would marry sooner or later (Duvall and Hill, 1948; Duvall 1957). This turned out to be right for those who married in the 1950s, when all but 5 percent eventually married. By contrast, projections indicate that twice that proportion, or about 10 percent, of the young adults today, are likely to remain unmarried throughout life (Glick, 1984). Perhaps more of those who are unsuited for marriage are foregoing it or, among other things, were just born at the wrong time to find an acceptable partner, as the following statement suggests.

One tangible demographic development that has affected the ability of the average woman born during the baby boom to find "Mr. Right" to marry has been called the "marriage squeeze" (Glick, Heer, and Beresford, 1963). This factor has its basis in the upward movement of the birth rate during the baby boom of the 1940s and 1950s and the tendency for women to marry men two or three years older than themselves. For example, a woman born in 1950, after the birth rate had gone up sharply, would ordinarily marry a man born two or three years earlier, when the birth rate was 10 to 20 percent lower. Hence, there was an excess of women born during the baby boom in relation to the number of men of the "right age" to marry. This created a squeeze on the women to find suitable men with whom to enter into first marriage. Accordingly, it has been estimated that the men born during the baby boom married one-half year younger, on the average, and women married one-half year older, on the average, than they otherwise would have married (Schoen, 1983).

Not very long ago, marital partners usually met at church or at school gatherings, but now that more young adults work longer before marriage, the more likely locale for finding that "one and only" is at the work place. And for those who wish to explore more widely for companionship that might lead to marriage, the commercial dating service has become increasingly popular in metropolitan areas since this author first discussed this service in a paper that was written during the 1960s (Glick, 1967).

A generation ago, nearly all women not only married but they either stayed married or remarried after their earlier marriage was dissolved. Specifically, in 1960 only 11 percent of the women 30 to 34 years old were not currently married. But by 1987, two and one-half times that many, or 27 percent, of the women 30 to 34 were not married. In this context, a recent study of attitudes toward marriage shows a steady decline between 1972 and 1986 in the relationship between being married and reported happiness (Glenn and Weaver, 1988). It found a decreasing proportion of reportedly happily married women and an increasing proportion of reportedly happy men who had never married. Women's gain from marriage has become less universal as more young women have become at least minimally capable of living independently, while more young men have found that life as a bachelor can be reasonably satisfying.

FEWER YOUNG CHILDREN AND MORE YOUNG ADULTS LIVE WITH THEIR PARENTS

The peak of the baby boom occurred before the decline in attitudes toward marriage set in. Thus, in the mid-1950s, the average number of children per U.S. woman (the total fertility rate) had climbed to 3.8, after which it went down almost continuously until it reached 1.8 children in the early 1970s and has remained at that level. Among the main reasons for the decline in the birth rate was a desire for fewer children so that they could be given a better start in life and the difficulty employed women would have in raising a large family. Two generations ago, only about one-tenth of the women went through life childless, but among young women today, 20 to 25 percent are likely to remain childless (Population Reference Bureau, 1982). Among U.S. couples who have already had all the children they want, all of 60 percent are now resorting to sterilization as the means of contraception. Much of the increase in the use of sterilization has come from those formerly using other effective types of contraception such as the Pill, the diaphragm, or abortion (Glick, 1988a).

An increasing proportion of families recognize the difficulty of rearing children under present conditions and of facing the mounting costs of raising children. A conservative estimate of the financial impact of rearing two children in an average middle-class family all the way from birth to college graduation is $400,000 in 1988 dollars (Espenshade, 1986). Yet the vast majority of couples will have at least one or two children for the pleasure they provide and for many other reasons. Incidentally, I returned a few years ago from a meeting of fertility experts with a lapel button reading "Onlies are OK," meaning, among other things, that children without siblings develop reasonably well and get along better with adults, on the average, than children from larger families.

Usually young adults leave their parental home for a period of bachelor life in an apartment before marriage. But back in 1940, at the end of the depression, fully one-half of those 20 to 24 years of age were still living with their parents (Glick and Lin, 1986; Heer, Hodge, and Felson, 1985). The marriage rate was low, and beginning jobs were scarce. But by 1960, near the end of the baby boom, relatively few young adults were living in their parents' home. The 1950s had been a period of prosperity and early marriage, and besides, it was a time when more homes were filling up with young children who were crowding out their young adult siblings. Later, by the mid-1980s, the situation had changed again. The proportion of young adults still at home or back home again with their parents had risen until it was nearly as high as it had been in 1940. Many of the beginning jobs were still being held by the large cohort of baby boomers, more of those who had married were returning home after divorce, and more young unwed mothers could not maintain a separate home. The situation remains essentially the same today as it was in 1980.

THE LEVEL OF DIVORCE HAS DECLINED BUT IS STILL HIGH

The divorce rate surged upward during the late 1960s and the 1970s but declined slightly during the early 1980s. Currently about one-half of the marriages of persons now in their thirties are likely to end in divorce, including those that have already done so (Glick, 1984). Moreover, about three of every five divorces involve young children. Therefore, about three of every ten marriages are likely to end in divorces that involve young children, but seven of every ten marriages are likely not to end in divorces that involve young children.

The high level of divorce seems likely to continue, because many of the factors that caused divorce to rise are likely to continue for years to come. Still, there may be pressure for the divorce rate to decline somewhat further during the next decade, for such reasons as increasing opportunities for the small cohort of adults born after the baby boom to find jobs and settle down, and a potentially growing concern about a forthcoming AIDS epidemic that could cause an increase in the extent and stability of marriage.

Few would disagree with the idea that a stable marriage between two happily adjusted partners is in the best interest of the adults and children involved and also in the best interest of society as well. By contrast, divorce generally is associated with negative social and economic consequences. A recent study shows that, on the average, the economic status of women during the first year after divorce is likely to decline by about 30 percent (Hoffman and Duncan, 1988). This finding provides a more moderate and reasonable appraisal of the effect of divorce than the 73 percent decline during the first year after divorce that is often cited (Weitzman, 1985). The most needy divorced women who remarry tend to do so as quickly as they can, while those in more favorable economic conditions tend to be more deliberate about whether or when to remarry (Glick and Lin, 1987). The fact remains that the divorce rate remains high. Evidently it takes much less of a disagreeable marriage now than a generation ago to cause one of the marital partners, about three-fourths of the time the wife, to take steps that lead to divorce.

THE LEVEL OF REMARRIAGE IS STILL DECLINING

Young adults who have become divorced are much more likely to marry again than persons of the same age are likely to marry for the first time. A 1987 study shows that in the United States an expected 72 percent of recently divorced women will eventually remarry (Bumpass, Sweet, and Castro, 1989). The level was higher (81 percent) for divorced women with no children and considerably lower for divorced mothers of three or more children (57 percent). Also, men are always more likely than women to remarry. But the remarriage rate has fallen sharply during the last 20 years and is still declining. There remains a question as to whether or not and when the remarriage rate will stabilize at least temporarily, or even move upward again as some believe it will.

As the situation now stands, nearly one-half (45 percent) of recent marriages involve a second or subsequent marriage for the bride, the groom, or both. But because of the numerous hassles that usually complicate remarriage, many are being discouraged from trying it again. By the way, a little more than one-half of the second marriages are ending in redivorce. More of the divorced adults are opting for cohabitation or for living entirely alone instead of remarrying. In this discussion, the analysis has mentioned only remarriage after divorce. Actually, nine-tenths of all those who marry again do so after divorce. Widowed persons more often feel less free to marry because of opposition from their sons or daughters or for other reasons.

NEARLY ONE-FOURTH OF ALL FAMILIES WITH CHILDREN ARE SINGLE-PARENT FAMILIES

An increasing proportion of families are maintained by one parent who has never married, who is in-between marriages, or who has decided never to remarry. In

1988, fully 23 percent of U.S. families with children under 18 were maintained by a single parent. Nearly one-half of these single-parent families were below the poverty level (46 percent). Currently, a majority of these families are headed by a separated or divorced parent, and one of every four are maintained by a parent who has never married. Among black families with young children, one-third are maintained by a never-married mother.

One of the favorable developments in single-parenting is the fact that the lone parents of today have a much higher average educational level than their counterparts a few years ago. To illustrate, about 40 percent of the increase in single-parent families between 1970 and 1987 occurred among those with at least some college education. This situation reflects not only a general increase in college attainment among young adults but also an increasing tendency for lone mothers with little education to marry and to do so more quickly than lone mothers with more education (Glick and Lin, 1987).

ONE-SEVENTH OF THE CHILDREN LIVING WITH TWO PARENTS ARE STEPCHILDREN

More often than not, children in single-parent families are moved into remarried families where they become stepchildren. The magnitude of the stepchild situation can be appreciated best if it is understood through the presentation of the following information. In 1987, about 10 million children under 18 years of age were in stepfamilies. Of these 10 million, 7 million were stepchildren, because they were born before the remarriage had occurred. The other 3 million were siblings of the stepchildren, because they were born after the remarriage (Glick, 1989b).

The 7 million stepchildren at the present time constitute one of every seven children under 18 years of age who are living in a home with two parents. But because some children now under 18 who have not been stepchildren yet will do so before they are 18, and still others who were previously stepchildren (living with two parents) are no longer classified as stepchildren because the stepparents have become separated or divorced before the children reached 18 years of age. Therefore, on the basis of previous research, it is reasonable to expect that one-third of the children now under 18 have already experienced being a stepchild in a two-parent family or will do so before they reach the age of 18 years (Glick, 1988b).

The entire number of persons in step situations include not only the stepparents and the young children living with them; it also includes the absent parents and their new families, if any. The term "binuclear families" has been given to this entire group of persons (Ahrons and Rodgers, 1986). The number of stepchildren would still be much larger if it were considered as covering also the sons and daughters over 18 years old whose parents had remarried after their children were born. This broad but not fanciful approach would result in an estimate that over one-half of today's young persons in the United States may be identified as stepsons or stepdaughters by the year 2000 (Glick, 1989b).

COUPLES ARE LIVING LONGER AND BETTER AFTER THEIR CHILDREN LEAVE HOME

The last child usually leaves home when his or her parents are in their 40s or 50s. Then the middle-aged couple enters into an empty nest period that has been lengthening substantially. It is worth repeating that a century ago, in 1890, the median age of women at first marriage was 22 years, and women who married at that age could expect, on the average, to have their marriage end by the death of one spouse or the other when the wife had reached the "ripe old age" of 53 years (Glick, 1947). But as already noted, the death rate was still high and families were still large a hundred years ago, therefore that event happened, on the average, two years before the expected marriage of their last child. Now the situation is different. Young people marry later, they have fewer children, and the death rate is much lower. Therefore, currently the median age of women at first marriage is 24 years, and women who marry at that age have a 50-50 chance of living until the age of 68 years before their death or that of their husband ends their marriage (Duvall and Miller, 1985; Glick, 1989a). Whether today's couples really enjoy that longer life together is a subject worth studying.

Before married couples reach old age, their income situation has reached a peak. Thus, if income is expressed in terms of the amount per family member, the highest level is reached for families in which the husband is 55 to 64 years old. This is likely to be the period between the launching of their children and the retirement of the employed parents. These are small families with a national average income of $14,250 per person, according to data for 1986. But later on, when the husband has reached 65 years old or over, family income falls to about the same average level as that for beginning families.

Information on the living arrangements of the elderly shows that typically those over 65 are still married. Actually, almost twice as many are currently married as are living alone (53 percent versus 30 percent in 1980). Moreover, almost one-half of the men who live to the age of 85 are living with their wife, but not always their first one. And almost one-half of the women who live to the age of 70 are living with their first or subsequent husband.

My own experience of living comfortably alone as an elderly widower for six years has provided insight about how satisfying that type of life can be. With no health problems, with neighbors and faculty colleagues who are friendly, with two sons living only a few miles away, with a daily routine that keeps me busy at interesting activities, eating most of my meals at a restaurant all alone being no problem, and being able to watch a few hours of television each day allows one to turn the TV off much more easily than one could "turn off" any relative that might be sharing the home. In other words, I am alone but not lonely. Of course, this experience may be typical of only a minority of widowed persons living alone, but at least it illustrates a type of life that is probably becoming more common among elderly persons who are widowed, divorced, or never married.

CHANGES IN FAMILY LIFE HAVE RESULTED FROM CHANGES IN SOCIAL CONDITIONS

If it were not for the vast changes in social and economic conditions during the last several decades, the typical family life cycle of today would resemble closely the pattern it followed before the changes occurred. And most of the developments are quite unlikely to be reversed. Among the more significant social and demographic changes affecting family life have been the remarkable increases in education, employment, and economic independence of women along with the associated improvement in the status of women. All of these changes have been occurring at the same time and will be discussed briefly.

In the process of becoming better educated, women have been exposed to the diffusion of new ideas about family formation and family limitation (Watkins, 1987). In addition, technological advancement has opened opportunities for women to work usually at some distance from their husband where they associate with other men. There they develop an expanded interest in consumerism that competes with marriage and parenting. This entire process has been reinforced as families became smaller, and more parents were able to give their daughters as well as their sons a college education. The situation can be documented by pointing out that U.S. women with the most education are those 35 to 39 years old, and that in 1985 one-fourth of them (24 percent) had completed four or more years of college; this is four times the corresponding proportion in 1960 (6 percent). The increase among men was smaller; in 1985 the proportion was two and one-half times as large as it had been in 1960 (33 percent versus 13 percent).

Women have typically been able during recent years to apply their high school or college education in the workplace before marriage. Having experienced the benefits (and costs) of working while single, more of them have continued to be employed outside the home after marriage and childbearing. The proportion of women 16 and over in the U.S. labor force was half-again as large in 1988 as in 1960 (56 percent versus 38 percent). Projections prepared by the U.S. Department of Labor indicate that the worker rate for women is expected to be only a little higher in 1995, when about 60 percent of the women, as compared with about 75 percent of the men, 16 and over are likely to be in the labor market. Corresponding rates for wives and mothers are about 10 percent higher than those for other women including the elderly, but the rate for divorced mothers is the highest (about 80 percent).

The kinds of work that women do have been upgraded in some sectors during recent years. Between 1970 and 1980, the proportion of U.S. executives and managers who were women increased from about 20 percent to 30 percent, and by 1980 women college graduates constituted a majority of persons in professional specialties who were working full time (Bianchi and Spain, 1986). However, the great majority of women are still employed in the types of occupations that have been dominated by women for a long time.

From the end of World War II until the early 1970s, average family income rose almost continuously, due in no small measure to the growing proportion of wives in the paid labor force. Real median family income reached a peak in 1973, at about $30,000 (in 1987 dollars) and has changed very little since that time. A continuing growth in the employment of wives was being offset by an upsurge of relatively low income families maintained by women.

The impact of this altered condition had a particularly negative effect on the average income of black families, more than one-third of which have an unmarried female householder.

When income was rising, the poverty rate was falling. Poverty was first measured in 1959, and at that time about 20 percent of all families and nearly 50 percent of black families were classified as below the poverty level. As might have been expected, the poverty rate reached its lowest point in 1973 (9 percent), coinciding with the peak of family income. Then as the number of one-parent families took a sharp upturn, the poverty rate for all families rose somewhat (to 11 percent) by 1987. At that time, the poverty rate was only about one-half as high as in 1960. But because many families move in and out of poverty, it was found that one-third of the nation's families experienced a period of poverty sometime during the 1970s (Duncan, 1987). A period of poverty is a time when it is hard to keep a family together.

Young adults today have been exposed to a wide range of social conditions that contrast sharply with those that their parents faced. But it is reasonable to believe that the situation will not become very different for the forthcoming generation. Urbanization has gone about as far as it can go, the birth rate is not expected to make wide fluctuations again, the educational level certainly will not rise as much in the near future as it did in the recent past, and the employment rate of women seems most unlikely to increase at the same fast pace as it has during the last few years. In this light, it seems likely that changes in family forms will also become more moderate in the years immediately ahead. But there needs to be a continual monitoring of the situation through research that is carefully designed for use in implementing social policies.

NOW, WHAT ABOUT AMERICAN FAMILIES, WHERE ARE THEY GOING?

When asked to comment on the state of American families, knowledgeable people express widely differing opinions (Glenn, 1987). At one extreme are those who believe that the negative aspects of current family life are largely offset by positive gains. At the other extreme are those who are convinced that the family system has undergone fundamental deterioration from which it is unlikely to rebound. In this concluding section, some of the pros and cons about where families are heading will be discussed.

On the one hand are those who see the family as undergoing a temporary state of confusion largely because of the suddenness of recent family changes that will be followed by more gradual change. This view holds that we are passing through a period of experimentation with various family forms, after which new family norms will be established (Macklin, 1987; Chilman, 1988). These observers see that marriage is still much more popular than nonmarriage among those in their middle years, even though it may be marriage the second time around (Raschke, 1987). Therefore, being divorced for a while is now regarded as an increasingly acceptable transition period for those who are involved with serious marital problems and who expect to remarry eventually (Spanier and Furstenberg, 1987).

In addition, some of the research on recent trends in family structure has led to the conclusion that the family system has been changing but not necessarily disintegrating. In particular, trends in children's behavior do reflect deterioration in some ways but improvement in other ways (Zill and Rogers, 1988). These trends have been influenced not only by changes in family stability but also by changes in peer culture and the media. Still other research supports the opinion that Americans continue to place a high value on marriage, on family life, and on the role of a spouse (Rodgers and Thornton, 1985). But marriage is not for everyone. Single life has been growing increasingly attractive, and, for those who choose it, the chances are that they will find their later life less problematic than it might have been if recent changes in social conditions had not occurred (Stein, 1981).

These are some of the opinions of observers who detect benefit as well as loss from the recent family changes, thus recognizing that both sides of the situation exist.

On the other hand are those who see more negative than positive consequences from the changes. The recent trend is seen by these observers as a move away from familism and toward individualism, a move that has weakened but not yet killed the ideal of permanence in marriage (Glenn, 1987). This process is regarded as a gain for men and a loss for women and children. Men are accused of more often being the one leaving the marriage, and women are accused of allowing them to do it, while neither accepts the responsibility for keeping the family intact (White, 1987). These critics say that modern lifestyles, including cohabitation, have loosened family ties and placed emphasis on personal values at the expense of family values (Hunt and Hunt, 1987).

In addition, some critical analysts of the current family situation find that young women are becoming increasingly uncertain about their chances of keeping a marriage intact and are therefore acquiring education and work experience that would help them become self-maintaining if their marriage should not last (Sweet and Bumpass, 1988). This situation is seen as a factor also in keeping the birth rate low, for fear that women may be required to have lone custody of their children between divorce and remarriage or until their children grow up. Especially among well-educated women, the task of taking care of one or two children is being considered as much less than a full-time job. So, these mothers return to the labor market soon after their children are born and all too frequently have to leave their children in lower quality child care than they would like.

These are some of the ways that the more critical observers are visualizing family life in America today. From time immemorial, of course, the pessimists have said that the younger generation was going to the dogs, and now these critics say that this time it is for real. But is it?

A balanced position would acknowledge that sound points are made by observers on each side of the issue. The immense changes in society have produced

immense changes in family life, and neither set of changes seems likely to be reversed very much. While the gains from marriage and family values may have diminished, there have been gains from enhanced lifestyle options and from greater
consumption of material comforts. It is therefore a question as to whether the
trade-off has been even or not.

Perhaps too many observers have been emphasizing one side of the situation
only. Note that one-half of the mothers are employed outside the home, but one-
half remain at home to take care of their children. Single-parenting and living
alone have doubled during the present generation, but yet nearly three-fourths of
the U.S. population live in the homes of married couples. One-half of marriages
end in divorce, but three-fourths of divorced adults remarry. The practice of cohabitation has skyrocketed, but it would probably have been as high a generation
or two ago if the young adults at that time thought they could get by with it. And no
one knows how many empty marriages of a short while back would have been
endured if the choice to end them had been culturally acceptable.

In this context, the family situation may not be as bleak as some people say or
as tolerable as other people say. In this writer's opinion, American families are, on
the average, somewhere in between the opposing positions and are likely to stay
that way for some time to come. This author says this as a research worker attempting to understand what has been happening. But those who want to improve the
situation would do well to concentrate on measures designed to help families and
individuals of all types to cope intelligently with their serious adjustment problems.

REFERENCES

Ahrons, C. A. & Rodgers, R. H. 1986. Divorced families: A multidisciplinary development
view. New York: W. W. Norton.

Bianchi, S. M., & Spain, D. 1986. American women in transition. New York: Russell Sage
Foundation.

Chilman, C. S., Nunnaly, E. W., & Cox, F. M. 1988. Variant Family Forms. Beverly Hills,
CA: Sage Publications.

Duncan, G. J. 1987. The volatility of family income over the life course. Paper presented at
the annual meeting of the Population Association of America in Chicago.

Duvall, E. M. 1957. Family development. Philadelphia: J. B. Lippincott.

Duvall, E. M., & Hill, R. L. 1948. Report of the committee on the dynamics of family
interaction. Working paper prepared for the National Conference on the Family,
Washington, D.C.

Duvall, E. M., & Miller, B. C. 1985. Marriage and family development. New York: Harper
and Row.

Espenshade, T. J. 1986. The dollars and cents of parenthood. Journal of Policy Analysis and
Management, 5, 813–817.

Glenn, N. D. 1987. A tentatively concerned view of American marriage. Journal of Family
Issues, 8, 350–354.

Glenn, N. D., & Weaver, C. N. 1988. The changing relationship of marital status to reported happiness. Journal of Marriage and the Family, 50, 317–324.

Glick, P. C. 1947. The family cycle. American Sociological Review, 12, 164–174.

Glick, P. C. 1967. Permanence of marriage. Population Index, 33, 517–526.

Glick, P. C. 1984. Marriage, divorce, and living arrangements: Prospectives changes. Journal of Family Issues, 5, 7–26.

Glick, P. C. 1988a. Fifty years of family demography: A record of social change. Journal of Marriage and the Family, 50, 861–873.

Glick, P. C. 1988b. The role of divorce in the changing family structure. Pages 3–34 in Wolchik, S., & Karoly, P. Eds., Children of Divorce: Empirical perspectives on adjustment. New York: Gilford Press.

Glick, P. C. 1989a. The family life cycle and social change. Family Relations, 38, 123–129.

Glick, P. C. 1989b. Remarried families, stepfamilies, and stepchildren. Family Relations, 38, 24–27.

Glick, P. C., Heer, D. M., & Beresford, J. C. 1963. Family formation and family composition: Trends and prospects. Pages 30–40 in Sussman, M. B. Ed. Sourcebook in marriage and the family, Boston: Houghton Mifflin.

Glick, P. C., & Lin, S. L. 1986. Recent changes in divorce and remarriage. Journal of Marriage and the Family, 48, 737–747.

Glick, P. C., & Lin, S. L. 1987. Remarriage after divorce: Recent changes and demographic variations. Sociological Perspectives, 30, 62–78.

Heer, D. M., Hodge, R. W., & Felson, M. 1985. The cluttered nest: Evidence that young adults are more likely to live at home than in the recent past. Sociology and Social Research, 69, 436–441.

Hoffman, S., & Duncan, G. J. 1988. What are the consequences of divorce? Demography, 25, 641–645.

Hunt, J. C., & Hunt, L. L. 1987. Here to play: From families to lifestyles. Journal of Family Issues, 8, 440–443.

Macklin, E. 1987. Nontraditional family forms. Pages 317–353 in Sussman, M. S., & Steinmetz, S. K. Eds., Handbook of marriage and the family. New York: Plenum Press.

Martin, T. C., & Bumpass, L. L. 1989. Recent trends in marital disruption. Demography, 26, 37–51.

Morgan, S. P., Lye, D. N., & Condran, G. A. 1988. Sons, daughters, and the risk of marital disruption. American Journal of Sociology, 94, 110–129.

Population Reference Bureau 1982. U. S. population: where we are; where we are going. Population Bulletin, 37, No. 2.

Raschke, H. J. 1987. Divorce. Pages 597–624 in Sussman, M. B., & Steinmetz, S. K. Eds., Handbook of marriage and the family. New York: Plenum Press.

Rodgers, W. L., & Thornton, A. 1985. Changing patterns of first marriage in the United States. Demography, 22, 265–279.

Schoen, R. 1983. Measuring the tightness of the marriage squeeze. Demography, 20, 61–78.

Spanier, G. B., & Glick, P. C. 1981. Marital instability in the United States: Some correlates and recent changes. Family Relations, 31, 329–338.

Spanier, G. B., & Furstenberg, F. F., Jr. 1987. Remarriage and reconstituted families. Pages 419–434 in Sussman, M. B., & Steinmetz, S. K. Eds., Handbook of marriage and the family. New York: Plenum Press.

Stein, P. J. 1981. Single life: Unmarried adults in social context. New York: St. Martin's Press.

Sweet, J. A., & Bumpass, L. L. 1988. American families and households. New York: Russell Sage Foundation.

Thornton, A. 1988. Cohabitation and marriage in the 1980s. Demography, 25, 497–508.

Watkins, S. C. 1987. The fertility transition: Europe and the Third World compared. Sociological Forum, 2, 645–673.

Weitzman, L. B. 1985. The divorce revolution: The unexpected social and economic consequences for women and children in America. New York: Free Press.

White, L. 1987. Freedom versus constraint: The new synthesis. Journal of Family Issues, 8, 468–470.

Zill, N., & Rogers, C. C. 1988. Recent trends in the well being of children in the United States and their implications for public health. Pages 31–115 in A. Cherlin Ed., The changing American family and public policy. Washington, D. C.: The Urban Institute Press.

Reading 8

The Modernization of Grandparenthood

Andrew J. Cherlin and Frank F. Furstenberg, Jr.

Writing a book about grandparents may seem an exercise in nostalgia, like writing about the family farm. We tend to associate grandparents with old-fashioned families—the rural, extended, multigenerational kind much celebrated in American mythology. Many think that grandparents have become less important as the nation has become more modern. According to this view, the shift to factory and office work meant that grandparents no longer could teach their children and grandchildren the skills needed to make a living; the fall in fertility and the rise in divorce weakened family ties; and the growth of social welfare programs meant that older people and their families were less dependent on each other for support. There is some truth to this perspective, but it ignores a powerful set of historical facts that suggest that grandparenthood—as a distinct and nearly universal stage of family life—is a post-World War II phenomenon.

Consider first the effect of falling rates of death. Much of the decline in mortality from the high preindustrial levels has occurred in this century. According to calculations by demographer Peter Uhlenberg, only about 37 percent of all males and 42 percent of all females born in 1870 survived to age sixty-five; but for those born in 1930 the comparable projections were 63 percent for males and 77 percent for females. The greatest declines in adult mortality have occurred in the last few decades, especially for women. The average number of years that a forty-year-old white woman could expect to live increased by four between 1900 and 1940; but between 1940 and 1980 it increased by seven. For men the increases have been smaller, though still substantial: a two-year increase for forty-year-old whites between 1900 and 1940 and a four-year increase between 1940 and 1980. (The trends for nonwhites are similar.) Consequently, both men and women can expect to live much longer lives than was the case a few decades ago, and more and more women are outliving men. In 1980, the average forty-year-old white woman could expect to live to age eighty, whereas the average forty-year-old white man could expect to live only to age seventy-four. As a result, 60 percent of all the people sixty-five and over in the United States in 1980 were women. Thus, there are many more grandparents around today than just a few decades ago simply because people are living longer—and a majority of them are grandmothers.

This decline in mortality has caused a profound change in the relationship between grandparents and grandchildren. For the first time in history, most adults live long enough to get to know most of their grandchildren, and most children have the opportunity to know most of their grandparents. A child born in 1900, according to Uhlenberg, had a better than nine-out-of-ten chance that two or more of his grandparents would be alive. But by the time that child reached age fifteen, the chances were only about one out of two that two or more of his grandparents would still be alive. Thus, some children were fortunate enough to establish relationships with grandparents, but in many other families the remaining grandparents must have died while the grandchild was quite young. Moreover, it was unusual for grandchildren at the turn of the century to know all their grandparents: only one in four children born in 1900 had four grandparents alive, and a mere one in fifty still had four grandparents alive by the time they were fifteen. In contrast, the typical fifteen-year-old in 1976 had a nearly nine-out-of-ten chance of having two or more grandparents still alive, a better than one-out-of-two chance of having three still alive, and a one-out-of-six chance of having all four still alive. Currently, then, nearly all grandchildren have an extended relationship with two or more grandparents, and substantial minorities have the opportunity for extended relationships with three or even all four.

Indeed, Americans take survival to the grandparental years pretty much for granted. The grandparents we spoke to rarely mentioned longer life when discussing the changes since they were children. *Of course* they were still alive and reasonably healthy; that went without saying. But this taken-for-grantedness is a new phenomenon; before World War II early death was a much greater threat, and far fewer people lived long enough to watch their grandchildren grow up.

Most people are in their forties or fifties when they first become grandparents. Some observers have mistakenly taken this as an indication that grandparents are younger today than in the past. According to one respected textbook:

> Grandparenting has become a phenomenon of middle age rather than old age. Earlier marriage, earlier childbirth, and longer life expectancy are producing grandparents in their forties.

But since the end of the nineteenth century (the earliest period for which we have reliable statistics) there has been little change in the average age at marriage. The only exception was in the 1950s, when ages at marriage and first birth did decline markedly but only temporarily. With the exception of the unusual 1950s, then, it is likely that the age when people become grandparents has stayed relatively constant over the past century. What has changed is the amount of time a person spends as a grandparent: increases in adult life expectancy mean that grandparenthood extends into old age much more often. In our national sample of the grandparents of teenagers, six out of ten had become grandparents while in their forties. When we interviewed them, however, their average age was sixty-six. Grandparenting has been a phenomenon of middle age for at least the past one hundred years. The difference today is that it is now a phenomenon of middle age *and* old age for a greater proportion of the population. To be sure, our notions of what constitutes old age also may have changed, as one woman in our study implied when discussing her grandmother:

> She stayed home more, you know. And I get out into everything I can. That's the difference. That is, I think I'm younger than she was at my age.

Moreover, earlier in the century some middle-aged women may have been too busy raising the last of their own children to think of themselves as grandmothers. Nevertheless, in biological terms, the average grandparent alive today is older, not younger, than the average grandparent at the turn of the century.

Consider also the effects of falling birth rates on grandparenthood. As recently as the late 1800s, American women gave birth to more than four children, on average. Many parents still were raising their younger children after their older children had left home and married. Under these conditions, being a grandparent often overlapped with being a parent. One would imagine that grandparenthood took a back seat to the day-to-day tasks of raising the children who were still at home. Today, in contrast, the birth rate is much lower; and parents are much more likely to be finished raising their children before any of their grandchildren are born. In 1900, about half of all fifty-year-old women still had children under eighteen; but by 1980 the proportion had dropped to one-fourth. When a person becomes a grandparent now, there are fewer family roles competing for his or her time and attention. Grandparenthood is more of a separate stage of family life, unfettered by child care obligations—one that carries its own distinct identification. It was not always so.

The fall of fertility and the rise of life expectancy have thus greatly increased the supply of older persons for whom grandparenthood is a primary intergenerational role. To be sure, there always have been enough grandparents alive so that everyone in American society (and nearly all other societies, for that matter) was familiar with the role. But until quite recently, an individual faced a considerable risk of dying before, or soon after, becoming a grandparent. And even if one was fortunate enough to become a grandparent, lingering parental obligations often took precedence. In past times, when birth and death rates were high, grandparents were in relatively short supply. Today, as any number of impatient older parents will attest, grandchildren are in short supply. Census data bear this out: in 1900 there were only twenty-seven persons aged fifty-five and over for every one hundred children fourteen and under; but by 1984 the ratio had risen to nearly one-to-one. In fact, the Bureau of the Census projects that by the year 2000, for the first time in our nation's history, there will be more persons aged fifty-five and over than children fourteen and under.

Moreover, technological advances in travel and long-distance communication have made it easier for grandparents and grandchildren to see or talk to each other. . . . [T]he grandparents at one senior citizen center had to remind us that there was a time within their memories when telephone service was not universal. We tend to forget that only fifty years ago the *Literary Digest* predicted a Landon victory over Roosevelt on the basis of responses from people listed in telephone directories—ignoring the crucial fact that telephones were to be found disproportionately in wealthier, and therefore more often Republican, homes. As late as the end of World War II, only half the homes in the United States had a telephone. The proportion rose quickly to two-thirds by the early 1950s and three-fourths by the late 1950s. Today, more than 97 percent of all homes have telephones. About one-third of the grandparents in our survey reported that they had spoken to the study child on the telephone once a week or more during the previous year.

Nor did most families own automobiles until after World War II, as several grandparents reminded us:

> I could be wrong, but I don't feel grandparents felt as close to grandchildren during that time as they do now. . . . Really back there, let's say during the twenties, transportation was not as good, so many people did not have cars. Fortunately, I can say that as far back as I remember my father always had a car, but there were many other people who did not. They traveled by horse and buggy and some even by wagons. And going a distance, it did take quite some time. . . .

Only about half of all families owned automobiles at the end of the war. Even if a family owned an automobile, long trips still could take quite some time:

> Well, I didn't see my grandmother that often. They just lived one hundred miles from us, but back then one hundred miles was like four hundred now, it's the truth. It just seemed like clear across the country. It'd take us five hours to get there, it's the truth. It was an all-day trip.

But in the 1950s, the Federal government began to construct the interstate highway system, which cut distances and increased the speed of travel. The total number of miles driven by passenger vehicles increased from about 200 million miles in the mid-1930s to about 500 million miles in the mid-1950s to over a billion miles in the 1980s. Not all of this increase represents trips to Grandma's house, of course; but with more cars and better highways, it became much easier to visit relatives in the next county or state.

But weren't grandparents and grandchildren more likely to be living in the same household at the turn of the century? After all, we do have a nostalgic image of the three-generation family of the past, sharing a household and solving their problems together. Surprisingly, the difference between then and now is much less than this image would lead us to believe. To be sure, there has been a drastic decline since 1900 in the proportion of older persons who live with their adult children. In 1900 the proportion was more than three out of five, according to historian Daniel Scott Smith; in 1962 it was one out of four; and by 1975 it had dropped to one in seven. What has occurred is a great increase in the proportion of older people who live alone or only with their spouses. Yet the high rates of co-residence in 1900 do not imply that most grandparents were living with their grandchildren—much less that most grandchildren were living with their grandparents. As Smith's data show, older persons who were married tended to live with unmarried children only; children usually moved out when they married. It was mainly widows unable to maintain their own households who moved in with married children. Consequently, according to Smith's estimates, only about three in ten persons sixty-five and over in 1900 lived with a grandchild, despite the great amount of co-residence between older parents and their adult children. What is more, because of the relative shortage of grandparents, an even lower percentage of grandchildren lived with their grandparents. Smith estimates that about one in six children under age ten in 1900 lived in the same household with someone aged fifty-five or over. Even this figure overestimates the number of children living with their grandparents, because some of these elderly residents were more distant kin, boarders, or servants.

There were just too many grandchildren and too few grandparents for co-residence to be more common. In the absence of more detailed analyses of historical censuses, however, the exact amount of change since 1900 cannot be assessed. Nor was our study designed to provide precise estimates of changes in co-residence. But it is still worth noting that just 30 percent of the grandparents in our sample reported that at least one of their grandparents ever lived with them while they were growing up. And 19 percent reported that the teenaged grandchild in the study had lived with them for at least three months. Undoubtedly, some of the grandparents in our study had shared a household with some of their own grandchildren, although we unfortunately did not obtain this information. Thus, although our study provides only imperfect and incomplete data on this topic, the responses are consistent with our claim that the change in the proportion of grand-parents and grandchildren who share a household has been more modest than the change in the proportion of elderly persons who share a household with an adult child.

Grandparents also have more leisure time today, although the trend is more pronounced for men than for women. The average male can now expect to spend fifteen years of his adult life out of the labor force, most of it during retirement. (The labor force comprises all persons who are working for pay or looking for work.) The comparable expected time was ten years in 1970, seven years in 1940, and only four years in 1900. Clearly, a long retirement was rare early in this century and still relatively rare just before World War II. But since the 1960s, workers have begun to leave the labor force at younger ages. In 1961, Congress lowered the age of eligibility for Social Security benefits from sixty-five to sixty-two. Now more than half of all persons applying for Social Security benefits are under sixty-five. Granted, some of the early retirees are suffering from poor health, and other retirees may have difficulty adjusting to their new status. Still, when earlier retirement is combined with a longer life span, the result is a greatly extended period during which one can, among other things, get to know and enjoy one's grandchildren.

The changes in leisure time for women are not as clear because women have always had lower levels of labor force participation than men. To be sure, women workers also are retiring earlier and, as has been noted, living much longer. And most women in their fifties and sixties are neither employed nor raising children. But young grandmothers are much more likely to be employed today than was the case a generation ago; they are also more likely to have aged parents to care for. Young working grandmothers, a growing minority, may have less time to devote to their grandchildren.

Most employed grandparents, however, work no more than forty hours per week. This, too, is a recent development. The forty-hour work week did not become the norm in the United States until after World War II. At the turn of the century, production workers in manufacturing jobs worked an average of fifty hours per week. Average hours dropped below forty during the depression, rose above forty during the war, and then settled at forty after the war. Moreover, at the turn of the century, 38 percent of the civilian labor force worked on farms, where long hours were commonplace. Even in 1940, about 17 percent of the civilian labor force worked on farms; but currently only about 3 percent work on farms. So even if they are employed, grandparents have more leisure time during the work week than was the case a few decades ago.

They also have more money. Living standards have risen in general since World War II, and the rise has been sharpest for the elderly. As recently as 1960, older Americans were an economically deprived group; now they are on the verge of becoming an economically advantaged group. The reason is the Social Security system. Since the 1950s and 1960s, Congress has expanded Social Security coverage, so that by 1970 nearly all nongovernment workers, except those in nonprofit organizations, were covered. And since the 1960s, Congress has increased Social Security benefits far faster than the increase in the cost of living. As a result, the average monthly benefit (in constant 1980 dollars, adjusted for changes in consumer prices) rose from $167 in 1960, to $214 in 1970, to $297 in 1980. Because of the broader coverage and higher benefits, the proportion of the elderly who are poor has plummeted. In 1959, 35 percent of persons sixty-five and over had incomes below the official poverty line, compared to 22 percent of the total population. By 1982 the disparity had disappeared: 15 percent of those sixty-five and over were poor, as were 15 percent of the total population. The elderly no longer were disproportionately poor, although many of them have incomes not too far above the poverty line. Grandparents, then, have benefitted from the general rise in economic welfare and, as they reach retirement, from the improvement in the economic welfare of the elderly.

Because of the postwar prosperity and the rise of social welfare institutions, older parents and their adult children are less dependent on each other economically. Family life in the early decades of the century was precarious; lower wages, the absence of social welfare programs, and crises of unemployment, illness, and death forced people to rely on their kin for support to a much greater extent than is true today. There were no welfare checks, unemployment compensation, food stamps, Medicare payments, Social Security benefits, or government loans to students. Often there was only one's family. Some older people provided assistance to their kin, such as finding a job for a relative, caring for the sick, or tending to the grandchildren while the parents worked. Sometimes grandparents, their children, and their grandchildren pooled their resources into a single family fund so that all could subsist. Exactly how common these three-generational economic units were we do not know; it would be a mistake to assume that all older adults were cooperating with their children and grandchildren at all times. In fact, studies of turn-of-the-century working-class families suggest that widowed older men—past their peak earning capacity and unfamiliar with domestic tasks as they were—could be a burden to the households of their children, while older women—who could help out domestically—were a potential source of household assistance. Nevertheless, these historical accounts suggest that intensive intergenerational cooperation and assistance was more common than it is today. Tamara Hareven, for example, studied the families of workers at the Amoskeag Mills in Manchester, New Hampshire, at the turn of the century. She found that the day-to-day cooperation of kin was necessary to secure a job at the mill, find housing, and accumulate enough money to get by. Cooperation has declined because it is not needed as often: social welfare programs now provide services that only the family formerly provided; declining rates of illness, death, and unemployment have reduced the frequency of family crises; and the rising standard of living—particularly of the elderly—has reduced the need for financial assistance.

The structure of the Social Security system also has lessened the feelings of obligation older parents and their adult children have toward each other. Social Security is an income transfer system in which some of the earnings of workers are transferred to the elderly. But we have constructed a fiction about Social Security, a myth that the recipients are only drawing out money that they put into the fund earlier in their lives. This myth allows both the younger contributors and the older recipients to ignore the economic dependency of the latter. The elderly are free to believe that they are just receiving that to which they are entitled by virtue of their own hard work. The tenacity of this myth—it is only now breaking down under the tremendous payment burden of our older age structure—demonstrates its importance. It allows the elderly to accept financial assistance without compromising their independence, and it allows children to support their parents without either generation openly acknowledging as much.

All of these trends taken together—changes in mortality, fertility, transportation, communications, the work day, retirement, Social Security, and standards of living—have transformed grandparenthood from its pre-World War II state. More people are living long enough to become grandparents and to enjoy a lengthy period of life as grandparents. They can keep in touch more easily with their grandchildren; they have more time to devote to them; they have more money to spend on them; and they are less likely still to be raising their own children.

GENDER AND SEX

INTRODUCTION

American society has experienced both a sexual revolution and a sex-role revolution. The first has liberalized attitudes toward erotic behavior and expression; the second has changed the roles and status of women and men in the direction of greater equality. Both revolutions have been brought about by the rapid social changes in recent years, and both revolutions also represent a belated recognition that traditional beliefs and norms did not reflect how people actually behaved and felt.

The conventional idea of sexuality defines sex as a powerful biological drive continually struggling for gratification against restraints imposed by civilization. The notion of sexual instincts also implies a kind of innate knowledge: A person intuitively knows his or her own identity as male or female, he or she knows how to act accordingly, and he or she is attracted to the "proper" sex object—a person of the opposite gender. In other words, the view of sex as biological drive pure and simple implies "that sexuality has a magical ability, possessed by no other capacity, that allows biological drives to be expressed directly in psychological and social behaviors" (Gagnon & Simon, 1970, p. 24).

The whole issue of the relative importance of biological versus psychological and social factors in sexuality and sex differences has been obscured by polemics. On the one hand, there are the strict biological determinists who declare that anatomy is destiny. On the other hand, there are those who argue that all aspects of sexuality and sex-role differences are matters of learning and social construction.

There are two essential points to be made about the nature-versus-nurture argument. By the 1970s, scientists understood that extreme positions overlook the connection between biology and experience:

> In the theory of psychosexual differentiation, it is now outmoded to oppose or juxtapose nature vs. nurture, the genetic vs. psychological, or the instinctive vs. the environmental, the innate vs. the acquired, the biological vs. the psychological, or the instinctive vs. the learned. Modern genetic theory avoids these antiquated dichotomies. (Money & Ehrhardt, 1972, p. 1)

A second and related point concerns a misconception about how biological forces work. Both biological determinists and their opponents assume that if a biological force exists, it must be overwhelmingly strong. But the most sophisticated evidence concerning both gender development *and* erotic arousal suggests that physiological forces are gentle rather than powerful. Acknowledging the possible effects of prenatal sex hormones on the brains of human infants, Robert Stoller (1972) thus warned against "biologizing":

> While the newborn presents a most malleable central nervous system upon which the environment writes, we cannot say that the central nervous system is neutral or neuter. Rather, we can say that the effects of these biological systems, organized prenatally in a masculine or feminine direction, are almost always . . . too gentle in humans to withstand the more powerful forces in human development, the first and most powerful of which is mothering. (p. 211)

Research into the development of sex differences thus suggests not an opposition between genetics and environment but an interaction. Gender identity as a child and occupation as an adult are primarily the product of social learning rather than anatomy and physiology.

In terms of scholarship, the main effect of the sex-role and sexual revolutions has been on awareness and consciousness. For example, much early social science writing was revealed to have been based on sexist assumptions. Many sociologists and psychologists took it for granted that women's roles and functions in society reflect universal physiological and temperamental traits. Since in practically every society women were subordinate to men, inequality was interpreted as an inescapable necessity of organized social life. Such analysis suffered from the same intellectual flaw as the idea that discrimination against nonwhites implies their innate inferiority. All such explanations failed to analyze the social institutions and forces producing and supporting the observed differences. In approaching the study of either the physical or the social relations between the sexes, it is therefore important to understand how traditional stereotypes have influenced both popular and professional conceptions of sexuality and sex differences.

Jessie Bernard's and William J. Goode's articles on male and female sex roles develop this theme in different ways, but generally examine how stereotyping influences and sets limits on male and female socialization. These limits rob both men and women of a broader potential—for example, gentleness for men, achievement for women. Stereotyping thus diminishes the capacity of both women and men to fulfill a broader potential than conventional sex roles dictate.

Yet, as Kathleen Gerson points out in her study of men's responses to gender and family change, some men flee from marriage and parenting altogether, while others cling to the traditional breadwinner role. Some men place family at the center of their lives and are able to combine male breadwinning with parenting—provided that they don't commit themselves heavily to breadwinning. Nevertheless, men are usually denied the option of choosing to be a full-time parent—an option that still remains open to women.

As gender and family roles have shifted, so have ideas about sexual norms and behavior. Prior to the 1960s, men and women were, ideally, to remain chaste before marriage. Nevertheless, premarital male sexual behavior was winked at, if not condoned. But nowhere, as Lillian Rubin asserts, do we find the effects of the sexual revolution more graphically illustrated and played out than in the sexual behavior—and sense of entitlement to sex—of today's teenagers. This represents a profound change, especially for girls.

Teenagers who are experiencing more sex are also having more pregnancies. Kristin Luker argues that, while teen pregnancy is indeed a problem, we define the problem wrongheadedly. It is not simply a problem of immorality, of young women out of control. Rather, she argues, it makes far more sense of reality to understand that teenage pregnancy reflects limited opportunities for personal achievement, fulfillment, and self-esteem.

REFERENCES

Gagnon, J. H. and Simon, W. 1970. *The Sexual Scene.* Chicago: Aldene.

Money, J. and Ehrhardt, A. A. 1972. *Man and Woman, Boy and Girl.* Baltimore: Johns Hopkins Press.

Stoller, R. J. 1972. "The Bedrock of Masculinity and Femininity: Bisexuality." *Archives of General Psychiatry,* 26, pp. 207–212.

Chapter
3

Gender and Equality

Reading 9

The Good-Provider Role: Its Rise and Fall

Jessie Bernard

ABSTRACT

The general structure of the "traditional" American family, in which the husband-father is the provider and the wife-mother is the housewife, began to take shape early in the 19th century. This structure lasted about 150 years, from the 1830s to 1980, when the U.S. Census no longer automatically denominated the male as head of the household. As "providing" became increasingly mediated by cash derived from participation in the labor force or from commercial enterprises, the powers and prerogatives of the provider role augmented, and those of the housewife, who lacked a cash income, declined. Gender identity became associated with the work site as well as with work. As affluence spread, the provider role became more and more competitive and escalated into the good-provider role. There were always defectors from the good-provider role, and in recent years expressed dissatisfaction with it increased. As more and more married women entered the labor force and thus assumed a

From *American Psychologist*, Vol. 36, No. 1, January 1981, pp. 1–12. Copyright © 1981 by the American Psychological Association. Reprinted by permission.

*share of the provider role, the powers and prerogatives of the good-provider
role became diluted. At the present time a process that Ralph Smith
calls "the subtle revolution" is realigning family roles. A host of
social-psychological obstacles related to gender identity have to be
overcome before a new social-psychological structure can be achieved.*

The Lord is my shepherd, I shall not want. He sets a table for me in the very sight
of my enemies; my cup runs over (23rd Psalm). And when the Israelites were
complaining about how hungry they were on their way from Egypt to Canaan, God
told Moses to rest assured: There would be meat for dinner and bread for break-
fast the next morning. And, indeed, there were quails that very night, enough to
cover the camp, and in the morning the ground was covered with dew that proved
to be bread (Exodus 16:12–13). In fact, in this role of good provider, God is sometimes almost synonymous with Providence. Many people, like Micawber, still wait
for him, or Providence, to provide.

Granted, then, that the first great provider for the human species was God the
Father, surely the second great provider for the human species was Mother, the
gatherer, planter, and general factotum. Boulding (1976), citing Lee and deVore,
tells us that in hunting and gathering societies, males contribute about one fifth of
the food of the clan, females the other four fifths (p. 96). She also concludes that by
12,000 B.C. in the early agricultural villages, females provided four fifths of human
subsistence (p. 97). Not until large trading towns arose did the female contribution
to human subsistence decline to equality with that of the male. And with the beginning of true cities, the provisioning work of women tended to become invisible.
Still, in today's world it remains substantial.

Whatever the date of the virtuous woman described in the Old Testament
(Proverbs 31:10–27), she was the very model of a good provider. She was, in fact, a
highly productive conglomerate. She woke up in the middle of the night to tend to
her business; she oversaw a multiple-industry household; *her* candles did not go
out at night; there was a ready market for the high-quality linen girdles she made
and sold to the merchants in town; and she kept track of the real estate market and
bought good land when it became available, cultivating vineyards quite profitably.
All this time her husband sat at the gate talking with his cronies.

A recent counterpart to the virtuous woman was the busy and industrious
shtetl woman:

> The earnings of a livelihood is sexless, and the large majority of women . . . participate
> in some gainful occupation if they do not carry the chief burden of support. The wife of
> a "perennial student" is very apt to be the sole support of the family. The problem of
> managing both a business and a home is so common that no one recognizes it as spe-
> cial. . . . To bustle about in search of a livelihood is merely another form of bustling
> about managing a home; both are aspects of . . . health and livelihood. (Zborowski &
> Herzog, 1952, p. 131)

In a subsistence economy in which husbands and wives ran farms, shops, or
businesses together, a man might be a good, steady worker, but the idea that he

was *the* provider would hardly ring true. Even the youth in the folk song who listed all the gifts he would bestow on his love if she would marry him—a golden comb, a paper of pins, and all the rest—was not necessarily promising to be a good provider.

I have not searched the literature to determine when the concept of the good provider entered our thinking. The term *provider* entered the English language in 1532, but was not yet male sex typed, as the older term *purveyor* already was in 1442. Webster's second edition defines the good provider as "one who provides, especially, colloq., one who provides food, clothing, etc. for his family; as, he is a good or an adequate provider." More simply, he could be defined as a man whose wife did not have to enter the labor force. The counterpart to the good provider was the housewife. However the term is defined, the role itself delineated relationships within a marriage and family in a way that added to the legal, religious, and other advantages men had over women.

Thus, under the common law, although the husband was legally head of the household and as such had the responsibility of providing for his wife and children, this provision was often made with help from the wife's personal property and earnings, to which he was entitled:

> He owned his wife's and children's services, and had the sole right to collect wages for their work outside the home. He owned his wife's personal property outright, and had the right to manage and control all of his wife's real property during marriage, which included the right to use or lease property, and to keep any rents and profits from it. (Babcock, Freedman, Norton, & Ross, 1975, p. 561)

So even when she was the actual provider, the legal recognition was granted the husband. Therefore, whatever the husband's legal responsibilities for support may have been, he was not necessarily a good provider in the way the term came to be understood. The wife may have been performing that role.

In our country in Colonial times women were still viewed as performing a providing role, and they pursued a variety of occupations. Abigail Adams managed the family estate, which provided the wherewithal for John to spend so much time in Philadelphia. In the 18th century "many women were active in business and professional pursuits. They ran inns and taverns; they managed a wide variety of stores and shops; and, at least occasionally, they worked in careers like publishing, journalism and medicine" (Demos, 1974, p. 430). Women sometimes even "joined the menfolk for work in the fields" (p. 430). Like the household of the proverbial virtuous woman, the Colonial household was a little factory that produced clothing, furniture, bedding, candles, and other accessories, and again, as in the case of the virtuous woman, the female role was central. It was taken for granted that women provided for the family along with men.

The good provider as a specialized male role seems to have arisen in the transition from subsistence to market—especially money—economies that accelerated with the industrial revolution. The good-provider role for males emerged in this country roughly, say, from the 1830s, when de Tocqueville was observing it, to the late 1970s, when the 1980 census declared that a male was not automatically to be assumed to be head of household. This gives the role a life span of about a century and a half. Although relatively short-lived, while it lasted the role was a seemingly rock-like feature of the national landscape.

As a psychological and sociological phenomenon, the good-provider role had wide ramifications for all of our thinking about families. It marked a new kind of marriage. It did not have good effects on women: The role deprived them of many chips by placing them in a peculiarly vulnerable position. Because she was not reimbursed for her contribution to the family in either products or services, a wife was stripped to a considerable extent of her access to cash-mediated markets. By discouraging labor force participation, it deprived many women, especially afflu-ent ones, of opportunities to achieve strength and competence. It deterred young women from acquiring productive skills. They dedicated themselves instead to winning a good provider who would "take care of" them. The wife of a more suc-cessful provider became for all intents and purposes a parasite, with little to do except indulge or pamper herself. The psychology of such dependence could be-come all but crippling. There were other concomitants of the good-provider role.

EXPRESSIVITY AND THE GOOD-PROVIDER ROLE

The new industrial order that produced the good provider changed not so much the division of labor between the sexes as it did the site of the work they engaged in. Only two of the concomitants of this change in work site are selected for com-ment here, namely, (a) the identification of gender with work site as well as with work itself and (b) the reduction of time for personal interaction and intimacy within the family.

It is not so much the specific kinds of work men and women do—they have always varied from time to time and place to place—but the simple fact that the sexes do different kinds of work, whatever it is, which is in and of itself important. The division of labor by sex means that the work group becomes also a sex group. The very nature of maleness and femaleness becomes embedded in the sexual division of labor. One's sex and one's work are part of one another. One's work defines one's gender.

Any division of labor implies that people doing different kinds of work will occupy different work sites. When the division is based on sex, men and women will necessarily have different work sites. Even within the home itself, men and women had different work spaces. The woman's spinning wheel occupied a differ-ent area from the man's anvil. When the factory took over much of the work for-merly done in the house, the separation of work space became especially marked. Not only did the separation of the sexes become spatially extended, but it came to relate work and gender in a special way. The work site as well as the work itself became associated with gender; each sex had its own turf. This sexual "territoriali-ty" has had complicating effects on efforts to change any sexual division of labor. The good provider worked primarily in the outside male world of business and industry. The homemaker worked primarily in the home.

Spatial separation of the sexes not only identifies gender with work site and work but also reduces the amount of time available for spontaneous emotional give-and-take between husbands and wives. When men and women work in an economy based in the home, there are frequent occasions for interaction. (Consider, for example, the suggestive allusions made today to the rise in the birth rate nine months after a blackout.) When men and women are in close proximity, there is always the possibility of reassuring glances, the comfort of simple physical presence. But when the division of labor removes the man from the family dwelling for most of the day, intimate relationships become less feasible. De Tocqueville was one of the first to call our attention to this. In 1840 he noted that

> almost all men in democracies are engaged in public or professional life; and . . . the limited extent of common income obliges a wife to confine herself to the house, in order to watch in person and very closely over the details of domestic economy. All these distinct and compulsory occupations are so many natural barriers, which, by keeping the two sexes asunder, render the solicitations of the one less frequent and less ardent—the resistance of the other more easy. (de Tocqueville, 1840, p.212)

Not directly related to the spatial constraints on emotional expression by men, but nevertheless a concomitant of the new industrial order with the same effect, was the enormous drive for achievement, for success, for "making it" that escalated the provider role into the good-provider role. De Tocqueville (1840) is again our source:

> The tumultuous and constantly harassed life which equality makes men lead [becoming good providers] not only distracts from the passions of love, by denying them time to indulge in it, but it diverts them from it by another more secret but more certain road. All men who live in democratic ages more or less contract ways of thinking of the manufacturing and trading classes. (p. 221)

As a result of this male concentration on jobs and careers, much abnegation and "a constant sacrifice of her pleasures to her duties" (de Tocqueville, 1840, p. 212) were demanded by the American woman. The good-provider role, as it came to be shaped by this ambience, was thus restricted in what it was called upon to provide. Emotional expressivity was not included in that role. One of the things a parent might say about a man to persuade a daughter to marry him, or a daughter might say to explain to her parents why she wanted to, was not that he was a gentle, loving, or tender man but that he was a good provider. He might have many other qualities, good or bad, but if a man was a good provider, everything else was either gravy or the price one had to pay for a good provider.

Lack of expressivity did not imply neglect of the family. The good provider was a "family man." He set a good table, provided a decent home, paid the mortgage, bought the shoes, and kept his children warmly clothed. He might, with the help of the children's part-time jobs, have been able to finance their educations through high school, and, sometimes, even college. There might even have been a little left over for an occasional celebration in most families. The good provider made a decent contribution to the church. His work might have been demanding, but he expected it to be. If in addition to being a good provider, a man was kind, gentle, generous, and not a heavy drinker or gambler, that was all frosting on the cake. Loving attention and emotional involvement in the family were not part of a woman's implicit bargain with the good provider.

By the time de Tocqueville published his observations in 1840, the general outlines of the good-provider role had taken shape. It called for a hard-working man who spent most of his time at his work. In the traditional conception of the role, a man's chief responsibility is his job, so that "by definition any family behaviors must be subordinate to it in terms of significance and [the job] has priority in the event of a clash" (Scanzoni, 1975, p. 38). This was the classic form of the good-provider role, which remained a powerful component of our societal structure until well into the present century.

COSTS AND REWARDS OF THE GOOD-PROVIDER ROLE FOR MEN

There were both costs and rewards for those men attached to the good-provider role. The most serious cost was perhaps the identification of maleness not only with the work site but especially with success in the role. "The American male looks to his breadwinning role to confirm his manliness" (Brenton, 1966, p. 194).[1] To be a man one had to be not only a provider but a *good* provider. Success in the good-provider role came in time to define masculinity itself. The good provider had to achieve, to win, to succeed, to dominate. He was a bread*winner.* He had to show "strength, cunning, inventiveness, endurance—a whole range of traits henceforth defined as exclusively 'masculine' " (Demos, 1974, p. 436). Men were judged as men by the level of living they provided. They were judged by the myth "that endows a money-making man with sexiness and virility, and is based on man's dominance, strength, and ability to provide for and care for 'his' woman" (Gould, 1974, p. 97). The good provider became a player in the male competitive macho game. What one man provided for his family in the way of luxury and display had to be equaled or topped by what another could provide. Families became display cases for the success of the good provider.

The psychic costs could be high:

> By depending so heavily on his breadwinning role to validate his sense of himself as a man, instead of also letting his roles as husband, father, and citizen of the community count as validating sources, the American male treads on psychically dangerous ground. It's always dangerous to put all one's psychic eggs into one basket. (Brenton, 1966, p. 194)

The good-provider role not only put all of a man's gender-identifying eggs into one psychic basket, but it also put all the family-providing eggs into one basket. One individual became responsible for the support of the whole family. Countless stories portrayed the humiliation families underwent to keep wives and especially

---

[1]Rainwater and Yancy (1967), critiquing current welfare policies, note that they "have robbed men of their manhood, women of their husbands, and children of their fathers. To create a stable monogamous family we need to provide men with the opportunity to be men, and that involves enabling them to perform occupationally" (p. 235).

mothers out of the labor force, a circumstance that would admit to the world the male head's failure in the good-provider role. If a married woman had to enter the labor force at all, that was bad enough. If she made a good salary, however, she was "co-opting the man's passport to masculinity" (Gould, 1974, p. 89) and he was effectively castrated. A wife's earning capacity diminished a man's position as head of the household (Gould, 1974, p. 99).

Failure in the role of good provider, which employment of wives evidenced, could produce deep frustration. As Komarovsky (1940, p. 20) explains, this is "because in his own estimation he is failing to fulfill what is the central duty of his life, the very touchstone of his manhood—the role of family provider."

But just as there was punishment for failure in the good-provider role, so also were there rewards for successful performance. A man "derived strength from his role as provider" (Komarovsky, 1940, p. 205). He achieved a good deal of satisfaction from his ability to support his family. It won kudos. Being a good provider led to status in both the family and the community. Within the family it gave him the power of the purse and the right to decide about expenditures, standards of living, and what constituted good providing. "Every purchase of the family—the radio, his wife's new hat, the children's skates, the meals set before him—all were symbols of their dependence upon him" (Komarovsky, 1940, pp. 74–75). Such dependence gave him a "profound sense of stability" (p. 74). It was a strong counterpoise vis-à-vis a wife with a stronger personality. "Whether he had considerable authority within the family and was recognized as its head, or whether the wife's stronger personality . . . dominated the family, he nevertheless derived strength from his role as a provider" (Komarovsky, 1940, p. 75). As recently as 1975, in a sample of 3,100 husbands and wives in 10 cities, Scanzoni found that despite increasing egalitarian norms, the good provider still had "considerable power in ultimate decision-making" and as "unique provider" had the right "to organize his life and the lives of other family members around his occupation" (p. 38).

A man who was successful in the good-provider role might be freed from other obligations to the family. But the flip side of this dispensation was that he could not make up for poor performances by excellence in other family roles. Since everything depended on his success as provider, everything was at stake. The good provider played an all-or-nothing game.

DIFFERENT WAYS OF PERFORMING THE GOOD-PROVIDER ROLE

Although the legal specifications for the role were laid out in the common law, in legislation, in legal precedents, in court decisions, and, most importantly, in custom and convention, in real-life situations the social and social-psychological specifications were set by the husband or, perhaps more accurately, by the community, alias the Joneses, and there were many ways to perform it.

Some men resented the burdens the role forced them to bear. A man could easily vent such resentment toward his family by keeping complete control over all expenditures, dispensing the money for household maintenance, and complaining about bills as though it were his wife's fault that shoes cost so much. He could, in effect, punish his family for his having to perform the role. Since the money he earned belonged to him—was "his"—he could do with it what he pleased. Through extreme parsimony he could dole out his money in a mean, humiliating way, forcing his wife to come begging for pennies. By his reluctance and resentment he could make his family pay emotionally for the provisioning he supplied.

At the other extreme were the highly competitive men who were so involved in outdoing the Joneses that the fur coat became more important than the affectionate hug. They "bought off" their families. They sometimes succeeded so well in their extravagance that they sacrificed the family they were presumably providing for to the achievements that made it possible (Keniston, 1965).[2]

The Depression of the 1930s revealed in harsh detail what the loss of the role could mean both to the good provider and to his family, not only in the loss of income itself—which could be supplied by welfare agencies or even by other family members, including wives—but also and especially in the loss of face.

The Great Depression did not mark the demise of the good-provider role. But it did teach us what a slender thread the family hung on. It stimulated a whole array of programs designed to strengthen that thread, to ensure that it would never again be similarly threatened. Unemployment insurance was incorporated into the Social Security Act of 1935, for example, and a Full Employment Act was passed in 1946. But there proved to be many other ways in which the good-provider role could be subverted.

ROLE REJECTORS AND ROLE OVERPERFORMERS

Recent research in psychology, anthropology, and sociology has familiarized us with the tremendous power of roles. But we also know that one of the fundamental principles of role behavior is that conformity to role norms is not universal. Not everyone lives up to the specifications of roles, either in the psychological or in the sociological definition of the concept. Two extremes have attracted research attention: (a) the men who could not live up to the norms of the good-provider role or did not want to, at one extreme, and (b) the men who overperformed the role, at the other. For the wide range in between, from blue-collar workers to professionals, there was fairly consistent acceptance of the role, however well or poorly, however grumblingly or willingly, performed.

---

[2]Several years ago I presented a critique of what I called "extreme sex role specialization," including "work-intoxicated fathers." I noted that making success in the provider role the only test for real manliness was putting a lot of eggs into one basket. At both the blue-collar and the managerial levels, it was dysfunctional for families. I referred to the several attempts being made even then to correct the excesses of extreme sex role specialization: rural and urban communes, leaving jobs to take up small-scale enterprises that allowed more contact with families, and a rebellion against overtime in industry (Bernard, 1975, pp. 217–239).

First the nonconformists. Even in Colonial times, desertion and divorce occurred:

> Women may have deserted because, say, their husbands beat them; husbands, on the other hand, may have deserted because they were unable or unwilling to provide for their usually large families in the face of the wives' demands to do so. These demands were, of course, backed by community norms making the husband's financial support a sacred duty (Scanzoni, 1979, pp. 24–25)

Fiedler (1962) has traced the theme of male escape from domestic responsibilities in the American novel from the time of Rip Van Winkle to the present:

> The figure of Rip Van Winkle presides over the birth of the American imagination; and it is fitting that our first successful home-grown legend should memorialize, however playfully, the flight of the dreamer from the shrew—into the mountains and out of time, away from the drab duties of home . . . anywhere to avoid . . . marriage and responsibility. One of the factors that determine theme and form in our great books is this strategy of evasion, this retreat to nature and childhood which makes our literature (and life) so charmingly and infuriatingly "boyish." (pp. xx–xxi)

Among the men who pulled up stakes and departed for the West or went down to the sea in ships, there must have been a certain proportion who, like their mythic prototype, were fleeing the good-provider role.

The work of Demos (1974), a historian, offers considerable support for Fiedler's thesis. He tells us that the burdens thrust on men in the 19th century by the new patterns of work began to show their effects in the family. When "the [spatial] separation of the work lives of husbands and wives made communication so problematic," he asks, "what was the likelihood of meaningful communication?" (Demos, 1974, p. 438). The answer is, relatively little. Divorce and separation increased, either formally or by tacit consent—or simply by default, as in the case of a variety of defaulters—tramps, bums, hoboes—among them.

In this connection, "the development of the notorious 'tramp' phenomenon is worth noticing," Demos (1974, p. 438) tells us. The tramp was a man who just gave up, who dropped out of the role entirely. He preferred not to work, but he would do small chores or other small-scale work for a handout if he had to. He was not above begging the housewife for a meal, hoping she would not find work for him to do in repayment. Demos (1974) describes the type:

> Demoralized and destitute wanderers, their numbers mounting into the hundreds of thousands, tramps can be fairly characterized as men who had run away from their wives. . . . Their presence was mute testimony to the strains that tugged at the very core of American family life. . . . Many observers noted that the tramps had created a virtual society of their own [a kind of counterculture] based on a principle of single-sex companionship. (p. 438)

A considerable number of them came to be described as "homeless men" and, as the country became more urbanized, landed ultimately on skid row. A large part of the task of social workers for almost a century was the care of the "evaded" women

they left behind.[3] When the tramp became wholly demoralized, a chronic alcoholic, almost unreachable, he fell into a category of his own—he was a bum.

Quite a different kettle of fish was the hobo, the migratory worker who spent
several months harvesting wheat and other large crops and the rest of the year in
cities. Many were the so-called Wobblies, or Industrial Workers of the World, who
repudiated the good-provider role on principle. They had contempt for the men
who accepted it and could be called conscientious objectors to the role. "In some
IWW circles, wives were regarded as the 'ball and chain.' In the West, IWW literature proclaimed that the migratory worker, usually a young, unmarried male, was
'the first specimen of American manhood . . . the leaven of the revolutionary labor
movement' " (Foner, 1979, p. 400). Exemplars of the Wobblies were the nomadic
workers of the West. They were free men. The migratory worker, "unlike the factory slave of the Atlantic seaboard and the central states, . . . was most emphatically 'not afraid of losing his job.' No wife and family cumbered him. The worker of
the East, oppressed by the fear of want for wife and babies, dared not venture
much" (Foner, 1979, p. 400). The reference to fear of loss of job was well taken;
employers preferred married men, disciplined into the good-provider role, who
had given hostages to fortune and were therefore more tractable.

Just on the verge between the area of conformity to the good-provider
role—at whatever level—and the area of complete nonconformity to it was the
non-good provider, the marginal group of workers usually made up of "the under-
educated, the under-trained, the under-employed, or part-time employed, as well
as the under paid, and of course the unemployed" (Snyder, 1979, p. 597). These
included men who wanted—sometimes desperately—to perform the good-provider role but who for one reason or another were unable to do so. Liebow (1966)
has discussed the ramifications of failure among the black men of Tally's corner:
The black man is

> under legal and social constraints to provide for them [their families], to be a husband
> to his wife and a father to his children. The chances are, however, that he is failing to
> provide for them, and failure in this primary function contaminates his performance as
> father in other aspects as well. (p. 86)

---

[3]In one department of a South Carolina cotton mill early in the century, "every worker was a grass
widow" (Smuts, 1959, p. 54). Many women worked "because their husbands refused to provide for their
families. There is no reason to think that husbands abandoned their duties more often than today, but
the woman who was burdened by an irresponsible husband in 1890 usually had no recourse save taking
on his responsibilities herself. If he deserted, the law-enforcement agencies of the time afforded little
chance of finding and compelling him to provide support" (Smuts, 1959, p. 54). The situation is not
greatly improved today. In divorce child support is allotted in only a small number of cases and enforced in even fewer. "Roughly half of all families with an absent parent don't have awards at all.
. . . Where awards do exist they are usually for small amounts, typically ranging from $7 to $18 per
child" (Jones, 1976, abstract). A summary of all the studies available concludes that "approximately 20
percent of all divorced and separated mothers receive child support regularly, with an additional 7
percent receiving it 'sometimes': 8 percent of all divorced and separated women receive alimony regularly or sometimes" (Jones, 1976, p. 23).

In some cases, leaving the family entirely was the best substitute a man could supply. The community was left to take over.[4]

At the other extreme was the overperformer. De Tocqueville, quoted earlier, was already describing him as he manifested in the 1830s. And as late as 1955 Warner and Ablegglen were adding to the considerable literature on industrial leaders and tycoons, referring to their "driving concentration" on their careers and their "intense focusing" on interests, energies, and skills on these careers, "even limiting their sexual activity" (pp. 48–49). They came to be known as workaholics or work-intoxicated men. Their preoccupation with their work even at the expense of their families was, as I have already noted, quite acceptable in our society.

Poorly or well performed, the good-provider role lingered on. World War II initiated a challenge, this time in the form of attracting more and more married women into the labor force, but the challenge was papered over in the 1950s with an "age of togetherness" that all but apotheosized the good provider, his house in the suburbs, his homebody wife, and his third, fourth, even fifth, child. As late as the 1960s most housewives (87%) still saw breadwinning as their husband's primary role (Lopata, 1971, p. 91).[5]

INTRINSIC CONFLICT IN THE GOOD-PROVIDER ROLE

Since the good-provider role involved both family and work roles, most people believed that there was no incompatibility between them or at least that there should not be. But in the 1960s and 1970s evidence began to mount that maybe something was amiss.

De Tocqueville had documented the implicit conflict in the American businessman's devotion to his work at the expense of his family in the early years of the 19th century; the Industrial Workers of the World had proclaimed that the good-provider role which tied a man to his family was an impediment to the great revolution at the beginning of the 20th century; Fiedler (1962) had noted that throughout our history, in the male fantasy world, there was freedom from the responsibilities of this role; about 50 years ago Freud (1930/1958) had analyzed the intrinsic conflict between the demands of women and the family on one side and the demands of men's work on the other:

> Women represented the interests of the family and sexual life, the work of civilization has become more and more men's business; it confronts them with ever harder tasks, compels them to sublimations of instinct which women are not easily able to achieve. Since man has not an unlimited amount of mental energy at his disposal, he must

---

[4]Even though the annals of social work agencies are filled with cases of runaway husbands, in 1976 only 12.6% of all women were in the status of divorce and separation, and at least some of them were still being "provided for." Most men were at least trying to fulfill the good-provider role.

[5]Although all the women in Lopata's (1971) sample saw breadwinning as important, fewer employed women (54%) than either nonemployed urban (63%) or suburban (64%) women assigned it first place (p. 91).

accomplish his tasks by distributing his libido to the best advantage. What he employs for cultural [occupational] purposes he withdraws to a great extent from women, and his sexual life; his constant association with men and his dependence on his relations with them even estrange him from his duties as husband and father. Woman finds herself thus forced into the background by the claims of culture [work] and she adapts an inimical attitude towards it. (pp. 50–51)

In the last two decades, researchers have been raising questions relevant to Freud's statement of the problem. They have been asking people about the relative satisfactions they derive from these conflicting values—family and work. Among the earliest studies comparing family–work values was a Gallup poll in 1940 in which both men and women chose a happy home over an interesting job or wealth as a major life value. Since then there have been a number of such polls, and considerable body of results has now accumulated. Pleck and Lang (1979) and Hesselbart (Note 1) have summarized the findings of these surveys. All agree that there is a clear bias in the direction of the family. Pleck and Lang conclude that "men's family role is far more psychologically significant to them than is their work role" (p. 29), and Hesselbart—however critical she is of the studies she summarizes—believes they should not be dismissed lightly and concludes that they certainly "challenge the idea that family is a 'secondary' valued role" (p. 14).[6] Douvan (Note 2) also found in a 1976 replication of a 1957 survey that family values retained priority over work: "Family roles almost uniformly rate higher in value production than the job role does" (p. 16).[7]

The very fact that researchers have asked such questions is itself interesting. Somehow or other both the researchers and the informants seem to be saying that all this complaining about the male neglect of the family, about the lack of family involvement by men, just is not warranted. Neither de Tocqueville nor Freud was right. Men do value family life more than they value their work. They do derive their major life satisfactions from their families rather than from their work.

It may well be true that men derive the greatest satisfaction from their family roles, but this does not necessarily mean they are willing to pay for the benefit. In any event, great attitudinal changes took place in the 1960s and 1970s.

---

[6]Pleck and Lang (1979) found only one serious study contradicting their own conclusions: "Using data from the 1973 NORC (National Opinion Research Center) General Social Survey, Harry analyzed the bivariate relationship of job and family satisfaction to life happiness in men classified by family life cycle stage. In three of the five groups of husbands . . . job satisfaction had a stronger association than family satisfaction to life happiness" (pp. 5–6).

[7]In 1978, a Yankelovich survey on "The New Work Psychology" suggested that leisure is now becoming a strict competitor for both family and work as a source of life satisfactions: "Family and work have grown less important than leisure; a majority of 60 percent say that although they enjoy their work, it is not their major source of satisfaction" (p. 46). A 1977 survey of Swedish men aged 18 to 35 found that the proportion saying that the family was the main source of meaning in their lives declined from 45% in 1955 to 41% in 1977; the proportion indicating work as the main source of satisfaction dropped from 33% to 17%. The earlier tendency for men to identify themselves through their work is less marked these days. In the new value system, the individual says, in effect, "I am more than my role. I am myself" (Yankelovich, 1978). Is the increasing concern with leisure a way to escape the dissatisfaction with both the alienating relations found on the work site and the demands for increased involvement with the family?

Douvan (Note 2), on the basis of surveys in 1957 and 1976, found, for example, a considerable increase in the proportion of both men and women who found marriage and parenthood burdensome and restrictive. Almost three fifths (57%) of both married men and married women in 1976 saw marriages as "all burdens and restrictions," as compared with only 42% and 47%, respectively, in 1957. And almost half (45%) also viewed children as "all burdens and restrictions" in 1976, as compared with only 28% and 33% for married men and married women, respectively, in 1957. The proportion of working men with a positive attitude toward marriage dropped drastically over this period, from 68% to 39%. Working women, who made up a fairly small number of all married women in 1957, hardly changed attitudes at all, dropping only from 43% to 42%. The proportion of working men who found marriage and children burdensome and restrictive more than doubled, from 25% to 56% and from 25% to 58%, respectively. Although some of these changes reflected greater willingness in 1976 than in 1957 to admit negative attitudes toward marriage and parenthood—itself significant—profound changes were clearly in process. More and more men and women were experiencing disaffection with family life.[8]

"ALL BURDENS AND RESTRICTIONS"

Apparently, the benefits of the good-provider role were greater than the costs for most men. Despite the legend of the flight of the American male (Fiedler, 1962), despite the defectors and dropouts, despite the tavern habitués "ball and chain" cliché, men seemed to know that the good-provider role, if they could succeed in it, was good for them. But Douvan's (Note 2) findings suggest that recently their complaints have become serious, bone-deep. The family they have been providing for is not the same family it was in the past.

Smith (1979) calls the great trek of married women into the labor force a subtle revolution—revolutionary not in the sense of one class overthrowing a status quo and substituting its own regime, but revolutionary in its impact on both the family and the work roles of men and women. It diluted the prerogatives of the good-provider role. It increased the demands made on the good provider, especially in the form of more emotional investment in the family, more sharing of household responsibilities. The role became even more burdensome.

However men may now feel about the burdens and restrictions imposed on them by the good-provider role, most have, at least ostensibly, accepted them. The tramp and the bum had "voted with their feet" against the role; the hobo or Wobbly had rejected it on the basis of a revolutionary ideology that saw it as enslaving

---

[8]Men seem to be having problems with both work and family roles. Veroff (Note 3), for example, reports an increased "sense of dissatisfaction with the social relations in the work setting" and a "dissatisfaction with the affiliative nature of work" (p. 47). This dissatisfaction may be one of the factors that leads men to seek affiliative-need satisfaction in marriage, just as in the 19th century they looked to the home as shelter from the jungle of the outside world.

men to the corporation; tavern humor had glossed the resentment habitués felt against its demands. Now the "burdens-and-restrictions" motif has surfaced both in research reports and, more blatantly, in the male liberation movement. From time to time it has also appeared in the clinicians' notes.

Sometimes the resentment of the good provider takes the form of simply wanting more appreciation for the life-style he provides. All he does for his family seems to be taken for granted. Thus, for example, Goldberg (1976), a psychiatrist, recounts the case of a successful businessman:

> He's feeling a deepening sense of bitterness and frustration about his wife and family. He doesn't feel appreciated. It angers him the way they seem to take the things his earnings purchase for granted. They've come to expect it as their due. It particularly enrages him when his children put him down for his "materialistic middle-class trip." He'd like to tell them to get someone else to support them but he holds himself back. (p. 124)

Brenton (1966) quotes a social worker who describes an upper-middle-class woman: She has "gotten hold of a man who'll drive himself mad to get money, and [is] denigrating him for being too interested in money, and not interested in music, or the arts, or in spending time with the children. But at the same time she's subtly driving him—and doesn't know it" (p. 226). What seems significant about such cases is not that men feel resentful about the lack of appreciation but that they are willing to justify their resentment. They are no longer willing to grin and bear it.

Sometimes there is even more than expressed resentment; there is an actual repudiation of the role. In the past, only a few men like the hobo or Wobbly were likely to give up. Today, Goldberg (1976) believes, more are ready to renounce the role, not on theoretical revolutionary grounds, however, but on purely selfish ones:

> Male growth will stem from openly avowed, unashamed, self-oriented motivation. . . . Guilt-oriented "should" behavior will be rejected because it is always at the price of a hidden build-up of resentment and frustration and alienation from others and is, therefore, counterproductive. (p. 184)

The disaffection of the good provider is directed to both sides of his role. With respect to work, Lefkowitz (1979) has described men among whom the good-provider role is neither being completely rejected nor repudiated, but diluted. These men began their working lives in the conventional style, hopeful and ambitious. They found a job, married, raised a family, and "achieved a measure of economic security and earned the respect of . . . colleagues and neighbors" (Lefkowitz, 1979, p. 31). In brief, they successfully performed the good-provider role. But unlike their historical predecessors, they in time became disillusioned with their jobs—not jobs on assembly lines, not jobs usually characterized as alienating, but fairly prestigious jobs such as aeronautics engineer and government economist. They daydreamed about other interests. "The common theme which surfaced again and again in their histories, was the need to find a new social connection—to reassert control over their lives, to gain some sense of freedom" (Lefkowitz, 1979, p. 31). These men felt "entitled to freedom and independence." Middle-class, educated, self-assured, articulate, and for the most part white, they knew they could talk themselves into a job if they had to. Most of them did not want to desert their families. Indeed, most of them "wanted to rejoin the intimate circle they felt they had neglected in their years of work" (p. 31).

Though some of the men Lefkowitz studied sought closer ties with their families, in the case of those studied by Sarason (1977), a psychologist, career changes involved lower income and had a negative impact on families. Sarason's subjects were also men in high-level professions, the very men least likely to find marriage and parenthood burdensome and restrictive. Still, since career change often involved a reduction in pay, some wives were unwilling to accept it, with the result that the marriage deteriorated (p. 178). Sometimes it looked like a no-win game. The husband's earlier career brought him feelings of emptiness and alienation, but it also brought financial rewards for the family. Greater work satisfaction for him in lower paying work meant reduced satisfaction with life-style. These findings lead Sarason to raise a number of points with respect to the good-provider role. "How much," he asks, "does an individual or a family need in order to maintain a satisfactory existence? Is an individual being responsible to himself or to his family if he provides them with little more than the bare essentials of living?" (p. 178). These [are] questions about the good-provider role that few men raised in the past.

Lefkowitz (1979) wonders how his downwardly mobile men lived when they left their jobs. "They put together a basic economic package which consisted of government assistance, contributions from family members who had not worked before and some bartering of goods and services" (p. 31). Especially interesting in this list of income sources are the "contributions from family members who had not worked before" (p. 31). Surely not mothers and sisters. Who, of course, but wives?

WOMEN AND THE PROVIDER ROLE

The present discussion began with the woman's part in the provider role. We saw how as more and more of the provisioning of the family came to be by way of monetary exchange, the woman's part shrank. A woman could still provide services, but could furnish little in the way of food, clothing, and shelter. But now that she is entering the labor force in large numbers, she can once more resume her ancient role, this time, like her male counterpart the provider, by way of a monetary contribution. More and more women are doing just this.

The assault of the good-provider role in the Depression was traumatic. But a modified version began to appear in the 1970s as a single income became inadequate for more and more families. Husbands have remained the major providers, but in an increasing number of cases the wife has begun to share this role. Thus, the proportion of married women aged 15 to 54 (living with their husbands) in the labor force more than doubled between 1950 and 1978, from 25.2% to 55.4%. The proportion for 1990 is estimated to reach 66.7% (Smith, 1979, p. 14). Fewer women are now full-time housewives.

For some men the relief from the strain of sole responsibility for the provider role has been welcome. But for others the feeling of degradation resembles the feeling reported 40 years earlier in the Great Depression. It is not that they are no longer providing for the family but that the role-sharing wife now feels justified in making demands on them. The good-provider role with all its prerogatives and perquisites has undergone profound changes. It will never be the same again.[9] Its death knell was sounded when, as noted above, the 1980 census no longer automatically assumed that the male member of the household was its head.

THE CURRENT SCENE

Among the new demands being made on the good-provider role, two deserve special consideration, namely, (1) more intimacy, expressivity, and nurturance—specifications never included in it as it originally took shape—and (2) more sharing of household responsibilities and child care.

As the pampered wife in an affluent household came often to be an economic parasite, so also the good provider was often, in a way, a kind of emotional parasite. Implicit in the definition of the role was that he provided goods and material things. Tender loving care was not one of the requirements. Emotional ministrations from the family were his right; providing them was not a corresponding obligation. Therefore, as de Tocqueville had already noted by 1840, women suffered a kind of emotional deprivation labeled by Robert Weiss "relational deficit" (cited in Bernard, 1976). Only recently has this male rejection of emotional expression come to be challenged. Today, even blue-collar women are imposing "a host of new role expectations upon their husbands or lovers. . . . A new role set asks the blue-collar male to strive for . . . deep-coursing intimacy" (Shostak, Note 4, p. 75). It was not only vis-à-vis his family that the good provider was lacking in expressivity. This lack was built into the whole male role script. Today not only women but also men are beginning to protest the repudiation of expressivity prescribed in male roles (David & Brannon, 1976; Farrell, 1974; Fasteau, 1974; Pleck & Sawyer, 1974).

Is there any relationship between the "imposing" on men of "deep-coursing intimacy" by women on one side and the increasing proportion of men who find marriage burdensome and restrictive on the other? Are men seeing the new emotional involvement being asked of them as "all burdens and restrictions"? Are they responding to the new involvements under duress? Are they feeling oppressed by them? Fearful of them?

From the standpoint of high-level pure-science research there may be something bizarre, if not even slightly absurd, in the growing corpus of serious research on how much or how little husbands of employed wives contribute to household chores and child care. Yet it is serious enough that all over the industrialized world

---

[9]Among the indices of the waning of the good-provider role are the increasing number of married women in the labor force; the growth in the number of female-headed families; the growing trend toward egalitarian norms in marriage; the need for two earners in so many middle-class families; and the recognition of these trends in the abandonment of the identification of head of household as a male.

such research is going on. Time studies in a dozen countries—communist as well as capitalist—trace the slow and bungling process by which marriage accommodates to changing conditions and by which women struggle to mold the changing conditions in their behalf. For everywhere the same picture shows up in research: an image of women sharing the provider role and at the same time retaining responsibility for the household. Until recently such a topic would have been judged unworthy of serious attention. It was a subject that might be worth a good laugh, for instance, as when an all-thumbs man in a cartoon burns the potatoes or finds himself bumbling awkwardly over a diaper, demonstrating his—proud—male ineptness at such female work. But it is no longer funny.

The "politics of housework" (Mainardi, 1970) proves to be more profound than originally believed. It has to do not only with tasks but also with gender—and perhaps more with the site of the tasks than with their intrinsic nature. A man can cook magnificently if he does it on a hunting or fishing trip; he can wield a skillful needle if he does it mending a tent or a fishing net; he can even feed and clean a toddler on a camping trip. Few of the skills of the homemaker are beyond his reach so long as they are practiced in a suitably male environment. It is not only women's work in and of itself that is degrading but any work on female turf. It may be true, as Brenton (1966) says, that "the secure man can wash a dish, diaper a baby, and throw the dirty clothes into the washing machine—or do anything else women used to do exclusively—without thinking twice about it" (p. 211), but not all men are that secure. To a great many men such chores are demasculinizing. The apron is shameful on a man in the kitchen; it is all right at the carpenter's bench.

The male world may look upon the man who shares household responsibilities as, in effect, a scab. One informant tells the interviewer about a conversation on the job: "What, are you crazy?" his hard-hat fellow workers ask him when he speaks of helping his wife. "The guys want to kill me. 'You son of a bitch! You are getting us in trouble.' . . . The men get really mad" (Lein, 1979, p. 492). Something more than persiflage is involved here. We are fairly familiar with the trauma associated with the invasion by women of the male work turf, the hazing women can be subjected to, and the male resentment of admitting them except into their own segregated areas. The corresponding entrance of men into the traditional turf of women—the kitchen or the nursery—has analogous but not identical concomitants.

Pleck and Lang (1979) tell us that men are now beginning to change in the direction of greater involvement in family life. "Men's family behavior is beginning to change, becoming increasingly congruent with the long-standing psychological significance of the family in their lives" (p. 1). They measure this greater involvement by way of the help they offer with homemaking chores. Scanzoni (1975), on the basis of a survey of over 3,000 husbands and wives, concludes that at least in households in which wives are in the labor force, there is the "possibility of a different pattern in which responsibility for households would unequivocally fall equally on husbands as well as wives" (p. 38). A brave new world indeed. Still, when we look at the reality around us, the pace seems intolerably slow. The responsibilities of the old good-provider role have attenuated far faster than have its prerogatives and privileges.

A considerable amount of thought has been devoted to studying the effects of the large influx of women into the work force. An equally interesting question is what the effect will be if a large number of men actually do increase their participation in the family and the household. Will men find the apron shameful? What if we were to ask fathers to alternate with mothers in being in the home when youngsters come home from school? Would fighting adolescent drug abuse be more successful if fathers and mothers were equally engaged in it? If the school could confer with fathers as often as with mothers? If the father accompanied children when they went shopping for clothes? If fathers spent as much time with children as do mothers?

Even as husbands, let alone as fathers, the new pattern is not without trauma. Hall and Hall (1979), in their study of two-career couples, report that the most serious fights among such couples occur not in the bedroom, but in the kitchen, between couples who profess a commitment to equality but who find actually implementing it difficult. A young professional reports that he is philosophically committed to egalitarianism in marriage and tries hard to practice it, but it does not work. He even feels guilty about this. The stresses involved in reworking roles may have an impact on health. A study of engineers and accountants finds poorer health among those with employed wives than among those with nonemployed wives (Burke & Wier, 1976). The processes involved in role change have been compared with those involved in deprogramming a cult member. Are they part of the increasing sense of marriage and parenthood as "all burdens and restrictions"?

The demise of the good-provider role also calls for consideration of other questions: What does the demotion of the good provider to the status of senior provider or even more coprovider do to him? To marriage? To gender identity? What does expanding the role of housewife to that of junior provider or even coprovider do to her? To marriage? To gender identity? Much will of course depend on the social and psychological ambience in which changes take place.

A PARABLE

I began this essay with a proverbial woman. I close it with a modern parable by William H. Chafe (Note 5), a historian who also keeps his eye on the current scene. Jack and Jill, both planning professional careers, he as doctor, she as lawyer, marry at age 24. She works to put him through medical school in the expectation that he will then finance her through law school. A child is born during the husband's internship, as planned. But in order for him to support her through professional training as planned, he will have to take time out from his career. After two years, they decide that both will continue their training on a part-time basis, sharing household responsibilities and using day-care services. Both find part-time positions and work out flexible work schedules that leave both of them time for child care and companionship with one another. They live happily ever after.

That's the end? you ask incredulously. Well, not exactly. For, as Chafe (Note 5) points out, as usual the personal is also political:

Obviously such a scenario presumes a radical transformation of the personal values that today's young people bring to their relationships as well as a readiness on the part of social and economic institutions to encourage, or at least make possible, the development of equality between men and women. (p. 28)

The good-provider role may be on its way out, but its legitimate successor has not yet appeared on the scene.

REFERENCE NOTES

1. Hasselbart, S. *Some underemphasized issues about men, women, and work.* Unpublished manuscript, 1978.
2. Douvan, E. *Family roles in a twenty-year perspective.* Paper presented at the Radcliffe Pre-Centennial Conference. Cambridge, Massachusetts, April 2–4, 1978.
3. Veroff, J. *Psychological orientations to the work role: 1957–1976.* Unpublished manuscript, 1978.
4. Shostak, A. *Working class Americans at home: Changing expectations of manhood.* Unpublished manuscript, 1973.
5. Chafe, W. *The challenge of sex equality: A new culture or old values revisited?* Paper presented at the Radcliffe Pre-Centennial Conference. Cambridge, Massachusetts, April 2–4, 1978.

REFERENCES

Babcock, B., Freedman, A. E., Norton, E. H., & Ross, S. C. *Sex discrimination and the law: Causes and remedies.* Boston: Little, Brown, 1975.

Bernard, J. *Women, wives, mothers.* Chicago: Aldine, 1975.

Bernard, J. Homosociality and female depression. *Journal of Social Issues,* 1976, 32, 207–224.

Boulding, E. Familial constraints on women's work roles. *SIGNS: Journal of Women in Culture and Society.* 1976, 1, 95–118.

Brenton, M. *The American male.* New York: Coward-McCann, 1966.

Burke, R., & Weir, T. Relationships of wives' employment status to husband, wife and pair satisfaction and performance. *Journal of Marriage and the Family,* 1976, 38, 279–287.

David, D. S., & Brannon, R. (Eds.). *The forty-nine percent majority: The male sex role.* Reading, Mass.: Addison-Wesley, 1976.

Demos, J. The American family in past time. *American Scholar,* 1974, 43, 422–446.

Farrell, W. *The liberated man.* New York: Random House, 1974.

Fasteau, M. F. *The male machine.* New York: McGraw-Hill, 1974.

Fiedler, L. *Love and death in the American novel.* New York: Meredith, 1962.

Foner, P. S. *Women and the American labor movement.* New York: Free Press, 1979.

Freud, S. *Civilization and its discontents.* New York: Doubleday-Anchor, 1958. (Originally published, 1930.)

Goldberg, H. *The hazards of being male.* New York: New American Library, 1976.

Gould, R. E. Measuring masculinity by the size of a paycheck. In J. E. Pleck & J. Sawyer (Eds.), *Men and masculinity.* Englewood Cliffs, N.J.: Prentice-Hall, 1974. (Also published in *Ms.*, June 1973, pp. 18ff.)

Hall, D., & Hall, F. *The two-career couple.* Reading, Mass.: Addison-Wesley, 1979.

Jones, C. A. *A review of child support payment performance.* Washington, D.C.: Urban Institute, 1976.

Keniston, K. *The uncommitted: Alienated youth in American society.* New York: Harcourt, Brace & World, 1965.

Komarovsky, M. *The unemployed man and his family.* New York: Dryden Press, 1940.

Lefkowitz, B. Life without work. *Newsweek,* May 14, 1979, p. 31.

Lein, L. Responsibility in the allocation of tasks. *Family Coordinator,* 1979, *28,* 489–496.

Liebow, E. *Tally's corner.* Boston: Little, Brown, 1966.

Lopata, H. *Occupational housewife.* New York: Oxford University Press, 1971.

Mainardi, P. The politics of housework. In R. Morgan (Ed.), *Sisterhood is powerful.* New York: Vintage Books, 1970.

Pleck, J. H., & Lang, L. Men's family work: Three perspectives and some new data. *Family Coordinator,* 1979, *28,* 481–488.

Pleck, J. H., & Sawyer, J. (Eds.), *Men and masculinity.* Englewood Cliffs, N.J.: Prentice-Hall, 1974.

Rainwater, L., & Yancy, W. L. *The Moynihan report and the politics of controversy.* Cambridge, Mass.: M.I.T. Press, 1967.

Sarason, S. B. *Work, aging, and social change.* New York: Free Press, 1977.

Scanzoni, J. H. *Sex roles, life styles, and childbearing: Changing patterns in marriage and the family.* New York: Free Press, 1975.

Scanzoni, J. H. An historical perspective on husband-wife bargaining power and marital dissolution. In G. Levinger & O. Moles (Eds.), *Divorce and separation in America.* New York: Basic Books, 1979.

Smith, R. E. (Ed.), *The subtle revolution.* Washington, D.C.: Urban Institute, 1979.

Smuts, R. W. *Women and work in America.* New York: Columbia University Press, 1959.

Snyder, L. The deserting, non-supporting father: Scapegoat of family non-policy. *Family Coordinator,* 1979, *38,* 594–598.

Tocqueville, A. de. *Democracy in America.* New York: J. & H. G. Hangley, 1840.

Warner, W. L., & Ablegglen, J. O. *Big business leaders in America.* New York: Harper, 1955.

Yankelovich, D. The new psychological contracts at work. *Psychology Today,* May, 1978, pp. 46–47; 49–50.

Zborowski, M., & Herzog, E. *Life is with people.* New York: Schocken Books, 1952.

Reading 10

Why Men Resist

William J. Goode

For many women, the very title of my essay is an exercise in banality, for there is no puzzle. To analyze the peculiar thoughtways of men seems unnecessary, since ultimately their resistance is that of dominant groups throughout history: they enjoy an exploitive position that yields them an unearned profit in money, power, and prestige. Why should they give it up?

That answer contains, of course, some parts of the truth, but we shall move more effectively toward equality only if we grasp much more of the truth than that bitter view reveals. If it were completely true, then the great power of men would have made all societies male-vanity cultures, in which women are kept behind blank walls and forced to work at productive tasks only with their sisters, while men laze away their hours in parasitic pleasure. In fact, one can observe that the position of women varies a good deal by class, by society, and over time, and no one has succeeded in proving that those variations are only the result of men's exploitation.

Indeed, there are inherent socioeconomic contradictions in any attempt by males to create a fully exploitative set of material advantages for all males. Moreover, there are inherent emotional contradictions in any effort to achieve full domination in that intimate sphere.

As to the first contradiction, women—and men, too, in the same situation, who are powerless, slavish, and ignorant are most easily exploitable, and thus there are always some male pressures to place them in that position. Unfortunately, such women (or men) do not yield much surplus product. In fact, they do not produce much at all. Women who are freer and are more in command of productive skills, as in hunting and gathering societies and increasingly in modern industrial ones, produce far more, but they are also more resistant to exploitation or domination. Without understanding that powerful relationship, men have moved throughout history toward one or the other of these great choices, with their built-in disadvantages and advantages.

As to emotional ties, men would like to be lords of their castle and to be loved absolutely—if successful, this is the cheapest exploitative system—but in real life

From *Rethinking the Family*. 1992. Barrie Thorne and Marilyn Valom (Eds.). Boston: Northeastern University Press.

this is less likely to happen unless one loves in return. In that case what happens is what happens in real life: men care about the joys and sorrows of the women to whom they are attached. Mutual caring reduces the degree to which men are willing to exploit their wives, mothers, and sisters. More interesting, their caring also takes the form of wanting to prevent other men from exploiting these women when they are in the outside world. That is, men as individuals know that they are to be trusted, and so should have great power, but other men cannot be trusted, and therefore the laws should restrain such fellows.

These large sets of contrary tensions have some effect on even those contemporary men who do not believe that the present relations between men and women are unjust. Both sets, moreover, support the present trend toward greater equality. In short, men do resist, but these and other tensions prevent them from resisting as fully as they might otherwise, and not so much as a cynical interpretation of their private attitudes would expect. On the other hand, they do resist somewhat more strenuously than we should predict from their public assertion in favor of, for example, equal pay, or slogans like "liberty and justice for all."

Why is that resistance so strenuous? My attempt here to answer that question is necessarily limited. Even to present the latest data on the supposed psychological traits of males would require more space than is available here. I shall try to avoid the temptation of simply describing men's reactions to the women's movement, although I do plan to inform you of men's attitudes toward some aspects of equality. I shall try to avoid defending men, except to the extent that explaining them may be a defense. And, as is already obvious, I shall not assert that we are on the brink of a profound, sudden change in sex-role allocations in the direction of equality, for we must never underestimate the cunning or the staying power of those in charge. Finally, because we are all observers of men, it is unlikely that I can bring forward many findings that are entirely unknown to you. At best, I can suggest some fruitful, perhaps new, ways of looking at male roles. Within these limitations, I shall focus on the following themes:

1. As against the rather narrow definition of men's roles to be found in the current literature on the topic, I want to remind you of a much wider range of traditionally approved roles in this and other cultures.
2. As against the conspiracy theory of the oppression of women, I shall suggest a modest "sociology of the dominant group" to interpret men's behavior and thinking about male roles and thus offer some robust hypotheses about why they resist.
3. I shall point to two central areas of role behavior, occupations and domestic tasks, where change seems glacial at present and men's resistance strong.
4. As against those who feel that if utopia does not arrive with the next full moon, we should all despair, I shall point to some processes now occurring that are different from any in recorded history and that will continue to press toward more fundamental changes in men's social positions and roles in this as well as other countries of the world.

THE RANGE OF SEX ROLES

Let me begin by reminding you of the standard sociological view about the alloca-tion of sex roles. First, although it is agreed that we can, with only small error, divide the population into males and females, the biological differences between the two that might affect the distribution of sex roles—which sex is supposed to do which social tasks, which should have which rights—are much too small to deter-mine the large differences in sex-role allocation within any given society or to ex-plain the curious doctrines that serve to uphold it. Second, even if some differ-ences would give an advantage to men (or women) in some tasks or achievements, the overlap in talent is so great that a large minority of women (or men)—perhaps even a majority—could do any task as well as could members of the other sex. Third, the biological differences are too fixed in anatomy and physiology to ac-count for the wide diversity of sex-role allocation we observe when we compare different societies over time and cultures.

Consequently, most of the sex-role allocation must be explained by how we rear children, by the sexual division of labor, by the cultural definitions of what is appropriate to the sexes, and by the social pressures we put on the two sexes to keep each in its place. Since human beings created these role assignments, they can also change them. On the other hand, these roles afford large advantages to men (e.g., opportunity, range of choices, mobility, payoffs for what is accom-plished, cultivation of skills, authority, and prestige) in this and every other society we know. Consequently, men are likely to resist large alterations in roles. They will do so even though they understand that in exchange for their privileges, they have to pay high costs in morbidity, mortality, and failure.[1] As a consequence of this fact about men's position, it can be supposed that they will resist unless their ability to rig the system in their favor is somehow reduced. It is my belief that this capacity is in fact being undermined somewhat, though not at a rapid rate.

A first glance at descriptions of the male role, especially as described in the literature on mass media, social stereotypes, family roles, and personality at-tributes, suggests that the male role is definite, narrow, and agreed upon. Males, we are told, are pressed into a specific mold. For example, "the male role pre-scribes that men be active, aggressive, competitive, . . . while the female role pre-scribes that women should be nurturant, warm, altruistic . . . and the like."[2] The male role requires the suppression of emotion: "the male role, as personally and socially defined, requires men to appear tough, objective, striving, achieving, un-sentimental. . . . If he weeps, if he shows weakness, he will likely be viewed as unmanly." Or: "Men are programmed to be strong and 'aggressive.' "[3] Those state-ments were published some time ago, but the flood of books since then has only elaborated that description.

We are so accustomed to reading such descriptions that we almost believe them, unless we stop to ask, first, how many men do we actually know who carry out these social prescriptions (i.e., how many are emotionally anesthetized, aggres-sive, physically tough and daring, unwilling or unable to give nurturance to a child)? Second, and this is the test of a social role, do they lose their membership cards in the male fraternity if they fail in these respects? If socialization and social pressures are so all-powerful, where are all the John Wayne types in our society? Or, to ask a more searching question, how seriously should we take such sex-role prescriptions if so few men live up to them? The recent creation of male groups chanting around a campfire, searching for the lost primitive hunter within each bosom, suggests that our generation can not even play the role anymore without a great deal of coaching.

The key fact is not that many men do not live up to such prescriptions; that is obvious. They never did. Rather, many other qualities and performances have always been viewed as acceptable or admirable, and this is true even among boys, who are often thought to be strong supporters of sex stereotypes. The macho boy is admired, but so is the one who edits the school newspaper, who draws cartoons, or who is simply a warm friend. There are at least a handful of ways of being an admired professor. Indeed, a common feminist complaint against the present system is that women are much more narrowly confined in the ways they are permitted to be professors, or members of any occupation.

But we can go further. A much more profound observation is that oppressed groups are *typically* given narrow ranges of social roles, while dominant groups afford their members a far wider set of behavior patterns, each qualitatively different but each still accepted or esteemed in varying degrees. One of the privileges granted, or simply assumed, by ruling groups, is that they can indulge in a variety of eccentricities while still demanding and getting a fair measure of authority or prestige. Consider in this connection, to cite only one spectacular example, the crotchets and quirks cultivated by the English upper classes over the centuries.

Moreover, if we enlarge our vision to encompass other times and places, the range becomes even greater. We are not surprised to observe Latin American men embrace one another, Arab or Indian boys walk together hand in hand, or seminary students being gentle. The male role prescriptions that commonly appear in the literature do not describe correctly the male ideal in Jewish culture, which embodies a love of music, learning, and literature; an avoidance of physical violence; an acceptance of tears and sentiment, nurturance, and a sensitivity to others' feelings. In the South that I knew half a century ago, young rural boys were expected to nurture their younger siblings, and male-male relations were ideally expected to be tender, supporting, and expressed ocassionally by embraces. Among my own kin, some fathers then kissed their school-age sons; among Greek Americans in New York City, that practice continues many decades later. Or, to consider England once more, let us remember the admired men of Elizabethan England. True enough, one ideal was the violent, daring Sir Francis Drake and the brawling poet Ben Jonson. But men also expressed themselves in kissing and embracing, writing love poems to one another, donning decorative (not to say gaudy and flamboyant) clothing, and studying flowers as well as the fiery heavens.

I assert, then, that men manage to be in charge of things in all societies but that their very control permits them to create a wide range of ideal male roles, with the consequence that large numbers of men, not just a few, can locate rewarding positions in the social structure. Thereby, too, they considerably narrow the options left for feminine sex roles. Feminists especially resent the narrowness of the feminine role in informal interaction, where they feel they are dealt with only as women, however this may be softened by personal warmth or affection. . . .

THE SOCIOLOGY OF SUPERORDINATES

That set of relationships is only part of the complex male view, and I want to continue with my sketch of the main elements in what may be called the "sociology of superordinates." That is, I believe there are some general principles or regularities to be found in the relationships between superordinates—here, the sex-class called males—and subordinates, in this instance women. Those regularities do not justify, but they do explain in some degree, the modern resistance of men to their social situation.[4] Here are some of them:

1. The observations made by either men or women about members of the other sex are limited and somewhat biased by what they are most interested in and by their lack of opportunity to observe behind the scenes of each others' lives.[5] However, far less of what men do is determined by women; what men do affects women much more. As a consequence, men are often simply less motivated to observe carefully many aspects of women's behavior and activity because women's behavior does not affect as much what men propose to do. By contrast, almost everything men do will affect what women *have* to do, and thus women are motivated to observe men's behavior as keenly as they can.

2. Since any given cohort of men know they did not create the system that gives them their advantages, they reject any charges that they conspired to dominate women.

3. Since men, like other dominants or superordinates, take for granted the system that gives them their status, they are not aware of how much the social structure, from attitude patterns to laws, pervasively yields small, cumulative, and eventually large advantages in most competitions. As a consequence, they assume that their greater accomplishments are actually the result of inborn superiority. Dominants are never satisfied with their rule unless they can also justify it.

4. As a corollary to this male view, when men weigh their situation, they are more aware of the burdens and responsibilities they bear than of their unearned advantages.

5. Superiors, and thus men, do not easily notice the talents or accomplishments of subordinates, and men have not in the past seen much wisdom in giving women more opportunities for growth, for women, in their view, are not capable of much anyway, especially in the areas of men's special skills. As is obvious, this is a self-validating process. Thus, few women have embarrassed men in the past by becoming superior in those areas. When they did, their superiority was seen, and is often still seen, as an odd exception. As a consequence, men see their superior position as a just one.

6. Men view even small losses of deference, advantages, or opportunities as large threats and losses. Their own gains, or their maintenance of old advantages, are not noticed as much.[6]

Although the male view is similar to that of superordinates generally, as the foregoing principles suggest, one cannot simply equate the two. The structural position of males is different from that of superordinate groups, classes, ethnic populations, or castes. Males are, first, not a group, but a social segment or a statistical aggregate within the society. They share much of a common destiny, but they share few if any group or collective goals (within small groups they may be buddies, but not with all males). Second, males share with certain women whatever gain or loss they experience as members of high or low castes, ethnic groups, or classes. For example, women in a ruling stratum share with their men a high social rank, deference from the lower orders, and so on; men in a lowly Indian caste share that rank with their women, too. In modern societies, men and women in the same family are on a more or less equal basis with respect to "inheritance, educational opportunity (at least undergraduate), personal consumption of goods, most rights before the law, and the love and responsibility of their children."[7] They are not fully equal, to be sure, but much more equal than are members of very different castes or social classes.

Moreover, from the male view, women also enjoy certain exemptions: "freedom from military conscription, whole or partial exemption from certain kinds of heavy work, preferential courtesies of various kinds." Indeed, men have generally believed, on the whole, that their own lot is the more difficult one.[8]

It is possible, however, that feminist cries of indignation have touched their hearts, and those of women too, in recent years. Without giving a breakdown by gender, Gallup announced "a remarkable shift of opinion" in 1989: almost half those polled asserted that men "have a better life" than women, compared with only 32 percent in 1975. Almost certainly many women have been convinced, since nearly two-thirds of younger women felt that way.[9] Fifty-nine percent of a 1990 *Times Mirror* sample of women aged eighteen to twenty-four agreed, but so did 65 percent of the men. . . .

DOMESTIC DUTIES AND JOBS

So far, the opinion data give some small cause for optimism. Nevertheless, all announcements of the imminent arrival of utopias are premature. Although men's approval of more equality for women has risen, the record in two major areas of men's roles—the spheres of home and occupation—gives some reason for optimism, but little for rejoicing. Here we can be brief, for though voluminous and complex data exist, the main conclusions can easily be summarized.[20] Changes have occurred, but they are not great if we consider the society as a whole and focus on changes in behavior. In short, men have gained great credit (in conformity with their higher ranking) for a few modest steps toward equality.

Let us consider first the domestic role of men. The many complex studies done during the past decade have at least shown how difficult it is to pin down the causes of the present division of labor in the home. Thus, a simple summary is not adequate, but I note some salient findings here.

Women who work full-time have reduced the hours they spend on household tasks—in some studies, by almost half, while the reduction is substantial even if only routine tasks are included.[21] Husbands do not do much more housework if their wives are employed full time; nevertheless, over time men have increased their contribution (especially in child care), although the increase must be measured by a few minutes per day. White men and men with high incomes are least likely to increase their contribution. About half of both husbands and wives believe they ought to share equally; four-fifths think this of child care.[22] This represents a substantial change among wives, since until the end of the 1970s only about one-fourth of wives stated that they thought their husband should work more, while the vanguard of opinion was led by the young, the educated, and African Americans.[23]

I have sometimes suggested that men generally decide they if they must contribute more equally to housework, then they begin to feel the seduction of doing it in a quicker, more slovenly fashion. One study of a highly educated sample suggests this relationship: both spouses at least express more satisfaction when the division is equal, but the two want different things. The man wants to spend only a few hours in household work, while the women wants the traditional chores (laundry, shopping, cooking) to be shared.[24] In the United States, as in other countries, men are quicker to express support for equality in that sphere than actually to practice it. They may be wise in doing so, for that is surely less costly, at least for the present.

Of course, there are some differences. If a child two years or younger is in the house, the father does more, especially in child care. Better-educated husbands do a bit more, and so do younger husbands. But the indisputable fact is that men's domestic contribution does not change much whether or not they work, and whether or not their wives work.

With reference to the second large area of men's roles, holding jobs, we observe two further general principles of the relations between superordinates and those at lesser ranks. One is that men do not, in general, feel threatened by competition from women if they believe that the competition is fair and that women do not have an inside track. (To be sure, against overwhelming evidence, many do believe women enjoy that preference, while many whites believe that Blacks also have the inside track.) Men still feel that they are superior and will do better if given the chance. Since no society has actually tried the radical notion of genuinely fair competition, they have little reason to fear as yet. Except in a few occupations, they have lost very little ground. Women's position (by some measures) did improve during the 1970s, but changed very little in the 1980s.[25]

The second general principle of superordination noted here is that those who hold advantaged positions in the social structure (men, in this case) can perceive or observe that they are being flooded by people they consider their inferiors— women, Blacks, or the lower classes—while the massive statistical fact is that only a few such people are rising by much. There are several causes of this seeming paradox.

First, the new arrivals are more visible, by being different from those who have held the jobs up to this time. The second cause is our perception of relative numbers. Since there are far fewer positions at higher job levels, only a few new arrivals constitute a fair-size minority of the total at that level. Third, the mass media emphasize the hiring of women in jobs that seem not to be traditional for them, for that is considered news. Men's structural position, then, causes them to perceive radical change here even when little has taken place, and they resist it.

Nevertheless, the general conclusion does not change much. There is progress, but it is not at all clear-cut. After all, as long as the entrance of a few women into good jobs is news, the reality is less rosy than one might hope. Here are a few details:

> The number of businesses owned by women increased by 63 percent between 1982 and 1987.[26]

> The percentage of physicians who were women rose to 20 percent by 1988, an increase of two-thirds from 1980.

> Women made almost no inroads into the skilled crafts.

> Women made up almost one-half of all bakers, but nearly all simply put the dough through the final process in retail stores.

> As buyers and as administrators or managers in education, auditing, personnel, and training, women occupied about one-half of the jobs by 1988. However, they made up only about 3 percent of the top executives in large U.S. companies by 1991, almost no change from 1980. In general, their earnings in this group of managerial jobs were about two-thirds of male salaries.[27]

> As bus drivers and bartenders, women had almost half of the jobs.

> Over the decade, women's salaries rose; instead of making two-thirds of men's wages, they were making 72 percent.

The strongest variable that determines the lower wages of women is occupational segregation by sex, and that changed very little in the 1980s.[28] The blunt fact is that women have been able to enter a given occupation easily only if men no longer defend that territory. Or, more dramatically, the common pattern of "feminization" in most occupations is simple: They are rising on an elevator in a crumbling building. The job itself is being downgraded. They get better wages than other women, perhaps, but lower wages than men once made in those occupations.

Although the mass figures are correct, we need not discount all our daily observation either. We do see women entering formerly masculine jobs, from garbage collecting to corporate management. That helps undermine sex stereotypes and thereby becomes a force against inequality. Although occupational segregation continues to be strong, it did decline in most professions (e.g., engineering, dentistry, science, law, medicine). That is, the percentage of women in those professions did rise. Generally they doubled or trebled in the period 1970–88.[29] Of course, the absolute percentages of women in such professions remain modest (4–22 percent), because in occupations where almost everyone was once male, it is not possible to recruit, train, and hire enough women to achieve equality within even a generation. Still, the trend seems clear.

A secondary effect of these increasing numbers should be noted. Percentages are important, but so are absolute numbers. When women lawyers increase from about seven thousand to more than a hundred thousand, they become a much larger social force, even though they still form no more than about 22 percent of the total occupation. When women medical students, while remaining a minority in their classes, increase in number so that they can form committees, petition administrators, or give solidarity to one another against any traditional masculine badgering and disesteem, they greatly increase their influence on discriminatory attitudes and behavior. That is, as their rise in numbers permits the formation of real groups in any occupation, their power mounts faster (except at the very start) than the numbers or the percentages. Thus, changes occur even when the percentage of the occupation made up of women is not really large.

BASES OF PRESENT CHANGES

Most large-scale, objective measures of men's roles show little change over the past decade, but men do feel now and then that their position is in question, and their security somewhat fragile. I believe they are right, for they sense a set of forces that lie deeper and are more powerful than the day-to-day negotiation and renegotiation of advantage among individual husbands and wives, fathers and children, or bosses and those who work for them. Men are troubled by this new situation.

The conditions we live in are different from those of any earlier civilization, and they give less support to men's claims of superiority than perhaps any other historical era. When these conditions weaken that support, men can rely only on previous tradition, on power, or on their attempts to socialize their children to shore up their faltering advantages. Such rhetoric is not likely to be successful against the new objective conditions and the claims of aggrieved women. Thus, men are correct when they feel they are losing some of their privileges, even if many continue to smile at the rhetoric of the women's liberation movement.

The new conditions can be listed concretely, but I shall also give you a theoretical formulation of the process. Concretely, because of the increased use of various mechanical gadgets and devices, fewer tasks require much strength. As to those that still require strength, most men cannot do them either. Women can now do more household tasks that men once felt only they could do, and still more tasks are done by repair specialists called in to do them. With the development of modern warfare, there are few if any important combat activities that only men can do. Even now, their "auxiliary" tasks take them in and around battle zones as a matter of course. Women are much better educated than before.

With each passing year, psychological and sociological research reduces the areas in which men are reported to excel over women and discloses far more overlap in talents, so that even when males still seem to have an advantage, it is but slight. It is also becoming more widely understood that the top posts in government and business are not best filled by the stereotypical aggressive male but by the people, male or female, who are sensitive to others' needs, adept at obtaining cooperation, and skilled in social relations. Indeed, had male management in a number of U.S. industries followed that truth over the past decade, their failure to meet Japanese competition would surely have been less. Finally, in one sphere after another, the number of women who try to achieve rises, and so does the number who succeed.

Although the pressure of new laws has its direct effect on these conditions, the laws themselves arise from an awareness of the foregoing forces. Phrased in more theoretical terms, the underlying shift is toward the decreasing marginal utility of males, and this I suspect is the main source of men's resistance to women's liberation. That is, fewer people believe that what the male does is indispensable, is nonsubstitutable, or adds such a special value to any endeavor that it justifies his extra "price" or reward. In past wars, for example, males enjoyed a very high value not only because it was felt that they could do the job better than women but also because they might well make the key or marginal difference between being conquered and remaining free. In many societies, their marginal utility came from their contribution of animal protein through hunting. As revolutionary heroes, explorers, hunters, warriors, and daring capitalist entrepreneurs, men felt, and doubtless their women did too, that their contribution was beyond anything women could do. Without question, this would not be true of all men, but it would have been true of men as a distinct group. Men thereby earned extra privileges of rank, authority, and creature services.

It is not then as individuals, as persons, that males will be deemed less worthy in the future or their contributions less needed. Rather, they will be seen as having no claims to extra rewards solely because they are members of the male sex-class. This is part of a still broader trend of our generation, which will also increasingly deny that being white or upper-class produces a marginally superior result and thus justifies extra privileges.

The relations of individuals are subject to continuous renegotiation as people try to gain or keep advantages or cast off burdens. They fail or succeed in part because one or the other person has special resources or deficits that are unique to that individual. Over the long run, however, the outcome of those negotiations depends on the deeper social forces I have been describing, which ultimately determine which qualities or performances are more or less valued.

Men now perceive that they may be losing some of their advantages and that more aspects of their social roles are subject to public challenge and renegotiation than in the past. They resist these changes, and we can suppose they will continue to do so. In all such changes, there are gains and losses. Commonly, when people at lower social ranks gain freedom, those at higher ranks lose some power or centrality. When those at the lower ranks also lose some protection, some support, those at the higher ranks lose some of the burden of responsibility. It is also true that the care or help given by any dominant group in the past was never as much as their members believed, and their loss in political power or economic rule was never as great as they feared.

On the other hand, I know of no instance when a group or social stratum gained its freedom or moved toward more respect and then its members decided that they did not want it. Therefore, although men will not joyfully give up their rank, in spite of its burdens, neither will women decide that they would like to get back the older feminine privileges, accompanied by the lack of respect and material rewards that went with those courtesies.

I believe that men perceive their roles as being under threat in a world that is different from any in the past. No society has yet come even close to equality between the sexes, but the modern social forces described here did not exist before, either. At the most cautious, we must concede that the conditions favoring a trend toward more equality are more favorable than at any previous time in history. If we have little reason to conclude that equality is at hand, let us at least rejoice that we are still marching in the right direction.

NOTES

1. Herbert Goldberg, *The Hazards of Being Male* (New York: Nash, 1976), and Patricia C. Sexton, *The Feminized Male: Classrooms, White Collars, and the Decline of Manliness* (New York: Random House, 1969). On the recognition of disadvantages, see J.S. Chafetz, *Masculine/Feminine or Human?* (Itasca, Ill.: Peacock, 1974), 56 ff.

2. Joseph H. Pleck, "The Psychology of Sex Roles: Traditional and New Views," in *Women and Men: Changing Roles, Relationships, and Perceptions*, ed. Libby A. Cater and Anne F. Scott (New York: Aspen Institute for Humanistic Studies, 1976), 182. Pleck has carried out the most extensive research on male roles, and I am indebted to him for special help in this inquiry.

3. Sidney M. Jourard, "Some Lethal Aspects of the Male Role," in *Men and Masculinity*, ed. Joseph H. Pleck and Jack Sawyer (Englewood Cliffs, N.J.: Prentice-Hall, 1974), 22, and Irving London, "Frigidity, Sensitivity, and Sexual Roles," in *Men and Masculinity*, ed. Pleck and Sawyer, 42. See also the summary of such traits in I.K. Braverman et al., "Sex-Role Stereotypes: A Current Appraisal," in *Women and Achievement*, ed. Martha T.S. Mednick, S.S. Tangri, and Lois W. Hoffman (New York: Wiley, 1974), 32–47.

4. Robert Bierstedt's "The Sociology of the Majority," in his *Power and Progress* (New York: McGraw-Hill, 1974), 199–220, does not state these principles, but I was led to them by thinking about his analysis.

5. Robert K. Merton, in "The Perspectives of Insiders and Outsiders," in his *The Sociology of Science* (Chicago: University of Chicago Press, 1973), 99–136, has analyzed this view in some detail.

6. This general pattern is noted at various points in my monograph *The Celebration of Heroes: Prestige as a Social Control System* (Berkeley and Los Angeles: University of California Press, 1979).

7. Erving Goffman, "The Arrangement between the Sexes," *Theory and Society* 4 (1977): 307.

8. Hazel Erskine, "The Polls: Women's Roles," *Public Opinion Quarterly* 35 (Summer 1971).

9. Linda DeStefano and Diane Colasanto, Gallup Organization press release, 5 February 1989. For the *Times Mirror* sample, see Times Mirror Center for the People and the Press, press release, September 1990, 5.

10. Goffman, "Arrangement between the Sexes," 308.
11. A simple analysis of these responses is presented in William J. Goode, *Principles of Sociology* (New York: McGraw-Hill, 1977), 359 ff.
12. See Joseph H. Pleck, "The Power of Men," in *Women and Men: The Consequences of Power*, ed. Dana V. Hiller and R. Sheets (Cincinnati: Office of Women's Studies, University of Cincinnati, 1977), 20. See also Colin Bell and Howard Newby, "Husbands and Wives: The Dynamic of the Deferential Dialectic," in *Dependence and Exploitation in Work and Marriage*, ed. Diana L. Barker and Sheila Allen (London: Longman, 1976), 162–63, as well as Richard Sennett and Jonathan Cobb, *The Hidden Injuries of Class* (New York: Vintage Books, 1973), 125. On the satisfaction of work, see Daniel Yankelovich, "The Meaning of Work," in *The Worker and the Job*, ed. Jerome Rosow (Englewood Cliffs, N.J.: Prentice-Hall, 1974), 19–49. Men now recognize that they cannot easily use this rhetoric in family arguments, but I suspect they still believe it.
13. Whatever other sacrifices women want from men, until recently a large majority did not believe men should do more housework. On this matter, see Joseph H. Pleck, *Working Wives, Working Husbands* (Newbury Park, Calif.: Sage, 1985). In the mid-1970s only about one-fourth of wives agreed with such a proposal.
14. Sennett and Cobb, *Hidden Injuries of Class*, 125.
15. Susan Faludi, *Backlash: The Undeclared War against American Women* (New York: Crown, 1991), also documents in some detail many of the different efforts made during the 1980s to put women "back in their place," but little of what Faludi describes is truly "backlash." Leaving aside the innocents whom she attacks, most of these efforts were carried out by people who never thought women should have left "their" place to begin with.
16. To date, the most complete published summary for that period is that by Erskine ("The Polls," 275–91). From the late 1970s onward, however, the documentation is much fuller.
17. Stephanie Greene, "Attitudes toward Working Women Have 'a Long Way to Go,'" Gallup Opinion Poll, March 1976, 33. A wide variety of related questions are to be found in *Public Opinion Quarterly 53* (1989): 265–76.
18. Harris Survey, 16 February 1978; see also Harris Survey, 11 December 1975.
19. Time Mirror Center for the People and the Press, press release, September 1990, 10.
20. By now, the research data on household tasks are voluminous, their conclusions complex, and by the time they are published they may be somewhat dated. For comparisons with other countries, see Jonathan Gershuny and John P. Robinson, "Historical Changes in the Household Division of Labor," *Demography 25* (1988): 537–52. See also Linda Thompson and Alexis J. Walker, "Gender in Families: Women and Men in Marriage, Work, and Parenthood," *Journal of Marriage and the Family 51* (1989): 845–71; Mary H. Benin and Joan Agostinelli, "Husbands' and Wives' Satisfaction with the Division of Labor," *Journal of Marriage and the Family 50* (1988): 349–61; and Beth A. Shelton, "The Distribution of Household Tasks," *Journal of Family Issues* 11 (1990): 115–35. Joseph Pleck was a leader in these studies during the 1970s and 1980s.
21. Shelton, "Distribution of Household Tasks," table 2, p. 124; Gershuny and Robinson, "Historical Changes," 550.
22. Thompson and Walker, "Gender in Families," 857.
23. Arland Thornton and Deborah S. Freedman, "Changes in the Sex Role Attitudes of Women, 1962–1977," *American Sociological Review* 44 (1979): 833.
24. Benin and Agostinelli, "Husbands' and Wives' Satisfaction," 360.
25. For an excellent analysis of the many complex processes involved in these changes, see Barbara F. Reskin and Patricia A. Roos, *Job Queues, Gender Queues* (Philadelphia: Temple University Press, 1990).

26. U.S. Department of Commerce, Bureau of the Census, *Statistical Abstract of the United States, 1991* (Washington, D.C.: GPO, 1992).

27. These and other related data were published in *U.S. News and World Report*, 17 June 1991, from a study of the "glass ceiling" conducted for the Department of Labor but not officially issued.

28. Reskin and Roos, *Job Queues, Gender Queues*, tables 1.7, 1.8. See especially the case studies of changes in occupational segregation in ibid., part 2. In the usual case of "desegregation," women move into men's jobs (bartending, in-store baking, bus driving, banking) when those jobs are downgraded, usually technologically, so that the wages no longer attract men. Most of the expansion of women's jobs has occurred in "female" jobs, service jobs at lower levels.

29. Ibid., 19. On the earlier period, see also Victor R. Fuchs, "A Note on Sex Segregation in Professional Occupations," *Explorations in Economic Research* 2, no. 1 (Winter 1975): 105–11.

Reading 11

Choosing between Privilege and Sharing: Men's Responses to Gender and Family Change

Kathleen Gerson

While the transformation in women's lives has garnered the most attention, significant changes have also occurred in men's family patterns. The primary breadwinner who emphasizes economic support and constricted participation in child rearing persists, but this model—like its female counterpart, the homemaker—no longer predominates. Alongside this pattern, several alternatives have gained ad-

Excerpted from Kathleen Gerson, "Coping with Commitment: Dilemmas and Conflicts of Family Life." In Alan Wolfe (Ed.). *America at Century's End*. 1991. Berkeley: University of California Press. pp. 35–57.

herents. An increasing proportion of men have moved away from family commitments—among them single and childless men who have chosen to forgo parenthood and divorced fathers who maintain weak ties to their offspring. Another group of men, however, has become more involved in the nurturing activities of family life. Although these "involved fathers" rarely assume equal responsibility for child rearing, they are nevertheless significantly more involved with their children than are primary breadwinners, past or present. Change in men's lives, while limited and contradictory, is nonetheless part of overall family change.

As with women's choices, men's family patterns reflect uneven exposure to structural change in family and work arrangements. In my research on men's changing patterns of parental involvement, I found that men who established employment stability in highly rewarded but demanding jobs, and who experienced unexpected marital stability with a domestically oriented spouse, were pushed and pulled toward primary breadwinning even when they had originally hoped to avoid such a fate. In contrast, men who experienced employment instability and dissatisfaction with the "rat race" of high-pressure, bureaucratically controlled jobs tended to turn away from primary breadwinning. When these experiences were coupled with instability in heterosexual relationships and dissatisfying experiences with children, many rejected parental involvement altogether—opting instead for personal independence and freedom from children. When declining work commitments were coupled with unexpected pleasure in committed, egalitarian heterosexual relationships and unexpected fulfillment through involvement with children, men tended to become oriented toward involved fatherhood. Thus, while about 36 percent of the respondents developed a primary breadwinning orientation, the remaining men did not. Unanticipated encounters in relationships with women and at the workplace encouraged these men to establish either greater distance from family life (about 30 percent of the sample) or, alternatively, to become more involved in parenthood than did primary breadwinners (about 34 percent of the sample).

As with women, these contrasting orientations among men represent reasonable, if often unexpected and typically unconscious, reactions to encounters with contrasting packages of constraints and opportunities in adulthood. They also reflect different responses to the trade-offs men face in their family choices. Although men do not typically have to choose between workplace participation and childbearing, they do confront conflicts and dilemmas. As women's lives have been transformed, men, too, are increasingly caught on the horns of a dilemma between preserving their historic privileges and taking advantage of expanded opportunities to share or reject the economic and social burdens of breadwinning. Among men (as among women), different experiences and orientations promote contrasting strategies to cope with the tensions between maintaining male privilege and easing traditional male burdens.

STRATEGIES OF PRIMARY BREADWINNING MEN

Just as domestically oriented women interpret the meaning of work through the lens of their family commitments, whether or not they are employed, so primary breadwinning men define their parental involvement in terms of income, whether or not their wives work. First, these men emphasize money, not time, in calculating their contributions to the household. For this surveyor, "good fathering" means being a good provider—that is providing financial support, not participating in child rearing:

> What is a good father? It's really hard to say. I always supported my children, fed them, gave them clothes, a certain amount of love when I had time. There was always the time factor. Maybe giving them money doesn't make you a good father, but not giving it probably makes you a bad father. I guess I could have done maybe a little more with them if financially I wasn't working all the time, but I've never hit my kids. I paid my daughter's tuition. I take them on vacation every year. Am I a good father? Yes, I would say so.

Even when their wives are employed, primary breadwinning men devalue the importance of wives' earnings. They define this income as "extra" and nonessential and thus also define a woman's job as secondary to her domestic responsibilities. Even though his wife worked hard as a waitress, this architect did not believe that she shared the duties of breadwinning:

> She took care of [our son], and I did all the breadwinning. When we got the house, she started working for extra money. She worked weekends, but her job doesn't affect us at all. Financially, my job takes care of everything plus. Her income is gravy, I guess you'd call it.

By defining fatherhood in terms of financial support and wives' income as supplementary and nonessential, primary breadwinners relieve themselves of the responsibility for domestic chores and of a sense of guilt that such an arrangement might generate. A park worker was proud to announce:

> I do nothing with the cooking or cleaning. I do no household, domestic anything. I could, but I won't, because I feel I shouldn't have to. If my wife's not sick, I see no reason why I should do it. I feel my responsibility is to bring home the money and her responsibility is to cook and clean.

And like the domestically oriented women who felt fortunate not to *have* to work, primary breadwinners see their wives as the fortunate recipients of personal freedom and material largess. The park worker continued:

> My wife's got it made. The cat's got it made, too. I'm very good to my wife. She drives a new car, has great clothes, no responsibilities. She's very happy to be just around the house, do what she wants. She's got her freedom; what more could you want?

Although primary breadwinning men, like domestically oriented women, have been relatively insulated from the social-structural incentives that promote nontraditional choices among others, they, too, are affected by changes in other's lives. Despite stable employment and marriages, these men fear the erosion of the material and ideological supports for male privilege that their fathers could take for granted. As women have fought for equal rights at the workplace and other men have moved away from family patterns that emphasize separate spheres, those who remain committed to the "good provider" ethic feel embattled and threatened. Even the small gains made by women at the workplace are perceived as unfair as the historic labor market advantages of men undergo reconsideration, if not drastic alteration. A plumber and father of five resented the incursions some women are making into his field of expertise:

> Women have it a little easier as far as job-related [matters] is concerned [*sic*]. The tests are getting easier, classifications are going down [to let women in]. From what I hear in plants with women, they *can't* do the job. This isn't chauvinistic guys talking; this is guys talking in general. We pick up a 250-pound motor, but there's no way a young lady will pick it up unless she's a gorilla, a brute. But when she's got to do the job, two other guys have got to come along to help. I'm not saying women can't handle the job, [but] a woman comes to work for us, and they [the bosses] have got five men covering for her. Usually it's a hardship, but the guys bend over backwards for her. If she can't handle her job, why should she be there?

Similarly, primary breadwinners make a distinction between their situation and that of other men—especially childless, single men who, presumably, do not share their heavy economic responsibilities. They define their interests not just in terms of being a man, but a particular type of man who sacrifices for the good of his family and therefore needs to protect his interests in a hostile, changing world. The park worker explained:

> Being a father is a responsibility. If you don't have a wife, don't have children—you get fired, who cares? When you have someone who's depending on your salary, you protect your interest on the job more. You become more afraid, and you become more practical. You realize you're out in the ocean, and nobody's going to help you. You're on your own, and you grow up real quick and start behaving like an adult.

In response to this perceived need to protect their interests, primary breadwinning men, like domestically oriented women, hold tightly to a set of social and political beliefs that emphasize the natural basis and moral superiority of gender differences and inequalities. Primary breadwinners argue that their own sexual division of labor is both natural and normal, as the plumber maintained:

> As far as bread and butter is concerned, the man should have a little more [of] the responsibility than the woman. I'm not chauvinistic or anything, but it's basic, normal [that] it's a man. There aren't many men where the wife works full-time.

> *Who should take care of the children?*

> Again, you go back to whoever's home and whoever's working. Primary would be the mother. It's natural; it comes natural. In my house, it's *my* wife. She's doing it all.

ALTERNATIVES TO PRIMARY BREADWINNING AMONG MEN

Men who eschew primary breadwinning have concluded that the privileges afforded "good providers" are not worth the price that privilege entails. They view breadwinning responsibilities as burdensome and constricting, but their rejection of breadwinning poses its own dilemmas. The loosening bonds of marriage allow these men greater latitude to avoid parental responsibilities, both economic and social. On the other hand, the increasing number of work-committed women encourages and, indeed, pressures some nontraditional men to become more involved in the noneconomic aspects of family life than was typical of men a generation ago. These two patterns—forgoing parental commitments and becoming involved in caretaking—represent increasingly popular, if quite different, responses to the search for an alternative to traditional masculinity amid a contradictory and ambiguous set of options.

Forgoing Parental Commitments

Like permanently childless women, some men have opted to forgo parental responsibilities. This group included childless men who do not wish or plan to become fathers and divorced fathers who have significantly curtailed their economic and social ties to their offspring in the wake of marital disruption. These men have come to value autonomy over commitment and to view children as a threat to their freedom of choice. A social service director, for example, was convinced that childlessness opened vocational options he would not have enjoyed as a breadwinning father:

> *What do you think things would be like if you did have kids?*

> Vocationally, I would have had to make other choices because the field I'm in just doesn't pay a terrific amount of money, and with children, you have expenses, and you have to look forward to a lot more future planning than I have to do with my current situation. So I've been able to sort of play with my career, and really just have a lot of fun in doing what I do, without having that responsibility.

Permanently childless men have decided that the potential benefits of fatherhood are not worth its risks. A childless psychologist admitted with some discomfort:

> *Does seeing other men with young children bring out any response in you?*

> Relief! [laughs] I don't just see the good parts; I see it all. I see the shit they have to wade through literally and figuratively, and very often I say to myself, "There but for the grace of God go I." It's a very ambivalent position I have about it.

This ambivalence toward fatherhood is not necessarily confined to childless men. Some divorced fathers also develop a relatively weak emotional and social attachment to their children. Whether their reaction is a defense against the pain of loss or an extension of their lack of involvement in child rearing prior to divorce, divorced fathers who become distant from their children tend to discount the importance of parenthood. A truck driver and divorced father of two, who sees his children and pays their child support sporadically, explained:

> *How would you feel if you had never had kids?*

> I don't think that would bother me. Being that I do have them, it's okay. I enjoy them when I see them. But if I never had them, I don't think I'd really miss them. I don't think it would be that important if they weren't there.

And even though this divorced dentist spent little time with his school-age daughter, who resided with her mother in another city, he envied his childless counterparts:

> Men who don't have any children just seem to have more time to do the things they want to do and don't have to deal with the trials and tribulations of raising a child.

In contrast to traditional women and men, these men agree with work-committed women that traditional arrangements are neither inherently superior nor more natural family forms. Instead, they argue that primary breadwinning is oppressive to men and harmful to society. . . .

[T]hese men support women's economic self-sufficiency, for their own ability to remain autonomous is closely linked to women's independence. A systems analyst who had never married declared:

> I'm not really big on women who stay at home and just raise kids. I think everybody should be a fully functioning, self-supporting adult and certainly economically that's a necessity now. I believe, in terms of women's issues, that if they prepared themselves for the idea that they have to assume their financial burdens and responsibilities, they won't have to be emotional hostages to toxic relationships. And men won't either.

This vision of economic and social equality does not, however, easily extend to the domestic sphere. Because these men place a high value on their freedom, they resist applying the principle of equality to child rearing. Indeed, the paradox of espousing the equal right to be free while resisting the equal responsibility for parenthood leads them to avoid parental commitments. The systems analyst feared he would be drawn into what he deemed the least attractive aspects of parenting:

> [If I had a child,] I could see that I would want to take a role in playing with the child, overseeing its training and schooling, providing that type of thing. I don't really see me wanting to do a lot in the way of getting up in the middle of the night, formulas, changing of diapers. I'm not at all into that.

And so, these men are able to resolve the dilemma between their support of some aspects of gender equality and their resistance to its more threatening implications only by forgoing both the burdens and the joys of raising a child.

Caretaking Fathers

A more equal sharing of both earning income and rearing children provides another alternative to primary breadwinning. While complete equality remains rare even among dual-earner couples, male participation in caretaking is nevertheless on the rise. Men who are married to work-committed women and divorced fathers who have retained either joint or sole custody of their children are particularly likely to participate in child rearing. In contrast to childless men, these men have placed family at the center of their lives. In contrast to primary breadwinners, they value spending time with their families as much as contributing money to them. A utility worker with a young daughter and a wife employed as a marketing manager insisted:

For me, being with my family is the major, the ultimate in my life—to be with them and share things with them. Money is secondary, but time with them is the important thing in life. That's why I put up with this job—because I can get home early. To me, spending time with [my daughter] makes up for it. I'm home at 3:40 and spend a lot of time with her, just like the long days when she was young and I was on unemployment.

Some involved fathers view the time spent in child care not as simply helping out, but as an incomparably pleasurable activity and an essential component of good parenting. This thirty-seven-year-old construction worker chose to work the night shift so that he could spend his days with his newborn daughter while his wife pursued a dancing career:

I take care of [my daughter] during the morning and the day. [My wife] takes care [of her] in the evenings. I work from three to eleven P.M. and wake up with the morning ahead of me, and that's important with a little one. Even if I'm pretty tired when I get up, all I have to do is look at that little face, and I feel good. It's not just a case of doing extra things. I'm not doing extra things. This is what has to be done when you have a baby. . . . You learn so much too. It's a thrill to watch the various senses start to come into play. She'll make a gurgling noise that's close to a vowel sound or an actual syllable, and I'll repeat it. I love the communication. The baby smiles more around me than she does around [her mother].

Unlike primary breadwinners or childless men, these "involved fathers" do not draw distinct boundaries between the tasks of mothers and fathers. The time constraints on their wives combine with their own need and preference for economic sharing to promote financial and social interdependence. Neither breadwinning nor nurturing is defined as one person's domain. . . .

These involved fathers come closest to embracing the "interdependent" vision of gender equality upheld by work-committed mothers. They see moral and practical advantages to shared caretaking. According to the construction worker quoted earlier, domestic as well as workplace equality is not only the most practical response to changed economic conditions but also the best way to avoid the resentment and conflict that too often occur between husbands and wives:

With the baby, we do everything even-steven. What other way can you go nowadays, the whole economy being what it is? But that's also the way it should be. Even if I had the money to take care of things [myself], [my wife] has a calling, a vocation, that she needs to fulfill and I want her to fulfill. We're in this together; we both want to be an influence on the child. The next logical step is for both of us to spend time with her. . . . I feel there won't be any of this women-against-men in our marriage.

If work-committed women face numerous obstacles in their search for ways to combine career and motherhood, then nurturing fathers also face deeply rooted structural barriers to full equality in parenting. Even when the desire to participate in parenting is strong, these men encounter significant constraints on implementing their preferences. Role reversal, for example, is rarely a realistic option, since men's wages remain essential to the survival of the vast majority of households and few couples are comfortable with an arrangement in which a woman supports a man. . . .

[W]hile women grapple with the choice between motherhood and committed employment, men are generally denied such a choice. Even when a man wishes to be an involved father, rarely is he able to trade full-time employment for parental involvement. The primary breadwinnning surveyor noted, with some envy, that although women remain disadvantaged, many still retain the option not to work—an option few men enjoy:

> Women can have the best of both worlds, whereas men can only have one choice. A woman has a choice of which way she wants to go. If she wants to be a successful lawyer, she has that choice. If she wants to stay home, she also has that choice most of the time. Women have doors opened for them and their meals paid for. They have the best of both worlds; men are just stuck with one.

Structural and ideological barriers to men's participation in child rearing inhibit the prospects for genuine equality in parental and employment options. Limits on men's options constrain even the most feminist men's ability and willingness to embrace genuine symmetry in gender relations. The truncated range of choices available to men restricts the options open to women as well.

Chapter
4

Sexuality

Reading 12 ~~10/20/94~~

The Culture of Adolescent Sexuality

Lillian B. Rubin

If there are two words that describe the sexual sensibility of today's youth, they are "tolerance" and "entitlement." *Nowhere are the effects of the sexual revolution more dramatically evident than in teenagers' sense of entitlement to make their own choices about sex and in their tolerance of all kinds of sexual behaviors, so long as they meet the current peer norms.* A sharp contrast to the young of earlier generations, among whom tolerance was limited and entitlement almost nonexistent.

It's the language of love and romance, not commitment and marriage, that defines the boundaries of sexuality for most teenagers today. No promises made, given or implied. "We love each other, so there's no reason why we shouldn't be making love," said 16-year-old Emily from Columbus, Ohio, her dark eyes fixing me with an intent gaze.

"Does that mean you've made a long-term commitment to each other?"

She hesitated and looked doubtful, then finally spoke: "I don't know what you mean by that. Do you mean are we going to get married? The answer is no. Or will

From Lillian B. Rubin, *Erotic Wars: What Happened to the Sexual Revolution?* 1990. New York: Harper-Collins. References have been deleted.

we be together next year? I don't know about that; that's a long time from now. Most kids don't stay together such a long time. But we won't date anybody else as long as we're together. That's a commitment, isn't it? Just because we don't expect to get married doesn't mean we're not in love, does it?"

Data on teenage sexual activity are inexact, to say the least. But most experts in the field agree that somewhere over 60 percent of American teenagers have had sexual intercourse by the time they finish high school. A Harris poll in 1986 found that 57 percent of the nation's 17-year-olds, 46 percent of the 16-year-olds and 29 percent of the 15-year-olds had had sexual intercourse. In a finely tuned analysis of the national data, demographer Sandra Hofferth estimates conservatively that 66 percent are sexually experienced by the time they reach their nineteenth birthday. Planned Parenthood puts the figure at 75 percent. And all agree that the age at which adolescents make their sexual debut continues to decline. A recent survey of eighth-grade students—that is, 14-year-olds—from three rural counties in Maryland revealed that 58 percent of the boys and 47 percent of the girls had experienced coitus.

Even among teenagers brought up in conservative Christian families, the proportion who are sexually experienced is very high. In mid-1987, eight evangelical denominations in the central and southern states conducted a study of teen sexual behavior. The findings could have given little comfort to the advocates of sexual abstinence in the teenage world. Forty-three percent of the young people surveyed, all of whom attended church regularly, had had sexual intercourse before their eighteenth birthday, and an almost equal number had experimented with sexual behaviors short of actual coitus. Equally unsettling for their parents and ministers, well over one-third of these students refused to brand sex outside marriage as morally unacceptable.

These impressive statistics speak to important changes in the culture of adolescent sexuality—changes that are especially profound for girls, since boys and men have always had more sexual leeway than girls and women. For boys, the big difference now is that, for the first time ever, their sexual exploration and activity need not be confined to "bad" girls only. No small change, it's true, but insignificant when compared with the shift for girls, who now have permission to be sexually active outside the context of love, marriage and commitment.

Still, there's something more to be said about the statistics we commonly cite about teenage sex. For while statistics may not lie, they often leave us with a distorted version of the truth. It isn't that the findings of the studies are wrong, but that, by the very nature of large-scale statistical surveys, they can get at only a small corner of reality. In the matter of adolescent sexual behavior, these studies ask such questions as: Have you ever had sexual intercourse? A yes puts the respondent into the sexually active category, a no into its opposite. But these are labels that tell us little about the reality of a young person's sexual experience, especially among the girls, even about whether they are sexually active or not.

Two-thirds of the teenagers I met had had sexual intercourse. Yet among those "sexually active" young people were several girls who, after trying it out once, decided to put the whole issue on hold. "It was with my boyfriend, who I'd been going out with for about seven or eight months," explained a 16-year-old Oakland girl, who looked around uncomfortably as she spoke. "We talked about it a lot, and we both decided we wanted to and, like, the time was right. It was the first time for both of us, and we decided we wanted to have sex for the first time with each other."

"And how did you feel about it afterwards?"

"It didn't affect me in the way I thought it would. I mean, I didn't sit around afterwards thinking: 'Gosh, I took this great, huge step.' I think I expected everything in the world to change, but the world just kept going on the next day just like it did the day before. But I do feel it was an important experience that maybe I should have done when I was older. I'm not sure. I don't have any regrets, but it wasn't exactly what I expected. I mean, it wasn't that bad, but it wasn't like it felt real good or anything. I'm glad the first time was with him, but I don't feel like rushing out and doing it again with him or anyone else, not in the near future anyway."

There are others who also would come up positive in the sexually active column yet who, on closer examination, turned out to have been abstinent for as long as a year or two at the time of our meeting. Seventeen-year-old Joanne, a high-school senior from Richmond, Virginia, had her first sexual experience about six months after her fourteenth birthday. "We had been together for four months, and he asked me to have sex. He didn't push me; he was very understanding. But we were really in love, and it felt like, why shouldn't we?"

"How was it for you?"

"It was fine. Everyone was saying, 'You'll be really scared the first time,' but I wasn't. I knew I really loved him a lot, and I knew he felt the same way about me. So it didn't bother me at all. I felt really close to him and I liked that, and I could tell he really felt close to me, too. It felt really nice. We went together for a year and a half, and since then I haven't had sex with anyone else."

"Do you want to?"

"No, not really, not now anyway. If I fall in love with someone, I'm sure I will—want to, I mean. But I haven't yet, and it's been over a year since we broke up."

Finally, there are those who had been quite sexually active, girls who at 14 or 15 had had more than one sexual experience, sometimes with several different partners, and in the process seemed to have scared themselves into celibacy. "I go to this Christian school, and a lot of the kids are into stuff they shouldn't be doing, you know, sex and drugs and things like that," said a 17-year-old New York suburbanite, the words rushing from her as if in a confessional. "It's not as bad as the public school in this town, but there's a lot of that stuff in my school, too. Anyway, I met this boy there who became my boyfriend for a little while. That was the first time I had sex.

"At the time, my parents and I weren't getting along, and I was rebelling against them. So sex and drugs and all that was a good way to do it. But I always felt guilty and stuff; I'd wake up the next morning and feel miserable. Then the headmaster of the school found out about what the kids were doing, and they really cleaned house and expelled a whole bunch of kids. I was so terrified that they'd get me, too, but I was one of the lucky ones."

Interrupting the flow of words for a moment, she planted her elbows on the table, cupped her face in her hands and said quietly, "I was so relieved. I was getting more and more scared, like I didn't know what was happening to me, or why I was doing what I was doing. It seemed like I was trying to find a way to stop but didn't know how. I found out that sex without marriage is more physically enjoyable than it is mentally. So now I'm saving myself for when I get married. Maybe that's why I'm looking forward to marriage so much."

"What do you mean when you say sex was more physically then mentally enjoyable?"

"You know, it was nice; it feels good; it's nice to be close like that to someone you care about. But then you have all the guilt."

"Did you have orgasms?"

"Not at first, but after we were doing it for a while, I did—not all the time, but a lot of times."

Just as the words "sexually active" do not define the experience of such young people, so it is a travesty to describe most of the rest as "not sexually active" simply because they have not had sexual intercourse. Among the teenagers I met, just over one-third would fall into the "not sexually active" category of most large-scale surveys. Yet only seven had never engaged in any sexual play at all—all of them 13–15 year olds.

Ironically, our historic and obsessive concern with virginity, which discourages sexual intercourse, unintentionally fosters behaviors no one thought to prohibit. Thus, most of those who had not yet had coitus engaged in all kinds of sexual practices, from genital fondling to mutual masturbation to oral sex. And the older they were, the more sophisticated the level of exploration and experimentation became. Indeed, by the time these "not sexually active" young people were finishing high school, fellatio and cunnilingus had become a significant part of sexual activity for close to half of them. "I don't mind giving a guy a blow job if he comes fast," said a Houston 17-year-old, fingering her long golden-highlighted brown hair as she spoke. "But with some guys it takes them a while to come, and my jaws lock, and that's not the most enjoyable thing in the world."

Anal sex, behavior that was almost unheard of among heterosexuals a couple of decades ago, also is part of the sexual discourse now, something kids talk about as a possibility, although only a few of them, whether they had had coitus or not, had tried it out before the end of high school. "I think whatever a couple does is their business; it's up to them," said 16-year-old Sara from Louisville. "There are things I won't do, like anal sex. My last boyfriend started to do it, and it hurt. It's terrible; I made him stop. But my best friend says she likes it, and if that's what she wants, that's okay. I don't think anyone has a right to judge what people do. It's nobody's business as long as the couple both agree."

Even the most conservative of the young people I met were firm in their belief that the choice about being sexual belongs to the individual alone. They make no judgments of others, and expect none to be made of them. "I have friends who are sexually active, and I think that's great for them," said 15-year-old Ying, a San Franciscan. "As far as I'm concerned, I think each person has to make their own decision about what they're going to do. If they're mature enough to handle it, that's fine; it's up to them. I can respect their decision, and I want people to respect mine. For me, I know I'm not ready, and I think it would be kind of dumb to do something I don't really want to do. But I don't know how I'll feel next year. If I meet somebody I really care about and it seems right, then I'd have sex."

"Do people respect your decision not be sexual now?"

"Yeah, mostly. I mean, if you go to a dance or a party, there's always some boy who'll try. But I don't go to those things a lot. And my real friends, they'd never pressure me about something like that. People mostly figure it's your business, and you'll do what you want."

The question of peer pressure is not quite so simple, of course. But generally it also is not the kind of direct, one-on-one pressure the adult world so often envisions. Instead, the pressure resides largely in the atmosphere itself—pressure that permeates all facets of teenage life, whether the style of dress, the language used, the music listened to or the initiation into sexual activity. The need to belong, to feel one with the world in which we live, is common to all of us, adolescents and adults. Why else do fashions sweep the country, influencing not just the clothes we buy and the books we read, but personal habits of health and leisure? If everybody's wearing it, reading it, listening to it, doing it, the temptation to conform, to share in the experiences of those around us, is almost irresistible.

For adolescents who are struggling to separate from the family, to find a self-in-the-world that's uniquely theirs, a reference group against which to judge and measure themselves is a must. The peer group is the place where the possibilities of a self-yet-to-become can find expression. But like the family before it, this new group has its own needs for conformity among its members and its own requirements for acceptance. Paradoxically, then, the very group that facilitates the separation from the family and its restrictions becomes another arbiter of behavior in equally powerful ways.

When it comes to sex, it's not just the need to belong that exerts pressure, it's the need to know as well. A member of the peer group is the first to take the plunge and talk about it. It's news; it's consequential. For those who have not yet had the experience, it's riveting. Someone close has actually done it, can describe it, can say what it feels like. The veil of silence is pierced. But for the uninitiated, the mystery deepens; the pressure to know grows.

Undoubtedly there are instances when peer pressure is more direct and specific. The girl who is the first among her friends to have sexual intercourse may need to convince others to join her in order to assuage whatever guilt or anxiety may accompany her behavior. "I have to admit I was glad when a couple of my friends did it, too. It made me feel better that I wasn't the only one," said Lorie, now 18, as she recalled her feelings when she had her first experience at 15. "I didn't exactly try to talk them into it, but I didn't not try either. I mean, I talked about it a lot, and maybe I even made it better than I really thought it was so they'd get jealous and do it."

Some adolescents are able to resist all such persuasions. Most of these boys and girls stand outside the mainstream of peer culture and identify themselves—sometimes with pain, sometimes with pride—as "not in with the popular kids at school." A few, however, manage to withstand the pressure, whether around sex, drugs or alcohol, while still sustaining an identification with friends and peers whose behavior differs from their own. These generally are young people who exhibit a kind of personal magnetism that's unusual at any stage of life and who also have serious commitments to career or sports—a boy who's a committed runner and bicyclist, a girl who expects a college basketball scholarship, another who not only knows she's going on to college, but already has chosen a career path that requires an advanced degree. Their personal charm helps them to maintain status in the peer group, while their special interests enable them to keep enough distance to oppose its pressures.

Once in a while, there's someone for whom the example of friends and peers inspires restraint rather than the kind of titillation that seeks mimicry. "Whatever I do, I do in moderation; I know my limits," said 16-year-old Valerie, a Los Angeles girl, who spoke in a quiet, firm voice that matched the controlled, poised manner she exhibited throughout the interview. "A lot of people feel like when they get to high school, they have to become 'unvirgined.' I have no hang-ups about that. I'm not sexually active yet. I figure when the time comes, it comes, and I'll know it. I watch some of my friends and see the trouble they're getting into—you know, they get pregnant, or they're doing so bad in school that they'll never be able to get into a decent college. A couple of kids I know even dropped out of school. It's not at all appealing to me."

But these are the rare ones. For the rest, even though they may never have an conscious awareness of the pressure, it's clear that the peer culture in which they live and with which they identify is a powerful influence in their decision making about sex.

Boys have always felt the urgency to be one of the guys, whether in doing sex or talking about it. For them, the difference between the present and the past is only in the timing. The age at which they come under pressure to conform sexually is substantially younger today than it was a few decades ago. "I was 15 the first time I had sex, and before that I lied about it, told people I did it when I didn't," said a 17-year-old Chapel Hill boy, the discomfort on his face contradicting the words that seemed to come so easily.

"Why did you feel you had to lie?"

"There was always a lot of pressure from the other guys to join in the action, and I didn't want them to think I was a wimp or a nerd. You know, they were always talking about it, whether this girl or that one is a good lay, or about some girl who's got great tits, or somebody who likes it in the ass. And you want to be a part of it all, so you lie."

Girls, too, have always lied to accommodate peer norms. But in earlier generations, the sexually active girl played the role of the naïve innocent. Today the innocent pretends to be the sexual sophisticate. "I haven't found someone I feel comfortable with, so I haven't felt the need to have sex yet," said Hannah, a 15-year-old from suburban Chicago. "I don't see the point in rushing anything; I'm young; I have time. But only my very best friend knows the truth. The other kids don't know because I lie and say I'm doing things I'm not. As long as you say what they want to hear, nobody bothers you. It's when you're different that they don't like it."

According to the standards of today's adolescent culture, both boys and girls are expected to have sex with only one person at a time and to be true to the relationship. For most sexually active teenagers, therefore, serial monogamy is the rule. The definition of relationship, however, can be very loose. "A relationship is when two people decide they're going together, even if it's only for a weekend," explained 15-year-old Rick.

Most relationships probably last more than a weekend, but a month is a long time, and a year an eternity. To the adult mind, this seems shocking. But to the 15-year-old, for whom a year is such a significant proportion of conscious life, it is a very long time indeed.

Ideally, the norm calling for serial monogamy applied to all, regardless of gender. But, as is the case in any complex part of life, change and stability live alongside each other, sometimes easily, sometimes not. Therefore, there's a great distance between their ideal statements and the reality with which these young people live. In the real world, the double standard of sexuality that has for so long defined our sexual consciousness has been wounded, but is not yet dead. Consequently, a boy still has very wide latitude before he's criticized or censured, while a girl who is involved with more than one boy at a time will soon acquire a "bad rep." For her, the word is "slut"—a term in common use in high schools and colleges all across the land and one of unequivocal derogation. In a rather dramatic shift from the past, however, the girls are no longer so quick to be the enforcers of the sexual rules. In fact, they're far less likely to do the censuring now than they were in the fifties.

I don't mean to suggest that adolescent girls no longer render judgments on their peers or that a girl won't use the word "slut" to describe the behavior of another. But to the degree that they do, the standards by which those judgments are made are likely to be far more diverse than they were in the past and, more important, not so totally derived from the ideals of sexual conduct that, historically, have been decreased by those in power.

Obviously, no one is immune to the impact of those edicts. Adolescent girls, like their adult sisters and mothers, know quite well that men retain at least some of their ancient power to name women's behavior, to define what is worthy and acceptable and what is not. But most girls and women no longer accept such labeling without question or contention. This, in fact, is one of the unheralded gains of the feminist movement. The changes it has wrought in women's conception of self—in their belief in their right to define themselves and, at the very least, to participate in setting their own behavioral standards—have been so deeply internalized by now that they seem natural to the adolescents of this generation, as if it were ever thus. Consequently, teenage girls today not only are tolerant of an extraordinarily wide range of sexual behaviors, they also believe that, just as their own behavior is no one else's business, so it is with another's.

As with any of us, belief and behavior don't always match, of course. But many of the girls I met are conscious of the conflict between the two and persist in trying to reduce the dissonance. Even when they can't or don't, however, the girl who offends group norms usually isn't turned into a pariah and thrown into exile as she was in the fifties. "You know, it doesn't seem right that a girl gets a bad name; the guys sleep around all the time, and nobody calls them anything," said a 16-year-old small-town Texas girl angrily.

"Well, how do you feel about girls who sleep around?"

"I don't believe in it, and I don't really think anybody should do it. But, I don't know, I guess it's not my business, and I don't think it should be theirs either," she concluded emphatically.

For most men, however, the power to name and label is not given up lightly. Here again, I'm not suggesting that a man consciously sets out to control female sexual behavior or that any given man is aware that he's doing it. Rather, I'm saying that it's so deeply ingrained a part of the social fabric that it seems almost as natural as breathing. "A guy's got to know what he's getting into when he starts up with a girl," cautioned a 17-year-old Pittsburgh boy, straightening himself in his chair as if to make sure that his body language matched the certainty in his voice. "If you're looking for a girlfriend, not just some quick and dirty sex, you don't want to get involved with a slut, you know, one of those girls who goes out with more than one guy at a time, or a girl who goes for those one-nighters. You want her to be one of the nice girls, you know, the kind of girl who only has sex with her boyfriend, and she makes sure he's her boyfriend before she does it."

While male condemnation of girls who violate the norm of monogamy is ubiquitous, I never heard anyone speak about a boy with equal disparagement. Indeed, if they wanted to, they would have had a hard time finding a way to express their feelings, since there are no words in the lexicon of teenage life that would give evidence that any serious stigma attaches to a sexually promiscuous male. For him, the favored term is "stud," a word that traditionally has carried far more approbation than opprobrium. But here, too, there are subtle changes to suggest that girls are taking to themselves some of the power to name and label. Thus, when a girl uses the word "stud" now, it often is said sarcastically, carrying negative connotations and designed to warn other girls to beware. Among boys, however, the word still has the power to evoke images of masculinity and feelings of envy.

Certainly there are plenty of boys today who are sensitive to relationship issues, who say they only really enjoy sex when it's with someone they care about, who wouldn't be proud to be called a stud. But the same boys also find themselves envious of the guy who has such a reputation, even though his behavior may be distasteful to them. "There's these guys at school who are real studs, and sometimes I look at them and wonder: 'How do they do it?' " said a 16-year-old Cincinnati boy with reluctant admiration. "I don't know, I guess you can't help envying guys who can always get any girl. I mean, I don't like the idea of degrading girls or anything like that, but, well, I don't know, it seems that those guys are the ones who get the prettiest girls in school."

Change and stability, coexisting together, living side by side so peacefully that most of the time we don't even notice the contradictions involved. The changes in the world of adolescent sex, especially for girls, are massive and real: A teenage girl can now be fully sexually active without risk to her reputation and, therefore, to her sense of self. But some things remain doggedly, intransigently, the same: The power to determine the limits of her behavior, to legislate who's fit to be girlfriend, wife, mother, remains in the hands of men. Courts still declare a woman an "unfit" mother and take custody of her children from her because of her sexual behavior. Who ever heard of the phrase "unfit father"? And what is it that would make him "unfit"? Certainly not the fact that he's having a sexual relationship with a woman.

Reading 13

Dubious Conceptions: The Controversy Over Teen Pregnancy

Kristin Luker

The conventional wisdom has it that an epidemic of teen pregnancy is today ruining the lives of young women and their children and perpetuating poverty in America. In polite circles, people speak regretfully of "babies having babies." Other Americans are more blunt. "I don't mind paying to help people in need," one angry radio talk show host told Michael Katz, a historian of poverty, "but I don't want my tax dollars to pay for the sexual pleasure of adolescents who won't use birth control."

By framing the issue in these terms, Americans have imagined that the persistence of poverty and other social problems can be traced to youngsters who are too impulsive or too ignorant to postpone sexual activity, to use contraception, to seek an abortion, or failing all that, especially if they are white, to give their babies up for adoption to "better" parents. Defining the problem this way, many Americans, including those in a position to influence public policy, have come to believe that one attractive avenue to reducing poverty and other social ills is to reduce teen birth rates. Their remedy is to persuade teenagers to postpone childbearing, either by convincing them of the virtues of chastity (a strategy conservatives prefer) or by making abortion, sex education, and contraception more freely available (the strategy liberals prefer).

Reducing teen pregnancy would almost certainly be a good thing. After all, the rate of teen childbearing in the United States is more similar to the rates prevailing in the poor countries of the world than in the modern, industrial nations we think of as our peers. However, neither the problem of teen pregnancy nor the remedies for it are as simple as most people think.

In particular, the link between poverty and teen pregnancy is a complicated one. We do know that teen mothers are poorer than women who wait past their

From *The American Prospect*, No. 5, Spring 1991, pp. 73–83. Copyright © 1991 by New Prospect, Inc. Reprinted by permission.

twentieth birthday to have a child. But stereotypes to the contrary, it is not clear whether early motherhood causes poverty or the reverse. Worse yet, even if teen pregnancy does have some independent force in making teen parents poorer than they would otherwise be, it remains to be seen whether any policies in effect or under discussion can do much to reduce teen birth rates.

These uncertainties raise questions about our political culture as well as our public choices. How did Americans become convinced that teen pregnancy is a major cause of poverty and that reducing one would reduce the other? The answer is a tale of good intentions, rising cultural anxieties about teen sex and family breakdown, and the uses—and misuses—of social science.

HOW TEEN PREGNANCY BECAME AN ISSUE

Prior to the mid-1970s, few people talked about "teen pregnancy." Pregnancy was defined as a social problem primarily when a woman was unmarried; no one thought anything amiss when an 18- or 19-year-old got married and had children. And concern about pregnancies among unmarried women certainly did not stop when the woman turned twenty.

But in 1975, when Congress held the first of many hearings on the issue of adolescent fertility, expert witnesses began to speak of an "epidemic" of a "million pregnant teenagers" a year. Most of these witnesses were drawing on statistics supplied by the Alan Guttmacher Institute, which a year later published the data in an influential booklet, *Eleven Million Teenagers*. Data from that document were later cited—often down to the decimal point—in most discussions of the teenage pregnancy "epidemic."

Many people hearing these statistics must have assumed that the "million pregnant teenagers" a year were all unmarried. The Guttmacher Institute's figures, however, included married 19-year-olds along with younger, unmarried teenage girls. In fact, almost two-thirds of the "million pregnant teenagers" were 18- and 19-year-olds; about 40 percent of them were married, and about two-thirds of the married women were married prior to the pregnancy.

Moreover, despite the language of epidemic, pregnancy rates among teenagers were not dramatically increasing. From the turn of the century until the end of World War II, birth rates among teenagers were reasonably stable at approximately 50 to 60 births per thousand women. Teen birth rates, like all American birth rates, increased dramatically in the period after World War II, doubling in the baby boom years to a peak of about 97 births per thousand teenaged women in 1957. Subsequently, teen birth rates declined, and by 1975 they had gone back down to their traditional levels, where, for the most part, they have stayed (see Figure 13.1).

Were teen births declining in recent decades only because of higher rates of abortion? Here, too, trends are different from what many people suppose. The legalization of abortion in January of 1973 made it possible for the first time to get reliable statistics on abortions for women, teenagers and older. The rate among teenagers rose from about 27.0 to 42.9 abortions per 1,000 women between 1974

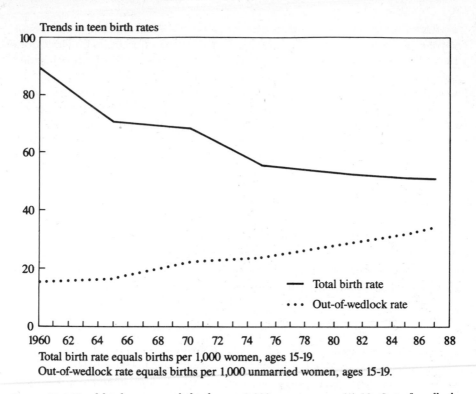

Trends in teen birth rates

Total birth rate equals births per 1,000 women, ages 15-19.
Out-of-wedlock rate equals births per 1,000 unmarried women, ages 15-19.

Figure 13.1 Total birth rate equals births per 1,000 women, ages 15–19. Out-of-wedlock rate equals births per 1,000 unmarried women, ages 15–19. *Sources:* National Center for Health Statistics, *Annual Vital Statistics,* and *Monthly Vital Statistics Reports;* U.S. DHEW, Vital and Health Statistics, "Trends in Illegitimacy, U.S. 1940–1965."

and 1980. Since 1980 teen abortion rates have stabilized, and may even have declined somewhat. Moreover, teenagers account for a declining proportion of all abortions: in the years just after *Roe v. Wade,* teenagers obtained almost a third of all abortions in the country; now they obtain about a quarter. A stable teen birth rate and a stabilizing teen abortion rate means that pregnancy rates, which rose modestly in the 1970s, have in recent years leveled off.

What has been increasing—and increasing dramatically—is the percentage of teen births that are out-of-wedlock (Figure 13.1). In 1970 babies born out of wedlock represented about a third of all babies born to teen mothers. By 1980 out-of-wedlock births were about half; and by 1986 almost two-thirds. Beneath these overall figures lie important racial variations. Between 1955 and 1988 the out-of-wedlock rate rose from 6 to 24.8 per thousand unmarried, teenage, white women, while for unmarried, nonwhite teenagers the rate rose from 77.6 to 98.3 per thousand. In other words, while the out-of-wedlock birth rate was rising 25 percent among nonwhite teens, it was actually quadrupling among white teens.

The immediate source for this rise in out-of-wedlock teen pregnancy might seem to be obvious. Since 1970 young women have increasingly postponed marriage without rediscovering the virtues of chastity. Only about 6 percent of teenagers were married in 1984, compared to 12 percent in 1970. And although estimates vary, sexual activity among single teenagers has increased sharply, probably doubling. By 1984 almost half of all American teenage women were both unmarried and sexually active, up from only one in four in 1970.

Yet the growth of out-of-wedlock births has not occurred only among teens; in fact, the increase has been more rapid among older women. In 1970 teens made up almost half of all out-of-wedlock births in America; at present they account for a little less than a third. On the other hand, out-of-wedlock births represent a much larger percentage of births to teens than of births to older women. Perhaps for that reason, teenagers have become the symbol of a problem that, to many Americans, is "out of control."

Whatever misunderstandings may have been encouraged by reports of a "million pregnant teenagers" a year, the new concept of "teen pregnancy" had a remarkable impact. By the mid-1980s, Congress had created a new federal office on adolescent pregnancy and parenting; 23 states had set up task forces; the media had published over 200 articles, including cover stories in both *Time* and *Newsweek;* American philanthropy had moved teen pregnancy into a high priority funding item; and a 1985 Harris poll showed that 80 percent of Americans thought teen pregnancy was a "serious problem" facing the nation, a concern shared across racial, geographic, and economic boundaries.

But while this public consensus has been taking shape, a debate has emerged about many of its premises. A growing number of social scientists have come to question whether teen pregnancy causes the social problems linked to it. Yet these criticisms have at times been interpreted as either an ivory-tower indifference to the fate of teen parents and their babies or a Panglossian optimism that teen childbearing is just one more alternate lifestyle. As a result, clarity on these issues has gotten lost in clouds of ideological mistrust. To straighten out these matters, we need to understand what is known, and not known, about the relation of teen pregnancy to poverty and other social problems.[1]

DISTINGUISHING CAUSES FROM CORRELATIONS

As the Guttmacher Institute's report made clear, numerous studies have documented an association between births to teenagers and a host of bad medical and social outcomes. Compared to women who have babies later in life, teen mothers are in poorer health, have more medically treacherous pregnancies, more stillbirths and newborn deaths, and more low-birthweight and medically compromised babies.

Later in life, women who have babies as teenagers are also worse off than other women. By their late 20s, women who gave birth as teenagers are less likely to have finished high school and thus not to have received any subsequent higher education. They are more likely to have routine, unsatisfying, and dead-end jobs, to be on welfare, and to be single parents either because they were never married or their marriage ended in divorce. In short, they often lead what the writer Mike Rose has called "lives on the boundary."

Yet an interesting thing has happened over the last twenty years. A description of the lives of teenage mothers and their children was transmuted into a causal sequence, and the often-blighted lives of young mothers were assumed to flow from their early childbearing. Indeed, this is what the data would show, if the women who gave birth as teenagers were the same in every way as women who give birth later. But they are not.

Although there is little published data on the social origins of teen parents, studies have documented the effects of social disadvantage at every step along the path to teenage motherhood. First, since poor and minority youth tend to become sexually active at an earlier age than more advantaged youngsters, they are "at risk" for a longer period of time, including years when they are less cognitively mature. Young teens are also less likely to use contraceptives than older teenagers. Second, the use of contraception is more common among teens who are white, come from more affluent homes, have higher educational aspirations, and who are doing well in school. And, finally, among youngsters who become pregnant, abortions are more common if they are affluent, white, urban, of higher socio-economic status, get good grades, come from two-parent families, and aspire to higher education. Thus, more advantaged youth get filtered out of the pool of young women at risk of teen parenthood.

Two kinds of background factors influence which teens are likely to become pregnant and give birth outside of marriage. First is inherited disadvantage. Young women from families that are poor, or rural, or from a disadvantaged minority, or headed by a single parent are more likely to be teen mothers than are their counterparts from more privileged backgrounds. Yet young mothers are not just disadvantaged; they are also discouraged. Studies suggest that a young woman who has other troubles—who is not doing well in school, has lower "measured ability," and lacks high aspirations for herself—is also at risk of becoming a teenaged mother.

Race plays an independent part in the route to teen motherhood. Within each racial group, according to Linda Waite and her colleagues at the Rand Corporation, teen birth rates are highest for those who have the greatest economic disadvantage and lowest academic ability. The effects of disadvantage, however, vary depending on the group. The Rand study found that among young high-ability, affluent black women from homes with two parents, only about one in a hundred become single, teenage mothers. For comparable whites, the risk was one in a thousand. By contrast, a poor, black teenager from a female-headed household who scores low on standardized tests has an astonishing one in four chance of becoming an unwed mother in her teens. Her white counterpart has one chance in twelve. Unwed motherhood thus reflects the intersecting influences of race, class, and gender; race and class each has a distinct impact on the life histories of young women.

Since many, if not most, teenage unwed mothers are already both disadvantaged and discouraged before they get pregnant, the poor outcomes of their pregnancies as well as their later difficulties in life are not surprising. Consider the health issues. As the demographer Jane Menken pointed out some time ago (and as many other studies have corroborated), the medical complications associated with teen pregnancy are largely due not to age but to the poverty of young mothers. As poor people, they suffer not from some biological risk due to youth, but from restricted access to medical care, particularly to prenatal care. (To be fair, some research suggests that there may be special biological risks for the very youngest mothers, those under age 15 when they give birth, who constitute about 2 percent of all teen mothers.)

Or, to take a more complicated example, consider whether bearing a child blocks teenagers from getting an education. In the aggregate, teen mothers do get less education than women who do not have babies at an early age. But teen mothers are different from their childless peers along exactly those dimensions we would expect independently to contribute to reduced schooling. More of them are poor, come from single-parent households, and have lower aspirations for themselves, lower measured ability, and more problems with school absenteeism and discipline. Given the nature of the available data, it is difficult to sort out the effects of a teen birth apart from the personal and social factors that predispose young women to both teen motherhood and less education. Few would argue that having a baby as a teenager enhances educational opportunities, but the exact effect of teen birth is a matter of debate.

Educational differences between teen mothers and other women may also be declining, at least in terms of graduating from high school. Legislation that took effect in 1975 forbade schools to expel pregnant teens. Contrary to current skepticism about federal intervention, this regulation seems to have worked. According to a study by Dawn Upchurch and James McCarthy, only 18.6 percent of teenagers who had a baby in 1958 subsequently graduated from high school. Graduation rates among teen mothers reached 29.2 percent in 1975; by 1986 they climbed to 55 percent. Teen mothers were still not graduating at a rate equal to other women (as of 1985, about 87 percent of women ages 25 to 29 had a high school diploma or its equivalent). But over the decade prior to 1986, graduation rates had increased more quickly for teen mothers than for other women, suggesting that federal policies tailored to their special circumstances may have made a difference.

Since education is so closely tied to later status, teasing out the relationship between teen pregnancy and schooling is critical. The matter is complicated, however, because young people do many things simultaneously, and sorting out the order is no easy task. In 1984 Peter Morrison of the Rand team reported that between a half and a third of teen mothers in high school and beyond dropped out before they got pregnant. Upchurch and McCarthy, using a different and more recent sample, found that the majority of female dropouts in their study left school before they got pregnant and that teens who got pregnant while still in school were not particularly likely to drop out. On the other hand, those teens who first drop out and then get pregnant are significantly less likely to return to school than other dropouts who do not get pregnant. Thus the conventional causal view that teens get pregnant, drop out of school, and as a result end up educationally and occupationally disadvantaged simply does not match the order of events in many people's lives.

THE SEXUAL ROOTS OF PUBLIC ANXIETY

Teen pregnancy probably would not have "taken off" as a public issue quite so dramatically, were it not for the fact it intersects with other recent social changes in America, particularly the emergence of widespread, anxiety-producing shifts in teen sex. Academics debate whether there has been a genuine "sexual revolution" among adults, but there is no doubt in regard to teenagers. Today, by the time American teenagers reach age 20, an estimated 70 percent of the girls and 80 percent of the boys have had sexual experiences outside of marriage. Virtually all studies confirm that this is a dramatic historical change, particularly for young women. (As usual, much less is known about the historical experiences of young men.) For example, Sandra Hofferth and her colleagues, using nationally representative data from the 1982 National Survey of Family Growth, found that women navigating adolescence in the late 1950s had a 38.9 percent chance of being sexually active before marriage during their teenage years. Women who reached their twentieth birthday between 1979 and 1981, in contrast, had a 68.3 percent likelihood.

Yet even these statistics do not capture how profoundly different this teen sexuality is from that of earlier eras. As sources such as the Kinsey Report (1953) suggest, premarital sex for many American women before the 1960s was "engagement" sex. The woman's involvement, at least, was exclusive, and she generally went on to marry her partner in a relatively short period of time. Almost half of the women in the Kinsey data who had premarital sex had it only with their fiances.

But as the age at first marriage has risen and the age at first intercourse has dropped, teen sexuality has changed. Not surprisingly, what scattered data we have about numbers of partners suggest that as the period of sexual activity before marriage has increased, so has the number of partners. In 1971, for example, almost two-thirds of sexually active teenaged women in metropolitan areas had had only one sexual partner; by 1979 fewer than half did. Data from the 1988 National Survey of Family Growth confirm this pattern for the nation as a whole, where about 60 percent of teens have had two or more partners. Similarly, for metropolitan teens, only a small fraction (about 10 percent) were engaged at the time of their first sexual experience, although about half described themselves as "going steady."

Profound changes in other aspects of American life have complicated the problem. Recent figures suggest that the average age at first marriage has increased to almost 24 years for women and over 25 years for men, the oldest since reliable data have been collected. Moreover, the age of sexual maturity over the last century has decreased by a little under six months each decade owing to nutritional and other changes. Today the average American girl has her first menstrual period at age 12½, although there are wide individual variations. (There is less research on the sexual maturity of young men.) On average, consequently, American girls and their boyfriends face over a decade of their lives when they are sexually mature and single.

As teenagers pass through this reproductive minefield, the instructions they receive on how to conduct themselves sexually are at best mixed. At least according to public opinion polls, most Americans have come, however reluctantly, to accept premarital sex. Yet one suspects that what they approve is something closer to Kinsey-era sex: sexual relations en route to a marriage. Present-day teenage sex, however, starts for many young people not when they move out of the family and into the orbit of what will be a new family or couple, but while they are still defined primarily as children.

When young people, particularly young women, are still living at home (or even at school) under the control, however nominal, of parents, sexual activity raises profound questions for adults. Many Americans feel troubled about "casual" sex, that is, sex which is not intimately tied to the process by which people form couples and settle down. Yet many teenagers are almost by definition disqualified as too young to "get serious." Thus the kinds of sexuality for which they are socially eligible—sex based in pleasure, not procreation, and in short-term relationships rather than as a prelude to marriage—challenge fundamental values about sexuality held by many adults. These ambiguities and uncertainties have given rise to broad anxieties about teen sexuality that have found expression in the recent alarm about teen pregnancy.

RAISING CHILDREN WITHOUT FATHERS

While Americans have had to confront the meaning and purpose of sexuality in the lives of teenagers, a second revolution is forcing them to think about the role—and boundaries—of marriage and family. Increasingly for Americans, childbearing and, more dramatically, childrearing have been severed from marriage. The demographer Larry Bumpass and his colleagues have estimated that under present trends, half or more of all American children will spend at least part of their childhood in a single-parent (mainly mother-only) family, due to the fact that an estimated 60 percent of recent marriages will end in divorce.

At the same time, as I indicated earlier, out-of-wedlock births are on the rise. At present, 26 percent of all births are to single women. If present trends continue, Bumpass and others estimate, almost one out of every six white women and seven out of ten black women will give birth to a child without being married. In short, single childbearing is becoming a common pattern of family formation for all American women, teenagers and older.

This reality intersects with still another fact of American life. The real value of inflation-adjusted wages, which grew 2.5 to 3.0 percent a year from the end of World War II to at least 1973, has now begun to stagnate and for certain groups decline; some recent studies point to greater polarization of economic well-being. Americans increasingly worry about their own standard of living and their taxes, and much of that worry has focused on the "underclass." Along with the elderly and the disabled, single women and their children have been the traditional recipients of public aid in America. In recent years, however, they have become especially visible among the dependent poor for at least two reasons. First, the incomes of the elderly have improved, leaving behind single mothers as a higher percentage of the poor; and second, the number of female-headed households has increased sharply. Between 1960 and 1984, households headed by women went from 9.0 percent to 12.0 percent of all white households, and from 22.0 percent to 43 percent of all black households. The incomes of about half of all families headed by women, as of 1984, fell below federal poverty levels.

Raising children as a single mother presents economic problems for women of all ages, but the problem is especially severe for teenagers with limited education and job experience. Partly for that reason, teenagers became a focus of public concern about the impact of illegitimacy and single parenthood on welfare costs. Data published in the 1970s and replicated in the 1980s suggested that about half of all families supported by Aid to Families with Dependent Children (AFDC) were started while the mother was still a teenager. One estimate calculated that in 1975 the costs for these families of public assistance alone (not including Medicaid or food stamps) amounted to $5 billion; by 1985, that figure increased to $8.3 billion.

Yet other findings—and caveats—have been ignored. For example, while about half of all AFDC cases may be families begun while the woman was still a teenager, teens represent only about 7 percent of the caseload at any one time. Moreover, the studies assessing the welfare costs of families started by teens counted any welfare family as being the result of a teen birth if the woman first had a child when under age 20. But, of course, that same woman—given her prior circumstances—might have been no less likely to draw welfare assistance if, let us say, she had a baby at age 20 instead of 19. Richard Wertheimer and Kristin Moore, the source of much of what we know about this area, have been careful to note that the relevant costs are the marginal costs—namely, how much less in welfare costs society would pay if teen mothers postponed their first births, rather than foregoing them entirely.

It turns out, not surprisingly, that calculated this way, the savings are more modest. Wertheimer and Moore have estimated that if by some miracle we could cut the teen birth rate in half, welfare costs would be reduced by 20 percent, rather than 50 percent, because many of these young women would still need welfare for children born to them when they were no longer teens.

Still other research suggests that most young women spend a transitional period on welfare, while finishing school and entering the job market. Other data also suggest that teen mothers may both enter and leave the welfare ranks earlier than poor women who postpone childbearing. Thus teen births by themselves may have more of an effect on the timing of welfare in the chain of life events than on the extent of welfare dependency. In a study of 300 teen mothers and their children originally interviewed in the mid-1960s, Frank Furstenberg and his colleagues found seventeen years later that two-thirds of those followed up had received no welfare in the previous five years, although some 70 percent of them had received public assistance at some point after the birth of their child. A quarter had achieved middle-class incomes, despite their poverty at the time of the child's birth.

None of this is to deny that teen mothers have a higher probability of being on welfare in the first place than women who begin their families at a later age, or that teen mothers may be disproportionately represented among those who find themselves chronically dependent on welfare. Given the disproportionate number of teen mothers who come from socially disadvantaged origins (and who are less motivated and perhaps less able students), it would be surprising if they were not overrepresented among those needing public assistance, whenever they had their children. Only if we are prepared to argue that these kinds of women should never have children—which is the implicit alternative at the heart of much public debate—could we be confident that they would never enter the AFDC rolls.

RETHINKING TEEN PREGNANCY

The original formulation of the teen pregnancy crisis seductively glossed over some of these hard realities. Teen motherhood is largely the province of those youngsters who are already disadvantaged by their position in our society. The major institutions of American life—families, schools, job markets, the medical system—are not working for them. But by framing the issue as teenage pregnancy, Americans could turn this reality around and ascribe the persistence of poverty and other social ills to the failure of individual teenagers to control their sexual impulses.

Framing the problem as teen pregnancy, curiously enough, also made it appear universal. Everyone is a teenager once. In fact, the rhetoric has sometimes claimed that the risk of teen pregnancy is universal, respecting no boundaries of class or race. But clearly, while teenage pregnancies do occur in virtually all walks of life, they do not occur with equal frequency. The concept of "teen pregnancy" has the advantage, therefore, of appearing neutral and universal while, in fact, being directed at people disadvantaged by class, race, and gender.

If focusing on teen pregnancy cast the problem as deceptively universal, it also cast the solution as deceptively simple. Teens just have to wait. In fact, the tacit subtext of at least some of the debate on teen pregnancy is not that young women should wait until they are past their teens, but until they are "ready." Yet in the terms that many Americans have in mind, large numbers of these youngsters will never be "ready." They have already dropped out of school and will face a marginal future in the labor market whether or not they have a baby. And as William J. Wilson has noted, many young black women in inner-city communities will not have the option of marrying because of the dearth of eligible men their age as a result of high rates of unemployment, underemployment, imprisonment, and early death.

Not long ago, Arline Geronimous, an assistant professor of public health at the University of Michigan, caused a stir when she argued that teens, especially black teens, had little to gain (and perhaps something to lose) in postponing pregnancy. The longer teenagers wait, she noted, the more they risk ill health and infertility, and the less likely their mothers are to be alive and able to help rear a child of theirs. Some observers quickly took Geronimous to mean that teen mothers are "rational," affirmatively choosing their pregnancies.

Yet, as Geronimous herself has emphasized, what sort of choices do these young women have? While teen mothers typically report knowing about contraception (which they often say they have used) and knowing about abortion, they tell researchers that their pregnancies were unplanned. In the 1988 National Survey of Family Growth, for example, a little over 70 percent of the pregnancies to teens were reported as unplanned; the teenagers described the bulk of these pregnancies as wanted, just arriving sooner than they had planned.

Researchers typically layer their own views on these data. Those who see teens as victims point to the data indicating most teen pregnancies are unplanned. Those who see teens as acting rationally look at their decisions not to use contraceptives or seek an abortion. According to Frank Furstenberg, however, the very indecisiveness of these young people is the critical finding. Youngsters often drift into pregnancy and then into parenthood, not because they affirmatively choose pregnancy as a first choice among many options, but rather because they see so few satisfying alternatives. As Laurie Zabin, a Johns Hopkins researcher on teen pregnancy, puts it, "As long as people don't have a vision of the future which having a baby at a very early age will jeopardize, they won't go to all the lengths necessary to prevent pregnancy."

Many people talk about teen pregnancy as if there were an implicit social contract in America. They seem to suggest that if poor women would just postpone having babies until they were past their teens, they could have better lives for themselves and their children. But for teenagers already at the margins of American life, this is a contract that American society may be hard put to honor. What if, in fact, they are acting reasonably? What can public policy do about teen pregnancy if many teenagers drift into childbearing as the only vaguely promising option in a life whose options are already constrained by gender, poverty, race, and failure?

The trouble is that there is little reason to think any of the "quick fixes" currently being proposed will resolve the fundamental issues involved. Liberals, for example, argue that the answer is more access to contraception, more readily available abortion, and more sex education. Some combination of these strategies probably has had some effect on teen births, particularly in keeping the teen pregnancy rate from soaring as the number of sexually active teens increased. But the inner logic of this approach is that teens and adults have the same goal: keeping teens from pregnancies they do not want. Some teens, however, do want their pregnancies, while others drift into pregnancy and parenthood without ever actively deciding what they want. Consequently, increased access to contraceptives, sex education, and abortion services are unlikely to have a big impact in reducing their pregnancies.

Conservatives, on the other hand, often long for what they imagine was the traditional nuclear family, where people had children only in marriage, married only when they could prudently afford children, and then continued to provide support for their children if the marriage ended. Although no one fully understands the complex of social, economic, and cultural factors that brought us to the present situation, it is probably safe to predict that we shall not turn the clock back to that vision, which in any event is highly colored by nostalgia.

This is not to say that there is nothing public policy can do. Increased job opportunities for both young men and young women; meaningful job training programs (which do not slot young women into traditional low-paying women's jobs); and child support programs[2] would all serve either to make marriage more feasible for those who wish to marry or to support children whose parents are not married. But older ages at first marriage, high rates of sex outside of marriage, a significant portion of all births out of wedlock, and problems with absent fathers tend to be common patterns in Western, industrialized nations.

In their attempts to undo these patterns, many conservatives propose punitive policies to sanction unmarried parents, especially unmarried mothers, by changing the "incentive structure" young people face. The new welfare reform bill of 1988, for example, made it more difficult for teens to set up their own households, at least in part because legislators were worried about the effects of welfare on the willingness to have a child out of wedlock. Other, more draconian writers have called for the children of unwed teen parents to be forcibly removed and placed into foster care, or for the reduction of welfare benefits for women who have more than one child out of wedlock.

Leave aside, for the moment, that these policies would single out only the most vulnerable in this population. The more troublesome issue is such policies often fall most heavily on the children. Americans, as the legal historian Michael Grossberg has shown, have traditionally and justifiably been leery of policies that regulate adult behavior at children's expense.

The things that public policy could do for these young people are unfortunately neither easy to implement nor inexpensive. However, if teens become parents because they lack options, public policy towards teen pregnancy and teenage childbearing will have to focus on enlarging the array of perceived options these young people face. And these must be changes in their real alternatives. Programs that seek to teach teens "future planning," while doing nothing about the futures they can expect, are probably doomed to failure.

We live in a society that continues to idealize marriage and family as expected lifetime roles for women, even as it adds on the expectation that women will also work and be self-supporting. Planning for the trade-offs entailed in a lifetime of paid employment in the labor market and raising a family taxes the skills of our most advantaged young women. We should not be surprised that women who face discrimination by race and class in addition to that of gender are often even less adept at coping with these large and contradictory demands.

Those who worry about teenagers should probably worry about three different dangers as Americans debate policies on teen pregnancy. First, we should worry that things will continue as they have and that public policy will continue to see teens as unwitting victims, albeit victims who themselves cause a whole host of social ills. The working assumption here will be that teens genuinely do not want the children that they are having, and that the task of public policy is to meet the needs of both society and the women involved by helping them not to have babies. What is good for society, therefore, is good for the individual woman.

This vision, for all the reasons already considered, distorts current reality, and as such, is unlikely to lower the teen birth rate significantly, though it may be effective in keeping the teen birth rate from further increasing. To the extent that it is ineffective, it sets the stage for another risk.

This second risk is that the ineffectiveness of programs to lower teen pregnancy dramatically may inadvertently give legitimacy to those who want more punitive control over teenagers, particularly minority and poor teens. If incentives and persuasion do not lead teenagers to conduct their sexual and reproductive lives in ways that adults would prefer, more coercive remedies may be advocated. The youth of teen mothers may make intrusive social control seem more acceptable than it would for older women.

Finally, the most subtle danger is that the new work on teen pregnancy will be used to argue that because teen pregnancy is not the linchpin that holds together myriad other social ills, it is not a problem at all. Concern about teen pregnancy has at least directed attention and resources to young, poor, and minority women; it has awakened many Americans to their diminished life chances. If measures aimed at reducing teen pregnancy are not the quick fix for much of what ails American society, there is the powerful temptation to forget these young women altogether and allow them to slip back to their traditional invisible place in American public debate.

Teen pregnancy is less about young women and their sex lives than it is about restricted horizons and the boundaries of hope. It is about race and class and how those realities limit opportunities for young people. Most centrally, however, it is typically about being young, female, poor, and non-white and about how having a child seems to be one of the few avenues of satisfaction, fulfillment, and self-esteem. It would be a tragedy to stop worrying about these young women—and their partners—because their behavior is the measure rather than the cause of their blighted hopes.

NOTES

1. Teen pregnancy affects both young men and young women, but few data are gathered on young men. The availability of data leads me to speak of "teen mothers" throughout this article, but it is important to realize that this reflects an underlying, gendered definition of the situation.
2. Theda Skocpol, "Sustainable Social Policy: Fighting Poverty Without Poverty Programs" *TAP,* Summer 1990.

PART
Three

COUPLING

INTRODUCTION

*T*o many people, the current state of marriage seems to provide the clearest
evidence that the family is falling apart. In the past three decades, marriage
rates have declined, divorce rates have risen, and increasing numbers of couples have come to live together without being married. Yet these changes do
not necessarily mean that people no longer want long-term commitments or
that they are psychologically incapable of forming deep attachments. Rather,
they reflect the fact that in the modern world, marriage is increasingly a personal relationship between two people. Over time, fewer and fewer reasons tie
couples to unsatisfactory relationships. As the standards for emotional fulfillment in marriage have risen, so have the levels of discontent.

In the preindustrial past, the least important aspect of marriage was the
emotional relationship between husband and wife. A marriage was an exchange
between kin groups, a unit of economic production, and a means of replenish-
ing populations with high death rates. In traditional societies, parents often
selected their children's mates. Parents were more interested in the practical
consequences of choice than in romantic considerations.

By contrast, people are supposed to marry for "love" in our modern society. They may marry for practical reasons or for money; nevertheless, they often follow their culture's rules and decide they are "in love." People may also
decide they are in love and want to live together but do not care to have their
union licensed by the state or blessed by the clergy.

Couple relationships are thus influenced by a new fluidity and openness
with regard to social norms in general and sexual behavior in particular. At one
time, a relationship between a man and a woman could be easily categorized:

179

it was either "honorable" or "dishonorable." An "honorable" relationship went through several distinct stages: dating, keeping company, going steady, agreeing to be married, announcing the engagement, and finally getting married, presumably for life. Divorce was regarded as a personal tragedy and social disgrace. Sexual relations before marriage were also shameful, especially for the woman, although the shame decreased as the marriage drew nearer.

Today the system of courtship has yielded to a new pattern of couple relationships—less permanent, more flexible, more experimental. Our cultural ideals of marital happiness and emotional fulfillment are often at odds with the realities of everyday married life. The article by John F. Cuber and Peggy Harroff reveals that enduring and satisfying marriages can vary a great deal from one another as well as from the ideals of happy marriage.

What makes for a happy or, more important, an enduring marriage? Based on a study of the long-married, Frances Klagsbrun concludes that eight factors, from an ability to change and tolerate change, to shared values, to sheer good luck—life stability, job stability, good health—all contribute to the longevity of marriage.

Although marriages can be long, prosperous, sexually fulfilling, and personally enriching, they can also be psychologically devastating, and even physically dangerous.

Family life can bring considerable strain. Violence within the family, while not quite as American as apple pie, is not so unusual either. In the article we reprint here, Murray A. Straus, Richard Gelles, and Suzanne Steinmetz explore the prevalence of and reasons for contemporary wife-beating. As might be expected, violence is reported more frequently in marriages ending in divorce.

Traditional societies do not necessarily have happier marriages or even lower divorce rates—some have rates higher than ours. Strong kin groups in traditional societies either keep couples together regardless of how they feel or make it easier for couples to break up without severe disruption. Nevertheless, traditional societies were quite conservative in their view of marriage, which was regarded as a permanent moral commitment that the church, and later the state, was to protect and preserve. Traditional marriage was also based on a division of labor between the sexes. The husband was to be head of the family and its chief provider; the wife was to provide services in the form of child care and housework. Divorce could be granted only through either the failure of one of the spouses to live up to his or her role or the betrayal of a spouse through adultery or cruelty.

The new divorce laws, as the article by Lenore J. Weitzman and Ruth B. Dixon points out, abolish this notion of fault or blame; instead, "irreconcilable differences" are grounds for the dissolution of marriage. Further, the new laws attempt to establish more equal rights and obligations between husband and wife, both during the marriage and at the time of divorce. While it is still too early to know the ultimate effects of the new laws on marriage as an institution, it is clear that they codify a very different conception of marriage and divorce than previously existed in the law.

As the piece by Terry Arendell suggests, despite the positive intentions of those who wrote the new laws, divorce often has a negative economic impact on middle-class women, a finding confirmed by Weitzman's research as well. Divorce touches 2 million children every year, and by 1990, it is expected to have been experienced by over half of American children under age 18. Researchers are coming to view divorce not as a single event, but as a complex chain of events—separation, property division, child custody—that unfolds across the child's life.

When divorce happens, fathers may disappear, or make only rare appearances. Why only about half of noncustodial fathers see their children after divorce is discussed by James R. Dudley, who interviewed 84 such fathers and elicited their views about why they have such limited involvement with their children.

Another effect of divorce is the possibility of remarriage by one or both spouses. Such remarriages generate interesting and problematic kinship structures and relationships that have scarcely been studied and for which we may not even have names. We know something about stepparents and stepchildren. But is there a difference between the way a father acts to his own children of his first marriage who live part of the time with his first wife, and the children of his second marriage who live full-time with him and his second wife? What of half-brothers, and -sisters? What of the relationship between a father's first-marriage children, second wife's first-marriage children, and children of both of the second marriage? The selection by Constance R. Ahrons and Roy H. Rodgers discusses the family complexities generated by divorce and modern remarriage.

Despite all its difficulties, marriage is not likely to go out of style in the near future. Ultimately we agree with Jessie Bernard (1972), who, after a devastating critique of marriage from the point of view of a sociologist who is also a feminist, said this:

> The future of marriage is as assured as any social form can be. . . . For men and women will continue to want intimacy, they will continue to want to celebrate their mutuality, to experience the mystic unity which once led the church to consider marriage a sacrament. . . . There is hardly any probability such commitments will disappear or that all relationships between them will become merely casual or transient. (p. 301)

REFERENCES

Bernard, Jessie. 1972. *The Future of Marriage.* New York: World.

Cherlin, Andrew. 1978. "Remarriage as an Incomplete Institution." *American Journal of Sociology,* 84, pp. 634–650.

Weitzman, Lenore J. 1985. *The Divorce Revolution.* New York: Free Press.

Chapter 5

Love and Marriage

Reading 14

10/27/94

Five Types of Marriage

John F. Cuber and Peggy B. Harroff

The qualitative aspects of enduring marital relationships vary enormously. The variations described to us were by no means random or clearly individualized, however. Five distinct life styles showed up repeatedly and the pairs within each of them were remarkably similar [in the ways in] which they lived together, found sexual expression, reared children, and made their way in the outside world.

The following classification is based on the interview materials of those people whose marriages had already lasted ten years or more and who said that they had never seriously considered divorce or separation. While 360 of the men and women had been married ten or more years to the same spouse, exclusion of those who reported that they had considered divorce reduced the number to 211. The discussion in this chapter is, then, based on 211 interviews: 107 men and 104 women.

The descriptions which our interviewees gave us took into account how they had behaved and also how they felt about their actions past and present. Examination of the important features of their lives revealed five recurring configurations of male-female life, each with a central theme—some prominent distinguishing psychological feature which gave each type its singularity. It is these preeminent characteristics which suggested the names for the relationship; the *Conflict-Habituated,* the *Devitalized,* the *Passive-Congenial,* the *Vital,* and the *Total.*

THE CONFLICT-HABITUATED

We begin with the conflict-habituated not because it is the most prevalent, but because the overt behavior patterns in it are so readily observed and because it presents some arresting contradictions. In this association there is much tension and conflict—although it is largely controlled. At worst, there is some private quarreling, nagging, and "throwing up the past" of which members of the immediate family, and more rarely close friends and relatives, have some awareness. At best, the couple is discreet and polite, genteel about it in the company of others—but after a few drinks at the cocktail party the verbal barbs begin to fly. The intermittent conflict is rarely concealed from the children, though we were often assured otherwise. "Oh, they're at it again—but they always are," says the high-school son. There is private acknowledgment by both husband and wife as a rule that incompatibility is pervasive, that conflict is ever-potential, and that an atmosphere of tension permeates the togetherness.

An illustrative case concerns a physician of fifty, married for twenty-five years to the same woman, with two college-graduate children promisingly established in their own professions.

> You know, it's funny; we have fought from the time we were in high school together. As I look back at it, I can't remember specific quarrels; it's more like a running guerrilla fight with intermediate periods, sometimes quite long, of pretty good fun and some damn good sex. In fact, if it hadn't been for the sex, we wouldn't have been married so quickly. Well, anyway, this has been going on ever since. . . . It's hard to know what it is we fight about most of the time. You name it and we'll fight about it. It's sometimes something I've said that she remembers differently, sometimes a decision—like what kind of car to buy or what to give the kids for Christmas. With regard to politics, and religion, and morals—oh, boy! You know, outside of the welfare of the kids—too much and that's just abstract—we don't really agree about anything. . . . At different times we take opposite sides—not deliberately; it just comes out that way.
>
> Now these fights get pretty damned colorful. You called them arguments a little while ago—I have to correct you—they're brawls. There's never a bit of physical violence—at least not directed to each other—but the verbal gunfire gets pretty thick. Why, we've said things to each other that neither of us would think of saying in the hearing of anybody else. . . .
>
> Of course we don't settle any of the issues. It's sort of a matter of principle *not* to. Because somebody would have to give in then and lose face for the next encounter. . . .
>
> When I tell you this in this way, I feel a little foolish about it. I wouldn't tolerate such a condition in any other relationship in my life—and yet here I do and always have. . . .
>
> No—we never have considered a divorce or separation or anything so clear-cut. I realize that other people do, and I can't say that it has never occurred to either of us, but we've never considered it seriously.

A number of times, there has been a crisis, like the time I was in the automobile accident, and the time she almost died in childbirth, and then I guess we really showed that we do care about each other. But as soon as the crisis is over, it's business as usual.

There is a subtle valence in these conflict-habituated relationships. It is easily missed in casual observation. So central is the necessity for channeling conflict and bridling hostility that these considerations come to preoccupy much of the interaction. Some psychiatrists have gone so far as to suggest that it is precisely the deep need to do psychological battle with one another which constitutes the cohesive factor insuring continuity of the marriage. Possibly so. But even from a surface point of view, the overt and manifest fact of habituated attention to handling tension, keeping it chained, and concealing it, is clearly seen as a dominant life force. And it can, and does for some, last for a whole lifetime.

THE DEVITALIZED

The key to the devitalized mode is the clear discrepancy between middle-aged reality and earlier years. These people usually characterized themselves as having been "deeply in love" during the early years, as having spent a great deal of time together, having enjoyed sex, and, most importantly of all, having had a close identification with one another. The present picture, with some variation from case to case, is in clear contrast—little time is spent together, sexual relationships are far less satisfying qualitatively or quantitatively, and interests and activities are not shared, at least not in the deeper and meaningful way they once were. Most of their time together now is "duty time"—entertaining together, planning and sharing activities with children, and participating in various kinds of required community responsibilities. They do as a rule retain, in addition to a genuine and mutual interest in the welfare of their children, a shared attention to their joint property and the husband's career. But even in the latter case the interest is contrasting. Despite a common dependency on his success and the benefits which flow therefrom, there is typically very little sharing of the intrinsic aspects of career—simply an acknowledgment of their mutual dependency on the fruits.

Two rather distinct subtypes of the devitalized take shape by the middle years. The following reflections of two housewives in their late forties illustrate both the common and the distinguishing features:

Judging by the way it was when we were first married—say the first five years or so—things are pretty matter-of-fact now—even dull. They're dull between us, I mean. The children are a lot of fun, keep us pretty busy, and there are lots of outside things—you know, like Little League and the P.T.A. and the Swim Club, and even the company parties aren't always so bad. But I mean where Bob and I are concerned—if you followed us around, you'd wonder why we ever got *married*. We take each other for granted. We laugh at the same things sometimes, but we don't really laugh together—the way we used to. But, as he said to me the other night—with one or two under the belt, I think—"You know, you're still a little fun now and then." . . .

Now, I don't say this to complain, not in the least. There's a cycle to life. There are things you do in high school. And different things you do in college. Then you're a young adult. And then you're middle-aged. That's where we are now. . . . I'll admit that I do yearn for the old days when sex was a big thing and going out was fun and I hung on to everything he said about his work and his ideas as if they were coming from a genius or something. But then you get the children and other responsibilities. I have the home and Bob has a tremendous burden of responsibility at the office. . . . He's completely responsible for setting up the new branch now. . . . You have to adjust to these things and we both try to gracefully. . . . Anniversaries though do remind you kind of hard. . . .

The other kind of hindsight from a woman in a devitalized relationship is much less accepting and quiescent:

I know I'm fighting it. I ought to accept that it has to be like this, but I don't like it, and I'd do almost anything to bring back the exciting way of living we had at first. Most of my friends think I'm some sort of a sentimental romantic or something—they tell me to act my age—but I do know some people—not very darn many—who are our age and even older, who still have the same kind of excitement about them and each other that we had when we were all in college. I've seen some of them at parties and other plac-es—the way they look at each other, the little touches as they go by. One couple has grandchildren and you'd think they were honeymooners. I don't think it's just sex ei-ther—I think they are just part of each other's lives—and then when I think of us and the numb way we sort of stagger through the weekly routine, I could scream. And I've even thought of doing some pretty desperate things to try to build some joy and excite-ment into my life. I've given up on Phil. He's too content with his balance sheets and the kids' report cards and the new house we're going to build next year. He keeps saying he has everything in life that any man could want. What do you *do?*

Regardless of the gracefulness of the acceptance, or the lack thereof, the com-mon plight prevails: on the subjective, emotional dimension, the relationship has become a void. The original zest is gone. There is typically little overt tension or conflict, but the interplay between the pair has become apathetic, lifeless. No se-rious threat to the continuity of the marriage is generally acknowledged, however. It is intended, usually by both, that it continue indefinitely despite its numbness. Continuity and relative freedom from open conflict are fostered in part because of the comforts of the "habit cage." Continuity is further insured by the absence of any engaging alternative, "all things considered." It is also reinforced, sometimes rather decisively, by legal and ecclesiastical requirements and expectations. These people quickly explain that "there are other things in life" which are worthy of sustained human effort.

This kind of relationship is exceedingly common. Persons in this circumstance frequently make comparisons with other pairs they know, many of whom are sim-ilar to themselves. This fosters the comforting judgment that "marriage is like this—except for a few oddballs or pretenders who claim otherwise."

While these relationships lack visible vitality, the participants assure us that there is "something there." There are occasional periods of sharing at least some-thing—if only memory. Even formalities can have meanings. Anniversaries can be celebrated, if a little grimly, for what they once commemorated. As one man said, "Tomorrow we are celebrating the anniversary of our anniversary." Even clearly substandard sexual expression is said by some to be better than nothing, or better than a clandestine substitute. "A good man" or a "good mother for the kids" may "with a little affection and occasional attention now and then, get you by." Many believe that the devitalized mode is the appropriate mode in which a man and woman should be content to live in the middle years and later.

THE PASSIVE-CONGENIAL

The passive-congenial mode has a great deal in common with the devitalized, the essential difference being that the passivity which pervades the association has been there from the start. The devitalized have a more exciting set of memories; the passive-congenials give little evidence that they had ever hoped for anything much different from what they are currently experiencing.

There is therefore little suggestion of disillusionment or compulsion to make believe to anyone. Existing modes of association are comfortably adequate—no stronger words fit the facts as they related them to us. There is little conflict, although some admit that they tiptoe rather gingerly over and around a residue of subtle resentments and frustrations. In their better moods they remind themselves (and each other) that "there are many common interests" which they both enjoy. "We both like classical music." "We agree completely on religious and political matters." "We both love the country and our quaint exurban neighbors." "We are both lawyers."

The wife of a prominent attorney, who has been living in the passive-congenial mode for thirty years, put her description this way:

> We have both always tried to be calm and sensible about major life decisions, to think things out thoroughly and in perspective. Len and I knew each other since high school but didn't start to date until college. When he asked me to marry him, I took a long time to decide whether he was the right man for me and I went into his family background, because I wasn't just marrying him; I was choosing a father for my children. We decided together not to get married until he was established, so that we would not have to live in dingy little apartments like some of our friends who got married right out of college. This prudence has stood us in good stead too. Life has moved ahead for us with remarkable orderliness and we are deeply grateful for the foresight we had. . . .
>
> When the children were little, we scheduled time together with them, although since they're grown, the demands of the office are getting pretty heavy. Len brings home a bulging briefcase almost every night and more often than not the light is still on in his study after I retire. But we've got a lot to show for his devoted effort. . . .
>
> I don't like all this discussion about sex—even in the better magazines. I hope your study will help to put it in its proper perspective. I expected to perform sex in marriage, but both before and since, I'm willing to admit that it's a much overrated activity. Now and then, perhaps it's better. I am fortunate, I guess, because my husband has never been demanding about it, before marriage or since. It's just not that important to either of us. . . .
>
> My time is very full these days, with the chairmanship of the Cancer Drive, and the Executive Board of the (state) P.T.A. I feel a little funny about that with my children already grown, but there are the grandchildren coming along. And besides so many of my friends are in the organizations, and it's so much like a home-coming.

People make their way into the passive-congenial mode by two quite different routes—by default and by intention. Perhaps in most instances they arrive at this way of living and feeling by drift. There is so little which they have cared about deeply in each other that a passive-congenial mode is a deliberately intended arrangement for two people whose interests and creative energies are directed elsewhere than toward the pairing—into careers, or in the case of women, into children or community activities. They say they know this and want it this way. These people simply do not wish to invest their total emotional involvement and creative effort in the male-female relationship.

The passive-congenial life style fits societal needs quite well also, and this is an important consideration. The man of practical affairs, in business, government service, or the professions—quite obviously needs "to have things peaceful at home" and to have a minimum of distraction as he pursues his important work. He may feel both love and gratitude toward the wife who fits this mode.

A strong case was made for the passive-congenial by a dedicated physician:

> I don't know why everyone seems to make so much about men and women and marriage. Of course, I'm married and if anything happened to my wife, I'd get married again. I think it's the proper way to live. It's convenient, orderly, and solves a lot of problems. But there are other things in life. I spent nearly ten years preparing for the practice of my profession. The biggest thing to me is the practice of that profession, to be of assistance to my patients and their families. I spend twelve hours a day at it. And I'll bet if you talked with my wife, you wouldn't get any of that "trapped housewife" stuff from her either. Now that the children are grown, she finds a lot of useful and necessary work to do in this community. She works as hard as I do.

The passive-congenial mode facilitates the achievement of other goals too. It enables people who desire a considerable amount of personal independence and freedom to realize it with a minimum of inconvenience from or to the spouse. And it certainly spares the participants in it from the need to give a great deal of personal attention to "adjusting to the spouse's needs." The passive-congenial menage is thus a mood as well as a mode.

Our descriptions of the devitalized and the passive-congenials have been similar because these two modes are much alike in their overt characteristics. The participants' evaluations of their *present situations* are likewise largely the same— the accent on "other things," the emphasis on civic and professional responsibilities; the importance of property, children, and reputation. The essential difference lies in their diverse histories and often in their feelings of contentment with their current lives. The passive-congenials had from the start a life pattern and a set of expectations essentially consistent with what they are now experiencing. When the devitalized reflect, however, when they juxtapose history against present reality, they often see the barren gullies in their lives left by the erosions of earlier satisfactions. Some of the devitalized are resentful and disillusioned; others, calling themselves "mature about it," have emerged with reasonable acceptance of their existing devitalized modes. Still others are clearly ambivalent. "I wish life would be more exciting, but I should have known it couldn't last. In a way, it's calm and quiet and reassuring this way, but there are times when I get very ill at ease—sometimes downright mad. Does it *have* to be like this?"

The passive-congenials do not find it necessary to speculate in this fashion. Their anticipations were realistic and perhaps even causative of their current marital situation. In any event, their passivity is not jarred when teased by memory.

THE VITAL

In extreme contrast to the three foregoing is the vital relationship. The vital pair can easily be overlooked as they move through their worlds of work, recreation, and family activities. They do the same things, publicly at least; and when talking for public consumption say the same things—they are proud of their homes, love their children, gripe about their jobs, while being quite proud of their career accomplishments. But when the close, intimate, confidential, empathic look is taken, the essence of the vital relationship becomes clear: the mates are intensely bound together psychologically in important life matters. Their sharing and their togetherness is genuine. It provides the life essence for both man and woman.

> The things we do together aren't fun intrinsically—the ecstasy comes from being *together in the doing*. Take her out of the picture and I wouldn't give a damn for the boat, the lake, or any of the fun that goes on out there.

The presence of the mate is indispensable to the feelings of satisfaction which the activity provides. The activities shared by the vital pairs may involve almost anything: hobbies, careers, community service. Anything—so long as it is closely shared.

It is hard to escape the word *vitality*—exciting mutuality of feelings and participation together in important life segments. The clue that the relationship is vital (rather than merely expressing the joint activity) derives from the feeling that it is important. An activity is flat and uninteresting if the spouse is not a part of it.

Other valued things are readily sacrificed in order to enhance life within the vital relationship.

> I cheerfully, and that's putting it mildly, passed up two good promotions, because one of them would have required some traveling and the other would have taken evening and weekend time—and that's when Pat and I *live*. The hours with her (after twenty-two years of marriage) are what I live for. You should meet her. . . .

People in the vital relationship for the most part know that they are a minority and that their life styles are incomprehensible to most of their associates.

> Most of our friends think we moved out to the country for the kids; well—the kids *are* crazy about it, but the fact of the matter is, we moved out for ourselves—just to get away from all the annoyances and interferences of other people—our friends actually. We like this kind of life—where we can have almost all of our time together. . . . We've been married for over twenty years and the most enjoyable thing either of us does—well, outside of the intimate things—is to sit and talk by the hour. That's why we built that imposing fireplace—and the hi-fi here in the corner. . . . Now that Ed is getting

older, that twenty-seven-mile drive morning and night from the office is a real burden, but he does it cheerfully so we can have our long uninterrupted hours together. . . . The children respect this too. They don't invade our privacy any more than they can help—the same as we vacate the living room when Ellen brings in a date, she tries not to intrude on us. . . . Being the specialized kind of lawyer he is, I can't share much in his work, but that doesn't bother either of us. The *big* part of our lives is completely mutual. . . .

Her husband's testimony validated hers. And we talked to dozens of other couples like them, too. They find their central satisfaction in the life they live with and through each other. It consumes their interest and dominates their thoughts and actions. All else is subordinate and secondary.

This does not mean that people in vital relationships lose their separate identities, that they may not upon occasion be rivalrous or competitive with one another or that conflict may not occur. They differ fundamentally from the conflict-habituated, however, in that when conflict does occur, it results from matters that are important to them, such as which college a daughter or son is to attend; it is devoid of the trivial "who said what first and when" and "I can't forget when you. . . ." A further difference is that people to whom the relationship is vital tend to settle disagreements quickly and seek to avoid conflict, whereas the conflict-habituated look forward to conflict and appear to operate by a tacit rule that no conflict is ever to be truly terminated and that the spouse must never be considered right. The two kinds of conflict are thus radically different. To confuse them is to miss an important differentiation.

THE TOTAL

The total relationship is like the vital relationship with the important addition that it is more multifaceted. The points of vital meshing are more numerous—in some cases all of the important life foci are vitally shared. In one such marriage the husband is an internationally known scientist. For thirty years his wife has been "his friend, mistress, and partner." He still goes home at noon whenever possible, at considerable inconvenience, to have a quiet lunch and spend a conversational hour or so with his wife. They refer to these conversations as "our little seminars." They feel comfortable with each other and with their four grown children. The children (now in their late twenties) say that they enjoy visits with their parents as much as they do with friends of their own age.

There is practically no pretense between persons in the total relationship or between them and the world outside. There are few areas of tension, because the items of difference which have arisen over the years have been settled as they arose. There often *were* serious differences of opinion but they were handled, sometimes by compromise, sometimes by one or the other yielding; but these outcomes were of secondary importance because the primary consideration was not who was right or who was wrong, only how the problem could be resolved without tarnishing the relationship. When faced with differences, they can and do dispose of the difficulties without losing their feeling of unity or their sense of vitality and centrality of their relationship. This is the mainspring.

The various parts of the total relationship are reinforcing, as we learned from this consulting engineer who is frequently sent abroad by his corporation.

She keeps my files and scrapbooks up to date. . . . I invariably take her with me to conferences around the world. Her femininity, easy charm and wit are invaluable assets to me. I know it's conventional to say that a man's wife is responsible for his success and I also know that it's often not true. But in my case I gladly acknowledge that it's not only true, but she's indispensable to me. But she'd go along with me even if there was nothing for her to do because we just enjoy each other's company—deeply. You know, the best part of a vacation is not *what* we do, but that we do it together. We plan it and reminisce about it and weave it into our work and other play all the time.

The wife's account is substantially the same except that her testimony demonstrates more clearly the genuineness of her "help."

It seems to me that Bert exaggerates my help. It's not so much that I only want to help him; it's more that I want to do those things anyway. We do them together, even though we may not be in each other's presence at the time. I don't really know what I do for him and what I do for me.

This kind of relationship is rare, in marriage or out, but it does exist and can endure. We occasionally found relationships so total that all aspects of life were mutually shared and enthusiastically participated in. It is as if neither spouse has, or has had, a truly private existence.

The customary purpose of a classification such as this one is to facilitate understanding of similarities and differences among the cases classified. In this instance enduring marriage is the common condition. The differentiating features are the dissimilar forces which make for the integration of the pair within each of the types. It is not necessarily the purpose of a classification to make possible a clear-cut sorting of all cases into one or another of the designated categories. All cannot be so precisely pigeon-holed; there often are borderline cases. Furthermore, two observers with equal access to the facts may sometimes disagree on which side of the line an unclear case should be placed. If the classification is a useful one, however, placement should *as a rule* be clear and relatively easy. The case is only relative because making an accurate classification of a given relationship requires the possession of amounts and kinds of information which one rarely has about persons other than himself. Superficial knowledge of public or professional behavior is not enough. And even in his own case, one may, for reasons of ego, find it difficult to be totally forthright.

A further caution. The typology concerns relationships, not personalities. A clearly vital person may be living in a passive-congenial or devitalized relationship and expressing his vitality in some other aspect of life—career being an important preoccupation for many. Or, possibly either or both of the spouses may have a vital relationship—sometimes extending over many years—with someone of the opposite sex outside of the marriage.

Nor are the five types to be interpreted as *degrees* of marital happiness or adjustment. Persons in all five are currently adjusted and most say that they are content, if not happy. Rather, the five types represent *different kinds of adjustment* and *different conceptions of marriage.* This is an important concept which must be emphasized if one is to understand the personal meanings which these people attach to the conditions of their marital experience.

Neither are the five types necessarily stages in a cycle of initial bliss and later disillusionment. Many pairings started in the passive-congenial stage; in fact, quite often people intentionally enter into a marriage for the acknowledged purpose of living this kind of relationship. To many the simple amenities of the "habit cage" are not disillusionments or even disappointments, but rather are sensible life expectations which provide an altogether comfortable and rational way of having a "home base" for their lives. And many of the conflict-habituated told of courtship histories essentially like their marriages.

While each of these types tends to persist, there *may* be movement from one type to another as circumstances and life perspectives change. This movement may go in any direction from any point, and a given couple may change categories more than once. Such changes are relatively *in*frequent however, and the important point is that relationship types tend to persist over relatively long periods.

The fundamental nature of these contexts may be illustrated by examining the impact of some common conditions on persons of each type.

Infidelity, for example, occurs in most of the five types, the total relationship being the exception. But it occurs for quite different reasons. In the conflict-habituated it seems frequently to be only another outlet for hostility. The call girl and the woman picked up in a bar are more than just available women; they are symbols of resentment of the wife. This is not always so, but reported to us often enough to be worth noting. Infidelity among the passive-congenial, on the other hand, is typically in line with the stereotype of the middle-aged man who "strays out of sheer boredom with the uneventful, deadly prose" of his private life. And the devitalized man or woman frequently is trying for an hour or a year to recapture the lost mood. But the vital are sometimes adulterous too; some are simply emancipated—almost bohemian. To some of them sexual aggrandizement is an accepted fact of life. Frequently, the infidelity is condoned by the partner and in some instances even provides an indirect (through empathy) kind of gratification. The act of infidelity in such cases is not construed as disloyalty or as a threat to continuity, but rather as a kind of basic human right which the loved one ought to be permitted to have—and which the other perhaps wants also for himself.

Divorce and separation are found in all five of the types, but the reasons, when viewed realistically and outside of the simplitudes of legalistic and ecclesiastical fiction, are highly individual and highly variable. For example, a couple may move from a vital relationship to divorce because for them the alternative of a devitalized relationship is unendurable. They can conceive of marriage only as a vital, meaningful, fulfilling, and preoccupying interaction. The "disvitality" of any other marriage form is abhorrent to them and takes on "the hypocrisy of living a public lie." We have accounts of marriages which were unquestionably vital or total for a period of years but which were dissolved. In some respects relationships of this type are more readily disrupted, because these people have become adjusted to such a rich and deep sharing that evidences of breach, which a person in another type of marriage might consider quite normal, become unbearable.

> I know a lot of close friendships occur between men and women married to someone else, and that they're not always adulterous. But I know Betty—and anyhow, I personally believe they eventually do become so, but I can't be sure about that. Anyway, when Betty found her self-expression was furthered by longer and longer meetings and conversations with Joe, and I detected little insincerities, not serious at first, you understand, creeping into the things we did together, it was like the little leak in the great dike. It didn't take very long. We weren't melodramatic about it, but it was soon clear to both of us that we were no longer the kind of pair we once were, so why pretend. The whole thing can go to hell fast—and after almost twenty years!

Husbands in other types of relationships would probably not even have detected any disloyalty on the part of the wife. And even if they had, they would tend to conclude that "you don't break up a home just because she has a passing interest in some glamorous writer."

The divorce which occurs in the passive-congenial marriage follows a different sequence. One of the couple, typically a person capable of more vitality in his or her married life than the existing relationship provides, comes into contact with a person with whom he gradually (or suddenly) unfolds a new dimension to adult living. What he had considered to be a rational and sensible and "adult" relationship can suddenly appear in contrast to be stultifying, shallow, and an altogether disheartening way to live out the remaining years. He is left with "no conceivable alternative but to move out." Typically, he does not do so impulsively or without a more or less stubborn attempt to stifle his "romanticism" and listen to well-documented advice to the effect that he should act maturely and "leave the romantic yearning to the kids for whom it is intended." Very often he is convinced and turns his back on his "new hope"—but not always.

Whether examining marriages for the satisfactions and fulfillments they have brought or for the frustrations and pain, the overriding influence of life style—or as we have here called it, relationship type—is of the essence. Such a viewpoint helps the observer, and probably the participant, to understand some of the apparent enigmas about men and women in marriage—why infidelities destroy some marriages and not others; why conflict plays so large a role for some couples and is so negligible for others; why some seemingly well-suited and harmoniously adjusted spouses seek divorce while others with provocations galore remain solidly together; why affections, sexual expression, recreation, almost everything observable about men and women is so radically different from pair to pair. All of these are not merely different objectively; they are perceived differently by the pairs, are differently reacted to, and differently attended to.

If nothing else, this article has demonstrated that realistic understanding of marital relationships requires use of concepts which are carefully based on perceptive factual knowledge. Unfortunately, the language by which relationships between men and women are conventionally expressed tends to lead toward serious and pervasive deceptions which in turn encourage erroneous inferences. Thus, we tend to assume that enduring marriage is somehow synonymous with happy marriage or at least with something comfortably called adjustment. The deception springs from lumping together such dissimilar modes of thought and action as the conflict-habituated, the passive-congenial, and the vital. To know that a marriage has endured, or for that matter has been dissolved, tells one close to nothing about the kinds of experiences, fulfillments, and frustrations which have made up the lives of the people involved. Even to know, for example, that infidelity has occurred, without knowledge of circumstances, feelings, and other essences, results in an illusion of knowledge which masks far more than it describes.

To understand a given marriage, let alone what is called "marriage in general," is realistically possible only in terms of particular sets of experiences, meanings, hopes, and intentions. This article has described in broad outline five manifest and recurring configurations among the Significant Americans.

Reading 15

Long-Term Marriages

Frances Klagsbrun

What are the characteristics of long, satisfying, happy marriages? . . . [T]here is no formula, no single recipe that when used in the right proportions will produce the perfect marriage, or even a working one. Rather, there are certain abilities and outlooks that couples in strong marriages have, not all of them at all times, but a large proportion a good part of the time. They fall, it seems to me, into eight categories:

1. AN ABILITY TO CHANGE AND TOLERATE CHANGE

Change is inevitable in marriage as in life. Partners become involved in work and pull back from work; children are born, go to school, leave home; spouses age, get sick, drop old interests, take on new ones, make new friends, live through the sorrows of old ones; parents get old and die; couples move from apartments to

---

houses and back to apartments, from one town to another. Changes bring anxieties and disequilibrium. Yet in the strongest marriages, each partner is able to make "midcourse corrections, almost like astronauts," as one psychiatrist put it. That is, they are able both to adapt to the change that is happening in the marriage or in the other partner and, when called for, to change themselves. . . .

In the marriages that have remained strong and viable, partners have had the flexibility to pick up what was useful to them from the barrage of slogans and confusions of "facts," and change their marriages and themselves to incorporate new ideals that made sense to them. Even the marriages that have kept the most traditional forms, as many have, have had to make concessions to the mood of the times, if not within the marriage itself then in the couple's outlook and their attitudes toward their children. The Flahertys, one of the most conventional couples interviewed, maintained that Peggy Flaherty's place was in her home, and her work the work of running the family finances and caring for her husband. Yet they strongly encouraged their two daughters to develop occupations—one is a dental technician, the other a nurse—and to continue working after they had families of their own. (True, these are typically "women's" occupations, but the very idea of a married women working had once been anathema to Tom Flaherty.) Although practicing Catholics themselves, they have succored and supported one daughter who is divorced, recognizing, they said, that she had a right to rid herself of a bad marriage and seek her own happiness.

Much greater changes have taken place in the couples who have shifted their life patterns as social values have shifted. The women who have gone to work or back to school years into their marriages have come to see themselves as different beings than they were in their earlier days. They have not discarded their old selves; they have developed a different part of them. But in doing so they have changed their marriages. Their husbands have accommodated to those changes— some more willingly than others—and in doing so, many have changed themselves. They have changed the way they behave by taking on household tasks they would not have dreamed of touching when they first married, and by rearranging their schedules to make room for their wives' schedules. More important, they have changed inwardly, many of them, truly acknowledging their wives' strivings, ambitions and accomplishments outside their homes. One tiny manifestation of these changes in long marriages are the numbers of no-longer-young men I see at dinner parties automatically getting up to clear the table or serve a course while their wives sit and chat with guests. They are not self-consciously carrying out some carefully formulated contract. They have incorporated this domestic behavior into their way of being. For them, such acts are not merely gestures; they represent an inner change.

But there is an attitude toward change in long marriages that goes far beyond the social issues. There is this: People who stay happily married see themselves not as victims of fate, but as free agents who make choices in life. Although, like everyone else, they are influenced by their own family backgrounds, for the most part they do not allow their lives together to be dominated by their earlier family lives apart. Because they choose to be married to one another, a choice they make again and again, they are open to changing themselves, pulling away from what *was* in order to make what *is* alive and vital. In other words, as much as they are able to, they try to control their lives, rather than drifting along as the patsies of destiny. . . .

2. AN ABILITY TO LIVE WITH THE UNCHANGEABLE

[This] means to live with unresolved conflict when necessary. The simultaneous acceptance of change and of lack of change in long marriages is summed up by the words of a shopkeeper, married thirty-eight years: "You have to know when to holler and you have to know when to look away."

A statement made by many couples when asked about the "secrets" of their happy marriage was, "We don't expect perfection," or some variation thereof. They would go on to explain that their marriage had areas that were far from perfect, qualities in one another that they wish could have changed but they have come to recognize as qualities that will never change. Still, they live with those unchangeable, and sometimes disturbing, qualities, because, as one woman said, "The payoff is so great in other areas." We have been so bombarded with advice books and articles about "solving" problems and "overcoming" adversity, about "improving" our marriages and becoming "ideal" mates that we often forget that it is possible also just to let things be, without solution or improvement.

On a superficial level, I think of a woman who described her misery early in her second marriage because of her husband's unbelievably ear-shattering snores. Night after night she lay awake listening to his nasal roars and wondering how she was going to survive this marriage. For a while she tried slipping out of bed in the middle of the night to sleep in the living room. But she didn't sleep well there, and, anyhow, she wanted to be in bed with her husband. Then she prevailed upon him to seek medical help to control the snoring. The doctors had nothing to offer, and the night sounds continued unabated. Finally, she stopped complaining and bought some ear plugs. They do not block out the noise completely, but they help. The snoring problem, she has decided, will never be solved, the plugs make it possible for her to live with it as best she can, and that is as much as she can do.

On a more serious level, long-married couples accept the knowledge that there are some deep-seated conflicts—about personality differences, habits, styles of dealing with things—that will never be solved. In the best of situations, they stop fighting about those issues and go about their lives instead of wasting their energies on a constant, fruitless struggle to settle differences "once and for all." Not long ago, at a time when marriage was under perpetual attack, this very quality of marriage, its imperfectability, was at the crux of the arguments against it. People spoke of marriage as a form of "settling" for something less than ideal, as "compromising" with what one wanted from life. Yet this ability to live with the imperfect is, it seems to me, the essence of maturity. Mature people are able to accept the limitations life places on them and work around them. And in the "working around," in finding ways to live with difficulties, they may experience some of the most creative moments of living. . . .

3. AN ASSUMPTION OF PERMANENCE

Most marriages, first, second or later, begin with the hope and expectation that they will last forever. In the marriages that do last, "forever" is not only a hope, but an ongoing philosophy. The mates do not seriously think about divorce as a viable option. Certainly there are "divorce periods," times of distancing and anger, but even if divorce itself crosses the minds of the couple, it is not held out as an escape from difficulties. One can argue that couples who got married more than fifteen or twenty years ago don't think about divorce because it was not as prevalent a part of our culture in earlier days as it is now. But that's not the complete story. Many couples married during those earlier days have divorced, and for many younger couples permanence is a built-in component of marriage, as it had been for their parents.

This attitude that a marriage will last, *must* last (not because some religious authority or family member says so, but because the marriage is that important to the couple), tempers a husband's and a wife's approach to conflicts and imperfections. They see the marriage as an entity in itself that must be protected. Or as family therapist Salvador Minuchin said, "A marriage is more than the sum of its parts. In marriage, one plus one doesn't equal two; it forms something different, something that is much more than two." And for the sake of that "something" that is the marriage, these couples are willing to make compromises and sacrifices when necessary. In today's terminology, they are committed to the marriage as well as to one another. . . .

4. TRUST

This is a word used again and again by couples, and it means many things. It means love, although people tend to use the word "trust" more often than they use "love." In part this is because "love" is an overused word, and one whose romantic meanings have overshadowed the deeper, more profound meaning of the love that binds married people. In larger part it is because feelings of love may wax and wane in the course of a marriage—in times of anger, for example, few people can keep in touch with those feelings—but trust is a constant; without it there is no true marriage. Trust also implies intimacy, or, rather, it forms the base for the closeness that couples in good marriages have established. But couples use the word "trust" more readily than "intimacy" or "love." And I believe they do because "trust" sums up much of the dynamic of a marriage, the back-and-forth interaction from which everything else grows. Trust in marriage allows for the sense of security and comfort that mark long and satisfying unions. Trust also makes possible the freedom marriage provides, the freedom and "right," in the words of psychiatrist Aaron Stein, "people have to be themselves and have their own feelings." Each partner trusts the other with his or her core self, trusts that that self will not be ridiculed or violated, trusts that it will be nurtured and protected—safe. And in that safety lies a special kind of freedom.

Intimacy, as I have said, is built around the trust partners allow themselves to have in one another. Once that trust exists, there is no set form intimacy must assume. I cannot say that every couple in a strong marriage communicate with one another as openly as the much-publicized communication ideals of our society would have them. Some do. Some are open and loose with one another, ventilating feelings and sensations freely. In other families, one partner, or both, may be more closed off, less able or willing to pour out heartsounds. But these marriages have their own ways of being intimate, which grow from the trust between partners. It may be that one partner is the expansive one while the second is more silent, relying on the other for emotional expressiveness. Or it may be that both act somewhat restrained in revealing sensitivities, yet they understand one another and feel comfortable with the more limited interchanges they have. I found many styles of relating among long-married couples, and no one seemed better than another as long as each couple was satisfied with their own style.

The trust that lies at the heart of happy marriages is also the foundation for sexual enjoyment among partners. When mates spoke about sexual loving, they almost always spoke about trusting feelings that had expanded over the years. "Sex is richer and deeper for us," said one woman. "We trust each other and we're not ashamed to get pleasure." Trust is also the reason invariably given for a commitment to monogamy, as in "I may be tempted, but I wouldn't want to violate our trust." When a partner has had a fling or brief affair, trust is the reason most often offered for having ended it or for avoiding further extramarital involvements. In short, trust is regarded by many couples as the linchpin of their marriage.

5. A BALANCE OF DEPENDENCIES

[This] is another way of saying a balance of power. I prefer "dependency," even though "power" is a sexier word, with its implied comparison between marriage and politics. I prefer "dependency" because it better conveys the way couples see and regard one another. They speak of needing each other and depending on each other, and in doing so, they are not speaking about the weaknesses of marriage, but about its strengths. In the best of marriages, partners are mutually dependent; interdependent is another way of saying that. They are aware of their dependencies and not ashamed to cater to them, acknowledging openly their debt to one another. . . .

Dependency, it needs to be added quickly, does not mean an obliteration of self. One thing I consistently became aware of was that no matter how close or how interdependent a couple, each spouse retained an individuality, a sense of self. If one or the other had lost that individuality and become completely submerged or exploited by the other, one or both partners usually expressed deep unhappiness in the marriage. Again, even in the most traditional marriages, where a woman's social identity may be tied to her husband's occupation or profession, the women who spoke most convincingly about the satisfactions of their marriages were women who viewed themselves as individuals, and who did not rely on their husbands to make them feel worthy. . . .

6. AN ENJOYMENT OF EACH OTHER

Wives and husbands in satisfying long marriages like one another, enjoy being together and enjoy talking to each other. Although they may spend evenings quietly together in a room, the silence that surrounds them is the comfortable silence of two people who know they do not *have* to talk to feel close. But mostly they do talk. For many couples conversations go on continually, whether the gossip of everyday living or discussions of broader events. And they listen to one another. I watched the faces of people I interviewed and watched each listening while the other spoke. They might argue, become irritated or jump in to correct each other, but they are engaged, and rarely bored.

They enjoy each other physically also, and sexual pleasures infuse many marriages for years and years. I could sense a sexual electricity between some partners. A different kind of warmth emanated from others, a feeling of closeness and affection. They held hands, they touched, they smiled and the spoke of sex as "warm and loving," as one woman said, "maybe not the wildness of our early marriage, but very pleasing."

They laugh at each other's jokes. Humor is the universal salve and salvation, easing tensions and marriage fatigue. "If you can laugh about it," everyone said, "you know it will be all right." And for them it is.

They find each other interesting, but they do not necessarily have the same interests. And that was a surprise. Far fewer couples than I expected spoke about sharing interests or hobbies. . . .

But if sharing interests is not a prerequisite for a rewarding marriage, sharing *values* is. Values refer to the things people believe in, the things they hold dear and worthy. The philosopher Bertrand Russell explained their importance in marriage well when he wrote, "It is fatal . . . if one values only money and the other values only good works." Such a couple will have trouble getting along, let alone enjoying one another's interests or ideas.

Mates who feel well-matched share a common base of values even when they disagree about other things. One couple described having their biggest arguments about money. He loves to spend whatever they have on clothes, records and the theater; she watches every cent, wearing the same dress again and again. Yet they had an instant meeting of minds when it came time to buy a cello for their musically gifted daughter. They bought the best they could afford, even using a good part of their savings, because they both valued their child's music education above anything else money could buy. Another couple, who love antique Oriental ceramics, think nothing of living in a dingy, run-down apartment while they spend their modest earnings on beautiful ceramic vases that they track down and buy together.

For some couples, religion is the value that informs everything else in life. Those couple were in a minority among the families I interviewed, as they are a minority in our secular society. But those who did value religion considered it the strongest bond in their lives, and many attributed the happiness and stability of their marriages to that bond. I found it interesting that marriages in which both partners valued religion, even if the partners were of different faiths, had fewer conflicts over religious issues than same-faith marriages, in which only one felt a religious commitment, especially if the other partner was disdainful of religion.

For all marriages, sharing values enhances the intimacy and mutual respect spouses feel, adding to their enjoyment of one another.

7. A SHARED HISTORY THAT IS CHERISHED

Every couple has a story, and couples in long marriages respect their own stories. They are connected to each other through those stories, and even the sadnesses they shared are a valued part of their history. "Our life is like a patchwork," one woman said. "We pull in red threads from here and blue threads from there and make them into one piece. Sometimes the threads barely hold, but you pull hard at them and they come together, and the patchwork remains whole."

The attachment couples have to their histories is not necessarily a sentimental or nostalgic attachment, but an affectionate one that sees significance in the past and in all the times spent together. George Gilbert said it nicely. His marriage, with one of the most troubled histories of all, had been filled with the traumas of manic-depressive illness and alcoholism until some years ago when he made himself stop drinking and his illness was brought under control by medication. "You know," he said, "you talk about this and you talk about that, and it sounds so chaotic, the alcohol and the rest. But still, in the midst of it all there were great moments. Once, at the height of my drinking, we went to Cape Cod with our three sons and we got an acre of land. We put out a camper and we rented a canoe and we had a glorious time. Sure, when you reflect you think of the bad things—the flashing lights and the arms wrapped around the porcelain in the bathroom when you're hung over and sick. But there was so much else, even then. There was still a lot of fun, still a lot of humor, still a lot of good loving for both of us." . . .

People in long marriages value their joint history. When their ties in the present get raggedy, they are able to look to the past to find the good that they shared, rather than give in to the disillusionments of the moment. Their sense of history also gives them a respect for time. They know, by looking backward, that changes take time and that angers vanish with time, and they know that there is time ahead for new understandings and new adventures.

8. LUCK

It has to be said, because everyone said it. With it all, the history and the trust, the willingness to change and to live without change, people need a little bit of luck to keep a marriage going.

You need luck, first of all, in choosing a partner who has the capacity to change and trust and love. In their book *Marriage and Personal Development*, psychiatrists Rubin Blanck and Gertrude Blanck make the case that marriages work best when both partners have reached a level of maturity before marriage that makes them ready for marriage. They are quite right. The only difficulty with their case is that few people are terribly mature when they marry, certainly not people in first marriages who marry young, and not even many people in second marriages. Yet many marriages work because partners mature together, over the years of matrimony. So, you need a little luck in choosing someone who will mature and grow while you, too, mature.

And you need a little luck in the family you come from and the friends that you have. A horrendous family background in which parents abuse their children or offer no love can set up almost insurmountable obstacles to the ability to sustain a marital relationship. Yet there are couples in long, happy marriages who did have devastating backgrounds. Often they were able to break the patterns they had known because of the encouragement of an aunt or an uncle, a grandparent, a teacher, a friend. They were lucky in finding the support they needed.

Then, you need a little luck with life. A marriage might move along happily and smoothly enough until a series of unexpected events rain down on it. A combination of illnesses or job losses, family feuds or personal failures might push the marriage off-course, when without these blows, it could have succeeded. Every marriage needs some luck in holding back forces that could crush it.

These aspects of luck may be out of our power to control. But the good thing about luck is that it is not all out of our control. Many people who considered themselves happy in marriage also spoke about themselves as being lucky. Since they seemed to have the same share of problems and difficulties as anyone else, sometimes even more than their share, I came to think that luck in marriage, as in life, is as much a matter of attitude as of chance. Couples who regard themselves as lucky are the ones who seize luck when they are able to. Instead of looking outside their marriage and assuming the luck is all there, in other people's homes, they look inside their marriage and find the blessings there. They are not blind to the soft spots of their marriages—nobody denied difficulties; they just consider the positives more important. So they knock wood and say they are lucky. And I guess they are. They have grabbed luck by the tail and have twisted it to their own purposes.

Reading 16

11/22/94

The Marriage License as a Hitting License

Murray A. Straus, Richard Gelles, and Suzanne Steinmetz

Wife-beating is found in every class, at every income level. The wife of the president of a midwestern state university recently asked one of us what she could do about the beatings without putting her husband's career in danger. Japan's former Prime Minister Sato, a winner of the Nobel Peace Prize, was accused publicly by his wife of many beatings in their early married life. Ingeborg Dedichen, a former mistress of Aristotle Onassis, describes his beating her till he was forced to quit from exhaustion. "It is what every Greek husband does, it's good for the wife," he told her.

What is at the root of such violent attacks? Proverbs such as "A man's home is his castle," go a long way in giving insights into human nature and society. The home belongs to the man. It is the woman who finds herself homeless if she refuses further abuse.

The image of the "castle" implies freedom from interference from outsiders. What goes on within the walls of the castle is shielded from prying eyes. And a modern home, like a medieval castle, can contain its own brand of torture chamber. Take the case of Carol, a Boston woman who called the police to complain that her husband had beaten her and then pushed her down the stairs. The policeman on duty answered, "Listen, lady, he pays the bills, doesn't he? What he does inside of his house is his business."

The evidence we documented . . . suggested that, aside from war and riots, physical violence occurs between family members more often than it occurs between any other individuals. At the same time we also pointed out the limitations of the data. In particular, no research up to now gives information on how often each of the different forms of family violence occurs in a representative sample of American families.

THE OVERALL LEVEL OF HUSBAND-WIFE VIOLENCE

Violence Rates

A first approach to getting a picture of the amount of violence between 2,143 husbands and wives in this study is to find out how many had engaged in any of the eight violent acts we asked about. For the year we studied this works out to be 16 per cent. In other words, every year about one out of every six couples in the United States commits at least one violent act against his or her partner.

If the period considered is the entire length of the marriage (rather than just the previous year), the result is 28 per cent, or between one out of four and one out of three American couples. In short, if you are married, the chances are almost one out of three that your husband or wife will hit you.

When we began our study of violence in the family, we would have considered such a rate of husbands and wives hitting each other very high. In terms of our values—and probably the values of most other Americans—it is still very high. But in terms of what we have come to expect on the basis of the pilot studies, this is a low figure. *It is very likely a substantial underestimate.*

Later in this article we will give the reasons for thinking it is an underestimate. But for now, let us examine the violent acts one by one. This is important if we are to get a realistic picture of the meaning of the overall rates of 28 per cent. One needs to know how much of the violence was slaps and how much was kicking and beating up. This information is given in Figure 16.1.

Slaps, Beatings, and Guns

Figure 16.1 shows that in almost seven of every hundred couples either the husband or the wife had thrown something at the other in the previous year, and about one out of six (16 per cent) had done this at some point in their marriage.

The statistics for *slapping* a spouse are about the same: 7 per cent in the previous year and 18 per cent at some time.

The figures for pushing, shoving, or grabbing during an argument are the highest of any of the eight things we asked about: 13 per cent had done this during the year, and almost one out of four at some time in the marriage.

At the other extreme, "only" one or two out of every hundred couples (1.5 per cent) experienced a *beating-up* incident in the previous year. But a "beating up" had occurred at some time in the marriages of one out of every twenty of the couples we interviewed.

The rates for actually *using a knife or gun* on one's spouse are one out of every two hundred couples in the previous year, and almost one out of twenty-seven couples at some point in the marriage.

We were surprised that there was not a bigger difference between the rate of occurrence for "mild" violent acts (such as pushing and slapping) and the severe acts of violence (such as beating up and using a knife or gun). This is partly because the rates for the more violent acts turned out to be greater than we expected, and

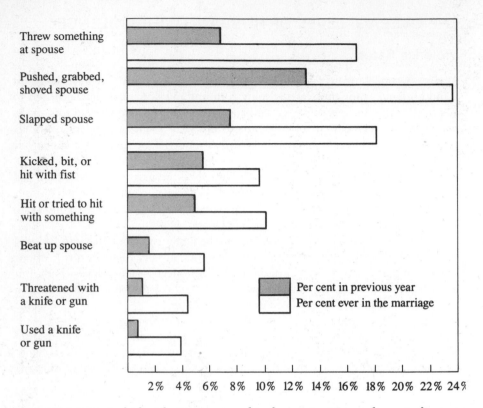

Figure 16.1 Rate at which violent acts occurred in the previous year and ever in the marriage

partly because the rates for the "ordinary" acts of husband-wife violence were less than expected. Whatever the reasons, it seems that couples are using more than slaps and shoves when violence occurs.

Indeed, the statistics on the number of husbands and wives who had ever "beaten up" their spouses or actually used a knife or gun are astoundingly high. The human meaning of these most extreme forms of violence in the family can be understood better if we translate the percentages into the total number of marriages affected. Since there were about 47 million couples living together in the United States in 1975, the rates just given mean that *over 1.7 million Americans had at some time faced a husband or wife wielding a knife or gun, and well over 2 million had been beaten up* by his or her spouse.

How Accurate Are the Statistics?

It is difficult to know how much confidence to put in these statistics because several different kinds of error are possible. First, these are estimates based on a sample. But the sample is reasonably large and was chosen by methods which should make it quite representative of the U.S. population. Comparisons with characteristics reported in the U.S. census show that this in fact is the case.

Still, there is the possibility of sampling error. So we computed what is known as the "standard error" for each of the rates in Figure 16.1. The largest standard error is for the overall violence index. Even that is low: there is a 95 per cent chance that the true percentage of couples *admitting to* ever having physically assaulted one another is somewhere between 26.8 and 28.8 per cent of all couples.

"Admitting to" was italicized to highlight a much more serious and more likely source of error, that of an underestimate. The 26.8 to 28.8 per cent figure assumes that everyone "told all." But that is very unlikely. Three of the reasons are:

1. There is one group of people who are likely to "underreport" the amount of violence. For this group a slap, push, or shove (and sometimes even more severe violence) is so much a normal part of the family that it is simply not a noteworthy or dramatic enough event always to be remembered. Such omissions are especially likely when we asked about things which had happened during the entire length of the marriage.
2. At the opposite end of the violence continuum, there is another group who fail to admit or report such acts because of the shame involved if one is the victim, or the guilt if one is the attacker. Such violent attacks as being hit with objects, bitten, beaten up, or attacked with a knife or gun go beyond the "normal violence" of family life and are often unreported.
3. A final reason for thinking these figures are drastic underestimates lies in the nature of the sample. We included only couples currently living together. Divorced people were asked only about their present marriage. Since "excessive" violence is often a cause of divorce, the sample probably omits many of the high-violence cases.

The sample was selected in this way because a major purpose of the study was to investigate the extent to which violence is related to other aspects of husband-wife interaction. Questions were limited to current marriages because of interview time limits and limits on what people could be expected to remember.

The figures therefore could easily be twice as large as those revealed by the survey. In fact, based on the pilot studies and informal evidence (where some of the factors leading to underreporting were not present), it seems likely that *the true rate is closer to 50 or 60 per cent of all couples than it is to the 28 per cent who were willing to describe violent acts to our interviewers.*

MEN AND WOMEN

Traditionally, men have been considered more aggressive and violent than women. Like other stereotypes, there is no doubt a kernel of truth to this. But it is far from the clear-cut difference which exists in the thinking of most people. This is also the case with our survey. About one out of eight husbands had carried out at least one violent act during the course of a conflict in the year covered by the survey, *and* about the same number of wives had attacked their husbands (12.1 per cent of the husbands versus 11.6 per cent of the wives).

Mutual Violence

One way of looking at this issue is to ask what percentage of the sample are couples in which the husband was the only one to use violence? What per cent were couples in which the only violence was by the wife? And in what percentage did both use violence?

The most common situation was that in which both had used violence.

One man, who found himself in the middle of a family battle, reported it this way:

It started sort of slowly . . . so I couldn't tell for sure if they were even serious. . . . In the beginning they'd push at each other, or shove, like kids—little kids who want to fight but they don't know how. Then, this one time, while I'm standing there not sure whether to stay or go, and them treating me like I didn't exist, she begins yelling at him like she did.

"You're a bust, you're a failure, I want you out of here, I can always get men who'll work, good men, not scum like you." And they're pushing and poking with their hands, like they were dancing. She pushes him, he pushes her, only she's doing all the talking. He isn't saying a word.

Then all of a sudden, she must have triggered off the right nerve because he lets fly with a right cross that I mean stuns. I mean she goes down like a rock! And he's swearing at her, calling her every name in the book. Jesus, I didn't know what the hell to do.

What I wanted to do was call the police. But I figured, how can I call the police and add to this guy's misery, because she was pushing him. . . . She was really pushing him. I'd have done something to her myself.

Of those couples reporting any violence, 49 per cent were of situations of this type, where both were violent. For the year previous to our study, a comparison of the number of couples in which only the husband was violent with those in which only the wife was violent shows the figures to be very close: 27 per cent violent husbands and 24 per cent violent wives. So, as in the case of the violence rates, there is little difference between the husbands and wives in this study.

Specific Violent Acts

Figure 16.2 compares the men and women in our study on each of the eight violent acts. Again, there is an overall similarity. But there are also some interesting differences, somewhat along the lines of the stereotype of the pot- and pan-throwing wife.

I got him good last time! He punched me in the face and I fell back on the stove. He was walking out of the kitchen and I grabbed the frying pan and landed it square on his head. Man, he didn't know what hit him.

The number of wives who threw things at their husbands is almost twice as large as the number of husbands who threw things at their wives. The rate for

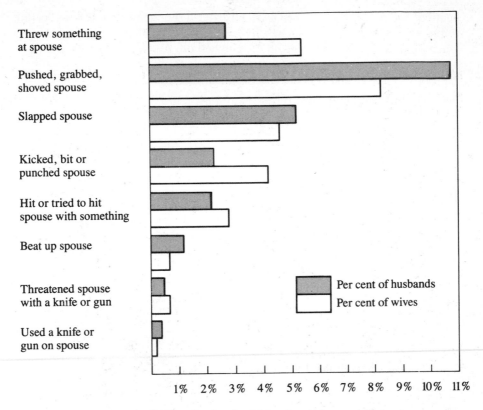

Figure 16.2 Comparison of husband and wife violence in previous year

kicking and hitting with an object is also higher for wives than for husbands. The husbands on the other hand had higher rates for pushing, shoving, slapping, beating up, and actually using a knife or gun.

WIFE-BEATING—AND HUSBAND-BEATING

Wife-beating has become a focus of increasing public concern in the last few years. In part this reflects the national anguish over all aspects of violence, ranging from the Vietnam war to the upward surge of assault and murder. Another major element accounting for the recent public concern with wife-beating is the feminist movement. Behind that are the factors which have given rise to the rebirth of the feminist movement in the late 1960s and early 1970s.

What Is Wife-Beating?

To find out how much wife-beating there is, one must be able to define it in a way which can be objectively measured. When this is tried, it becomes clear that "wife-beating" is a political rather than a scientific term. For some people wife-beating refers only to those instances in which severe damage is inflicted. Less severe violence is not considered violence or it is laughed off. A joke one of us heard while driving across northern England in 1974 is no doubt familiar to many readers of this book. It goes like this in the BBC version: One woman asks another why she feels her husband doesn't love her any more. The answer: "He hasn't bashed me in a fortnight." Or take the following letter to Ann Landers:

> *Dear Ann Landers:*
> Come out of the clouds, for Lord's sake, and get down here with us humans. I am sick to death of your holier-than-thou attitude toward women whose husbands give them a well deserved belt in the mouth.
> Don't you know that a man can be pushed to the brink and something's got to give? A crack in the teeth can be a wonderful tension-breaker. It's also a lot healthier than keeping all that anger bottled up.
> My husband hauls off and slugs me every few months and I don't mind. He feels better and so do I because he never hits me unless I deserve it. So why don't you come off it?—REAL HAPPY.

> *Dear Real Happy:*
> If you don't mind a crack in the teeth every few months, it's all right with me. I hope you have a good dentist.

So a certain amount of violence in the family is "normal violence." In fact, most of the violent acts which occur in the family are so much a part of the way family members relate to each other that they are not even thought of as violence.

At what point does one exceed the bounds of "normal" family violence? When does it become "wife-beating"? To answer this question, we gathered data on a series of violent acts, ranging from a slap to using a knife or gun. This allows anyone reading this article to draw the line at whatever place seems most appropriate for his or her purpose.

Measuring Wife-Beating

This "solution," however, can also be a means of avoiding the issue. So in addition to data on each violent act, we also combined the most severe of these into what can be called a Severe Violence Index. If these are things done by the husband, then it is a "Wife-beating Index." The Wife-beating Index consists of the extent to which the husband went beyond throwing things, pushing or grabbing, and slapping and attacking his wife by kicking, biting, or punching; hitting with some object; beating her up; threatening her with a gun or knife; or using a knife or gun (the last five behaviors in Figure 16.1).

Why limit the Wife-beating Index to "only" the situations where the husband went beyond throwing things, pushing, grabbing, and slapping? Certainly we don't want to imply that this reflects our conception of what is permissible violence. None of these are acceptable for relationships between husband and wife—just as they are unacceptable between student and teacher, minister and parishioner, or colleagues in a department. In short, we follow the maxim coined by John Valusek: "People are not for hitting."

What then is the basis for choosing kicking, biting, or punching; hitting with an object; beating up; threatening with a knife or gun; and using a knife or gun for the Wife-beating Index? It is simply the fact that these are all acts which carry with them a high risk of serious physical injury.

What Percentage Are Beaten?

How many husbands and wives experience the kind of attack which is serious enough to be included in the Wife-beating and Husband-beating Indexes? A remarkably large number. In fact, since our survey produced a rate of 3.8 per cent, this means that about one out of twenty-six American wives get beaten by their husbands every year, or a total of almost 1.8 million per year.

Staggering as are these figures, the real surprise lies in the statistics on husband-beating. These rates are slightly higher than those for wife-beating! Although such cases rarely come to the attention of the police or the press, they exist at all social levels. Here is an example of one we came across:

> A wealthy, elderly New York banker was finally granted a separation from his second wife, 31 years his junior, after 14 years of marriage and physical abuse. According to the presiding judge, the wife had bullied him with hysteria, screaming tantrums and vicious physical violence.
>
> The husband wore constant scars and bruises. His ear had once been shredded by his wife with her teeth. She had blackened his eyes, and on one occasion injured one of his eyes so badly that doctors feared it might be lost.

From 4.6 per cent of the wives in the sample admitted to or were reported by their husbands as having engaged in an act which is included in the Husband-beating Index. That works to be about one out of twenty-two wives who attacked their husbands severely enough to be included in this Husband-beating Index. That is over 2 million very violent wives. Since three other studies of this issue also found high rates of husband-beating, some revision of the traditional view about female violence seems to be needed.

How Often Do Beatings Happen?

Let us look at just the couples for which a violent incident occurred during the year previous to our study. Was it an isolated incident? If not, how often did attacks of this kind occur?

It was an isolated incident (in the sense that there was only one such attack during the year) for only about a third of the violent couples. This applies to both wife-beating and husband-beating. Almost one out of five of the violent husbands and one out of eight wives attacked his or her partner this severely twice during the year. Forty-seven per cent of the husbands who beat their wives did so three or more times during the year, and 53 per cent of the husband-beaters did so three or more times. So, for about half the couples the pattern is that if there is one beating, there are likely to be others—at least three per year! In short, violence between husbands and wives, when it occurs, tends to be a recurrent feature of the marriage.

Was There Ever a Beating?

A final question about how many beatings took place can be answered by looking at what happened over the entire length of the marriage. Did something that can be called a beating *ever* happen in the marriage?

There are several reasons why even a single beating is important. First, even one such event debases human life. Second, there is the physical danger involved. Third is the fact that many, if not most, such beatings are part of a struggle for power in the family. It often takes only one such event to fix the balance of power for many years—or perhaps for a lifetime.

Physical force is the ultimate resource which most of us learn as children to rely on if all else fails and the issue is crucial. As a husband in one of the families interviewed by LaRossa said when asked why he hit his wife during an argument:

> . . . She more or less tried to run me and I said no, and she got hysterical and said, "I could kill you!" And I got rather angry and slapped her in the face three or four times and I said, "Don't you ever say that to me again!" And we haven't had any problem since.

Later in the interview, the husband evaluated his use of physical force as follows:

> You don't use it until you are forced to it. At that point I felt I had to do something physical to stop the bad progression of events. I took my chances with that and it worked. In those circumstances my judgment was correct and it worked.

Since greater size and strength give the advantage to men in such situations, the single beating may be an extremely important factor in maintaining male dominance in the family system.

We found that one out of eight couples (12.6 per cent) experienced at least one beating incident in the course of marriage. That is approximately a total of 6 million beatings. However, as high as that figure is, the actual statistics are probably higher. This is because things are forgotten over the years, and also because (as we pointed out earlier) the violent acts in question are only about the current marriage. They leave out the many marriages which ended in divorce, a large part of which were marked by beatings.

Wives and Husbands as Victims

This study shows a high rate of violence by *wives* as well as husbands. But it would be a great mistake if that fact distracted us from giving first attention to wives *as victims* as the focus of social policy. There are a number of reasons for this:

1. The data in Figure 16.2 show that husbands have higher rates of the most dangerous and injurious forms of violence (beating up and using a knife or gun).
2. Steinmetz found that abuse by husbands does more damage. She suggests that the greater physical strength of men makes it more likely that a woman will be seriously injured when beaten up by her husband.

3. When violent acts are committed by a husband, they are repeated more often than is the case for wives.
4. The data do not tell us what proportion of the violent acts by wives were in self-defense or a response to blows initiated by husbands. Wolfgang's study of husband-wife homicides suggests that this is an important factor.
5. A large number of attacks by husbands seem to occur when the wife is pregnant, thus posing a danger to the as yet unborn child. This isn't something that happens only on Tobacco Road:

> The first time Hortense Barber's husband beat her was the day she told him she was pregnant with their first child. "He knocked out my two front teeth and split open my upper lip," the 32 year old honors graduate told a New York Senate Task Force on Women. Later Mrs. Barber's husband regularly blacked her eyes during her pregnancy and threw a knife at her "in jest," cutting her knee.

6. Women are locked into marriage to a much greater extent than men. Women are bound by many economic and social constraints, and they often have no alternative to putting up with beatings by their husbands. The situation is similar to being married to an alcoholic. Nine out of ten men leave an alcoholic wife, but only one out of ten women leave an alcoholic husband.

Most people feel that social policy should be aimed at helping those who are in the weakest position. Even though wives are also violent, they are in the weaker, more vulnerable position in respect to violence in the family. This applies to both the physical, psychological, and economic aspects of things. That is the reason we give first priority to aiding wives who are the victims of beatings by their husbands.

At the same time, the violence *by* wives uncovered in this study suggests that a fundamental solution to the problem of wife-beating has to go beyond a concern with how to control assaulting husbands. It seems that violence is built into the very structure of the society and the family system itself. . . . Wife-beating . . . is only one aspect of the general pattern of family violence, which includes parent-child violence, child-to-child violence, and wife-to-husband violence. To eliminate the particularly brutal form of violence known as wife-beating will require changes in the cultural norms and in the organization of the family and society which underlie the system of violence on which so much of American society is based.

NORMS AND MEANINGS

Just as we need to know the extent to which violent *acts* occur between husbands and wives, parents and children, and brothers and sisters, it is also important to know how family members feel about intrafamily violence. Just how strongly do they approve or disapprove of a parent slapping a child or a husband slapping a wife? To what extent do people see violence in the family as one of those undesirable but necessary parts of life?

It is hard to find out about these aspects of the way people think about family violence. One difficulty is there are contradictory rules or "norms." At one level there are norms strongly opposed to husbands and wives hitting each other. But at the same time, there also seem to be implicit but powerful norms which permit and even encourage such acts. Sometimes people are thinking of one of these principles and sometimes the other.

Another thing is that violence is often such a "taken for granted" part of life that most people don't even realize there are socially defined rules or norms about the use of violence in the family.

The existence of these implicit norms are illustrated by the case of a husband who hit his wife on several occasions. Each time he felt that it was wrong. He apologized—very genuinely. But still he did it again. The husband explained that he and his wife got so worked up in their arguments that he "lost control." In his mind, it was almost involuntary, and certainly not something he did according to a rule or norm which gives one the right to hit his wife.

But the marriage counselor in the case brought out the rules which permitted him to hit his wife. He asked the husband why, if he had "lost control," he didn't stab his wife! This possibility (and the fact that the husband did not stab his wife despite "losing control") shows that hitting the wife was not just a bubbling over of a primitive level of behavior. Although this husband did not realize it, he was following a behavioral rule or norm. It seems that the unrecognized but operating norm for this husband—and for millions of other husbands—is that it is okay to hit one's wife, but not to stab her.

There is other evidence which tends to support the idea that the marriage license is also a hitting license. For example, "Alice, you're going to the moon," was one of the standard punch lines on the old Jackie Gleason "Honeymooners" skits which delighted TV audiences during the 1950s, and which are currently enjoying a revival. Jokes, plays, such as those of George Bernard Shaw, and experiments which show that people take less severe actions if they think the man attacking a woman is her husband are other signs.

It has been suggested that one of the reasons neighbors who saw the attack didn't come to the aid of Kitty Genovese in the 1964 Queens murder case was because they thought it was a man beating his wife!

Or take the following incident:

Roy Butler came over to help his bride-to-be in preparations for their wedding, which is why the wedding is off.

Roy, 24, made the mistake of going to a stag party first.

On the way to fiancée Anthea Higson's home, he dropped the wedding cake in the front garden.

In the shouting match that followed, he dropped Anthea's mother with a right cross to the jaw.

Anthea, 21, promptly dropped Roy. She said the wedding was off and she never wanted to see him again.

"*If he had hit me instead of my mother, I probably would have married him all the same,*" [italics added] she said yesterday after a court fined Butler $135 for assaulting Mrs. Brenda Higson.

"But I'm not having any man hitting my mum," Anthea said.

Interesting as are these examples, none of them provide the kind of systematic and broadly representative evidence which is needed. That is what we attempted to get in this study.

Measuring the Meaning of Violence

To find out how our sample felt about violence in the family, we used the "semantic differential" method. For husband-wife violence, we asked subjects to rate the phrase "Couples slapping each other." They were asked to make three ratings: unnecessary . . . necessary; not normal . . . normal; and good . . . bad.

How many of the husbands and wives rated "Couples slapping each other" as "necessary," "normal," or "good"? Over all just under one out of four wives and one out of three husbands (31.3 and 24.6 per cent) saw this type of physical force between spouses as at least somewhat necessary, normal, or good.

These statistics are remarkably close to those from a national sample studied by the U.S. Violence Commission. The Violence Commission found that about one quarter of the persons interviewed said they could think of circumstances in which it would be all right for a husband to hit his wife or a wife to hit her husband. This is slightly lower than the percentages for our sample. But if the Violence Commission survey data had been analyzed in the way we examined our data, the results could well have been almost identical.

The separate ratings for violence being necessary, normal, or good are interesting in the contrast they provide with each other and in the way men and women think about violence. On the other hand, there are big differences in the percentage of husbands as compared to wives who could see some situations in which it is necessary for a husband or wife to slap each other (see Figure 16.3). There is also a larger percentage of husbands who could see some situations in which this would not be a bad thing to do. In fact, for both these ratings, twice as many husbands as wives felt this way.

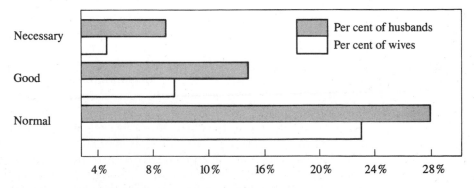

Figure 16.3 Percent of husbands and wives who rated "A couple slapping each other" as at least somewhat necessary, good, or normal

On the other hand, the percentages for the not normal . . . normal rating are particularly interesting because they are larger and because there is little difference between men and women. The figures in the chart show that a large proportion of American husbands and wives see violence as a normal part of married life. It may not be good, and it may not be necessary, but it is something which is going to happen under normal circumstances. The marriage license is a hitting license for a large part of the population, and probably for a much greater part than could bring themselves to rate it as "normal" in the context of this survey.

SUMMING UP

We are reasonably confident that the couples in the study are representative of American couples in general. But we suspect that not everyone told us about all the violence in his or her family. In fact, the pilot studies and informal evidence suggest that the true figures may be double those based on what people were willing to admit in a mass survey such as this. If this is the case, then about a third of all American couples experience a violent incident every year, and about two thirds have experienced such an incident at least once in the marriage.

Of course, a large part of these "violent incidents" are pushes and slaps, but far from all of them. A large portion are also actions which could cause serious injury or even death. We know from the fact that so many murderers and their victims are husband and wife that this is not just speculation. For the couples in this sample, in fact, almost one out of every twenty-five had faced an angry partner with a knife or gun in hand.

If the "dangerous violence" is not limited solely to use of a knife or gun, and includes everything *more serious* than pushing, grabbing, shoving, slapping, and throwing things, the rate is three times as high. In short, almost one out of every eight couples admitted that at some point in the marriage there had been an act of violence which could cause serious injury.

Another way of grasping this is to compare the rates of wife-beating and husband-beating in our survey with assaults which are reported in official statistics. The Uniform Crime Reports on "aggravated assault" are given in rate per 100,000. But the rates in this article are percentages, i.e., rates per 100, not per 100,000.

We can translate the rates for this survey into rates per 100,000 per year. They are 3,800 per 100,000 for assaults on wives, 4,600 for assaults on husbands, and a combined rate of 6,100 per 100,000 couples. Compare this with the roughly 190 per 100,000 aggravated assaults of all kinds known to the police each year.

Of course, many crimes are not reported to the police. So there have been surveys asking people if they were the victims of a crime. The rate of aggravated assault coming out of the National Crime Panel survey is very high: 2,597 per 100,000. But our rate for wife-beating and husband-beating of 6,100 per 100,000 is almost two and a half times higher. Also, since the Uniform Crime Reports, and especially the National Crime Panel data, include many within-family assaults, the amount by which husband-wife assault exceeds any other type of assault is much greater than these rates suggest.

Leaving aside the fact that our figures on husband-wife violence are probably underestimates, and even leaving aside the psychological damage that such violence can produce, just the danger to physical health implied by these rates is staggering. If any other crime of risk to physical well-being involved almost 2 million wives and 2 million husbands per year, plus a much larger amount at some point in the marriage, a national emergency would probably be declared.

Chapter
6

Divorce and Remarriage

Reading 17

The Transformation of Legal Marriage Through No-Fault Divorce

Lenore J. Weitzman and Ruth B. Dixon

INTRODUCTION

Divorce and family breakdown constitute one of the major social problems in the United States today. In 1975 alone over 3 million men, women and minor children were involved in a divorce.[1] In the future it is likely that one-third to one-half of all the adults in the United States, and close to one-third of the minor children under

18 will be affected by a divorce or dissolution.[2] These data reflect not only the numerical importance of divorce, but its increased social significance as well. While divorce may have been considered a "deviant family pattern" in the past, it is rapidly becoming accepted as a possible (though not yet probable) outcome of marriage.

Since 1970 there has been a major reform in divorce law which attempts to institutionalize fundamental social changes in family patterns. Commonly referred to as no-fault divorce, this new legislation seeks to alter the definition of marriage, the relationship between husbands and wives, and the economic and social obligations of former spouses to each other and to their children after divorce.

In 1970, California instituted the first no-fault divorce law in the United States. Since then fourteen other states have adopted "pure" no-fault divorce laws[3] and an additional thirteen states have added no-fault grounds to their existing grounds for divorce.[4] No-fault divorce has been praised as the embodiment of "modern" and "enlightened" law, and heralded as the forerunner of future family law in the United States. It has also been strongly attacked for "destroying the family" and for causing irreparable harm to women. This article aims at analyzing the effects of this new legislation on both marriage and divorce.

The laws governing divorce tell us how a society defines marriage and where it sets the boundaries for appropriate marital behavior. One can generally examine the way a society defines marriage by examining its provisions for divorce, for it is at the point of divorce that a society has the opportunity to reward the marital behavior it approves of, and to punish spouses who have violated its norms.[5] In addition, in virtually all societies which allow divorce, it is assumed that people who were once married continue to have obligations to each other; and these obligations reflect the rights and duties of marriage itself.

This article is divided into three sections. It begins with a discussion of traditional legal marriage followed by a review of traditional divorce law. The last section examines the aims of the no-fault legislation and its implications for traditional family roles.

TRADITIONAL LEGAL MARRIAGE

The origins of Anglo-American family law[6] may be traced to the tenth or eleventh century, when Christianity became sufficiently influential in Britain to enable the Church to assert its rules effectively. (Clark, 1968) Traditionally legal marriage was firmly grounded in the Christian conception of marriage as a holy union between a man and woman. Marriage was a sacrament, a commitment to join together for life: "to take each other to love and to cherish, in sickness and in health, for better, for worse, until death do us part."

The nature of the marital relationship, and the legal responsibilities of the spouses were specified by law—by statute, case law and common law. While a thorough analysis of legal marriage is obviously beyond the scope of this paper (but see Clark, 1968; Kay, 1974; Weitzman, 1979), five important features may be briefly summarized as follows: First, legal marriage was limited to a single man and a single woman; bigamy, polygamy and homosexual unions were prohibited. Second, legal marriage was monogamous. The spouses were to remain sexually faithful to each other and adultery was explicitly prohibited. Third, marriage was for procreation. One of the major objects of matrimony was the bearing and rearing of (legitimate) children. (Reynolds v. Reynolds, 1862)

Fourth, legal marriage established a hierarchical relationship between the spouses: the husband was the head of the family, with his wife and children subordinate to him. The husband's authority was based on the common-law doctrine of coverture which established the legal fiction that a husband and wife took a single legal identity upon marriage—the identity of the husband. At common law a married woman became a *femme covert,* a legal nonperson, under her husband's arm, protection and cover. (Blackstone, 1765)

Although most of the disabilities of coverture were removed by the Married Women's Property Acts in the nineteenth century—the common-law assumption that the husband was the head of the family remained firmly embodied in statutory and case law in the United States. The married woman's subordination was most clearly reflected in rules governing her domicile and name. In both cases the married woman assumed her husband's identity—taking his name and his domicile as her own. This basic assumption of traditional legal marriage has, of course, been challenged in recent years.

The fifth, and most important feature of traditional legal marriage, was its sex-based division of family roles and responsibilities. The woman was to devote herself to being a wife, homemaker and mother in return for her husband's promise of lifelong support. The husband was given the sole responsibility for the family's financial welfare, while he was assured that his home, his children and his social-emotional well-being would be cared for by his wife. Professor Homer Clark, a noted authority on family law, summarizes the legal obligations of the two spouses as follows:

> Specifically, the courts say that the husband has a duty to support his wife, that she has a duty to render services in the home, and that these duties are reciprocal. . . . The husband is to provide the family with food, clothing, shelter and as many of the amenities of life as he can manage, either (in earlier days) by the management of his estates, or (more recently) by working for wages or a salary. The wife is to be mistress of the household, maintaining the home with resources furnished by the husband, and caring for children. A reading of contemporary judicial opinions leaves the impression that these roles have changed over the last two hundred years. (Clark, 1968)

All states, even those with community property systems, placed the burden of the family support on the husband; he was legally responsible for providing necessities for his wife and his children. Similarly, all states made the wife responsible for domestic and child care services: her legal obligation was to be a companion, housewife and mother. As one court enumerated the services a man could legally expect from his wife:

> (she had a duty) to be his helpmate, to love and care for him in such a role, to afford him her society and her person, to protect and care for him in sickness, and to labor

faithfully to advance his interest . . . (she must also perform) her household and domestic duties . . . A husband is entitled to the benefit of his wife's industry and economy. (Rucci v. Rucci, 1962)

The wife was also assigned responsibility for child care, both during marriage
and after divorce, as the law viewed her as the "natural and proper" caretaker of
the young.

While no one would claim that the law was responsible for the traditional
division of labor in the family, it did serve to legitimate, sanction, and reinforce
these traditional family roles. For example, the law reinforced the wife's subordinate status—and her economic dependency—by defining the husband as the only
person who was responsible for (and capable of) supporting the family. (Kay, 1974)

By promising the housewife lifelong support, the law provided a disincentive
for women to develop their economic capacity and to work in the paid labor force.
In addition, by making them legally responsible for domestic and child care services, it reinforced the primacy of these activities in their lives, leaving them with
neither time nor incentive to develop careers outside of the home.

The law similarly reinforced the traditional male role by directing the husband
away from domestic and childcare activities. While the law did legitimate the husband's power and authority in the family, it also encouraged a single-minded ded-
ication to work, and to earning a living, for it made it clear that his sole responsibility was his family's economic welfare.

TRADITIONAL DIVORCE LAW

Since marriage was regarded as an indissoluble union, it could be ended only by
the death of one of the parties. (Rheinstein, 1972) "Divorce, in the modern sense
of a judicial decree dissolving a valid marriage, and allowing one or both partners
to remarry during the life of the other, did not exist in England until 1857." (Kay,
1970)[7]

A rare exception, originating in the late 17th century, allowed divorce (on the
sole ground of adultery) by special act of Parliament. As a practical matter, however, a few of these divorces were granted—and they were available only to the
very rich, and to men. (Clark, 1968) The Church also permitted divorce *a mensa et
thoro,* literally a divorce from bed and board, which allowed the parties to live
apart. But this legal separation did not sever the marital bond.

The Ecclesiastical Courts retained their exclusive jurisdiction over marriage
and divorce in England until 1857, when divorce jurisdiction was transferred to the
Civil Court System, and divorces were authorized for adultery. But the underlying
premise of divorce law remained the same: Marriage was still regarded as a permanent and cherished union which the Church—and then the state—had to protect
and preserve. And it was still assumed that the holy bond of matrimony would best
be protected by restricting access to divorce. As Clark observed:

(They believed) that marital happiness is best secured by making marriage indissoluble
except for very few causes. When the parties know that they are bound together for

life, the argument runs, they will resolve their differences and disagreements and make an effort to get along with each other. If they are able to separate legally upon less serious grounds, they will make no such effort, and immorality will result. (Clark, 1968)

It should also be noted that these early divorce laws established a different standard for men and women: "wives . . . could obtain a divorce only if the husband's adultery was aggravated by bigamy, cruelty or incest, while the husband could get his divorce for adultery alone." (Clark, 1969)[8]

Divorce laws in the United States were heavily influenced by the English tradition. In the middle and southern Colonies, divorces were granted by the legislature, and were rare. However, New England allowed divorce more freely. The Protestant doctrines (and the absence of any system of Ecclesiastical Courts) resulted in statutes which authorized divorce for adultery, desertion, and, in some cases, cruelty—sometimes by the courts and sometimes by acts of the Legislature.

Although some diversity in the divorce laws of the states continued, in nineteenth century most states gave the courts the jurisdiction to dissolve marriages on specified grounds (Kay, 1968), and by 1900 most states had adopted what we shall refer to as the four major elements of traditional divorce laws.

First, *traditional divorce law perpetuated the sex-based division of roles and responsibilities in traditional legal marriage.* As we noted above, in legal marriage the woman presumably agreed to devote herself to being a wife, homemaker and mother in return for her husband's promise of lifelong support. Although traditional family law assumed that the husband's support would be provided in a lifelong marriage, if the marriage did not endure, and if the wife was virtuous, she was nevertheless guaranteed alimony—a means of continued support. Alimony perpetuated the husband's responsibility for economic support, and the wife's right to be supported in return for her domestic services. It thus maintained the reciprocity in the legal marriage contract.

Traditional divorce laws also perpetuated the sex-based division of roles with respect to children: the husband remained responsible for their economic support, the wife for their care. All states, by statute or by case law tradition, gave preference to the wife as the appropriate custodial parent after the divorce; and all states gave the husband the primary responsibility for their economic support.

Second, *traditional divorce law required grounds for divorce.* Divorce could be obtained only if one party committed a marital offense, giving the other a legal basis or ground for the divorce. Since marriage was supposed to be a permanent lifelong union, only serious marital offenses such as adultery, cruelty, or desertion could justify a divorce. As Professor Herma Hill Kay explains:

> The state's interest in marital stability, thus delegated to the courts, was to be guarded by the judge's diligence in requiring that evidence clearly established the ground relied on for a divorce, that the defendant had no valid defense to the plaintiff's suit, and that the parties had not conspired to put on a false case. (Kay, 1970: 221)

The standards for judging appropriate grounds also reflected the sex-typed expectations of traditional legal marriage. While the almost ritualistic "evidence" of misbehavior varied from state to state, husbands charged with cruelty were often alleged to have caused their wives bodily harm, while wives charged with cruelty were more typically charged with neglecting their husbands (showing lack of affection, belittling him); or their homes (leaving the home in disarray, neglecting dinner), impuning their husband's self-respect or reputation (denigrating or insulting him in front of business associates or friends); or ignoring their wifely duties (what Clark calls the country club syndrome in which the wife "is entirely preoccupied with club and social life, is extravagant, drinks heavily, and wholly disregards the husband's desires for affection and comfort"). (Clark, 1968)

Cruelty was the most commonly used grounds for divorce followed by desertion, which accounted for less than 18% of all divorces (Jacobson, 1959). Adultery was rarely used outside of New York, where it was the only permissible ground for divorce until 1967. While the standards for desertion also varied from state to state, two sex-based standards were common to most: (1) If a wife refused to live in the domicile chosen by her husband, she was held responsible for desertion in the divorce action. In addition, if the husband moved and she refused to accompany him, *she* was considered to have deserted *him,* since he had the legal right to choose the family home. She would then be the guilty party in the divorce, and that had important economic consequences which are discussed below. Second, a spouse's withdrawal from his or her marital roles might be considered desertion, and the standards for these withdrawals were clearly sex-typed. For example, a wife who showed "lack of affection" for the husband, had a relationship with another man (but did not commit adultery), refused to do housework, and nagged her husband, would be guilty of desertion (see, for example, Anton v. Anton, 1955) but a husband who acted in a similar fashion would not—unless he also stopped supporting his wife financially.

Over time, in actual practice many divorcing couples privately agreed to an uncontested divorce where one party, usually the wife, would take the *pro forma* role of plaintiff. Supported by witnesses, she would attest to her husband's cruel conduct and he would not challenge her testimony. But even if these allegations involved collusion and perjury, as many of them did, the type of behavior reported as grounds for divorce nevertheless reflected what the courts considered "appropriate violations" of the marriage contract. The husband, supposed to support and protect his wife, was sanctioned for nonsupport and physical abuse. The wife, obligated to care for her home and husband, was sanctioned for neglecting her domestic responsibilities.

Third, traditional legal divorce *was based on adversary proceedings.* The adversary process required that one party be guilty, or responsible for the divorce, and that the other be innocent. The plaintiff's success in obtaining a divorce depended on his or her ability to prove the defendant's fault for having committed some marital offense. Divorces had to be "won" by the innocent party against the guilty party. As the Tennessee Supreme Court (Brown v. Brown, 1955) stated "divorce is conceived as a remedy for the innocent against the guilty." If a spouse who was found guilty could prove the other was also at fault, or that the other had colluded in or condoned their behavior, the divorce thus might not be granted in order to punish both parties.

Finally, traditional divorce law *linked the financial terms of the divorce to the determination of fault.* Being found "guilty" or "innocent" in the divorce action had important financial consequences.

For example, alimony, or a "suitable allowance for support and maintenance" could be awarded only to the *innocent* spouse "for his or her life, or for such shorter periods as the courts may deem 'just' as a judgment *against* the guilty spouse." (California Civil Code 139). Thus a wife found guilty of adultery was typically barred from receiving alimony, while a husband found guilty of adultery or cruelty could be ordered to pay for his transgressions with alimony and property. And many attorneys believed that justice was served by using alimony as a lever against a promiscuous husband, or as a reward for a virtuous wife. As Eli Bronstein, a New York matrimonial lawyer, put it: "If a woman has been a tramp, why reward her? By the same token, if the man is alley-catting around town, shouldn't his wife get all the benefits she had as a married woman?" (Wheeler, 1974)

Property awards were similarly linked to fault. In most states, the court had to award more than half of the property to the "innocent" or "injured" party.[9] This standard easily led to heated accusations and counter-accusations of wrongs in order to obtain a better property settlement. (Hogoboom, 1971) It also allowed a spouse who did not want a divorce to use the property award as a lever in the negotiations. In practice, since the husband was more likely to be the party who wanted the divorce, the wife was more likely to assume the role of the innocent plaintiff (Friedman and Percival, 1976); and she was therefore more likely to be awarded a greater share of the property. Of course, the proportion of her share (and the extent of the inequality) was related to both the amount and type of property involved: significantly unequal awards were most likely to occur in cases in which the only family asset was the house, as the (innocent) wife was typically awarded the family home. (Weitzman, Kay & Dixon, 1979)

Custody awards could also be influenced by findings of fault. A woman found guilty of adultery or cruelty might be deprived of her preference as the custodial parent—especially if her behavior indicated that she was an "unfit" mother.[10]

By linking both the granting of the divorce and the financial settlements to findings of fault, the law gave the "aggrieved" spouse, particularly an "innocent" wife who wanted to stay married, a considerable advantage in the financial negotiations. In return for her agreement to the divorce, her husband was typically willing to be the guilty defendant (in a noncontested divorce) and to give her, as the innocent plaintiff, alimony and more than half of the property.

In summary, traditional divorce law helped sanction the spouses' roles and responsibilities in marriage—by both punishment and reward. On the negative side, if a wife was found guilty of adultery, cruelty or desertion, she would have to pay for her wrongdoing by being denied alimony (and sometimes custody and property as well). And if the husband was at fault, he would be "punished" through awards of property, alimony and child support to his ex-wife.

On the positive side, traditional divorce law promised "justice" for those who fulfilled their marital obligations. It guaranteed support for the wife who devoted herself to her family, thus reinforcing the desirability and legitimacy of the wife's role as homemaker, and the husband's role as supporter. And it assured the husband that he would not have to support a wife who betrayed or failed him. Justice in this system was the assurance that the marriage contract will be honored. If not, the "bad" spouse would be punished, the "good" spouse rewarded, and the husband's obligation to support his wife (if she was good) enforced.

NO-FAULT DIVORCE

In 1970 California instituted the first law in the Western world to abolish completely any requirement of fault as the basis for marital dissolution. (Hogoboom, 1971) The no-fault law provided for a divorce upon *one* party's assertion that "irreconcilable differences have caused the irremediable breakdown of the marriage." In establishing the new standards for marital dissolution, the California State Legislature sought to eliminate the adversarial nature of divorce and thereby to reduce the hostility, acrimony and trauma characteristics of fault-oriented divorce.

The California no-fault divorce law marked the beginning of a nationwide trend toward legal recognition of "marital breakdown" as a sufficient justification for divorce. The new law not only eliminated the need for evidence of misconduct; it eliminated the concept of fault itself. And it thereby abolished the notion of interpersonal justice in divorce. With this seemingly simple move, the California legislature dramatically altered the legal definition of the reciprocal rights of husbands and wives during marriage and after its dissolution.

Proponents of the divorce law reform had several aims. They sought to eliminate the hypocrisy, perjury and collusion "required by courtroom practice under the fault system" (Kay, 1968); to reduce the adversity, acrimony and bitterness surrounding divorce proceedings; to lessen the personal stigma attached to the divorce; and to create conditions for more rational and equitable settlements of property and spousal support. (Hogoboom, 1970; Kay, 1970; Krom, 1970) In brief, the new law attempted to bring divorce legislation into line with the social realities of marital breakdown in contemporary society. It recognized that marital conduct and misconduct no longer fit rigid categories of fault. And it eliminated the punitive element of moral condemnation that had pervaded Western thought for centuries.

The no-fault legislation changed each of the four basic elements in traditional divorce law. First, *it eliminated the fault-based grounds for divorce.* No longer did one spouse have to testify to the other's adultery, cruelty or desertion. And no longer were witnesses necessary to corroborate their testimony.

By replacing the old fault-based grounds for divorce with a single new standard of "irreconcilable differences," the legislature sought to eliminate both the artificial grounds for the breakdown of a marriage, and the artificial conception that one party was "responsible" for the breakdown. Further, the criterion of "irreconcilable differences" recognized that whatever the reasons for marital failure, they were best left out of the proceedings because they were irrelevant to an equitable settlement. Now the divorce procedure could begin with a neutral "petition for dissolution," with no specific acts or grounds needed as a justification.

Second, *the new laws eliminated the adversary process.* Divorce reformers believed that at least some of the trauma of a fault-based divorce resulted from the legal process itself, rather than from the inherent difficulties of dissolving a marriage. (See, for example, Rheinstein, 1972.) They assumed that husbands and wives who were dissolving their marriages were potentially "amicable," but that the *legal process generated hostility and trauma* by forcing them to be antagonists. The reformers assumed that if fault and the adversary process were eliminated from the legal proceedings, "human beings who are entitled to divorces could get them with the least possible amount of damage to themselves and to their families" (Proceedings from the California Assembly Committee on the Judiciary, 1964).

Each aspect of the legal process was therefore changed to reflect the new nonadversary approach to divorce: "Divorce" became "dissolution"; "plaintiffs" and "defendants" became "petitioners" and "respondents"; "alimony" became "spousal support"; and the court records read "*in re* the Marriage of Doe" instead of "Doe vs. Doe."[11] Standard printed forms written in plain English replaced the archaic legalistic pleadings. Residence requirements were reduced from one year to six months in the state before filing, and the minimum period between filing and the final decree was shortened from one year to six months. These revisions were designed in part to smooth the progress of a marital dissolution through the courts and to avoid some of the unnecessary legal wrangling and personal hostilities engendered by the adversarial model.

Third, *the financial aspects of the divorce were to be based on equity, equality and economic need* rather than on either fault or sex-based role assignments. Proponents of no-fault divorce contended that it was outmoded to grant alimony and property as a reward for virtue, and to withhold them as punishment for wrongdoing. Instead, they advocated more realistic standards for alimony and property awards—standards based on the spouses' economic circumstances and a new principle of equality between the sexes. They argued that justice for both the wife and husband would be better served by considering their economic situations, rather than by weighing their guilt or innocence. And they believed that men and women should no longer be shackled by the weight of traditional sex roles; new norms were necessary to bring the law into line with modern social reality.

With regard to the new economic criteria for awards, the no-fault law aimed at making the financial aspects of the divorce more equitable to facilitate the post-divorce adjustment of both men and women. Substantively, guidelines for financial settlements were changed to remove evidence of misconduct from consideration. For example, while alimony under the old law could only be awarded to the "injured party," regardless of that person's financial need, under the new law, it was to be based on the financial needs and financial resources of both spouses.

With regard to the new norm of equality between the sexes, the advocates of the divorce law reform pointed to the changing position of women in general, and to their increased participation in the labor force in particular, and urged a reformulation of alimony and property awards which recognized the growing ability of women to be self-supporting. With a reformist zeal they assumed that the employment gains of women had already eliminated the need for alimony as a means of continued support after divorce. Ignoring the fact that even full-time year-round female workers earn less than 60 percent of what men earn, some advocates went so far as to declare that "it does seem somewhat anachronistic, in an era of increasing feminine [sic] equality, that the statutes providing for alimony have remained on the books for as long as they have" (Brody, 1970).

The legislators also challenged the anachronistic assumption that the husband had to continue to support his wife—for life. They pointed to the difficulty that men face in supporting two households if they remarry, and argued that the old law had converted "a host of physically and mentally competent young women into an army of alimony drones who neither toil nor spin and become a drain on society and a menace to themselves." (Hofstadter and Levittan, 1967) Thus while the reformers were willing to consider support for the older housewife, they did not believe that the younger housewife deserved continued support; instead they saw her as a potential "alimony drone" who ought to be self-supporting.

Under the new law, California judges setting alimony are directed to consider "the circumstances of the respective parties, including the duration of the marriage, and the ability of the supported spouse to engage in gainful employment without interfering with the interests of the children of the parties in the custody of each spouse." (Civil Code 4801) California's no-fault divorce law is thus typical of new alimony legislation: It is concerned primarily with financial criteria and, while it specifically mentions the custodial spouse and the wife in a marriage of long duration, the thrust of the law is to encourage the divorced woman to become self-supporting (by engaging in gainful employment).

The implicit aim of the new alimony was to encourage (some would say force) formerly dependent wives to assume the responsibility for their own support. With the elimination of fault as the basis for alimony, the new standard explicitly excluded the granting of support awards to women just because they had been wives, or just because their husbands had left them, or just because they had spent years as homemakers. The new law recognized, in theory, the need for transitional support, support for the custodial parent, and support for the older housewife who could not become self-supporting.

Property awards under no-fault are also to be based on equity and equality and are no longer limited to findings of fault. For example, in California the community property *must be divided equally*.[12] Underlying the new law is a conception of marriage as a partnership, with each person having made an equal contribution to the community property and therefore deserving an equal share.

The standards for child custody also reflect the new equality between the spouses. The preference for the mother (for children of tender years) has been replaced by a sex-neutral standard which instructs judges to award custody in the "best interest of the child."[13] Finally, the new law makes both husbands and wives responsible for child support.

Fourth, *no-fault divorce re-defined the traditional responsibilities of husbands and wives by instituting a new norm of equality between the sexes.*

Instead of the old sex-typed division of family responsibilities the new law has attempted to institutionalize sex-neutral obligations which fall equally upon the husband and the wife. No longer is the husband the head of the family—both spouses are now presumed to be equal partners in the marriage. Nor is the husband alone responsible for support, or the wife alone obligated to care for the home and children.

Each of the provisions of the new law discussed above reflect these new assumptions about appropriate spousal roles. The new standards for alimony indicate that a woman is no longer supposed to devote herself to her home and family—rather, she now bears an equal responsibility for her own economic support. For the law has clearly established a new norm of economic self-sufficiency for the divorced woman. Similarly, the new standards indicate that men will no longer be held responsible for their wives' (and ex-wives') lifelong support.

The criterion for dividing property also reflects the new norm of equality between the sexes. There is no preference or protection for the older housewife—or, even for the custodial mother (although some states do have a preference for the custodial parent to retain the family home while the children are living there). Instead, the two spouses are treated equally—each one receives an equal share of the property.

Finally, the expectations for child support are sex-neutral. Both parents are equally responsible for the financial welfare of their children after divorce. What was previously considered the husband's responsibility is now shared equally by the wife.

In summary, traditional divorce law and no-fault reflect two contrasting visions of "justice." The traditional law sought to deliver a moral justice which rewarded the good spouse and punished the bad spouse. It was a justice based on compensation for *past* behavior, both sin and virtue. The no-fault law ignores both moral character and moral history as a basis for awards. Instead it seeks to deliver a fairness and equity based on the financial *needs* and upon equality of the two parties.

The law is based on the assumption that divorced women can be immediately self-supporting. This assumption stands in contrast to the Uniform Marriage and Divorce Act which specifies that the court should consider the time necessary to acquire sufficient education or training to enable the party seeking temporary maintenance to find appropriate employment. Under this provision, a husband whose wife has supported him during his graduate education or professional training may be required to finance her education or training in order to place her in a position more nearly akin to the one she could have achieved. (Kay, 1972). The lack of such provisions in the no-fault divorce laws adopted by most states, such as California, may incur a heavier burden on the wife and make post-divorce adjustment especially difficult for women.

Thus, while the aims of the no-fault laws, i.e., equality and sex-neutrality, are laudable, the laws may be instituting equality in a society in which women are not fully prepared (and/or permitted) to assume equal responsibility for their own and their children's support after divorce. Public policy then becomes a choice between temporary protection and safeguards for the transitional woman (and for the older housewife in the transitional generation) to minimize the hardships incurred by the new expectations, versus current reinforcement of the new equality, with the hope of speeding the transition, despite the hardships this may cause for current divorcees.

NOTES

1. In 1975, for the first time in U.S. history, there were over *one million* divorces in a twelve-month period (Carter and Glick, 1976: 394), and the number of divorces is expected to rise.

2. Preston estimates that 44 percent of all current marriages will end in divorce (Preston, 1974: 435), while the more conservative estimate of Carter and Glick (1976: 396) is that at least one-third of all the first marriages of couples under 30 will end in divorce.

3. As of June, 1976, the fourteen states that adopted "pure" no-fault divorce statutes (in which irretrievable breakdown is the only grounds for the dissolution of the marriage) are Arizona, California, Colorado, Delaware, Florida, Iowa, Kentucky, Michigan, Minnesota, Missouri, Montana, Nebraska, Oregon and Washington.

4. The thirteen states that have added no-fault grounds to their existing fault-based grounds for divorce are Alabama, Connecticut, Georgia, Hawaii, Idaho, Indiana, Maine, Massachusetts, Mississippi, New Hampshire, North Dakota, Rhode Island and Texas. Most of the remaining states have recently added a provision allowing divorce for those "living separate and apart" for a specified period of time, which is an even more modified version of no-fault. Only three states, Illinois, Pennsylvania and South Dakota, retain fault as the *only* basis for divorce (Foster and Freed, 1977, Chart B1).

5. Today more citizens come into contact with the legal system in family law cases than in any other type of litigation (with the possible exception of traffic court) as matrimonial actions now comprise over fifty percent of all civil cases at the trial court level in most cities and states. (Friedman and Percival, 1976: 281–83)

6. We are referring explicitly to divorce, or "the legal termination of a valid marriage," (Clark 1968: 280) as distinguished from an annulment, which is a declaration that a purported marriage has been invalid from its beginning.

7. Adultery remained the only grounds for divorce in England until 1937 when the Matrimonial Causes Act added desertion, cruelty and some other offenses as appropriate grounds for divorce. (Clark, 1968: 282)

8. In contrast, Maxine Virtue's observations of a Chicago court (1956) indicated identical standards for cruelty among husbands and wives. As she notes (Virtue, 1956: 86–89), "The number of cruel spouses in Chicago, both male and female, who strike their marriage partner in the face exactly twice, without provocation, leaving visible marks, is remarkable."

9. Thirty-six states (twenty-eight common-law jurisdictions and eight community property states) allow the court to divide the property upon divorce. (Krause, 1976: 980) The remaining 14 states all have common law property systems which allow each person to retain the property in his or her name. However, there is a considerable impetus for reforms in these states. Legal scholars, such as Foster and Freed, have called the maintenance of the separate property system at the time of divorce obsolete, archaic and shockingly unfair. The strongest argument against it is that "in its application it ignores the contribution wives make to the family." (Foster and Freed, 1974: 170) This argument has also been the major objection of feminist groups to the common-law property system. For example, the Citizen's Advisory Council on the Status of Women (1974: 6) has advocated the importance of changing the law "to recognize explicitly the contribution of the homemaker . . . and to give courts the authority to divide property (owned by both spouses) upon divorce."

10. Of all the financial aspects of the divorce, only child support was, in theory, unaffected by fault—as it was based on the needs of the children (and the father's financial status).

11. The new language was not always easy to adopt, however. When film star Linda Lovelace was divorced, the newspapers reported that she had "charged her husband with irreconcilable differences."

12. The court may make an unequal award if community property has been deliberately misappropriated, or if immediate equal division will incur an extreme or unnecessary hardship. Property may also be divided unequally in a private agreement between the two parties.

13. In California this was changed in 1972 but was part of the original recommendations from the governor's commission which initiated the no-fault legislation.

REFERENCES

Anton v. Anton. 1955. 49 Del. 431, 118 A.2d 605. (Supp. 1955).

Blackstone, William. 1765. Commentaries on the Laws of England.

Brody, Stuart. 1970. "California's Divorce Reform: Its Sociological Implication" Pacific Law Journal, 1.

Brown v. Brown. 1955. 198 Tenn. 600, 381 S.W. 2d 492.

Carter, Hugh, and Paul C. Glick. 1970. Marriage and Divorce: A Social and Economic Study. Cambridge, Mass.: Harvard.

——————— 1976. Marriage and Divorce: A Social and Economic Study. Cambridge, Mass.: Harvard (Revised Ed.).

Clark, Homer. 1968. Domestic Relations. St. Paul, Minn.: West.

Citizens' Advisory Council on the Status of Women. 1974. Recognition of Economic Contribution of Homemakers and Protection of Children in Divorce and Practice. Washington, D.C.: U.S. Government Printing Office.

Foster, Henry H., and Doris Jonas Freed. 1974. "Marital Property Reform in New York: Partnership of Co-Equals?" Family Law Quarterly. Vol. 8; pp. 169–205.

——————— 1977. Family Law: Cases and Materials. Boston: Little, Brown (3rd ed.)

Friedman, Lawrence M., and Robert V. Percival. 1976a. "Who Sues for Divorce? From Fault Through Fiction to Freedom." Journal of Legal Studies 5 (1): 61–82.

——————— 1976b. "A Tale of Two Courts: Litigation in Alameda and San Benito Counties." Law and Society Review 10 (2): 267–303.

Hofstadter, Samuel H., and Shirley R. Levittan. 1967. "Alimony—A Reformulation." Journal of Family Law 7:51–60.

Hogoboom, William P. 1971. "The California Family Law Act of 1970: 18 Months' Experience." Journal of Missouri Bar: 584–589.

Kay, Herma Hill. 1970. A Family Court: The California Proposal in Paul Bohannan (ed.) Divorce and After. Garden City, New York: Doubleday.

——————— 1974. "Sex-Based Discrimination in Family Law" in Kenneth M. Davidson, Ruth G. Ginsburg and Herma Hill Kay, Sex-Based Discrimination Text, Cases and Materials. St. Paul, Minn.: West.

Krause, Harry D. 1976. Family Law: Cases and Materials. St. Paul, Minn.: West.

Reynolds v. Reynolds. 1862. 85 Mass. (3 Allen) 605 (1862).

Rheinstein, Max. 1972. Marriage Stability, Divorce and the Law. Chicago: University of Chicago.

Rucci v. Rucci. 1962. 23 Conn. Supp. 221, 181 A.2d 125.

Weitzman, Lenore. 1979. The Marriage Contract. Englewood Cliffs, N.J.: Prentice-Hall.

Weitzman, Lenore, and Ruth B. Dixon. 1976. "The Alimony Myth." Paper read at the meeting of the American Sociological Association.

——————— 1979. "Child Custody Standards and Awards." Journal of Social Issues, Forthcoming.

Weitzman, Lenore J., Herma Hill Kay, and Ruth B. Dixon. 1979. No Fault Divorce: The Impact of Changes in the Law and the Legal Process. California Divorce Law Research Project, Center for the Study of Law and Society. University of California, Berkeley.

Wheeler, Michael. 1974. No-Fault Divorce. Boston: Beacon Press.

Reading 18 *12/1/94*

Mothers and Divorce: Downward Mobility

Terry Arendell

[The women in this study°] had assumed that after divorce they would somehow be able to maintain a middle-class life-style for themselves and their children. Those in their twenties and thirties had been confident that they could establish themselves as capable employees and find positions that would provide sufficient

---

°Arendell's study, begun in 1983, is based on interviews with 60 divorced women, ranging in age from 26 to 58, in 8 counties of Northern California. All of the women had custody of children whose ages ranged from 3 to 18. All had lived at a middle-class economic level before the divorce.

†From *Mothers and Divorce: Legal, Economic, and Social Dilemmas* by Terry Arendell, pp. 36–53. Copyright © 1986 The Regents of the University of California. Reprinted by permission of the University of California Press. References and footnotes have been omitted.

incomes. Most of the older women, who had been out of the work force longer, had been less confident about their earning abilities, but they had assumed that the difference between the former family income and their own earnings would be adequately compensated for by court-ordered child support and spousal support payments. In fact, virtually all of the women had assumed that family management and parenting efforts, which had kept most of them from pursuing employment and career development while they were married, would be socially valued and legally recognized in their divorce settlements. What had worried them most was not economic difficulty but the possible psychological effects of divorce on themselves and their children. Still, they had believed that they would probably recover from the emotional trauma of divorcing in a matter of months and would then be able to reorganize their lives successfully.

DRASTICALLY REDUCED INCOMES

But even the women who had worried most about how they would manage financially without their husbands' incomes had not imagined the kind of hardship they would face after divorce. All but two of the sixty women had to cope with a substantial loss of family income. Indeed, 90 percent of them (fifty-six out of sixty) found that divorce immediately pushed them below the poverty line, or close to it. As wives and mothers, they had been largely dependent on their husbands, who had supplied the family's primary income.° Without that source of income, they suffered a drastic reduction in standard of living—an experience not shared by their ex-husbands. Like women generally, they were "declassed" by divorce.

The economic decline experienced by these sixty women, all of whom remained single parents, was not temporary. With caution and careful spending, most could meet their essential monthly expenses. But few had any extra money for dealing with emergencies or unexpected demands, and some continued to fall further behind, unable even to pay their monthly bills. One of them, divorced for nearly eight years, described her experience this way:

> I've been living hand to mouth all these years, ever since the divorce. I have no savings account. The notion of having one is as foreign to me as insurance—there's no way I can afford insurance. I have an old pickup that I don't drive very often. In the summertime I don't wear nylons to work because I can cut costs there. Together the kids and I have had to struggle and struggle. Supposedly struggle builds character. Well, some things simply aren't character building. There have been times when we've scoured the shag rug to see if we could find a coin to come up with enough to buy milk so we could have cold cereal for dinner. That's not character building.

°According to Lee Rainwater (1984) and the U.S. Bureau of the Census (1985), the earnings of working married wives contribute only 22 percent of the average family's total income. For this reason, poverty, which occurs in only one of nineteen husband-wife families and in only one of nine families maintained by a single father, afflicts almost one of every three families headed by a woman.

Although they had been living for a median period of over four years as divorced single parents, only *nine* of these sixty women had managed to halt the economic fall prompted by divorce; four of these nine had even managed to reestablish a standard of living close to what they had had while married. Thus the remaining majority—fifty-one women—had experienced no economic recovery. Few had any savings, and most lived from paycheck to paycheck in a state of constant uncertainty. One of them, a woman in her late forties and divorced more than four years, told me:

> I can't go on like this. There's no way. I can manage for another year, maybe a year and a half, but no more. I don't have the stamina. It's not that I don't have a job. My problem is money, plain and simple. That's all that counts in this situation.

This group of recently divorced mothers was by no means unique. All female-headed households experience high rates of economic hardship, and the gap in median income between female-headed families and other types of families has actually widened between 1960 and 1983.° Part of the reason is obvious: certain fixed costs of maintaining a family—such as utility bills and home mortgages or rent—do not change when the family size declines by one, and many other expenses, such as food and clothing, do not change significantly. Additionally, in most cases when the mother obtained employment, it provided a low income that was substantially reduced by new expenses, such as the costs of transportation and child care.†

These women understood how their economic dependency in marriage had contributed to their present economic situation. One of them, who had been married nearly twenty years before divorcing, said:

> Money does wonders in any situation. I'm sure women with more education and better jobs don't have situations quite as desperate as mine. But I quit school when I married and stayed home to raise my children.

Unfortunately, they arrived at such understanding the hard way, through experience. Before divorcing, they had expected to receive "reasonable" child support

---

°Between 1960 and 1983, the median income of female-headed families with no husband present dropped by the following percentages: from 61 to 57 percent of the median income of male-headed families with no wife present, from 43 to 41 percent of the median income of married couples, and from 51 to 38 percent of the median income of married-couple families in which the wife was also employed. In 1983, the median income for female-headed families was $11,484; for male-headed families with no wife present, $20,140; for married-couple families, $26,019; and for married couples in which the wife was employed, $30,340 (U.S. Bureau of the Census, 1985).

†From his Michigan study, David Chambers (1979) concludes that the custodial parent needs 80 percent of the predivorce income to maintain the family's standard of living. The total income of most family units of divorced women and children falls below 50 percent of their former family income. Sweden, in fact, has determined that single-parent families actually need more income than others and provides cash supports that give them incomes comparable to those of two-parent families (Cassetty, 1983a).

and had thought they could probably find jobs that paid "reasonable" wages. They had only the vaguest understanding of other women's divorce experiences. Thus two of them said:

> Friends of mine had ended up divorced with children, and they would tell me some of these things. But I had no empathy at all. I might say, "Gee, that doesn't seem fair" or "Gee, that's too bad." But it never *really* hit me how serious it is until it happened to me. So I think there must be a lot of people out there who don't have the foggiest idea what it feels like.
>
> I had no idea how *much* money it takes. You don't have the [husband's] income, but you still have your family. There's the rub.

Their experiences led them to conclude that in America today, divorced women generally must accept a reduced standard of living. And as women with children, they were keenly aware that only remarriage could offer a quick escape from economic hardship.* A mother of three told me:

> I have this really close friend. She was a neighbor and often kept my daughter until I got home from school. She and her husband had two darling little kids. One day he just up and left. Surprised us all—he married his secretary eventually. My friend hadn't worked before, so I helped her get some typing skills. She worked for two weeks and said, "No more." She called me and said, "Well, I'm not going through what you did. I'm getting married." That was like a slap in the face. Gosh, did I look that bad? I started to doubt myself. Was I doing that bad a job? Should I have gone the marriage route? Gone out and gotten a job and then married somebody? I still wonder about that. Things would have been a lot easier financially. The kids would have had a father. And I would have done what society looks at favorably. I don't know. I still don't know what to do.

Economically these women lost their middle-class status, but socially their expectations of themselves and their children remained the same. They still identified with the middle class, but their low incomes prevented them from participating in middle-class activities. This contradiction created many dilemmas and conflicts:

> I went to a CETA workshop, and I started crying when all they talked about was how to get a job. A woman came after me in the hallway, and I just bawled. I'd been searching for a job for months. I had a degree and teaching credential, and here I was being told how to fill out a stupid job application. And I had three kids at home that I didn't know how I was going to feed that week and a lovely home I couldn't afford.
>
> I moved here after the divorce because the school had a particularly good program for gifted children. Kids were classed by ability and not just by grade level. So my

---

*Research supports the commonsense belief that the surest way to reverse the economic decline resulting from divorce is to remarry (Sawhill, 1976; Duncan and Morgan, 1974, 1979; Johnson and Minton, 1982). Do women remarry because they conclude, pragmatically, that being a single woman is too costly, for themselves and perhaps also for their children? Would fewer women remarry if they could successfully support themselves? The answers to such questions will have interesting political implications.

kid was in a really good spot for what he needed. I didn't realize at the time that I was the only single parent in that group. One reason those kids can achieve at that level is because they have a very stable home life, two parents to work with every child on the enrichment and the projects and the homework. I hate to say this, but it's all socioeconomic. Every kid in there belonged to a high socioeconomic group. Oh, they can rationalize that it's not really like that, but it's completely WASPish, all two-parent families where the mothers don't work. Mothers are available to take kids to music lessons, soccer lessons, gymnastic lessons, and all of that whenever it's needed. I had to take my son out of that class. I couldn't keep up the level of activity required of the kids and the parents. The gap was growing greater and greater. If I'd lived like this a long time, I might have known how to cope, but this was all new. And it all came down to money.

The women resented their precarious positions all the more because they knew that their former husbands had experienced no loss in class status or standard of living and could have eased their struggles to support the children:

Five hundred dollars here and there—or taking over the orthodontist's bills—anything like that would have meant a lot. I don't see why this kid should have to live with jaw and tooth problems because I got a divorce. His jaw had to be totally realigned, so it wasn't just cosmetic. His father could easily have paid that monthly [orthodontist] bill and deducted it. That would have made a tremendous difference. But he wouldn't. By making me suffer, he made his child suffer too.

When the children retained some access to middle-class activities through involvement with their fathers, their mothers had ambivalent feelings. They were grateful that their children were not neglected by their fathers and could enjoy some enriching and entertaining activities with them; but they found their former husbands' greater financial resources a painful reminder of how little they themselves could provide. One woman, who had to let her child get free meals through the subsidized school lunch program, despite her many efforts to make more money, told me this:

His father seldom buys him anything. But his stepmother sometimes does. She can give him all these nice things. She's given him nice books, a stereo headset. I have no idea what her motivation is, but it's a very funny feeling to know that I can't go and buy my son something he would love to have, but this perfect stranger can. And how will that affect my son ultimately? He must know how difficult things are here, and that I'm not deliberately depriving him. But it's kind of ironic—I helped establish that standard of living, but I end up with none of it, and she has full access to it.

EXPENSES AND ECONOMIZING

Living with a reduced budget was a constant challenge to most of these women because they had no cushion to fall back on if expenses exceeded their incomes. Their savings were depleted soon after they divorced; only twelve of the sixty women I talked to had enough money in savings to cover a full month's expenses. Most said they had radically cut back their spending. The major expenses after divorce were housing, food, and utilities. The women with young children also had substantial child care expenses, and several had unusually high medical bills that were not covered by health insurance.

Within a short time after their divorces, more than one-third of the women—sixteen women living in homes they owned and seven living in rented places—had to move to different housing with their children in order to reduce their expenses. Two of the women had moved more than four times in the first two years after their divorces, always for financial reasons. During marriage, forty-nine of the sixty women had lived in homes owned with their husbands. After divorce, only nine of them retained ownership of the family home. Of these nine, six were able to acquire ownership by buying out their husbands as part of the community property settlement (five of them only because they were able to get financial assistance from their parents); two retained the home by exchanging other community assets for it; and one received the home according to the dictates of the religion she and her husband shared.

Home ownership brought with it many expenses besides mortgage payments. Several women neglected upkeep and repairs for lack of money. A woman who was in her fifties reported this common dilemma:

> I owe $16,000 on this house. I could get about $135,000 for it, so I have a large equity. But it would have taken all of that to get that condominium I looked at, and my payments would still have been about $400 a month. I don't know how I'll be able to keep up the house, financially or physically. The house needs painting, and I can't keep up the yard work. I'd like to move. I'd like a fresh start. But the kids don't want to move, and I can't imagine how I'll handle all of this once they're gone. When the alimony [spousal support] stops, there'll be no way I can manage a move. I'm stuck here now. The mortgage is really low and the interest is only 5 percent.

Two of the mothers reduced expenses by moving their children from private to public schools. Two others were able to keep their children in private schools only after administrators waived the tuition fees. Seven mothers received financial assistance for preschoolers' child care costs, five from private and two from public agencies. One of these women, who worked full-time, had this to say about her expenses:

> I'm buying this house. I pay $330 a month for it. Child care for my two kids runs to almost $500 a month. Since I bring home only a little more than $900, there's no way I could make it without the child care assistance. There'd be nothing left.

About half of these women had economic situations so dire that careful budgeting was not enough, and they continued to fall further behind economically. Those living close to the margin managed by paying some bills one month and others the next. Their indebtedness increased, and opportunities for reversing the situation did not appear:

> I'm so far in debt. Yes indeed. I keep thinking, why should I worry about the bills? I'll never get out of debt! All I can do is juggle. Without my charge cards, my kids would be bare-assed naked. And school is coming up again. What am I going to do for school clothes? And they've all grown fast this year. . . . I probably owe $3,000 on charge

cards, and I still owe rent—I haven't paid this month or last. The landlord I have has been very understanding. He's let us go along as best he can. We've been here four years, and he knows what I'm going through. Over the years, he's given me several eviction notices, but this last time he hired a lawyer and everything. I decided I'd just pitch my tent on the capitol mall in Sacramento and say, "Here I am." I've written my congressman again, because I qualify for subsidized housing. But it'll take forever to get any action on that.

For many, however, even the persistent realities of economic hardship could not extinguish middle-class hopes:

My husband liked really good food and always bought lots and the best. So when he left, it was really hard to cut the kids back. They were used to all that good eating. Now there's often no food in the house, and everybody gets really grouchy when there's no food around. . . . I think I've cut back mostly on activities. I don't go to movies anymore with friends. We've lost $150 a month now because my husband reduced the support. It gets cut from activities—we've stopped doing everything that costs, and there's nowhere else to cut. My phone is shut off. I pay all the bills first and then see what there is for food. . . . I grew up playing the violin, and I'd wanted my kids to have music lessons—piano would be wonderful for them. And my older two kids are very artistic. But lessons are out of the question.

Obtaining credit had been a real problem for many, for the reasons given by this woman, who had worked during the marriage while her husband attended school:

My kids and I were very poor those first years after the divorce. I had taken care of our finances during marriage. But I didn't have accounts in my own name, so I couldn't get credit. I got a job as soon as I could. I was getting $65 a month for child support and paying $175 a month for rent. Between the rent and the child care and the driving to work, I was absolutely broke. I really didn't have enough to live on. I had no benefits either, with my first job. I was living dangerously, and with children. I could barely pay the basic bills. There wasn't enough money for food lots of times. I cried many times because there wasn't enough money. I couldn't get any credit. [When I was married] my husband could get any credit he wanted, but it was on the basis of *my* job, which had the higher income. He couldn't even keep his checkbook balanced, but now I'm the one who can't get credit! It was a hard lesson to learn. Now whenever I get a chance, I tell women to start getting a credit rating.

The woman who told me this, incidentally, had managed to overcome initial impoverishment and gain a middle-class income from her job.

Some women regarded personal possessions such as jewelry, furniture, and cars as things they might sell to meet emergencies or rising indebtedness:

I sold jewelry to have my surgery, to pay for the part that wasn't covered. I still have some silver, and I have some good furniture, which could probably bring something. That's probably what I'd do in an emergency, sell those things. What else do people do?

Teenaged children helped by earning money through odd jobs and babysitting. Older teenagers changed their college plans, and several entered community colleges instead of universities. One woman's daughter was already in the Navy, pursuing her schooling in languages and working as a translator, and the daughter of another was considering military service as a way of saving money for a college education.

Most women compared their own hardship and forced economizing to the economic freedom enjoyed by their ex-husbands. For example:

> I know my ex-husband goes somewhere almost every weekend, and he usually takes a friend along. I wonder how he can do that. How can he go somewhere every weekend? The only way I could do that is find a rich man! I couldn't possibly work enough hours to pay for that much stuff. I'd be doing well to finance a [twenty-mile] trip to San Francisco!

There were some exceptions to the general pattern of economic decline. Nine of the sixty women had regained some latitude for discretionary spending, though only three of them had managed this economic reversal without help. These nine were a distinct subgroup; the others did not share their higher standards of living or their feelings and approaches to the future. Still, only two of these nine women had not experienced a major decline in income immediately upon divorcing (or separating). One had been living on welfare because her husband's excessive drinking and erratic behavior had prevented him from holding a job; she found employment immediately after separating from him. The other one had been the primary family wage earner during her marriage.[*] Four of the women whose incomes had dropped significantly had managed to stop and even reverse the economic decline very soon after divorce because they were granted temporary spousal support awards and acquired some money and assets from their community property settlement; two of them, who had been divorced after more than twenty years of marriage, also received substantial amounts of money from their parents. Although these four did not experience the degree of hardship shared by the others, they did not fully recover their formerly high income levels and therefore also had to alter their life-styles. As one of them said:

> Essentially, I took an $80,000 drop in annual income. And I had to borrow again last year. This year I finally sold the house, and that was really the only way I've made it. My change in life-style has been *tremendous.* Just my heating and electricity bill for our home was $350 a month. We just barely got by on $2,000 a month. I stopped buying household things; I stopped buying clothes for myself. And I rented out a room in the house. It was a huge house, and that helped out. I let the cleaning woman and the gardener go. I didn't paint. I let the property taxes go until I sold the house and paid them then. I quit taking trips. This house I'm in now has much lower operating expenses. My son doesn't have the same things he'd had. His grandparents buy most of his shoes and clothes now. He used to have lots and lots, so it's been a change for him.

---

[*]A recent study by Lee Rainwater (1984: 84) shows how economic dependency in a previous marriage makes it difficult for a woman to recover economically from divorce: "By the fourth year that they headed their own families, women who had regular work experience before becoming female heads had family incomes equal to 80 percent of their average family income while a wife. Women who had not worked at all had incomes slightly less than half that of their last married years."

Of the other five women who succeeded in improving their economic situations after a few years, three did so entirely through their own work efforts, and the other two managed with help from their former husbands—one took in the child for more than a year while his ex-wife worked at several jobs, and the other accepted a shared parenting arrangement.

EMOTIONAL RESPONSES TO ECONOMIC LOSS

None of the nine women who had experienced substantial economic recovery reported suffering serious emotional changes. Forty-four of the others, however, spoke of frequent struggles with depression and despair. Every one of them attributed these intense feelings, which often seemed overwhelming, directly to the financial hardships that followed divorce. This woman spoke for many others in describing the effects that economic loss had had on her:

> I think about money a great deal. It's amazing. I used to get so bored by people who could only talk about money. Now it's all I think about. It's a perpetual thought, how to get money—not to invest, or to save, but just to live. The interesting thing is that you develop a poverty mentality. That intrigues me. I would never have thought that could happen. But if I had had money, several times in the last year I would have fought what was happening to me in a way I no longer think of fighting. You tend to accept what's coming because there's so much you *have* to accept. You get so you accept everything that comes your way. For example, I accepted at first what I was told about treating this cancer on my face: that the only surgery possible would leave my face disfigured with one side paralyzed. I knew it would ruin any possibility of my teaching if they did that to my face, but I would have just accepted it if a friend hadn't gotten me to go to someone else for consultation. I wouldn't have done that on my own. That's not how I would have behaved at other times in my life. I think it must happen to a lot of divorced women. It was only this year that I realized how strange this has become. I'm educated, I've come through a wealthy phase of my life, and now here I am, being shuttled around and not even fighting. It continues to fascinate me. After a while, you develop a begging mentality in which you'd like to squeeze money out of anybody. I guess I'm somewhere in the realm of poverty. I know there are poorer people, but I'm pretty well down near the bottom. If I were to lose this job—which is always possible, there's no security to it—I'd be finished. Finished. I'd lose my house. I'd lose everything. There's no way I could survive.

The first year of divorce was traumatic for most, especially because legal uncertainties were mixed with other fears. A vicious circle was common: anxieties brought sleepless nights, and fatigue made the anxieties sharper. Although economic hardship remained, by the end of the first year most of the women had learned to control some of the anxiety surrounding it.°

°Various studies argue that the first year or so after divorce is the most stressful and traumatic (Hetherington, Cox, and Cox, 1976; Wallerstein and Kelly, 1979, 1980; Weiss, 1979a, 1979b). Additionally, both Pett (1982) and Buehler and Hogan (1980) found that financial concerns were among the factors that limited divorced mothers' emotional recovery from divorce. None of these studies, however, attempts to distinguish the effects of economic uncertainty from more generalized separation emotions.

Depression overtook a majority of these women at some time or other. Their feelings of despair over financial troubles were worsened by concerns for their children. One of them said:

> I thought about running away, but who would I have turned my kids over to? I also thought about suicide—especially when the youngest was still a baby and I had so much trouble with child care and it cost me so much. I kept thinking that if I were gone, it would take a major burden off of everybody.

In fact, such despair was a common experience: twenty-six of the sixty women volunteered that they had contemplated suicide at some time after divorce. They mentioned various contributing factors, such as emotional harassment from their husbands and uncertainty about their own abilities and identities, but all said that economic hardship was *the* primary stress that pushed them to the point of desperation.

One mother gave a very detailed account of her experience with suicidal depression, which occurred at a time when she had been barely managing for several months. She would drag herself to work and then collapse in bed when she got home. When she would get out of bed, she told me, the sight of her ten-year-old son sitting in front of the television set, alone in a cold room and eating cold cereal, would send her back to bed, where her exhaustion and despair would be exacerbated by hours of crying. She went on:

> I came home to an empty house that night—it was February. I had gotten my son's father to take him that weekend so I could go to my class—the one about learning to live as a single person again. I'd hoped that by getting some encouragement, I'd be able to pull myself out of this and find a way to make a better living. About eleven o'clock, I just decided this was no way to live. I couldn't take care of this child. I'd gone to Big Brothers, and they wouldn't take him because he had a father. But his father wasn't seeing him. Family Services weren't any help. The woman there did try to help, I think. She cared. But she'd been married more than twenty-five years, and just didn't understand. All I could do in the fifty-minute appointment with her was cry. My attorney wasn't giving me any help or getting me any money. My mother was mad at me—she said it was my fault for leaving my husband.
>
> I just couldn't see it ever being any different, so I decided to kill myself. I'm sure that's not a unique thing. It was the most logical thing in the world. I knew exactly how I was going to do it. I was going to fill the bathtub with warm water and cut my wrists. It would be fine then—that thought was the only thing that made me feel any better. Nothing was as bad as the thought of getting up the next day. So I called my son's father—he was going to bring him back the next day—and I asked him if he thought he could take care of him. I didn't think I gave any evidence [of my feelings] or anything—it wasn't a desperate call for help, or a threatening call, or anything like that, because I'd already made up my mind. I just didn't want him to bring my son in here and find me like that. I wanted him to make some kind of arrangements to take care of him. He didn't say anything on the phone, but in about twenty minutes the doorbell rang. Two young men in blue uniforms were standing there. They wanted to take me to an emergency room. It was a crisis place, they said. They were young and scared themselves and acted like they didn't know what to do.
>
> I guess the shock of realizing how far I'd gone was enough to snap me out of it. I'd spent those twenty minutes [after the phone call] piddling around taking care of some

last-minute things, tidying up and so on. It seems that once I made the decision, it gave me such inner peace, such a perfect reconciliation. It seemed the most logical, practical thing in the world. Then their coming stopped me from doing it. I didn't go with them, but they gave me a phone number and told me there were people there who would come and get me anytime.

I've only recently put into perspective what happened. It wasn't so much my inability to cope as it was the convergence of everything in my situation. That person at Family Services did help, actually, when she pointed out that some people who've never had trouble dealing with anything don't know what else to do when they feel like they can't cope. That fit. I'd never had a crisis I couldn't deal with in some way. I'd gotten myself into bad situations before, but I could always see cause-and-effect relationships, and I'd always felt like I could make some changes right away that would change things in my life. In this case, I couldn't figure anything out. I don't even know how to tell you what I thought.

This woman had been divorced before and had not suffered depression; but she had had no child then, no one else for whom she was responsible.

These women who were new to poverty had no ideas about how to cope in their new situations, and they found little help in the society at large. Some of the most desperate were unable to afford professional counseling. One of them said:

At one point during the eviction, I was getting hysterical. I needed help. So I called a program called Women's Stress. Good thing I wasn't really suicidal, because they kept me on hold a long time. They said, "Well, this program is just for women with an alcohol or drug problem. Does that fit you?" I said, "No, but if I don't get help, it will." They said they'd send me a pamphlet, which they did. It cost twenty-five dollars to join. I never did find any help.

The worst personal pain these women suffered came from observing the effects of sudden economic hardship on their children. Here is one woman's poignant account:

I had $950 a month, and the house payment was $760, so there was hardly anything left over. So there we were: my son qualified for free lunches at school. We'd been living on over $4,000 a month, and there we were. That's so humiliating. What that does to the self-esteem of even a child is absolutely unbelievable. And it isn't hidden: everybody knows the situation. They knew at his school that he was the kid with the free lunch coupons. . . . My son is real tall and growing. I really didn't have any money to buy him clothes, and attorneys don't think school clothes are essential. So he was wearing these sweatshirts that were too small for him. Then one day he didn't want to go to school because the kids had been calling him Frankenstein because his arms and legs were hanging out of his clothes—they were too short. That does terrible things to a kid, it really does. We just weren't equipped to cope with it.

But the need to cut costs—on food, clothing, and activities for the children—was not the only source of pain. Most of the mothers reported that their parenting approaches changed and that their emotions became more volatile, and even unstable, in periods of great financial stress. Mothers who went to work full-time resented the inevitable loss of involvement in their children's lives:

I wish I could get over the resentment. [In the first years after the divorce] I spent half the time blaming myself and the other half blaming their father. Because I was so preoccupied, I missed some really good years with them, doing things I'd looked forward to and wanted to do. Those years are gone now.

Some of the mothers also thought the experience of economic hardship after divorce might eventually affect the society at large, as more and more women and children come to share it. For example:

It's not just the mother [who's affected]. It's a whole generation of kids who don't even know how to use a knife and a fork, who don't sit at a table to eat, who don't know how to make conversation with people of different ages. There are so many awful possibilities, and it's a whole society that's affected. I'm not talking about people who have lived for years in poverty. We planned and lived one way with no idea of the other reality. Then this harsh reality hits, and everything becomes a question of survival. I think it must be different if that's all you've experienced. At least then your plans fit your responsibilities—that sort of thing. You can't spend your whole day trying to survive and then care anything about what's going on in the world around you. You really can't. . . . Maybe it's going to take 50 percent of the population to be in this shape before we get change. But some of us have to be salvaged, just so we can fight. We can't all be so oppressed by trying to survive that we can't do anything at all.

Although their despair was worsened by concern for their children, it was the children who gave these women their strongest incentive to continue the struggle:

Sure, I think about suicide. And I'm a smart lady who's been creative and able to do some things to change our situation. But I'm tired—*tired*. And it's real hard. What keeps me alive is my kid. I may be boxed in, but if I give up, what will happen to her? She doesn't deserve that.

Most of these women also admitted to having lost a sense of the future. A fifty-year-old woman, who said she wondered if she would someday become a bag lady, told me:

That's what I started to say at the beginning—*I don't have a future.* I can sit around and cry about that for a while, but then I have to move on and ask, what am I going to do about it? And there's not much I can do. What career can I start at my age? How do I retrieve all those years spent managing a family?

And another somewhat younger woman said:

The worst poverty is the poverty of the spirit that sets in when you've been economically poor too long, and it gets to the point where you can't see things turning around.

To avoid this sense of hopelessness, a majority of the sixty women tried not to think about the future and made only short-term plans:

I learned very quickly that I couldn't think too far into the future or I'd drive myself crazy. The future became, "What will I do next month?" I learned I had to go day to day and just do the best I could. That's been my major technique for coping, and I learned it right away. I've built up some retirement and Social Security through work, thank heavens. But I have to live right now. I just can't think about the future. The worst that can happen is that the state will take care of me, and I'll end up in a crappy old folks' home. But I don't think about that.

Ten of the sixty women—a unique subgroup—said they had not experienced serious depression or despair after divorce. But the reasons they gave simply reemphasize the central importance of economic loss in the lives of divorced women. Four of these ten had various sources of income that protected them from poverty and enabled them to work actively toward improving their situation. Two of them were using income from the divorce property settlement to attend graduate school, and they hoped to regain their former standard of living by pursuing professional careers. Two were receiving financial support from their parents while they sought employment and planned for the possible sale of their homes as part of the property settlement. The remaining six said they were generally optimistic *in spite of* their poor economic positions. Like the others, they found the financial hardships imposed by divorce surprising and difficult to handle; they simply found these hardships easier to cope with than the despair they had known in their marriages.

In summary, these women discovered that the most important change brought about by divorce was an immediate economic decline, which for most of them had not been reversible. Despite their economizing efforts and dramatically altered life-styles, many of them continued to lose ground financially. In addition, economic circumstances had a powerful effect on their emotional lives. Only a very few escaped feelings of despair and hopelessness. Most found that economic uncertainties fostered depression, discouragement, and despair, and nearly all said they had endured periods of intense anxiety over the inadequacy of their income and its effects on the well-being of their children. Most of them felt trapped in their present circumstances and said they had no sense of the future.

Reading 19

12/1/94

Fathers Who Have Infrequent Contact with Their Children

James R. Dudley

Currently, the parenting role of divorced fathers varies considerably in our society. A small percentage of divorced fathers are custodial parents, and a growing percentage are sharing custody with their former spouses. However, the vast majority are noncustodial, and a large portion of these noncustodial fathers have infrequent or no contact with their children. One study, using a representative sample of divorced children ages 7 to 11, reported that approximately half of all noncustodial fathers had not seen their children during the past year (Furstenberg, Nord, Peterson, & Zill, 1983).

Increasing attention has been given to divorced fathers in the literature. However, most studies still focus on mother-custody families; and even in these studies, fathers' views are often not included (Greif & Bailey, 1990). As a result, family-oriented professionals, policymakers, and the general public often do not have adequate knowledge about divorced fathers. More knowledge is needed about the effects of divorce on fathers and the reasons why so many of them are not more active parents.

This article is intended for professionals who wish to help divorced fathers remain active or become more active in their children's lives. The findings of a study of 84 fathers with infrequent contact are presented to increase our understanding of this population of men. This study is unusual because it comprises a

This study was supported by a grant from Temple University. The author also wishes to thank Dr. John Franklin for supporting this research.

James R. Dudley is Professor, Department of Sociology, Anthropology, and Social Work, University of North Carolina at Charlotte, Charlotte, NC 28223.

From *Family Relations,* 1991 40 279–285.

group of fathers whose views are seldom, if ever, included in studies of divorced families. The focus is on their views about why their involvement is limited, an area which is usually overlooked by researchers and professionals. The study also examines the influence of several variables related to their divorce proceedings.

The negative effects of divorce on all family members have been extensively documented (Jacobs, 1982; Pearce & McAdoo, 1983; Wallerstein & Kelly, 1980). Children are usually hurt the most. This is most likely to occur when the noncustodial parent withdraws from their lives, or when the parents persistently engage in high levels of conflict with each other (Emery, 1982; Hetherington, Cox, & Cox, 1979; Roman & Haddad, 1978). Custodial parents, who are usually women, typically experience increased stress from the added demands on their parental and occupational roles (Brandwein, Brown, & Fox, 1974; Glasser & Navarre, 1965). They also usually suffer from substantially reduced incomes (Albrecht, 1980; Cassetty, 1978; Duncan, 1984).

Noncustodial parents, who are usually men, are likely to be negatively affected in psychological ways. A most pervasive problem is suffering caused by the feeling that they have lost their children. This occurs because they may no longer see their children on a regular basis or they must "visit" in a way that is quite different than what they were used to when they lived with their children (Grief, 1979; Keshet & Rosenthal, 1978). These noncustodial fathers also are likely to experience feelings of guilt about the marital breakup and feelings of inadequacy about their role as a parent (Dominic & Schlesinger, 1980). They also often experience intense conflicts with their former spouses, and these conflicts typically interfere with their on-going parent-child relationships (Moreland & Schwebel, 1981; Tepp, 1983; Wallerstein & Kelly, 1980).

Even though we do not know enough about why so many fathers have infrequent contact with their children, several possible explanations have been offered. Some of the reasons have their origins in the marital relationship. Most divorcing couples are in conflict at the time of separation, and a significant proportion do not settle these disputes for several years after the divorce, if ever (Johnston, Campbell, & Tall, 1985; Lamb, 1986). Knowledge is limited as to how and why such conflicts do not resolve themselves more quickly. Most important, these continued conflicts are often associated with fathers decreasing their contact with their children.

Too little attention has been given to the negative effects of divorce proceedings on paternal involvement. Adversarial proceedings are commonly known to exacerbate existing conflicts between divorcing parents, as well as create new conflicts. It has been suggested that litigated divorces, in particular, are likely to exacerbate relations with a former spouse. Also, it has been suggested that litigated proceedings result in less paternal contact with children than other types of proceedings (Elkin, 1987; Koch & Lowery, 1984).

As Clingempeel and Reppucci (1982) report, family courts and legal procedures vary considerably in the extent to which they encourage or discourage cooperation between divorcing parents. Mediation, which is offered by some courts and not others, has been reported to provide a more cooperative outcome than adversarial proceedings. Specifically, mediation is more likely than the adversarial approach to facilitate a favorable postdivorce adjustment and an active role by noncustodial fathers (Bahr, 1981; Ebel, 1980; Girdner, 1985).

The custody arrangements in divorce agreements also are likely to have a direct influence over the extent of paternal contact. While most states now have the options of shared legal and shared physical custody, the extent to which they are awarded varies (Folberg, 1984). Numerous studies have investigated shared custody arrangements to discern how they work, the effects on children, and the circumstances under which they are not thought to be in the children's best interest (Clingempeel & Repucci, 1982; Folberg, 1984). Generally, these studies indicate that the arrangement provides more advantages and fewer disadvantages than sole custody arrangements (Buehler, 1989). However, most of these studies have involved small samples and have focused on voluntary arrangements agreed upon by both parents. Few studies have focused on families in which one parent contested their shared custody arrangement (Johnston, Kline, & Tschann, 1989).

Several studies have attempted to identify the family and other demographic characteristics predicting how active noncustodial fathers are. Fathers with less education, financial instability, and lower socioeconomic status tended to be less active than those with more education, higher incomes, and a higher socioeconomic status (Furstenberg et al., 1983). In terms of children's characteristics, Wallerstein and Kelly (1980) found that children between 2 and 8 years of age saw their fathers the most. Those between the ages of 9 and 10 saw them the least, with adolescents having a frequency of visits somewhere in between. They also reported that boys had more father contact than girls soon after the divorce; however the sex of the child was no longer significantly associated with the amount of contact 18 months after the divorce. In another study, fathers' contact with daughters decreased rapidly over time (Hess & Camara, 1979). Others have reported no relationship between characteristics of the children and contact with the noncustodial father (Furstenberg et al., 1983; Koch & Lowery, 1984; Tepp, 1983).

When fathers have remarried, they have been found to have less contact with their children than those who remained single (Furstenberg et al., 1983; Tepp, 1983). Similarly, when divorced mothers have remarried, noncustodial fathers have had less contact than when the divorced mother did not remarry. Also, the geographic distance between the noncustody father and his children was found to be inversely related to the frequency of his visits (Furstenberg et al., 1983; Koch & Lowery, 1984).

The purpose of this research is to examine why some divorced fathers have infrequent or no contact with their children. The study does this in two ways. First, the fathers' stated reasons for their infrequent contact are examined, based on open-ended questions. Second, the influence of several other variables are examined during both the time of divorce proceedings and at the time that they completed the questionnaire. These variables include the type of divorce proceedings, the custody arrangement, the father's perceptions of his relationship with his former spouse, the extent to which he wants more time with his children, and several demographic characteristics.

METHOD

Characteristics of the 84 Fathers

This study focused on 84 divorced fathers who were part of a larger sample of 255 divorced fathers. These 84 fathers have considerably less frequent contact with their children than the other 171 fathers. The 84 fathers currently report having only occasional overnight contact, occasional day contact, or no contact with their children during the past year. In contrast, the contact of the other 171 fathers varies from one overnight visit each month to every night.

Seventy of these 84 fathers are white, 12 are African American, 1 is Hispanic, and 1 is Asian American. They have a mean age of 43 years ($SD = 6.8$), and the mean age of their former spouses is 40 years ($SD = 5.7$). Most of these fathers are middle-income wage earners, with only 15 having incomes of $20,000 or less and 43 having incomes over $30,000. Similarly, their educational levels are relatively high, with only 16 having a high school diploma or less, and 43 having at least a college degree.

Thirty-one of the fathers have only male children and 37 have only female children. The remaining fathers have both male and female children. Six of the fathers have children under 5 years of age, and the remaining 78 fathers only have children between the ages of 5 and 18 years.

These 84 fathers obtained their divorces in a range of ways. Most of them used the adversarial approach, with 21 being decided by a judge, and 32 being settled out of court by attorneys representing each parent. Seventeen fathers used mediation, and 9 settled their divorce without outside assistance beyond filing procedures. Five did not respond to this question.

Several types of custody arrangements were negotiated by the time of divorce. The former spouses of most of the fathers (59) were awarded sole custody. Fifteen fathers were awarded joint legal custody, with their former wives being awarded physical custody. Five fathers had joint physical and joint legal custody. Five did not indicate their custody arrangement.

These fathers have been divorced for a mean of 6 years ($SD = 4.5$), with 39 being divorced for 5 years or less and 43 being divorced for over 5 years. Two did not respond to this question. Thirty-three of the 84 fathers and 30 of their former spouses have remarried.

Sampling Approach

The intent of the overall study was to develop a relatively large sample that was as representative as possible of divorced fathers living in a large metropolitan area. The fathers were selected based on three criteria: They had to be divorced, have at least one child under 19 years of age, and reside in Philadelphia or one of its Pennsylvania suburban counties.

Using a purposive sampling approach, any father meeting these three criteria was encouraged to participate. They were identified from numerous and varied sources, including fathers' groups, Parents Without Partners, day-care programs, schools, churches, a police league, divorce mediators, human service professionals, other fathers who were respondents of the study, and media announcements. Efforts were made to maintain a high response rate by calling each respondent before sending him a questionnaire. The response rate was 64%, based on this procedure.

The sampling approach was not entirely successful in creating a sample of divorced fathers who reflect the population of a large urban area. African American and other minority fathers are underrepresented even though special efforts were made to involve them. Also, fathers with less formal education and those with low to moderate incomes are underrepresented.

Questionnaire

A questionnaire was mailed to each participant. Questions were asked about the divorce proceedings and divorce agreement, including the father's time schedule with his children at the point of divorce. The fathers were also asked if they had to return to court at a later time.

Several questions focused on the fathers' perceptions of their relationship with their former spouse. They were asked how much conflict there was between the couple both when they separated and immediately after the divorce. Also, the respondents were asked how cooperative their former spouse was in helping them implement their time schedule with their children. These questions on perceptions were constructed with Likert scale response categories.

Also, open-ended questions were asked to elicit the fathers' views, in their own words, about their circumstances. They were asked what they perceived to be their most important current obstacle, if any, to having more frequent contact with their children. Other open-ended questions were also included to elicit understanding of their current fathering role and the past and present circumstances which have affected it. These questions included: What they thought was the major reason for the marital breakup, why they thought they were currently seeing their children less often than when they got divorced (if this was the case), and a section for general comments.

The responses to the question on the father's perception of the most important obstacle to more active parenting were analyzed using content analysis to determine more general types of responses. Criteria were set up to guide this content analysis process. If a response was not totally clear, the responses to other open-ended questions were also examined to add clarity. Also, if more than one obstacle was identified without a ranking of the most important one, the other open-ended questions were reviewed in determining an overall issue that seemed to predominate.

RESULTS

In response to the question of what they perceived to be their most important obstacle to more active parenting, four different types of obstacles were identified that were mutually exclusive of each other. Thirty-three fathers identified their former spouse as their obstacle, and 22 identified personal problems or circumstances. Thirteen fathers explained that their children were older and too busy to see them, and 12 indicated that the primary barrier was that their children lived a long distance away. Four additional fathers did not fit into any of these four groupings.

A closer examination of the qualitative responses of the participants revealed some important differences among these four groups of fathers. In addition, a crosstabulation of these four groups with several other variables further distinguished these groups, particularly the group identifying their former spouse as their barrier from the other three groups (see Table 19.1).

Former Spouse as Obstacle

The first group of fathers identified their former spouse as their major obstacle to having more frequent contact with their children. This group of fathers was the largest, numbering 33. These fathers described their former spouse's interference in different ways. Twenty-two of them focused on current conflicts. Some of them accused their former spouses of directly interfering with visitation arrangements that were established. Others indicated that her interference was more indirect;

Table 19.1   PERCEPTIONS AND CIRCUMSTANCES OF THE FATHERS BY EXPRESSED OBSTACLE (IN PERCENT)

	Group				
Circumstances	Former spouse ($n = 33$)	Father's issue ($n = 22$)	Children older ($n = 13$)	Long distance ($n = 12$)	Total group ($n = 80$)
Adversarial proceedings (Judge or two attorneys)	84%	39%	85%	75%	72%*
Has had to return to court at a later time	69	36	46	58	54
Considerable conflict at separation	85	72	84	50	76
Much more conflict immediately after divorce	50	19	8	33	32*
Ex-Wife uncooperative with visits at divorce	83	36	23	42	53**
Ex-Wife uncooperative with visits now	88	32	15	42	54**
Father wanted considerably more time at divorce	64	18	23	33	39*
Father wants considerably more time now	72	35	15	73	52*

*$p < .01$. **$p < .001$.

she would say negative things to the children about their father which affected the children's attitudes towards visits. The perceived reasons for her interference with the visitation arrangement were not usually identified, except that one father mentioned that he thought it was because he was gay, and another said that he was falsely charged with child abuse. None of these 21 fathers explicitly referred to the divorce proceedings as being responsible for their conflicts.

The other 11 fathers in this group directly mentioned that the earlier divorce proceedings were related to why their former spouse was an obstacle. Decisions and events of the proceedings were identified as being problematic, for example, a custody decision or a hearing with a judge that seemed to disregard their testimony. In a variety of ways these 11 fathers expressed hostility and cynicism toward the family courts because they perceived them as biased in favor of the mother and insensitive to fathers' needs and rights. The courts' failure to enforce or expand their visitation agreements were a frequently mentioned complaint.

As Table 19.1 indicates, this group of 33 fathers was similar to and different from the other three groups. Like most of the other fathers, most in this group experienced considerable conflict with their wives when they separated. Also, like most of the other fathers, the men in this group were most likely to use adversarial divorce proceedings. But, about half of them perceived that there was much more conflict with their former spouse immediately after the divorce than when they separated. This was a relatively high percentage compared to the other three groups [χ^2 (12, $N = 78$) = 31.23, $p < .01$]. Also, a considerably higher percentage than the other groups perceived their former wife as uncooperative in implementing their schedule with their children both at the time of divorce [χ^2 (12, $N = 76$) = 41.81, $p < .001$] and currently [χ^2 (12, $N = 76$) = 38.13, $p < .001$].

Two thirds of this group also had to return to court since the divorce, suggesting that such issues as visitation and child support had not been fully resolved. Also, most of these fathers wanted considerably more time with their children at the time of divorce than what they actually had, in contrast to the other three groups [χ^2 (6, $N = 75$) = 19.4, $p < .01$]. Most of these fathers also wanted considerably more time with their children currently than what they had, which distinguished them from the groups with personal issues and older children, but not from those with distance as a barrier [χ^2 (6, $N = 73$) = 22.9, $p < .01$].

Fathers' Own Issues or Problems

Twenty-two of the fathers identified personal reasons for why they were not more active. None of them made references to their former spouse as an obstacle. The personal problems or issues that they identified varied considerably.

Five fathers admitted that a substance abuse problem interfered with their parenting. Two of these five fathers reported that they were recovering from their abuse problem and wanted to reenter their children's lives. These two fathers revealed a need for help in reconnecting with their children. As one of them explained,

> I have been addicted for over 20 years—all of my son's life. Most of that time I could hardly take care of myself. Now that I am slowly getting my life together, I don't know how to reenter my son's life and I am afraid of rejection.

Two fathers said that the demands of their job prevented them from becoming more active parents. Another respondent admitted that his personal leisure was his "excuse." Two others identified personal health problems as the most important obstacle. One of them said that he was a disabled veteran and the other explained that he had a heart condition.

Two fathers said that they voluntarily agreed to discontinue contacting their children to avoid confusing them with having both a father and a stepfather. One of these fathers was adamant in his explanation,

> It is my belief that it is better for my son to not be confused by two daddies. I was a child who didn't see his father from 3 to 33 and have NO hard feelings. I have raised two wonderful stepchildren as my own kids for the past 14 years and I have by design given up my right as a father so as not to confuse my son. I believe that his development is more important than my rights.

In two other cases, the father's girlfriend was identified as taking preference over their children. One of these fathers explained his conflict as follows: "The woman I love requires a lot of time and attention. I know I would lose her if I spend more time with my kids. I dread going back out there into the singles' bar and dating scene."

While 8 of the 22 fathers in this group have remarried, none of them explicitly mentioned that their new wife or family was a barrier to having more frequent contact. However, in four instances, time limitations in general were mentioned, and 2 of these fathers have remarried.

One father in this group reported that he is gay. While his former spouse was unable to understand and cope with his lifestyle, he indicated that it was his decision to have no contact at all with either his son or daughter since the divorce. Another father explained that his barrier to more active parenting was his fear of making mistakes with his children. He did not elaborate on this.

Another father who has two sons and two daughters indicated that it was difficult to be with all of his children at the same time. Their age and gender differences made it difficult to find activities that all of them would enjoy. One additional father explained that he had an estranged relationship with his children because the children still blamed the divorce on him. There was no indication that his former spouse was discouraging his children from seeing their father.

This group of fathers is different from the other groups in a few ways (see Table 19.1). A considerably smaller percentage of this group compared to the other three groups obtained their divorces using adversarial proceedings [χ^2 (9, N = 75) = 24.43, $p < .01$]. Also, most of these 22 fathers did not experience greater conflict with their former spouses after the divorce than when they separated.

Two thirds of these fathers perceived their former spouse as cooperative or neutral with regard to their visitation arrangement both at the time of divorce and currently. Also, most reported being satisfied with the frequency of their contact with their children both when they got divorced and currently.

The Children Growing Older

Thirteen of the 84 fathers reported that they were not in more frequent contact with their children primarily because of their children's ages. In these cases, they reported that their children had grown older and were no longer able to find much time to be with their fathers. They reported that their children preferred to be with their friends and some had jobs that demanded much of their time. All of these children were in their late teens (16 to 18 years). Also, all of these fathers reported that they were more active in their children's lives at the time of the divorce than they currently were.

Five of these fathers pointed out that their greatest loss was not living in the same household as their children. The absence of this daily contact excluded them from some of the daily happenings and decisions that they wished that they could share with them. As one father explained,

> The loss of physical contact and therefore normal influence over my child has been the greatest heartbreak imaginable. My son has had many problems directly caused by not having his dad when he needed him.

Only one of this group of fathers experienced greater conflict with his former spouse after his divorce than when he separated, even though most used adversarial proceedings. Most of these fathers reported that their former spouse was cooperative or neutral with their visitation arrangements, and most were satisfied with the frequency of their contact with their children both at the time of divorce and currently.

Long Distance as an Obstacle

Twelve of the fathers were distinguished from the other fathers based on the barrier of geographic distance between them and their children. The average distance between these fathers and their children is 946 miles, ranging from 150 to 3,000 miles. In some of these cases the mother and children moved away from the father, and in other cases the father moved away.

While all of these fathers reported having very little contact with their children, most of them have made numerous efforts to stay connected. Telephone calls and short summer vacations of a week or less are examples.

Usually, these fathers had more frequent contact with their children when they lived closer. Also, some continued to have frequent contact for awhile after the move. One example is a father who traveled to see his child 350 miles away every other weekend. His routine was to travel by train and spend the weekend with his child in a hotel room. When his son grew older, their contacts eventually diminished to occasional visits during the year.

The anguish felt by many of these fathers because of their separation from their children is evident in some of their comments. One father said, "I deeply love my children. They are God's gift to me. I would never walk away from my responsibilities to them. But it has been made considerably more difficult with the move." Another long-distance father said,

> I have been an attentive father. I spent a lot of my nonworking time with my children (before the move). They are a large part of who I am. At times the guilt that I feel in not being with them is overwhelming. I feel as though part of me has been amputated.

And another father shared, "I communicate with them as often as possible. Even at times when they stopped communicating with me, I kept letting them know that I love them, miss them, and always will be concerned about everything that is in their lives."

Like the first group, most of these fathers want considerably more time with their children at the present time. However, they are different from the first group in that the geographic distance appears to be their principal obstacle to more frequent parental contact. While most of their proceedings were adversarial and reported to be problematic, this was often in direct response to a long-distance move that separated these fathers from their children. Also, in instances when a move occurred after the divorce, court proceedings were often initiated to renegotiate custody, visitation, and child support decisions.

This group of fathers needs to be distinguished from fathers with another set of circumstances. In the case of 4 of the 84 fathers in the sample, a long-distance move was deliberately initiated by the custodial mother to get away from the father and in one of these cases to even hide from him. These 4 fathers are included in the first group because they more closely fit that group's profile. They identified their former spouse as their major obstacle.

Demographic Differences Among the Four Groups

The fathers in these four groups were significantly different based on their ages [F (3, 76) = 3.1, $p < .05$]. Fathers who perceived the age of their children as their major barrier had a mean age of 47 years ($SD = 5.1$), while the other groups had mean ages ranging from 40 to 42 (SDs ranging from 6.2 to 6.9). Similarly, the former spouses of the fathers identifying the age of their children as a barrier were older than the former spouses of the other fathers [F (3, 76) = 3.8, $p < .05$].

In terms of the geographic distance between the fathers and their children, the fathers with long distance as the perceived obstacle lived a longer distance from their children than the other three groups [F (3, 74) = 12.4, $p < .001$]. They lived a mean distance away of 946 miles ($SD = 768$). The fathers identifying their former spouse as their obstacle lived a mean distance away of 156 miles ($SD = 546$). The other two groups lived very close to their children, having a mean distance of about 15 miles ($SD = .16$).

No other demographic characteristics distinguished these four groups of fathers, including their income level, race, characteristics of their children, number of years that the fathers were married and divorced, and whether or not they or their former wives had remarried. The custody arrangement also was not significantly different for these four groups.

IMPLICATIONS FOR PRACTICE

In considering the implications of these findings for other fathers, it is important for the reader to keep in mind the limitations of the sample and research design. While efforts were made to select as representative a sample of divorced fathers as possible, some groups of fathers were noticeably underrepresented. Also, the views of the former spouses were not elicited. This needs to be noted because some research studies have shown that divorced fathers and mothers often differ in their reporting on many topics, even in the reported frequency of the father's contact with his children (Goldsmith, 1980).

The findings pertaining to the different types of fathers with infrequent contact reminds us that this social problem cannot be explained by any one phenomenon. Rather, it could result from any of a number of factors. Professionals who serve families will need to be informed and sensitive to the various legal, psychological, and familial issues faced by divorced fathers if they are to be effective in helping them (Jacobs, 1982).

The fathers in this study were initially differentiated, based on their explanations for why they were not more active in their children's lives. The reasons that they gave were helpful in explaining their infrequent contact. Also, these reasons correlated with other variables that help to formulate profiles of these four groups.

The group of 33 fathers who view their former spouse as their most important obstacle were, in most cases, in conflict with their former spouse over an extended period of time. They experienced considerable conflict when they separated. Also, they reported that the conflict continued and, in many cases, intensified after the divorce.

Most of these 33 fathers obtained their divorce using adversarial proceedings, with almost half of them being decided in court by a judge. Also, most had to return to court for changes in their agreements. The nature of their proceedings probably exacerbated the conflicts that they had had with their former spouses as well as created new ones (Moreland & Schwebel, 1981; Tepp, 1983; Wallerstein & Kelly, 1980). The comments of some of these fathers, presented in the Results section, support this conclusion. This suggests that future research should focus more on ways to avoid adversarial divorce proceedings, particularly litigation (Girdner, 1985; Johnston et al., 1985).

Family counselors should be cognizant of the possibility that divorced fathers still have intense anger toward their former spouse long after a divorce is final (Fox, 1985). Moving fathers toward an eventual resolution of the volatile residues of these conflicts may be critical if the father is to continue his involvement in the family. In this regard, such fathers will likely need to ventilate their feelings and explain their views of the events that occurred. They will need help in recognizing the impact of attorneys, judges, and other parties on their family relationships in order to disengage from these conflicts (Johnston et al., 1985). In some cases, they will need encouragement to seek expanded visitation arrangements or to take steps to get their present visitation agreement enforced. It may help to refer them to a local divorced fathers' rights group to pursue their visitation concerns.

The variables that distinguished fathers in conflict with their former wives from the other three groups could be viewed as topics to explore in helping divorced fathers to unravel their difficulties. For example, counselors could ask a father to talk about the state of his relationship with his former wife and children at the time of separation. This could be followed by an exploration of how the divorce proceedings and the decisions of these proceedings may have altered these relationships. Hopefully, such examinations could open up new ways of perceiving what happened as well as create new options to consider in increasing the father's involvement. Others have developed more comprehensive formats to be used by counselors in understanding the father's divorce-related difficulties (Ferreiro, Warren, & Konanc, 1986).

The group of 22 fathers who reported having personal problems had very different circumstances from each other and require different kinds of assistance. However, attorneys and family counselors should be careful not to falsely assume that any of these reported problems necessarily precludes a father from becoming more active. Otherwise, helping professionals could be inadvertently discouraging fathers from considering more active roles which may be in the best interests of the father and his children. Each case needs to be evaluated on an individualized basis.

Gay fathers are an example of this. These fathers may be discouraged from being active parents if attorneys and other professionals hold some of the popular myths about them. Examples of such myths are that gay fathers will molest their male children, or children will become gay if they are raised by their gay fathers (Bozett, 1985; Miller, 1979).

Divorced fathers who have a substance abuse problem may pose a more complicated situation. Clearly, other family members must be protected from any harmful effects of the addicted member. But, some addicted fathers may have the most hope of recovering if they can be in a healthy relationship with their children (Lewis, 1989). Various types of family-based interventions have been successful in helping addicts to recover. Also, support groups like Alcoholic Anonymous can be effective both in the recovery process and in improving family relationships. Some fathers with a variety of emotional problems may be more likely to recover if the professional assistance that they are given focuses on helping them to maintain and improve their relationships with their children (Jacobs, 1982).

Another type of divorced father with personal issues is the father who does not want to interfere with the parenting of a stepfather. Two fathers in the study agreed to discontinue having contact with their children because they were persuaded that it would be best for their children to have only one active father figure. Undoubtedly, having both a biological father and a stepfather can be confusing to a child and difficult for the parents and stepparents to work out. However, biological parents have a bond with their children that will always exist; physical separation is not likely to mean that children will forget their father (Cohen, 1989; Wylder, 1982). Professionals should be prepared to help biological parents to remain in their children's lives if this is what they want. Visher and Visher (1989), for example, offer the concept of "parenting coalitions" as a therapeutic intervention in behalf of families with two households. These coalitions strive to minimize competition between the mother's and father's households, and to replace it with efforts to support the activities of the other household.

When asked how satisfied they were with the frequency of their visitations with their children, most of these 22 fathers indicated that they were satisfied. This may seem peculiar since all of them had little or no contact with their children. This question may be a useful one for family professionals to ask in an attempt to explore, in more depth, a father's motivations and circumstances. If he appears to be satisfied with having very little time with his children, he may feel inadequate in his parental role. Or he may be discouraged from being an active parent by his present wife or an important friend. Or he could feel that other things like his job or his leisure are more important than his children. Or he may believe that it is best for his children if he is not involved. Whatever the response, it could identify some important underlying issues that may need counseling attention.

Another group of fathers must cope with long distances that separate them from their children. Because this may become an eventual outcome for numerous divorcing parents, provisions should be considered in divorce agreements for potential long-distance parenting arrangements. Considering such a plan before a move is even contemplated could be helpful. Both parents would have to think seriously about the effects of long-distance on the relationships between the children and the parents. Also, it may be easier to work out logistical and financial issues based on a hypothetical situation.

Cohen (1989) devotes an entire book to the joys and difficulties of long-distance parenting. She offers creative ways to stay in touch with children who are far away, and ways to cope with some of the difficulties.

Sometimes a long-distance separation between a father and his children can be a barrier that is not identified to a family professional. The first group of fathers lived, on the average, quite far from their children. Surprisingly, only a few of these fathers mentioned this as a problem. Therefore, when exploring the obstacles to more active parenting, it could be helpful to ask about several potential obstacles in addition to exploring the ones identified by a father.

The last group of fathers in the study reminds us that the children's ages can be perceived as a barrier to more active parenting. In this case, teenage children may have a tendency to reduce their time spent with a noncustodial father because of the increasing importance of their peers and social life. While this seems logical, none of the other cited studies found that fathers with teenage children had less frequent contact than those with younger children.

Nevertheless, family professionals may need to encourage noncustodial fathers to continue their involvement with their children when they become adolescents, even though this may require more initiative on the father's part. Fathers have much to offer to their adolescent children in many areas, including their career development, moral development, and sex role identification (Martin, 1985).

This age factor also suggests that noncustodial fathers should be encouraged to give priority time to their children when they are younger. This earlier period may be the only time that they can have regular opportunities to spend large blocks of time with their children.

In considering help for all four types of fathers in the study, the important potential role of support groups should not be overlooked. One fourth of these fathers indicated that they were active with a support group, and most of them found these groups to be helpful to them as parents. Men tend to avoid seeking help from other men who are experiencing similar problems (Goldberg, 1976). Because of this tendency, a men's support group can be an important vehicle for facilitating problem solving and networking among fathers.

In conclusion, it is important that we explore with divorced fathers why they have infrequent contact with their children. As this study indicates, there are numerous factors that could explain their circumstances. These factors also provide clues for helping them to become more involved if this is what they want.

As fathers work on ways to become more active in their children's lives, they will need help in understanding the circumstances of their former spouse. Hopefully, they will also be helped to develop a cooperative alliance with her. Former spouses will also need to be helped to understand the circumstances facing a noncustodial father, as they can be critical to the father's continued involvement (Fox, 1985).

Perhaps, a large proportion of fathers would become increasingly active in response to appropriate professional intervention. Also, it seems that the pattern of infrequent contact of numerous noncustodial fathers could possibly be averted, particularly at the time of divorce proceedings. Professionals working in and with the family court system need to be viewed as having an important influence over the divorced father's long-term parental role.

REFERENCES

Albrecht, S. L. (1980). Reactions and adjustments to divorce: Differences in the experiences of males and females. *Family Relations, 29,* 59–68.

Bahr, S. J. (1981). An evaluation of court mediation for divorce cases with children. *Journal of Family Issues, 2,* 39–60.

Bozett, F. W. (1985). Gay men as fathers. In S. M. Hanson & F. W. Bozett (Eds.), *Dimensions of fatherhood* (pp. 327–352). Beverly Hills, CA: Sage.

Buehler, C. (1989). Influential factors and equity issues in divorce settlements. *Family Relations, 38,* 76–82.

Brandwein, R. A., Brown, C. A., & Fox, E. M. (1974). Women and children last: The social situation of divorced mothers and their families. *Journal of Marriage and the Family, 36,* 498–514.

Cassetty, J. (1978). *Child support and public policy; Securing support from absent fathers.* Lexington, MA: Lexington Books.

Clingempeel, W. G., & Reppucci, N. D. (1982). Joint custody after divorce: Major issues and goals for research. *Psychological Bulletin, 91,* 102–127.

Cohen, M. G. (1989). *Long-distance parenting.* New York: New American Library.

Dominic, K. T., & Schlesinger, B. (1980). Weekend fathers: Family shadows. *Journal of Divorce, 3,* 241–247.

Duncan, G. P. (1984). *Years of poverty, years of plenty: The changing economic fortunes of American workers and families.* Ann Arbor: University of Michigan, Institute for Social Research.

Ebel, D. M. (1980). Bar programs—Other ways to resolve disputes. *Ligitation, 6,* 25–28.

Elkin, M. (1987). Joint custody: Affirming that parents and families are forever. *Social Work, 32,* 18–24.

Emery, R. E. (1982). Interparental conflict and the children of discord and divorce. *Psychological Bulletin,* 92, 310–330.

Ferreiro, B. W., Warren, N. J., & Konanc, J. T. (1986). ADAP: A divorce assessment proposal. *Family Relations,* 35, 439–449.

Folberg, C.H. (Ed.). (1984). *Joint custody and shared parenting.* Washington, DC: Association of Family and Conciliation Courts.

Fox, G. L. (1985). Noncustodial fathers. In S. M. Hanson & F. W. Bozett (Eds.), Dimensions of fatherhood (pp. 393–415). Beverly Hills, CA: Sage.

Furstenberg, F. F., Nord, C. W., Peterson, J. L., & Zill, N. (1983). The life course of children of divorce: Marital disruption and parental conflict. *American Sociological Review,* 8, 656–668.

Girdner, L. (1985). Adjudication and mediation: A comparison of custody decision-making processes involving third parties. *Journal of Divorce,* 9, 33–47.

Glasser, P., & Navarre, E. (1965). Structural problems of the one-parent family. *Journal of Social Issues,* 21, 98–109.

Goldberg, H. (1976). *The hazards of being male: Surviving the myth of masculine privilege.* New York: New American Library.

Goldsmith, J. (1980). Relationships between former spouses: Descriptive findings. *Journal of Divorce,* 4, 1–20.

Greif, G. L., & Bailey, C. (1990). Where are the fathers in social work literature. *Families in Society,* 71, 88–92.

Griel, J. B. (1979). Fathers, children, and joint custody. *American Journal of Orthopsychiatry,* 49, 311–319.

Hess, R. D., & Camara, K. A. (1979). Post-divorce relationships as mediating factors in the consequences of divorce for children. *Journal of Social Issues,* 35, 79–96.

Hetherington, E. M., Cox, M., & Cox, R. (1979). Family interaction and the social, emotional and cognitive development of children following divorce. In V. Vaughan & T. Brazelton (Eds.). *The family: Setting priorities* (pp. 71–87). New York: Science and Medicine.

Jacobs, J. W. (1982). The effect of divorce on fathers: An overview of the literature. *American Journal of Psychiatry,* 139, 1235–1241.

Johnston, J. R., Campbell, L. E., & Tall, M.C. (1985). Impasses to the resolution of custody and visitation disputes. *American Journal of Orthopsychiatry,* 55, 112–129.

Johnston, J. R., Kline, M., & Tschann, J. T. (1989). Ongoing postdivorce conflict: Effects on children of joint custody and frequent access. *American Journal of Orthopsychiatry,* 59, 576–592.

Keshet, H., & Rosenthal, K. (1978). Fathering after marital separation. *Social Work,* 23, 11–18.

Koch, M. A., & Lowery, C. R. (1984). Visitation and the noncustodial father. *Journal of Divorce,* 8, 47–65.

Lamb, M. E. (1986). The changing roles of fathers. In M. E. Lamb (Ed.), *The father's role: Applied perspectives* (pp. 3–27). New York: John Wiley & Sons.

Lewis, R. A. (1989). The family and addictions: An introduction. *Family Relations,* 38, 254–257.

Martin, D. H. (1985). Fathers and adolescents. In S. M. Hanson & F. W. Bozett (Eds.), *Dimensions of fatherhood* (pp. 170–195). Beverly Hills, CA: Sage.

Miller, B. (1979). Gay fathers and their children. *The Family Coordinator,* 28, 544–552.

Moreland, J., & Schewebel, A. I. (1981). A gender role transcendent perspective on father-ing. *The Counseling Psychologist,* 9, 45–52.

Pearce, D., & McAdoo, H. (1983). *Women and children: Alone and in poverty.* Report to the National Advisory Council on Economic Opportunity, reprinted by Catholic University Law School, Washington, DC.

Roman, M., & Haddad, W. (1978). *The disposable parent: The case for joint custody.* New York: Holt, Rinehart & Winston.

Tepp, A. V. (1983). Divorced fathers: Predictors of continued paternal involvement. *American Journal of Psychiatry,* 140, 1465–1469.

Visher, E. B., & Visher, J. S. (1989). Parenting coalitions after remarriage: Dynamics and therapeutic guidelines. *Family Relations,* 38, 65–70.

Wallerstein, J. S., & Kelly, J. B. (1980). *Surviving the break-up: How children and parents cope with divorce.* New York: Basic Books.

Wylder, J. (1982). Including the divorced father in family therapy. *Social Work,* 27, 479–482.

Reading 20   12/1/94

The Remarriage Transition

Constance R. Ahrons and Roy H. Rodgers

The family change process set in motion by one marital disruption boggles one's mind. It frequently requires complex computation to chart and understand the kinship relationships. Even though the current remarriage rates show a continuing decline . . . , the vast majority of divorced families will move through the series of stressful transitions and structural changes brought about by the expansion of the family postdivorce. The structural changes in remarriage give rise to a host of disruptions in roles and relationships, and each transition may be mastered with varying amounts of stress and turmoil.

Projections from the current trends indicate that between 40 and 50 percent of the children born in the 1970s will spend some portion of their minor years in a one-parent household. Given the current remarriage rates it is also projected that approximately 25 to 30 percent of American children will live for some period of time in a remarried household. Although we do not have as adequate cohabitation information as we would like, we can assume that many of these children will also live for some period of time in a cohabiting household, which may or may not become a remarriage household. This means that at least 25 to 30 percent of the children will have more than two adults who function simultaneously as parents. Rates of redivorce are also increasing, resulting in even more complex kinship structures.

Consider the following case example of the Spicer/Tyler/Henry binuclear family. . . .

When Ellen was eight and David ten, their parents separated. They continued to live with their mother, Nancy, spending weekends and vacations with their father, Jim. Two years after the divorce their father married Elaine, who was the custodial parent of her daughter, Jamie, aged six. Ellen and David lived in a one-parent household with their mother for three years, at which time their mother remarried. Their new stepfather, Craig, also had been divorced, and he was the joint-custodial parent of two daughters, aged six and 11. His daughters spent about ten days each month living in his household. Within the next four years, Ellen and David's father and stepmother had two children of their own, a son and a daughter.

When Ellen and David are 15 and 17, their family looks like this: They have two biological parents, two stepparents, three stepsisters, a half-brother and a half-sister. Their extended family has expanded as well: They have two sets of step-grandparents, two sets of biological grandparents, and a large network of aunts, uncles, and cousins. In addition to this complex network of kin, they have two households of "family. . . ."

BINUCLEAR FAMILY REORGANIZATION THROUGH EXPANSION: AN OVERVIEW

The expansion of the binuclear family through remarriage involves the addition of new family members in all three generations. The recoupling of one of the former spouses requires another reorganization of the former spouse subsystem and each of the parent-child subsystems; a recoupling of the other former spouse requires still another reorganization of the whole system. Each of these transitions has the potential of being highly stressful for family members. The way in which the family reorganizes itself will determine whether the binuclear family emerges as a functional or dysfunctional system. . . .

We are very much hindered by the inadequacy of current language in our discussion of the binuclear family in remarriage. For most of the relationships between family members in this expanded system there are no formal labels or role titles. What does one call one's former mate's new spouse? Or the children or parents of the new mate who have a relationship with one's child? Even the former spouse relationship has no current title, which requires that we continue to speak of it as a past relationship. Although ex-spouses with children may refer to each other as "my daughter's (or son's) father (or mother)," this does not capture the ongoing nonparental relationship between the divorced couple. So, of necessity, as we struggle to analyze some of the components of this complex system, our language suffers from being cumbersome and we will occasionally resort to inadequate terms that have emerged in the process of studying these families.

Former Spouse Subsystem

The former spouse relationship, with its many possible relational variations, becomes even more complex when one or both partners remarry. The timing of the remarriage further complicates the dynamics of this highly ambiguous post-divorce relationship. In McCubbin and Patterson's theoretical formulation of the pathways and mediating factors leading from stress to crisis, accumulating stressors, or "pileup," increase the potential for crisis. Consequently, if one of the ex-spouses remarries before the binuclear family has adequate time to establish new patterns for its reorganized structure, the potential for dysfunctional stress is high. Given the statistic that about 62 percent of men and 61 percent of women remarry within two years after divorce . . . , many families will experience the added stress of incorporating new family members in the midst of struggling with the complicated changes produced by the divorce.

Even if remarriage is delayed until the divorced family has had sufficient time to reorganize and stabilize, shifting of roles and relationships is necessary when a new member is introduced into the family system by remarriage. The family has to struggle with the role of the new family member while allegiances, loyalties and daily relationship patterns undergo transition. For many families, just as they are adjusting to one new member, the other ex-spouse remarries, which causes another transition requiring a shift in the family's tentative equilibrium. The length of time between one ex-spouse's remarriage and the second remarriage will influence the severity of stress experienced by all family members as they are required once again to cope with reorganization.

For the single ex-spouse, the remarriage of a former mate irrespective of the timing, may stimulate many of the feelings unresolved in the emotional divorce. If there are any lingering fantasies of reconciliation, the remarriage brings the sharp reality that reunion is no longer a possibility. It is not unusual for the single ex-spouse to feel a temporary loss of self-esteem as he or she makes comparisons to the new partner. Feelings of jealousy and envy are normal, even for those who thought they had worked through these feelings at the time of the divorce. Seeing an ex-spouse "in love" with someone else often rekindles the feelings of the early courtship and romantic phase of the first married relationship and a requestioning of the reasons for divorce. For a single ex-spouse who did not want the divorce, the remarriage has the potential of creating a personal crisis that closely resembles the experiences of the divorce. But even for those ex-spouses who may have initiated the divorce, the remarriage usually stimulates old feelings and resentments.

> NANCY: When Jim told me he was getting married I reacted with a cutting comment, saying I hoped she was better prepared for long evenings alone than I was. But what I was really scared about was that he would be different with her than he was with me. What if he had *really* changed? I realized that I wanted his marriage to fail. Then I would know that I was right in divorcing him.

Jim's remarriage resulted in Nancy's returning to therapy to work through many of the unresolved issues of the divorce. Jim's new wife was younger than Nancy and had one child by a previous marriage. Nancy and Jim had become cooperative colleagues in their divorced parenting relationship and she was fearful that she would have to give up many of the conveniences of their shared parenting as Jim took on the responsibilities of a new family.

The remarriage of one or both of the former spouses might be expected to decrease the amount of coparenting between former spouses, since a person involved in a new relationship may have less time to spend, or interest in, relating to his or her former spouse, or may perhaps feel pressure from the new spouse to decrease his or her involvement with the first spouse. For Jim, the conflicts were many.

> JIM: When Elaine and I decided to get married I felt guilty and like I needed to tell Nancy immediately. I dreaded telling her. When I did tell her she didn't say much but I knew she was feeling upset. I wanted the kids to be part of the wedding and I knew Nancy was going to feel jealous and left out. I'd feel much better if she had someone else in her life. Elaine's relationship with her ex-husband is nothing like my relationship with Nancy and she didn't understand my wanting to ease Nancy's pain by not flaunting my new life at her.

Jim's marriage to Elaine initiates a complex cycle of changes for all participants. Nancy needs to adjust to Jim's sharing of his life with a new partner and a child, while both Jim and Elaine need to cope with two ex-spouses who will continue to be part of their future lives. Six months after Jim's marriage to Elaine, Nancy summarized it this way:

> NANCY: Things have changed a lot since Jim remarried. He's less willing to accommodate when I need to change plans around the kids. He always has to check with Elaine first. I really resent that—the kids should come first. I invited Jim to Ellen's birthday party but he couldn't come because of plans he had made with Elaine and her child. And I feel uncomfortable calling him at home about anything. Elaine usually answers the phone and I feel like she's listening the whole time. Jim has asked to take the kids on a week's vacation to visit Elaine's parents over Easter. I know it's his time with the kids but I think he should give them some special time and not make them spend it with Elaine's family.

For Nancy it is difficult for her to see her children's family extending to include more members not directly related to her. And in these early stages of his remarriage Jim is having difficulty coping with the conflicting demands that his increasing family membership causes.

JIM: I knew Nancy would be upset about our plans for the Easter vacation. Sometimes I wish I could just go off with the kids skiing like we did the first year after the divorce, but I know Elaine wants to visit her parents. There's no way I can please everyone.

Nancy and Jim's relationship is in the process of undergoing considerable change. They talk less frequently and anger sparks up more often now as they try to make decisions about the kids. Jim feels more anger at Nancy now because she is "not understanding" his new responsibilities, and Nancy feels more anger as she has less access to Jim. They are traveling the bumpy road of this transition as they redefine their relationship again, dealing with the changes brought about by Elaine's entry into the family system.

In Ahrons' Binuclear Family Study a deterioration in coparental relations after remarriage did occur among the respondents. This was especially true if only the husband had remarried. For instance, the number and frequency of childrearing activities shared between the former spouses were highest where neither partner had remarried and lowest if only the husband had remarried. The amount of support in coparental interaction was highest and conflict lowest where neither partner had remarried, while conflict was highest and support lowest if only the husband had remarried. Also, if neither former spouse had remarried, they were most likely to spend time together with each other and their children, and least likely if only the husband had remarried. . . .

Remarried Couple Subsystem

The transition to remarriage after a divorce of one or both partners is markedly different from the transition to a first marriage. Not only do the new spouses bring their families of origin into their extended system, but they also have relationships with their first married families which need to be integrated in some way. Remarried couples overwhelmingly report that they are unprepared for the complexities of remarried life. Their model for remarriage is often based on a first marriage model. In contrast to the relatively impermeable boundary that surrounds a nuclear family, permeable boundaries are needed in households within the binuclear family system. These facilitate the exchange of children, money, and decision-making power. If one of the partners has not been previously married, he or she is particularly vulnerable to the dream of the ideal traditional family. . . .

When Elaine and Jim decided to get married, they talked about their divorce histories and their current relationships with their ex-spouses and brought their respective children together for brief periods of time. They fantasized about their plans for blending their family and perhaps adding a new child of their own to the picture. Although they were both aware of some potential problems, they felt able to cope because of the strong bond they had developed between themselves. But as they actually made the transition to remarriage many of the problems created more stress than they had anticipated.

> ELAINE: When Jim and I decided to get married I was surprised by his feeling guilty about Nancy. I didn't have any of those feelings about my ex, Tom. When Tom remarried last year it didn't make much difference in my life. He hadn't seen much of Jamie anyway and he just saw her less after he remarried. It was a relief not to have much to do with him. So, after living alone with Jamie for three years, I was really excited to have a family again and give Jamie more of a dad. But it's not working out that way. Jamie is angry a lot about not having time alone with me, which ends up with Jim and me fighting a lot. Jim feels badly about not spending enough time with his kids and when the kids are together, it just seems to be everyone fighting over Jim. And I feel resentful at not having enough time alone with Jim. Between every other weekend with his kids and the long hours we both work we never seem to have time alone together. Last Friday we were finally spending an evening all alone and, just as I was putting dinner on the table, Nancy called. Jim and I spent the next two hours talking about Nancy. It ended up spoiling our whole evening.

Elaine's feelings are not uncommon for second spouses within a complex binuclear family. The stresses of accommodating the existing bonds of first married relationships into the new stepfamily subsystem often turn the traditional "honeymoon stage" of marriage into an overwhelming cast of characters who share the marital bed. The reorganization required in moving from a one-parent household to a two-parent one often involves more adjustment than the single parent expected. Roles and relationships require realignment and the addition of a new person in some type of parent role is stressful for all the family participants. A frequent complaint in new remarriages is the lack of time and privacy for the newly remarried partners. Jim expressed his disillusionment this way:

> JIM: Maybe we shouldn't have gotten married. When we were dating we made time for each other and spent many days and evenings enjoying things together. But after we got married Elaine felt guilty leaving Jamie with her mother or a babysitter very often. Jamie is very demanding—she always seems to want Elaine to do something for her. And Elaine can't seem to say no. Whenever I try to suggest to Elaine that Jamie should learn to play alone more, Elaine seems to get moody and quiet. Her resentment of the time I spend with my kids is hard for me to deal with. Sometimes I think she wishes I would stop seeing them or see them as little as Tom sees Jamie.

When the remarriage partners have been previously married, it is difficult for them not to compare their respective relationships with their ex-spouses. Their own former spouse relationship becomes the model for their new spouse's former spouse relationship. Elaine's expectation that Jim would have a similar relationship with Nancy as she had with Tom was shattered as she realized that Nancy was still very much a part of Jim's life.

The rise of dual-career marriages has resulted in a time problem for first marriages which is only exacerbated in the dual career remarriage. Add to this children and an ex-spouse or two and the issue of time becomes a very real problem. The usual marital issues of power and regulation of distance and intimacy are multiplied in the complex binuclear family. . . .

As with divorce, and with marriage as well, the first year of remarriage has the most potential for crisis. The rate for divorce after remarriage is even higher than that for divorce in first marriages. Glick calculates that 54 percent of women and 61 percent of men who remarry will divorce. The timing of redivorce also differs from that of a first divorce. Remarriages have a 50 percent greater probability of redivorce in the first five years than first marriages.

Current empirical work also suggests that remarriage satisfaction is highly dependent on stepparent-stepchild relationships. How the crises are handled by the remarriage pair will depend on many past experiences and will define the future functioning of the family. Over time, and perhaps with some professional help, Elaine and Jim may be able to find ways to cope with their overcrowded lives. They will need to devise ways to protect and nourish their relationship without damaging the existing parent-child bonds. This will require developing a new model of familying which includes more flexibility, compromise, and fluidity of boundaries than they may have expected originally. . . .

Sibling Subsystems: Step and Half

The child development literature notes the stresses of adding children to the family with its normalizing of "sibling rivalry." In the remarriage family with children of both partners, the joining of the new sibling subsystems is a difficult transition for the children—acquiring an "instant sibling" can pose a threat to even the most secure child. The new remarriage partners have their marriage at stake and, therefore, need their respective children to like each other. Given a host of factors, such as the age and temperament of the children, the blending of two households of unrelated children requires major adjustments. Few newly blended families resemble the "Brady Bunch," but many have this as their model for this transition!

The usual competitive struggles among siblings often become major battles in remarried families, as children must adapt to sharing household space and parental time with new siblings. . . . [T]he remarriage of Ellen and David's father included a new "kid sister" for them. That was followed a year later by their mother's remarriage, which included two more "kid sisters" who shared their home with them for one-third of every month. And, a few years down the line, they had to incorporate two half siblings when their father and stepmother had a son and a daughter. . . .

Empirical research on the effects of remarriage on children is not as easily summarized as the literature on the effects of divorce. Although research is steadily increasing, we still lack major longitudinal studies identifying the stresses and developmental phases of adding new members to the binuclear family. And sibling relationships in binuclear families have been a sadly neglected area of study. But it is our guess that for many children the transition to remarriage is more stressful than the transition to divorce. The addition of new family members can also mean more loss than gain for many children—if not permanent losses, then at least temporary relationship loss in the transition period. The changes children need to make when a parent inherits new children as part of his or her remarriage are numerous and difficult. And the newly remarried parent, who so frequently feels overwhelmed, may have her or his energies absorbed more in the new mate than in facilitating the child's transition.

Mother/Stepmother—Father/Stepfather Subsystems

Now we are faced with describing baffling relationships with a wordiness created by our current language deficits. We are hampered further in our efforts by the lack of clinical or empirical research on these relationships. Nevertheless, we will attempt here to describe some of the stressful aspects of these relationships, which form such an integral part of the remarriage transition.

In fact, these first and second spouses do have some bearing on each other's lives. For some second spouses, the "ghost" of the first spouse is ever present. For many, the first spouse can be an unwanted interloper, creating conflict between the remarriage pair. In other remarriage couples the first spouse is a uniting force on whom the new spouses place blame for all the problems of a dysfunctional family. This type of scapegoating is the subject of much humor and provides the basis for many of the prevalent negative stereotypes of this relationship.

Obviously, even in one family system, the relationships between current and former spouses can be quite different, depending on the type of relationship between the former spouse pairs and all the individual personalities. . . .

The possibilities and complexities in these types of relationships are vast, and our knowledge of them is almost nonexistent. But clearly the type of relationship style adopted by the former spouses is a major factor determining the relationship between first and second spouses. In many remarried binuclear systems the former spouse relationship is likely to diminish in importance over time, especially when there are no minor children to bind the parents together. As this happens, the need for first and second spouses to relate also diminishes. . . .

Functional and Dysfunctional Remarriage Relationships

Our definition of functional and dysfunctional systems in remarriage is very similar to that of functional and dysfunctional divorces. . . . Developing new roles and relationships in remarriage which take into account the existence and losses of divorced family relationships is critical to enhancing remarried family functioning. The addition of new family members can result in dysfunctional binuclear family systems if prior kin relationships are severed. If remarriage subsystems try to model nuclear families—that is, if they insist upon "instant" family and try to establish traditional parenting roles—they will experience resistance and distress. A functional binuclear family system needs to have permeable boundaries which permit children and adults to continue prior family relationships while slowly integrating the new remarried subsystem. This, of necessity, causes transitory stresses and strains created by the conflict between new and old alliances. Remarriage is still another transition, with even more possibilities for stress than divorce.

As we emphasized in the divorce transition, the clear delineation of boundaries is critical to successful functioning. The remarried husband coparent, for example, must clarify his role vis-à-vis his biological and stepchildren, and his first and second spouses. He and his ex-spouse need to renegotiate what is appropriate and inappropriate in his continuing role as coparent. Coparenting agreements that may have been satisfactory prior to his remarriage are likely to have implications for his current spouse. For example, if it has been agreed that he needs to spend more time with his eight-year-old son, who wants and needs his father's attention, this takes time away from his marriage. His responsibilities as a parent and his spousal responsibilities come into conflict. This can be exacerbated by opinions expressed by his current partner that the "boy is spoiled and demanding and needs to learn that his father can't always be there." Or she may feel that the former spouse is using the child as a way of hanging on to her ex-husband. And, of course, she may also be concerned about the time taken away from her and the children she has brought to this new marriage. But the new partner must also be sensitive to the degree that expression of such thoughts violates important boundaries between the new marriage and the old.

While he will be wise not to pass these opinions of his new partner on to the former spouse (these are clearly outside the boundaries of the former spouse relationship), unless the husband coparent is able to deal effectively with his ex-spouse around these conflicting pressures, crisis may result. His former wife may see him as withdrawing from the coparental relationship they have agreed upon. And she, not having remarried, may have a renewed sense of abandonment resulting from the remarriage of her former spouse. Given their agreements concerning coparenting, she has legitimate call upon her former spouse. At the same time, the remarried spouse has equally legitimate expectations related to their marriage. Without explicit negotiation of arrangements and reasonable expectations from both sides, thus establishing clear boundaries for his actions in both subsystems, he is destined to fall short in both.

The single former spouse also may experience considerable distress in adjusting to the expanded system. Noncustodial parents will feel some resentment at losing some of their former responsibilities in both division of labor and decision-making. They may also feel that the new spouse interferes in their relationship with the former spouse and their children. A custodial parent, usually the mother, will often experience a loss of services when her former spouse remarries. She may no longer be able to call on him for help, as many of her demands—except as they are related to the coparenting relationship—begin to fall outside the legitimate boundaries of the former spouse relationship. Clearly, agreements and court orders with respect to financial child support are legitimate. However, expectations that the former husband will perform repairs or maintenance on the home of the former spouse may have to be rejected. This may be difficult, since that home is likely to be his former home, in which he may feel some residual investment, and in some cases may still retain some financial investment. However, resistance from the new partner to continuing such tasks is likely to severely restrict any such activity. All of this may be softened or made more difficult, depending upon the kind of postdivorce relationship style which has developed.

Remarriage restructures the division of labor developed in the postdivorce reorganization. New spouses of custodial parents take on many of the day-to-day responsibilities for care of children and household tasks formerly handled alone by the custodial parent or carried out by one of the children from time to time. As we have seen, this may lead to some genuine friction, as children resent the new step-parent's "taking over" or displacing them in some valued responsibility. If the new spouse attempts to assume responsibilities which the noncustodial parent may have continued, this is another source of potential stress. The former spouse may resent it, the stepchildren may resent it, and even the new spouse may have difficulty in accepting it.

Decision-making and the power structure implications carry similar potential stress. This will be especially true around decisions concerning the stepchildren, but may be true in other areas as well. If a new spouse has been used to having his or her former spouse participate and be involved in decisions concerning the children, the new spouse can easily be seen as "interfering," both by the other biological parent and the child. For example, as we have seen in the case presented in this chapter, Nancy resented Elaine's parenting involvement.

The style of the postdivorce ex-spouse relationship may either ease these adjustments . . . or make them more difficult. . . . If former spouses are insecure and competitive about their parenting relationships with their children, . . . the addition of a new parent figure will intensify those feelings during the transition. An ex-spouse may feel threatened by the "new family" of the remarried spouse, anticipating that the children will prefer this new household to the one-parent household where they currently live.

When parents—both biological and step—are unclear about their roles, children are likely to use the ambiguity to manipulate the new stepparent, their custodial parent, and the noncustodial parent. During the early stages of the remarriage transition it is not unusual for children to play one parent off against another for some personal gain. For example, in the Spicer-Tyler-Henry family, Ellen, after spending a weekend at her father's house, might very well tell her mother that Elaine, her new stepmother, "lets me watch TV until 10 p.m." Ellen's hope, of course, is that her mother will respond by permitting her to stay up later than her usual bedtime. Sometimes, new stepparents will be more lenient with their stepchildren in the hopes of being liked and accepted by them. Consciously, or perhaps unconsciously, the new stepparent is competing with the other biological parent for the child's affections.

Although former spouses may have worked out consistent rules for discipline, etc., during the divorce transition, these are likely to need renegotiation when a new parent enters the family. Only now, the renegotiation is more complicated, as three parents become part of the process instead of the original two. And if the other ex-spouse remarries, there may be a replay of some of the issues as the system accommodates to a fourth parent. As we noted earlier, however, this may be an easier transition. Not only are the parents familiar now with many of the problems of adjustment but the system itself is in better balance. There are now two stepfamily households, with each biological parent having an ally.

The remarried binuclear family faces a unique problem in controlling intimacy in the family. Incest taboos, which are assumed between blood kin in first marriage nuclear families (though, as is now being revealed, more often violated than many have known), become an important issue. The function of such taboos, of course, is to maintain unambiguous and appropriate intimate relationships in families. The potential for sexual feelings and possible abuse between non-blood parents and children, as well as between adolescent stepsiblings, is high. Therefore, establishment of clearly defined boundaries in this highly charged emotional area is essential.

A situation observed by one of the authors in family therapy illustrates how dysfunctional failure to establish such boundaries can be. In the course of the session, an adolescent stepdaughter revealed that she had been sexually involved with the son of her stepfather, i.e., her stepbrother. There were indications that this involvement was involuntary on her part. The mother of the young woman became very angry. At this point, the two biological daughters of the stepfather, who no longer lived in the household, confronted their stepmother with their sexual experiences some years before with her son—their stepbrother. They were extremely angry with the stepmother for not having the same reactions to their experiences, of which they believed the stepmother to be aware. These revelations, of course, provided some understanding of the kinds of conflicts in this stepfamily that had prompted the request for therapeutic treatment. The issues extended far beyond the matter of sexual abuse to include the entire range of emotional relationships which had developed in this remarried family over several prior years. Failure to have defined appropriate intimacy boundaries in the reorganization of this binuclear family had contributed to an extremely dysfunctional situation.

Relationships with extended kin find new stresses facing them upon the remarriage of one or both ex-spouses. Children may be particularly puzzled by suddenly finding their access to one set of grandparents or a favored aunt or uncle severely restricted or cut off. The nature of those relationships may also be changed, even if they are continued, by the inability of the extended kin to keep their feelings about the ex-spouse from contaminating their interactions with the children. Further, the introduction of new extended kin can also be confusing and stress-producing for children.

The new relationships with the spouse's extended family are not of the same character as those of first married couples. They often carry residual elements from the former marriage, particularly since these are not just in-laws, but also grandparents, uncles, and aunts. In addition, in many cases there are also associations to be worked out with the former spouse of the new partner. Until new relationships with extended family are established, they tend to be mediated through the new marital relationship.

CONCLUSION

. . . The study of even one remarried subsystem alone presents sufficient complexities to cause many social scientists to return to studying individuals rather than family systems. Our lack of both language and analytic tools, as well as the difficulties in conceptualizing the totality of these complex systems, creates frustration in both the writer and the reader.

All of this brings into sharp relief the importance of developing a new set of meanings for the relationships between former spouses, with the new spouse, between former and current spouses, between stepparents and stepchildren, between step and half siblings, and with extended kin. If the expanded binuclear family structure is to survive and function in an effective manner, then all parties must develop clear understandings of what these meanings are in the new remarriage situation. These meanings are most likely to center on the coparenting responsibilities that the ex-spouses share, but they go well beyond this.

Clearly delineating a precise definition of functional and dysfunctional remarriage binuclear families is not possible, given our current lack of knowledge. Although we can comfortably conclude that remarriage subsystems must be open systems with permeable boundaries, we cannot say what degree of openness is optimal. Remarriage subsystems need to be able to develop their own sense of connectedness and independence, while simultaneously functioning as interdependent units. Stepparents have a confusing and difficult role. In most families they need to develop new parenting type roles that supplement, rather than replace, biological parents. And they need to do so expecting resistance and a long developmental process of integration. What is required is a new model of familying that encompasses an expanded network of extended and quasi-kin relationships.

PART
FOUR

CHILDREN IN THE FAMILY

INTRODUCTION

No aspect of childhood seems more natural, universal, and changeless than relationships between parents and children. Yet historical and cross-cultural evidence reveals major changes in conceptions of childhood and adulthood and in the psychological relationships between children and parents. As Robert LeVine and Merry White point out in their article here, the shift from agrarian to industrial society over the past 200 years has revolutionized parent-child relations and the conditions of child development.

Among the changes associated with this transformation of childhood are: the elimination of child labor; the fall in infant mortality; the spread of literacy and mass schooling; and a focus on childhood as a distinct and valuable stage of life. As a result of these changes, industrial-era parents bear fewer children, make greater emotional and economic investments in them, and expect less in return than their agrarian counterparts. Agrarian parents were not expected to emphasize emotional bonds or the value of children as unique individuals. Parents and children were bound together by economic necessity: children were a necessary source of labor in the family economy and a source of support in old age. Today, almost all children are economic liabilities. But they now have profound emotional significance. Parents hope offspring will provide intimacy, even genetic immortality. Although today's children have become economically worthless they have become emotionally "priceless" (Zelizer, 1985).

Shifting to a shorter time frame, David H. Demo examines the impact on children of the dramatic changes in family life over the past three decades. Demo agrees with other researchers who have found a decline in some of the major indicators of children's well-being over this period. But he argues that the effects of working mothers, divorce, and single-parent families have been greatly exaggerated. The key factors in children's lives are the amount of conflict between parents, economic hardship, and above all, the emotional quality of parent-child relationships.

In their article, Frank F. Furstenberg and Andrew J. Cherlin take a more detailed look at the effects of divorce on children's adjustment. They find that divorce is a long process, not a single event. Like Demo, they find that much of the negative impact of divorce on children stems from conflict between the parents. Indeed, there is evidence that children from divorcing families begin to have problems well before the parents separate. A key factor in children's well-being after divorce is the quality of the child's relationship with the custodial parent, usually the mother.

THE NEW PARENTHOOD

No matter how eagerly the first child is awaited, becoming a parent is usually experienced as one of life's major "normal" crises. In a classic article Alice Rossi (1968) was one of the first to point out that the transition to parenthood is often one of life's difficult passages. Since Rossi's article first appeared over two decades ago, a large research literature has developed, most of which supports her view that the early years of parenting can be a period of stress and change as well as joy.

Parenthood itself has changed since Rossi wrote. As Carolyn and Philip Cowan observe, becoming a parent may be more difficult now that it used to be. The Cowans studied couples before and after the births of their first children. Because of the rapid and dramatic social changes of the past decades, young parents today are like pioneers in a new, uncharted territory. For example, the vast majority of today's couples come to parenthood with both husband and wife in the work force, and most have expectations of a more egalitarian relationship than their own parents had. But the balance in their lives and their relationship has to shift dramatically after the baby is born. Most couples cannot afford the traditional pattern of the wife staying home full time; nor is this arrangement free of strain for those who try it. Young families thus face more burdens than in the past, yet the supportive family policies that exist in other countries, such as visiting nurses, paid parental leave, and the like, are lacking in the United States.

Mothers are still the principal nurturers and caretakers of their children, but the norms of parenthood have shifted—as the growing use of the term "parenting" suggests. Views of fatherhood in the research literature are changing along with the actual behavior of fathers and children in real life. Until recently, a father could feel he was fulfilling his parental obligations merely by supporting his family. He was expected to spend time with his children when his work schedule permitted, to generally oversee their upbringing, and to discipline them when necessary. Even scholars of the family and of child development tended to ignore the role of the father except as breadwinner and role model. His family participation did not call for direct involvement in the daily round of childrearing, especially when the children were babies. By contrast, scholars expressed the extreme importance of the mother and the dangers of maternal deprivation. Today, however, the role of father is beginning to demand much more active involvement in the life of the family, especially with regard to childrearing. Countering this trend, however, is the rising divorce rate of recent years, which for many children means a greatly reduced amount of life with father.

Frank Furstenberg examines these two faces of fatherhood in his article here. The old breadwinner model of fatherhood, he argues, has been replaced by two new models—the good father and bad father. The good dad is like Bill Cosby—warm, nurturant, and "as adept at changing diapers as changing tires." The bad dads are ones who duck out of their parental obligations—dropping out of their children's lives, failing to make support payments. Dads are more likely to be bad after divorce or when childbearing occurs outside of marriage. Furstenberg concludes that it is important for men to be involved in nurturing their children, and they should be encouraged do so in a variety of ways.

SINGLE MOTHERS

The rise in the divorce rate is the main reason for the dramatic increase in single-parent families since the 1970s. The vast majority of single-parent families are headed by women, and as Martha T. Mednick observes in her article here, the term "feminization of poverty" was coined to describe this segment of the population. Mednick reviews and criticizes current research on single mothers from the point of view of the mothers themselves. In the past, the single-parent family was treated as a pathological family type that had a uniform set of bad effects. Today many researchers recognize that single mothers are a diverse group and that single motherhood need not inevitably lead to negative personal or social consequences. For example, much of the depression and stress experienced by these women may be due to poverty rather than single-parent status per se. But poverty is not the only problem that confronts single mothers. Having to take over the traditionally male role of supporting and heading the family may be incongruent with assumptions about women's roles. Further, raising children as a single mother can be stressful, especially if the children are boys. Finally, even though this family form is more accepted than it used to be, the assumption that the nuclear family is the "hallmark of normality" still affects research as well as the mothers themselves.

CHILD ABUSE

While the stable two-parent family remains the ideal norm, marital conflict and divorce can be understood as one of the hazards of family life—a "normal" problem. Child abuse, by contrast, seems to be a violation of the very nature of family bonds. Yet as researchers have discovered, most child abusers are not pathological monsters, and most incidents of child abuse seem to be an exaggeration of everyday family life, rather than something apart from it. The line between "normal" punishment and abuse is sometimes hard to draw.

In their article here, Richard Gelles and Murray Strauss discuss the effect on children's lives of growing up in a violent family. Apart from the physical and emotional pain children experience in abusive households, children are at risk for having other difficulties—failing in school, getting into fights with children and adults, drinking, and drug use. Whether family violence is the cause of all these difficulties or not, they all seem to be part of a cycle of trouble and violence that occurs in all too many homes. Nevertheless, growing up in a violent family does not always produce such difficulties, and the notion that abused children are doomed to grow up to become abusive parents themselves is a great exaggeration of the truth. Many people "survive" maltreatment and go on to lead normal and productive lives.

REFERENCES

Rossi, A. Transition to Parenthood. *Journal of Marriage and the Family*, 1968, 30:26–39.

Zelizer, V.A. *Pricing the Priceless Child*. NY: Basic Books, 1985.

Chapter
7

Children

Reading 21 11/10/94

The Social Transformation of Childhood

Robert A. LeVine and Merry White

INTRODUCTION

During the past 200 years the conditions of child development in much of the world have changed more drastically than they had in millennia—perhaps since the spread of agrarian conditions after 7000 B.C. The history of this recent change can be traced numerically, with school enrollments rising and infant mortality rates falling as countries industrialized, populations moved to the city, and families reduced their fertility. It can be told as a moral tale, with the elimination of child labor and illiteracy, when parents and public policymakers alike recognized the rights and expanded the opportunities of children. It can be, and often is, looked upon as a struggle for the welfare of children that is not yet won, particularly since many of the conditions abolished in the industrial countries (e.g., high infant mortality, illiteracy, and child labor) still exist in the Third World.

However one regards this shift, it represents a fundamental change not only in the means by which children are raised but in the reasons for which they are brought into the world and the goals they pursue during their lives. It is a change that is only beginning to be understood in terms of its history, its causes, and its contemporary directions. This chapter provides an overview of its major elements, particularly in the West, and considers its implications for the comparative analysis of parenthood and child development. The social changes reviewed here have undermined traditional agrarian conceptions of the life span, particularly the centrality of fertility and filial loyalty in the social identities of men and women. This shift has occurred in the industrial countries of the West, Eastern Europe, and Japan. It has been occurring, and continues, in certain countries of the Third World, although not uniformly within those countries. That the shift deserves to be called "revolutionary" can hardly be disputed; the question is whether it should be thought of as one revolution or many. Are all the socioeconomic, demographic, educational, and ideological changes involved but different aspects of one comprehensive process of social transformation (for example, "modernization"), or separable processes that happen to be linked in particular historical cases? Are the sequences and outcomes of recent change—particularly in Japan and the Third World—replicating those of the past, particularly of nineteenth century Europe and the United States?

This question, even in specific regard to family life, has long concerned sociologists, but many chose to answer it by assuming there was a unitary process driving history in a single direction. More empirical knowledge, however, has made theories of global modernization, like the classical Marxist stages of history, seem examples of what Hirschman (1971) has called "paradigms as a hindrance to understanding": Sociologists prevented taking diversity seriously enough, until documentation of diversity overwhelmed the very theories that had denied their importance. Fortunately, social scientists have brought a wealth of new evidence to bear on questions of historical change in family life and the conditions of child development in social and cultural settings throughout the world. This points to a history of the family adapting to specific local conditions rather than moving in one preordained direction.

The abandonment of unilinear evolution as a conceptual framework for analyzing social change in family life does not mean the denial of recurrent trends that can be documented and are clearly significant. On the contrary, those broad trends must be the starting point for our inquiry. This article begins with a brief consideration of the radically diverse perspectives from which children are viewed in the contemporary world, both in the private contexts of family life and in the public contexts of national and international policy. Then questions follow: How did it come to be this way? How did human societies develop such differing perspectives on children? This amounts to asking how—given a world with primary agrarian perspectives only two centuries ago—did some societies move so far from these perspectives?

THE MEANINGS OF CHILDREN: DIFFERENCES AND SIMILARITIES IN THE CONTEMPORARY WORLD

In contrast with agrarian values common to much of the world two centuries ago, the cultures of contemporary industrialized countries, particularly their middle-class subcultures, tend to value parent-child relationships that provide unilateral support—economic, emotional, and social—to children, with parents not expected to receive anything tangible in return. The period of such support in Western societies has been lengthening, from childhood through adolescence into adulthood, and the proportion of family resources devoted to children has been increasing.

The current state of the evidence has been summarized by Hoffman and Manis (1979):

> [The] economic value of children is particularly salient among rural parents and in countries where the economy is primarily rural. In addition, children are often seen as important for security in old age. Children are valued for this function, particularly in an age where there is no official, trusted, and acceptable provision for the care of the aged and disabled.
>
> In a highly industrialized country like the United States, however, with a government-sponsored social security system, children are less likely to have economic utility. Even their utility in rural areas might be lessened because of rural mechanization and the greater availability of hired help. And, since the cost of raising children is higher in the more urban and industrially advanced countries, children are not likely to be seen as an economic asset (p. 590).

When a national sample of Americans was asked about the advantages of having children, only 3.1% of the white mothers with more than 12 years of schooling gave answers involving economic utility (Hoffman and Manis, 1979, p. 585). The rest of that subsample mentioned a variety of social, emotional, and moral benefits. The responses of East Asian mothers to this question help to place the American figure in a global context (Table 21.1).

In the industrial countries, Japan and Taiwan, the proportion of urban middle-class respondents mentioning the economic utility of children is virtually identical

Table 21.1   ADVANTAGES OF HAVING CHILDREN: PERCENTAGE MENTIONING ECONOMIC UTILITY[a]

	Urban middle class	Rural
Japan	2	11
Taiwan	3	36
Philippines	30	60

[a] *Source:* Arnold, 1975, Table 4.4.

to that of the more educated white mothers in the United States, despite differences in culture. In the Philippines, a largely agrarian country, the proportion of the urban middle class perceiving economic benefits in children is ten times higher. Within each of the three Asian countries, with national policies of old-age assistance held constant, the rural proportion is at least twice as high as that of the urban middle class. While such figures from one limited question are only suggestive, they show the magnitude of the differences in attitudes and their powerful association with agrarian life both within and between contemporary countries.

The fact that the majority of middle-class parents in industrial countries expect no tangible return from children can be seen as paradoxical, not only from the perspective of utilitarian economics, which assumes that substantial investment must be motivated by the expectation of material return, but also from the viewpoint of agrarian cultures, in which reciprocity between the generations is a basic principle of social life. It does not seem paradoxical to most contemporary Westerners, who take it for granted that the parent-child relationship is exempted from ideas of material return and long-term reciprocation.

Indeed, the Western notion that the welfare of children should represent the highest priority for society as well as parents and that children should be unstintingly supported without calculation of reward—a revolutionary idea in world history—has established itself as an unchallengeable principle of international morality. The most fervent support for the idea, however, continues to come from northwestern Europe and the United States, where the public defense of children is an established cultural tradition, religious and secular, generating symbols used to arouse intense emotions, mobilize voluntary activity, and subsidize programs of action.

What is most remarkable about this basically Western ideology that has been accepted in international forums as a universal moral code is that it entails a passionate concern with the welfare of *other people's children.* In other words, it presumes that the current well-being and future development of children are the concern and responsibility not only of their parents but of a community—local, national, and international—that is not based on kinship. Westerners are proud, for example, of the long and ultimately successful campaign against child labor waged by reformers in their own countries, but their ideology requires that such benefits be extended to all children everywhere. In some Western countries such as Sweden, the Netherlands, and Canada, there is more concern with and activity on behalf of poor children in Third World societies than there is among the privileged segments of the latter societies. This gap in cultural values belies the apparent consensus embodied in United Nations declarations and points to the radical disagreement about practices such as child labor that would emerge if Western reformers tried harder to implement their ideas as global programs of action. How did the West acquire its contemporary cultural ideals concerning parent-child relationships and other people's children? That is the question to be explored in this chapter, in terms of four topics: (1) the shift from agrarian to urban-industrial institutions, (2) the demographic transition, (3) mass schooling, and (4) the rise of a public interest in children.

THE SHIFT FROM AGRARIAN TO URBAN-INDUSTRIAL INSTITUTIONS

The industrialization of Europe and North America made its primary impact on the family through the rise of wage labor and bureaucratic employment as alternatives to agricultural and craft production, the consequent separation of the workplace from the home and of occupational from kin-based roles and relationships, the migration from rural villages to concentrated settlements where jobs were available, and the penetration of labor market values into parental decisions regarding the future of children. Each of these channels needs to be analyzed in terms of how it operated to alter the assumptions on which agrarian parents had based their conceptions of childhood.

The rise of wage labor and bureaucratic employment meant first that an increasing number of children would make their future living through jobs that were unfamiliar to their parents and which the latter could not teach them. This was in itself a break with the agrarian tradition, in which the work roles of one generation largely replicated that of its forebears: If a parent had not himself mastered the skills his child would live by, he had kin, neighbors, or friends who had. Under the new conditions, however, increasing numbers of parents would have to acknowledge that they lacked not only the specific competencies required by their children for future work, but also the social connections with others who had the skills.

This decline in the parental capacity to provide training for subsistence was accompanied by a loss of supervisory control, as children and adults worked in factories, shops, and offices under other supervisors. The dual role of the agrarian parents as nurturers and supervisors of their immature and adult children working at home—a role they could transfer to foster parents through apprenticeship in domestically organized craft workshops—was not possible when employers and foremen had no social ties with the parents of their laborers. This set the stage for the abuses of child labor that ultimately led to its abolition.

Equally significant, however, was the liberation of adult workers from parental supervision in domestic production, even as they were exploited by industrial employers. Industrialism in the West cast off the kinship model of relationships that had prevailed in craft production in favor of a rationalistic and contractual model of work relationships now thought of as bureaucratic. Industrial paternalism was not unknown, but the polarization of work versus family roles and relationships rose with increasing mass production, labor migration, and the creation of a heterogeneous work force that lacked preexisting social ties or common origins. The workplace required of employees not only skills but conformity to a new code of social behavior not foreshadowed in the domestic group; it resocialized workers and gave them new identities distinct from those of birth and marriage. But since work for a particular firm was often not permanent, identification with it as an object of loyalty and idealization was the exception rather than the rule. Industrial employment was contractual, and the social identities of workers came to incorporate this sense of contractual distance from the firm. Sprung loose from the permanence of agrarian kin and community affiliations and from the parental control involved in domestic production, the more mobile industrial workers found new identities in religious sects, nationalism, voluntary associations—and in the ideals of organizations like trade unions and professional associations that were organized by occupation but offered membership more permanent than employment with any firm was likely to be. Whether one views this trend as facilitating personal autonomy or promoting anomie and social disintegration, it meant the greater salience of models of behavior that were not based on domestic relationships. It also meant a decline in parental control as an expectable concomitant of work roles.

Large-scale industrialization draws people from the countryside into concentrated settlements, either large cities with many functions or specialized industrial communities such as mining and mill towns, and this relocation is likely to have a great impact on the family. This does not mean the breakup of family and kin networks, for social historians and anthropologists have shown how resourceful rural migrants were and are in preserving these ties after moving to the city. But urbanization eroded many of the premises on which agrarian family values rested. The availability of residential housing, wild game, and assistance from neighbors, for example, had been taken for granted in many rural areas, but the migrant to the city found such resources to be commodities that had to be purchased, and at a steep price. Many more consumer goods were available in urban centers, and material aspirations quickly rose, but migrants had to develop a new awareness of what things cost in relation to their limited incomes. Thus, urbanization encouraged families to examine the choices in their lives in explicitly economic terms.

The family's recognition of having moved from country to city in order to better its economic position through employment was another important, if indirect, influence on the parent-child relationship. In the rural areas it had been possible to see one's residence, occupation, and social position as simply inherited together from the past and therefore fixed, but the knowledge of having moved to where jobs were inevitably gave subjective priority to occupation and earnings as the source of the family's position, and it encouraged the younger generation to think of improving their lives through maximizing their incomes.

In the cities and increasingly even outside them, the influence of the labor market on parental thinking and family decision-making grew. Childhood was seen as a time for offspring to acquire whatever skills would enhance their future employability in a competitive labor market where workers outnumbered jobs. The uncertainties inherent in this situation brought new anxieties to parents. In the agrarian past, the future position and livelihood of a son was preordained through inheritance of land and an inherited role in domestic production, that of a daughter through marriage. Parents helped their children marry and start a household, but (except where primogeniture was the rule) did not have to find occupations for their sons. The rise of industrial employment eroded the predictability inherent in this agrarian situation, forced parents to concern themselves more broadly with what would become of their children once they grew up, and offered hope for success in the future labor market only through adequate preparation in childhood. The domestic group, once the setting for the entire life cycle in its productive as well as relational dimensions, became a temporary nest for the nurturance of fledglings who would leave to wrest a living from an uncertain and competitive outside world. Parent-child relations, once conceived as a lifelong structure of reciprocity, were increasingly thought of as a support and nurturance system provided by adults to their immature offspring, leaving the future relationship ambiguous.

By moving to cities, European families in the 19th century were moving closer to expanding urban school systems and enhancing the likelihood that their children would become enrolled. As the population of each country became more concentrated through urbanization, the difficulties of distributing formal education were reduced and literacy grew. Urban populations were in fact generally more exposed than rural ones to the laws and programs of increasingly active and bureaucratized national governments, and schooling provided children contact with the symbols and doctrines of the national state.

Urbanization became a mass phenomenon in the 19th century as European villagers migrated to cities and towns in Europe, North and South America, Australia, and New Zealand, and they have continued to do so throughout the present century. In 1800 only 7.3% of the population of all these regions (including in South America only Argentina, Chile, and Uruguay) lived in settlements of at least 5000 people; by 1900 it was 26.1% and in 1980 it was 70.2%. Western Europe urbanized earliest and most heavily. Great Britain had by 1850 become the first major country with more than half its population residing in cities; by 1900 the figure was 77%, and by 1980 it was 91%. The major industrial cities of England and Germany grew to ten times their size and those of France grew by five times in the course of the 19th century alone. These figures show how large was the proportion of families affected by industrial employment. Urban migrants did not necessarily lose their kin ties nor the significance of kinship in their lives, but their livelihoods and those of their children depended on the labor market. This was an irreversible change, and it reached into the countryside, commercializing work relationships in agriculture and inducing even rural parents to regard wage labor as a major alternative way of life for their children.

Thus, industrialization and urbanization changed the economic basis of family life (i.e., the role of the family as a productive unit) and replaced the local age-sex hierarchy of rural communities with new social identities and sources of motivation centered on the urban occupational structure. This trend has long been known in general terms, but it is only in recent decades that social historians have investigated whether and how particular Western countries fit into the general picture. Did they all start at the same place? Did they change in the same ways in terms of sequence and intensity? Did they arrive at the same outcomes in terms of resultant patterns of family life and child development? While the evidence is far from complete, the answer to all these questions is no.

It has been shown, for example, that contractualism in property relations within and outside the family, as well as the separation of adolescent and preadolescent children from their parents, has a much longer history in England than on the Continent, and MacFarlane (1977) argues that these patterns antedate even England's preindustrial economic development, representing a cultural tradition that sets England apart from the rest of Europe. While his cultural argument is subject to controversy, there is no dispute concerning English primacy in industrial development and urbanization and in the utilitarian ideology of market relationships that social scientists have seen as an integral part of the urban-industrial transformation. In other words, England, along with its American colonies and the Calvinist communities of the Netherlands, Geneva, and Scotland, may in the 17th century have had many of the social and psychological characteristics that the rest of Europe did not acquire until the urban-industrial transformation of the mid-19th century.

Similarly, the preindustrial family structures of the Western countries were far from identical, and some of them can plausibly be seen as preparing rural families for urban life under industrial conditions. Wherever the rules of inheritance did not permit the division of family land, for example, the "stem family" in rural populations assured only the heirs of a future on the parental land and created for the other sons something closer to the uncertainty of the industrial labor market. This situation in Sweden and Ireland was a factor in early (i.e., pre-19th century) migration of rural labor to urban markets at home and abroad. The United States, with its lack of a feudal tradition and expanding rural as well as urban settlements, provided more opportunities for migration into newly established communities that were less dominated by inherited kinship and status relationships than those of Europe. Thus, the Western countries, far from being homogeneous in culture and family structure before major industrial and urban development, were significantly varied in ways that bore directly on how they would enter and experience that historical transition.

It is equally clear that the processes of industrial and urban development were not the same throughout the West. France, for example, never became urbanized to the extent that England did. A much larger proportion of Frenchmen remained in rural villages, participating in agriculture. In Italy and the United States, urban growth and industrialization were heavily concentrated in the northern regions, leaving the south rural and "under-developed" down to the present, but this was not the case in smaller and more densely populated countries like the Netherlands. Hence, the suddenness of the shift from agrarian to urban-industrial conditions, the proportions of the population that were uprooted from rural areas and absorbed in the urban labor force, the continuity of urban centers with a preindustrial culture, and many other factors were variable among (and within) the Western countries and are highly relevant to family life and the raising of children.

Do such historical variations make a difference in terms of late 20th century outcomes? Not if outcomes are measured only by economic indicators such as gross national product per capita and demographic indicators such as birth and death rates for all the countries of the contemporary world. In these comparisons, the Western countries stand out (with Japan) at the high end economically and the low end demographically—particularly in contrast with the Third World. There are major differences among the Western countries, however, in the results of industrial and urban development, especially in regard to the quality of life.

The contrast between the United States and virtually all of Europe in residential mobility, for example, is enormous and of great significance in how occupational identities and local ties affect childhood and adult experience. Divorce, female participation in the work force, and the extent of government welfare entitlements are other widely varying quantitative factors that affect both the individual life course and family life among the Western countries. On the qualitative side, the salience of social class divisions, trade union affiliations, and religious participation represent other variables that create differing contexts for life experience in the several countries of the West.

It is clear, then, on the basis of available evidence that industrial and urban development has not simply homogenized Western countries as social environments for the development of children. These countries did not enter the transition from agrarian life at the same places, did not undergo quite the same historical experiences, and did not arrive at identical destinations in terms of the conditions of family life and childhood. Their similarities in the urban-industrial transitions are well established, particularly in comparison with other parts of the world, but neither the process nor the outcome of the transition should be considered uniform.

THE DEMOGRAPHIC TRANSITION

Between the late 18th and mid-20th centuries Western birth and death rates declined drastically, eliminating the agrarian expectations of natural fertility and a relatively short life as normal features of the human condition. The impact on family life was as great as that of the more or less concomitant decline in domestic production and child labor. So many conditions affecting the family were changing during that time, however, that the connections between socioeconomic and demographic change are matters of theoretical controversy rather than straightforward fact. "Demographic transition theory" (Caldwell, 1982, pp. 117–133) includes all historical formulations that assume the inevitability and irreversibility of declining birth and death rates and the coupling of those declines to each other and to other socioeconomic trends, regardless of those factors to which the change is attributed. From this chapter's perspective, demographic transition theory is interesting not only because it attempts to make sense of secular trends affecting parents, but because it explicitly suggests parallels between 19th century Europe and the contemporary Third World. Recent research in historical demography makes possible comparisons between what happened in the West and Japan and what is now happening in the rest of the world.

The basic facts have been succinctly summarized by van de Walle and Knodel (1980, p. 5):

> In the first half of the 19th century, there were two general levels of birth rates in Europe. West of an imaginary line running from the Adriatic to the Baltic Sea, birth rates were under 40 per 1,000 persons per year—the result of late marriage and wide spread celibacy—and death rates were in the '20s. East of the line, universal and early marriage made for birth rates above 40 per 1000—not unlike those in much of Asia and Africa today—while death rates were in the '30s. Now, at the end of the transition, most birth rates are under 15 per 1000 in Western Europe and only a little higher in Eastern Europe. And death rates on both sides of the line are down to about 10 per 1000.

The magnitude of these shifts, particularly if they are considered irreversible, deserves to be emphasized: Contemporary Europeans bear only one-third as many children and have a death rate only half as high as Europeans in the early 19th century. The decline in infant mortality was even more precipitous, from early 19th century rates of about 200 infant deaths in every 1000 births to about 10 at present; contemporary Europeans thus lose only 1/20th as many infants as their forebears in 1800. Similar changes occurred at roughly the same time in North America and Australia.

The timing, sequence, and socioeconomic concomitants of these shifts are important to an understanding of how they might have affected, and been affected by, parental attitudes. Crude death rates, though not infant mortality, dropped moderately and gradually throughout the 19th century, then more steeply after 1900. The onset of mortality decline, probably in the late 18th century, was well in advance of improvements in medicine and has been attributed by McKeown (1976) to the greater availability of potatoes and maize, which improved the diet of ordinary people and made them more resistant to infection. Fertility, having increased in the late 18th century, began to decline around 1880 (much earlier in France, Switzerland, and the United States), had dropped substantially by 1920, and continued its decline in the mid-20th century. Infant mortality declined little in the 19th century, except in Sweden, but dropped precipitously between 1900 and 1920 (due to improved water and sanitation and the pasteurization of milk), continuing its decline thereafter.

When European parents started to limit the number of their children, they had not yet experienced the enhanced probability of infant survival that came with the 20th century. Thus, the *onset* of fertility decline cannot be attributed to the greater parental confidence in child survival that follows reduced infant mortality. Whatever their reasons for limiting births (which are still a matter of speculation), they accomplished it through abstinence and withdrawal—methods theoretically available to all humans—rather than through advances in contraceptive technology. Parents in the 19th century were healthier on the average and living longer than their forebears, and they had large families that were less likely to be disrupted by the death of a parent during the reproductive years. The drop in infant mortality that followed the onset of fertility decline probably strengthened the trend but could not have instigated it.

Deliberate birth limitation on the scale that occurred in Europe and North America in the late 19th and early 20th centuries was unprecedented in human history, and seems to have marked a turning point in concepts and conditions of child development. The small-family ideal that emerged represented a departure from agrarian values toward a view of parent-child relations attuned to an urban-industrial economy, one in which each child signified increased costs and reduced contributions.

The relations of fertility decline to the urban-industrial transition and the spread of schooling are discussed below. At this point it should be noted that each of the major demographic trends of the 19th and 20th centuries seems to have been instigated by changes in socioeconomic conditions and subsequently amplified by use of new medical technologies rather than the other way around. Thus, the decline in crude death rates around 1800 may have resulted from an improved diet due to the more abundant and nutritious food supply of early capitalistic economies, though the trend was certainly strengthened later on by better medical care. Fertility decline began because married couples decided to limit births and used existing techniques, though their efforts were later facilitated by the availability of contraceptive technology. Infant mortality may have begun to decline after fertility was limited due to better parental care for each of fewer children, though the trend was powerfully strengthened by public sanitation (water and sewerage), the pasteurization of milk, immunization, and more effective drugs. In other words, demographic transition should not be seen as the simple result of changes in biotechnology but rather as the outcome of parental responses to changing socioeconomic conditions.

The West, Eastern Europe, and Japan arrived at roughly the same demographic destination by the last quarter of the 20th century, with only a few exceptions. Their birth and death rates are low and vary within a narrow range. They did not begin the demographic transition at the same place, however, and did not move along identical pathways to their present positions. In other words, it would be a mistake to conclude that their current similarities in comparison with Third World societies are the outcomes of the same historical process or represent a shared historical background. This is particularly important to bear in mind when attempting to generalize from their past patterns of change in order to forecast what is possible and probable for the Third World.

As historical demography is pursued in greater depth, more country-specific patterns—including features of the pretransitional social order—are identified as having been crucial to the process of demographic transition. Wrigley (1983), for example, argues that household formation in England from the 17th century was sensitive to the cost of living. Couples postponed marriage—and therefore childbearing—when prices were high, thus reducing the birth rate. The customary practices by which families regulated the establishment of reproductive unions in response to economic conditions constitute a type of influence on fertility prior to the industrial revolution that might have facilitated the English fertility transition at a later date.

In France and the United States the secular decline in birth rates began before 1800—perhaps a century before the rest of Europe—and probably for different reasons. In both countries, however, the decline was initiated before industrialization and urbanization. This is particularly noteworthy because neither France nor the United States became as urban in the proportions of their populations living in cities as England and some of the other industrial countries. In other words, the forefront of fertility decline in the 19th century occurred in settings characterized by agrarian, or at least predominantly rural, conditions, contradicting the view that fertility decline is inexorably linked to urbanization.

A recent comparison of fertility decline in Japan and Sweden also emphasizes the influence of country-specific pretransitional characteristics—in this case the patriarchal stem family, which is shared by those two countries but not by others in their respective regions (Mosk, 1983). Here again the evidence points to the conclusion that the demographic transition encompasses varied trajectories to the same destinations.

MASS SCHOOLING

There were schools in Europe from ancient times, but until the 19th century a relatively small proportion of children attended them. In the 50 years between 1840 and 1890 primary school attendance was enormously broadened and became compulsory in Western Europe, North America, and Australia. This marks one of the most radical shifts in the parent-child relationship in human history. Mass schooling must be seen as both a reflection of powerful antecedent trends in social, political, and economic conditions and a determinant of subsequent changes in reproduction and family life. The extension of schooling in the individual life span and its expansion across the globe have proved to be irresistible and apparently irreversible tendencies, fundamentally altering the way children are regarded.

How did mass schooling affect the parent-child relationship? First, it kept children out of full-time productive work and minimized their economic contributions to the family. It furthermore established in a public and unavoidable way that childhood was dedicated to preparation for adult roles outside the family. It gave children a certain kind of power vis-à-vis their parents, either because the latter saw their better educated children as bearers of potentially higher social status or because the children themselves, having gained access to a new world of valuable skills and information, asserted themselves more within the family. Assertive, school-going children cost more than compliant children who work under parental supervision in domestic production; they required a larger share of family resources for their clothes, for space in which to study, and for the satisfaction of the consumer tastes they acquired outside the home. Their demands, implicit and actual, were strongly supported by the wider society, particularly after compulsory school legislation, which had the effect of informing parents that the state had officially determined how their offspring should spend their time during childhood.

The parental response to this revolutionary change was initially to minimize its impact, then to devise strategies to maximize the advantages it offered. At first children enrolled in school were frequently kept home when their work was needed, as attested by daily attendance figures. In 1869–1870, for example, although 57% of the United States population aged 5 to 17 was enrolled in school, only 35% attended daily. Even those children who did attend daily were probably required to perform chores at home and to "make themselves useful" to their parents. Caldwell (1982, pp. 117–131) has argued that so long as this was the case, parents could realistically consider numerous offspring advantageous even if they were not directly involved in domestic production. Eventually, however, the advantages of children in performing household chores must have been outweighed by their rising costs to the family, particularly if parents could not count on benefiting from their children's future wages, thus creating an economic incentive for birth control. According to Caldwell's theory, however, this shifting cost-contribution ratio was subjectively experienced in terms of parental ideology rather than economic calculation.

A new model of parenthood arose, with the goal of optimizing life chances for each of a few children through extended education and a measure of adult attention that had formerly been reserved for heirs to the throne. "Quality" replaced "quantity" as the focus of child-rearing efforts, first in the middle classes but with a rapid spread into other classes.

The new model was effective as a strategy for optimizing the competitive position of offspring in a labor market that increasingly favored more education and personal autonomy, but what did it do for parents? Not very much in material terms, for economic "returns" to parents were usually unfavorable. The code of filial reciprocity that had prevailed in agrarian communities was no longer binding on adult children, at least to a dependable degree. But something happened which cannot be accounted for in strictly economic terms; parents came to identify with the children in whom they had invested so much of themselves as well as their resources, and they were able to derive subjective satisfaction from the economic and reproductive careers of their children even in the absence of material support. The history of ideological sources of this subjective satisfaction is considered in the following section.

The history of schooling in the West varied from one country to another. Before 1800 schooling (often limited to literacy acquisition) was widespread in England, Scotland, the United States, the Netherlands, and Prussia. In these countries, between 40 and 60% of the entire male population attended school, if only for a few years, and became literate. In the rest of Europe smaller proportions ever attended school or became literate. Thus, the nineteenth century opened with major differences in educational development among the countries of Europe.

Schooling was extended through diverse forms of organization. Prussia pioneered the development of a governmentally planned and hierarchically organized school system, and France also built a centrally controlled national network of schools. England, on the other hand, had a wide and unregulated variety of religious and private schools, many of them of poor quality, until late in the 19th century, and never imposed the bureaucratic controls found in France. In the United States schools were built and managed under state and local control (and financing), with a degree of decentralization unknown in Europe. These institutional variations affected long-range outcomes, for variability in school quality by social class in England and by locality (which is correlated with social class) in the United States have remained strong into present times. Hence, the relations of schools to the central government and to the national system of social status have varied widely across Western countries.

THE RISE OF PUBLIC INTEREST IN CHILDREN

There can be no doubt that European attitudes toward children changed radically during the 19th century, but the changes had so many expressions and concomitants that they are not simple to describe or explain. Furthermore, ideas spread more quickly from one country to another than economic, demographic, and institutional patterns, and became harder to isolate for analysis. Most of the revolutionary ideas of the 19th century had been formulated in earlier centuries, and questions remain as to when their impact was fully felt. Stone (1977) and Plumb (1980) trace some of these ideas to the second half of the 17th century in England. On the Continent, the ideas formulated by Rousseau in *Emile* early in the 18th century were basic to the changing concepts of child development and education a century and more later. Pestalozzi, the 18th century Swiss educator, spread these concepts to Prussia before 1800.

This complex intellectual and social history is still being investigated by professional historians and remains an area of controversy. From a comparative perspective, however, its outlines are clear. Western conceptions of childhood after 1500 reflected a growing and changing debate over freedom, individualism, and authority. At first this debate was conducted in religious terms and was associated with the rise of Protestant Christianity. Calvinism conceptualized the child as born with a will of its own, but viewed this as symptomatic of original sin, to be subdued by parental authority in the interests of moral virtue and divinely sanctioned moral order. Later, philosophers such as Locke and Rousseau proposed the natural goodness of the child and an acceptance of the child's playful impulses as beneficial for education and individual development. Such ideas grew in influence during the eighteenth century, particularly in the arts (e.g., the poetry of William Blake) and in philosophical discourse on education (e.g., Pestalozzi). During the same period liberal political theory—emphasizing individual freedom rather than obedience to authority—not only developed but was dramatically promulgated through the American and French revolutions. In the nineteenth century literary and artistic romanticism established an emotional climate on which the struggle for children's rights as a form of political liberation could draw. It was during the nineteenth century, then, that the sentimental idealization of childhood combined with the liberal notion that children had enforceable rights, was expressed in such cultural phenomena as the novels of Dickens and the legislative struggle against child labor.

Much of the complexity of this history derives from the fact that the debate over freedom versus constraint in childhood has not led to a final resolution but continues even today, in issues specific to contemporary contexts. Furthermore, the Western countries represent a variety of experiences with this debate in terms of the particular sequences of intellectual discourse, public policy, and effects on family life. What distinguishes the Western ideology as a whole from that of many non-Western cultures is not so much the preference for freedom, even for children, as the definition of freedom as liberation from authority—a polarity that pits options (freedom to choose) against ligatures (social constraints) in the struggle for a better life. This struggle, this morality play on behalf of children, provided the basic terms in which the modern European conceptions of the child emerged during the 19th century.

The new ideas were hostile to agrarian models of obedience and reciprocity. Focusing on childhood as a distinct and valuable phase of life, they emphasized autonomy and the child's development as a separate and equal human being, supported and protected, by loving parents as he developed his capacities to make free and intelligent choices. In philosophy, literature, and the arts, these ideas were advanced and elaborated. In psychology and child study they were justified on scientific grounds. In politics they inspired legislation to defend children against exploitation in factories and to restrict parental control. And in the family they inspired an emotional commitment that knew no precedent except in the rearing of royal princes.

The relationship of these ideas to the socioeconomic trends reviewed above and to the larger cultural ideologies from which they were derived deserves more intensive research. It is clear that these ideas were important in forming the emotional attitudes of parents and policymakers alike and thus had an important impact. It also seems true, however, that the emotional component, and particularly the sense of a struggle for children against those who do them harm, was stronger in some countries than in others. In some European countries, then, the cause of children gained a political constituency of reformers crusading against the status quo, while in others reforms were enacted, perhaps somewhat later and more peacefully as simply necessary steps required of every civilized society.

All these trends focused more public and private attention on childhood and the development of children than had previously been the case in European societies and in agrarian societies generally. Children were as never before depicted as valuable, lovable, innocent but intelligent individuals, to be cherished, protected, defended, and developed. Public and private poles of this general tendency might seem to have been in conflict, for the public laws prohibiting child labor and compelling school attendance embodied the assumption that the citizenry bore a collective responsibility for other people's children in addition to their own offspring, while romantic sentimentalism promoted an intensification of the parent-offspring bond in the most private and exclusive terms. Both poles, however, were based on the notion that every individual child was uniquely valuable to his own parents *and* to the wider society—an idea compatible with Western traditions but newly applied to children in the context of a secular national state.

The ideological complementarity of these two poles can be seen in the presumption that parents who cherished their own children would be able to support the public cause of all children through a process of identification, i.e., by imagining how they would feel if their own children were the victims of neglect or exploitation. Similarly, the argument that the development of children represented a national resource for public investment was expected to evoke in parents a complementary "investment" in the educational and occupational aspirations of their own offspring. In the larger cultural ideology that emerged, then, the potential conflict between public and private interests in children was not only conceptually reconciled but embedded in the idea of their convergence to the benefit of children.

CONCLUSIONS

All the trends reviewed above favor the bearing of *fewer* children receiving *more* attention (and other resources) over a *longer* period of their lives than was typical in agrarian societies. Changing economic, demographic, and structural conditions led Western parents in the late 19th century to perceive the allocation of greater resources to each child as enhancing the future advantage of the child in an increasingly competitive environment. Changing ideological conditions motivated their willingness to commit resources to each child without expecting a material return and to define their commitment in emotional and moral terms from which economic considerations were expunged. Similar trends have been observed in Japan and in some Third World countries as they have moved from agrarian to urban-industrial conditions.

This brief overview has also indicated differences among Western countries in the conditions of family life and child development before 1800, in the processes and sequences of change during the 19th and 20th centuries, and in the outcomes as of the present time. European countries were not homogeneous to begin with and are not homogeneous today, however much they contrast with other countries in the world. Moreover, their advances in formal education and the regulation of birth and death were not achieved by taking the same steps in the same order, but through various pathways reflecting the diversity of their socioeconomic and cultural conditions. This historical record suggests that family change will continue to reflect the diversity of settings in which it occurs. Those who formulate policy will have to pay close attention to the unique resources and limits of each setting rather than assume a universal series of prerequisites for replicating progress.

In attempting to explain how the West was transformed from its agrarian condition, it is not only diversity in local settings that must be taken into account but temporal diversity in the circumstances under which each major change occurred in a given country. Each secular trend showed at least two surges, often 80 or 100 years apart. Fertility began its major decline in the 19th century but fell sharply after World War I. Infant mortality dropped after 1900 but continued to decline thereafter until it reached present levels. The spread of primary schooling was a 19th century phenomenon, but secondary schooling as a mass process did not occur until the 20th century. New concepts of the child and education arose between the mid-17th and early 19th centuries but did not have their major institutional impact until much later. In each case the socioeconomic and ideological conditions affecting the consciousness of parents were different by the time the later surge occurred, and different social forces were mobilized to advance the trend. This makes it possible for largely economic factors to have determined the first surge and largely ideological factors the second, or vice versa. It means that secular trends cannot be treated as single historical events and that the telescoping of historical process in "late developing countries" cannot be treated as replicating lengthy European antecedents.

The general shift from "quantity" to "quality" as objectives of parental behavior is somewhat analogous to the contrast between r-selection and K-selection among animal species: r-selected species, adapted to dispersion in relatively unexploited habitats, bear numerous offspring at one time, provide minimal postpartum care, and have high rates of offspring mortality; K-selected species, adapted to more densely occupied and competitive environments, bear few offspring, provide lengthy and attentive parental care, and have low rates of offspring mortality (Wilson, 1975). There is a similarity between animal ecology and human history in the inverse relationship or "trade-off" between number of offspring and amount of parental energy expended per individual offspring as generating distinctive (and equally successful) strategies for adapting to different levels of competition.

The analogy is a limited one, however, and not only because it leaves out the distinctive channels through which adaptation is accomplished in each case: genetic and embryological mechanisms in animal ecology and the impact of social processes on parental consciousness for human history. In the human situation, the quantity-quality trade-off as an abstraction fails to capture the fact that parents in agrarian and industrial societies (unlike animals of different species) do not share a single set of reproductive goals: The economic utility of children as young labor and future old-age support, so important in agrarian settings, is minimized in industrial populations. In other words, offspring are not experienced as fulfilling the same goals for all humans. Furthermore, the parental commitment differs not only in its distribution over time and number of offspring but in other ways that need to be specified: for example, the confident expectation by agrarian parents of filial reciprocation, the emotional intensity of unilateral commitment by parents in industrial societies. In both cases, their concepts of child care are related to broader cultural ideologies not specific to the parent-child relationship, for example, the ideologies of patrilineal kinship and humanitarian liberalism. Finally, the analogy between animal adaptation and human history, however useful it is as a starting point, implies a greater uniformity of adaptive responses to environmental competitiveness than is shown by the available historical and ethnographic evidence. A theoretical model that encompasses the broad historical shift from quantity to quality in human parenthood, and cultural diversity in the ends and means of parenthood within each historical phase, is needed.

The following formulation can be proposed. For every society there is probably an optimal strategy of parental investment, i.e., a most efficient way of maximizing culture-specific parental goals through regulation of fertility and amount of parental energy expended per child. The optimal strategy is a function of: (1) the expectable lifetime costs and contributions of each child to parents (a concept similar to Caldwell's net flow of wealth between generations, but extended to include as costs and contributions anything that counts as such in a particular culture), and (2) the means available to enhance the lifetime cost-contribution ratio of a child from the average parent's point of view. The expectable cost-contribution ratio and the means available for its enhancement are in turn conditioned by prevalent socioeconomic and demographic parameters such as labor market dependence, child labor laws, compulsory schooling, urbanization, birth and infant mortality rates—plus an array of options and constraints specific to certain societies, e.g., rural landholding and inheritance patterns, white-collar employment.

The optimal strategy of parental investment for a society may not be formulated as such by its members, but it is recognized by them in their concepts of parental success and failure. The African polygynous husband with six wives and fifty children approximates an ideal in a certain kind of agrarian society, while the barren woman or man without descendants constitutes a recognizable case of failure there. Conversely, the couple raising two highly educated children is an ideal image for a Western urban society in which failure is represented by a woman with ten neglected children. Thus, the optimum strategy, though a hypothetical construct, is represented in parental consciousness through prevalent cultural models.

Insofar as there are optimal strategies of parental investment adapted to broad categories of societies, such as agrarian and industrial societies, they should be thought of as containing variation in the cultural models of parenthood within each category but not determining the symbolic content that motivates parents to commit themselves to implementing the strategy. Each society provides the symbolic content from its own traditions and prepares its members from their early years to become emotionally responsive to the symbols involved. This results in diverse implementations of a given strategy in different societies of a particular category. A cultural model of parenthood, then, reflects both a general strategy of parental investment and culture-specific prototypes for the symbolic action of parents.

At their extremes, agrarian societies contrast with industrial societies in their optimal strategy of parental investment along a quantity-quality dimension. Agrarian societies can be defined to include those in which the majority live by domestic food production involving child labor and are characterized by high birth and death rates and little schooling. Industrial societies can be defined as not only meaning a majority living by wage labor in cities but with low birth and death rates and children going to school instead of work. With such a polarized comparison it is possible to claim that for all agrarian societies the optimal strategy is to maximize the number of offspring because they contribute more than they cost and are in any event unlikely to survive in numbers exceeding demand. Similarly, one can claim that for industrial societies the optimal strategy is to minimize the number of offspring because they cost more than they contribute and have excellent—hence economically excessive—survival chances, and to provide each one with intensive and extended preparation for competition in the labor market. The evidence indicates, however, that variations in cultural models of parenthood within each of these two polar types, while not incompatible with these claims, are not trivial. Among agrarian societies parental attitudes and practices varied between preindustrial England and continental Europe (MacFarlane, 1977) and between what might be called the patriarchal cultures of Africa, the Middle East, India, and China, and the less patriarchal cultures of Southeast Asia and the Pacific.

Among industrial societies there are significant variations that can be illustrated by contemporary Japan and the United States. Despite their common commitment to minimizing the number of births and maximizing schooling, Japanese and American married couples differ in the means they typically adopt to enhance the life chances of their children. Japanese mothers become intensively involved in their young children's learning of school subjects, so they can help them with homework and preparation for exams as part of their broader definition of their identity as primary caretakers of their children. They are less likely than American mothers to work outside the home during their children's school years. American families, however, are more likely to devote themselves to their children's futures through residential mobility, i.e., moving to communities reputed to have less crime and better schools, even when the costs involved mean mothers must work for the family to afford them. There is a difference in family priorities, in concepts of what children need and who should provide it. Although middle-class Japanese and Americans could be said to share an optimal strategy of parental investment, the social conditions in which they live (for example, availability of housing, frequency of crime, variability in the standards of schools) and their cultural models of learning (see White and LeVine, 1985) differ sufficiently to lead to different styles of parental commitment. Each style incorporates a central feature derived from the respective traditions of the two countries: for Japan, the intense devotion of women to domestic tasks of economic value; for the United States, the residential mobility of the family in search of a better life. Thus, styles of parental commitment are not simply predictable from optimal strategies of parental investment, at least as broadly defined for agrarian and industrial societies. There is no reason to believe that the continuing global transformation of family life will eliminate diversity in models of parenthood or their realization in differing styles of parental commitment.

CHANGES IN THE LIFE COURSE

The changes in parenthood and the family on which this article has focused are related to a different structure of the life course in agrarian and urban-industrial societies. Here a distinction must be made between what parents want *for* their children and what they want *from* them. Parents in all societies want similar things for their children: health, economic security, and the optimization of local cultural values. Differing customary patterns of parental behavior can be seen as cultural responses to the jeopardy in which particular environments put the attainment of these goals (LeVine, 1974). Thus, peoples with high infant and child mortality will have parental practices designed to protect health and survival; those with competitive or unstable economies will have customs focused heavily on the early development of economic skills, and so forth. Parents do not differ fundamentally in the hopes that they have for their children, but in their perceptions—conditioned by folk knowledge—of the chances that the hopes will be fulfilled. Perceiving different hazards, they devise local solutions that become traditional prescriptions for parental behavior. Since traditions often change slowly or partially, the parental practices of two peoples like the Japanese and Americans are likely to vary even after the major environmental parameters that helped shape them are no longer sources of difference.

When it comes to what parents want *from* their children, however, there are the fundamental differences between agrarian and urban-industrial societies with which this chapter began. Agrarian parents want, and consider themselves entitled to, economic returns in the short run (child labor) and the long term (old-age security). These goals, and the expectation that they will be fulfilled, are predicated on a different conception of the life course than that prevailing in urban-industrial societies. Where the family depends on child labor for economic subsistence, parents are strongly motivated to continue bearing children as long as possible, that is, until the woman reaches menopause and even longer in polygynous societies where men may take younger wives to prolong their own reproductive careers. Thus, being the parent of a young child is seen as a property of adulthood in general, not only young adulthood or any other limited period within the adult life course. In contrast with the expectation of urban-industrial parents for low fertility and confinement of childbearing to young adulthood, the agrarian expectation is that the raising of children is a normal accompaniment of family life in all its phases.

The restricted period of parenthood within the life course of adults in urban-industrial societies is a major change from the agrarian past, and one that both reflects and reinforces the diminished salience of the parent-child relationship and other kin ties as defining attributes of social identity in those societies. This is clearly seen with respect to the issue of old-age security. In the agrarian context, the parental expectation of being helped by children in old age was not based on a hope of filial generosity. On the contrary, it was predicated on a social organization that connected children and parents in active relationships throughout the life span. Where there was domestic production, significant family property, and residential stability, at least some of the children were likely to be neighbors and co-workers of their parents until the latter died. Where there were also corporate descent groups, the parent-child relationship was publicly embedded in a system of intergenerational continuity and reciprocity that included a code of mutual assistance and conferred a social identity on each person.

In other words, the self-definition of a person in an agrarian society was likely to be based on kinship ties in which parentage was salient—not only when children were young but in their adulthood as well. Where parents did look to their children for assistance in old age—and this was not universal, particularly among the preindustrial societies of the West—it was as part of a local organization of relationships that defined each person's participation in society. The urban-industrial transformation was a growth of new forms of social participation not defined by kin and locality and not necessarily involving parentage, thus reducing the salience of those relationships in the social identities and self-evaluation of adults. Concepts of the parent-child relationships as a lifelong bond between adults gave way to a concept of parenthood as the raising of offspring to an autonomous maturity in which their future relationship was optional. Where parents had seen their old age as the time when the benefits of parenthood—in social respect from the community as well as kin—were most expectable, it came to be seen as the time when, for many, the nest was empty and parenthood was largely finished. The prolongation of the life span and the institutional provision of old-age pensions have also contributed to urban-industrial conceptions of the adult life course in which parenthood is an intermediate phase of adulthood, with an increasingly salient postparental phase.

REFERENCES

Arnold F., Bulatao, R., Burikpakdi, C., Chung, B., Fawcett, J., Iritani, T., Lee, S., and Wu, T. *The Value of Children. Vol. I: Introduction and Comparative Analysis.* Honolulu, HI: East-West Population Institute, 1975.

Caldwell, J. *Theory of Fertility Decline.* NY: Academic Press, 1982.

Caldwell, J. Direct economic costs and benefits of children. In R. Bulatao and R. Lee (Eds.), *Determinants of Fertility in Developing Countries,* NY: Academic Press, 1983.

Hirschman, A. O. *A Bias for Hope.* Princeton, NJ: Princeton University Press, 1971.

Hoffman, L., and Manis, J. The value of children in the United States: a new approach to the study of fertility. *Journal of Marriage and the Family,* 1979, 41:583–96.

LeVine, R. A. Parental goals: A cross-cultural view. *Teachers College Record,* 1974, 76; 226–239.

MacFarlane, A. *The Origins of English Individualism.* Cambridge, MA: Cambridge University Press, 1977.

McKeown, T. *The Modern Rise of Population.* NY: Academic Press, 1976.

Mosk, C. *Patriarchy and Fertility: Japan and Sweden, 1880–1960.* NY: Academic Press, 1983.

Plumb, J. The new world of children in eighteenth century England. In V. Fox and M. Quitt (Eds.), *Loving, Parenting and Dying.* NY: Psychohistory Press, 1980.

Stone, L. *The Family, Sex and Marriage in England, 1500–1800.* NY: Harper & Row, 1977.

van de Walle, E., and Knodel, J. Europe's fertility transition: new evidence and lessons for today's developing world. *Population Bulletin,* 1980, 34(6).

White, M., and LeVine, R. "What is an li ko?" In H. Stevenson and K. Hakuta (Eds.), *Child Development in Japan and the United States.* Philadelphia, PA: Witt, Freeman, 1985.

Wilson, E. *Sociobiology: The New Synthesis.* Cambridge, MA: Harvard University Press, 1975.

Wrigley, E. The growth of population in eighteenth century England: a conundrum resolved. *Past and Present,* 1983, 98: 121–150.

Reading 22

Parent-Child Relations: Assessing Recent Changes

David H. Demo

. . . Several dramatic structural changes have occurred in American marriage and family life over the past three decades: in the proportion of births occurring out of wedlock, the proportion of marriages ending in divorce, postponed marriage and childbearing, smaller family size, single-parent families, stepfamilies, and dual-earner marriages. One important question is how these changes have influenced parent-child relations and children's well-being. Furstenberg, Nord, Peterson, and Zill (1983) assert that "the experience of growing up has probably changed as much in the past several decades as in any comparable period in American history" (p. 667). The popular literature and media frequently blame the family for high rates of teenage sexual activity, pregnancy, delinquency, and alcohol and drug use, often citing low levels of parent-child interaction and high levels of family conflict and "broken homes." Family scholars have empirically documented that rapidly changing values, social roles, behavioral patterns, and household arrangements have negatively influenced parent-child relations.

Neal, Groat, and Wicks (1989) observe that negative and even hostile attitudes toward children are common in the United States today and that young married couples report considerable ambivalence about having and rearing children. Nock and Kingston (1988) report that dual-earner parents spend considerably less time with their children than their single-earner ("traditional") counterparts. Numerous studies find that marital dissolution and reconstitution disrupt primary bonds between parents and children and cause short-term emotional and behavioral problems for children (Hetherington, Camara, & Featherman, 1983; Kinard & Reinherz, 1984, 1986). Two recent reviews (Demo & Acock, 1988; McLanahan & Booth, 1989) document consistent empirical evidence that single parents (mostly mothers) are less involved in their children's school work, exert less parental influence, and find it more difficult to supervise and discipline their children, family processes that lead adolescents in single-parent families to exhibit significantly higher rates of deviant behavior.

From *Journal of Marriage and the Family* 54 (February 1992): 104–117.

But despite the accumulating evidence, two limitations prevent a fuller under-standing of exactly how parent-child relations have changed: (a) research in this area is ahistorical (Gecas & Seff, 1990); and (b) family research continues to be guided by traditional notions of family normality and deviance. The objective of this paper is to determine how parent-child relations have changed from the tradi-tional American family of the 1950s, and how these changes have influenced the social and psychological well-being of American children. First I examine recent structural changes in children's living arrangements, in the domestic division of labor, and in parental child-rearing values. Then I assess how the frequency and quality of parent-child interaction have been affected by maternal employment, dual-earner families, divorce, and single-parent families. I conclude by assessing the current state of parent-child interaction and the implications for children's well-being. It will be argued that, although children's well-being has declined over the past three decades (Uhlenberg & Eggebeen, 1986), the negative consequences attributed to divorce single-parent family structure, and maternal employment have been greatly exaggerated.

THE TRADITIONAL AMERICAN FAMILY AND RECENT CHANGES

The traditional American family consisted of a husband and wife married for the first time, rearing their biological children, with the male serving as the provider and the female as wife, mother, and homemaker. This ideal continues to serve as a reference point against which contemporary families are judged, despite the fact that many families did not conform to these ideals even during the nostalgic 1950s and early 1960s. In 1960, less than half (43%) of American families conformed to the traditional ideal of single-earner married couples, and nearly one fourth (23%) were dual-earner couples (Masnick & Bane, 1980). In other respects, however, children's living arrangements were quite consistent with the traditional norm. As Table 22.1 illustrates, in 1960 the vast majority (nearly 88%) of children under age 18 lived with two parents, only 9% with one parent, and 3% with neither parent. Among blacks, two thirds (67%) of children lived with two parents and 20% lived in mother-only households.

The percentage of single-parent, predominantly female-headed households has increased steadily since the end of World War II. But the most important changes have been in the events and processes associated with the formation and composition of single-parent families. Table 22.2 indicates that in 1959, the pre-ponderance of single-parent families were headed by widows (45%), three times the percentage headed by divorced parents. These patterns changed quickly over the ensuing three decades. In 1989, the largest percentage (39%) of single-parent families were precipitated by divorce, nearly one third (31%) were headed by never-married parents, one fourth (24%) were characterized as spouse-absent (usually separated), and only 6% were headed by widowed parents. Changes in children's living arrangements have been much more pronounced among blacks.

Table 22.1   LIVING ARRANGEMENTS OF CHILDREN UNDER 18,
BY RACE AND HISPANIC ORIGIN

Living arrangement	1960	1970	1980	1989
All races (1,000s)	63,727	69,162	63,427	63,637
Percentage living with:				
Two parents	87.7	85.2	76.7	73.1
One parent	9.1	11.9	19.7	24.3
Mother only	8.0	10.8	18.0	21.5
Father only	1.1	1.1	1.7	2.8
Other relatives	2.5	2.2	3.1	2.1
Nonrelatives only	0.7	0.7	0.6	0.4
White (1,000s)	55,077	58,790	52,242	51,134
Percentage living with:				
Two parents	90.9	89.5	82.7	79.6
Mother only	6.1	7.8	13.5	16.1
Father only	1.0	0.9	1.6	2.7
Other	1.9	1.8	2.2	1.6
Black (1,000s)	8,650	9,422	9,375	9,835
Percentage living with:				
Two parents	67.0	58.5	42.2	38.0
Mother only	19.9	29.5	43.9	51.1
Father only	2.0	2.3	1.9	3.4
Other	11.1	9.7	12.0	7.5
Hispanic (1,000s)	—	4,006	5,459	6,973
Percentage living with:				
Two parents	—	77.7	75.4	67.0
Mother only	—	—	19.6	27.8
Father only	—	—	1.5	2.7
Other	—	—	3.5	2.5

Sources: U.S. Bureau of the Census, *Marital Status and Living Arrangements,* Current Population Reports, Series P-20. March 1988, No. 433, Table A-4; and March 1989, No. 445, Table 4.

Notes: Excludes persons under 18 years old who were maintaining households or families. Blacks compiled as nonwhites in 1960. Persons of Hispanic origin may be of any race. Some figures for Hispanics in 1960 and 1970 are not available.

In 1989, never-married parents constituted the largest proportion (53%) of black single parents, 23% were spouse-absent, 19% were divorced, and less than 5% were widowed.

In addition to these changes in single-parent families, the structure and dynamics of two-parent families also have changed in that a sizable number of children are living in stepfamilies, without one of their biological parents. Today, only 7% of American households comprise traditional married couples with an employed father, housewife mother, and two or more school-age children (Otto, 1988). In short, there is now much greater diversity in family structure than 30 years ago. But perhaps more consequential for parent-child relations have been

Table 22.2   NUMBER AND PERCENTAGE OF CHILDREN UNDER
18 LIVING WITH ONLY ONE PARENT, BY MARITAL
STATUS OF PARENT, RACE, AND HISPANIC ORIGIN

	1959	1989
All children living with one parent (1,000s)	9,165	15,493
Percentage living with single parent who is:		
Never married	—	30.9
Spouse absent	38.7	23.8
Widowed	45.4	6.4
Divorced	14.8	38.9
White children living with one parent (1,000s)	6,466	9,626
Percentage living with single parent who is:		
Never married	—	18.9
Spouse absent	30.2	23.8
Widowed	50.7	7.0
Divorced	17.5	50.3
Black children living with one parent (1,000s)	2,699	5,362
Percentage living with single parent who is:		
Never married	—	53.1
Spouse absent	59.0	23.2
Widowed	32.9	4.6
Divorced	8.1	19.1
Hispanic children living with one parent (1,000s)	—	2,129
Percentage living with single parent who is:		
Never married	—	31.8
Spouse absent	—·	35.7
Widowed	—	5.0
Divorced	—	27.5

Sources: U.S. Bureau of the Census, Current Population Reports, Series P-20. *Family Characteristics of Persons:* March 1959, No. 112, Table 2; and *Marital Status and Living Arrangements*, March 1989, No. 445, Table 5.

Notes: Blacks compiled as nonwhites in 1959. Persons of Hispanic origin may be of any race. Some 1959 figures for Hispanics are not available.

the changes in the factors precipitating different family types, namely changing social values, teenage childbearing, divorce, remarriage, and maternal employment.

To assess the impact of these changes, however, we need to understand typical family experiences and relationships during the baseline period of the 1960s. In what ways were traditional family roles evident during this period, and how have they changed?

The Domestic Division of Labor

In the 1960s, husbands spent an average of 11 hours per week on child care and housework, while wives invested 35 to 40 hours weekly (Coverman & Sheley,

1986; Walker & Woods, 1976). Thus men spent between one third and one fourth the amount of time on domestic labor as their wives, and this pattern persisted regardless of number of ages of children or of wives' employment status. More specific to the focus of this paper of the 11 hours per week men spent in household labor, only 15 minutes per day (or less than 2 hours per week) were devoted to child care, compared to 54 minutes per day (or more than 6 hours per week) among women (Coverman & Sheley, 1986).

Some modest changes occurred during the 1970s. A number of studies report no overall changes in men's housework and child care time between the 1960s and 1970s, but there were significant decreases in the time women spent on housework (Coverman & Sheley, 1986; Sanik, 1981). There were also noteworthy increases in domestic labor among particular categories of men. Coverman and Sheley found that men under age 30 spent significantly more time in housework in 1975 than in 1965, and men with preschool children increased their child care time significantly. They suggest that changes in this younger segment of the married population may reflect a pattern of changing gender-role socialization. Pleck (1979) reported that by 1977 husbands of employed wives spent a few more hours per week on housework and child care than husbands of nonemployed wives. An analysis of data collected in 1985 indicates further increases in men's housework involvement (Robinson, 1988), but married women continue to spend twice as much time as their husbands on housework and 50% more time in child care (Barnett & Baruch, 1987).

In a study using detailed time diary data collected from married couples with children in 1981, Nock and Kingston (1988) demonstrate the importance of examining parents' work commitments in trying to understand time spent with children. On average workdays, unemployed mothers with preschoolers spend nearly 9 hours each day with their children, more than twice the time of their employed counterparts. The differences are smaller, but still substantial, among families with only school-age children: Unemployed mothers' contact with children averages 6 hours on workdays, compared to a little less than 4 hours for employed mothers. Fathers' contact with children is lower than that of mothers in all family types, averaging 2.5 hours per working day in single-earner and dual-earner families. Corroborating and clarifying the findings of Coverman and Sheley (1986), Nock and Kingston found that in families with young children, fathers with an employed wife spend considerably more time with their children on weekends than fathers with an unemployed wife. As one would expect, employed mothers also spend more time with their children on weekend days than on workdays, partially compensating for loss of time with children during the workweek.

Child-Rearing Values

We also know there have been substantial changes in parental socialization values over the past few decades, with parents in the 1950s and 1960s stressing the importance of obedience in their children and parents in the 1970s and 1980s emphasizing greater personal autonomy and responsibility (Alwin, 1986, 1990). Further, the changes occurred across American families of different religioethnic and socioeconomic categories (Alwin, 1986), and similar changes in parental values have been observed in other industrialized societies (Tromsdorff, 1983). These findings are important because, as discussed below, changes in parent-child relationships are partly due to shifting cultural values regarding traits desired in children.

An important area receiving relatively scarce attention has been the orientation of children toward their parents. Sebald (1986) observed a marked decline in adolescents' orientation toward parents between 1963 and 1976, and a corresponding increase in peer influence over the same period. By 1982 there was a very modest recovery in the valuation of parental opinions, but a continually strengthening trend toward adolescents making decisions independent of parental or peer advice. Sebald concludes that much of the overall decline in importance attached to parental opinions may be attributed to the countercultural movement of the late 1960s and early 1970s, and this is certainly a plausible, albeit partial, explanation. Another, perhaps equally important, explanation is that this is the same period during which parents were attributing greater significance to personal autonomy. Viewed in this manner, it is understandable that parental advice is sought (and followed) less frequently, although adolescents continue to seek parental advice on the most important issues, as discussed below.

In sum, children were much more likely to live with two parents in 1960 than in 1990, and contemporary children living in single-parent families are more likely to be children of unwed mothers or to have experienced family disruption. Children of all ages are more likely to have employed mothers, but women continue to spend significantly more time than their husbands on housework and child care. The traditional American family, to whatever degree it may have existed in the past, is now conspicuous by its absence.

In the next section I consider two of the most important structural changes over the past three decades and how they have influenced parent-child relations. Popular opinion holds that each of these developments has had deleterious consequences for children by reducing the amount of time parents and children spend together. First I consider the consequences of maternal employment for parent-child interaction and children's well-being, then the effects of divorce and single-parent family structure.

MAJOR DEVELOPMENTS RESTRUCTURING PARENT-CHILD RELATIONSHIPS

Maternal Employment and Dual-Earner Families

Although a recent study shows that most Americans believe that working mothers are detrimental to aspects of children's development and well-being (Greenberger, Goldberg, Crawford, & Granger, 1988), reviews of the effects of maternal employment on children demonstrate that mother's employment per se has very few adverse effects and there are, in fact, some positive effects on children's development (e.g., see Bianchi & Spain, 1986; Menaghan & Parcel, 1990; Spitze, 1988a). Importantly, many of the observed effects may be mediated by other variables, notably children's age, sex, social class, and personality characteristics; quality of substitute care (see Belsky, 1990); and mothers' occupational status (Acock, Barker, & Bengtson, 1982; Macke & Morgan, 1978).

Still, there are a number of consistent findings. Maternal employment expands role models for children, fosters egalitarian gender-role attitudes among both sons and daughters, and promotes more positive attitudes toward women and women's employment (Kiecolt & Acock, 1988; Mortimer & Sorensen, 1984; Powell & Steelman, 1982). There are also benefits of employment for mothers' self-esteem, personal efficacy, and overall well-being (Mirowsky & Ross, 1986; Rosenfield, 1989), yielding indirect benefits for children. Children, especially adolescents, often have to assume more personal and domestic responsibilities when their mothers work, which may enhance children's maturity and sense of self-reliance (Amato & Ochiltree, 1986; Hoffman, 1974). An improved standard of living resulting from maternal employment has numerous advantages, especially for children in lower socioeconomic classes. As adults, daughters of employed women are more likely to be employed and to have jobs similar to their mothers' (Stevens & Boyd, 1980).

Indeed, the evidence is sufficiently consistent and persuasive to wonder whether we are asking the most important question. That is, we continue to explore the consequences of mother's employment status in the face of compelling evidence that what is more important for children is the conditions under which mothers and fathers work, namely, substantive complexity of work, levels of supervision, work stress, and role overload (Menaghan & Parcel, 1990). Further, it is often assumed that single mothers must work to support themselves and their children (implying that employment is optional for other women). Regardless of their reasons for working, however, single, employed mothers generally have much lower family income than employed mothers in dual-earner families. The more relevant question in this case (and others) would seem to be the consequences for children of mothers not working, but unfortunately, research on the consequences of maternal employment generally ignores single parents (Spitze, 1988a).

A related question in systematically examining maternal employment concerns the short- and long-term consequences of maternal unemployment in two-parent families. In many cases the wife's income raises the family's status above poverty or from lower- to middle-class (Spitze, 1988b). In addition to social, psychological, and financial benefits stemming from steady employment, there is the preparation, security, and financial stability it provides married women in the event divorce follows, as it often does.

Regarding the quantity or frequency of parent-child interaction, the research evidence described above confirms the popular belief that employed women spend less total time with their children than nonemployed women. However, the amount of time employed mothers spend interacting directly with their children, and the quality of care they provide, are comparable to nonemployed mothers (Nock & Kingston, 1988; Stith & Davis, 1984). Further, both employed women and their husbands spend more time with their children on the weekends than their counterparts in families where the wife is not employed (Nock & Kingston, 1988). Frequently, employed women make time for their children by sacrificing time they would otherwise devote to housework or leisure (Hill & Stafford, 1980). Each of these patterns may be viewed as an indicator of parental support and concern.

Even considering lower overall levels of mother-child interaction among employed mothers, it cannot be assumed that this pattern has uniformly deleterious consequences for children. Stated differently, higher levels of interaction between nonemployed mothers and their children may become strenuous for parents and unhealthy for children. Research in the area of family violence, for example, indicates that women employed full-time are less likely to be violent toward their children than mothers with part-time jobs and mothers who are not employed (Gelles, 1987). Employment per se, of course, is a crude indicator of family relations. A more meaningful variable is the level of work and household responsibility. Gelles found that across different employment conditions (part-time, full-time, housewives), "women who reported excess domestic responsibilities had higher rates of violence and abuse than mothers with the same work status who said they had equal or less responsibility than they desired" (p. 94). Viewed in this manner, the problem of mother-child violence may be more accurately described as a function of excessive responsibilities (role strain) rather than one of employment per se.

Further evidence of this interpretation is that full-time employed mothers with nonemployed husbands, women strained by a series of demanding responsibilities, are especially likely to be violent toward their children. Considering fathers, those with employed wives are less likely to be violent, and much less likely to be abusive toward their children, compared to fathers married to nonemployed women. Gelles (1987) suggests that one explanation for this pattern may be that men with nonemployed wives hold traditional beliefs dictating that the man is head of the household and responsible for being the enforcer and disciplinarian, beliefs that often eventuate in violent behavior.

These findings also can be viewed as consistent with the hypothesis that a detached style of parental support has beneficial consequences for children, that is, that parents who are employed spend less time interacting with their children and therefore are at a reduced risk of being violent during the periods when they are with their children. Gelles (1987) found some support for what he termed the *time at risk hypothesis:* Rates of child abuse were highest among women who would normally spend the most time with their children—housewives with preschool children—and lowest among those assumed to spend the least time with their children—mothers with full-time jobs.

In sum, despite the fervor with which Americans cling to traditional notions of maternal responsibility for children, children of employed mothers fare no worse on a number of measures of well-being, and in many cases fare better, than children of nonemployed mothers.

Divorce and Single-Parent Families

It is clear that children in the 1990s are much more likely to experience the disruption of their parents' marriage and to live with a single parent than children in the 1960s. Although about one fifth of children in mother-only families have never-married mothers, most children (two thirds) in these families are living with a separated or divorced parent (Sweet & Bumpass, 1987). For many, living with one parent will be a long-term arrangement. Over half of the children whose parents divorce spend at least 6 years with only one parent, and the majority of children in single-parent families will live out their childhood without ever entering a second family (Bumpass & Sweet, 1989; Sweet & Bumpass, 1987.) For black children, most will spend the majority of their childhood years in a one-parent family (Sweet & Bumpass, 1987).

Recent reviews of the effects of divorce (Demo & Acock, 1988; Emery, 1982) and single-parent family structure (Cashion, 1984; McLanahan & Booth, 1989) indicate that these developments have some adverse effects on children, but that the effects attributable to divorce or living in a single-parent family (rather than to other factors) are not nearly as dramatic or as permanent as popularly believed. Further, divorce and living in a single-parent family are two different experiences for children and affect them in different ways.

Although popular and clinical impressions suggest that children of divorce suffer long-term deleterious effects, research on nonclinical populations consistently shows that children experience short-term emotional adjustments and that older children typically have an easier time adjusting than younger children (Hetherington et al., 1983). In addition, there is abundant evidence that levels of family conflict are more important than type of family structure for understanding children's adjustment, self-esteem, and other measures of psychological well-being (Berg & Kelly, 1979; Emery, 1982; Raschke & Raschke, 1979). Other studies indicate that children's physical well-being is unaffected by divorce, that frequent marital and family conflict in so-called intact families is detrimental to children's physical health, and that divorce may, in fact, insulate some children and adolescents from prolonged exposure to health-threatening family interactions (Gottman & Katz, 1989; Mechanic & Hansell, 1989). Of course, the term *intact* itself may be just as accurate in describing many one-parent families, particularly those with no history (or recent history) of marital disruption.

Nonetheless, children living in mother-only families fare worse on measures of intellectual performance and educational attainment (Hetherington et al., 1983; Keith & Finlay, 1988; McLanahan, 1985) and exhibit higher rates of sexual and delinquent activity. One explanation for the latter finding is that levels of parental supervision and control are lower in single-parent families, allowing adolescents more opportunities to make decisions independent of parental input (Dornbusch et al., 1985; Newcomer & Udry, 1987). In addition, Nock (1988) proposes that the absence of generational boundaries and hierarchical authority relations in single-parent families represents socialization deficits that result in lower educational and occupational attainment as adults.

The most serious consequences, however, are those related to severe and often long-lasting financial problems suffered by women and children in single-parent families. Compared to children living with both parents, those in mother-only families are five times as likely to be living below the poverty threshold (47% versus 9%); for black children, three of every five in mother-child families are living in poverty (Sweet & Bumpass, 1987). Further, and of central importance to the focus of this paper, since 1967 the economic well-being of mother-only families has worsened vis-à-vis other family types (McLanahan & Booth, 1989). Economic hardship has dire consequences for parents and children, including lower levels of parental nurturance, inconsistent discipline, and adolescent distress (Lempers, Clark-Lempers, & Simons, 1989).

Again, recognizing that methodological limitations restrict our understanding of the processes most directly impinging on children in single-parent families (see Blechman, 1982; Demo & Acock, 1988), the accumulated evidence is sufficiently consistent to wonder whether we, as researchers, are asking the most important questions, or whether we, like the families we are trying to study, are more strongly influenced by traditional notions of family normality. A substantial amount of effort has been expended trying to isolate the effects of divorce and single-parent family structure, but relatively little effort has been expended trying to understand the correlates and consequences of persistent marital and family conflict across family types and across stages of individual and family development. Indeed, reviews of the literature demonstrate that it is precisely these experiences, conflict in marital and parent-child relationships, that mediate the effect of family structure on children's well-being (Demo & Acock, 1988; Emery, 1982; also see Booth & Edwards, 1989, for an empirical illustration). Whether living with one parent or two, and whether living with biological parents or stepparents, family processes are critical to children's development and well-being.

One such family process is parental supervision and control. The documented pattern of lower levels of parental supervision in single-parent families is both important and understandable, but how are we to interpret it? Often these findings are interpreted as problems inherent in single-parent families, inevitable consequences of deviation from traditional marriage and family patterns. Viewed from a different perspective, however, the key to understanding these families and the consequences for children may be by examining processes such as participation and support by absent fathers. Long-term single parenting, usually performed by employed women, is a chronic stressor (Thompson & Ensminger, 1989). Yet visitation, involvement, and financial support by absent fathers are minimal. Using national survey data, Furstenberg, Morgan, and Allison (1987) report that more than two fifths of absent, biological fathers had no contact with their children in the preceding year, and three fifths provided no financial support (also see Seltzer & Bianchi, 1988). Importantly, in families where paternal economic support was provided, the likelihood of adolescent problem behavior was reduced.

In short, the pattern of findings described here provides compelling evidence that children, although certainly affected by divorce and single-parent family structure, are more profoundly influenced by socioeconomic resources and by the degree of involvement, support, and discipline provided by their parents. Many of our research questions and concepts continue to reflect traditional notions of marriage and family, blurring our understanding of the linkages between family structure, family interaction, and child outcomes. Divorce and single-parent families have been dramatic developments over the past three decades, but the evidence at hand suggests they may not be as important for children's well-being as paternal abandonment, neglect, and failure to pay child support.

Having addressed some of the major developments restructuring parent-child relationships, I now assess the current state of these relationships in terms of the regularity and quality of interaction.

CURRENT STATE OF PARENT-CHILD INTERACTION

Has the rapid pace of social and demographic change over the past three decades created profound discontinuities between the values of parents and children? How do parents view their children, and how do children perceive their parents? How much time do parents and children spend together, and is it *quality* time? In families where fathers are present, has their involvement in parenting changed? How pervasive are conflict and violence in contemporary parent-child relations?

Values and Attitudes

Contrary to popular myth, the bulk of evidence indicates that parents continue to value children positively, that children provide meaningful sources of happiness and social support, and that parents remain very influential in the transmission of values, especially on important issues (Bachman, Johnston, & O'Malley, 1987; Offer, Ostrov, Howard, & Atkinson, 1988; Sebald, 1986). In fact, as Acock and Bengtson (1980) have observed, the "generation gap" may be considered a social construction of reality in the sense that perceived differences between the attitudes of parents and children are much greater than actual differences. However, it appears that children generally acquire the values and attitudes they attribute to their parents, or attitudes that parents wish to instill or communicate, which may or may not correspond to parents' actual values and attitudes.

Studying a sample of parents, Meredith, Stinnett, and Cacioppo (1985) found that the majority judged parenting to be a very positive and satisfying experience. Among the greatest sources of satisfaction reported by parents were watching children grow and develop, loving their children, taking pride in their achievements, sharing experiences, passing on values, and experiencing the feeling of being part of a family. A similarly strong pattern of parental satisfaction was observed 30 years ago by Miller and Swanson (1958).

Adolescents' perceptions of parents also tend to be positive. Recent data indicate that between two thirds and three fourths of adolescents feel close to their parents, identify with them, and are satisfied with the way they get along (Bachman et al., 1987; Steinberg, Elmen, & Mounts, 1989). However, parents view the relationships as more positive and the conflicts as less severe than adolescents (Montemayor, 1986; Smetana, 1989). It is widely documented that disagreements occur regularly, especially in mid-adolescence, but that they tend to be minor and to concern mundane, everyday issues (Montemayor, 1986; also see Collins, 1990, for an excellent review). Furthermore, disagreements of this type may be viewed as adaptive in the sense that relationships are renegotiated regularly, facilitating adolescent adjustment and individuation (Holmbeck & O'Donnell, 1991).

Parental Involvement

In assessing actual parenting behavior, researchers have distinguished three types of parental involvement: engagement (direct, one-on-one interaction), accessibility (being nearby and available to meet a child's need), and responsibility (being accountable for the child's care and welfare) (Lamb, Pleck, Charnov, & Levine, 1987; LaRossa, 1988). In general, the data indicate low levels of parental engagement. The one exception, as discussed earlier, is mothers who are not employed outside the home; they have roughly twice the amount of direct contact with their children compared to employed mothers. Across family types, fathers' time with children is roughly two thirds that of mothers. Although most studies of paternal interaction involve infants and toddlers, there is evidence that children's age has an important influence on the proportion of time fathers spend in activities with their children. Studies consistently find very low levels of paternal engagement with infants (e.g., Frodi & Lamb, 1978; LaRossa & LaRossa, 1981), more frequent direct interaction with school-age children, and about the same amount of time interacting with adolescents as mothers spend, which is usually 1 hour per day (Montemayor, 1982).

However, these findings conceal more dramatic differences in parenting behavior. First, mothers continue to bear most of the child care responsibilities for young children (age 5 and under). Nock and Kingston (1988) show that fathers of preschoolers, who average 2.5 to 3 hours per workday in contact with their children, spend only about 15 minutes per day in child care; on weekends it doubles to about 30 minutes per day. Mothers of preschoolers, on the other hand, average 1 to 1.5 hours each day directly caring for young children.

With older (school-age) children, however, child care is an almost insignificant aspect of parent-child interaction, involving no more than 30 minutes for mothers or fathers. Among these families, there are only modest mother-father differences in amount of time spent in various parent-child activities. On a typical weekend day, mothers and fathers each spend about 2 hours having fun with children at museums, movies, and so forth, an hour watching television with them, and between 30 minutes and an hour eating meals with them. On average, mothers and fathers engage in no more than 10 minutes per day of direct conversation with their older children, and no more than 16 minutes talking with their preschool children.

Further, mothers spend substantially more time alone with children than fathers do. In a study of parents of kindergartners and fourthgraders, Barnett and Baruch (1987) observe that fathers spend an average of 30 hours per week in total interaction time with children, and mothers spend 45 hours (or 50% more). In terms of time alone with children, however, fathers average only 5.5 hours per week while mothers average 19.5 hours (or 350% more).

Thus, as LaRossa (1988) has observed, there has not been as much change in fathering behavior as there has been in the *culture of fatherhood*, that is, the norms, values, and beliefs concerning fathering. In most contemporary families it is the mothers who are more directly involved in childrearing responsibilities. Rather than signifying recent changes in parenting, these patterns signify the continuation of structural arrangements dating back to the late 18th and early 19th centuries whereby mothers (or female substitutes) are primarily responsible for childhood care and socialization (Vinovskis, 1987).

Violence Between Parents and Children

Straus and Gelles (1986) estimated that in 1975, nearly 4% of children aged 3 to 17 living with two parents, or approximately 1.5 million children, were abused by their parents. By 1985, they reported a 47% decline in the most severe violent acts. Although overall rates of violence did not change over the 10-year period, the researchers speculate that significant decreases in the most severe forms of violence indicate that parents' consciousness has been raised concerning the inappropriateness of abusive behavior.

Some categories of children remain vulnerable, however. Young children and children in poor and disadvantaged families are more likely to be victimized (Straus & Gelles, 1986). While violence toward children in the general (predominantly white) sample declined significantly from 1975 to 1985, among blacks minor and severe parent-to-child violence increased slightly (Hampton, Gelles, & Harrop, 1989). In addition, most cases of sexual abuse of children are perpetrated by parents, most often biological fathers victimizing their daughters (Finkelhor, 1979; VanderMey & Neff, 1984).

Another grim reflection on parent-child relations is the occurrence of child-to-parent violence. Using 1975 data on two-parent households, Gelles (1987) conservatively estimated that each year at least 9% of parents of children aged 10 to 17 (or nearly 3 million parents) are victims of violence perpetrated by their own children. Mothers were more likely than fathers to be victims, especially in cases of severe violence and parent abuse (also see Agnew & Huguley, 1989).

Reflecting the intergenerational transmission of violence, the severity of violence directed toward parents is directly related both to the severity of violence experienced by the child and to the severity of interspousal violence the child has observed (Gelles, 1987). Gelles interprets these findings as evidence that mothers are at greater risk of violence because they spend more time with their children than fathers do, because they lack the physical and social resources to defend themselves, and, perhaps most importantly, because children have observed their mothers being abused by their fathers and they "learn that mothers are an appropriate and acceptable target for intrafamily violence" (p. 165).

TOWARD A RECONCEPTUALIZATION OF PARENTAL SUPPORT

Across diverse family structures and across numerous domains of parent-child relations, the evidence reviewed above suggests a consistent pattern of *supportive detachment* in contemporary parent-child relationships. There are two noteworthy exceptions to this pattern: abusive parents and absent fathers. Most parents, however, are highly supportive in that they love their children, consider their children to be important, invest years of nurturance, protection, and guidance in rearing and disciplining their children, and typically succeed quite well in transmitting norms and values from one generation to the next, especially values regarding important issues. On the other hand, however, parents also tend to be detached from their children in the sense that direct interaction is severely restricted by the substantial periods of time children spend in day-care settings, schools, before- and after-school programs, and camps; the time children spend with peers and babysitters and the countless hours they spend simply watching television (or playing video games); and by the physical absence of parents (most often fathers). The result is that although parents typically support their children, both emotionally and financially, for extended periods of the life course, the child-rearing years are characterized by low levels of face-to-face participation in shared activities.

Although contact between parents and children is reduced by the high incidence of divorce and single-parent families (most importantly, low rates of visitation by nonresident fathers), by maternal and paternal employment, and by reliance on child care by nonrelatives, the detachment in general is not an uncaring or uninvolved detachment. Parents in modern society spend substantial amounts of time at work to provide for the financial needs of the family, and mothers especially are expected to complete various domestic tasks in their strenuous triple role of wife, mother, and homemaker (Menaghan & Parcel, 1990). LeMasters and De-Frain (1989) note that American mothers are in addition expected to be home managers, community liaisons, and family decision makers, and that as a result of ever-increasing demands and responsibilities, they are generally overcommitted. It is also clear that parental support and influence are exerted indirectly through structuring children's relationships in extrafamilial contexts, as illustrated in parental monitoring of friendship choices, peer activities, and dating patterns, decisions to live in certain neighborhoods so that children will attend particular schools, or selection of day-care environments.

Popular claims that parents do not care about their children also are misleading. The evidence suggests that most parents care deeply, although often from a distance. Greenberger and O'Neill (1990) report that employed parents' concerns about their children (concerns about the consequences of maternal employment, perceived quality of child care, and their children's problem behaviors) have adverse effects on parental feelings about work and general well-being (role strain, depression, and physical health). Unexpectedly, they find that fathers are more strongly influenced than mothers by concerns about their children. Although child-related concerns clearly operate as stressors for both men and women, the concerns vary in nature and consequences. Greenberger and O'Neill document that quality of child care is a better predictor of women's well-being, that men in dual-earner households are more likely than women to believe that maternal employment has negative consequences for children (also see Greenberger et al., 1988), and that men are particularly vulnerable to role strain, depression, and ill health when they view their children's behavior as problematic.

The position taken here is that supportive detachment is a useful concept for understanding parent-child interaction. Rather than viewing the parental role as dichotomous—either parents are concerned, supportive, devoted, and conscientious, or they are uncaring, uninvolved, and abusive—the evidence suggests that parental support has taken on a new meaning in American society and that often it is executed in a detached rather than a direct, face-to-face manner. Further, supportive detachment as a child-rearing and socialization process is likely to be associated with certain positive and negative consequences for children, just as other child-rearing processes have desirable and undesirable outcomes. To illustrate, at the same time that parents work to support themselves and their family, they simultaneously foster self-regulation in children and adolescents who will depend on such attributes for life in the family and the larger society in which they will live as adults. As discussed above, parents are much more likely now than 30 years ago to emphasize autonomy for their children and to de-emphasize conformity. Parents are also likely to adhere to new norms supporting their own adult development and self-fulfillment (Bellah, Sullivan, Swidler, & Tipton, 1985; Schnaiberg & Goldenberg, 1989). These well-documented changes in American cultural and parenting values are consistent with parenting behaviors and childhood role experiences that socialize children for independence and self-reliance (see Youniss & Smollar, 1985).

CONCLUSIONS

It seems clear that the well-being of American children has declined since 1960. Uhlenberg and Eggebeen (1986) observe that between 1960 and 1980, academic achievement scores dropped, while rates of delinquency, illegitimacy, abortion, and alcohol and drug use increased dramatically. During the same period, adolescent mortality rates increased, largely as a result of sharp increases in death rates due to homicide, suicide, and other violent causes. Like many others, the authors attribute these patterns to the declining commitment of parents, increased labor force participation, divorce, and a general "erosion of the bond between parent and child" (Uhlenberg & Eggebeen, 1986, p. 38).

The evidence reviewed here suggests that this conclusion, while partially accurate, is vastly overstated. To be sure, parental support is weakened by low levels of direct interaction with children. As a result, children are disadvantaged. Of particular concern in this regard is the widespread occurrence of paternal abandonment and neglect, the latter commonly occurring both in father-absent and father-present families. However, there is persuasive evidence that maternal employment and parental divorce can not be equated with lack of parental commitment, and that both have been exaggerated as causes of distress and maladjustment in children.

The ever-increasing diversity of American families requires that we broaden our research agenda beyond traditional concepts and notions of family normality. Children's well-being depends much more on enduring parental support and satisfying family relationships than it does on a particular family structure. Classifications relying on the number of parents in the household, or the number of employed parents, provide, at best, crude indicators of family relations and the larger social context. As one illustration, children living with a single parent, especially black children, are much more likely than children in two-parent families to have other relatives living with them (Sweet & Bumpass, 1987). Dornbusch et al. (1985) found that the presence of an additional adult facilitated supervision and control of adolescent behavior in mother-only households, reducing rates of delinquent behavior. Another explanation is that in such households the presence of another adult creates a more hierarchical authority structure within which children learn deference and conformity (Nock, 1988).

More consequential than family type for children's well-being is the quality of parent-child and other family relationships. Lack of parental supervision and control, persistent parent-child conflict, marital conflict, and family violence have lasting deleterious consequences for children of all family types. Yet it seems clear that, with the exception of marital conflict, these patterns are more common in single-parent families, and that they are precipitated by economic hardship. The linkages between socioeconomic resources, family processes, and child outcomes require much more systematic attention from researchers.

The extent and degree of parent-child conflict are widely exaggerated. Adolescents generally report close and satisfying relationships with parents, and they routinely turn to parents for advice and guidance on important decisions. Parents, in turn, tend to be concerned about their children's welfare; they report that some stages and events in parenthood are stressful, but they maintain that it is a satisfying experience. Even during the empty nest phase, parents' life satisfaction depends on frequent contact with their children (White & Edwards, 1990).

Perhaps one reason parents and adolescents report generally favorable relationships is that they spend very little time together, often no more than 1 hour per day of direct interaction. It may be that more time together is not always and necessarily better for children, or for their families. The restructuring of work and family roles over the past few decades has ushered in a more detached but still supportive role for contemporary parents. Compared to parents a generation earlier, adults today spend less time rearing dependent-aged children but more time caring for their elderly parents. In sum, although other work and family expectations have expanded, there has been no corresponding delimitation of the parental role.

Parent-child relations have changed, but not as significantly as many assume and not all for the worse. Socialization processes involving supportive detachment prepare children for the changing society in which they will live as adults. Childhood experiences in single-parent families and stepfamilies and with extended kin provide socialization for experiences in reciprocal roles later in the life course. There is every indication that parenthood continues to be highly valued. But it is equally clear that parents and children need to find more time to spend with each other if they are to reap the many benefits of close parent-child relations.

Note

I would like to thank Alan C. Acock, John N. Edwards, and two anonymous reviewers for helpful comments on an earlier version of this article.

REFERENCES

Acock, A. C., Barker, D., & Bengtson, V. L. (1982). Mother's employment and parent-youth similarity. *Journal of Marriage and the Family, 44,* 441–455.

Acock, A. C., & Bengtson, V. L. (1980). Socialization and attribution processes: Actual versus perceived similarity among parents and youth. *Journal of Marriage and the Family,* *43,* 501–515.

Agnew, R., & Huguley, S. (1989). Adolescent violence towards parents. *Journal of Marriage and the Family, 51,* 699–711.

Alwin, D. F. (1986). Religion and parental child-rearing orientations: Evidence of a Catholic-Protestant convergence. *Journal of Marriage and the Family, 92,* 412–440.

Alwin, D. F. (1990). Cohort replacement and changes in parental socialization values. *Journal of Marriage and the Family, 52,* 347–360.

Amato, P. R., & Ochiltree, G. (1986). Family resources and the development of child competence. *Journal of Marriage and the Family, 48,* 47–56.

Bachman, J. G., Johnston, L. D., & O'Malley, P. M. (1987). *Monitoring the future: Questionnaire responses from the nation's high school seniors, 1986.* Ann Arbor: University of Michigan, Institute for Social Research.

Barnett, R. C., & Baruch, G. K. (1987). Determinants of fathers' participation in family work. *Journal of Marriage and the Family, 49,* 29–40.

Bellah, R. N., Sullivan, W. M., Swidler, A., & Tipton, S. M. (1985). *Habits of the heart: Individualism and commitment in American life.* New York: Harper and Row.

Belsky, J. (1990). Parental and nonparental child care and children's socioemotional development: A decade in review. *Journal of Marriage and the Family, 52,* 885–903.

Berg, B., & Kelly R. (1979). The measured self-esteem of children from broken, rejected, and accepted families. *Journal of Divorce, 2,* 363–369.

Bianchi, S. M., & Spain, D. (1986). *American women in transition.* New York: Russell Sage Foundation.

Blechman, E. A. (1982). Are children with one parent at psychological risk? A methodological review. *Journal of Marriage and the Family, 44,* 179–195.

Booth, A., & Edwards, J. N. (1989). Transmission of marital and family quality over the generations: The effect of parental divorce and unhappiness. *Journal of Divorce, 13,* 41–58.

Bumpass, L. L., & Sweet, J. A. (1989). Children's experience in single-parent families: Implications of cohabitation and marital transitions. *Family Planning Perspectives, 21,* 256–260.

Cashion, B. G. (1984). Female-headed families: Effects on children and clinical implications. In D. H. Olson & B. C. Miller (Eds.), *Family studies review yearbook* (pp. 481–489). Beverly Hills, CA: Sage.

Collins, W. A. (1990). Parent-child relationships in the transition to adolescence: Continuity and change in interaction, affect, and cognition. In R. Montemayor, G. R. Adams, & T. P. Gullotta (Eds.), *Advances in adolescent development: From childhood to adolescence: A transitional period?* (pp. 85–106). Newbury Park, CA: Sage.

Coverman, S., & Sheley, J. F. (1986). Change in men's housework and child-care time, 1965–1975. *Journal of Marriage and the Family, 48,* 413–422.

Demo, D. H., & Acock, A. C. (1988). The impact of divorce on children. *Journal of Marriage and the Family, 50,* 619–648.

Dornbusch, S. M., Carlsmith, J. M., Bushwall, S. J. Ritter, P. L., Leiderman, H., Hastorf, A. H., & Gross, R. T. (1985). Single parents, extended households, and the control of adolescents. *Child Development, 56,* 326–341.

Emery, R. E. (1982). Interparental conflict and the children of discord and divorce. *Psychological Bulletin, 92*, 310–330.

Finkelhor, D. (1979). *Sexually victimized children.* New York: The Free Press.

Frodi, A. M., & Lamb, M. E. (1978). Sex differences in responsiveness to infants: A developmental study of psychophysiological and behavioral responses. *Child Development, 49*, 1182–1188.

Furstenberg, F. F., Morgan, P., & Allison, P. D. (1987). Paternal participation and children's well-being after marital dissolution. *American Sociological Review, 52*, 695–701.

Furstenberg, F. F., Jr., Nord, C. W., Peterson, J. L., & Zill, N. (1983). The life course of children of divorce: Marital disruption and parental contact. *American Sociological Review, 48*, 656–668.

Gecas, V., & Seff, M. A. (1990). Families and adolescents: A review of the 1980s. *Journal of Marriage and the Family, 52*, 941–958.

Gelles, R. J. (1987). *Family violence.* Newbury Park, CA: Sage.

Gottman, J. M., & Katz, L. F. (1989). Effects of marital discord on young children's peer interaction and health. *Developmental Psychology, 25*, 373–381.

Greenberger, E., Goldberg, W. A., Crawford, T., & Granger, J. (1988). Beliefs about the consequences of maternal employment for children. *Psychology of Women Quarterly, 12*, 35–59.

Greenberger, E. & O'Neil, R. (1990). Parents' concerns about their child's development: Implications for fathers' and mothers' well-being and attitudes toward work. *Journal of Marriage and the Family, 52*, 621–635.

Hampton, R. L., Gelles, R. J., & Harrop, J. W. (1989). Is violence in black families increasing? A comparison of 1975 and 1985 national survey rates. *Journal of Marriage and the Family, 51*, 969–980.

Hetherington, E. M., Camara, K. A., & Featherman, D. L. (1983). Achievement and intellectual functioning of children in one-parent households. In J. T. Spence (Ed.), *Achievement and achievement motives: Psychological and sociological appraoches* (pp. 205–284). San Francisco: Freeman.

Hill, C. R., & Stafford, F. (1980). Parental care of children: Time diary estimates of quantity, predictability, and variety. *Journal of Human Resources, 15*, 219–239.

Hoffman, L. W. (1974). Effects on child. In L. W. Hoffman & F. I. Nye (Eds.), *Families and work* (pp. 126–166). Philadelphia: Temple University Press.

Holmbeck, G. N., & O'Donnell, K. (1991). Discrepancies between perceptions of decision-making and behavioral autonomy. In R. L. Paikoff & W. A. Collins (Eds.), *Parent-adolescent disagreements in the family: New directions for child development* (pp. 51–69). San Francisco: Jossey-Bass.

Keith, V. M., & Finlay, B. (1988). The impact of parental divorce on children's educational attainment, marital timing, and likelihood of divorce. *Journal of Marriage and the Family, 50*, 797–809.

Kiecolt, K. J., & Acock, A. C. (1988). The long-term effects of family structure on gender-role attitudes. *Journal of Marriage and the Family, 50*, 709–717.

Kinard, E. M., & Reinherz, H. (1984). Marital disruption: Effects of behavioral and emotional functioning in children. *Journal of Family Issues, 5*, 90–115.

Kinard, E. M., & Reinherz, H. (1986). Effects of marital disruption on children's school aptitude and achievement. *Journal of Marriage and the Family, 48*, 285–293.

Lamb, M. E., Pleck, J. H., Charnov, E. L., & Levine, J. A. (1987). A biosocial perspective on paternal behavior and involvement. In J. B. Lancaster, J. Altmann, A. S. Rossi, & L. R. Sherrod (Eds.), *Parenting across the lifespan: Biosocial dimensions* (pp. 111–142). New York: Aldine de Gruyter.

LaRossa, R. (1988). Fatherhood and social change. *Family Relations, 37,* 451–457.

LaRossa, R., & LaRossa, M. M. (1981). *Transition to parenthood: How infants change families.* Beverly HIlls, CA: Sage.

LeMasters, E. E., & DeFrain, J. (1989). *Parents in contemporary America: A sympathetic view,* Belmont, CA: Wadsworth.

Lempers, J. D., Clark-Lempers, D., & Simons, R. L. (1989). Economic hardship, parenting, and distress in adolescence. *Child Development, 60,* 25–39.

Macke, A., & Morgan, W. R. (1978). Maternal employment, race, and work orientation of high school girls. *Social Forces, 57,* 187–204.

Masnick, G., & Bane, M. J. (1980). *The nation's families: 1960–1990.* Boston: Auburn House.

McLanahan, S. (1985). Family structure and the reproduction of poverty. *American Journal of Sociology, 90,* 873–902.

McLanahan, S., & Booth, K. (1989). Mother-only families: Problems, prospects, and politics. *Journal of Marriage and the Family, 51,* 557–580.

Mechanic, D., & Hansell, S. (1989). Divorce, family conflict, and adolescents' well-being. *Journal of Health and Social Behavior, 30,* 105–116.

Menaghan, E. G., & Parcel, T. L. (1990). Parental employment and family life: Research in the 1980s. *Journal of Marriage and the Family, 52,* 1079–1098.

Meredith, W. H., Stinnett, N., & Cacioppo, B. F. (1985). Parent satisfactions: Implications for strengthening families. In R. Williams, H. Lingren, G. Rowe, S. Van Zandt, P. Lee, & N. Stinnett, (Eds.), *Family strengths 6: Enhancement of interaction* (pp. 143–150). Lincoln: University of Nebraska.

Miller, D. R., & Swanson, G. E. (1958). *The changing American parent.* New York: Wiley.

Mirowsky, J., & Ross, C. E. (1986). Social patterns of distress. *Annual Review of Sociology, 12,* 23–45.

Montemayor, R. (1982). The relationship between parent-adolescent conflict and the amount of time adolescents spend alone and with parents and peers. *Child Development, 53,* 1512–1519.

Montemayor, R. (1986). Family variation in parent-adolescent storm and stress. *Journal of Adolescent Research, 1,* 15–31.

Mortimer, J., & Sorensen, G. (1984). Men, women, work, and family. In K. M. Borman, D. Quarm, & S. Gideonse (Eds.), *Women in the workplace: The effects on families* (pp. 139–167). Norwood, NJ: Ablex.

Neal, A. G., Groat, H. T., & Wicks, J. W. (1989). Attitudes about having children: A study of 600 couples in the early years of marriage. *Journal of Marriage and the Family, 51,* 313–328.

Newcomer, S., & Udry, J. R. (1987). Parental marital status effects on adolescent sexual behavior. *Journal of Marriage and the Family, 49,* 235–240.

Nock, S. L. (1988). The family and hierarchy. *Journal of Marriage and the Family, 50,* 957–966.

Nock, S. L., & Kingston, P. W. (1988). Time with children: The impact of couples' work-time commitments. *Social Forces, 67*, 59–85.

Offer, D., Ostrov, E., Howard, K. I., & Atkinson, R. (1988). *The teenage world. Adolescents' self-image in ten countries.* New York: Plenum.

Otto, L. B. (1988). America's youth: A changing profile. *Family Relations, 37*, 385–391.

Pleck, J.H. (1979). Men's family work: Three perspectives and some new data. *The Family Coordinator, 28*, 481–488.

Powell, B., & Steelman, L. C. (1982). Testing an undertested comparison: Maternal effects on sons' and daughters' attitudes toward women in the labor force. *Journal of Marriage and the Family, 44*, 349–355.

Raschke, H. J., & Raschke, V. J. (1979). Family conflict and the children's self-concepts. *Journal of Marriage and the Family, 41*, 367–374.

Robinson, J. P. (1988, December). Who's doing the housework? *American Demographics,* pp. 24–28, 63.

Rosenfield, S. (1989). The effects of women's employment: Personal control and sex differences in mental health. *Journal of Health and Social Behavior, 30*, 77–91.

Sanik, M. M. (1981). Division of household work: A decade comparison, 1967–1977. *Home Economics Research Journal, 10*, 175–180.

Schnaiberg, A., & Goldenberg, S. (1989). From empty nest to crowded nest: The dynamics of incompletely-launched young adults. *Social Problems, 36*, 251–266.

Sebald, H. (1986). Adolescents' shifting orientation toward parents and peers: A curvilinear trend over recent decades. *Journal of Marriage and the Family, 48*, 5–13.

Seltzer, J. A., & Bianchi, S. M. (1988). Children's contact with absent parents. *Journal of Marriage and the Family, 50*, 663–677.

Smetana, J. G. (1989). Adolescents' and parents' reasoning about actual family conflict. *Child Development, 60*, 1052–1067.

Spitze, G. (1988a). Women's employment and family relations: A review. *Journal of Marriage and the Family, 50*, 595–618.

Spitze, G. (1988b). The data on women's labor force participation. In A. H. Stromberg & S. Harkess (Eds.), *Women working: Theories and facts in perspective* (2nd ed., pp. 42–60). Mountain View, CA: Mayfield.

Steinberg, L., Elmen, J. D., & Mounts, N. (1989). Authoritative parenting, psychosocial maturity, and academic success among adolescents. *Child Development, 60*, 1424–1436.

Stevens, G., & Boyd, M. (1980). The importance of mother: Labor force participation and intergenerational mobility of women. *Social Forces, 59*, 186–199.

Stith, S. M., & Davis, A. J. (1984). Employed mothers and family day care substitute caregivers: A comparative analysis of infant care. *Child Development, 55*, 1340–1348.

Straus, M. A., & Gelles, R. J. (1986). Societal change and change in family violence from 1975 to 1985 as revealed by two national surveys. *Journal of Marriage and the Family, 48*, 465–479.

Sweet, J. A., & Bumpass, L. L. (1987). *American families and households.* New York: Russell Sage Foundation.

Thompson, M. S., & Ensminger, M. E. (1989). Psychological well-being among mothers with school age children: Evolving family structures. *Social Forces, 67*, 715–730.

Tromsdorff, G. (1983). Value change in Japan. *International Journal of Intercultural Relations, 7,* 337–360.

Uhlenberg, P., & Eggebeen, D. (1986). The declining well-being of American adolescents. *The Public Interest, 82,* 25–38.

Vander Mey, B. J., & Neff, R. L. (1984). Adult-child incest: A sample of substantiated cases. *Family Relations, 33,* 549–557.

Vinovskis, M. A. (1987). Historical perspectives on the development of the family and parent-child interactions. In J. B. Lancaster, J. Altmann, A. S. Rossi, & L. R. Sherrod (Eds.), *Parenting across the lifespan: Biosocial dimensions* (pp. 295–312). New York: Aldine de Gruyter.

Walker, K., & Woods, M. (1976). *Time use: A measure of household production of family goods and services.* Washington, DC: American Home Economics Association.

White, L., & Edwards, J. N. (1990). Emptying the nest and parental well-being: An analysis of national panel data. *American Sociological Review, 55,* 235–242.

Youniss, J., & Smollar, J. (1985). *Adolescent relations with mothers, fathers, and friends.* Chicago: University of Chicago Press.

Reading 23

Children's Adjustment to Divorce

Frank F. Furstenberg and Andrew J. Cherlin

As Helen watched, Sally, then three, walked over to where her six-year-old brother was playing and picked up one of his toy robots. Mickey grabbed the robot out of her hand, shouted "No!" and pushed her away. The little girl fell backward and began to cry. Helen had just finished another frustrating phone call with Herb, who had told her that he could no longer afford to pay as much child support as

Reprinted by permission of the publishers from *Divided Families: What Happens to Children When Parents Part* by Frank F. Furstenberg and Andrew J. Cherlin, Cambridge, Mass.: Harvard University Press, Copyright © 1991 by the President and Fellows of Harvard College.

they had agreed. She was grateful to her parents for allowing her and the kids to live with them temporarily, but the crowded household was beginning to strain everyone's patience. She rushed over to her daughter, picked her up, and shouted at her son, "Don't you hit her like that!" "But it was mine," he said, whereupon he took another robot and threw it on the floor near his mother's feet. She grabbed his arm and dragged him to his room, screaming at him all the way.

Then she sat down in the living room, with Sally in her lap, and reflected on how often scenes such as this were occurring. Ever since the separation eight months earlier, she had had a hard time controlling Mickey. He disobeyed her, was mean to his sister, and fought with friends in school. And when he talked back to her, she lost her temper. But that just made him behave worse, which in turn made her angrier, until he was sent to his room and she sat down, distraught.

Helen's problems with her son fit a pattern familiar to psychologists who study the effects of divorce on children, an escalating cycle of misbehavior and harsh response between mothers and sons. But not all parents and children become caught up in these so-called coercive cycles after the breakup of a marriage. Studies show a wide range of responses to divorce. Some children do very well; others fare poorly. In this chapter we will examine these differences and inquire into why they occur.

We tend to think of divorce as an event that starts when a husband or wife moves out of their home. But it is often more useful to think of divorce as a process that unfolds slowly over time, beginning well before the separation actually occurs. In many cases it is preceded by a lengthy period of conflict between the spouses. It is reasonable to expect that this predisruption conflict, and the corresponding emotional upset on the part of the parents, may cause problems for children.

For example, when things began to heat up between Mickey and his mother, Helen naturally assumed that the problems between them were largely the result of the divorce. Perhaps she was right. But her guilty feelings made Helen conveniently forget that Mickey had had behavioral problems for several years—ever since the quarreling between his parents became severe. Almost two years before the separation, Mickey's preschool teacher had asked Helen if things were going all right at home. Mickey had displayed unusual fits of temper with his classmates and seemed distracted during play periods. If you had asked Mickey's teacher, she would have predicted that Mickey, although bright enough, was going to have adjustment problems in kindergarten. And so he did. True, Mickey's problems did get worse the year that his parents separated, but it is not obvious that his difficulties in school would have been avoided even if his parents had managed to remain together.

In fact, there is evidence that some children show signs of disturbance months, and sometimes even years, before their parents separate. In 1968 a team of psychologists began to study three-year-olds at two nursery schools in Berkeley, California. The psychologists followed these children and their families, conducting detailed personality assessments at ages four, five, seven, eleven, and fourteen. When the study started, 88 children were living with two married parents. Twenty-nine of these children experienced the breakup of their parents marriages by the time they were fourteen. Curious as to what the children were like before the breakup, the psychologists paged backward through their files until they found the descriptions of the children eleven years earlier, when they were age three.

The results were quite dramatic for boys. Years before the breakup, three-year-old boys whose families eventually would disrupt were more likely to have been described as having behavioral problems than were three-year-old boys whose families would remain intact. According to the researchers, Jeanne H. Block, Jack Block, and Per F. Gjerde, three-year-old boys who would eventually experience family disruption already were rated as more "inconsiderate of other children, disorderly in dress and behavior," and "impulsive" and more likely to "take advantage of other children." Moreover, their fathers were more likely to characterize themselves as often angry with their sons, and both fathers and mothers reported more conflict with their sons. Much smaller differences were found among daughters.

Had the Berkeley researchers started their study when the children were age fourteen, they surely would have found some differences between the adolescents from the 29 disrupted families and the adolescents from the 59 intact families. And they probably would have attributed these differences to the aftermath of the disruption, as most other researchers do. But because they could look back eleven years, they saw that some portion of the presumed effects of divorce on children were present well before the families split up.

Why is this so? It is, of course, possible that some children have behavioral problems that put stress on their parents' marriages. In these instances divorce, rather than *causing* children's problems, may be the *result* of them. But it is doubtful that inherently difficult children cause most divorces. The Berkeley researchers suggest, rather, that conflict between parents is a fundamental factor that harms children's development and produces behavioral problems. In many families, this conflict—and the harm it engenders—may precede the separation by many years.

There are many other characteristics of divorce-prone families that might affect children. For example, people who divorce are more likely to have married as teenagers and to have begun their marriages after the wife was pregnant. They also are less religious. It is possible that these families may provide a less stable and secure environment and therefore cause children more problems even while the family is intact. But no researcher would suggest that all of the effects of divorce are determined before the actual separation. Much of the impact depends on how the process unfolds after the separation and how the children cope with it. Nearly all children are extremely upset when they learn of the breakup. For most, it is an unwelcome shock. Judith Wallerstein and Joan Kelly found that young children seemed surprised even in families where the parents were openly quarreling and hostile. Although young children certainly recognize open conflict—and indeed may be drawn into it—they usually can't grasp the long-term significance and don't envisage the separation. Moreover, parents typically don't inform their children of the impending separation until shortly before it occurs.

When children do learn of the breakup, their reactions vary according to their ages. Preschool-age children, whose ability to understand the situation is limited, are usually frightened and bewildered to find that their father or mother has moved out of the house. Preschoolers see the world in a very self-centered way, and so they often assume that the separation must be their fault—that they must have done something terribly wrong to make their parent leave. Three-year-old Sally promised never to leave her room a mess again if only Daddy would come home. Older children comprehend the situation better and can understand that they are not at fault. But they still can be quite anxious about what the breakup will mean for their own lives. And adolescents, characteristically, are more often intensely angry at one or both of their parents for breaking up their families.

SHORT-TERM ADJUSTMENT

The psychologists P. Lindsay Chase-Lansdale and E. Mavis Hetherington have labeled the first two years following a separation as a "crisis period" for adults and children. The crisis begins for children with shock, anxiety, and anger upon learning of the breakup. (But as was noted, the harmful effects on children of marital conflict may begin well before the breakup.) For adults, too, the immediate aftermath is a dismaying and difficult time. It is especially trying for mothers who retain custody of the children, as about nine in ten do.

Helen, for example, faced the task of raising her two children alone. Even when she was married, Helen had taken most of the responsibility for raising the children. But Herb had helped out some and had backed her up when the children were difficult. Now responsibility fell solely on her. What's more, she was working full time in order to compensate for the loss of Herb's income. And all this was occurring at a time when she felt alternately angry at Herb, depressed about the end of her marriage, and anxious about her future. Harried and overburdened, she was sometimes overwhelmed by the task of keeping her family going from day to day. Dinner was frequently served late, and Sally and Mickey often stayed up past their bedtime as Helen tried to complete the household chores.

Children have two special needs during the crisis period. First, they need additional emotional support as they struggle to adapt to the breakup. Second, they need the structure provided by a reasonably predictable daily routine. Unfortunately, many single parents cannot meet both of these needs all the time. Depressed, anxious parents often lack the reserve to comfort emotionally needy children. Overburdened parents let daily schedules slip. As a result, their children lose some of the support they need.

A number of psychological studies suggest that the consequences of the crisis period are worse for boys than for girls; but it may be that boys and girls merely react to stress differently. Developmental psychologists distinguish two general types of behavior problems among children. The first—externalizing disorders—refers to heightened levels of problem behavior directed outward, such as aggression, disobedience, and lying. The second—internalizing disorders—refers to heightened levels of problem behaviors directed inward, such as depression, anxiety, or withdrawal. Boys in high-conflict families, whether disrupted or intact, tend to show more aggressive and antisocial behavior. Hetherington studied a small group of middle-class families, disrupted and intact, for several years. She found coercive cycles between mothers and sons, like the ones between Helen and

Mickey, to be prevalent. Distressed mothers responded irritably to the bad behavior of their sons, thus aggravating the very behavior they wished to quell. Even as long as six years after the separation, Hetherington observed this pattern among mothers who hadn't remarried and their sons.

The findings for girls are less consistent, but generally girls appear better behaved than boys in the immediate aftermath of a disruption. There are even reports of overcontrolled, self-consciously "good" behavior. But we should be cautious in concluding that girls are less affected. It may be that they internalize their distress in the form of depression or lowered self-esteem. And some observers suggest that the distress may produce problems that only appear years after the breakup.

It is also possible that boys do worse because they typically live with their opposite-sex parent, their mother. A number of studies report intriguing evidence that children may fare better if they reside with a same-sex parent after a marital disruption. Families in which single fathers become the custodial parent, however, are a small and select group who may be quite different from typical families. Until recently, sole custody was awarded to fathers mainly in cases in which the mother had abandoned the children or was an alcoholic, drug abuser, or otherwise clearly incompetent. Until there is more evidence from studies of broad groups of children, we think it would be premature to generalize about same-sex custody.

To sum up, researchers agree that almost all children are moderately or severely distressed when their parents separate and that most continue to experience confusion, sadness, or anger for a period of months and even years. Nevertheless, the most careful studies show a great deal of variation in the short-term reactions of children—including children in the same family. Most of this variation remains unexplained, although differences in age and gender account for some of it. Part of the explanation, no doubt, has to do with differences in children's temperaments. Some probably are more robust and better able to withstand deprivation and instability. They may be less affected by growing up in a one-parent family, and they may also cope better with a divorce. In addition, clinicians have speculated that some children draw strength from adults or even peers outside of the household, such as grandparents, aunts, or close friends. But we are far from certain just how important each of the sources of resiliency is to the child's ability to cope with divorce.

LONG-TERM ADJUSTMENT

Even less is known about the long-term consequences of divorces than about the short-term consequences. Within two or three years, most single parents and their children recover substantially from the trauma of the crisis period. Parents are able to stabilize their lives as the wounds from the breakup heal. With the exception of some difficulties between single mothers and their sons, parent–child relationships generally improve. And the majority of children, it seems, return to normal development.

But over the long run there is still great variation in how the process of divorce plays out. Without doubt, some children suffer long-term harm. It is easy, however, to exaggerate the extent of these harmful effects. In their widely read book that reports on a clinical study of 60 recently divorced middle-class couples from the San Francisco suburbs and their 131 children, aged two to eighteen, Judith Wallerstein and Sandra Blakeslee paint a picture of a permanently scarred generation. "Almost half of the children," they write, "entered adulthood as worried, underachieving, self-deprecating, and sometimes angry young men and women." Are these difficulties as widespread among children of divorce as the authors suggest? Despite their claim that the families were "representative of the way normal people from a white, middle-class background cope with divorce," it is highly likely that the study exaggerates the prevalence of long-term problems. Its families had volunteered to come to a clinic for counseling, and many of the parents had extensive psychiatric histories. Moreover, there is no comparison group of intact families: instead, all of the problems that emerged after the break-up are blamed on the divorce.

We do not doubt that many young adults retain painful memories of their parents' divorce. But it doesn't necessarily follow that these feelings will impair their functioning as adults. Had their parents not divorced, they might have retained equally painful memories of a conflict-ridden marriage. Imagine that the more troubled families in the Wallerstein study had remained intact and had been observed ten years later. Would their children have fared any better? Certainly they would have been better off economically; but given the strains that would have been evident in the marriages, we doubt that most would have been better off psychologically.

Studies based on nationally representative samples that do include children from intact marriages suggest that the long-term harmful effects of divorce are worthy of concern but occur only to a minority. Evidence for this conclusion comes from the National Survey of Children, which interviewed parents and children in 1976 and again in 1981. For families in which a marital disruption had occurred, the average time elapsed since the disruption was eight years in 1981. James L. Peterson and Nicholas Zill examined parents' 1981 responses to the question, "Since January 1977 . . . has [the child] had any behavior or discipline problems at school resulting in your receiving a note or being asked to come in and talk to the teacher or principal?" Peterson and Zill found that, other things being equal, 34 percent of parents who had separated or divorced answered yes, compared with 20 percent of parents in intact marriages.

Is this a big difference or a small difference? The figures can be interpreted in two ways. First, the percentage of children from maritally disrupted families who had behavior or discipline problems at school is more than half-again as large as the percentage from intact families. That's a substantial difference, suggesting that children from disrupted families have a noticeably higher rate of misbehaving seriously in school. (Although some of these children might have misbehaved even if their parents had not separated.) Second, however, the figures also demonstrate that 66 percent of all children from maritally disrupted homes *did not* misbehave seriously at school. So one also can conclude that most children of divorce don't have behavior problems at school. Both conclusions are equally valid; the glass is either half full or half empty, depending on one's point of view. We think that in order to understand the broad picture of the long-term effects of divorce on children, it's necessary to keep both points of view in mind.

The same half-full and half-empty perspective can be applied to studies of the family histories of adults. Based on information from several national surveys of adults, Sara McLanahan and her colleagues found that persons who reported living as a child in a single-parent family were more likely subsequently to drop out of high school, marry during their teenage years, have a child before marrying, and experience the disruption of their own marriages. For example, the studies imply that, for whites, the probability of dropping out of high school could be as high as 22 percent for those who lived with single parents, compared with about 11 percent for those who lived with both parents, other things being equal. Again, the glass is half-empty: those who lived with a single parent are up to twice as likely to drop out of high school. And it is half-full: the overwhelming majority of those who lived with a single parent graduated from high school.

In addition, the NSC data demonstrate that children in intact families in which the parents fought continually were doing no better, and often worse, than the children of divorce. In 1976 and again in 1981, parents in intact marriages were asked whether they and their spouses ever had arguments about any of nine topics: chores and responsibilities, the children, money, sex, religion, leisure time, drinking, other women or men, and in-laws. Peterson and Zill classified an intact marriage as having "high conflict" if arguments were reported on five or more topics or if the parent said that the marriage, taking things all together, was "not too happy." They found that in 1981, children whose parents had divorced or separated were doing no worse than children whose parents were in intact, high-conflict homes. And children whose parents' marriages were intact but highly conflicted in both 1976 and 1981 were doing the worst of all: these children were more depressed, impulsive, and hyperactive, and misbehaved more often.

To be sure, even if only a minority of children experience long-term negative effects, that is nothing to cheer about. But the more fundamental point—one that all experts agree upon—is that children's responses to the breakup of their parents' marriages vary greatly. There is no ineluctable path down which children of divorce progress. What becomes important, then, is to identify the circumstances under which children seem to do well.

WHAT MAKES A DIFFERENCE?

A critical factor in both short-term and long-term adjustment is how effectively the custodial parent, who usually is the mother, functions as a parent. We have noted how difficult it can be for a recently separated mother to function well. The first year or two after the separation is a difficult time for many mothers, who may feel angry, depressed, irritable, or sad. Their own distress may make it more difficult to cope with their children's distress, leading in some cases to a disorganized household, lax supervision, inconsistent discipline, and the coercive cycles between mothers and preschool-aged sons that have been identified by Hetherington and others. Mothers who can cope better with the disruption can be more effective parents. They can keep their work and home lives going from day to day and can better provide love, nurturing, consistent discipline, and a predictable routine.

Quite often their distress is rooted in, or at least intensified by, financial problems. Loss of the father's income can cause a disruptive, downward spiral in which children must adjust to a declining standard of living, a mother who is less psychologically available and is home less often, an apartment in an unfamiliar neighborhood, a different school, and new friends. This sequence of events occurs at a time when children are greatly upset about the separation and need love, support, and a familiar daily routine.

A second key factor in children's well-being is a low level of conflict between their mother and father. This principle applies, in fact, to intact as well as disrupted families. Recall the finding from the NSC that children who live with two parents who persistently quarrel over important areas of family life show higher levels of distress and behavior problems than do children from disrupted marriages. Some observers take this finding to imply that children are better off if their parents divorce than if they remain in an unhappy marriage. We think this is true in some cases but not in others. It is probably true that most children who live in a household filled with continual conflict between angry, embittered spouses would be better off if their parents split up—assuming that the level of conflict is lowered by the separation. And there is no doubt that the rise in divorce has liberated some children (and their custodial parents) from families marked by physical abuse, alcoholism, drugs, and violence. But we doubt that such clearly pathological descriptions apply to most families that disrupt. Rather, we think there are many more cases in which there is little open conflict, but one or both partners finds the marriage personally unsatisfying. The unhappy partner may feel unfulfilled, distant from his or her spouse, bored, or constrained. Under these circumstances, the family may limp along from day to day without much holding it together or pulling it apart. A generation ago, when marriage was thought of as a moral and social obligation, most husbands and wives in families such as this stayed together. Today, when marriage is thought of increasingly as a means of achieving personal fulfillment, many more will divorce. Under these circumstances, divorce may well make one or both spouses happier; but we strongly doubt that it improves the psychological well-being of the children.

A possible third key factor in children's successful adjustment is the maintenance of a continuing relationship with the noncustodial parent, who is usually the father. But direct evidence that lack of contact with the father inhibits the adjustment of children to divorce is less than satisfactory. A number of experts have stressed the importance of a continuing relationship, yet research findings are inconsistent. The main evidence comes from both the Hetherington and Wallerstein studies, each of which found that children were better adjusted when they saw their fathers regularly. More recently, however, other observational studies have not found this relationship.

And in the NSC, the amount of contact that children had with their fathers seemed to make little difference for their well-being. Teenagers who saw their fathers regularly were just as likely as were those with infrequent contact to have problems in school or engage in delinquent acts and precocious sexual behavior. Furthermore, the children's behavioral adjustment was also unrelated to the level of intimacy and identification with the nonresidential father. No differences were observed even among the children who had both regular contact and close relations with their father outside the home. Moreover, when the children in the NSC were reinterviewed in 1987 at ages 18 to 23, those who had retained stable, close ties to their fathers were neither more nor less successful than those who had had low or inconsistent levels of contact and intimacy with their fathers.

Another common argument is that fathers who maintain regular contact with their children also may keep paying child support to their children's mothers. Studies do show that fathers who visit more regularly pay more in child support. But it's not clear that they pay more *because* they visit more. Rather, it may be that fathers who have a greater commitment to their children both visit and pay more. If so, then the problem is to increase the level of commitment most fathers feel, not simply to increase the amount of visiting.

These puzzling findings make us cautious about drawing any firm conclusions about the psychological benefits of contact with noncustodial parents for children's adjustment in later life. Yet despite the mixed evidence, the idea that continuing contact with fathers makes a difference to a child's psychological well-being is so plausible and so seemingly grounded in theories of child development that one is reluctant to discount it. It may be that evidence is difficult to obtain because so few fathers living outside the home are intimately involved in childrearing. It is also likely that, even when fathers remain involved, most formerly married parents have difficulty establishing a collaborative style of childrearing. We remain convinced that when parents are able to cooperate in childrearing after a divorce and when fathers are able to maintain an active and supportive role, children will be better off in the long run. But we are certain that such families are rare at present and unlikely to become common in the near future.

DOES CUSTODY MAKE A DIFFERENCE FOR CHILDREN?

The belief that the family's involvement is beneficial to children was an important reason why many states recently adopted joint-custody statues. Supporters argued that children adjust better when they maintain a continuing relationship with both parents. They also argued that fathers would be more likely to meet child-support obligations if they retained responsibility for the children's upbringing. Were they correct? Joint custody is so recent that no definitive evidence exists. But the information to date is disappointing.

Joint *legal* custody seems to be hardly distinguishable in practice from maternal sole custody. A recent study of court records in Wisconsin showed no difference in child-support payments in joint-legal-custody versus mother-sole-custody families, once income and other factors were taken into account. The Stanford study found little difference, three and one-half years after separation, between joint-legal-custody (but not joint-physical-custody) families and mother-sole-custody families. Once income and education were taken into account, fathers who had joint legal custody were no more likely to comply with court-ordered child-support awards than were fathers whose former wives had sole legal and physical custody. They did not visit their children more often; they did not cooperate and communicate more with their former wives; and they didn't even participate more in decisions about the children's lives. The investigators concluded that joint legal custody "appears to mean very little in practice."

The handful of other small-scale studies of joint legal custody show modest effects, at most. It appears that joint legal custody does not substantially increase the father's decision-making authority, his involvement in childrearing, or the amount of child support he pays. Why is it so hard to increase fathers' involvement after divorce? For one thing . . . many men don't seem to know how to relate to their children except through their wives. Typically, when married, they were present but passive—not much involved in childrearing. When they separate, they carry this pattern of limited involvement with them; and it is reinforced by the modest contact most have with their children. Uncomfortable and unskilled at being an active parent, marginalized by infrequent contact, focused on building a new family life, many fathers fade from their children's lives.

Less is known about joint physical custody. But a few recent studies suggest that it isn't necessarily better for children's adjustment than the alternatives. Among all families in the Stanford Study in which children still were seeing both parents about two years after the separation, parents in dual-resistance families talked and coordinated rules more; but they quarreled about the children just as much as did parents in single-residence families. Several colleagues of Wallerstein followed 58 mother-physical-custody families and 35 joint-physical-custody families for two years after the families had been referred to counseling centers in the San Francisco area. Many of the parents were disputing custody and visitation arrangements. Children from the joint-physical-custody families were no better adjusted than children from the mother-physical-custody families: their levels of behavioral problems, their self-esteem, their ease at making friends were very similar. What did make a difference for the children was the depression and anxiety levels of their parents and the amount of continuing verbal and physical aggression between them, regardless of the custody arrangement. The authors suggest that children whose parents are having serious disputes may have more behavior problems, lower self-esteem, and less acceptance by friends if they shuttle between homes. They are exposed to more conflict, and their movement back and forth may even generate it.

The admittedly limited evidence so far suggests to us that custody arrangements may matter less for the well-being of children than had been thought. It is, of course, possible that when more evidence is available, joint custody will be shown to have important benefits for some families. As with father involvement, the rationale for joint custody is so plausible and attractive that one is tempted to disregard the disappointing evidence and support it anyway. But based on what is known now, we think custody and visitation matter less for children than the two factors we noted earlier: how much conflict there is between the parents and how effectively the parent (or parents) the child lives with functions. It is likely that a child who alternates between the homes of a distraught mother and an angry father will be more troubled than a child who lives with a mother who is coping well and who once a fortnight sees a father who has disengaged from his family. Even the frequency of visits with a father seems to matter less than the climate in which they take place.

For now, we would draw two conclusions. First, joint physical custody should be encouraged only in cases where both parents voluntarily agree to it. Among families in which both parents shared the childrearing while they were married, a voluntary agreement to maintain joint physical custody probably will work and benefit the children. Even among families in which one parent did most of the childrearing prior to the divorce, a voluntary agreement won't do any harm—although we think the agreement likely will break down to sole physical custody over time. But only very rarely should joint physical custody be imposed if one or both parents do not want it. There may be a few cases in which the father and mother truly shared the childrearing before the divorce but one of them won't agree to share physical custody afterward. These difficult cases call for mediation or counseling, and they may require special consideration. But among the vastly larger number of families in which little sharing occurred beforehand and one or both parents doesn't want to share physical custody afterward, imposing joint physical custody would invite continuing conflict without any clear benefits. Even joint legal custody may matter more as a symbol of fathers' ties to their children than in any concrete sense. But symbols can be important, and joint legal custody seems, at worst, to do no harm. A legal preference for it may send a message to fathers that society respects their rights to and responsibilities for their children.

Our second conclusion is that in weighing alternative public policies concerning divorce, the thin empirical evidence of the benefits of joint custody and frequent visits with fathers must be acknowledged. All of the findings in this chapter have implications for the way in which we as a society confront the effects of divorce on children. A question we will examine later is: Which public policies should have priority? What outcomes are most important for society to encourage and support? In some cases, such as the economic slide of mothers and children, the problem is clear, and alternative remedies readily come to mind. In other cases, the problems are complex and the remedies unclear. . . .

. . . [H]owever, we must note that a divorce does not necessarily mark the end of change in the family lives of children. A majority will see a new partner move into their home. A remarriage, or even a cohabiting relationship, brings with it the potential both to improve children's lives and to complicate further their adjustment. . . .

Reading 24

The Impact of
Intimate Violence

Richard J. Gelles and
Murray A. Straus

Bill was hardly a model husband or father. Indeed, if he promised his wife Allison and daughter Cindy a rose garden, you may be certain that they got not the roses but the thorns—and worse. His violent outbursts were sporadic, but they could be intensely cruel. He began to hit and batter his wife during her first pregnancy. At first he pushed or slapped Allison when he was angry. After a while, he escalated the violence to kicks and punches. In Allison's eyes there seemed to be no rhyme or reason behind the outbursts. One day it happened because Bill could not find his new shirt. Another day he exploded when he was served fish and not the fried chicken he expected. On this occasion he hurled his plate at Allison and then picked up the kitchen table and threw it across the room. Soon he began to purchase guns—first a shotgun, then a rifle, then two handguns. He would often threaten Allison with one or another of the weapons. She never did know whether they were loaded or not.

Cindy remembers seeing her father hit her mother on many occasions. Bill rarely spanked Cindy. When he did, it was rather mild. But his other punishments were extraordinarily cruel. Cindy's clearest childhood memory was of her father shooting her pet cat. The cat had tracked mud onto Bill's easy chair. In a rage, Bill carried the cat to his closet, took out a rifle, and stomped outside—all the while yelling to Cindy what he planned to do. He threw the cat into the corner of the fenced-in front yard, and shot the trapped animal in full view of Cindy and Allison. When finished, Bill picked up the carcass and ceremoniously dumped it into the garbage can.

One afternoon, when Cindy was seventeen years old, her father arrived home drunk. He began to make sexual advances toward her. He wrapped her in a giant hug, and when she tore free, he began to grab and tear at her clothes. With his

From *Intimate Violence* by Richard J. Gelles and Murray A. Straus, published by Simon & Schuster, Inc. © 1988 by Richard J. Gelles and Murray A. Straus. Reprinted by permission.

attention totally focused on Cindy, he did not hear Allison open the hall closet door and remove a shotgun. Allison stood quietly in the hall as the tumult in the living room went on. Finally, Cindy tumbled into the hall. Bill staggered out after her. Allison calmly emptied both barrels of the shotgun into her husband's chest. She put down the shotgun and called the police. "I've just killed my husband," she reported.

No brief written description, television drama, or full-length book can do justice to the experience of living in an abusive household. We can describe the shape and form the physical and mental abuse take, but words are not adequate to capture what life must be like for the victims of domestic abuse. What went on in the mind of six-year-old Cindy as she watched her father shoot her pet cat? How did Allison cope with the violence she experienced, her own psychological distress, and the aftermath of her attempted suicide? More importantly, how did she cope with the uncertainty of not knowing when or why the next violent outburst would take place? Most people would assume that Cindy and Allison could never be normal after enduring the violence and cruelty they experienced. It is generally assumed by professionals and laymen alike that abuse victims sustain lifelong scars.

GROWING UP AMIDST VIOLENCE: THE IMPACT ON CHILDREN

The belief that battered and abused children grow up to become abusive parents is widely shared and accepted by professionals and the general public. Yet, among students of child maltreatment there is heated controversy over the validity of the claim that abuse leads to abuse. On the one side of the debate are those who see childhood experiences with abuse as a major and direct cause of later violent behavior. Henry Kempe and Barton Schmitt claimed that "untreated abused children frequently grow up to be delinquents, murderers, and batterers of the next generation of children." On the other side is the child development expert Edward Zigler of Yale University who, after a review of the major research studies on the link between abuse experienced as a child and abusive behavior as an adult, concluded that "the majority of abused children do not become abusive parents" and ". . . the time has come for the intergenerational myth to be placed aside."

The most careful review of research on the intergenerational link finds that between 18 and 70 percent of those individuals who grew up in violence will recreate that behavior as adults. Zigler and his colleague Joan Kaufman believe that the most accurate estimate within this wide range is that the rate of intergenerational transmission is about 30 percent. They conclude that this means that the link between being maltreated and becoming abusive is far from inevitable; thus they advocate abandoning the notion of abused children growing up to be abusive.

Kaufman and Zigler's dismissal of the intergenerational link may be as misleading as the zealots who claim that all abused children grow up to be abusive. Kaufman and Zigler are correct on two counts. First, the best available evidence indicates that *most* battered children do not become abusive. Second, it would be incorrect and unfair for individuals who experienced violence as children to see themselves as walking time bombs. Worse, such an incorrect self-image might lead to a self-fulfilling prophecy in which the self-concept, and not the experiences, may induce violent outbursts. Yet, to totally dismiss the experiences of violence as one of the causes of later violence is also misleading and wrong. While a rate of intergenerational transmission of 30 percent is not even a majority, it is far greater than the average rate of abusive violence which is less than 3 percent for the general population. In short, while one could not always predict future violence based on knowing past history, past history is important enough as a causal factor to warrant explanation and clinical intervention.

Since all battered children do not grow up to become abusers, Kaufman and Zigler believe that the most important question to answer is not, "Do abused children become abusive parents?" but rather, "Under what circumstances is the transmission of abuse most likely to occur?"

The researchers Rosemary Hunter and Nancy Kilstrom reported that the parents who did not repeat the cycle of abuse shared a number of characteristics. These nonabusive parents had more extensive social supports and fewer ambivalent feelings about their pregnancies. Their babies were healthier. The parents also displayed more open anger about their own abusive experiences and were able to describe these traumas more freely. If they had been abused, it was by one parent, while the other parent served as a supportive life raft in a sea of trouble and pain.

The psychologist Byron Egeland has also examined factors that enhance or reduce the chances that a violent childhood will lead to adult violence. He cautions that his conclusions are suggestive, since he has not yet subjected his data to rigorous analysis.

One finding is obvious. The more severe the maltreatment experienced by a mother, the more likely it is she will re-create it when she becomes a parent. Those mothers who were severely abused but who did not abuse their children had a number of characteristics in common. First, despite the abuse they had grown up with, they had at least one parent or foster parent who provided some love and support. As adults, their home situation was more stable than that of the abusing mothers. They had supportive husbands and a regular source of income.

The conclusion that we can draw from both studies is that the recreation of past abuse seems avoidable if present support is available. One of the subjects in Egeland's research appropriately demonstrates this point. The mother came from one of the most abusive backgrounds in the study. She was one of ten children. Her mother beat her often, using a belt one time, a book another, and once a hot iron. She had been emotionally battered as well as deprived of proper medical or dental attention until the time she was placed in a foster home. Despite her background, the woman in the study has not recreated the physical or emotional environment she experienced. She has married, and both she and her husband are regularly employed. In addition to the support she receives from her husband, the woman was also open and articulate about her past, unlike mothers who grew up to be abusive and who spoke of their violent experiences with little emotion or detail. Egeland concluded his case discussion by noting: "With the support she receives from her husband and the help he provides in child care, she is able to provide adequate care to her children."

While much of the research, and most of the public attention, has focused on the question of whether or not abuse experienced as a child leads to violent behavior later in life, less attention has been given to the more subtle developmental consequences of violence. Victims of child maltreatment are thought of as innocent and defenseless. Those who are harmed by the abuse do not remain innocent and defenseless for long. The image of the cute and cuddly battered baby is a myth. Therapists and foster parents have found these children to suffer from numerous deficits which often make them extremely difficult children to raise and nurture.

An example is the case of Frank, Jane, and their son Ben. Frank and Jane already had a son, Danny, who was eight years old when they adopted Ben, who was four. He had been placed in foster care after being removed from the care of his mother. Ben's mother was seventeen years old when Ben was born. She had routinely used severe and harsh punishment. At the time he was adopted, Ben's back was still marked by the scars of numerous cigarette burns and beatings inflicted by his mother. Ben was initially aloof and withdrawn when adopted. He gradually opened up, but remained quiet and wary of strangers. As is common with children who grow up in unpredictable and deprived homes, Ben hid food, even though Frank and Jane's refrigerator was always well stocked. Ben's first eight years in the home were relatively calm, marked by the normal parent/child conflicts and a handful of violent outbursts, but the situation deteriorated markedly when Ben entered adolescence. His withdrawal increased, as did his aggression. When challenged by Jane or Frank, Ben responded with a torrent of obscenities. Once, he confronted Jane with Frank's hunting rifle. He ran away from home often, experimented with drugs, and was truant from school. Frank and Jane's vision of providing a healthy and warm home for a needy child was shattered by the reality of the many and varied demands made by a child whose first six years of life were marked by emotional and physical damage.

Our knowledge about the long-term effects of abuse during the early years of life is quite limited. In almost no case has an investigator followed abused infants and children from early childhood through adolescence and into adult life. Most of what we know comes from studies that obtain retrospective histories from older children, teenagers, and adults who speak of past abuse and present troubles.

Despite the methodological limitations, a number of investigators have collected data that suggest that growing up in a violent home compromises the intellectual development of abused children. Children who have experienced violence and neglect are reported to have achieved lower scores on formal intelligence tests than peers from nonabusive homes. In addition, other researchers have found that abused and maltreated children exhibit learning problems. There is some evidence that maltreatment experiences translate into poorer school performance and lower grades. Research conducted by Roy and Ellen Herrenkohl of Lehigh University found that children from families in which a child welfare agency had found indications of physical abuse were more likely to have experienced academic failure, to have attended special classes, and to have learning disabilities.

Among the most obvious personality traits of children from violent homes is aggressiveness. It has been our experience, and the experience of many clinicians, that children from violent homes are not only aggressive and oppositional, they are also extremely wary. A social worker who treats battered children described a first session with a battering victim.

> We did not exactly start off on the proper foot. I was just finishing my lunch when I took the elevator up to the outpatient clinic where I was to meet the family. My cotherapist had already introduced herself to the state welfare worker and the child. I walked up to all three of them. I had a doughnut on a plate that was to be my dessert. The child (a ten-year-old boy) grabbed the doughnut off my plate and stuffed it into his mouth. Things went downhill from here. I did manage to get him to come with me to the office where we were to meet for therapy. Once in the office he was all over the place. He moved sporadically from one chair to the next, from one toy to another. He would glance or glare at me from time to time, but never directly responded to my attempts to start a conversation. Nor was he interested in any nonverbal interaction—such as a game or playing with a toy. After about fifteen minutes of frenetic behavior, he discovered the window and the fact that we were on the tenth floor. He jumped up onto the inside windowsill and stood flush against the window—first facing me, then facing out. The window was sealed, the building is air-conditioned, but it did not give me a secure feeling to see him pressed against the window staring down. When our fifty-minute session was over I was hungry, exhausted, and frustrated. I had failed to make any real contact with him at all.

Researchers and clinicians list several characteristics that have been found among abused children, including symptoms such as bed-wetting, poor self-concept, a tendency to withdraw and become isolated, and a pattern of hyperactivity and tantrums. E. Milling Kinard reviewed much of the literature on the psychological consequences of abuse and found other traits such as an inability to trust others, difficulties relating to both peers and adults, and a generalized unhappiness. The psychiatrist Brandt Steele notes that many abused children see themselves as ugly, stupid, inept, clumsy, or somehow defective.

Our own experiences with battered children reflect much of what we read in the scholarly literature. The most vivid and sad presentations were the pictures drawn by battered children. Many of the self-portraits drawn by abused children portray them as minute specks, apart from the other members of the family. Abused children frequently draw themselves without arms and hands, a clinical manifestation of their fear of their own anger and aggression. The pictures present sad images of withdrawn children with shattered self-concepts and, in other pictures, aggressive children with violent fantasies and fears.

In short, growing up in an abusive house can dramatically compromise the developmental and personal competence of the children. Many, if not most, maltreated children enter adolescence with severe personal deficits. It should be no great surprise that many of these children are prone to juvenile delinquency.

A variety of data points to the fact that abused children, especially boys, have a much greater chance of becoming involved in juvenile crime than children from nonabusive homes. A number of social scientists point to the fact that what we call juvenile delinquency, including acts such as running away, is a logical form of expression for the maltreated child who has a damaged self-concept and a persistent need to belong to something or do something that will improve the shattered ego.

Running away serves the important function of fleeing maltreatment, even though technically it is a status offense and a delinquent act. Delinquent groups and gangs can provide approval. Delinquent and antisocial acts are a form of direct and indirect revenge against maltreating caretakers or a society that is powerless to protect the injured child.

One investigation in New York State tracked children who had contact with official agencies for child maltreatment in the 1950s. The investigators examined records of juvenile justice agencies to see if the maltreated children had later contact for delinquency. A second group of juveniles who had contact for delinquency in 1970 were traced backward in time to determine if they had prior contact for child maltreatment. Overall, the records of more than four thousand children were examined, tracked, and traced. The investigators found that one in five children with contact for maltreatment had later reported instances of delinquency. Similarly, one in five delinquents had prior contact for maltreatment. More importantly, the kind of maltreatment related to the form of delinquency. If the maltreatment was physical abuse, the delinquency tended toward violent crime rather than status offenses such as running away or truancy.

The most unusual events are often the most sensational. The rarest form of intimate violence is children killing parents or siblings. Of the more than two thousand family homicides recorded by the Federal Bureau of Investigation in 1984, 504 (11.4 percent) involved a child killing a parent—fathers were the most likely victim; 403 cases (9.1 percent) involved a child killing a sibling—81 percent of the victims were brothers. The official statistics overestimate the actual number of children who kill, since the FBI uses the term "child" to refer to a family relationship, not an age group. Thus, a forty-year-old son who kills his father is categorized along with ten-year-olds or teenagers.

Two of the more sensational recent instances of children killing parents support the claim that growing up in a violent home increases the risk of fatal violence. Yet these cases have been sensational and controversial because of a darker aspect of the killings. In both cases the children claimed they killed to protect themselves or a sibling from an abusive parent.

Late in 1982 Richard Jahnke, a thirty-eight-year-old Internal Revenue Service agent, stepped out of his car and opened his garage door. As he opened the door, he was ambushed by a shotgun-wielding assailant. Jahnke died instantly in his driveway. The killing was the first homicide in six months in Jahnke's hometown of Cheyenne, Wyoming. Twelve hours after the murder, Jahnke's son Richard, sixteen, and daughter Deborah, seventeen, were arrested and charged with murder.

Sixteen-year-old Richard Jahnke held his father's twelve-gauge shotgun and waited for his father to open the garage door. Deborah waited in the living room, backing up her brother with a thirty-caliber automatic carbine. The children's defense for their acts was that they were protecting themselves from a brutal and abusive father. The elder Jahnke was known by his neighbors to be a severe and harsh disciplinarian. The children, speaking before and during the trial, told of their futile attempts to enlist local child protection agencies to protect them from their abusive father.

Three and one-half years after Richard Jahnke was murdered, James Pierson, a forty-two-year-old electrician, was about to leave his Long Island home for work when he was shot to death in the doorway to his kitchen. The killer was the seventeen-year-old son of a former New York City policeman. The killer had been paid $400 by Pierson's sixteen-year-old daughter's boyfriend. The daughter, Cheryl, claimed that she had been sexually abused by her father for some time. She had paid to have her father killed because she feared that he was about to begin molesting her eight-year-old sister. Cheryl Pierson was found guilty and sentenced to six months in jail and five years probation.

Did violence beget violence? Was violence used as the ultimate form of self-defense by the desperate victims of private violence who could find no help and no escape from their brutalization? Or did the children use a convenient excuse for their own brutality? The evidence from these cases is unclear. Cheryl Pierson's aunt denies the scenario painted by her niece, and suggests that the killing may have been motivated by Pierson's half-million-dollar estate.

Irrespective of the legal issues involved in the Jahnke and Pierson cases, both cases underscore the deadly and tragic impact of children growing up amidst violence. Richard Jahnke was slain by his own gun. The isolation in which the Jahnke and Pierson families lived insulated them from outside control, and cut off their children from protection and intervention. Faced with no outside help and having grown up in a violent home, fatal violence may be the tragic solution opted for by desperate children. As one of Richard Jahnke's neighbors said to a *Time* magazine reporter, "What those children did, it made terrible sense."

We attempted to add to our knowledge about the impact of growing up in a violent home in our Second National Family Violence Survey. We interviewed 3,206 parents of children under seventeen years of age who were living at home. After asking parents about their use of violence toward children in the past year and over the course of the child's lifetime, we asked whether there were any "special difficulties" with the child in the past twelve months. We presented the following list of difficulties:

1. Trouble making friends
2. Temper tantrums
3. Failing grades in school
4. Disciplinary problems
5. Misbehavior and disobedience at home
6. Physical fights with kids who live in your house
7. Physical fights with kids who do not live in your house
8. Physical fights with adults who live in your house
9. Physical fights with adults who do not live in your house
10. Deliberately damaging or destroying property
11. Stealing money or something else
12. Drinking
13. Using drugs
14. Got arrested for something

We found consistent relationships between experiencing severe or abusive violence and all of the difficulties. More importantly, the risk of troubles for children who grew up in violent homes was nearly twice that of those children whose child-hoods were free of violence. Overall, more than four out of ten children from violent homes had some trouble at school, were aggressive, and/or had troubles with drugs or alcohol in the past year. This compares with 22.9 percent of the children from nonviolent homes.

Assessing the more than three thousand children slightly *underestimates* the difficulties they experienced, since the group includes infants, toddlers, and pre-school children. Confining our analysis to only school-aged children from violent homes, we find that 44 percent experienced one or more problems in the past year. For children thirteen years of age or older, this figure rises to more than half (50.7 percent).

Across the board, children from violent homes are more likely to have personal troubles—temper tantrums, trouble making friends, school problems—failing grades, discipline problems, and aggressive and violent flare-ups with family members and people outside the home. These children are three to four times more likely than children from nonviolent homes to engage in illegal acts—vandalism, stealing, alcohol, and drugs—and to be arrested.

The research approach we used cannot tell us whether the violence actually *causes* the personal, school, aggression, and delinquency problems. Our survey only studied families at one point in time, and asked about both the troubles and violence. We cannot know from this survey, for instance, whether it was the trouble that led to the severe violence—as when a child is severely beaten because he steals, uses drugs, is failing at school, or fights with a sibling—or whether the violence led to the trouble.

A plausible interpretation of our results, along with the findings from other research on the impact of growing up amidst violence, is that a cycle of violence, troubles, and violence is created in many homes. Violent experiences set the stage for the individual and social traits that lead to trouble. The trouble is responded to with more violence.

One of the least discussed and most surprising aspects of an examination of the impact of growing up amidst violence is that not all children who experience severe physical and emotional abuse go on to have difficult lives. Cindy, the teen-ager described in this chapter's introduction, seems to have escaped the lifelong scars that many would predict for her. In spite of growing up in a tense, explosive environment, being sexually molested by her father, and witnessing her father's murder, Cindy seems to be headed for a relatively normal adult life. She endured her mother's trial and ultimate acquittal for murder, enrolled in college, and grad-uated with honor grades and a major in psychology. She is a vivacious, articulate, poised, lovely young adult who survived a family holocaust.

History is full of "survivors" of unhappy childhoods. Brandt Steele notes that many famous figures in the world had bad experiences with maltreatment early in their lives and yet amounted to something very important. The list includes French philosopher Jean Jacques Rousseau who grew up in a foster home with a punitive aunt during his youth in the 1700s. Mary Wollstonecraft was badly beaten and maltreated by her father, and went on to write "A Vindication of the Rights of Woman" in 1792, a manuscript that marked the beginning of the women's rights movement. Steele lists Rudyard Kipling, Richard Nixon, Eleanor Roosevelt, and George Orwell among the other familiar names who became successful despite significantly unhappy childhoods.

What insulates the survivors? What makes them invulnerable children? We can only speculate. Based on the results of work such as the research conducted by Byron Egeland, we suspect that one major factor in the lives of survivors is the presence of a nurturing adult. For Cindy, this was clearly her mother. For others it may be a relative, foster family, or friend. The nurturance can be personal and economic. Survivors not only need to have their personal and psychological needs met, they need to grow up in an environment that meets their needs for consistent shelter, food, and medical care. Timely, appropriate, and effective intervention also can change the equation for these children from a bleak cycle of violence and abuse to a more hopeful and productive life.

Chapter
8

Parents

Reading 25   11/10/94

Becoming a Parent

Carolyn P. Cowan and
Phillip A. Cowan

SHARON: I did a home pregnancy test. I felt really crummy that day, and I stayed home from work. I set the container with the urine sample on a bookcase and managed to stay out of the room until the last few minutes. Finally, I walked in and it looked positive. And I went to check the information on the box and, sure enough, it *was* positive. I was so excited. Then I went back to look and see if maybe it had disappeared; you know, maybe the test was false. Then I just sat down on the sofa and kept thinking, "I'm pregnant. I'm really pregnant. I'm going to have a baby!"

DANIEL: I knew she was pregnant. She didn't need the test as far as I was concerned. I was excited too, at first, but then I started to worry. I don't know how I'm going to handle being there at the birth, especially if anything goes wrong. And Sharon's going to quit work soon. I don't know when she's going to go back, and we're barely making it as it is.

SHARON: My mom never worked a day in her life for pay. She was home all the time, looking after *her* mother, and us, and cleaning the house. My dad left all of that to her. We're not going to do it that way. But I don't know how we're supposed to manage it all. Daniel promised that he's going to pitch in right along with me in taking care of the baby, but I don't know whether that's realistic. If he doesn't come through, I'm going to be a real bear about it. If I put all my energy into Daniel and the marriage and something happens, then I'll have to start all over again and that scares the hell out of me.

Sharon is beginning the third trimester of her first pregnancy. If her grandmother were to listen in on our conversation with Sharon and her husband, Daniel, and try to make sense of it, given the experience of her own pregnancy fifty years ago, she would surely have a lot of questions. Home pregnancy tests? Why would a woman with a newborn infant *want* to work if she didn't have to? What husband would share the housework and care of the baby? Why would Sharon and Daniel worry about their marriage not surviving after they have a baby? Understandable questions for someone who made the transition to parenthood five decades ago, in a qualitatively different world. Unfortunately, the old trail maps are outmoded, and there are as yet no new ones to describe the final destination. They may not need covered wagons for their journey, but Sharon and Daniel are true pioneers.

Like many modern couples, they have two different fantasies about their journey. The first has them embarking on an exciting adventure to bring a new human being into the world, fill their lives with delight and wonder, and enrich their feeling of closeness as a couple. In the second, their path from couple to family is strewn with unexpected obstacles, hazardous conditions, and potential marital strife. Our work suggests that, like most fantasy scenarios, these represent extreme and somewhat exaggerated versions of what really happens when partners become parents. . . .

THE FIVE DOMAINS OF FAMILY LIFE

The responses of one couple to our interview questions offer a preview of how the five domains in our model capture the changes that most couples contend with as they make their transition to parenthood. Natalie and Victor have lived in the San Francisco Bay Area most of their lives. At the time of their initial interview, Natalie, age twenty-nine, is in her fifth month of pregnancy. Victor, her husband of six years, is thirty-four. When their daughter, Kim, is six months old, they visit us again for a follow-up interview. Arranged around each of the five domains, the following excerpts from our second interview reveal some universal themes of early parenthood.

Changes in Identity and Inner Life

After settling comfortably with cups of coffee and tea, we ask both Natalie and Victor whether they feel that their sense of self has shifted in any way since Kim was born. As would be typical in our interviews, Mother and Father focus on different aspects of personal change:

NATALIE: There's not much "me" left to think about right now. Most of the time, even when I'm not nursing, I see myself as attached to this little being with only the milk flowing between us.

VICTOR: I've earned money since I was sixteen, but being a father means that I've become the family breadwinner. I've got this new sense of myself as having to go out there in the world to make sure that my wife and daughter are going to be safe and looked after. I mean, I'm concerned about advancing in my job—and we've even bought insurance policies for the first time! This "protector" role feels exciting *and* frightening.

Another change that often occurs in partners' inner lives during a major life transition is a shift in what C. Murray Parkes (1971) describes as our "assumptive world." Men's and women's assumptions about how the world works or how families operate sometimes change radically during the transition from couple to family.

NATALIE: I used to be completely apathetic about political things. I wasn't sure of my congressman's name. Now I'm writing him about once a month because I feel I need to help clean up some of the mess this country is in before Kim grows up.

VICTOR: What's changed for me is what I think families and fathers are all about. When we were pregnant, I had these pictures of coming home each night as the tired warrior, playing with the baby for a little while and putting my feet up for the rest of the evening. It's not just that there's more work to do than I ever imagined, but I'm so much more a part of the action every night.

Clearly, Natalie and Victor are experiencing qualitatively different shifts in their sense of self and in how vulnerable or safe each feels in the world. These shifts are tied not only to their new life as parents but also to a new sense of their identities as providers and protectors. Even though most of these changes are positive, they can lead to moments when the couple's relationship feels a bit shaky.

Shifts in the Roles and Relationships within the Marriage

VICTOR: After Kim was born, I noticed that something was bugging Natalie, and I kept saying, "What is bothering you?" Finally we went out to dinner without the baby and it came out. And it was because of small things that I never even think about. Like I always used to leave my running shorts in the bathroom . . .

NATALIE: He'd just undress and drop everything!

VICTOR: . . . and Nat never made a fuss. In fact she *used* to just pick them up and put them in the hamper. And then that night at dinner she said, "When you leave your shorts there, or your wet towel, and don't pick them up—I get furious." At first I didn't believe what she was saying because it never used to bother her at all, but now I say, "OK, fine, no problem. I'll pick up the shorts and hang them up. I'll be very conscientious." And I have been trying.

NATALIE: You have, but you still don't quite get it. I think my quick trigger has something to do with my feeling so dependent on you and having the baby so dependent on me—and my being stuck here day in and day out. You at least get to go out to do your work, and you bring home a paycheck to show for it. I work here all day long and by the end of the day I feel that all I have to show for it is my exhaustion.

In addition to their distinctive inner changes, men's and women's roles change in very different ways when partners become parents. The division of labor in taking care of the baby, the household, the meals, the laundry, the shopping, calling parents and friends, and earning the money to keep the family fed, clothed, and sheltered is a hot topic for couples (C. Cowan and P. Cowan 1988; Hochschild 1989). It seems to come as a great surprise to most of them that changes in some of their major roles affect their feelings about their overall relationship.

In a domino effect, both partners have to make major adjustments of time and energy as individuals during a period when they are getting less sleep and fewer opportunities to be together. As with Natalie and Victor, they are apt to find that they have less patience with things that didn't seem annoying before. Their frustration often focuses on each other. For couples who thought that having a baby was going to bring them closer together, this is especially confusing and disappointing.

NATALIE: It's strange. I feel that we're much closer *and* more distant than we have ever been. I think we communicate more, because there's so much to work out, especially about Kim, but it doesn't always feel very good. And we're both so busy that we're not getting much snuggling or loving time.

VICTOR: We're fighting more too. But I'm still not sure why.

Victor and Natalie are so involved in what is happening to them that even though they can identify some of the sources of their disenchantment, they cannot really make sense of all of it. They are playing out a scenario that was very common for the couples in our study during the first year of parenthood. Both men and women are experiencing a changing sense of self *and* a shift in the atmosphere in the relationship between them. The nurturance that partners might ordinarily get from one another is in very short supply. As if this were not enough to adjust to, almost all of the new parents in our study say that their other key relationships are shifting too.

Shifts in the Three-Generational Roles and Relationships

VICTOR: It was really weird to see my father's reaction to Kim's birth. The week before Natalie's due date, my father all of a sudden decided that he was going to Seattle, and he took off with my mom and some other people. Well, the next day Natalie went into labor and we had the baby, and my mother kept calling, saying she wanted to get back here. But my dad seemed to be playing games and made it stretch out for two or three days.

Finally, when they came back and the whole period was past, it turned out that my father was *jealous* of my mother's relationship with the baby. He didn't want my mother to take time away from him to be with Kim! He's gotten over it now. He holds Kim and plays with her, and doesn't want to go home after a visit. But my dad and me, we're still sort of recovering from what happened. And when things don't go well with me and Dad, Natalie sometimes gets it in the neck.

NATALIE: I'll say.

For Victor's father, becoming a first-time grandfather is something that is happening *to* him. His son and daughter-in-law are having a baby and he is becoming a grandfather, ready or not. Many men and women in Victor's parents' position have mixed feelings about becoming grandparents (Lowe 1991), but rarely know how to deal with them. As Victor searches for ways to become comfortable with his new identity as a father, like so many of the men we spoke to, he is desperately hoping that it will bring him closer to his father.

As father and son struggle with these separate inner changes, they feel a strain in the relationship between them, a strain they feel they cannot mention. Some of it spills over into the relationship between Victor and Natalie: After a visit with his parents, they realize, they are much more likely to get into a fight.

Changing Roles and Relationships Outside the Family

NATALIE: While Victor has been dealing with his dad, I've been struggling with my boss. After a long set of negotiations on the phone, he reluctantly agreed to let me come back four days a week instead of full-time. I haven't gone back officially yet, but I dropped in to see him. He always used to have time for me, but this week, after just a few minutes of small talk, he told me that he had a meeting and practically bolted out of the room. He as much as said that he figured I wasn't serious about my job anymore.

VICTOR: Natalie's not getting much support from her friends, either. None of them has kids and they just don't seem to understand what she's going through. Who ever thought how lonely it can be to have a baby?

Although the burden of the shifts in roles and relationships outside the family affects both parents, it tends to fall more heavily on new mothers. It is women who tend to put their jobs and careers on hold, at least temporarily, after they have babies (Daniels and Weingarten 1982, 1988), and even though they may have more close friends than their husbands do, they find it difficult to make contact with them in the early months of new parenthood. It takes all of the energy new mothers have to cope with the ongoing care and feeding that a newborn requires and to replenish the energy spent undergoing labor or cesarean delivery. The unanticipated loss of support from friends and co-workers can leave new mothers feeling surprisingly isolated and vulnerable. New fathers' energies are on double duty too. Because they are the sole earners when their wives stop working or take maternity leave, men often work longer hours or take on extra jobs. Fatigue and limited availability means that fathers too get less support or comfort from co-workers or friends. This is one of many aspects of family life in which becoming a parent seems to involve more *loss* than either spouse anticipated—especially because they have been focused on the gain of the baby. Although it is not difficult for us to see how these shifts and losses might catch two tired parents off guard, most husbands and wives fail to recognize that these changes are affecting them as individuals and as a couple.

New Parenting Roles and Relationships

Natalie and Victor, unlike most of the other couples, had worked out a shared approach to household tasks from the time they moved in together. Whoever was available to do something would do it. And when Kim was born, they just continued that. During the week, Victor would get the baby up in the morning and then take over when he got home from work. Natalie put her to bed at night. During the weekends the responsibilities were reversed.

It was not surprising that Natalie and Victor expected their egalitarian system—a rare arrangement—to carry over to the care of their baby. What is surprising to us is that a majority of the couples predicted that they would share the care of their baby much more equally than they were sharing their housework and family tasks *before* they became parents. Even though they are unusually collaborative in their care of Kim, Natalie and Victor are not protected from the fact that, like most couples, their different ideas about what a baby needs create some conflict and disagreement:

VICTOR: I tend to be a little more . . . what would you say?

NATALIE: Crazy.

VICTOR: A little more crazy with Kim. I like to put her on my bicycle and go for a ride real fast. I like the thought of the wind blowing on her and her eyes watering. I want her to feel the rain hitting her face. Natalie would cover her head, put a thick jacket on her, you know, make sure she's warm and dry.

NATALIE: At the beginning, we argued a lot about things like that. More than we ever did. Some of them seemed trivial at the time. The argument wouldn't last more than a day. It would all build up, explode, and then be over. One night, though, Victor simply walked out. He took a long drive, and then came back. It was a bad day for both of us. We just had to get it out, regardless of the fact that it was three A.M.

VICTOR: I think it was at that point that I realized that couples who start off with a bad relationship would really be in trouble. As it was, it wasn't too pleasant for us, but we got through it.

Despite the fact that their emotional focus had been on the baby during pregnancy and the early months of parenthood, Victor and Natalie were not prepared for the way their relationship with the baby affected and was affected by the changes they had been experiencing all along as individuals, at work, in their marriage, and in their relationships with their parents, friends, and co-workers—the spillover effects. They sometimes have new and serious disagreements, but both of them convey a sense that they have the ability to prevent their occasional blowups from escalating into serious and long-lasting tensions.

As we follow them over time, Victor and Natalie describe periods in which their goodwill toward each other wears thin, but their down periods are typically followed by genuine ups. It seems that one of them always finds a way to come back to discuss the painful issues when they are not in so much distress. In subsequent visits, for example, the shorts-in-the-bathroom episode, retold with much laughter, becomes a shorthand symbol for the times when tensions erupt between them. They give themselves time to cool down, they come back to talk about what was so upsetting, and having heard each other out, they go on to find a solution to the problem that satisfies both of their needs. This, we know, is the key to a couple's stable and satisfying relationship (Gottman and Krokoff 1989).

Compared to the other couples, one of the unusual strengths in Natalie and Victor's life together is their ability to come back to problem issues after they have calmed down. Many couples are afraid to rock the boat once their heated feelings have cooled down. Even more unusual is their trust that they will both be listened to sympathetically when they try to sort out what happened. Because Natalie and Victor each dare to raise issues that concern them, they end up feeling that they are on the same side when it comes to the most important things in life (cf. Ball 1984). This is what makes it possible for them to engage in conflict and yet maintain their positive feelings about their relationship.

Most important, perhaps, for the long-term outcome of their journey to parenthood is that the good feeling between Victor and Natalie spills over to their daughter. Throughout Kim's preschool years and into her first year of kindergarten, we see the threesome as an active, involved family in which the members are fully engaged with one another in both serious and playful activities.

WHAT MAKES PARENTHOOD HARDER NOW

Natalie and Victor are charting new territory. They are trying to create a family based on the new, egalitarian ideology in which both of them work *and* share the tasks of managing the household and caring for their daughter. They have already embraced less traditional roles than most of the couples in our study. Although the world they live in has changed a great deal since they were children, it has not shifted sufficiently to support them in realizing their ideals easily. Their journey seems to require heroic effort.

Would a more traditional version of family life be less stressful? Couples who arrange things so that the woman tends the hearth and baby and the man provides the income to support them are also showing signs of strain. They struggle financially because it often takes more than one parent's income to maintain a family. They feel drained emotionally because they rely almost entirely on their relationship to satisfy most of their psychological needs. Contemporary parents find themselves in double jeopardy. Significant historical shifts in the family landscape of the last century, particularly of the last few decades, have created additional burdens for them. As couples set foot on the trails of this challenging journey, they become disoriented because society's map of the territory has been redrawn. Becoming a family today is more difficult than it used to be.

In recent decades there has been a steady ripple of revolutionary social change. Birth control technology has been transformed. Small nuclear families live more isolated lives in crowded cities, often feeling cut off from extended family and friends. Mothers of young children are entering the work force earlier and in ever larger numbers. Choices about how to create life as a family are much greater than they used to be. Men and women are having a difficult time regaining their balance as couples after they have babies, in part because the radical shifts in the circumstances surrounding family life in America demand new arrangements to accommodate the increasing demands on parents of young children. But new social arrangements and roles have simply not kept pace with these changes, leaving couples on their own to manage the demands of work and family.

More Choice

Compared with the experiences of their parents and grandparents, couples today have many more choices about whether and when to bring a child into their lives. New forms of birth control have given most couples the means to engage in an active sex life with some confidence, though no guarantee, that they can avoid unwanted pregnancy. In addition, despite recent challenges in American courts and legislatures, the 1973 Supreme Court decision legalizing abortion has given couples a second chance to decide whether to become parents if birth control fails or is not used.

But along with modern birth control techniques come reports of newly discovered hazards. We now know that using birth control pills, intrauterine devices, the cervical cap, the sponge, and even the diaphragm poses some risk to a woman's health. The decision to abort a fetus brings with it both public controversy and the private anguish of the physical, psychological, and moral consequences of ending a pregnancy (see Nathanson 1989). Men and women today may enjoy more choice about parenthood than any previous generation, but the couples in our studies are finding it quite difficult to navigate this new family-making terrain.

Sharon, who was eagerly awaiting the results of her home pregnancy test when we met her at the beginning of this reading, had not been nearly as eager to become a mother three years earlier.

> SHARON: Actually, we fought about it a lot. Daniel already had a child, Hallie, from his first marriage. "Let's have one of our own. It'll be easy." he said. And I said, "Yeah, and what happened before Hallie was two? You were out the door."

DANIEL: I told you, that had nothing to do with Hallie. She was great. It was my ex that was the problem. I just knew that for us a baby would be right.

SHARON: I wasn't sure. What was I going to do about a career? What was I going to do about me? I wasn't ready to put things on hold. I wasn't even convinced, then, that I wanted to become a mother. It wouldn't have been good for me, and it sure wouldn't have been good for the baby, to go ahead and give in to Daniel when I was feeling that way.

In past times, fewer choices meant less conflict between spouses, at least at the outset. Now, with each partner expecting to have a free choice in the matter, planning a family can become the occasion for sensitive and delicate treaty negotiations. First, couples who want to live together must decide whether they want to get married. One partner may be for it, the other not. Second, the timing of childbirth has changed. For couples married in 1950–54, the majority (60 percent) would have a baby within two years. Now, almost one-third of couples are marrying *after* having a child, and those who marry before becoming parents are marrying later in life. Only a minority of them have their first child within two years. Some delay parenthood for more than a decade (Teachman, Polonko, and Scanzoni 1987).

Couples are also having smaller families. The decline in fertility has for the first time reduced the birthrate below the replacement level of zero population growth—less than two children per family.° And because couples are having fewer children and having them later, more seems to be at stake in each decision about whether and when to have a child. What was once a natural progression has become a series of choice points, each with a potential for serious disagreement between the partners.

Alice is in the last trimester of her pregnancy. In our initial interview, she and Andy described a profound struggle between them that is not over yet.

ALICE: This pregnancy was a life and death issue for me. I'd already had two abortions with a man I'd lived with before, because it was very clear that we could not deal with raising a child. Although I'd known Andy for years, we had been together only four months when I became pregnant unexpectedly. I loved him, I was thirty-four years old, and I wasn't going to risk the possibility of another abortion and maybe never being able to have children. So when I became pregnant this time, I said, "I'm having this baby with you or without you. But I'd much rather have it with you."

ANDY: Well, I'm only twenty-seven and I haven't gotten on track with my own life. Alice was using a diaphragm and I thought it was safe. For months after she became pregnant, I was just pissed off that this was happening to me, to us, but I gradually calmed down. If it was just up to me, I'd

---

° There are indications, however, that the birthrate in the United States is now on the rise.

wait for a number of years yet because I don't feel ready, but I want to be with her, and you can hear that she's determined to have this baby.

Clearly, more choice has not necessarily made life easier for couples who are becoming a family.

Isolation

The living environments of families with children have changed dramatically. In 1850, 75 percent of American families lived in rural settings. By 1970, 75 percent were living in urban or suburban environments, and the migration from farm to city is continuing.

We began our own family in Toronto, Canada, the city we had grown up in, with both sets of parents living nearby. Today we live some distance from our parents, relatives, and childhood friends, as do the majority of couples in North America. Increasingly, at least in the middle- and upper-income brackets, couples are living in unfamiliar surroundings, bringing newborns home to be reared in single-family apartments or houses, where their neighbors are strangers. Becoming a parent, then, can quickly result in social isolation, especially for the parent who stays at home with the baby.

John and Shannon are one of the younger couples in our study. He is twenty-four and she is twenty-three.

> JOHN: My sister in Dallas lives down the block from our mother. Whenever she and her husband want a night out, they just call up and either they take the baby over to Mom's house or Mom comes right over to my sister's. Our friends help us out once in a while, but you have to reach out and ask them and a lot of times they aren't in a position to respond. Some of them don't have kids, so they don't really understand what it's like for us. They keep calling us and suggesting that we go for a picnic or out for pizza, and we have to remind them that we have this baby to take care of.

> SHANNON: All the uncles, aunts, and cousins in my family used to get together every Sunday. Most of the time I don't miss that because they were intrusive and gossipy and into everybody else's business. But sometimes it would be nice to have someone to talk to who cares about me, and who lived through all the baby throw-up and ear infections and lack of sleep, and could just say, "Don't worry, Shannon, it's going to get better soon."

Women's Roles

Since we began our family thirty years ago, mothers have been joining the labor force in ever-increasing numbers, even when they have young babies. Women have always worked, but economic necessity in the middle as well as the working classes, and increased training and education among women, propelled them into the work force in record numbers. In 1960, 18 percent of mothers with children under six were working at least part-time outside the home. By 1970, that figure had grown to 30 percent, and by 1980 it was 45 percent. Today, the majority of women with children under *three* work at least part-time, and recent research suggests that this figure will soon extend to a majority of mothers of one-year-olds (Teachman, Polonko, and Scanzoni 1987).

With the enormous increase in women's choices and opportunities in the work world, many women are caught between traditional and modern conceptions of how they should be living their lives. It is a common refrain in our couples groups.

JOAN: It's ironic. My mother knew that she was supposed to be a mom and not a career woman. But she suffered from that. She was a capable woman with more business sense than my dad, but she felt it was her job to stay home with us kids. And she was *very* depressed some of the time. But I'm *supposed* to be a career woman. I feel that I just need to stay home right now. I'm really happy with that decision, but I struggled with it for months.

TANYA: I know what Joan means, but it's the opposite for me. I'm doing what I want, going back to work, but it's driving me crazy. All day as I'm working, I'm wondering what's happening to Kevin. Is he OK, is he doing some new thing that I'm missing, is he getting enough individual attention? And when I get home, I'm tired, Jackson's tired, Kevin's tired. I have to get dinner on the table and Kevin ready for bed. And then I'm exhausted and Jackson's exhausted and I just hit the pillow and I'm out. We haven't made love in three months. I know Jackson's frustrated. *I'm* frustrated. I didn't know it was going to be like this.

News media accounts of family-oriented men imply that as mothers have taken on more of a role in the world of paid work, fathers have taken on a comparable load of family work. But this simply hasn't happened. As Arlie Hochschild (1989) demonstrates, working mothers are coming home to face a "second shift"—running the household and caring for the children. Although there are studies suggesting that fathers are taking on a little more housework and care of the children than they used to (Pleck 1985), mothers who are employed full-time still have far greater responsibility for managing the family work and child rearing than their husbands do (C. Cowan 1988). It is not simply that men's and women's roles are unequal that seems to be causing distress for couples, but rather that they are so clearly discrepant from what both spouses expected them to be.

Women are getting the short end of what Hochschild calls the "stalled revolution": Their work roles have changed but their family roles have not. Well-intentioned and confused husbands feel guilty, while their overburdened wives feel angry. It does not take much imagination to see how these emotions can fuel the fires of marital conflict.

Social Policy

The stress that Joan and Tanya talk about comes not only from internal conflicts and from difficulties in coping with life inside the family but from factors outside the family as well. Joan might consider working part-time if she felt that she and her husband could get high-quality, affordable child care for their son. Tanya might consider working different shifts or part-time if her company had more flexible working arrangements for parents of young children. But few of the business and government policies that affect parents and children are supportive of anything beyond the most traditional family arrangements.

We see a few couples, like Natalie and Victor, who strike out on their own to make their ideology of more balanced roles a reality. These couples believe that they and their children will reap the rewards of their innovation, but they are exhausted from bucking the strong winds of opposition—from parents, from bosses, from co-workers. Six months after the birth of her daughter, Natalie mentioned receiving a lukewarm reception from her boss after negotiating a four-day work week.

NATALIE: He made me feel terrible. I'm going to have to work *very* hard to make things go, but I think I can do it. What worries me, though, is that the people I used to supervise aren't very supportive either. They keep raising these issues, "Well, what if so-and-so happens, and you're not there?" Well, sometimes I wasn't there before because I was traveling for the company, and nobody got in a snit. Now that I've got a baby, somehow my being away from the office at a particular moment is a problem.

VICTOR: My boss is flexible about when I come in and when I leave, but he keeps asking me questions. He can't understand why I want to be at home with Kim some of the time that Natalie's at work.

It would seem to be in the interest of business and government to develop policies that are supportive of the family. Satisfied workers are more productive. Healthy families drain scarce economic resources less than unhealthy ones, and make more of a contribution to the welfare of society at large. Yet, the United States is the only country in the Western world without a semblance of explicit family policy. This lack is felt most severely by parents of young children. There are no resources to help new parents deal with their anxieties about child rearing (such as the visiting public health nurses in England), unless the situation is serious enough to warrant medical or psychiatric attention. If both parents want or need to work, they would be less conflicted if they could expect to have adequate parental leave when their babies are born (as in Sweden and other countries), flexible work hours to accommodate the needs of young children, and access to reasonably priced, competent child care. These policies and provisions are simply not available in most American businesses and communities (Catalyst 1988).

The absence of family policy also takes its toll on traditional family arrangements, which are not supported by income supplements or family allowances (as they are in Canada and Britain) as a financial cushion for the single-earner family. The lack of supportive policy and family-oriented resources results in increased stress on new parents just when their energies are needed to care for their children. It is almost inevitable that this kind of stress spills over into the couple's negotiations and conflicts about how they will divide the housework and care of the children.

The Need for New Role Models

Based on recent statistics, the modern family norm is neither the Norman Rockwell *Saturday Evening Post* cover family nor the "Leave It to Beaver" scenario with Dad going out to work and Mom staying at home to look after the children. Only about 6 percent of all American households today have a husband as the sole breadwinner and a wife and two or more children at home—"the typical American family" of earlier times. Patterns from earlier generations are often irrelevant to the challenges faced by dual-worker couples in today's marketplace.

After setting out on the family journey, partners often discover that they have conflicting values, needs, expectations, and plans for their destination. This may not be an altogether new phenomenon, but it creates additional strain for a couple.

JAMES: My parents were old-school Swedes who settled in Minnesota on a farm. It was cold outside in the winters, but it was cold inside too. Nobody said anything unless they had to. My mom was home all the time. She worked hard to support my dad and keep the farm going, but she never really had anything of her own. I'm determined to support Cindy going back to school as soon as she's ready.

CINDY: My parents were as different from James's as any two parents could be. When they were home with us, they were all touchy-feely, but they were hardly ever around. During the days my mom and dad both worked. At night, they went out with their friends. I really don't want that to happen to Eddie. So, James and I are having a thing about it now. He wants me to go back to school. I don't want to. I'm working about ten hours a week, partly because he nags at me so much. If it were just up to me, I'd stay home until Eddie gets into first grade.

Cindy and James each feel that they have the freedom to do things differently than their parents did. The problem is that the things each of them wants to be different are on a collision course. James is trying to be supportive of Cindy's educational ambitions so his new family will feel different than the one he grew up in. Given her history, Cindy does not experience this as support. Her picture of the family she wanted to create and James's picture do not match. Like so many of the couples in our study, both partners are finding it difficult to establish a new pattern because the models from the families they grew up in are so different from the families they want to create.

Increased Emotional Burden

The historical changes we have been describing have increased the burden on both men and women with respect to the emotional side of married life. Not quite the equal sharers of breadwinning and family management they hoped to be, husbands and wives now expect to be each other's major suppliers of emotional warmth and support. Especially in the early months as a family, they look to their marriage as a "haven in a heartless world." Deprived of regular daily contact with extended family members and lifelong friends, wives and husbands look to each other to "be there" for them—to pick up the slack when energies flag, to work collaboratively on solving problems, to provide comfort when it is needed, and to share the highs and lows of life inside and outside the family. While this mutual expectation may sound reasonable to modern couples, it is very difficult to live up to in an intimate relationship that is already vulnerable to disappointment from within and pressure from without.

The greatest emotional pressure on the couple, we believe, comes from the culture's increasing emphasis on self-fulfillment and self-development (Bellah et al. 1985). The vocabulary of individualism, endemic to American society from its beginnings, has become even more pervasive in recent decades. It is increasingly difficult for two people to make a commitment to each other if they believe that ultimately they are alone, and that personal development and success in life must be achieved through individual efforts. As this individualistic vocabulary plays out within the family, it makes it even more difficult for partners to subordinate some of their personal interests to the common good of the relationship. When "my needs" and "your needs" appear to be in conflict, partners can wind up feeling more like adversaries than family collaborators.

The vocabulary of individualism also makes it likely that today's parents will be blamed for any disarray in American families. In the spirit of Ben Franklin and Horatio Alger, new parents feel that they ought to be able to make it on their own, without help. Couples are quick to blame themselves if something goes wrong. When the expectable tensions increase as partners become parents, their tendency is to blame each other for not doing a better job. We believe that pioneers will inevitably find themselves in difficulty at some points on a strenuous journey. If societal policies do not become more responsive to parents and children, many of them will lose their way.

Reading 26

11/10/94

Good Dads–Bad Dads: Two Faces of Fatherhood

Frank F. Furstenberg, Jr.

Bill Cosby's bestselling *Fatherhood* was no fluke. It is one of a growing list of volumes on the rewards of paternity with titles like *The Father's Book, The Nurturing Father,* and *The Wonderful Father Book.* Treatises on how to be a good dad are by no means unprecedented but the popularity and profusion of father self-help books in the 1980s are. There is no question about it: fatherhood is in vogue. Men enter fatherhood consciously and perform their fatherly duties self-consciously.

Television, magazines, and movies herald the coming of the modern father— the nurturant, caring, and emotionally attuned parent. Cosby is the prototype. No longer confined to their traditional task of being the good provider, men have broken the mold. The new father is androgynous; he is a full partner in parenthood. Today's father is at least as adept at changing diapers as changing tires.

There is another side to fatherhood, a darker side. More fathers than ever before are absent from the home. A growing proportion of men fathering children deny paternity or shirk their paternal obligations. This darker side of fatherhood has also entered our cultural consciousness through the mass media. We are bombarded with research data detailing the rising number of single mothers, inadequately supported by the men who fathered their children. A TV documentary on the breakdown in the black family, hosted by Bill Moyers, presents a young father boasting about the number of women he has impregnated. The nation is outraged. Deadbeat fathers—men who refuse to support their children—have become a political issue. The level of child support is so low that federal and state laws have been enacted to try to enforce paternal obligations.

Reconciling or at least making sense of these seemingly conflicting trends is the aim of this article. The simultaneous appearance of the good father and the bad father are two sides of the same cultural complex. Both patterns can be traced to the declining division of labor in the family. To advance this argument, the first section of this article briefly recounts the historical change in the role of fathers.

The second part examines varied sources of data that have mapped recent trends in the attitudes and behavior of fathers and points out some of the consequences of change. This examination is intended to uncover some indications of future trends in the paternal role. Is the pattern of polarization that has yielded two distinct paternal styles likely to continue? Answering this question involves considering how current public and private policies affect the distribution of paternal styles. The concluding section speculates about how some of these policies could shape the future of fatherhood.

Lest the reader expect more from this ambitious agenda than will be forthcoming, let me emphasize that this article primarily summarizes and interprets existing research. Evidence on fatherhood, though far more abundant now than a few years ago, is still sparse, especially when it comes to trend data (Lewis 1986; Parke and Tinsley 1984; Stein 1984). In any event, this article is not intended to be a review of existing research on fathers; several excellent reviews and compilations of reviews have already summarized the fragmentary literature (Lamb 1987; Lewis and Sussman 1986; Parke and Tinsley 1984). I draw on these reviews and certain seminal studies to present an impression of the changing character of fatherhood and to render a sociological reading of present trends and possible futures. On this latter matter, I am unabashedly, but I hope not recklessly, speculative.

A BRIEF HISTORY OF FATHERHOOD IN AMERICA

John Demos (1986) begins his recent essay on the social history of fatherhood by commenting, "Fatherhood has a very long history, but virtually no historians." Apparently, family historians and feminist scholars have written much about patriarchy while largely ignoring the role of the patriarch (Bloom-Feshbach 1981). Relying heavily on the work of several of his students, Demos briefly outlines the changing role of fathers over the past several centuries.

The story that Demos tells sounds familiar to readers acquainted with other features of family history. The pattern of change has not been completely linear, and much of the action has occurred in the twentieth century (Filene 1986; Parke and Tinsley 1984). After all, the changing role of fathers is part and parcel of a larger configuration of changes in the American family. (For a succinct summary of these changes, see Cherlin 1981; Thornton and Freedman 1983.)

Fathers played a dominant role in the lives of their children in the Colonial period. Fathers assumed a broad range of responsibilities, defining and supervising the children's development. Domestic control largely resided in the hands of men; wives were expected to defer to their husbands on matters of child rearing. According to E. Anthony Rotundo (1985, p. 9), a student of Demos, who has surveyed the history of fatherhood:

> Colonial fathers often showed a keen interest in the infants and toddlers of the household, but it was the mothers who fed the little ones, cared for them, and established intimate bonds with them. When children reached an age where they could understand what their parents told them (probably around age three) the lines of parent-child connection changed. Fathers began to tutor all their children in moral values at this point.

A father's moral role persisted throughout childhood, indeed into adult life; his influence was pervasive, usually exceeding the mother's responsibilities over the child. This was especially true for sons. Demos illustrates this point by noting that typically sons, when serving as apprentices, would write to their fathers, asking only to be remembered to their mothers. Both Demos and Rotundo argue that the dominant position of fathers can be traced to their economic role as landowners. (See also Greven 1970.)

At least one source of the erosion of paternal control over children was a shortage of land in New England and the shift away from an agrarian to an industrial mode of production in the beginning of the nineteenth century. However, European scholars argue that from the late eighteenth century, and perhaps earlier, an increase of affective ties within the family reshaped the nature of parenthood and parent-child relations (Shorter 1975; Stone 1979). A general decline of patriarchy, indeed, of parental authority, initiated the emergence of modern fatherhood. As men's economic roles increasingly drew them outside the home and into the marketplace, women extended their sphere of domestic influence (Filene 1986; Lasch 1977).

In a wonderfully provocative essay on the rise and fall of the "good provider" role, Jessie Bernard (1981) provides a similar account of the shift in the balance of power within the family. She observes that by the time that Tocqueville visited America in the 1830s, the nineteenth century pattern of a sharp family and parental division of labor was plainly evident. Tocqueville (1840, p. 212) portrays, as did scores of other foreign travelers (Furstenberg 1966), the contours of the modern nuclear family when he wrote that the public responsibility of men "obliges a wife to confine herself to the house, in order to watch in person and very closely over the details of domestic economy."

The spatial separation of work and home, the hallmark of an urbanized and industrialized economy, was revising both marriage and parent roles. For fathers, it meant the beginning of an almost exclusive emphasis on economic responsibilities, which curtailed the men's day-to-day contact with their children. Demos (p. 51) tells us that the consequences of the uncoupling of work and family life for men cannot be exaggerated. "Certain key elements of pre-modern fatherhood dwindled and disappeared (e.g., father as pedagogue, father as moral overseer, father as companion), while others were transformed (father as psychologist, father as example)."

Rotundo reports that men still continued to act as disciplinarians in the family, but their removal from the home meant that they "stood outside the strongest currents of feeling that flowed between generations in a family." The father as "instrumental leader," as he was later dubbed by sociologists, derived his status from the outside world, that is from his position in the marketplace. A man's occupational standing established his authority in the home and his worthiness as a husband and father. This movement from ascription to achievement, which occurred throughout the nineteenth century, signaled a profound erosion in the role of fathers. And this transformation is one source of the good father-bad father complex that becomes more evident in the twentieth century.

The strength of the evidence for this historical account is not great, however. True, as Demos and Rotundo observe, the nineteenth-century advice books reveal a growing tendency to speak to mothers exclusively about child-rearing matters, apparently acknowledging the shrinking role of fathers. A more convincing bit of evidence is provided by changing custody practices. Until the middle of the nineteenth century, custody following marital disruption was typically awarded to fathers, who, after all, were assumed to maintain control over marital property (of which the children were a part). By the end of the century, with the growth of family specialization, children increasingly remained with their mothers when marriages dissolved. Early in the twentieth century, the practice of granting custody to mothers was enshrined in the doctrine of "the tender years," which holds that the children's interests are best served when they are raised by their mothers, who ordinarily possess superior parental skills.

Yet, it is easy to overdraw the picture of change. Most available evidence is derived from the middle class. Then, too, accounts of family life in the nineteenth century, not to mention earlier times, are so sketchy that it is difficult to tell how much confidence to place in the existing evidence. As Demos points out, fathers retained considerable authority throughout the nineteenth century, while some may even have increased their affective involvement in child rearing. We should, therefore, assume only that a change occurred in the modal family type, or perhaps in the degree of cultural support for a more detached and distant style of child rearing. But as is true today, some fathers were unwilling to cede so much of the supervision of their offspring to their wives and became involved in the day-to-day upbringing of their children. It seems likely, however, that the number of these actively involved fathers may well have declined in the nineteenth century (Filene 1986). Jessie Bernard, among others, has contended that the more restrictive role of fathers ("good providers") accompanies the development of the privatized nuclear family, the "haven in a heartless world" (cf. Lasch 1977).

The image of the father as good provider remained securely in place—except, perhaps, during the Depression years, when many men could not make good on their end of the bargain (Benson 1968)—until the middle of the twentieth century. The Great Depression literature contains abundant evidence that the strict division of labor was necessarily violated, as women frequently were forced or permitted to assume a more dominant economic role and men occasionally were compelled to pick up domestic tasks in the wake of these changes (Komarovsky 1940). Women's economic roles were also expanded during the war years, as they demonstrated a capacity to fill positions in the job market. Despite these changes, there is little reason to believe that the legitimacy of the existing domestic order was seriously challenged until the 1960s. Indeed, the early post-World War II era appeared to restore the so-called traditional family by strengthening the gender-based division of labor in the family. Perhaps, participation in war enhanced the relative position of males in society and undermined gender stratification within the family. In any event, the post-war period appears to have been the heyday of the nuclear family.

Yet it was becoming clear that discontents on the part of both sexes were producing fault lines in this family form. Feminist scholars have made a strong case that the domestic accord regulating the division of labor within the family was problematic even before Betty Frieden's proclamation of grievances in 1963 issued in *The Feminine Mystique*. Barbara Ehrenreich (1983), in a fascinating cultural account of the changing male role, forcefully argues that concurrent with, if not prior to, the reawakening of feminist consciousness, men were experiencing their own resentments about the burdens of the good-provider role. She contends that in the 1950s men gradually began to retreat from the breadwinning role because they felt imprisoned both socially and emotionally by the sharply delineated masculine role. (See also Filene 1986.) So men had an independent interest in shucking the exclusive responsibilities of providing for their families. Ehrenreich (1983, p. 116) writes:

> The promise of feminism—that there might be a future in which no adult person was either a "dependent creature" or an overburdened breadwinner—came at a time when the ideological supports for male conformity were already crumbling.

What followed, Ehrenreich argues, was a male revolt that occurred in tandem with the feminist revolution of the 1970s. Both movements helped reorder domestic life, producing a family form singularly different from the traditional model that had emerged in the nineteenth century. The collapse of the breadwinner role and the simultaneous entrance of women into the labor force are twin products of twin discontents, according to Ehrenreich.

Ehrenreich gives far more weight to cultural discontents than do economists, who argue that it was the economic expansion of service jobs and the growth of wage rates for female employment that ultimately drew women into the labor force. Similarly, demographers and sociologists might provide other accounts for the disintegration of the strict, gender-based division of labor in the family. Declining fertility and high rates of divorce figured into changing opportunities or requirements for women to assume a larger economic role. And economists, demographers, and sociologists all might argue that rising educational levels of women made work outside the home more attractive than full-time mothering.

It is probably not useful to try to separate the cultural from the structural determinants of family change. They are really part and parcel of the events in the 1960s and 1970s that transformed the family. The decline of the good-provider role and of the father as instrumental leader came about when ideology and social structural change converged. The changes in the family that took place during the past two decades were, in effect, sociologically "overdetermined."

The cultural and structural accounts of change strike a common theme: the strict division of labor in the family that predominated for a century or more was precarious from the start. This family arrangement lasted for a time because gender roles were clear and men and women were mutually dependent, owing to their trained incapacity to share tasks. But its demise was predetermined because it set such rigid conditions for successful performance. Ultimately, neither men nor women were willing to uphold their end of the bargain. Women insisted on a larger role in the outside world, and men, it seems, demanded a larger role inside the family. Or, did they? On this point the evidence is much less clear-cut and consistent.

The next section of this article examines in greater detail the experiences of men over the past decade as they have presumably relinquished their responsibilities as sole providers and presumably taken up more of the slack in the home.

MEN IN THE HOME: CURRENT PATTERNS
OF FATHERING

Our consideration of fathers in the home begins on a discordant note. There are two sides to male liberation. As men have escaped from the excessive burdens of the good provider role, they have been freed to participate more fully in the family. They have also been freed from family responsibilities altogether. This contradiction emerges directly from the history of fatherhood just reviewed.

The "flight from commitment," as Barbara Ehrenreich describes the process of male liberation, is the inevitable process of the breakdown of the gender bargain that prevailed until the middle of the twentieth century. Ehrenreich (1983, p. 181), citing statistics of the rising reluctance of males to enter and maintain marital arrangements, is deeply skeptical about men's willingness to support women:

> If we accept the male revolt as a historical fait accompli and begin to act on its economic consequences for women—which I have argued that we must do—are we not in some way giving up on men . . . ? Are we acquiescing to a future in which men will always be transients in the lives of women and never fully members of the human family?

Hedging just a bit on the answer to this unsettling question, Ehrenreich concludes that in all probability men will not change and that women must rely on their own economic power with the support of an expanded welfare state.

Jessie Bernard, analyzing the changing role of the good-provider, arrives at a similar conclusion, although she is less prepared to abandon the possibility that men may find a way back into the family. The good-provider role is on its way out, she tells us, but "its legitimate successor has not yet appeared on the scene." She compares the reconstruction of gender and family roles to the deprogramming of a cult member. It has been far easier to convince husbands to share economic responsibilities with their wives than to assume domestic and child care responsibilities.

Historians Demos and Rotundo, in their individual assessments of the future of fatherhood, express similar apprehensions. Rotundo, in particular, is alarmed about the growing trend toward fathers' absence from families and the apparent unwillingness, when living apart from their children, to assume economic responsibility for their support. Rotundo comments, "Although this failure (of divorced fathers to pay child support) represents a dramatic defiance of the ideas of Modern Fatherhood, it is consistent with an extreme strain of male individualism that reacts to family responsibility as a quiet form of tyranny." He, too, questions whether androgynous fatherhood will emerge as the predominant pattern, even in the middle class where it has been championed, at least in some quarters. In sum, Rotundo expresses many of the same doubts that were voiced by feminists like Ehrenreich and Bernard about the willingness of males to remain involved in the family, now that the gender-based division of labor is no longer in place.

Let us have a closer look at the evidence they find so disturbing—the retreat from paternal obligations. Then we shall turn to the data on the other side: are fathers becoming more involved and, if so, what are the likely consequences for their spouses and their offspring?

In drawing any conclusions about trends in paternal involvement, we must be aware that the time we choose to begin our examination will to some extent affect the results. Most comparisons of demographic changes in the family begin in the 1950s and 1960s, in part because data from that period are abundant and the contrasts are almost invariably dramatic. Yet it is important to recognize, as Cherlin (1981) and others have pointed out, that comparisons between today and the baby boom era invariably exaggerate the amount of change. Even taking into account this tendency to magnify the patterns of change, it is hard to dispute that in some important respects, fathers do indeed seem to be receding from the family.

Eggebeen and Uhlenberg (1985), two demographers, have provided a descriptive overview of the declining involvement of men in families during the period from 1960 to 1980. Using data from the decennial censuses in 1960 and 1970 and the 1980 Current Population Survey, they calculate the amount of time men spend in family environments living with children. Later marriage, a decline in fertility, and increasing rates of marital dissolution all have contributed to a sharp decline—43 percent between 1960 and 1980—in the average number of years that men between ages 20 to 49 spend in families where young children live (falling from 12.34 years on average in 1960 to just 7.0 in 1980).

The decline is most evident for more educated males and is much sharper for blacks than whites. Eggebeen and Uhlenberg interpret these results to mean that the opportunity costs for entering fatherhood may be growing as the social pressure for men to become parents declines. In short, fatherhood is becoming a more voluntary role that requires a greater degree of personal and economic sacrifice.

An interesting corollary of this observation is that as fewer men assume the role, those who do will be selected among the most committed and dedicated. If this is true, one might expect to find that fathers today are fulfilling their paternal obligations more, not less, conscientiously. Fathers may be becoming a more differentiated population, with only more highly committed males entering their ranks.

This reassuring observation is, however, not entirely consistent with much of the available evidence on the entrance to fatherhood. Trends on the resolution of premarital pregnancies show a growing proportion of couples electing not to marry (O'Connell and Rogers 1984). Of course, women may be less eager than formerly to enter marriage. Social pressure and pressure from sexual partners have both declined, freeing males from entering marriage in order to make "honest women" of their partners or to "give their child a name." This more elective response to unplanned parenthood has been accompanied by a widespread reluctance of unmarried males to assume economic responsibility for their offspring. Data are unavailable to document whether or not the proportion of unmarried men who contribute to the support of their children has decreased during the past several decades, but most experts would probably agree that it has.

First, many males today do not report their children in social surveys. Fertility histories from males are notoriously unreliable because many men simply "forget" children living outside the household. My own study of unmarried youth in Baltimore showed strikingly higher reports of offspring among females than males, and recent reports indicate that many males are simply reluctant to acknowledge children they do not see or support.

Of course, it is possible to argue that such findings are not discrepant with a trend toward a more voluntaristic notion of parenthood. After all, men are increasingly selective in their willingness to assume the responsibilities of parenthood. But once they do, they may be counted on for support. Not so. A growing body of evidence suggests that adherence to child support is very undependable, even among men who are under a court agreement.

More than half of all men required to pay child support do not fully comply. Moreover, a substantial number of males leave marriage without a child support agreement. In all, only a third of all children living in fatherless homes receive paternal assistance. Among those receiving economic aid, the level is usually so low that it only rarely lifts children out of poverty. The average amount of child support paid to divorced women was $2,220 in 1981 (this figure excludes women due but not receiving support). The amount of child support measured in real dollars actually dropped from 1979 to 1981 (Weitzman 1985, ch.9). Several studies show that divorced men typically spend a much lower proportion of their postmarital income on child support than do their ex-wives. According to Weitzman (p. 295):

> Most fathers could comply with court orders and live quite well after doing so. Every study of men's ability to pay arrives at the same conclusion: the money is there. Indeed, there is normally enough to permit payment of significantly higher awards than are currently being made.

Many authorities believe that the main reason why men do not pay child support is limited enforcement. In 1984, Congress enacted legislation empowering and encouraging states to adopt stricter provisions for collecting child support. It is still too soon to tell whether the new procedures will significantly alter the level of compliance.

My own hunch is that the issue cannot be solved merely by stricter enforcement measures, although they are certainly a step in the right direction. The more intractable problem stems from the fact that many, if not most, noncustodial fathers are only weakly attached to their children. Data from the 1981 National Survey of Children revealed some alarming statistics on the amount of contact between noncustodial fathers and their offspring (who were between the ages of 11 and 16 at the time of the interview). Close to half of all children in mother-headed households had not seen their biological father during the 12 months preceding the survey, and another sixth of the sample had seen him only once or twice in the past year. And, only a sixth of the children saw their fathers as often as once a week on the average (Furstenberg et al. 1983).

Contact between children and their noncustodial fathers drops off sharply with the length of time since separation. Only about a third of the children in marriages that broke up 10 years earlier have seen their fathers in the past year. The provision of child support is closely related to the amount of contact maintained, which, in turn, is strongly associated with men's socioeconomic position.

Less educated and lower income males are less likely to remain connected to their children than those with more resources. Significantly, the figures for support by and contact with never-married fathers are almost as high as the figures for men who were wed to the mothers. It appears, then, that matrimony confers little advantage in maintaining bonds between noncustodial fathers and their offspring.

In general, these figures, along with the child support statistics, provide a dismal picture of the commitment of fathers to their children—at least to those not living in the home. Of course, we cannot completely dismiss the accounts of some noncustodial fathers who report that they are, in effect, "locked out" of a relationship with their offspring by their former wives, who resist their efforts to play a larger role in child rearing. Such men often say they are unwilling to provide child support when they are not permitted to see their offspring regularly.

Some of these responses, no doubt, are credible. More often, it seems, custodial mothers complain that they cannot interest their former husbands in seeing their children. In the National Survey of Children, 75 percent of the women stated that they thought that the children's fathers were too little involved in child care responsibilities, and most stated that they wished the fathers would play a larger role in the children's upbringing.

Having sifted through evidence from this survey and from a smaller and more qualitative study I carried out with Graham Spanier in Central Pennsylvania, the women's accounts are generally more accurate (Furstenberg and Spanier 1984). Fathers typically are unwilling or unable to remain involved with their children in the aftermath of divorce. Instead, men often assume child-rearing responsibilities in a new household after remarriage. This curious arrangement resembles a pattern of "child swapping," whereby many men relinquish the support of biological children from a first marriage in favor of biological or stepchildren in a successive union.

Interestingly, children in stepfamilies report roughly comparable levels of interaction with parents as children in families with two biological parents. Although they are less content with their stepfather's attentions, most acknowledge that their stepfathers are indeed involved in their upbringing—almost as involved as biological fathers in never-divorced families (Furstenberg 1987). It seems, then, that fatherhood is a transient status for many men. Paternal obligations are dictated largely by residence. This is not to say that some men do not maintain enduring ties with biological children when they move apart, especially with sons (Morgan, Lye and Condran 1987), but a substantial number seem to give equal or greater allegiance to their stepchildren.

This picture of men migrating from one family to the next modifies to some extent the proposition that a growing number of men are retreating from fatherhood. Just as they return to marriage, many men who have abandoned their biological children ultimately assume paternal responsibilities for a new set of offspring. Over their life course, most men will spend time raising children, if not their own, then someone else's. Yet it is clear that, from the children's point of view, this more transient notion of fatherhood may be less secure and satisfying.

Current estimates reveal that more than half of all children growing up today will spend at least part of their childhood in a single-parent household, usually headed by a woman. For many of these children, contact with and support from their biological fathers will be sporadic, at best. Although most will in time acquire stepfathers, these men will often be imperfect surrogates for missing biological fathers. They will be less constant in their attentions and, at least from the children's perspective, less often role models for adulthood. Researchers are divided over the issue of how much permanent emotional damage to children is created by marital disruption, but virtually all studies show that spells of paternal absence inevitably place children at a severe economic disadvantage in later life.

Unquestionably, then, the dark side of fatherhood, which I discussed at the beginning of this chapter, casts a large shadow over the sanguine reports of a rising interest in fatherhood. In the breakdown of the good-provider role, a large number of men, in Jessie Bernard's words, have become "role rejectors," men who retreat from family obligations. As she observes, the retreat from fatherhood is not new. Family desertion has always occurred and appeared to be common during the Depression. Then and now, a disproportionate share of the role rejectors are drawn from the ranks of the economically disadvantaged. What may be new is the number of middle-class men who are reneging on their paternal obligations—men who presumably have the resources but not the commitment to perform their fatherly responsibilities. In the concluding section of this chapter, I return to a consideration of what can or should be done to bolster the involvement of these derelict dads.

Despite the ominous rise in the number of transient fathers, it is impossible not to acknowledge that the decline of the good-provider role has, as so many observers have claimed, also brought about a more felicitous trend—the expansion of fatherhood to permit greater emotional involvement in child care. When I asked my barber, a father of two young children, whether he thought that dads were different today, he said, "They've got to be. They are there right at the beginning, don't you think?" he replied with a question back to me, the expert. When I asked him to elaborate he said, "You are right there when the baby is born. That's got to make a difference, don't you think?" he repeated.

I have not collected any statistics on the presence of men in childbirth classes and the delivery room, but I suspect that my barber is correct. Making childbirth and early infant care an important event for fathers conveys a powerful symbolic message: men are no longer on the outside, looking in; they are now part of the birth process. Whether that early contact has enduring "bonding effects," as some have argued, is a much less interesting and important question than the general impact of permitting, indeed expecting, fathers to be involved (Parke and Tinsley 1984). Unquestionably, as a number of leading developmental psychologists have observed, the shifting emphasis on paternal participation in early child care has created opportunities for a new and expanded definition of fatherhood (Lamb 1987).

The burgeoning developmental literature on fatherhood has focused largely on the consequences of new role responsibilities, especially during infancy and early childhood, for children's relations to their fathers and for their cognitive and emotional gains. Because this research is not central to the theme of this article, I merely note in passing that the seemingly obvious proposition that fathers' involvement in child care consistently and substantially benefits the child has not been well established. Existing evidence suggests that the relationship between paternal involvement and children's well-being is mediated by a number of conditions—the mother's attitude toward paternal participation, her ability to collaborate with the father, the father's skill in establishing a warm relationship to his offspring, and the child's needs, among others. The fact that increasing paternal involvement in child care does not automatically result in improved outcomes for children is not altogether surprising, especially to skeptics of simplistic proposals to enhance family functioning. Nonetheless this discovery has disappointed some of the proponents of the new fatherhood movement (Lamb 1982).

Fathers, it seems, neither matter so much emotionally as some wishful observers claim, nor so little as other skeptics contend. When fathers are strongly committed to playing a major role in their children's upbringing their impact can be large, especially when mothers are a less conspicuous presence in the family. Ordinarily, this is not what happens: mothers are the preeminent figures, and the added impact of paternal involvement in shaping the child's emotional development seems rather small.

But a growing body of research indicates that in certain circumstances fathers do play a central role in child rearing, a role that greatly benefits the cognitive and emotional development of young children. Despite some people's reservations (Rossi 1985), fathers, it seems, can be perfectly capable caretakers of young infants. The notion that mothers possess special or unique talents for child care has not been substantiated (Russell 1986). Fathers do characteristically perform child care duties differently, according to Michael Lamb and others who have investigated infant care by men. In particular, fathers tend to engage in more play and roughhousing. Yet Lamb (1987, p. 13) observes that the emotional tone of the paternal relationship is what matters: "As far as influence on children is concerned, there seems to be little about the gender of the parent that is distinctively important. The characteristics of the father as a parent rather than the characteristics of the father as a man appear to influence child development."

Moreover, it is likely that active paternal participation has broader consequences for family functioning. Lois Hoffman (1983), for example, has assembled evidence showing that greater involvement by fathers in household and child care duties reduces the role strain experienced by working mothers. On the basis of fragmentary data, Hoffman speculates that easing the burdens of employed wives enhances marital well-being, which, in turn, contributes to children's adjustment. If fathers assumed an equal parental role, children would be less likely to acquire gender conceptions that restrict the future family performance of males and occupational performance of females. More immediately, however, conjugal bonds might be strengthened when couples share parental tasks.

Hoffman's assessment of the possible benefits of greater paternal participation is not uniformly rosy, however. She notes that the expansion of fatherhood can and has encroached on the prerogatives of women in the home. A breakdown of the traditional division of labor can erode women's power, create greater conflict when parents do not share similar definitions of desirable parental behavior, and dilute the satisfactions of motherhood for women. Hoffman also observes that as men become more competent parents, they may be more willing to divorce, knowing that they have the skills to claim custodial rights. I arrived at a similar conclusion in a study of divorce and remarriage in Central Pennsylvania. When fathers assumed a more active parental role before divorce, the possibility of postmarital conflict over rights and responsibilities for the children tended to increase.

On balance neither I nor, probably, Hoffman would claim that the costs of greater paternal participation outweigh the potential benefits for children. Most women are only too happy to see their husbands play a greater role in child care and would gladly yield territory in the home to increase their power outside the household. The greater involvement of men in child care probably does more to contribute to marital contentment than it does to increase the risk of conflict and divorce.

What is more open to serious question is the extent to which fathers today actually involve themselves in child care. Here again I turned to my barber for an opinion. How much child care does he, as a liberated father, actually do? "Well, I give my wife some relief, but she naturally does most of it," he volunteered. "I really don't have that much time to help out." He is not unique. The preponderance of data from a variety of sources indicates that most fathers still do very little child care, especially when their children are very young.

The extent to which fathers' roles have changed in recent years cannot easily be measured, for researchers simply did not think to ask about paternal involvement in child care even a decade or so ago. This fact itself might be taken as an index of change. Yet it is possible that fathers in the recent past did more than they got credit for and today do less than we like to think. The consensus of most scholars who have studied the question of role change is that modest change has taken place in both the attitude and the behavior of fathers. The change that has occurred is linked to a general shift in less gender-specific family roles (Thornton and Freedman 1983; Stein 1984). Recent data from the Virginia Slims Survey of American Women, times-series data on women's issues collected by Roper, reveal similar shifts on a range of gender-related attitudes, although limited information was collected specifically on paternal obligations. From 1974 to 1985, women significantly increased (from 46 to 57 percent) their preference for a marriage in which husband and wife shared responsibility for work, household duties, and child care more equitably. Similarly, the Virginia Slims Survey recorded a sharp rise in wives desire to be paid by their husbands for household work (1985 Virginia Slims American Women's Opinion Poll). Although men were not asked these specific questions, their opinions on other related matters indicated that they, too, had greatly increased their support for more egalitarian marriages.

Whether these attitudinal changes are matched by parallel shifts in behavior is doubtful, though clearly some realignment of marital and child care roles has taken place. Joseph Pleck (1985), who has done the most extensive research on the question, concludes that most of these changes have been relatively modest.

The most recent data on changing patterns of paternal involvement were assembled by Juster and Stafford (1985) of the Institute for Survey Research at the University of Michigan. Juster, in a brief analysis of time spent in family activities, traces changes from 1975 to 1981. Using time diaries, he is able to show that men decreased hours spent at work in favor of home activities while women followed the opposite course. This change was especially marked for younger people. Further evidence of domestic change could be seen in the amount of time men spent in "female" types of activities—household duties that have traditionally been performed by women. Between the mid-1970s and the early 1980s, a distinct realignment in roles occurred, with women relegating more domestic tasks to men. This is further evidence of a movement toward greater equality between the sexes, a movement that Juster believes is likely to accelerate in years to come.

Unfortunately, Juster does not break out the data on child care separately or analyze the changes by the presence or absence of children in the home. Pleck's analysis of time diaries reveals that fathers spend substantially more time in domestic and child care duties in households when mothers are employed, but the men still fall far short of assuming an equal load. Moreover, men in families with young children do less than those in households with no children or older offspring. Clearly, these analyses confound a number of related variables—age, cohort, the number and age of children, and the labor force status of mothers. Unless these separate components of paternal participation in child care are disentangled, it is difficult to get a clear picture of the magnitude of the changes in patterns of child care by men and women.

Lamb and Pleck draw interesting distinctions in paternal child care that involves time spent interacting, time spent being available (being the parent on duty), and time spent being responsible, that is making child care arrangements. Apparently, much of the increase in paternal activity has been in the first realm—fathers as babysitters. The least change has occurred in the sphere as father as orchestrator of the child's activities. In this respect, it appears that fathers are still pinch hitters or part-time players rather than regulars.

Evidence from studies of father's role after divorce or separation shows much the same pattern. Fathers are even more marginal. Despite the considerable attention given to joint-custody arrangements in the mass media, in fact, such agreements are rare and often short-lived. Typically, fathers, even when they remain on the scene, play a recreational rather than instrumental role in their children's lives.

In conclusion, evidence of change is compelling, and some researchers believe that the pace of change may be picking up. But fathers, except in rare circumstances, have not yet become equal partners in parenthood. This is not to say that androgynous fatherhood could not happen, only that it has not happened and is not likely to happen in the near future.

Michael Lamb, Joseph Pleck, and their colleagues have analyzed some of the sources of resistance to change. They mention four in particular: motivation, skills and self-confidence, social support, and institutional practices. Motivation represents the willingness of men to change. (William Goode [1982] has written most cogently on the subtle barriers to changing male prerogatives.) Clearly, further change requires a growing number of men to accept an expanded family role. Unless they acquire the skills to assume a greater scope of parental responsibilities, they are likely to confine their attentions to traditional male tasks. The restructuring of the father role requires support and encouragement from wives. Presumably, some wives are reluctant to give up maternal prerogatives. Finally, a number

of institutional practices contribute to the maintenance of the status quo by denying fathers the resources to assume a greater share of child care responsibilities.
Entrenched social practices continue to convey the message that parenting is
mainly women's work.

Lamb argues that unless there is movement on all four of these fronts, fathers
are likely to continue to play a relatively marginal role in the family. Clearly, however, these four components overlap and are interconnected. Although Lamb con-
ceives of them as hierarchical, they are probably better thought of as isomorphic.
Change in any one will have ramifications for the others. Shifts at the personal and
interpersonal level are likely to create social and political demands for widening
opportunities for fathers to become active caretakers, just as changes in women's
attitudes and the views of men have created change in the marketplace. But political and economic change—sometimes loosely referred to as structural change—
can, by the same token, drastically alter personal and interpersonal expectations.
In the next and concluding section, which explores the link between public policy
and change in paternal practices, I assume that change may be instituted in a variety of ways. I am primarily interested in the prospects for change, ways that change
could come about, and some possible consequences for the future of the family.

PUBLIC POLICY AND PATERNAL PRACTICES

Up to now, I have largely avoided the political question of whether the breakdown
of the good-provider role was desirable. But I cannot entirely ignore this issue if I
am going to discuss the potential effects of future policy initiatives to further
equalize parental responsibilities. After all, many people wish to restore the gender-based division of labor that served as the mainspring of the nuclear family until
the middle part of this century.

I suppose that if I believed that the costs involved in this transformation of
family form greatly exceeded the benefits derived, I would be obligated to try, at
least, to imagine ways of returning to the status quo ante. Some costs may exist,
especially for children, who have probably been somewhat ill-served by the rapid-
ity of change. This is not to say that children, girls particularly, have not benefited
from the collapse of the gender-based division of labor. But we have not managed
to protect children as well as we might have if we regarded their welfare as a
collective, rather than merely family-based, obligation.

Change has not been cost-free for women, either. Restrictions on divorce provided social and material protections for women, albeit of a paternalist type. Certainly, the declining economic circumstances of divorced women constitute a serious penalty in the quest for equality. Furthermore, as women have entered the
marketplace, they have become susceptible to greater occupational stress, leading
in some instances to an increase of mental and physical maladies. Finally, some
people have argued that the sexual liberation has placed women at greater, not
lesser, risk of sexual exploitation by men. Rises in venereal diseases, pregnancy,
abortion, and possibly sexual abuse and rape could be seen as adverse side effects
of freer sexual relations.

Yet if one examines the sentiments of both men and women, admittedly imperfectly captured in public opinion surveys, most Americans, men and women alike, seem to endorse the changes that have occurred in recent decades. When asked whether they favored or opposed most of the efforts to strengthen and change women's status in society, only 40 percent of women and 44 percent of men were supportive in 1970. Today, 73 percent of women and 69 percent of men sanction continued efforts to improve the status of women. Both men and women anticipate further changes in women's roles, while only a tiny minority believe that traditional roles will be restored. Most important of all, the vast majority of women believe that they have gained respect in the process (1985 Virginia Slims). Possibly these sentiments should be counted as mere rationalizations, but I am inclined to interpret them as strong support for changes that have occurred. Even after experiencing the costs associated with family change, most Americans desire continued movement toward gender equality.

In any event, it is difficult to imagine a scenario that would restore the family form common a generation ago. The collapse of the good-provider role resulted from a combination of economic changes and ideological discontents. What is the possibility of reversing these changes? Engineering the withdrawal of women from the labor force and persuading men to pick up the economic slack would be somewhat like putting Humpty Dumpty together again.

Indeed, there is every reason to believe that we are in for more change of the type that we have seen. The proportion of working mothers with young children continues to climb, putting more pressure on fathers to shoulder more of the child care. Men's attitudes and behavior, whether willingly or grudgingly, may well fall into line, as they are increasingly pressured by their partners and society at large to help out more (Goode 1982). Open support for patriarchical privilege has receded in the middle class and may be on the wane in the working class as well. It is unacceptable to make sexist comments in public arenas and unfashionable to do so in private circles. Sexism, like racism, has been forced underground.

Proponents of change have called for a variety of policies that might hasten the process of accommodation to the new family order: parent education to prepare men for future paternal roles, paternity leave to allow them to accept a fuller measure of care for infants, and flex time to enable them to invest more time in child-rearing and domestic duties.

The limited evidence for the efficacy of such programs does not persuade me that any of these measures is likely to substantially increase the level of paternal involvement. Parent education classes may enhance the motivation and skills of young men who want to assume a larger paternal role, but they are not likely to produce many converts to the cause. They are somewhat like watered-down job training programs, which have had little or no effect in increasing occupational prospects. In Sweden, where paternity leave has been available for a number of years, only a small fraction of fathers use the benefit. There is little evidence that Swedish men, who are also exposed to more parent education, have developed more egalitarian child care patterns than American fathers. Finally, experiments to implement more flexible work schedules seem to have had a negligible effect on the participation of fathers in child care.

I do not dismiss these programs out of hand; they may not have had a full and fair chance to show effects. There is some evidence that many parents manage to get by with no outside day care when husbands and wives are able to work separate shifts (Presser and Cain 1983). Possibly, as some have argued, flex-time programs do not go far enough. The same can be said for measures such as education in parenthood or paternity leave. Besides, it might be argued that these provisions convey an important symbolic message to men that they have the right and the obligation to become more involved. Thus, these programs may have important indirect effects on men by changing the normative climate in society at large rather than by directly affecting the men who participate in them.

General family support services such as day care or preschool programs, which relieve the burden of child care for both employed parents, may do as much to foster paternal involvement as do categorical programs directed at fathers alone. Specialized programs can serve only a limited number of fathers—probably, largely the men who are already ideologically receptive. Systems designed to assist parents, regardless of gender, draw from a larger base and attract more public support. Thus, the arena for change may be played out in Parent-Teacher Associations, church groups, professional organizations, and the like. The degree to which these groups welcome or resist gender change within the family is a sensitive barometer to the transformation of family roles.

Enticing fathers in two-parent families to assume a greater share of child care responsibilities may be much less difficult than gaining their involvement when childbearing occurs out-of-wedlock, or retaining their involvement after marriages break up. As we saw earlier, some feminists are prepared to give up on men and turn to a more benign and generous welfare system for support. Building an economic support system that further weakens paternal obligation is questionable policy on several grounds. First, it is not clear how generous we are prepared to be in providing for the children of single mothers. And even if we raise the economic situation of female heads of families, their children are not going to be on a par with children in two-parent families. Furthermore, policies that let men off the hook are bound to contribute further to the retreat of men from the family. That is bad for women, bad for children, and bad for men as well. It is difficult to argue that black women, children, or even men, for that matter, have benefited from the retreat of males from participation in family life. Everyone seems to have lost as the ability of black males to contribute economically has been eroded over the past two decades. Some might say that the same trends are beginning to occur among poorer whites, as males increasingly offer little economic support to women and children. The rising rates of nonmarital childbearing among young white women may be an ominous harbinger.

As mentioned, vigorous efforts have recently been made to increase the contribution of males to children they have fathered but are not living with. This hard-line policy is intended to make men feel responsible for their children, but whether a more aggressive approach to the collection of child support produces a greater sense of paternal obligation remains to be seen.

The "stick" approach is worth trying, but should we not also be conjuring up a few carrots—programs designed to create incentives to paternal participation? In a recent article in the Public Interest, Vinovskis and Chase-Lansdale (1987) question whether teenage marriages ought to be discouraged. Citing a mixed bag of evidence, they assert that at least some fathers are capable of supporting their children and young mothers might do better if they were to enter marriage—even if the likelihood of the marriage's survival is low. Without discussing the validity of their claim, it is discouraging to discover that the authors of this provocative thesis suggest no policies for encouraging men to enter marriage other than to say that social scientists have been overly pessimistic about the merits of matrimony. Can we not conceive of ways to make marriage more attractive and to discourage single parenthood?

Previously I have argued, along with Wilson (Wilson and Neckerman 1985) and many others, that marriage is increasingly inaccessible to many low-income youth because males simply do not have the economic prospects to provide females with an incentive for entering marriage. The income-maintenance experiments notwithstanding, I am also persuaded that for many low-income couples, unemployment and poor future earnings weaken conjugal bonds and contribute to the especially high rates of marital instability among poorer Americans. Despite the demise of the good-provider role, men are more likely to move out of a marriage to which they do not contribute and women are less likely to want them to remain even if men are so inclined.

This situation probably could not be immediately remedied even if the unemployment rates were to return to the 1960s levels. With the breakdown of the division of labor within marriage, the value of men's economic contributions probably counts for less today than it once did, and the emotional exchange probably counts for more. Yet material contributions still matter, and a healthier economy would probably reduce, or at least slow down, the retreat from marriage and make remarriage more attractive, especially among disadvantaged populations.

There are probably other ways of making marriage more economically appealing to couples. Eliminating the residual marriage penalty and creating tax incentives for marriage, especially for poor people with children, might have some modest effects by at least reducing the disincentives to marrying. It might also be feasible to devise a program of family assistance linked to Social Security payments. Couples who contribute to the support of children might receive added payments during retirement. Although such a plan might not directly hold couples together, it would certainly encourage fathers to contribute to child support. It might be possible to provide bonus payments to households with two earners or two parents, or both.

Such programs are costly, and, judging from efforts designed to promote pronatalist policies, we should not look for large effects on nuptial behavior from incentive schemes. In some instances, though, even modest results might be cost-effective, given the very real price tag to society associated with single parenthood and the absence of child support. Moreover, as I have contended throughout this chapter, programs tailored to promote paternal involvement bolster the norm that it is desirable for men to participate in the family and support their offspring. As such they may produce indirect effects consistent with the aim of increasing paternal participation in the family.

Finally, it is reasonable to suppose that marital stability may be enhanced, at least slightly, by the diffusion of cultural norms permitting and promoting more child care involvement among fathers. Scattered evidence from a variety of studies, as I mentioned earlier, reveals that marital stress is relieved when men assume a larger burden of child care. Also, greater emotional investment in children by men appears to increase marital stability, reducing the risk that fathers will withdraw from the family (cf. Morgan, Lye, and Condran 1987).

CONCLUSION

Ordinarily it is difficult to predict future family trends. Forecasting changes in the father role is extremely hazardous, as we are witnessing a confluence of conflicting trends. About one thing we can be fairly certain—further attenuation of the good-provider role is likely to take place as fewer women count on their husbands to provide economic support without women's aid and fewer men expect women to manage the household and children without men's assistance. Whether the gender-based division of labor that characterized families until the middle of the twentieth century will disappear altogether is highly questionable. But if I am correct that the breakdown of the good-provider role for men is ultimately responsible for the rise of the good dad–bad dad complex, the bifurcation of fatherhood could continue unabated, creating both more fathers that are closely involved with their children and more that are derelict. Even if two discrete male populations are formed, men, as noted earlier, may migrate from one category to the other during their lifetime.

Some of the conditions that might reduce the number of men who are retreating from fatherhood involve normative shifts that encourage greater participation of fathers in child rearing; these shifts are not easily susceptible to policy manipulation. I nonetheless remain rather sanguine about the prospects of further change if only because the cultural climate appears to be increasingly receptive to this trend.

One set of policies that has been mentioned here involves creating larger incentives to contribute to children and disincentives to withhold support. Experimental programs may provide indications of the results to be expected from the judicious use of the carrot and stick. We probably should not expect too much from policy interventions, if only because we are not prepared to build either a very large carrot or stick. The crux of the problem is that men looking at marriage today may sense that it offers them a less good deal than it once did. This is the inevitable result of reducing male privileges, female deference to men, and a range of services that were customarily provided as part of the conjugal bargain. The loss of these privileges has persuaded some men to opt out of family life altogether.

Those who have not done so now expect more emotional gratification from marriage; more than ever before, intimacy has become the glue of family life. Recently, men have begun to realize a second source of benefits from family life—the gratifications of parenthood and the satisfactions of close ties with their children. These men have become the "new fathers" who are more emotionally invested in parenthood. It is too early to tell whether this new form of fatherhood will enhance stability in family life. Are these more involved fathers more committed to family life, more willing to endure marital discontents in order to remain with their children, and more prepared to sacrifice their own emotional needs in the interests of their offspring? I am not so certain, but time will tell. In the meantime, it may be necessary to devise all the means we can muster to produce more nurturant males, in the hope that they will help to strengthen our present imperfect and tenuous forms of marriage and parenthood.

BIBLIOGRAPHY

Benson, Leonard. 1968. *Fatherhood: A Sociological Perspective.* New York: Random House.

Bernard, Jessie. 1981. "The Good Provider Role: Its Rise and Fall." *American Psychologist* 36: no. 1:1–12.

Bloom-Feshbach, J. 1981. "Historical Perspectives on the Father's Role." In *The Role of the Father in Child Development,* 2nd ed., edited by Michael E. Lamb. New York: John Wiley & Sons.

Cherlin, Andrew J. 1981. *Marriage, Divorce, Remarriage.* Cambridge, Mass.: Harvard University Press.

Demos, John. 1986. *Past, Present and Personal: The Family and the Life Course in American History.* New York: Oxford University Press.

Eggebeen, David, and Peter Uhlenberg. 1985. "Changes in the Organization of Mens' Lives: 1960–1980." *Family Relations* 34, no. 2:251–57.

Ehrenreich, Barbara. 1983. *The Hearts of Men: American Dreams and the Flight from Commitment.* New York: Anchor Press.

Filene, Peter G. 1986. *Him/Her/Self: Sex Roles in Modern America.* Baltimore: The Johns Hopkins Press.

Frieden, Betty. 1963. *The Feminine Mystique.* W. W. Norton and Company, Inc.

Furstenberg, Frank F., Jr. 1966. "Industrialization and the American Family: A Look Backward." *American Sociological Review* 31:326–37.

Furstenberg, Frank F., Jr. 1987. "The New Extended Family: Experiences in Stepfamilies." In *Remarriage and Step-parenting Today,* edited by Kay Pasley and Marilyn Ihinger-Tallman: 42–61. New York: Guilford Press.

Furstenberg, Frank F., Jr., Christine Winquist Nord, James L. Peterson, and Nicholas Zill. 1983. "The Life Course of Children of Divorce: Marital Disruption and Parental Contact." *American Sociological* Review 48, no. 10:656–68.

Furstenberg, Frank F., Jr., and Graham B. Spanier. 1984. *Recycling the Family: Remarriage After Divorce.* Beverly Hills: Sage Publications.

Goode, William J. 1982. "Why Men Resist." In *Family in Transition,* edited by Arlene S. Skolnick and Jerome H. Skolnick: 201–18. Boston: Little, Brown and Company.

Greven, Phillip. 1970. *Four Generations: Population, Land and Family in Colonial Andover, Massachusetts.* Ithaca, N.Y.: Cornell University Press.

Hoffman, Lois Wladis. 1983. "Increasing Fathering: Effects on the Mother." In *Fatherhood and Family Policy,* edited by Michael E. Lamb and Abraham Sagi, 167–90. Hillsdale, N.J.: Lawrence Erlbaum Associates.

Juster, Thomas F., and Frank B. Stafford. 1985. *Time, Goods and Well-Being.* Ann Arbor: Institute for Survey Research.

Komarovsky, Mirra. 1940. *The Unemployed Man and His Family.* New York: Dryden Press.

Lamb, Michael E., ed. 1982. *Nontraditional Families: Parenting and Child Development.* Hillsdale, N.J.: Lawrence Erlbaum Associates.

Lamb, Michael E., ed. 1987. *The Father's Role: Applied Perspectives.* New York: John Wiley & Sons.

Lamb, Michael E. ed. 1987. *The Father's Role: Cross Cultural Perspectives.* Hillsdale, N.J.: Lawrence Erlbaum Associates.

Lasch, Christopher. 1977. *Haven in a Heartless World: The Family Besieged.* New York: Basic Books.

Lewis, Robert A. 1986. "Men's Changing Roles in Marriage and the Family." In *Men's Changing Roles in the Family,* edited by Robert A. Lewis and Marvin B. Sussman. New York: Haworth Press.

Lewis, Robert A., and Marvin B. Sussman, eds. 1986. *Men's Changing Roles in the Family.* New York: Haworth Press.

Morgan, S. Philip, Diane Lye, and Gretchen Condran. Forthcoming. "Sons, Daughters and Divorce: The Effect of Children's Sex on Their Parent's Risk of Marital Disruption." *American Journal of Sociology.*

O'Connell, Martin, and Carolyn C. Rogers. 1984. "Out-of-Wedlock Births, Premarital Pregnancies, and Their Effect on Family Formation and Dissolution." *Family Planning Perspectives* 16, no. 4:157–62.

Parke, Ross D., and Barbara R. Tinsley. 1984. "Fatherhood: Historical and Contemporary Perspectives." In *Life Span Developmental Psychology: Historical and Cohort Effects,* edited by K. A. McCluskey and H. W. Reese. New York: Academic Press.

Pleck, Joseph. 1985. *Working Wives Working Husbands.* Beverly Hills: Sage Publications.

Presser, H. B., and V. Cain. 1983. "Shift Work Among Dual-Earner Couples with Children." *Science* 219:876–79.

Rossi, Alice S. 1985. "Gender and Parenthood." In *Gender and the Life Course,* edited by Alice S. Rossi. New York: Aldine Publishing Company.

Rotundo, E. Anthony. 1985. "American Fatherhood: A Historical Perspective." *American Behavioral Scientist,* 29, no. 1:7–25.

Russell, Graeme. 1986. "Primary Caretaking and Role Sharing Fathers." In *The Father's Role: Applied Perspectives,* edited by Michael E. Lamb: 29–57. New York: John Wiley & Sons.

Shorter, Edward. 1975. *The Making of the Modern Family.* New York: Basic Books.

Stein, Peter J. 1984. "Men in Families." *Marriage and Family Review* 7, no. 3:143–62.

Stone, Lawrence. 1979. *The Family, Sex and Marriage in England 1500–1800.* New York: Harper & Row.

Thornton, Arland, and Deborah Freedman. 1983. "The Changing American Family." *Population Bulletin* 38, no. 4:2–44.

Tocqueville, Alexis de. 1954. *Democracy in America,* 2 vols. New York: Vintage Books.

Vinovskis, Maris A. P., and Lindsay Chase-Lansdale. 1987. "Should We Discourage Teenage Marriage?" *Public Interest* 87:23–37.

The 1985 Virginia Slims American Women's Opinion Poll. A Study conducted by the Roper Organization, Inc.

Weitzman, Lenore J. 1985. *The Divorce Revolution: The Unexpected Social and Economic Consequences for Women and Children in America.* New York: Free Press.

Wilson, William Julius, and Kathryn M. Neckerman. 1985. "Poverty and Family Structure: The Widening Gap between Evidence and Public Policy Issues." In *Fighting Poverty: What Works and What Doesn't,* edited by Sheldon H. Danziger and Daniel H. Weinberg: 232–59. Cambridge, Mass.: Harvard University Press.

Reading 27

Single Mothers: A Review and Critique of Current Research

Martha T. Mednick

The single mother of minor children has been a subject of considerable public attention since the early 1970s. This group of women was then recognized as a growing segment of the population, and one that would continue to grow. Now, in the mid-1980s, this forecast has been proven correct, and public discussion has focused on the impoverished condition of women raising young children alone. Indeed, the term "feminization of poverty" was coined to characterize this group (Pearce, 1978).

The problems encountered by these women constitute a social issue that needs constructive study by applied social psychologists. My purpose in this [pa-

From *Family Processes and Problems: Social Psychological Aspects, (Applied Social Psychology Annual 7).* Copyright 1987 by the Society for the Psychological Study of Social Problems, Inc. Reprinted by permission of Sage Publications, Inc. Cross-references to within the original have been omitted.

per] is to set a direction for such work by critically reviewing the psychological research on divorced, separated, or never-married women who are raising one or more children on their own. I have excluded studies of teenage pregnancy, of divorce process and trauma, and ones that examine only effects on children.

This review of the research of the past decade begins with demographics that give a sense of the dimensions of the problem. I then discuss the values that have framed the research in this area. Next is a review and critique of the research, and, finally, conclusions, some suggestions for future work, and a comment on public policy.

A DEMOGRAPHIC FRAME OF REFERENCE

Incidence and Economic Status

Reports based on the 1980 census, as well as on subsequent counts and projections, show a marked increase in the number and proportion of single mothers heading their own households.[1] In 1970, the percentage of female-headed households was 8.7%; by 1983, it was 11.3%. More pertinent is the fact that, by 1981, 18.8% of all families with minor children were female-headed. For blacks the rates were higher; by 1981, 47.5% of black families with minor children present were headed by women, up from 30.6% in 1970 (U.S. Commission on Civil Rights, 1983). Female-headed families and the millions of children living in these families became progressively poorer, even as the economy improved. In 1980, about 40% of single mothers were below national poverty levels; by 1983, this figure had increased to 47% (U.S. Commission on Civil Rights, 1983).

Single mothers tend to be in and out of the labor force and are more subject to unemployment and underemployment. Even with full-time employment, women heading their own families have a poverty rate that is two and one-half times that of two-parent families; and part-time and unemployed women workers are even worse off.

Family poverty rates by ethnicity, employment status, and family size are presented in Table 27.1. The negative impact of the presence of children, and of being black or Hispanic, on women's economic status is profound. Table 27.2 compares family income for various family structures and employment patterns in 1970 and 1981 and shows the impoverishing effects of being a female head of household. Black women in this category are particularly disadvantaged.

For many women, full-time employment does not raise their economic status much, if any, above the level of poverty, because women's work does not provide an income at all comparable to men's work. This is due to a multiplicity of factors, including occupational sex segregation, sex discrimination, poor education and training, sex role stereotyping, and the general devaluation of women's work (Mednick, 1982). "Employment is generally considered the key to economic independence in our society, but it does not unlock the door for many women" (U.S. Commission on Civil Rights, 1983)—a fact that has a particularly strong impact on the situation of the single mother.

Table 27.1   PERCENTAGE OF FEMALE HOUSEHOLDERS
BELOW THE U.S. POVERTY LEVEL, 1981

Ethnicity and employment status	Number of children under age 18			
	Zero	One	Two	Three
White female head	12.7%	31.3%	38.8%	58.8%
no earners	26.9	86.0	89.1	92.9
head only earner	11.5	25.1	27.3	47.5
Black female head*	35.8	45.1	61.2	72.6
no earners*	66.2	88.7	96.0	97.7
head only earner*	37.1	26.4	42.1	57.2
Hispanic female head	30.5	47.8	60.1	76.8
no earners	64.3	—	—	—
head only earner	25.0	30.4	—	—

Source: U.S. Commission on Civil Rights (1983, p. 3).

— Base less than 75,000.

* It is possible for the overall poverty rate for all black female-headed households to be lower than the poverty rate for black female-headed households where the head is the only earner because some such households have two or more adult earners.

FAMILY AND MOTHERHOOD VALUES

The values that have typically framed research in this area are that legitimate power and authority are the father's role, that the husband should be the sole or major economic provider, that marriage and family life must be structured in terms of separate roles and activities with a strict and proper division of labor, that all other family forms are deviant, and that single mothers are in a transitional state anyway.

The biasing effect of such values on the research on single mothers was delineated in an important review by Brandwein, Brown, and Fox (1974). Their search of the psychological, sociological, and social welfare literature revealed the limitations imposed by the assumption that the single-mother family form is deviant and pathological, and they concluded that more had been revealed about the effects of stigmatization than about the female-headed families under study. The corpus of work they reviewed had overlooked economic issues, the nature and effect of the authority shift from fathers to mothers, and the extent to which mothers' increased responsibilities and stress might be the important determinants of familial well-being.

Are Single Mothers in Transition?

Another part of the ideology that influenced earlier work was the view that the single-mother status is a transitional one (e.g., Ross & Sawhill, 1975). The impact of this view began with sample characteristics: Rarely was information provided

Table 27.2   MEDIAN FAMILY INCOME, BY RACE AND TYPE
OF FAMILY

Type of family	$ 1970	$ 1981	% Increase 1970–1981
Husband-wife families	$10,516	$25,065	138%
wife in labor force	12,276	29,247	138
Female householder, no husband present	5,093	10,960	115
Male householder, no wife present	—	19,889	—
White Families			
Husband-wife families	10,723	25,474	138
wife in labor force	12,543	29,713	137
Female householder, no husband present	5,754	12,508	117
Male householder, no wife present	—	20,421	—
Black Families			
Husband-wife families	7,816	19,624	151
wife in labor force	9,721	25,040	158
Female householder, no husband present	3,576	7,506	110
Male householder, no wife present	—	14,489	—

Source: U.S. Commission on Civil Rights (1983, p. 6).

about how long the subjects had been single, and there was almost no longitudinal research. Studies of effects of divorce and postdivorce adjustment typically covered only one or two years, as it was assumed that the effects of divorce trauma are over by then and that most women remarry. However, only longitudinal studies can address the vital question of how various single mothers manage their work and family lives during the entire course of their childrearing years.

REVIEW OF THE RESEARCH

Some Methodological and Conceptual Concerns

In the past, the mere fact of single status was treated as though it invariably produced a particular kind of experience that accounted for differences observed between single and married parents. The experience itself was rarely studied. Newer studies have begun to show that this is a heterogeneous population, with various types of single mothers. For example, race, culture, and class all affect the meaning and consequences of single parenthood, but such subgroups have been largely unstudied. It is only in recent years that nonracist and nonsexist writing about the black family has begun to appear at all (Carr, 1982; Engram, 1982; McAdoo, 1981), and most of the studies reviewed herein are of majority women. The exceptions are noted below.

Another problem is that the research is mainly about divorced and separated mothers; the never-married are rarely studied except as teenagers. It may seem reasonable to assume that, aside from the trauma of divorce and separation per se, many of the issues and problems of solo parenting are very similar for these different groups, but we do not really know the extent of generalizability. The research reviewed herein includes a few studies of different types of single-mother families, but most research was not designed to make comparison possible, so differential conclusions cannot be reached.

There is now less focus on deviant and clinical populations of single mothers (Belle, 1982; Kohen, Brown, & Feldberg, 1979). More studies have looked at women as they function in the community, and also at ones who have been in this status for longer than a year or two. There are still few efforts to look at families longitudinally, although several studies have been intensive and have extended over a brief period (Belle, 1982; Colletta, 1978). Finally, as will be seen, very little of the research is programmatic, nor has any of it been stimulated by systematic application of psychological theory.

Depression and Stress

Depression and stress are central to many of these women's lives, particularly for those who are poor (Belle, 1982; Pearlin & Johnson, 1977). Depression is the number one mental health problem for women under 45 (Merekengas, 1985; Walker, 1982). Various levels of depression, feelings of guilt and worthlessness, helplessness, despair, retarded activity, and change in eating or sleeping patterns were found by Belle and her colleagues (1982) in their study of poor women, two-thirds of whom were single parents. This depression apparently was caused by impoverishment and powerlessness, rather than marital status per se. The women viewed the mental health establishment as no real help, and the help they did receive appeared to reinforce self-blame, hardly a way out of depression (Belle & Dill, 1982). Similar findings were reported by Verbrugge (cited by Sales & Frieze, 1984), who found that role reduction and lack of control over life situations led to poor health and to depression.

It is hardly surprising that money problems have been found to be stressors (Pett, 1982). Keith and Schafer (1982) found that depression, even for employed divorced women, was linked to a low income level. Colletta (1979) compared the stress levels of low- and middle-income employed single mothers of preschoolers. These women reported many more areas of stress than a married control group, but income level made an impressive difference in their reported amount and source of stress and in the general quality of their lives. The single women with more income, even though it was an amount that hardly lifted them above the poverty level, said that they were very satisfied with their work and reported less stress than the low-income group.

Bould (1977) found that level of personal control was related to income. She studied a sample of families for whom single-mother status was a relatively permanent condition and who had had some time to adjust financially and psychologically. She found that the extent to which their income was controllable, stable, and free of stigmatization was more strongly predictive of level of personal control than was amount of income. "The mother who fully assumed both roles and earned her family's support was more likely to be better off than the mother who stayed home" (p. 348). This conclusion held for the black as well as the white women in her sample. Other investigators have reported that single mothers feel relatively powerless (Smith, 1980), a finding that suggests why welfare in its present form has negative personal consequences. Marshall (1985) reported that poor women typically consider all other alternatives before turning to AFDC welfare support.

Sense of control over income and feelings of efficacy as self-supporters have been found to be significant predictors of life satisfaction and absence of stress (Colletta, 1979; Kazak & Linney, 1983; Makosky, 1982; McAdoo, 1983; Ritchie, 1980). Kohen et al. (1979), in an intensive qualitative study, found that a sense of power and authority in her own domain was a positive factor for the female head of household.

The Michigan Panel Study of Income Dynamics longitudinal data were used by McLanahan (1983) to study the relationship of stress and family structure.[2] Three types of stress—the presence of chronic life strains, the occurrence of major life events, and the absence of social and psychological supports—were compared in male-headed and single-parent families. There was a higher incidence of major life events for single than for married families. These included decrease in family income, voluntary and involuntary job changes, household moves, and illness. McLanahan also found striking differences in amount of psychological support, with single mothers reporting much lower levels; in addition, they had lower self-esteem, lower feelings of efficacy, and greater pessimism. Furthermore, as the years passed, stressful life events increased, most notably after three years. Black women were more likely than white women to remain single, as were those who were less educated, illustrating the greater vulnerability of these groups.

The stress of life conditions as well as of life events was examined by Makosky (1982) as part of the Harvard Stress and Families Project (Belle, 1982). To a standard life-events survey, she added items germane to women's lives, such as rape, having an abortion, change in childcare arrangements, and going on welfare. The Revised Life Events Measure produced a life-events score for this sample that was significantly higher than any previously reported score. In addition, life conditions, such as low and unpredictable income, especially when these had been experienced for the previous two years, were found to be more predictive of stress, depression, anxiety, and poor self-esteem than were life events.

The loosely related group of studies that have looked at determinants of stress and depression indicate that, although single mothers are at risk, some experience positive outcomes. The favorable outcomes seem to relate to level of income and to other conditions that allow them to reduce the sense of powerlessness and increase areas of control in their lives.

Social Supports and Social Networks

Available help from relatives reduces the effects of stressors on single-mother families (Giovanni & Billingsley, cited by McAdoo, 1985). However for divorced single mothers, under some circumstances, support may also have negative consequences. Belle and her colleagues (1982) found that for low-income mothers, "social ties proved to be a two-edged sword, associated with important forms of assistance and emotional support and yet also associated with worries, upset and concern" (p. 142). Belle attributed part of the strain to the unalterable dependency involved. Thus, to the extent that low-income women must depend on relatives for support, she argued, they find such support to be a source of stress as well. If relatives and friends are supportive emotionally as well as materially, their presence and proximity do have a positive effect; but otherwise, such social ties can cause additional stress.

Colletta (1979) found that low-income mothers' satisfaction with support was related to their perceptions of need and of amount of stress in their lives, rather than to amount of support per se. Perceived support from community services was greater for these women than perceived social support; they especially appreciated help with daily coping and with finances.

Other studies of single mothers have found that perceived size of and satisfaction with their social network and social support predicts their social adjustment (Pett, 1982), but not maternal role satisfaction (Bowen, 1982). McLanahan, Wedemeyer, and Adelberg (1981) reported on the varied nature of networks and supports. Weinraub and Wolf's (1983) study of middle-class families concluded that single mothers were more socially isolated, received less emotional support, and had less stable social networks than their married counterparts. But support availability enhanced parental effectiveness, regardless of marital status.

Eger, Sarkissian, Brady, and Hartmann (1985) found that mothers living in an isolated Australian suburb, whether single or not, were depressed, passive, and had low self-esteem. The creation of a political-action support network radically changed the quality of life and level of psychological well-being for women in this study.

In sum, studies of social support and social networks appear to point to their generally positive features, although the type of support and extent of control over the process make a difference in their effects. . . .

Work and the Single Parent

The consistent association of income level with indicators of well-being, satisfaction, and lack of depression or stress is, as we have seen, moderated by psychological factors, most notably controllability, stability, and feelings of self-sufficiency. As the best way to be in control of the source of one's income and to feel self-sufficient is to have good employment, we should look next at studies that have examined work issues and the single mother.

The economic consequences of mothers being single, or of leaving a marriage, and the effect of welfare on labor-market behavior and marital stability have been of great concern, especially to economists, demographers, and other social researchers with an interest in public policy (Danziger, Jakobson, Schwartz, & Smolensky, 1982; Hoffman, 1977; Levitan & Belous, 1981; Mudrick, 1978; Schorr & Moen, 1984). Few of these economic studies raise psychological questions about work, but they contain some striking findings, such as that women chose work over welfare (Hoffman, 1977), and that 80% of the divorced and separated women in the Michigan Panel Study sample were employed, a figure that was similar for white and black respondents. The significance of work was also stressed by Bergmann and Roberts (1984), who developed a model that predicted that women would be less likely to be on AFDC and more likely to work if the federal government enforced fathers' child support payments. In their view, the enactment of such government enforcement in 1985 is important because it recognizes that fathers, as well as mothers, have economic responsibility for their children.

The conclusion that a *predictable* source of income and meaningful work lead to positive mental health consequences for single mothers is unavoidable. Yet apart from effects of level and source of income, we know very little about the meaning of work for single mothers. We have little idea how the kind of work, structure of worklife patterns, motivation, aspiration, or satisfaction on the job relate to the quality of their lives. Although many investigators have indicated that their women respondents were employed, detailed questions about psychological aspects of their work have rarely been asked. . . .

Tebbets (1982), as part of the aforementioned Harvard Stress and Families Project (Belle, 1982), found that even its sample of poor women had great interest and involvement in their work. Their work patterns varied; participation was tied to timing of births and number of children, and past and current work status was contingent upon other life commitments and experiences. For instance, women were more likely to be working currently if they were older when they had their first child, if they had fewer children, fewer preschoolers, and higher levels of education. Work was important for their emotional as well as financial health. Women who had held more jobs, had worked more in recent years, or were currently working were less depressed than those who wanted to work but were unemployed. Sales and Frieze (1984) stressed the positive consequences of work, especially for mothers of young children. These women were found to be less depressed and less lonely if they had employment outside the home (Stewart & Salt, 1981, cited by Sales & Frieze, 1984).

Other studies have found that single mothers thrive in rewarded and rewarding work roles in spite of their other life problems. Baruch et al. (1984) found employment to be good for women's sense of well-being and life satisfaction. The single parents in their study—in spite of great role overload and role conflict—were as satisfied with life as married women were. Monaghan-Leckband's (1978) single mothers, who reported role conflict in relation to "instrumental leadership of the family," did not report that work was a source of such strain. Although employed single mothers were found by Keith and Shafer (1982) to be depressed by work-family role strain, assistance with domestic tasks and childcare served as buffers.

Kazak and Linney (1983) reported that the "self-supporter" role is an important factor in level of life satisfaction of employed divorced mothers of minor children. The length of time since divorce enhanced this relationship; for those divorced more than three years, the self-supporter role was a more potent contributor to reported life satisfaction than either parenting or social roles.

Yet there are work circumstances that are stressful. McAdoo (1985) found, for employed black single mothers with a modal income at the poverty level, that work was a source of stress. Specifically, the mother role and work role were often reported as being in conflict. However, the stress level was reduced when mothers used a coping style that involved a redefinition of employers' expectations (e.g., refusing to work overtime because a child had to be picked up from daycare by a certain time). This method of coping, which increased level of control over a particular condition, was more effective than coping that involved relinquishing one of the roles (see also Harrison & Minor, 1982).

In a major survey of employed working mothers, Michelson (1983) found that mothers who felt that they had been forced into full-time employment were tense and unhappy. For others, tensions were due to the logistics of getting to work and of arranging for childcare. Time-pressure stress was found to be less for single mothers *"due to the absence of demands from a spouse"* (italics added, p. xi); and even with greater daily household responsibility and less relative overall satisfaction than married women, their self-image still benefited from employment.

Baruch et al. (1983) found, for the middle-class single mothers they studied, that amount of money earned and how well a woman felt she could support herself were important determinants of well-being. These women felt their careers and education had benefited by their divorce, and their employment appeared to buffer stress. Although concerned about loneliness and social isolation, they were positive about themselves in terms of mastery, growth in skills, and competence.

In sum, these few studies show how single mothers can benefit from having meaningful work, even though their daily life may become more complex and strained.

Gender Roles

Most of the research we have been discussing indirectly touches on gender roles, yet few studies have directly assessed single mothers' views about such roles or about gender identity.

Expectations about marital roles were examined by Ganvold, Pedler, and Schellie (1979) in a study of employed women. They found that egalitarian marriage role expectations were related to high acceptance of self and low levels of social anxiety for single mothers. Wedemeyer and Johnson (1982), studying gender role beliefs and post-divorce adjustment, found that traditional views generally prevailed. Thus, custodial mothers were more interested in their children than their work, whereas the reverse held for custodial fathers. Yet the women derived pleasure from the autonomy that work provided, even in the face of reduced financial circumstances.

Autonomy, authority, and power are not congruent with traditional family roles for women, yet these characteristics have been cited as an important source of positive feelings for single mothers (Baruch et al., 1983; Belle, 1982; Kohen et al., 1979; Ritchie, 1980; Weiss, 1979). As mentioned earlier, Kazak and Linney (1983) found that perceived competence as a self-supporter was a stronger predictor of life satisfaction than perceived competence in the parenting role. At the same time, the self-supporter role was also an area of low perceived competence, reflecting the fact that the role of economic provider was not traditional for these women and was therefore fraught with concerns. Still, as one of Baruch et al.'s (1983) single mothers stated, "There's one thing for sure. Every woman has to think absolutely like a man. She has to be prepared to support herself and others because the reality is that we still have the babies—and we will have to be able to support ourselves" (p. 198).

My search unearthed only two reports that applied the much-studied concept of androgyny. Custodial mothers of children aged 10–19 were more likely to be androgynous on the Bem Sex Role Inventory (BSRI) than a college student normative group, and were more likely to score high on the BSRI masculinity scale than married mothers. The researchers suggested that the demands of single-parent functioning may explain these scores (Kundek & Siesky, 1980). An androgynous self-concept was found to be related to the role satisfaction of single mothers by Ballard (1981).

Carr (1982), as part of a study of the development of achievement motivation in young black children, found that black single mothers, regardless of class, were more likely to report atypical sex-role socialization of their children than were married mothers. Mothers of boys reported more conventional attitudes than mothers of girls.

These issues are significant because the struggle with the common assumptions about legitimate power in the family and in relation to society is a central task for these women, one that involves serious incongruence with women's sex role stereotyping. Typically, society perceives women to be

> deficient in those qualities that are required for leadership . . . such as . . . rational thinking, assertiveness, competitiveness and aggression. . . . Such an ideology supports the relegation of women to supportive roles and creates negative expectations of their abilities to function in circumstances requiring . . . "male qualities." (Engram, 1982, p. 73)

Single mothers are probably particularly undermined by gender role expectations, and these issues have hardly been touched.

Parenting Role

Colletta (1979) found single mothers of sons or of two children to be the most stressed in her sample. The debilitating effect of boys on solo mothers has also been reported by Hetherington, Cox, and Cox (1979), who showed that recently divorced mothers of boys were less in control of the children's behavior than were girls' mothers or married mothers. They summarized,

The divorced mother is harassed by her children, particularly her sons. . . . Her children in the first year don't obey, affiliate or attend to her. . . . The aggression of boys with divorced mothers peaks at one year (after divorce) . . . then drops significantly, but it is still higher than that of boys in intact families at two years. (p. 35)

These authors speak of the role of divorced mothers as being intrinsically that of victim, particularly when there are problems and a consequent loss of control over outcomes.

Draper's (1982) study examining personal locus of control has some bearing on this. He found that older single mothers with several children, including a son under three years of age, were more external than married mothers or than single mothers of girls. He speculated that boys' aggressivity may affect the mothers' emotional well-being and that son-rearing is thus harder than daughter-rearing. He further suggested that fathers are needed to check their sons' aggression. Hetherington et al. (1979) cite a study by Patterson that suggests an alternative explanation, one less rooted in gender-based beliefs about boys' immutable aggressivity and mothers' inability to "check it." Patterson found that mothers and children get involved in a vicious cycle of coercion:

The lack of management skills of the mother accelerates the child's aversive behavior, of which she is the main instigator and target. This is reciprocated by increased coercion in the mother's parenting behavior and induces feelings of helplessness, depression, anger, and self-doubt in the mother. (Hetherington et al., 1979, p. 121)

These authors tested the Patterson hypothesis with their mothers and found that children's behavior, especially sons' aggression, resulted in more trait and state anxiety, low feelings of competence, low self-esteem, depression, and feelings of external control.

There is some evidence that mothers are rewarded less by their children than are fathers. Ambert (1982) found that children differ in their attitude about custodial mothers and fathers and are much more likely to express appreciation of fathers than of mothers.

The hopeful view that stress in parenting is not inevitable and that it subsides over time was emphasized by Kohen et al. (1979). They concluded that for their sample, the conflict-free nature of the divorced mother's authority in the family had led to improved mother-child relationships.

In spite of increased and changed responsibilities and the need to manage parenting in a nontraditional manner, single parents like being parents, are generally satisfied, and feel competent (Baruch et al., 1983; Belle, 1982; Kazak & Linney, 1983; Kohen et al., 1979; Weiss, 1979). A study by Fine et al. (1985) compared maternal satisfaction for different groups of employed mothers. On their Reactions to Motherhood Scale, they found that white single mothers were less satisfied with their motherhood experience than black single mothers or married mothers; their study was unenlightening about why this might be, but it should be noted that the general level of satisfaction was high.

These studies provide a few ideas about single mothering, but much more research is needed. A recent reviewer of family interaction research noted that no studies have compared time spent with children in two-parent and single-parent families. Her radical suggestion that children get more undivided attention in single-parent households, and may therefore do better, remains a hypothesis that begs to be tested (Scarr, 1984).

Another virtually untested set of questions concerns the effects of societal prejudice upon the single mother's role as a parent. Even though stigmatization is on the decline (Baruch et al., 1983; Weiss, 1979), the poor women interviewed by Belle (1982) and Colletta (1979) spoke of problems with bias in the social system. Work by Santrock and Tracy (1978) suggests that this perception may be based on reality. They had teachers view videotapes of the social interactions of an eight-year-old boy. His behavior was rated less positively when the teachers were told he was from a single-parent home than when he was described as being from a two-parent home. A question that must also be asked is how mothers, who must deal with teachers and other school authorities, are affected by the messages they receive in such contacts. Social psychologists who study attitudes, prejudice, stigma, and discrimination can play an important role here. The hypothesis that, like sexism and racism, dogmas of motherism and familism create hostile social environments for single mothers, and add to the mentally unhealthy and uncontrollable character of their lives, needs to be tested.

CONCLUSIONS

The past decade has produced research that reflects changing beliefs and values about single mothers, and investigators with nontraditional views about women's place and the meaning of family have made a contribution. Studies have moved from assumptions about deviant family forms and psychopathology to consideration of the hypothesis that good adjustment, well-being, and satisfaction with life are possible for single mothers. Furthermore, the determinants of good outcomes are being explored (Belle, 1982; Kohen et al., 1979). Recognition that many of these women are not in a transition stage, and that they are not one homogeneous group, has also had an impact. The category "female single parent" is now less likely to be confounded with other person variables, such as race and class. This unconfounding has led to new interpretations, as when depression or stress is understood as the result of poverty and all of its concomitants, rather than simply being due to single-parent status per se (Belle, 1982; Colletta, 1979). We also know there are many other sources of variation in single mothers' adjustment, such as coping styles (Belle, 1982; Harrison & Minor, 1982; McAdoo, 1985), life conditions (Makosky, 1982), and type and source of social support networks.

Yet social and personal views about gender roles and gender identity are deeply embedded and continue to affect what is studied. For instance, although a number of studies have found that good employment enhances well-being and that the meaning of work in single mothers' lives is an important factor in adjustment, relatively few studies have considered work and work attitudes as an important class of psychological variables, nor has any research attention been paid to the possibility that under some circumstances women will choose single-mother status as a positive alternative. It appears that gender role assumptions, especially about "mother at home," "husband as economic provider," and "nuclear family as the hallmark of normalcy," are still affecting research approaches. Nevertheless, research on parenting has finally begun to move to a new and more differentiated set of questions about sex-role socialization, about the effects of mothers and children on each other, about differences in the mothering of boys and girls, and about parenting efficacy and authority.

The future agenda of psychological study of the family must, of course, include the single-mother family form. This review has suggested that at least a portion of such work should be planned as a systematic exploration of the usefulness of control, efficacy, and gender-role concepts in explaining outcomes in two major role areas, that of parent and of self-supporter. Adequate research on single mothers demands methodology and conceptualizations that take account of the social context in which single mothers live.

Policy Implications

Finally, we should remember that research on single mothers had important public policy implications; it does not take place in a social vacuum. Schorr and Moen (1984) showed how public policy about single mothers has been shaped by the same biases that have affected the research. Thus, AFDC and workfare programs for the poor (mothers) are also grounded in the assumption that women's place is in the home and that families should be kept intact or reconstituted. As we have seen, the reality for many women, especially for those over 30 and for black women, is that remarriage is unlikely. Such policies also ignore the idea that, given a real choice economically, many women would not choose to remarry.

The research and findings based on alternative assumptions about the family can direct a search for alternative policy recommendations. The recognition that single motherhood is a fact of life and not necessarily one with negative personal or social consequences has already affected recent research on single mothers. It should be brought to bear more fully in future work, and it may perhaps lead to more appropriate policy recommendations.

NOTES

1. A family household is defined by the U.S. Census Bureau as one that has two or more related persons, one of whom owns or rents the living quarters. A female-headed household is so designated when there is no husband present (U.S. Department of Commerce, 1983, p. 1). In this [paper], we are concerned with female-headed households with minor children present.
2. The Michigan Panel Study data used in this way must be interpreted with caution, as only men were interviewed in the first round.

REFERENCES

Ambert, A. (1982). Differences in children's behavior toward custodial mothers and custodial fathers. *Journal of Marriage and the Family, 44,* 73–86.

Ballard, B. (1981). *Role satisfaction of divorced mothers in single parent families as a function of social networks and sex-role orientation.* Unpublished doctoral dissertation, California School of Professional Psychology, Berkeley.

Baruch, G., Barnett, R., & Rivers, C. (1983). *Lifeprints: New patterns of love and work for today's women.* New York: McGraw-Hill.

Belle, D. (1982). *Lives in stress: Women and depression.* Beverly Hills, CA: Sage.

Belle, D., & Dill, D. (1982). Research methods and sample characteristics. In D. Belle (Ed.), *Lives in stress: Women and depression.* Beverly Hills, CA: Sage.

Bergmann, B. R., & Roberts, M. D. (1984). *Income for the single parent: Work, child support, and welfare* (Working paper 84-12). Department of Economics, University of Maryland.

Bould, S. (1977). Female-headed families: Personal fate control and the provider role. *Journal of Marriage and the Family, 39,* 339–349.

Bowen, G. L. (1982). Social networks and the maternal role satisfaction of formerly-married mothers. *Journal of Divorce, 5,* 77–85.

Brandwein, A., Brown, A., & Fox, M. (1974). Women and children last: The social situation of divorced mothers and their families. *Journal of Marriage and the Family, 36,* 498–514.

Burlage, D. (1978). *Divorced and separated mothers: Combining the responsibilities of breadwinning and child rearing.* Unpublished doctoral dissertation, Harvard University.

Carr, P. (1982). *Family background and the socialization of achievement motivation in girls and boys.* Unpublished doctoral dissertation, Howard University.

Colletta, N. D. (1979). The impact of divorces: Father absence or poverty. *Journal of Divorce, 3,* 27–34.

Danziger, S., Jakobson, G., Schwartz, S., & Smolensky, E. (1982). Work and welfare as determinants of female poverty and household headship. *Quarterly Journal of Economics,* 320–334.

Draper, T. W. (1982). Sons, mothers, and externality: Is there a father effect? *Child Study Journal, 12,* 271–280.

Eger, R., Sarkissian, W., Brady, D., & Hartmann, L. (1985). Reviewing the Australian suburban dream: A unique approach to neighborhood change with the family support scheme. In M. Safir, M. T. Mednick, D. Izraeli, J. Bernard (Eds.), *Women's worlds: From the new scholarship.* New York: Praeger.

Engram, E. (1982). *Science, myth, reality: The black family in one-half century of research.* Westport, CT: Greenwood.

Fine, M. A., Schwebel, A. I., & Myers, C. J. (1985). The effects of world view on adaption to single parenthood among middle-class women. *Journal of Family Issues, 6,* 107–127.

Granvold, D. K., Pedler, C. M., & Schellie, S. G. (1979). A study of sex role expectancy and female post divorce adjustment. *Journal of Divorce, 2,* 283–293.

Harrison, A. O., & Minor, J. H. (1982). Interrole conflict, coping strategies, and role satisfaction among single and married employed mothers. *Psychology of Women Quarterly, 6,* 354–360.

Hetherington, E. M., Cox, M., & Cox, R. (1979). Stress and coping in divorce: A focus on women. In J. Gullahorn (Ed.), *Psychology and women in transition.* Washington, DC: Winston.

Hoffman, S. (1977). Marital instability and the economic status of women. *Demography, 14,* 67–76.

Kazak, A. E., & Linney, J. A. (1983). Stress, coping, and life-changes in the single-parent family. *American Journal of Community Psychology, 11,* 207–220.

Keith, P. M., & Schafer, R. B. (1982). A comparison of depression among employed single-parent and married women. *Journal of Psychology, 110,* 239–247.

Kohen, J. A., Brown, C. A., & Feldberg, R. (1979). Divorced mothers: The costs and benefits of family controlling. In G. Levinger & O. C. Moles (Eds.), *Divorce and separation.* New York: Basic Books.

Kundek, C. A., & Siesky, A. E., Jr. (1980). Sex role self-concepts of single divorced parents and their children. *Journal of Divorce, 3,* 249–261.

Levitan, S., & Belous, R. S. (1981). *What's happening to the American family?* Baltimore: Johns Hopkins University Press.

Makosky, V. P. (1982). Sources of stress: Events or conditions? In D. Belle (Ed.), *Lives in stress: Women and depression.* Beverly Hills, CA: Sage.

Marshall, N. (1985, March). *Welfare mothers.* Paper presented at Henry A. Murray Research Center, Radcliffe College.

McAdoo, H. P. (1981). *Black families.* Beverly Hills, CA: Sage.

McAdoo, H. P. (1985, May). *Stress levels and coping strategies used by single mothers.* Paper presented at Radcliffe College Conference on Women's Mental Health in Social Context.

McLanahan, S. S. (1983). Family structure and stress: A longitudinal comparison of two-parent and female-headed families. *Journal of Marriage and the Family, 45,* 347–357.

McLanahan, S. S., Wedemeyer, N. V., & Adelberg, T. (1981). Network structure, social support and psychological well-being in the single parent family. *Journal of Marriage and the Family, 43,* 601–612.

Mednick, M. T. (1982). Women and the psychology of achievement: Implications for personal and social change. In J. H. Bernardin (Ed.), *Women in the work force.* New York: Praeger.

Merekengas, K. (1985, May). *Sex differences in depression.* Paper presented at Radcliffe College Conference on Women's Mental Health in Social Context.

Michelson, W. (1983). *The logistics of maternal employment: Implications for women and their families* (Child in the City Report No. 18). Toronto: Ministry of National Health and Welfare.

Monaghan-Leckband, K. (1979). *Role adaptations of single parents: A challenge of the pathological view of male and female single parents.* Unpublished doctoral dissertation. New York University.

Mudrick, N. R. (1978). Note on policy and practice: The use of AFDC by previously high and low income households. *Social Service Review,* 107–115.

Pearce, D. (1978). The feminization of poverty: Women, work and welfare. *Urban and Social Change, 2,* 24–36.

Pearlin, L. T., & Johnson, J. (1977). Marital status, life strains, and depression. *American Sociological Review, 42,* 704–715.

Pett, M. G. (1982). Predictors of satisfactory social adjustment of divorced single parents. *Journal of Divorce, 5,* 1–17.

Ritchie, J. (1980). Characteristics of a sample of solo mothers. *New Zealand Medical Journal, 349–352.*

Ross, H. C., & Sawhill, I. V. (1975). *Time of transition: The growth of families headed by women.* Washington, DC: Urban Institute.

Sales, E., & Frieze, I. H. (1984). Women and work: Implications for mental health. In L. E. Walker (Ed.), *Women and mental health policy.* Beverly Hills, CA: Sage.

Santrock, J. W., & Tracy, R. L. (1978). The effects of children's family structure status on the development of stereotypes by teachers. *Journal of Education Psychology, 70,* 754–757.

Scarr, S. (1984). *Mother care, other care.* New York: Basic Books.

Schorr, A. C., & Moen, P. (1984). The single parent and public policy. In P. Voydanoff (Ed.), *Work and family: Changing roles of men and women.* Palo Alto, CA: Mayfield.

Smith, M. J. (1980). The social consequences of single parenthood: A longitudinal perspective. *Family Relations, 29,* 75–81.

Tebbets, R. (1982). Work: Its meaning for women's lives. In D. Belle (Ed.), *Lives in stress: Women and depression.* Beverly Hills, CA: Sage.

U.S. Commission on Civil Rights. (1983). *A growing crisis: Disadvantaged women and their children.* Washington, D.C.: Clearinghouse Publications.

U.S. Department of Commerce, Bureau of the Census. (1983). *Households, families, marital status and living arrangements* (Series P-20, no. 382). Washington, DC: Author.

Walker, L. E. (1984). *Women and mental health policy.* Beverly Hills, CA: Sage.

Wedemeyer, N. V., & Johnson, J. M. (1982). Learning the single-parent role: Overcoming marital-role influence. *Journal of Divorce, 5,* 41–53.

Weinraub, M., & Wolf, B. M. (1983). Effects of stress and social supports on mother-child interactions in single- and two-parent families. *Child Development, 54,* 1297–1311.

Weiss, R. S. (1979). *Going it alone: The family life and social situation of the single parent.* New York: Basic Books.

PART
FIVE

FAMILIES IN SOCIETY

INTRODUCTION

During the 1950s and 1960s, family scholars and the mass media presented an image of the typical, normal, or model American family. It included a father, a mother, and two or three children, living a middle-class existence in a single-family home in an area neither rural nor urban. Father was the breadwinner, and mother was a full-time homemaker. Both were, by implication, white.

No one denied that many families and individuals fell outside the standard nuclear model. Single persons, one-parent families, two-parent families in which both parents worked, three-generation families, and childless couples abounded. Three- or four-parent families were not uncommon, as one or both divorced spouses often remarried. Many families, moreover, neither white nor well-off, varied from the dominant image. White and seemingly middle-class families of particular ethnic, cultural, or sexual styles also differed from the model. The image scarcely reflected the increasing ratio of older people in the empty nest and retirement parts of the life cycle. But like poverty before its "rediscovery" in the mid-1960s, family complexity and variety existed on some dim fringe of semi-awareness.

When noticed, individuals or families departing from the nuclear model were analyzed in a context of pathology. Studies of one-parent families or working mothers, for example, focused on the harmful effects to children of such situations. Couples childless by choice were assumed to possess some basic personality inadequacy. Single persons were similarly interpreted, or else thought to be homosexual. Homosexuals symbolized evil, depravity, and degradation.

385

As Marvin Sussman (1971) noted early on, "This preoccupation with the model nuclear family pattern and efforts to preserve it at all costs prevented sociologists from describing what was becoming obvious to non-sociological observers of the American scene: a pluralism in family forms existing side by side with members in each form having different problems to solve and issues to face" (p. 42). Curiously, although social scientists have always emphasized the pluralism of American society in terms of ethnic groups, religion, and geographic region, the concept of pluralism had rarely been applied to the family.

In the wake of the social upheavals of the 1960s and 1970s, middle-class "mainstream" attitudes toward women's roles, sexuality, and the family were transformed. Despite the conservative backlash that peaked in the 1980s, the traditional family did not return. American families became increasingly diverse, and Americans were increasingly willing to extend the notion of pluralism to family life. The selections in this part of the book examine this diversity in its various aspects.

In Chapter 9, the links between the economy, work, and family life are considered. Katherine Newman's article discusses the impact of the hidden and dark side of the American dream—the slide *down* the economic ladder—on middle-class families. What happens when a successful breadwinner loses his job and the family must suffer the loss of a formerly comfortable, middle-class lifestyle? The result is often a severe loss of status and self-respect for the father, a radical change in family bonds, and the withdrawal of the family from the rest of the community. For middle-class families, the pain of downward mobility is not just the loss of status and material comfort; it is also, Newman argues, a "broken covenant"; it represents a profound violation of American cultural expectations—that if we work hard we will succeed; that we, not economic forces beyond our control, shape our own fate, and that the future will be better than the past.

Maxine Baca Zinn discusses the chronic problems of unemployment that prevail in America's inner cities, and their impact on families. Why have we witnessed over the past two decades the growth of a seemingly permanent "underclass" in America—a population of unmarried mothers, "illegitimate" children, and jobless men? Baca Zinn summarizes and evaluates the leading explanations. Many commentators blame the swelling underclass on a self-perpetuating "culture of poverty"—a value system that rejects hard work and achievement and accepts female-headed families. Cultural explanations come in a number of versions, but they all see family disintegration as the source of poverty.

There is, however, a different causal view. This interpretation, rooted in a large body of theory and research, stresses the import of transformations in the American economy and its opportunity structure, rather than culture, as the foundation of the poverty of the underclass. Baca Zinn concludes that the evidence best supports the structural explanation. But she also contends that most writers who present the structural view, in their emphasis on the need to increase employment opportunities for inner city males, overlook the changes in women's roles in recent years.

The other articles in this chapter discuss the revolution in women's roles that has taken place during the past two decades. The two-parent family, in which both parents work, is the form that now comes closest to being the "typical American family." In the 1950s, the working mother was considered deviant, even though many women were employed in the labor force. It was taken for granted that maternal employment must be harmful to children; much current research on working mothers still takes this "social problem" approach to the subject.

But as Sandra Scarr, and her colleagues, argue here, such fears are based not on research evidence but on traditional assumptions about how mothers' roles influence children. For example, the notion that a full-time mother at home is always the best form of child care is simply insupportable. The research literature shows that whether a mother works is not in itself a major factor in her child's development. Rather, the circumstances surrounding the family, the attitudes and expectations of fathers and mothers, and the amount of social support the mother receives make the difference. Scarr et al. consequently argue for increasing the availability of quality child care and for more participation by fathers in the raising of their children.

Hochschild and Machung take a closer look at what happens to the emotional dynamics inside the family when both parents work full-time and the "second shift"—the work of caring for children and maintaining the home—is not shared equitably. The selection from their book portrays a painful dilemma shared by many couples in their study: The men saw themselves as having equal marriages; they were doing more work around the house than their fathers had done and more than they thought other men did. The women, whose lives were different from their own mothers', saw their husbands' contributions as falling far short of true equality. They resented having to carry more than their share of the "second shift," yet stifled their angry feelings in order to preserve their marriages. Still, this strategy took its toll on love and intimacy.

Chapter 10 deals with family variation along a range of dimensions—racial, ethnic, lifestyle, life span. Paulette Moore Hines and her coauthors discuss the influence of ethnicity on family relationships. Originally written for family therapists, this article provides insights into the emotional dynamics of African-American, Hispanic, Irish, Asian-American, and Jewish families. As the authors point out, their portraits of each group are highly general and do not reflect the great variation that exists *within* each group.

The article by Taylor et al. is a review of research on black families in the past decade. Researchers are increasingly aware of great diversity among black families; they also recognize that lower income black family patterns can be resilient and adaptive—even when they differ from those in the white or black middle class. Nevertheless, in the research literature as well as the media, there is an unfortunate tendency to focus too much on "problem black families" and thus to see them as typifying "*the* black family."

One of the most striking cultural changes of recent years is the increased recognition of homosexual relationships as an alternative form of family. The number of children being raised by homosexual parents ranges from 6 to 14

million. What are the effects of such an upbringing? As Daniel Goleman's article points out, an array of recent students come to the same conclusion: Contrary to earlier assumptions that being raised in such "deviant" environments
must be harmful to children, growing up in a gay home seems to result in no
more psychological problems than being raised in a more conventional family.

In the last article in this chapter, Matilda White Riley discusses the new
variations of family life resulting from the "revolution in longevity." During this
century, life expectancy has risen from under 50 to over 70 years of age—and
is continually rising. This sharp increase in life expectancy is accompanied by a
greatly expanded kinship structure persisting through time. People used to
have lots of relatives, and they didn't live so long. Now people begin with
smaller families, but these persist and accrete through marriage, procreation,
and remarriage. Kinship structures used to look like short, stubby, ephemeral
bushes. Now they have sprouted into long, slender trees, with many branches.
Riley argues optimistically that the new kinship structure offers more choice
for selecting relationships individuals deem more significant.

How should we think about different visions of the family? This is the
question addressed by the articles in our final chapter. We call it "The Cultural
Politics of Family Life" because we recognize that change in the family, like all
social change, calls forth different reactions in people with different values and
different visions of the good society.

For example, the abortion debate, argues Kristin Luker in the first selection, is not so much about the fate of the embryo as about the meaning of
women's lives. Working women who are educated, affluent, and liberal tend to
be "pro-choice." "Pro-life" women, by contrast, have already arranged their
lives to support traditional concepts of women as wives and mothers. Thus,
pro-life and pro-choice women live in different evaluative worlds that offer different and conflicting definitions of motherhood—and public policy.

There are four ways to avoid having unwanted pregnancies, only one of
which is through surgical abortion. Another is by taking an abortifacient drug
like RU486, the use of which is opposed by the National Right to Life Committee, but which could shift the terms of the abortion debate in America.
RU486 has been used under strict guidelines in government clinics in France,
Britain and Sweden, and has proved to be safe and highly effective (96%).
With a pro-choice President in the White House, RU486 may well become a
major alternative to surgical abortion in the United States.

Abstinence is, of course, another way to avoid pregnancy. But abstinence
obviously does not work for sexually active fertile women. The methods that do
mostly work are such contraceptives as the pill, barrier methods, and condoms.
But they work only if used. Unfortunately, many women forget or are disin-
clined to take pills or don't always carry a barrier device, while many men are
reluctant to use condoms.

The Norplant system, as it is called, overcomes these problems of avoidance, forgetfulness or impulsivity by the surgical implantation, in the upper
arm, of six matchstick-sized capsules that slowly release a low dosage of a synthetic hormone similar to those used in birth control pills.

Norplant is as effective as pills in preventing pregnancy for up to five years (but has no effect in preventing venereal diseases.) Prevented pregnancies never result in abortion. Yet, as Barbara Kantrowitz and Pat Wingert show, Norplant has become increasingly controversial, especially over the issue of whether poor women should be urged—or forced—not to have more children.

Single mothers with children, single fathers with children, cohabiting couples whether straight or gay, all are increasingly prevalent forms of domestic relations. And all raise problems about the legal definition of a "family." David M. Rosen's article discusses how courts have struggled to decide whether and how to recognize such arrangements.

When Dan Quayle castigated TV's Murphy Brown for becoming a single mother, he was spearheading a battle in what James Davison Hunter calls "culture wars," or the contest to define what America stands for. Hunter argues that, in this competition, the definition of the family may be the decisive battleground. Each side clashes about different conceptions of the place, role, and structure of the family.

Yet the meaning of family life may always be problematic in a multicultural and multiethnic society. Families are not havens isolated from the surrounding society. In societies marked by scarcity, insecurity, inequalities of goods and power, anxiety over status, fear, and hatred, family life will bear the impact of these qualities.

Chances are that, even in a relatively untroubled society, family life will still be problematic because of the special psychology of close relationships. The family, as one writer put it, is where you are dealing with life-and-death voltages. No matter what form the family takes, the distinctive intimacy and commitment of family life provide the source of both the joy and its discontents.

Chapter
9

The Economy, Work, and Family Life

Reading 28 11/22/94

The Downwardly Mobile Family

Katherine S. Newman

Brutal though it can be, the damage downward mobility does to a displaced manager is only the beginning of a longer story. Like a storm gathering force, failure in the work world engenders further havoc, first buffeting relations between breadwinner and spouse, then spreading to the children. Economic foundations are wrenched out from under the family, and emotional bonds are stretched to the breaking point. In the end, even children's values and plans for the future are drawn into the maelstrom as they struggle to reconcile the teachings of meritocratic individualism with their parents' glaring inability to prove their worth in the world.

As unwilling refugees from the middle class, children of downwardly mobile managers offer a unique window into the world they have left behind. Most had

Reprinted with permission of The Free Press, a Division of Macmillan, Inc. from *Falling From Grace* by Katherine S. Newman. Copyright © 1988 by Katherine S. Newman.

391

taken their old affluent life-style for granted and did not understand the significance of what they had had until after it was gone.

For Penny Ellerby, who was fifteen when the great crash came, the most immediate and troubling impact was the change it wrought upon the father she looked up to:

> The pressure on my Dad was intense. From my point of view he just seemed to be getting irrational. He would walk around the house talking to himself and stay up all night, smoking cigarettes in the dark.
>
> When things started to fall apart no one would tell my sister or me anything about what was happening. So all I perceived is that somebody who used to be a figure of strength was behaving strangely: starting to cry at odd times . . . hanging around the house unshaven in his underwear when I would bring dates home from high school. In the absence of any understanding of what was going on, my attitude was one of anger and disgust, like "Why don't you get your act together? What's the matter with you?"

Penny's father had been a successful show business promoter. He had invested most of the family's assets in a talent show that ran successfully for four years until its sponsors pulled the plug and sent his career into a tailspin. Penny remembers the spectacular crash that followed:

> We went from one day in which we owned a business that was worth probably four or five million dollars in assets and woke up the next day to find that we were personally probably a half million in debt. Creditors called at the house and started to send threatening notes.
>
> First he started a novel, but that didn't last more than two months. Then he went back into a public relations project, which also didn't work out. Then he tried to put together a series of college film festivals. Nothing worked.

Penny's adolescence came to an abrupt end at that point. Her father was unable to find a professional position of any kind. Tension between her parents rose to unbearable heights. Her dad finally left home, one step ahead of the bill collectors. She had not seen him for nearly ten years; for most of that time he has lived on the streets in San Francisco. Penny's mother managed to find a low-level clerical job but it could not begin to sustain the life-style she had known as the wife of a promoter. Today she lives in one of New York's tougher public housing projects and faces problems familiar to many a marginal wage earner: how to make ends meet and how to face the prospect of poverty-level retirement.

Downward mobility can occur as the result of a precipitous crash whose effects are felt immediately. Indeed, Penny's story demonstrates how rapidly, and how completely, downward mobility can undermine a family. But for most managerial families, the process is one of gradual erosion. Occupational dislocation may occur suddenly, but its consequences can take six or seven years to become fully evident, depending upon the resources the families can tap.

When occupational disaster strikes, the first impulse is typically to contain the damage to the work world, and to continue as far as possible to maintain a sense of normalcy in the family realm. Hence families continue to pay the mortgage and send the kids off to school. But as months elapse without reemployment, and bank balances plummet, the attempt to maintain a normal life-style falters. What begins as a principled commitment to avoid defeatism and get on with life takes on a new character—the family starts to dissemble and hide its problems from the outside world, starting with small cover stories. Paul Armand instructed his son on how to describe his Dad's unemployment to his friends at boarding school: "In his school, everybody's father is the head of this and that. So I said, 'You just tell them your Dad was VP of a company and he just refused to go on an overseas assignment. . . .' I told him if anybody asks, tell them I started my own firm." This was, at best, a shading of the truth. Paul had created a "firm" on paper, but it was not engaged in any money-making enterprises.

The impetus to conceal, if not lie, sometimes comes from adolescent children. The world of the middle-class adolescent is consumerist, elitist, and exceptionally unforgiving of divergence from the norm. Teenagers want to look like, act like, and think like their friends. The paradox of middle-class adolescents is that they must achieve individuality first and foremost by learning to look and sound just like "everyone else" their own age. Dress style and musical taste are only part of the cultural baggage American adolescents bring to the task of peer consolidation. Children of affluence—the sons and daughters of the managerial middle class— also rely upon their families' social position in seeking peer acceptance. Their fathers' occupation, and the life-style that it makes possible, is part and parcel of a cultural image they attempt to project.

When David Patterson moved his wife and two teenage children from California to Long Island, his children complained at first that they were looked upon, with some degree of suspicion, as "transients." To overcome the ill-will and cultivate new friends, Patterson's son boasted his father's status as an executive. The scheme worked, for local families were highly attuned to occupational prestige. Consequently, when Patterson received his pink slip, it threatened to undermine his teenagers' public identity and put their social acceptance by peers at risk. The children reacted with shame and with secrecy: They stopped bringing acquaintances home; they avoided discussing the family crisis with peers or school counselors. They became overwhelmed by the feeling that if their father's downward mobility became public knowledge, their own social standing would be destroyed.

The downwardly mobile managerial family jealously guards its public face, even if this means that everyone must eat a dreary diet so that the children can have some stylish clothes for school. They cherish central symbols of belonging, like the family home, and families make considerable sacrifices in other domains to hold on to these valued possessions. Large houses are rarely traded in for something more modest until there is no other alternative.

Families avoid bankruptcy, both because they look upon it as the coward's way out of a disaster and as a too-public admission of failure and surrender. Dierdre Miller's father inherited a family firm that ran aground in the late 1960s. By the time Dierdre was a teenager, the firm was near collapse and the creditors began to hound Mr. Miller to pay up on his bills. It was clear to Dierdre's mother that they needed to declare bankruptcy to protect the family's remaining assets. But as Dierdre tells it, this was unthinkable:

My dad wouldn't hear of the idea of declaring bankruptcy or of selling the family business. He felt he had a reputation to protect and that if he went bankrupt it would be destroyed. He used to tell me that you just have to meet your obligations, that you can't just walk out on people and companies you owe money to. I think he felt that if he declared bankruptcy he'd never be able to recover. It would be the end because no one would respect him.

Joan deLancy, a Wall Street lawyer, remembers that her father—whose career as an engineer bit the dust in the wake of defense department cutbacks in the early 1970s—felt the same way:

My father did earn money through various consulting jobs and short-term positions of one kind or another, but we didn't see much of it. It went toward paying off their debts. He could have walked away from them by declaring bankruptcy, but he thought that would really seal his fate. Bankruptcy was too final, too much an admission of failure. Besides, it is not part of his character to walk away from responsibilities. As bad as things were financially, I think my parents were proud of the fact that they didn't take the easy way out.

As the financial slide worsens, the task of keeping up appearances becomes more difficult. Dierdre Miller's family lived in one of California's wealthiest suburbs before their troubles and continued to hold on after the crisis. She remembers that her mother would drive miles out of her way to spend the family allotment of food stamps in neighborhoods where her face was unknown. Though the Miller family was in serious financial trouble, with no money coming in to speak of, the mother's primary concern was maintaining face: "My mother wouldn't go down and apply for the food stamps. She made my father do all of that. She wouldn't have anything to do with [it]. She was real ashamed." Mrs. Miller's strategy worked. For many years, outward appearances provided no clue that her family was poor enough to qualify for public assistance. The Miller children stopped bringing their friends home and virtually never talked about their family troubles to anyone.

Eventually however, most downwardly mobile families find themselves in such financial straits that they can no longer camouflage their situation. Children begin to feel uncomfortable about the increasing visibility of the material differences between themselves and their peers, a problem that exacerbates the stigma of their fathers ending up in low status jobs.

The Boeing company was Seattle's largest employer up until the late 1960s. In 1968, it shut down a large part of its operations, throwing thousands of engineers, draftsmen, and technicians onto a weak labor market. The Boeing slump spread like a wave through the supplier industries in the area, compounding the disaster. Alice Pendergast's father was a sales manager in a firm that made precision tools; their biggest client was Boeing. By the time Alice was thirteen, five years after the crash, the depth of the Pendergast family disaster had become clear, especially by comparison to her more fortunate friends:

My junior high school was situated right under this big hill where all the Seattle executives lived, and so I started going to school with their kids. It ended up that my best friend's father was the vice president of the biggest bank in town. She lived in this house that seemed like the most beautiful place I'd ever seen. I remember feeling really awful because she had so much stuff.

I guess our standard of living was all right, given the bad money situation. But I always felt we were quite poor because I couldn't go out and buy new clothes like all my friends at school. Instead of shopping at Nordstrom's, the high-class department store, we used to go to K-Mart or Penney's. When I was a kid, trying to impress my peers, it was awful. I remember going to school every day and thinking, "Well, I got this new shirt but I got it because it was on sale at K-Mart."

Alice's dilemma is shared, in part, by all poor kids who rub shoulders with the more affluent. But she suffered an additional humiliation: She used to shop in exclusive stores, and therefore fully understood the disdain the Benetton set have for K-Mart kids.

It took a number of years before John Steinberg's family sank under the weight of prolonged income loss. In the good old days, John had enjoyed summers at the local country club, winter vacations in the Caribbean, and family outings to fancy restaurants. The Steinbergs lived in a magnificent three-story house atop a hill, a stately place fronted by a circular drive. Five years into the disaster, and with no maintenance budget to speak of, it was becoming visibly run down.

John remembers that by the time he was a college sophomore, the paint was peeling badly on the outside. The massive garden, long since bereft of a professional landscaper, was so overgrown he could no longer walk to the back of it. The inside of the house was a study in contrasts. Appliances that were standard issue for the managerial middle class—dishwashers, washing machines, dryers, televisions—stood broken and unrepaired. The wallpaper grew dingy, and the carpet on the stairs became threadworn. The antique chairs in the dining room were stained, the silk seat cushions torn. Chandeliers looked vaguely out of place in the midst of this declining splendor. The whole household had the look of a Southern mansion in the aftermath of the Civil War—its structure reflected a glorious past, but its condition told of years of neglect.

The family car was a regulation station wagon, the kind designed to haul a mob of kids. It aged well, but as John neared the end of high school the car developed signs of terminal mechanical failure. By this time, John's mother had taken a factory job in a nearby town and was dependent on the old wagon to travel to work. The starter motor went out at a particularly bad moment and, for nearly six months, the car could only function by being pushed out of the driveway and rolled down the hill until it picked up enough speed to jump-start in second gear. John remembers being grateful they lived on such a steep incline.

The Steinberg children had, in years past, accompanied their mother on her weekly shopping trips, for the fun of the outing and to make sure special treats found their way home. They would walk up and down the main street of their Connecticut town, stopping at the various specialty stores lining the prosperous commercial strip. Meat came from a butcher shop, bread from a fancy bakery, treats from the handmade candy shop, and staples from an independent, small grocery store. By the time John was in his late teens, the specialty stores were a thing of the past:

I remember the first time I went with my mother to a big supermarket, a chain store we hadn't been to much before. She went to the meat counter and there were these precut packages of meat in plastic wrap. I had never seen meat set out that way before. We had always gone to the butcher and he cut the meat to order for us and wrapped it in small white packages.

There are many people in the United States and around the world who would be more than satisfied to eat at the table of the downwardly mobile managerial family. None of these people were hungry or malnourished. But food has greater significance than the vitamins it provides. That middle-class families can open the refrigerator and eat their fill is a demonstration of their freedom from want. The recent proliferation of "designer" foods and fancy delicatessens reveals the additional role of food as fashion and of gastronomy as tourism. And not least, food is a symbol of social status.

For affluent adolescents wolfing down pizza, the connection between diet and fortune is obscure. They devote little energy to thinking about how the food they see on their own tables compares to the fare consumed by other, less fortunate families. Downwardly mobile children *do* learn about how high income underwrites a refrigerator stocked with goodies—when these items disappear. John Steinberg again:

My family was the real meat and potatoes type. We used to have roast beef and steak all the time. After a few years we couldn't afford it and it was just hamburger and more hamburger. That didn't bother me or my sisters. We were teenagers and we were perfectly happy with it. But I can remember one time my mother went out and splurged on what must have been a fairly cheap roast. It wouldn't hold up under my Dad's carving knife. It just fell apart. He was so disgusted he just walked out of the dining room, leaving my mother to face the kids. He was mad about having to eat that way.

Food, appliances, vacations, clothes, and cars—these basics of middle-class existence are transformed under the brunt of downward mobility. The loss of these items is not just a matter of inconvenience or discomfort. The lack of wheels whittles down each family member's freedom of movement and underlines a new dependency upon others. Dietary changes symbolize a shrinkage in the family's realm of choice. In a culture that lionizes independence, discretion, and autonomy, these material transformations become dramatic emblems of the family's powerlessness to affect its own fate.

But it is the loss of the home, the most tangible symbol of a family's social status, that is the watershed event in the life cycle of downward mobility. In one act, years of attachment to a neighborhood and a way of life are abruptly terminated. The blow is a hard one to withstand, for at least since the era of the GI mortgage, owning a house has defined membership in the middle class. Home ownership is America's most visible measure of economic achievement. Adults who have lost their homes—to foreclosure or distress sales—have truly lost their membership card in the middle class.

It took nearly eight years from the time John Steinberg's father lost his job to the time they lost the house. But when it finally happened, the family was grief-stricken:

Letting go of that house was one of the hardest things we ever had to do. We felt like we were pushed out of the place we had grown up in. None of the rental houses my family lived in after that ever felt like home. You know, we had a roof over our heads, but losing that house made us feel a little like gypsies.

Distress sales can free up capital and provide some cash reserves to draw on, but the financial relief is often short lived. The house is usually the last thing to go and debts have ordinarily piled high before that occurs. Hence the profits are already earmarked for debt relief. Moreover, the need to relocate finds the downwardly mobile family facing the same escalating housing costs that enabled them to pull a profit from their own home. Rental accommodations anywhere near the family's original homestead are frequently costly. Indeed, rents can be much higher than the house payments on the old home, simply because it was purchased years ago, in the days of low mortgages and reasonable prices. These market factors ultimately lead the downwardly mobile in the direction of lower-income neighborhoods, where their dollars go farther but where the atmosphere is comparatively déclassé.

The sliding standard of living the downwardly mobile endure constitutes a drift away from normal middle-class expectations and behavior. The family is growing more deviant over time—its resemblance to the "precrisis" era becomes increasingly faint. Some of the slide can be hidden through dissembling, lies, or cover-ups. The whole family goes "into the closet"—hiding the real situation from the outside world, trying to appear "straight" to their neighbors—while behind the scenes its life steadily draws farther and farther away from the middle-class norm. But there is a psychological cost to living in the closet: Relations between family members grow more intense, and new, sometimes arduous, demands are placed upon children.

Reading 29

9/8/94

Family, Race, and Poverty in the Eighties

Maxine Baca Zinn

The 1960s Civil Rights movement overturned segregation laws, opened voting booths, created new job opportunities, and brought hope to Black Americans. As long as it could be said that conditions were improving, Black family structure and life-style remained private matters. The promises of the 1960s faded, however, as the income gap between whites and Blacks widened. Since the middle 1970s, the Black underclass has expanded rather than contracted, and along with this expansion emerged a public debate about the Black family. Two distinct models of the underclass now prevail—one that is cultural and one that is structural. Both of them focus on issues of family structure and poverty.

THE CULTURAL DEFICIENCY MODEL

The 1980s ushered in a revival of old ideas about poverty, race, and family. Many theories and opinions about the urban underclass rest on the culture-of-poverty debate of the 1960s. In brief, proponents of the culture-of-poverty thesis contend that the poor have a different way of life than the rest of society and that these cultural differences explain continued poverty. Within the current national discussion are three distinct approaches that form the latest wave of deficiency theories.

The first approach—culture as villain—places the cause of the swelling underclass in a value system characterized by low aspirations, excessive masculinity, and the acceptance of female-headed families as a way of life.

The second approach—family as villain—assigns the cause of the growing underclass to the structure of the family. While unemployment is often addressed, this argument always returns to the causal connections between poverty and the disintegration of traditional family structure.

From *Signs: Journal of Women in Culture and Society* 1989, vol. 14, no. 4 © 1989 by The University of Chicago. Reprinted by permission.

The third approach—welfare as villain—treats welfare and antipoverty programs as the cause of illegitimate births, female-headed families, and low motivation to work. In short, welfare transfer payments to the poor create disincentives to
work and incentives to have children out of wedlock—a self-defeating trap of poverty.

Culture as Villain

Public discussions of urban poverty have made the "disintegrating" Black family
the force most responsible for the growth of the underclass. This category, by
definition poor, is overwhelmingly Black and disproportionately composed of female-headed households. The members are perceived as different from striving,
upwardly mobile whites. The rising number of people in the underclass has provided the catalyst for reporters' and scholars' attention to this disadvantaged category. The typical interpretation given by these social commentators is that the
underclass is permanent, being locked in by its own unique but maladaptive culture. This thinking, though flawed, provides the popular rationale for treating the
poor as the problem.

The logic of the culture-of-poverty argument is that poor people have distinctive values, aspirations, and psychological characteristics that inhibit their achievement and produce behavioral deficiencies likely to keep them poor not only within
generations but also across generations, through socialization of the young.[1] In this
argument, poverty is more a function of thought processes than of physical environment.[2] As a result of this logic, current discussions of ghetto poverty, family
structure, welfare, unemployment, and out-of-wedlock births connect these conditions in ways similar to the 1965 Moynihan Report.[3] Because Moynihan maintained that the pathological problem within Black ghettos was the deterioration of
the Negro family, his report became the generative example of blaming the victim.[4] Furthermore, Moynihan dismissed racism as a salient force in the perpetuation of poverty by arguing that the tangle of pathology was "capable of perpetuating itself without assistance from the white world."[5]

The reaction of scholars to Moynihan's cultural-deficiency model was swift
and extensive although not as well publicized as the model itself. Research in the
sixties and seventies by Andrew Billingsley, Robert Hill, Herbert Gutman, Joyce
Ladner, Elliot Leibow, and Carol Stack, to name a few, documented the many
strengths of Black families, strengths that allowed them to survive slavery, the en-
closures of the South, and the depression of the North.[6] Such work revealed that
many patterns of family life were not created by a deficient culture but were instead "a rational adaptational response to conditions of deprivation."[7]

A rapidly growing literature in the eighties documents the disproportionate
representation of Black female-headed families in poverty. Yet, recent studies on
Black female-headed families are largely unconcerned with questions about adaptation. Rather, they study the strong association between female-headed families
and poverty, the effects of family disorganization on children, the demographic
and socioeconomic factors that are correlated with single-parent status, and the
connection between the economic status of men and the rise in Black female-

headed families.[8] While most of these studies do not advance a social-pathology explanation, they do signal a regressive shift in analytic focus. Many well-meaning academics who intend to call attention to the dangerously high level of poverty in Black female-headed households have begun to emphasize the family structure and the Black ghetto way of life as contributors to the perpetuation of the underclass.

The popular press, on the other hand, openly and enthusiastically embraced the Moynihan thesis both in its original version and in Moynihan's restatement of the thesis in his book *Family and Nation*.[9] Here Moynihan repeats his assertion that poverty and family structure are associated, but now he contends that the association holds for Blacks and whites alike. This modification does not critique his earlier assumptions; indeed, it validates them. A profoundly disturbing example of this is revealed in the widely publicized television documentary, CBS Reports' "The Vanishing Family."[10] According to this refurbished version of the old Moynihan Report, a breakdown in family values has allowed Black men to renounce their traditional breadwinner role, leaving Black women to bear the economic responsibility for children.[11] The argument that the Black community is devastating itself fits neatly with the resurgent conservatism that is manifested among Black and white intellectuals and policymakers.

Another contemporary example of the use of the culture of poverty is Nicholas Lemann's two-part 1986 *Atlantic Monthly* article about the Black underclass in Chicago.[12] According to Lemann, family structure is the most visible manifestation of Black America's bifurcation into a middle class that has escaped the ghetto and an underclass that is irrevocably trapped in the ghetto. He explains the rapid growth of the underclass in the seventies by pointing to two mass migrations of Black Americans. The first was from the rural South to the urban North and numbered in the millions during the forties, fifties, and sixties; the second, a migration out of the ghettos by members of the Black working and middle classes, who had been freed from housing discrimination by the civil rights movement. As a result of the exodus, the indices of disorganization in the urban ghettos of the North (crime, illegitimate births) have risen, and the underclass has flourished.[13] Loose attitudes toward marriage, high illegitimacy rates, and family disintegration are said to be a heritage of the rural South. In Lemann's words, they represent the power of culture to produce poverty:

> The argument is anthropological, not economic; it emphasizes the power over people's behavior that culture, as opposed to economic incentives, can have. Ascribing a society's condition in part to the culture that prevails there seems benign when the society under discussion is England or California. But as a way of thinking about black ghettos it has become unpopular. Twenty years ago ghettos were often said to have a self-generating, destructive culture of poverty (the term has an impeccable source, the anthropologist Oscar Lewis). But then the left equated cultural discussions of the ghetto with accusing poor blacks of being in a bad situation that was of their own making. . . . The left succeeded in limiting the terms of the debate to purely economic ones, and today the right also discusses the ghetto in terms of economic "incentives to fail," provided by the welfare system. . . . In the ghettos, though, it appears that the distinctive culture is now the greatest barrier to progress by the black underclass, rather than either unemployment or welfare.[14]

Lemann's essay, his "misreading of left economic analysis, and cultural anthropology itself"[15] might be dismissed if it were atypical in the debate about the culture of poverty and the underclass. Unfortunately, it shares with other studies the problems of working "with neither the benefit of a well-articulated theory about the impact of personality and motivation on behavior nor adequate data from a representative sample of the low-income population."[16]

The idea that poverty is caused by psychological factors and that poverty is passed on from one generation to the next has been called into question by the University of Michigan's Panel Study of Income Dynamics (PSID), a large-scale data collection project conceived, in part, to test many of the assumptions about the psychological and demographic aspects of poverty. This study has gathered annual information from a representative sample of the U.S. population. Two striking discoveries contradict the stereotypes stemming from the culture-of-poverty argument. The first is the high turnover of individual families in poverty and the second is the finding that motivation cannot be linked to poverty. Each year the number of people below the poverty line remains about the same, but the poor in one year are not necessarily the poor in the following year. "Blacks from welfare dependent families were no more likely to become welfare dependent than similar Blacks from families who had never received welfare. Further, measures of parental sense of efficacy, future orientation, and achievement motivation had no effects on welfare dependency for either group."[17] This research has found no evidence that highly motivated people are more successful at escaping from poverty than those with lower scores on tests.[18] Thus, cultural deficiency is an inappropriate model for explaining the underclass.

The Family as Villain

A central notion within culture-of-poverty arguments is that family disintegration is the source and sustaining feature of poverty. Today, nearly six out of ten Black children are born out of wedlock, compared to roughly three out of ten in 1970. In the 25–34-year age bracket, today the probability of separation and divorce for Black women is twice that of white women. The result is a high probability that an individual Black woman and her children will live alone. The so-called "deviant" mother-only family, common among Blacks, is a product of "the feminization of poverty," a shorthand reference to women living alone and being disproportionately represented among the poor. The attention given to increased marital break-ups, to births to unmarried women, and to the household patterns that accompany these changes would suggest that the bulk of contemporary poverty is a family-structure phenomenon. Common knowledge—whether true or not—has it that family-structure changes cause most poverty, or changes in family structure have led to current poverty rates that are much higher than they would have been if family composition had remained stable.[19]

Despite the growing concentration of poverty among Black female-headed households in the past two decades, there is reason to question the conventional thinking. Research by Mary Jo Bane finds that changes in family structure have less causal influence on poverty than is commonly thought.[20] Assumptions about the correlation and association between poverty and family breakdown avoid harder questions about the character and direction of causal relations between the two phenomena.[21] Bane's longitudinal research on household composition and poverty suggests that much poverty, especially among Blacks, is the result of already-poor, two-parent households that break up, producing poor female-headed households. This differs from the event transition to poverty that is more common for whites: "Three-quarters of whites who were poor in the first year after moving into a female-headed or single person household became poor simultaneously with the transition; in contrast, of the blacks who were poor after the transition, about two-thirds had also been poor before. Reshuffled poverty as opposed to event-caused poverty for blacks challenges the assumption that changes in family structure have created ghetto poverty. This underscores the importance of considering the ways in which race produces different paths to poverty."[22]

A two-parent family is no guarantee against poverty for racial minorities. Analyzing data from the PSID, Martha Hill concluded that the long-term income of Black children in two-parent families throughout the decade was even lower than the long-term income of non-Black children who spent most of the decade in mother-only families: "Thus, increasing the proportion of Black children growing up in two-parent families would not by itself eliminate very much of the racial gap in the economic well-being of children; changes in the economic circumstances of the parents are needed most to bring the economic status of Black children up to the higher status of non-Black children."[23]

Further studies are required if we are to understand the ways in which poverty, family structure, and race are related.

Welfare as Villain

An important variant of the family-structure and deficient-culture explanations, one especially popular among political conservatives, is the argument that welfare causes poverty. This explanation proposes that welfare undermines incentives to work and causes families to break up by allowing Black women to have babies and encouraging Black men to escape family responsibilities. This position has been widely publicized by Charles Murray's influential book, *Losing Ground*.[24] According to Murray, liberal welfare policies squelch work incentives and thus are the major cause of the breakup of the Black family. In effect, increased AFDC benefits make it desirable to forgo marriage and live on the dole.

Research has refuted this explanation for the changes in the structure of families in the underclass. Numerous studies have shown that variations in welfare across time and in different states have not produced systematic variation in family structure.[25] Research conducted at the University of Wisconsin's Institute for Research on Poverty found that poverty increased after the late sixties due to a weakening economy through the seventies. No support was found for Murray's assertion that spending growth did more harm than good for Blacks because it increased the percentage of families headed by women. Trends in welfare spending increased between 1960 and 1972, and declined between 1970 and 1984; yet there were no reversals in family-composition trends during this period. The percentage of these households headed by women increased steadily from 10.7 percent to 20.8 percent between 1968 and 1983.[26]

Further evidence against the "welfare-dependency" motivation for the dramatic rise in the proportion of Black families headed by females is provided by William Darity and Samuel Meyers. Using statistical causality tests, they found no short-term effects of variations in welfare payments on female headship in Black families.[27]

Other research draws similar conclusions about the impact of welfare policies on family structure. Using a variety of tests, David Ellwood and Lawrence Summers dispute the adverse effects of AFDC.[28] They highlight two facts that raise questions about the role of welfare policies in producing female-headed households. First, the real value of welfare payments has declined since the early 1970s, while family dissolution has continued to rise. Family-structure changes do not mirror benefit-level changes. Second, variations in benefit levels across states do not lead to corresponding variations in divorce rates or numbers of children in single-parent families. Their comparison of groups collecting AFDC with groups that were not, found that the effects of welfare benefits on family structures were small.[29] In sum, the systematic research on welfare and family structure indicates that AFDC has far less effect on changes in family structure than has been assumed.

OPPORTUNITY STRUCTURES IN DECLINE

A very different view of the underclass has emerged alongside the popularized cultural-deficiency model. This view is rooted in a substantial body of theory and research. Focusing on the opportunity structure of society, these concrete studies reveal that culture is not responsible for the underclass.

Within the structural framework there are three distinct strands. The first deals with transformations of the economy and the labor force that affect Americans in general and Blacks and Hispanics in particular. The second is the transformation of marriage and family life among minorities. The third is the changing class composition of inner cities and their increasing isolation of residents from mainstream social institutions.

All three are informed by new research that examines the macrostructural forces that shape family trends and demographic patterns that expand the analysis to include Hispanics.

Employment

Massive economic changes since the end of World War II are causing the social marginalization of Black people throughout the United States. The shift from an economy based on the manufacture of goods to one based on information and services has redistributed work in global, national, and local economies. While these major economic shifts affect all workers, they have more serious consequences for Blacks than whites, a condition that scholars call "structural racism."[30]

Major economic trends and patterns, even those that appear race neutral, have significant racial implications. Blacks and other minorities are profoundly affected by (1) the decline of industrial manufacturing sectors and the growth of service sectors of the economy; and (2) shifts in the geographical location of jobs from central cities to the suburbs and from the traditional manufacturing cities (the rustbelt) to the sunbelt and to other countries.

In their classic work *The Deindustrialization of America,* Barry Bluestone and Bennett Harrison revealed that "minorities tend to be concentrated in industries that have borne the brunt of recent closing. This is particularly true in the automobile, steel, and rubber industries."[31] In a follow-up study, Bluestone, Harrison, and Lucy Gorham have shown that people of Color, particularly Black men, are more likely than whites to lose their jobs due to the restructuring of the U.S. economy and that young Black men are especially hard hit.[32] Further evidence of the consequences of economic transformation for minority males is provided by Richard Hill and Cynthia Negrey.[33] They studied deindustrialization in the Great Lakes region and found that the race-gender group that was hardest hit by the industrial slump was Black male production workers. Fully 50 percent of this group in five Great Lakes cities studied lost their jobs in durable-goods manufacturing between 1979 and 1984. They found that Black male production workers also suffered the greatest rate of job loss in the region and in the nation as a whole.

The decline of manufacturing jobs has altered the cities' roles as opportunity ladders for the disadvantaged. Since the start of World War II, well-paying blue-collar jobs in manufacturing have been a main avenue of job security and mobility for Blacks and Hispanics. Movement into higher-level blue-collar jobs was one of the most important components of Black occupational advancement in the 1970s. The current restructuring of industries creates the threat of downward mobility for middle-class minorities.[34]

Rather than offering opportunities to minorities, the cities have become centers of poverty. Large concentrations of Blacks and Hispanics are trapped in cities in which the urban employment base is shifting. Today inner cities are shifting away from being centers of production and distribution of physical goods toward being centers of administration, information, exchange, trade, finance, and government service. Conversely, these changes in local employment structures have been accompanied by a shift in the demographic composition of large central cities away from European white to predominantly Black and Hispanic, with rising unemployment. The transfer of jobs away from central cities to the suburbs has created a residential job opportunity mismatch that literally leaves minorities behind in the inner city. Without adequate training or credentials, they are relegated to low-paying, nonadvancing exploitative service work or they are unemployed. Thus, Blacks have become, for the most part, superfluous people in cities that once provided them with opportunities.

The composition and size of cities' overall employment bases have also changed. During the past two decades most older, larger cities have experienced substantial job growth in occupations associated with knowledge-intensive service industries. However, job growth in these high-skill, predominantly white-collar industries has not compensated for employment declines in manufacturing, wholesale trade, and other predominantly blue-collar industries that once consti-tuted the economic backbone of Black urban employment.[35]

While cities once sustained large numbers of less skilled persons, today's ser-vice industries typically have high educational requisites for entry. Knowledge and information jobs in the central cities are virtually closed to minorities given the required technological education and skill level. Commuting between central cit-ies and outlying areas is increasingly common; white-collar workers commute daily from their suburban residences to the central business districts while streams of inner-city residents are commuting to their blue-collar jobs in outlying nodes.[36]

An additional structural impediment inner-city minorities face is their in-creased distance from current sources of blue-collar and other entry-level jobs. Because the industries that provide these jobs have moved to the suburbs and nonmetropolitan peripheries, racial discrimination and inadequate incomes of in-ner-city minorities now have the additional impact of preventing many from mov-ing out of the inner city in order to maintain their access to traditional sources of employment. The dispersed nature of job growth makes public transportation from inner-city neighborhoods impractical, requiring virtually all city residents who work in peripheral areas to commute by personally owned automobiles. The severity of this mismatch is documented by John Kasarda: "More than one half of the minority households in Philadelphia and Boston are without a means of per-sonal transportation. New York City's proportions are even higher with only three of ten black or Hispanic households having a vehicle available."[37]

This economic restructuring is characterized by an overall pattern of uneven development. Manufacturing industries have declined in the North and Midwest while new growth industries, such as computers and communications equipment, are locating in the southern and southwestern part of the nation. This regional shift has produced some gains for Blacks in the South, where Black poverty rates have declined. Given the large minority populations in the sunbelt, it is conceivable that industrial restructuring could offset the economic threats to racial equality. How-ever, the sunbelt expansion has been based largely on low-wage, labor-intensive enterprises that use large numbers of underpaid minority workers, and a decline in the northern industrial sector continues to leave large numbers of Blacks and His-panics without work.

Marriage

The connection between declining Black employment opportunities (especially male joblessness) and the explosive growth of Black families headed by single women is the basis of William J. Wilson's analysis of the underclass. Several recent studies conducted by Wilson and his colleagues at the University of Chicago have established this link.[38] Wilson and Kathryn Neckerman have documented the re-lationship between increased male joblessness and female-headed households. By devising an indicator called "the index of marriageable males," they reveal a long-term decline in the proportion of Black men, and particularly young Black men, who are in a position to support a family. Their indicators include mortality and incarceration rates, as well as labor-force participation rates, and they reveal that the proportion of Black men in unstable economic situations is much higher than indicated in current unemployment figures.[39]

Wilson's analysis treats marriage as an opportunity structure that no longer exists for large numbers of Black people. Consider, for example, why the majority of pregnant Black teenagers do not marry. In 1960, 42 percent of Black teenagers who had babies were unmarried; by 1970 the rate jumped to 63 percent and by 1983 it was 89 percent.[40] According to Wilson, the increase is tied directly to the changing labor-market status of young Black males. He cites the well-established relationship between joblessness and marital instability in support of his argument that "pregnant teenagers are more likely to marry if their boyfriends are working."[41] Out-of-wedlock births are sometimes encouraged by families and absorbed into the kinship system because marrying the suspected father would mean adding someone who was unemployed to the family's financial burden.[42] Adaptation to structural conditions leaves Black women disproportionately separated, divorced, and solely responsible for their children. The mother-only family structure is thus the consequence, not the cause, of poverty.

Community

These changes in employment and marriage patterns have been accompanied by changes in the social fabric of cities. "The Kerner Report Twenty Years Later," a conference of the 1988 Commission on the Cities, highlighted the growing isolation of Blacks and Hispanics.[43] Not only is inner-city poverty worse and more persistent than it was twenty years ago, but ghettos and barrios have become isolated and deteriorating societies with their own economies and with increasingly isolated social institutions, including schools, families, businesses, churches, and hospitals. According to Wilson, this profound social transformation is reflected not only in the high rates of joblessness, crime, and poverty but also in a changing socioeconomic class structure. As Black middle-class professionals left the central city, so too did working-class Blacks. Wilson uses the term "concentration effects" to capture the experiences of low-income families who now make up the majority of those who live in inner cities. The most disadvantaged families are disproportionately concentrated in the sections of the inner city that are plagued by joblessness, lawlessness, and a general milieu of desperation. Without working-class or middle-class role models these families have little in common with mainstream society.[44]

The departure of the Black working and middle classes means more than a loss of role models, however. As David Ellwood has observed, the flight of Black professionals has meant the loss of connections and networks. If successfully employed persons do not live nearby, then the informal methods of finding a job, by which one worker tells someone else of an opening and recommends her or him to the employer, are lost.[45] Concentration and isolation describe the processes that systematically entrench a lack of opportunities in inner cities. Individuals and families are thus left to acquire life's necessities though they are far removed from the channels of social opportunity.

THE CHANGING DEMOGRAPHY OF RACE AND POVERTY

Hispanic poverty, virtually ignored for nearly a quarter of a century, has recently captured the attention of the media and scholars alike. Recent demographic and economic patterns have made "the flow of Hispanics to urban America among the most significant changes occurring in the 1980s."[46]

As the Hispanic presence in the United States has increased in the last decade, Hispanic poverty rates have risen alarmingly. Between 1979 and 1985, the percentage of Latinos who were poor grew from 21.8 percent to 29.0 percent. Nationwide, the poverty rate for all Hispanics was 27.3 percent in 1986. By comparison, the white poverty rate in 1986 was 11 percent; the Black poverty rate was 31.1 percent.[47] Not only have Hispanic poverty rates risen alarmingly, but like Black poverty, Hispanic poverty has become increasingly concentrated in inner cities. Hispanics fall well behind the general population on all measures of social and economic well-being: jobs, income, educational attainment, housing, and health care. Poverty among Hispanics has become so persistent that, if current patterns continue, Hispanics will emerge in the 1990s as the nation's poorest racial-ethnic group.[48] Hispanic poverty has thus become a trend to watch in national discussions of urban poverty and the underclass.

While Hispanics are emerging as the poorest minority group, poverty rates and other socioeconomic indicators vary widely among Hispanic groups. Among Puerto Ricans, 39.9 percent of the population lived below the poverty level in 1986. For Mexicans, 28.4 percent were living in poverty in 1986. For Cubans and Central and South Americans, the poverty rate was much lower: 18.7 percent.[49] Such diversity has led scholars to question the usefulness of this racial-ethnic category that includes all people of Latin American descent.[50] Nevertheless, the labels Hispanic or Latino are useful in general terms in describing the changing racial composition of poverty populations. In spite of the great diversity among Hispanic nationalities, they face common obstacles to becoming incorporated into the economic mainstream of society.

Researchers are debating whether trends of rising Hispanic poverty are irreversible and if those trends point to a permanent underclass among Hispanics. Do macrostructural shifts in the economy and the labor force have the same effects on Blacks and Latinos? According to Joan W. Moore, national economic changes do affect Latinos, but they affect subgroups of Latinos in different ways:

> The movement of jobs and investments out of Rustbelt cities has left many Puerto Ricans living in a bleak ghetto economy. This same movement has had a different effect on Mexican Americans living in the Southwest. As in the North, many factories with job ladders have disappeared. Most of the newer Sunbelt industries offer either high paying jobs for which few Hispanics are trained or low paying ones that provide few opportunities for advancement. Those industries that depend on immigrant labor (such as clothing manufacturing in Los Angeles) often seriously exploit their workers, so the benefits to Hispanics in the Southwest of this influx of industries and invest-

ments are mixed. Another subgroup, Cubans in Miami, work and live in an enclave economy that appears to be unaffected by this shift in the national economy.[51]

Because shifts in the subregional economies seem more important to Hispanics than changes in the national economy, Moore is cautious about applying William Wilson's analysis of how the underclass is created.

Opportunity structures have not declined in a uniform manner for Latinos. Yet Hispanic poverty, welfare dependence, and unemployment rates are greatest in regions that have been transformed by macrostructural economic changes. In some cities, Puerto Rican poverty and unemployment rates are steadily converging with, and in some cases exceeding, the rates of Blacks. In 1986, 40 percent of Puerto Ricans in the United States lived below the poverty level and 70 percent of Puerto Rican children lived in poverty.[52]

Family structure is also affected by economic dislocation. Among Latinos, the incidence of female-headed households is highest for Puerto Ricans—43.3 percent—compared to 19.2 percent for Mexicans, 17.7 for Cubans, and 25.5 percent for Central and South Americans.[53] The association between national economic shifts and high rates of social dislocation among Hispanics provides further evidence for the structural argument that economic conditions rather than culture create distinctive forms of racial poverty. . . .

NOTES

1. Mary Corcoran, Greg J. Duncan, Gerald Gurin, and Patricia Gurin, "Myth and Reality: The Causes and Persistence of Poverty," *Journal of Policy Analysis and Management* 4, no. 4 (1985): 516–36.

2. Mary Corcoran, Greg J. Duncan, and Martha S. Hill, "The Economic Fortunes of Women and Children: Lessons from the Panel Study of Income Dynamics," *Signs: Journal of Women in Culture and Society* 10, no. 2 (Winter 1984): 232–48.

3. Daniel P. Moynihan, "The Negro Family: The Case for National Action," in *The Moynihan Report and the Politics of Controversy*, ed. L. Rainwater and W. L. Yancy (Cambridge, Mass.: MIT Press, 1967), 39–132.

4. Margaret Cerullo and Marla Erlien, "Beyond the 'Normal Family': A Cultural Critique of Women's Poverty," in *For Crying Out Loud*, ed. Rochelle Lefkowitz and Ann Withorn (New York: Pilgrim Press, 1986), 246–60.

5. Moynihan, 47.

6. Leith Mullings, "Anthropological Perspectives on the Afro-American Family," *American Journal of Social Psychiatry* 6, no. 1 (Winter 1986): 11–16; see the following revisionist works on the Black family: Andrew Billingsley, *Black Families in White America* (Englewood Cliffs, N.J.: Prentice-Hall, 1968); Robert Hill, *The Strengths of Black Families* (New York: Emerson-Hall, 1972); Herbert Gutman, *The Black Family in Slavery and Freedom* (New York: Pantheon, 1976); Joyce Ladner, *Tomorrow's Tomorrow: The Black Woman* (New York: Doubleday, 1971); Elliot Leibow, *Talley's Corner: A Study of Negro Street Corner Men* (Boston: Little, Brown, 1967); Carol Stack, *All Our Kin* (New York: Harper & Row, 1974).

7. William J. Wilson and Robert Aponte, "Urban Poverty," *Annual Review of Sociology* 11 (1985): 231–58, esp. 241.

8. For a review of recent studies, see ibid.

9. Daniel Patrick Moynihan, *Family and Nation* (San Diego: Harcourt, Brace, Jovanovich, 1986).

10. "The Vanishing Family: Crisis in Black America," narrated by Bill Moyers, Columbia Broadcasting System (CBS) Special Report, January 1986.

11. "Hard Times for Black America," *Dollars and Sense*, no. 115 (April 1986), 5–7.

12. Nicholas Lemann, "The Origins of the Underclass: Part 1," *Atlantic Monthly* (June 1986), 31–55; Nicholas Lemann, "The Origins of the Underclass: Part 2," *Atlantic Monthly* (July 1986), 54–68.

13. Lemann, "Part 1," 35.

14. Ibid.

15. Jim Sleeper, "Overcoming 'Underclass': More Jobs Are Still the Key," *In These Times* (June 11–24, 1986), 16.

16. Corcoran et al. (n. 1 above), 517.

17. Martha S. Hill and Michael Ponza, "Poverty and Welfare Dependence Across Generations," *Economic Outlook U.S.A.* (Summer 1983), 61–64, esp. 64.

18. Anne Rueter, "Myths of Poverty," *Research News* (July–September 1984), 18–19.

19. Mary Jo Bane, "Household Composition and Poverty," in *Fighting Poverty*, ed. Sheldon H. Danziger and Daniel H. Weinberg (Cambridge, Mass.: Harvard University Press, 1986), 209–31.

20. Ibid.

21. Betsy Dworkin, "40% of the Poor Are Children," *New York Times Book Review* (March 2, 1986), 9.

22. Bane, 277.

23. Martha Hill, "Trends in the Economic Situation of U.S. Families and Children, 1970–1980," in *American Families and the Economy*, ed. Richard R. Nelson and Felicity Skidmore (Washington, D.C.: National Academy Press, 1983), 9–53, esp. 38.

24. Charles Murray, *Losing Ground* (New York: Basic, 1984).

25. David T. Ellwood, *Poor Support* (New York: Basic, 1988).

26. Sheldon Danziger and Peter Gottschalk, "The Poverty of *Losing Ground*," *Challenge* 28 (May/June 1985): 32–38.

27. William A. Darity and Samuel L. Meyers, "Does Welfare Dependency Cause Female Headship? The Case of the Black Family," *Journal of Marriage and the Family* 46, no. 4 (November 1984): 765–79.

28. David T. Ellwood and Lawrence H. Summers, "Poverty in America: Is Welfare the Answer or the Problem?" in *Fighting Poverty* (n. 19 above), 78–105.

29. Ibid., 96.

30. "The Costs of Being Black," *Research News* 38, nos. 11–12 (November–December 1987): 8–10.

31. Barry Bluestone and Bennett Harrison, *The Deindustrialization of America* (New York: Basic, 1982), 54.

32. Barry Bluestone, Bennett Harrison, and Lucy Gorham, "Storm Clouds on the Horizon: Labor Market Crisis and Industrial Policy," 68, as cited in "Hard Times for Black America" (n. 11 above).

33. Richard Child Hill and Cynthia Negrey, "Deindustrialization and Racial Minorities in the Great Lakes Region, U.S.A.," in *The Reshaping of America: Social Consequences of the Changing Economy,* ed. D. Stanley Eitzen and Maxine Baca Zinn (Englewood Cliffs, N.J.: Prentice-Hall, 1989), 168–77.

34. Elliot Currie and Jerome H. Skolnick, *America's Problems: Social Issues and Public Policy* (Boston: Little, Brown, 1984), 82.

35. John D. Kasarda, "Caught in a Web of Change," *Society* 21 (November/December 1983): 41–47.

36. Ibid., 45–47.

37. John D. Kasarda, "Urban Change and Minority Opportunities," in *The New Urban Reality,* ed. Paul E. Peterson (Washington, D.C.: Brookings Institution, 1985), 33–68, esp. 55.

38. William J. Wilson with Kathryn Neckerman, "Poverty and Family Structure: The Widening Gap between Evidence and Public Policy Issues," in *The Truly Disadvantaged,* by William J. Wilson (Chicago: University of Chicago Press, 1987), 63–92.

39. Ibid.

40. Jerelyn Eddings, "Children Having Children," *Baltimore Sun* (March 2, 1986), 71.

41. As quoted in ibid., 71.

42. Noel A. Cazenave, "Alternate Intimacy, Marriage, and Family Lifestyles among Low-Income Black Americans," *Alternative Lifestyles* 3, no. 4 (November 1980): 425–44.

43. "The Kerner Report Updated" (Racine, Wis.: Report of the 1988 Commission on the Cities, March 1, 1988).

44. Wilson, *The Truly Disadvantaged* (n. 38 above), 62.

45. Ellwood (n. 25 above), 204.

46. Paul E. Peterson, "Introduction: Technology, Race, and Urban Policy," in *The New Urban Reality,* ed. Paul E. Peterson (Washington, D.C.: Brookings Institution, 1985), 1–35, esp. 22.

47. Jennifer Juarez Robles, "Hispanics Emerging as Nation's Poorest Minority Group," *Chicago Reporter* 17, no. 6 (June 1988): 1–3.

48. Ibid., 2–3.

49. Ibid., 3.

50. Alejandro Portes and Cynthia Truelove, "Making Sense of Diversity: Recent Research on Hispanic Minorities in the United States," *Annual Review of Sociology* 13 (1987): 359–85.

51. Joan W. Moore, "An Assessment of Hispanic Poverty: Does a Hispanic Underclass Exist?" *Tomás Rivera Center Report* 2, no. 1 (Fall 1988): 8–9.

52. Robles, 3.

53. U.S. Bureau of the Census, *Current Population Reports,* Series P-20, nos. 416, 422 (Washington, D.C.: Government Printing Office, March 1987).

54. Adolph Reed, Jr., "The Liberal Technocrat," *Nation* (February 6, 1988), 167–70.

55. Ellwood (n. 25 above), 133.

56. Clyde W. Franklin 11, "Surviving the Institutional Decimation of Black Males: Causes, Consequences, and Intervention," in *The Making of Masculinities*, ed. Harry Brod (Winchester, Mass.: Allen & Unwin, 1987), 155–69, esp. 155.

57. See Maxine Baca Zinn, "Minority Families in Crisis: The Public Discussion," Working Paper no. 6 (Memphis, Tenn.: Memphis State University, Center for Research on Women, 1987), for an extended critique of the culture-of-poverty model.

Reading 30   9/8/94

Working Mothers and Their Families

Sandra Scarr, Deborah Phillips, and Kathleen McCartney

"A woman's work is never done," or so goes the old adage about women's responsibilities to the home. Women who are mothers of babies and young children spend even more hours on their family roles than do non-mothers or mothers with older children. If one adds to home care and motherhood full-time employment in the labor force, a mother's job requires 50% more hours than that of working fathers and single people without children (Nock & Kingston, in press; Rexroat & Shehan, 1987).

Women all over the world work longer hours than men (Tavris & Wade, 1984). Mothers work longer hours than anyone else because their family responsibilities to household and children are not equally shared by fathers—anywhere. In industrialized countries, whether in the Western or Eastern worlds, mothers do the majority of the shopping, house cleaning, cooking, laundry, and child care, in addition to their paid employment. Whereas fathers in these societies work an

From *American Psychologist*, vol. 44, no. 11, November 1989. Copyright © 1989 by the American Psychological Association, Inc. Reprinted by permission.

average of 50 hours per week in combined employment and household work, mothers work an average of 80 hours per week at the same tasks (Cowan, 1983).

The degree to which most fathers do not share the family work with their wives is vividly demonstrated by Rexroat and Shehan (1987) in a study of 1,618 White couples from the 1976 wave of the Panel Study of Income Dynamics. Whereas in the case of childless working couples and empty nesters, wives worked an average of 5 to 9 hours more per week than their husbands in combined employment and housework, in families with infants and preschool children, mothers worked 16 to 24 hours more per week than did fathers. The actual total hours per week worked by employed mothers of children under age three was 90!

Despite the enormous number of hours worked by most mothers in the world, the self-reports of mothers who are also employees demonstrate that their multiple roles are often not experienced as more stressful than the lives experienced by women with fewer roles and obligations (Crosby, 1987). These seemingly contradictory observations of actual workload and self-perceptions of well-being need to be resolved (Coleman, Antonucci, & Adelmann, 1987; Gove & Zeiss, 1987). Either the Puritans were right that hard work is good for the soul, or there is some self-selection of healthy women into complicated and demanding roles (Epstein, 1987; Reppetti, Matthews & Waldron, 1989, pp. 1394–1401).

In this article, we consider the implications of parental, particularly maternal, employment for family relationships and family well-being.

WHY DO MOTHERS WORK?

Most women in the labor force work primarily because the family needs the money and secondarily for their own personal self-actualization. Because of the decline in real family income from 1973 to 1988 (Congressional Budget Office, 1988), most families find it essential for both parents to work to support them at a level that used to be achieved by one wage-earner, and in many families two earners are required to keep the family out of poverty. Most divorced, single, and widowed mothers must work to avoid poverty.

However, most would not leave their paid employment, even if the family did not need the money (DeChick, 1988). Indeed, 56% of full-time homemakers say that they would choose to have a career if they had it to do all over again, and only 21% of working mothers would leave their current jobs to stay at home with the children (DeChick, 1988). Professional career women are a small but vocal minority of women who value the social and political equality of women's employment, and their endorsement of mothers' employment is consistent with their position. Surveys of working class mothers, with jobs as waitresses, factory workers, and domestics, show that these women are quite committed to their jobs (Hiller & Dyehouse, 1987), satisfied with their diverse roles, and would not leave the labor force even if they did not need the money. The social psychology of the workplace, with its social support, adult companionship, and contacts with the larger world, may explain the phenomenon (Repetti, Matthews, & Waldron, 1989). Like most men, most women want to participate in the larger society.

Several recent studies of mothers of newborns and infants show that returning to work soon after a birth is primarily a function of previously high involvement in the labor force and positive attitudes about mothers' employment, even among families who are economically marginal (Avioli, 1985; Greenstein, 1986; Pistrang, 1984). Mothers who are not employed during their child's infancy are less likely to have been employed prior to the birth and are more likely to have negative attitudes about maternal employment, regardless of the economic situation of the family. For more affluent mothers, attitudes carried more weight than any other factor (Greenstein, 1986). Thus, economic necessity may propel most women into the labor force, but other factors entice them to reenter after having a baby and to stay employed.

Regardless of the reasons, working mothers are here to stay. The Department of Labor projects that by 1995 roughly two thirds of all new labor force entrants will be women (Johnston, 1987), and 80% of those in their childbearing years are expected to have children during their work life. Yet, we as a nation are still ambivalent about mothers who work and whose children's care is delegated to others, and about their diminished time for responsibilities to husbands whose careers are generally presumed to be preeminent.

The major issues discussed in this article are the impact of mothers' employment on their marital relationships and on their children.

WORKING MOTHERS' MARITAL RELATIONSHIPS

Like other adults, mothers vary in their career ambitions, their sex-role expectations, and the degree to which they receive spousal support for their employment. Many reviews of research on mothers' employment show that such mediating factors are crucial to interpreting any effects of maternal employment on family relationships (Anderson-Kulman & Paludi, 1986; Locksley, 1980; Simpson & England, 1982; Smith, 1985). For women, spousal support is a key to the success of dual-career families; it is not maternal employment per se that affects marital satisfaction, but "the law of husband cooperation" (Bernard, 1974, p. 162). Husband cooperation includes positive attitudes toward maternal employment and cooperation with household and child care tasks (Bernardo, Shehan, & Leslie, 1987; Gilbert, 1985, 1988). Mothers who receive little or no spouse support, in either attitudes toward their employment or in participation in child care and household tasks, are indeed stressed by their multiple roles (Anderson-Kulman & Paludi, 1986; Pleck, 1985). Mothers who receive a great deal of positive spouse support feel positive about their spouses and their lives. For mothers, the quality of their roles matters more than how many or how seemingly stressful they are (Baruch & Barnett, 1987).

Husbands' appreciation for and enjoyment of their wives' employment depended both on their degree of participation in family affairs and on their own perceptions of work and family life (Pleck, 1985; Simpson & England, 1982). Gilbert (1985) found that men with children in dual-career families can be classified as traditional, participant, and role-sharing, depending on the degree to which they share household and child-care responsibilities.[1] Men who participate more in the family claim to be content with, even proud of, their wives employment (Wortman, 1987), but outside pressures also affect their support of their wives' careers.

> The responses from men in the study indicate that for men who do experience role conflict, the tension often centers around wanting to support their spouses' career aspirations and to be involved in parenting and household roles while at the same time wanting to have their own career aspirations put first. Being highly competitive, experiencing high work demands, and working in an environment hostile to men's involvement in family roles . . . all contribute to the tension (Gilbert, 1985, p. 104).

For dual-career parents, their satisfactions as couples often depend on their socialization experiences and current attitudes about male and female roles (Aldous, 1982; Pepitone-Rockwell, 1980). Role-sharing and participatory men are more likely to see maternal employment as opportunities for the wife to have greater independent identity, more social interaction, and greater intellectual companionship, opportunities that are less often cited by traditional men. Because of their more egalitarian beliefs about gender roles and women's rights, such fathers appreciate and applaud their wives' careers, even though they also perceive family costs.

Costs of maternal employment more often cited by nontraditional men include decreased leisure time, increased time spent on household tasks, and decreased sexual activity due to fatigue and lack of time (Gilbert, 1985; Voyandoff & Kelly, 1984). Traditional arrangements in which the father is less involved with child care and household responsibilities have some perceived advantages for fathers, but even traditional men acknowledge the contribution of maternal employment to increased family income. That they do not share family responsibilities has a negative effect on wives' perceptions of the marital relationship, but not evidently on theirs (Bernardo et al., 1987; Gilbert, 1988; Pleck, 1985).

The costs and benefits of maternal employment have a positive balance for both husbands and wives in most working families (see Crosby, 1987; Gilbert, 1985; Wortman, 1987). Satisfactions and dissatisfactions of marital partners depend on attitudes toward gender roles and the degree to which they can manage time and effort (Voyandoff & Kelly, 1984). For mothers, satisfactions also depend on spouse support for their household and maternal roles and on their work commitment prior to becoming mothers; mothers with previously high work commitments who stay home for five or more months after a birth report greater irritability, greater depression, decreased marital intimacy, and lower self-esteem than mothers with previously low work commitments (Pistrang, 1984). For men, satisfactions depend primarily on the degree to which they are inconvenienced by maternal employment in exchange for larger family income (Gilbert, 1985, 1988).

MATERNAL EMPLOYMENT AND CHILD DEVELOPMENT

National concerns about the possible plight of children of working mothers prompted a large review of research in 1982 by the National Academy of Sciences

(Kamerman & Hayes, 1982). A distinguished panel of social scientists reviewed all of the evidence and concluded that there were no consistent effects of maternal employment on child development. Rather, they said, maternal employment cannot have a single set of consistent effects on children because mothers work for various reasons and begin or interrupt work when their children are at various ages; furthermore, their employment is in contexts of various families and communities that support or do not support mothers' multiple roles.

Lois Hoffman (1984) reviewed 50 years of research on maternal employment, most of it predicated on the assumption that maternal employment should have negative effects on child development. Indeed, some of the investigators found that young sons were slightly disadvantaged by the loss of maternal attention in the early years. Of course, they were presumably in some form of day care, which may not have been of high quality.

Her reexamination of the data showed that daughters of employed mothers were often reported to be more self-confident, to achieve better grades in school, and to more frequently pursue careers themselves than were the daughters of non-employed mothers. Whereas most sons had role models of competent, employed fathers, daughters of employed mothers also had such a model of achievement. Hoffman also noted that few investigators asked how maternal employment could benefit children by higher family income, higher self-esteem for mothers, a less sharp distinction between male and female roles, and a more positive role model for both sons and daughters for later in their own lives (Gottfried & Gottfried, 1987; Weinraub, Jaeger, & Hoffman, 1988).

When both parents in families with preschool children are employed, the fathers *do not* spend significantly more time on child care or household chores than do fathers in single-earner families (Bernardo et al., 1987; Nock & Kingston, in press). In fact, employed mothers also reduce their household work hours, primarily in categories of homemaking chores, rather than in child care activities (Nock & Kingston, in press). Thus, when both parents of preschool children are employed, both fathers and mothers spend about the same total amount of time in direct interaction with their children as do parents in families in which only fathers are employed. The biggest differences between the two-earner and one-earner families with preschool children are the distribution of time spent with children on weekdays versus weekends and in time spent on non-child care chores (Nock & Kingston, in press). Both parents in one-earner families have more leisure time for themselves.

Differences between one-earner and two-earner families with school-age children and adolescents are less pronounced but also involve a decrease in the amount of time spent on homemaking chores, for both employed fathers and mothers (Nock & Kingston, in press).

All in all, the question of what effects (if any) maternal employment has on children is not a productive one because it ignores the many contextual features of family life that moderate the effects of maternal employment (Grossman, Pollack, & Golding, 1988). We do know that

the straightforward results of bad emotional, social, and intellectual outcomes for children of working mothers were not found, but no research can rule out yet unstudied subtleties. All we know is that the school achievement, IQ test scores, and emotional and social development of working mothers' children are every bit as good as that of children whose mothers do not work (Scarr, 1984, p. 25).

WORKING FAMILIES AND CHILD CARE

Child care is *not* a women's issue; it is a family issue. However, the lack of high-quality, affordable child care has more impact on working mothers than on any others. Not only is there a critical shortage of high-quality child care in this country, but there also is such ambivalence about providing child care that we have a shameful national dilemma: More than 50% of American mothers of infants and preschool children are now in the labor force and require child care services, but there is no coherent national policy on parental leaves or on child care services for working parents.

With the exception of federal child care provided during the Great Depression and World War II, public provision of child care has been reserved for non-mainstream, generally poor families (Phillips & Zigler, 1987; Steinfels, 1973). Day care began in settlement houses in the 1850s for poor mothers who had to work because their husbands were inadequate providers or because they were not married. Early education, on the other hand, was begun by middle and upper class mothers who sponsored nursery schools and kindergartens to give their advantaged children good social and intellectual experiences (Scarr & Weinberg, 1986).

Today, the historical split between early education and day care is no longer tenable. Middle and upper class women have the same needs for work-related, full-day child care as do minority, poor, and single mothers. As of 1986, 51% of married mothers and 49% of single mothers were working (Kahn & Kamerman, 1987). Similarly, by 1985, 62% of both Black and White young children had working mothers. As a consequence, high rates of employment are now common to mothers of all races and marital statuses.

In sum, working mothers have become an everyday part of children's lives, of family life, and of our economic structure (Scarr, Phillips, & McCartney, 1988). Prior distinctions in the degree of child care use by children of different ages and in patterns of use by women with different demographic characteristics have merged into a universal pattern of extensive use. However, even this extensive, mainstream reliance on child care has not ensured that the child care needs of working families are adequately addressed (Hewlett, 1986; McCartney & Phillips, 1989). Kahn and Kamerman (1987) estimated that direct federal funding for child care programs actually decreased by 18% in real dollars between 1980 and 1986.

HOW DOES THE UNITED STATES COMPARE?

The U.S. policies on child care and maternal leaves are an anomaly among industrialized countries. The United States, among 100 countries, is the sole exception to the rule of providing paid, job-protected maternal leaves as national policy (Kamerman, 1986, 1989). Only five states require employers to provide temporary disability insurance, and federal law requires that pregnant women be eligible for these disability benefits. Even among private businesses that provide maternity benefits, this generally means an unpaid leave with no guarantee of reinstatement.

All other industrialized countries have some maternal leave policy. Sweden has one of the most extensive policies: Mothers and fathers have the right to a leave following childbirth that is paid at 90% of one parent's wages for 9 months, followed by a fixed minimum benefit for 3 additional months. Swedish parents may also take an unpaid, but job-protected, leave until their child is 18 months old and may work a six-hour day until their child is eight years old. In Italy, women are entitled to a 6-month job-protected leave, paid at a flat rate equal to the average wage for women workers. At the conclusion of this period, an unpaid, job-protected leave is also available for one year. In France, a job-protected maternity leave of 6 weeks before childbirth and 10 weeks after is provided.

Other countries also have much more systematic child care policies in conjunction with parental leave policies. As of 1986, Sweden had placed 38% of preschoolers with working mothers in subsidized child care programs (Leijon, 1986). France, Italy, Spain, and all of the Eastern European countries have more than half of their infants, toddlers, and preschool children in subsidized child care because their mothers are in the labor force. France, for example, maintains a system of preschools, open to all children two to six years old, and partially subsidized care is available for children under age two. Comparable figures concerning children in subsidized child care in the United States are not available, itself a sign of inattention.

WHY THE POLICY GAP?

Cherished beliefs about maternal care have led us historically as a nation to favor marginal support for mothers to stay home with their babies, through paternal employment and through Aid to Families with Dependent Children (AFDC), rather than support for women's attainment of economic independence. Until the last few years, when employment and training opportunities for women on AFDC were begun as an experiment in several states, poor women with young children had no option but to accept the degradation of poverty-on-the-dole. Now poor mothers are captives of a system that is moving from AFDC to Workfare, which, even in the best of circumstances, does not sustain support for child care for more than one year after these mothers achieve the minimum-wage jobs for which they are being trained.

Working parents need options. One option currently under congressional consideration is an *unpaid* parental (read that as 95% maternal)[2] leave. Many mothers cannot afford to take months off from their jobs, especially without pay; unpaid leaves for divorced and single mothers and for women married to men who earn the minimum wage are not very useful.

Even among mothers who can afford the unpaid leaves, not all *want* to be away from their careers for more than a few months after the birth of a child. Upon serious and honest reflection, they consider themselves to be better parents when they work and mother, rather than attempt only one role, or their careers are such that there are professional costs for taking four to six months out of the office. These women do not want extended maternal leaves; they want high-quality child care, and some want fulfilling, well-compensated, part-time work opportunities.

Policies that create strong incentives for mothers to stay at home for extended periods or that require them to go to work soon after a birth are based on conflicting assumptions about the nature of women's participation in the society and assumptions about infants' needs. There are many reasons that most women would prefer to remain in close contact with their newborns. For one, many women need a rest period after a birth, especially if the pregnancy or the birth was difficult. For another, many new mothers need two or more months to establish reliable breast-feeding and to allow their babies to settle into a reasonably predictable routine. How long should a maternal leave be for either the mother's or the infant's benefit? Neither a mandatory child care nor a mandatory maternal leave policy suits all families. What we need are equally attractive options so that families can choose how best either to take advantage of quality child care while parents work or to arrange an extended leave for parents, usually the mother, to care for the baby. Still, many families (and policymakers) suffer great guilt and anxiety about mothers' return to work and placing infants and toddlers in child care. Psychological research has addressed their fears.

EFFECTS OF CHILD CARE ON CHILDREN

In psychological research, child care is often treated as a uniform arrangement that can be objectively characterized as "nonmaternal care" by investigators who in fact rarely study child care settings. By the same illogic, "home care" is treated uniformly as though all families were alike and is assumed to be preferred to other child care arrangements. Child care settings vary from babysitters in one's own home, to family day care in another's home, to centers that care for more than 100 infants and young children. The quality of these settings varies enormously in terms of their abilities to promote children's development and to provide support for working parents. Families also vary from abusive and neglectful of children's needs to supportive and loving systems that promote optimal development. So it is with other child care settings.

Recent reviews of the child care literature by psychologists of different theoretical persuasions agree that high-quality child care has no detrimental effects on intellectual or language development (Belsky, 1986; Clarke-Stewart, 1989; Scarr et al., 1988). In fact, high-quality day care settings have been shown to compensate for poor family environments (Ramey, Bryant, & Suarez, 1985) and to promote better intellectual and social development than children would have experienced in their own homes. The media and parents are most concerned about the possible effects of child care on attachments of infants to their mothers and on children's possible social deviance. The earliest research questioned whether child caregivers replaced mothers as children's primary attachment figure. Concerns that daily separations from mother might weaken the mother–child bond were a direct heritage of the work on children in orphanages (e.g., Spitz, 1945). Early evidence provided no suggestion that nonmaternal child care constitutes a milder form of full-time institutionalization. Attachment was not adversely affected by enrollment in the university-based child care centers that provided the early child care samples. Bonds formed between children and their caregivers did not replace the mother–child attachment relationship (Belsky & Steinberg, 1978; Etaugh, 1980; Kagan, Kearsley, & Zelazo, 1978).

Now that infant day care is the modal middle-class experience, a new debate about infant day care and attachment has arisen. The critics question whether full-time nonmaternal care in the first year of life increases the probability of insecure attachments between mothers and infants (Belsky & Rovine, 1988). Although the new literature has many limitations (Clarke-Stewart, 1989; Clarke-Stewart & Fein, 1983; McCartney & Galanopoulos, 1988; Phillips, McCartney, Scarr, & Howes, 1987; Scarr et al., 1988), there is near consensus among developmental psychologists and early childhood experts that child care per se does not constitute a risk factor in children's lives; rather poor quality care and poor family environments can conspire to produce poor developmental outcomes (Alliance for Better Child Care, 1988; Howes, Rodning, Galluzzo, & Myers, 1988).

Research on the effects of child care on children's social development has yielded contradictory findings. Although some studies report no differences in social behavior between children with and without child care experience (Golden et al., 1978; Kagan et al., 1978), others show that children who had nonmaternal child care are more socially competent (Clarke-Stewart, 1984; Gunnarsson, 1978; Howes & Olenick, 1986; Howes & Stewart, 1987; Phillips, McCartney, & Scarr, 1987; Ruopp, Travers, Glantz, & Coelen, 1979), and others suggest lower levels of social competence (Haskins, 1985; Rubenstein, Howes, & Boyle, 1981). Positive outcomes include teacher and parent ratings of considerateness and sociability (Phillips et al., 1987), observations of compliance and self-regulation (Howes & Olenick, 1986), and observations of involvement and positive interactions with teachers (McCartney, 1984; Ruopp et al., 1979; Vandell & Powers, 1983). Haskins's (1985) study of a high-quality child care program for disadvantaged infants and preschool children found that, at kindergarten, teachers rated these children higher on scales of aggression than children with community-based child care or no nonmaternal care experience. (Behavior management training of caregivers in the day care center decreased aggression by 80% for later cohorts of children in this program; Finkelstein, 1982). However, children who spent comparable amounts of time in community-based child care programs were the least aggressive children in the study, so that the relationship of aggression to day care experience was not established.

WHAT IS QUALITY CHILD CARE?

Working parents are necessarily concerned about "what is quality?" in child care. Researchers have found that child care quality, operationalized by a number of policy-relevant variables, is important to young children's development. The most important of these factors are small child-caregiver ratio, small group size, caregiver training in child development, and stability of the child's care experience (see Bruner, 1980; Phillips, 1987; Ruopp et al., 1979; Scarr et al., 1988). These variables, in turn, appear to exert their influence by facilitating constructive and sensitive interactions among caregivers and children, which, in turn, promote positive social and cognitive development.

CONCLUDING COMMENTS

In our opinion, many of the fears about child care are not based on scientifically demonstrated facts but socially determined theories about mothers' roles and obligations to their families (Scarr et al., 1988). Of course, it is important for parents to arrange competent care for their children while they work, but it is not clear that mothers have to provide this care on a continuous basis during the entire first year, either for infants' well-being or for their own.

Critics of child care sometimes write as though working parents do not function as parents at all. For example, the term, "maternal absence," was used to describe employed mothers in the title of a recent article in the prestigious journal, *Child Development* (Barglow, Vaughn, & Molitor, 1987). The terms "maternal absence" and "maternal deprivation" seem uncomfortably close to and conjure up the specter of neglected, institutionalized infants.[3] Some seem to forget that employed mothers are typically with their babies in the mornings, evenings, weekends, and holidays, which for most fully employed workers constitutes about half of the child's waking time.[4] Furthermore, when the child is ill, mothers are more likely than other family members to stay at home with the child (Hughes & Galinsky, in press).

The quality of maternal care, just like other child care arrangements, depends on many aspects of the home situation and mothers' mental health. The fantasy that mothers at home with young children provide the best possible care neglects the observation that some women at home full time are lonely, depressed, and not functioning well (see Crosby, 1987; Pistrang, 1984). Home care does not promise quality child care.

WORKING FAMILIES OF THE FUTURE

For the children of working families, the most pressing issue for the future is quality of care—care that will encourage and support all aspects of child development. In most cases, families will provide quality care themselves and try to buy it for their children while they work. Unfortunately, quality care costs more than inadequate care, and many parents today cannot afford good care without employer or public support.

For working parents, the most pressing family issues are shared family responsibilities, spousal support, and the affordability and availability of consistent, dependable child care. Working parents, especially mothers on whom most of the household and child care burdens fall, are constantly threatened psychologically by makeshift child care arrangements that fail unexpectedly and by the high cost of quality child care. Reluctance, even among high-income families, to hire household help means that mothers work more hours than they would need to if some income was invested in household help, rather than in consumer goods (Cowan, 1983; Scarr, 1984).

For policymakers at federal and state levels, the most pressing issues are how to fund a system of quality child care, regulate those aspects of quality that can be legislated and enforced, and coordinate efforts with the private sector and at all levels of government. If one could point to one "magic bullet" to improve the child care system in the United States, it would have to be money—more funding for every aspect of the child care system. Until the United States recognizes the rights of women to participate fully in the life of the society, through motherhood, employment, and political life, we will continue to fail to make appropriate provisions for the care of children of working families.

If statistical projections are correct, nearly 70% of mothers with infants and young children will be employed, most full-time, by the mid-1990s (Hofferth & Phillips, 1987). Such women will be devoted to their families, as they are now, but they will continue to be overworked and harassed by inadequate family supports, especially child care. One hopes that through concerted advocacy for women's rights and child care, there will be some improvements in their lives and in those of their families. Here are our suggestions:

1. Fathers should assume more personal responsibility for planning and implementing family life. At present, many fathers are willing to "fill in" or "help out" with family chores that they and the society consider the mother's responsibility. Indeed, such men are often heard to congratulate themselves on their efforts to aid their wife in her chores (Gilbert, 1985; Wortman, 1987). Fathers today "babysit" their children. Have you ever heard a mother say that she is "babysitting" her children? Even the U.S. Bureau of Census counts father-care as a form of child care alongside nonrelative care and child care centers. Attitudes must change to make the lives of working mothers more tolerable. One would not be likely to see an article on the effects of paternal employment on marital relations and child development, unless the father were unemployed.

2. Children have traditionally been the individual responsibility of families in this society, regardless of inequities in their life chances. Children's fates have been tied exclusively to the fates of their parents, unless there were legal infractions of neglect and abuse statues, in which case society has stepped in tentatively and temporarily. Can we not as a society recognize that children are also a community responsibility? They are the next generation for all of us, regardless of who their parents are. Many countries have family allowances that compensate parents for the extraordinary financial costs of rearing children. Child care costs can be subsidized by the society, just as public educational costs are shared by all. Few citizens to-

day object to public support of education for children from ages 5 to 18. Why should they object to child care and early education for children from age 1 to 5?

3. We must recognize changes in American families that make sole support for children more difficult than it has been in the past. Changes in the earning capacity of service workers, who cannot support a family on a full-time job, means that most families will require more than one worker. Increasing diversity in family composition means that children will be cared for in a variety of settings that may or may not include their biological parents. Single parents, mostly mothers who have been divorced or never married, are poor and cannot pay the full costs of child care while they work. They must be subsidized for child care, or they will have to live on welfare.

4. We can encourage employers to take more responsibility for the necessary balance of family and work life of their employees. Recently, in both Britain and the United States, some companies have recognized the shrinking labor pool projected for the 1990s and proposed measures to assist working families, and thereby they have become more attractive employers (Gardner, 1988a, 1988b). Proposals include now-familiar assistance with finding child care, provision of subsidies or on-site child care, and novel approaches (for these countries) such as paid and job-guaranteed maternal leaves for extended periods. Given the opposition of the National Chamber of Commerce to even an unpaid maternal leave for only 12 weeks, these changes may not come in the foreseeable future. Federal legislation will be required for paid, extended parental or maternal leaves to become a reality for most workers.

5. In Europe, North America, and most other parts of the world, mothers are economically disadvantaged compared with men and with non-mothers, especially if they are single parents. In the United States, more than 50% of single mothers and their young children are poor; in Australia, 65% of single mothers and their children are poor. These figures compare to poverty rates for single mothers of 35% to 39% for most of Europe and only 8.6% in Sweden (Smeedling & Torrey, 1988). Poverty rates for all families with children vary from a low of 5.1% in Sweden to a high of 17.1% in the United States (with Australia next to the bottom at 16.9%).

Employed women in the United States earn about 70% of men's wages. Even in Sweden, where women's earnings per hour are more than 90% of men's earnings, women work an average of 10 hours less per week than men and fill virtually all the part-time jobs (Leijon, 1986). Moreover, Swedish women are found in a much narrower band of occupations than are men, primarily concerned with "nursing, care, and services" (Leijon, 1986). It appears that, even when helpful options of parental leaves and subsidized child care are available, many mothers are economically disadvantaged, unless supported by a male worker. Rather than pursuing demanding, well-paid careers, they have part-time, lower status jobs. The combined responsibilities of motherhood and paid employment are an enormous burden that needs to be shared more equitably by fathers and by society as a whole.

NOTES

1. Traditional husbands do little to support their wives' employment by participating in family affairs. Participatory fathers take some responsibility for child care but do not do household chores. Role-sharing husbands take more responsibility for both children and home, but few (even in the university community studied) were found to share equally with the wife.
2. Sweden pays parents 90% of their salaries for one parent to take off nine months with a new infant. In practice, 95% of the leave is taken by mothers, even though there is an additional incentive for the parents to share the leave time with the baby.
3. Research on maternal deprivation reached an emotional climax in the 1950s, when Spitz (1945), Bowlby (1951), and others claimed that institutionalized infants wasted away for want of maternal care. Reanalyses of the evidence (Ernst, 1988; Yarrow, 1961) found that lack of sensory and affective stimulation in typical institutions of the day caused infants to languish both intellectually and emotionally. Longitudinal studies of institutionalized children showed that their later adjustment problems owed more to their continued deprivation throughout childhood than to deprived infant care (Ernst, 1988).
4. Consider five working days/week for 49 weeks of the year: 1.5 hours in the morning and 3 hours of the child's waking time in the late afternoon and evening, for a sum of 4.5 of the approximately 14 hours of the child's daily waking time. The caregiver accounts for approximately 9 hours, 2 hours of which the child typically spends in a nap. (A half hour is allocated for transportation.) The sum of work week hours of parents employed full time is 1,102; for caregivers, 1,715.

   To the parental sum, add weekends (2 days/work week) for 49 weeks, a sum of 1,274. To that, add three weeks of vacation time and 10 days of personal and sick leave (for self and child) during the work weeks, a sum of 455.

   By these calculations, the typical, fully employed parents spend 2,831 hours with the child; caregivers spend approximately 1,715.

REFERENCES

Aldous, J. (1982). *Two paychecks: Life in dual-earner families.* Beverly Hills, CA: Sage.

Alliance for Better Child Care. (1988, March). *Statement in support of the ABC Child Care Bill.* Washington, DC: Author.

Anderson-Kulman, R. E., & Paludi, M. A. (1986). Working mothers and the family context: Predicting positive coping. *Journal of Vocational Behavior, 28,* 241–253.

Avioli, P. S. (1985). The labor-force participation of married mothers of infants. *Journal of Marriage and the Family, 47,* 739–745.

Barglow, P., Vaughn, B. E., & Molitor, N. (1987). Effects of maternal absence due to employment on the quality of infant–mother attachment in a low-risk sample. *Child Development, 58,* 945–954.

Baruch, G. K., & Barnett, R. C. (1987). Role quality and psychological well-being. In F. J. Crosby (Ed.), *Spouse, parent, worker: On gender and multiple roles* (pp. 91–108). New Haven, CT: Yale University Press.

Belsky, J. (1986). Infant day care: A cause for concern? *Zero to Three, 6*(5), 1–9.

Belsky, J., & Rovine, M. J. (1988). Nonmaternal care in the first year of life and the security of infant–parent attachment. *Child Development, 59,* 157–176.

Belsky, J., & Steinberg, L. D. (1978). The effects of daycare: A critical review. *Child Development, 49,* 929–949.

Bernard, J. (1974). *The future of motherhood.* New York: Dial Press.

Bernardo, D. H., Shehan, C. L., & Leslie, G. R. (1987). A residue of tradition: Jobs, careers, and spouses' time in housework. *Journal of Marriage and the Family, 49,* 381–390.

Bowlby, J. (1951). *Maternal care and mental health.* Geneva, Switzerland: World Health Organization.

Bruner, J. (1980). *Under five in Britain.* London: Oxford University Press.

Clarke-Stewart, A. (1984). Day care: A new context for research and development. In M. Perlmutter (Ed.), *The Minnesota Symposia on Child Psychology: Vol. 17. Parent–child interaction and parent–child relations in child development* (pp. 61–100). Hillsdale, NJ: Erlbaum.

Clarke-Stewart, A. (1989). Infant day care: Malignant or maligned? *American Psychologist, 44,* 266–273.

Clarke-Stewart, A., & Fein, G. (1983). Early childhood programs. In M. Haith & J. Campos (Eds.), *Handbook of child psychology: Vol. 2. Infancy and developmental psychobiology* (pp. 917–1000). New York: Wiley.

Coleman, L. M., Antonucci, T. C., & Adelmann, P. K. (1987). Role involvement, gender, and well-being. In F. J. Crosby (Ed.), *Spouse, parent, worker: On gender and multiple roles* (pp. 138–153). New Haven, CT: Yale University Press.

Congressional Budget Office. (March, 1988). *New report on family income.* Washington, DC: Author.

Cowan, R. S. (1983). *More work for mother: The ironies of household technology from the open hearth to the microwave.* New York: Basic Books.

Crosby, F. J. (Ed.). (1987). *Spouse, parent, worker: On gender and multiple roles.* New Haven, CT: Yale University Press.

DeChick, J. (1988, July 19). Most mothers want a job, too. *USA Today,* p. D1.

Epstein, C. F. (1987). Multiple demands and multiple roles: The conditions of successful management. In F. J. Crosby (Ed.), *Spouse, worker, parent: On gender and multiple roles* (pp. 23–25). New Haven, CT: Yale University Press.

Ernst, C. (1988). Are early childhood experiences overrated? A reassessment of maternal deprivation. *European Archives of Psychiatry and Neurological Sciences, 237,* 80–90.

Etaugh, C. (1980). Effects of nonmaternal care on children: Research evidence and popular views. *American Psychologist, 35,* 309–319.

Finkelstein, N. (1982). Aggression: Is it stimulated by daycare? *Young Children, 37,* 3–9.

Gardner, M. (1988a, June 9). Home with the kids—job break without penalty. *Christian Science Monitor,* p. 23.

Gardner, M. (1988b, June 30). Family-friendly corporations. *Christian Science Monitor,* p. 32.

Gilbert, L. A. (1985). *Men in dual-career families: Current realities and future prospects.* Hillsdale, NJ: Erlbaum.

Gilbert, L. A. (1988). *Sharing it all: The rewards and struggles of two-career families.* New York: Plenum Press.

Golden, M., Rosenbluth, L., Grossi, M. T., Policare, H. J., Freeman, H., Jr., & Brownlee, E. M. (1978). *The New York City Infant Day Care Study.* New York: Medical and Health Research Association of New York City.

Gottfried, A., & Gottfried, A. (Eds.). (1987). *Maternal employment and children's development: Longitudinal research.* New York: Plenum.

Gove, W. R., & Zeiss, C. (1987). Multiple roles and happiness. In F. J. Crosby (Ed.), *Spouse, parent, worker: On gender and multiple roles* (pp. 125–137). New Haven, CT: Yale University Press.

Greenstein, T. N. (1986). Social-psychological factors in perinatal labor force participation. *Journal of Marriage and the Family, 48,* 565–571.

Grossman, F. K., Pollack, W. S., & Golding, E. (1988). Fathers and children: Predicting the quality and quantity of fathering. *Developmental Psychology, 24,* 82–91.

Gunnarsson, L. (1978). *Children in day care and family care in Sweden* (Research Bulletin No. 21). Gothenburg, Sweden: University of Gothenburg.

Haskins, R. (1985). Public aggression among children with varying day care experience. *Child Development, 57,* 689–703.

Hewlett, S. (1986). *A lesser life.* New York: Morrow.

Hiller, D. V., & Dyehouse, J. (1987). A case for banishing "dual-career marriages" from the research literature. *Journal of Marriage and the Family, 49,* 787–795.

Hofferth, S. L., & Phillips, D. A. (1987). Child care in the United States, 1970 to 1995. *Journal of Marriage and the Family, 49,* 559–571.

Hoffman, L. W. (1984). Work, family, and the socialization of the child. In R. D. Parke (Ed.), *Review of child development research* (Vol. 7, pp. 223–281). Chicago: University of Chicago Press.

Howes, C., & Olenick, M. (1986). Family and child care influences on toddlers' compliance. *Child Development, 57,* 202–216.

Howes, C., Rodning, C., Galluzzo, D., & Myers, L. (1988). Attachment and child care: Relationships with mother and caregiver. *Early Childhood Research Quarterly, 3,* 403–416.

Howes, C., & Stewart, P. (1987). Child's play with adults, toys, and peers: An examination of family and child-care influences. *Developmental Psychology, 23,* 423–430.

Hughes, D., & Galinsky, E. (in press). Relationships between job characteristics, work/family interference, and marital outcomes. *Early Childhood Research Quarterly.*

Johnston, W. B. (1987). *Workforce 2000: Work and workers for the 21st century.* Indianapolis, IN: Hudson Institute.

Kagan, J., Kearsley, R. B., & Zelazo, P. R. (1978). *Infancy: Its place in human development.* Cambridge, MA: Harvard University Press.

Kahn, A. J., & Kamerman, S. B. (1987). *Child care: Facing the hard choices.* Dover, MA: Auburn House.

Kamerman, S. (1986). Maternity, paternity, and parenting policies: How does the United States compare. In S. A. Hewlett, A. S. Ilchman, & J. J. Sweeney (Eds.), *Family and work: Bridging the gap* (pp. 53–66). Cambridge, MA: Ballinger.

Kamerman, S. (1989). Child care, women, work and the family: An international overview of child care services and related policies. In J. Lande, S. Scarr, & N. Gunzenhauser (Eds.), *The future of child care in the United States* (pp. 93–110). Hillsdale, NJ: Erlbaum.

Kamerman, S., & Hayes, C. D. (Eds.). (1982). *Families that work: Children in a changing world.* Washington, DC: National Academy Press.

Leijon, A. (1986). The origins, progress, and future of Swedish family policy. In S. A. Hewlett, A. S. Ilchman, & J. J. Sweeney (Eds.), *Family and work: Bridging the gap* (pp. 31–38). Cambridge, MA: Ballinger.

Locksley, A. (1980). On the effects of wives' employment on marital adjustment and companionship. *Journal of Marriage and the Family, 42,* 337–346.

McCartney, K. (1984). The effects of quality of day care environment upon children's language development. *Developmental Psychology, 20,* 244–260.

McCartney, K., & Galanopoulos, A. (1988). Child care and attachment: A new frontier the second time around. *American Journal of Orthopsychiatry, 58,* 16–24.

McCartney, K., & Phillips, D. (1989). Motherhood and child care. In B. Birns & D. Haye (Eds.), *Different faces of motherhood* (pp. 157–183). New York: Plenum.

Nock, S. L., & Kingston, P. W. (in press). Time with children: The impact of couples' work-time commitments. *Social Forces.*

Pepitone-Rockwell, F. (1980). *Dual-career couples.* Beverly Hills, CA: Sage.

Phillips, D. (Ed.). (1987). *Quality in child care: What does research tell us?* Washington, DC: National Association for the Education of Young Children.

Phillips, D., McCartney, K., & Scarr, S. (1987). Child care quality and children's social development. *Developmental Psychology, 23,* 537–543.

Phillips, D., McCartney, K., Scarr, S., & Howes, C. (1987). Selective review of infant day care research: A cause for concern! *Zero to Three, 7*(1), 18–21.

Phillips, D., & Zigler, E. (1987). The checkered history of federal child care regulations. In E. Rothkops (Ed.), *Review of research in education* (pp. 3–41). Washington, DC: American Educational Research Association.

Pistrang, N. (1984). Women's work involvement and experience of new motherhood. *Journal of Marriage and the Family, 46,* 433–447.

Pleck, J. H. (1985). *Working wives/working husbands.* Beverly Hills, CA: Sage.

Ramey, C. T., Bryant, D. M., & Suarez, T. M. (1985). Preschool compensatory education and the modifiability of intelligence: A critical review. In D. Detterman (Ed.), *Current topics in human intelligence (pp. 247–296).* Norwood, NJ: Ablex.

Repetti, R. L., Matthews, K. A., & Waldron, I. (1989). Effects of paid employment on women's mental and physical health. *American Psychologist, 44,* 1394–1401.

Rexroat, C., & Shehan, C. (1987). The family life cycle and spouses' time in housework. *Journal of Marriage and the Family, 49,* 737–750.

Rubenstein, J., Howes, C., & Boyle, P. (1981). A two year follow-up of infants in community based day care. *Journal of Child Psychology and Psychiatry, 22,* 209–218.

Ruopp, R., Travers, J., Glantz, F., & Coelen, C. (1979). *Children at the center: Final results of the National Day Care Study.* Boston, MA: Abt Associates.

Scarr, S. (1984). *Mother care/other care.* New York: Basic Books.

Scarr, S., Phillips, D., & McCartney, K. (1988). *Facts, fantasies and the future of child care in America.* Unpublished manuscript.

Scarr, S., & Weinberg, R. A. (1986). The early childhood enterprise: Care and education of the young. *American Psychologist, 41,* 1140–1146.

Simpson, I. H., & England, P. (1982). Conjugal work roles and marital solidarity. In J. Aldous (Ed.), *Two paychecks: Life in dual-earner families.* Beverly Hills, CA: Sage.

Smeedling, T. M., & Torrey, B. B. (1988). Poor children in rich countries. *Science, 242,* 873–877.

Smith, D. S. (1985). Wife employment and marital adjustment: A cumulation of results. *Family Relations, 34,* 483–490.

Spitz, R. (1945). Hospitalism: An inquiry into the genesis of psychiatric conditions in early childhood. *Psychoanalytic Studies of the Child, 1,* 53–74.

Steinfels, M. (1973). *Who's minding the children: The history and politics of day care in America.* New York: Simon & Schuster.

Tavris, C., & Wade, C. (1984). *The longest war: Sex differences in perspective.* New York: Harcourt Brace Jovanovich.

Vandell, D. L., & Powers, C. P. (1983). Day care quality and children's free play activities. *American Journal of Orthopsychiatry, 53,* 493–500.

Voyandoff, P. & Kelly, R. F. (1984). *Journal of Marriage and the Family, 46,* 881–892.

Weinraub, M., Jaeger, E., & Hoffman, L. (1988). Predicting infant outcome in families of employed and non-employed mothers. *Early Childhood Research Quarterly, 3,* 361–378.

Wortman, C. (1987, October). Coping with role overload among professionals with young children. In K. P. Matthews (Chair), *Workshop on Women, Work and Health.* Workshop conducted at the meeting of the MacArthur Foundation, Hilton Head, SC.

Yarrow, L. (1961). Maternal deprivation: Toward an empirical and conceptual evaluation. *Psychological Bulletin, 58,* 459–490.

Reading 31

11/22/99

The Second Shift: Working Parents and the Revolution at Home

Arlie Hochschild, with Anne Machung

Between 8:05 A.M. and 6:05 P.M., both Nancy and Evan are away from home, working a "first shift" at full-time jobs. The rest of the time they deal with the varied tasks of the second shift: shopping, cooking, paying bills; taking care of the car, the garden, and yard; keeping harmony with Evan's mother who drops over quite a bit, "concerned" about Joey, with neighbors, their voluble baby-sitter, and each other. And Nancy's talk reflects a series of second-shift thoughts: "We're out of barbecue sauce. . . . Joey needs a Halloween costume. . . . The car needs a wash. . . ." and so on. She reflects a certain "second-shift sensibility," a continual attunement to the task of striking and restriking the right emotional balance between child, spouse, home, and outside job.

When I first met the Holts, Nancy was absorbing far more of the second shift than Evan. She said she was doing 80 percent of the housework and 90 percent of the childcare. Evan said she did 60 percent of the housework, 70 percent of the childcare. Joey said, "I vacuum the rug, and fold the dinner napkins," finally concluding, "Mom and I do it all." A neighbor agreed with Joey. Clearly, between Nancy and Evan, there was a "leisure gap": Evan had more than Nancy. I asked both of them, in separate interviews, to explain to me how they had dealt with housework and childcare since their marriage began.

One evening in the fifth year of their marriage, Nancy told me, when Joey was two months old and almost four years before I met the Holts, she first seriously raised the issue with Evan. "I told him: 'Look, Evan, it's not working. I do the housework, I take the major care of Joey, *and* I work a full-time job. I get pissed.

This is *your* house too. Joey is *your* child too. It's not all *my* job to care for them.' When I cooled down I put to him, 'Look, how about this: I'll cook Mondays, Wednesdays, and Fridays. You cook Tuesdays, Thursdays, and Saturdays. And we'll share or go out Sundays.' "

According to Nancy, Evan said he didn't like "rigid schedules." He said he didn't necessarily agree with her standards of housekeeping, and didn't like that standard "imposed" on him, especially if she was "sluffing off" tasks on him, which from time to time he felt she was. But he went along with the idea in principle. Nancy said the first week of the new plan went as follows: On Monday, she cooked. For Tuesday, Evan planned a meal that required shopping for a few ingredients, but on his way home he forgot to shop for them. He came home, saw nothing he could use in the refrigerator or in the cupboard, and suggested to Nancy that they go out for Chinese food. On Wednesday, Nancy cooked. On Thursday morning, Nancy reminded Evan, "Tonight it's your turn." That night Evan fixed hamburgers and french fries and Nancy was quick to praise him. On Friday, Nancy cooked. On Saturday, Evan forgot again.

As this pattern continued, Nancy's reminders became sharper. The sharper they became, the more actively Evan forgot—perhaps anticipating even sharper reprimands if he resisted more directly. This cycle of passive refusal followed by disappointment and anger gradually tightened, and before long the struggle had spread to the task of doing the laundry. Nancy said it was only fair that Evan share the laundry. He agreed in principle, but anxious that Evan would not share, Nancy wanted a clear, explicit agreement. "You ought to wash and fold every other load," she had told him. Evan experienced this "plan" as a yoke around his neck. On many weekdays, at this point, a huge pile of laundry sat like a disheveled guest on the living-room couch.

In her frustration, Nancy began to make subtle emotional jabs at Evan. "I don't know *what's* for dinner," she would say with a sigh. Or "I can't cook now, I've got to deal with this pile of laundry." She tensed at the slightest criticism about household disorder; if Evan wouldn't do the housework, he had absolutely *no* right to criticize how she did it. She would burst out angrily at Evan. She recalled telling him: "After work *my* feet are just as tired as *your* feet. I'm just as wound up as you are. I come home. I cook dinner. I wash and I clean. Here we are, planning a second child, and I can't cope with the one we have."

About two years after I first began visiting the Holts, I began to see their problem in a certain light: as a conflict between their two gender ideologies. Nancy wanted to be the sort of woman who was needed and appreciated both at home and at work—like Lacey, she told me, on the television show "Cagney and Lacey." She wanted Evan to appreciate her for being a caring social worker, a committed wife, and a wonderful mother. But she cared just as much that she be able to appreciate *Evan* for what *he* contributed at home, not just for how he supported the family. She would feel proud to explain to women friends that she was married to one of these rare "new men."

A gender ideology is often rooted in early experience, and fueled by motives formed early on and such motives can often be traced to some cautionary tale in early life. So it was for Nancy. Nancy described her mother:

My mom was wonderful, a real aristocrat, but she was also terribly depressed being a housewife. My dad treated her like a doormat. She didn't have any self-confidence. And growing up, I can remember her being really depressed. I grew up bound and determined not to be like her and not to marry a man like my father. As long as Evan doesn't do the housework, I feel it means he's going to be like my father—coming home, putting his feet up, and hollering at my mom to serve him. That's my biggest fear. I've had *bad* dreams about that.

Nancy thought that women friends her age, also in traditional marriages, had come to similarly bad ends. She described a high school friend: "Martha barely made it through City College. She had no interest in learning anything. She spent nine years trailing around behind her husband [a salesman]. It's a miserable marriage. She hand washes all his shirts. The high point of her life was when she was eighteen and the two of us were running around Miami Beach in a Mustang convertible. She's gained seventy pounds and she hates her life." To Nancy, Martha was a younger version of her mother, depressed, lacking in self-esteem, a cautionary tale whose moral was "if you want to be happy, develop a career and get your husband to share at home." Asking Evan to help again and again felt like "hard work" but it was essential to establishing her role as a career woman.

For his own reasons, Evan imagined things very differently. He loved Nancy and if Nancy loved being a social worker, he was happy and proud to support her in it. He knew that because she took her caseload so seriously, it was draining work. But at the same time, he did not see why, just because she chose this demanding career, *he* had to change *his own* life. Why should her personal decision to work outside the home require him to do more inside it? Nancy earned about two-thirds as much as Evan, and her salary was a big help, but as Nancy confided, "If push came to shove, we could do without it." Nancy was a social worker because she loved it. Doing daily chores at home was thankless work, and certainly not something Evan needed her to appreciate about him. Equality in the second shift meant a loss in his standard of living, and despite all the high-flown talk, he felt he hadn't *really* bargained for it. He was happy to help Nancy at home if she needed help; that was fine. That was only decent. But it was too sticky a matter "committing" himself to sharing.

Two other beliefs probably fueled his resistance as well. The first was his suspicion that if he shared the second shift with Nancy, she would "dominate him." Nancy would ask him to do this, ask him to do that. It felt to Evan as if Nancy had won so many small victories that he had to draw the line somewhere. Nancy had a declarative personality; and as Nancy said, "Evan's mother sat me down and told me once that I was too forceful, that Evan needed to take more authority." Both Nancy and Evan agreed that Evan's sense of career and self was in fact shakier than Nancy's. He had been unemployed. She never had. He had had some bouts of drinking in the past. Drinking was foreign to her. Evan thought that sharing housework would upset a certain balance of power that felt culturally "right." He held the purse strings and made the major decisions about large purchases (like their house) because he "knew more about finances" and because he'd chipped in more inheritance than she when they married. His job difficulties had lowered his self-respect, and now as a couple they had achieved some ineffable "balance"—tilted in his favor, she thought—which, if corrected to equalize the burden of chores, would result in his giving in "too much." A certain driving anxiety behind Nancy's strategy of actively renegotiating roles had made Evan see agreement as "giving in." When he wasn't feeling good about work, he dreaded the idea of being under his wife's thumb at home.

Underneath these feelings, Evan perhaps also feared that Nancy was avoiding taking care of *him*. His own mother, a mild-mannered alcoholic, had by imperceptible steps phased herself out of a mother's role, leaving him very much on his own. Perhaps a personal motive to prevent that happening in his marriage—a guess on my part, and unarticulated on his—underlay his strategy of passive resistance. And he wasn't altogether wrong to fear this. Meanwhile, he felt he was "offering" Nancy the chance to stay home, or cut back her hours, and that she was refusing his "gift," while Nancy felt that, given her feelings about work, this offer was hardly a gift.

In the sixth year of her marriage, when Nancy again intensified her pressure on Evan to commit himself to equal sharing, Evan recalled saying, "Nancy, why don't you cut back to half time, that way you can fit everything in." At first Nancy was baffled: "We've been married all this time, and you *still* don't get it. Work is important to me. I worked *hard* to get my MSW. Why *should* I give it up?" Nancy also explained to Evan and later to me, "I think my degree and my job has been my way of reassuring myself that I won't end up like my mother." Yet she'd received little emotional support in getting her degree from either her parents or in-laws. (Her mother had avoided asking about her thesis, and her in-laws, though invited, did not attend her graduation, later claiming they'd never been invited.)

In addition, Nancy was more excited about seeing her elderly clients in tenderloin hotels than Evan was about selling couches to furniture salesmen with greased-back hair. Why shouldn't Evan make as many compromises with his career ambitions and his leisure as she'd made with hers? She couldn't see it Evan's way, and Evan couldn't see it hers.

In years of alternating struggle and compromise, Nancy had seen only fleeting mirages of cooperation, visions that appeared when she got sick or withdrew, and disappeared when she got better or came forward.

After seven years of loving marriage, Nancy and Evan had finally come to a terrible impasse. Their emotional standard of living had drastically declined: they began to snap at each other, to criticize, to carp. Each felt taken advantage of: Evan, because his offering of a good arrangement was deemed unacceptable, and Nancy, because Evan wouldn't do what she deeply felt was "fair."

This struggle made its way into their sexual life—first through Nancy directly, and then through Joey. Nancy had always disdained any form of feminine wiliness cr manipulation. Her family saw her as "a flaming feminist" and that was how she saw herself. As such, she felt above the underhanded ways traditional women used to get around men. She mused, "When I was a teen-ager, I vowed I would *never* use sex to get my way with a man. It is not self-respecting; it's demeaning. But when Evan refused to carry his load at home, I did, I used sex. I said, 'Look, Evan, I would not be this exhausted and asexual every night if I didn't have so much to face every morning.' " She felt reduced to an old "strategy," and her modern ideas made her ashamed of it. At the same time, she'd run out of other, modern ways.

The idea of a separation arose, and they became frightened. Nancy looked at the deteriorating marriages and fresh divorces of couples with young children around them. One unhappy husband they knew had become so uninvolved in family life (they didn't know whether his unhappiness made him uninvolved, or whether his lack of involvement had caused his wife to be unhappy) that his wife left him. In another case, Nancy felt the wife had "nagged" her husband so much that he abandoned her for another woman. In both cases, the couple was less happy after the divorce than before, and both wives took the children and struggled desperately to survive financially. Nancy took stock. She asked herself, "Why wreck a marriage over a dirty frying pan?" Is it really worth it?

UPSTAIRS-DOWNSTAIRS: A FAMILY MYTH AS "SOLUTION"

Not long after this crisis in the Holts' marriage, there was a dramatic lessening of tension over the issue of the second shift. It was as if the issue was closed. Evan had won. Nancy would do the second shift. Evan expressed vague guilt but beyond that he had nothing to say. Nancy had wearied of continually raising the topic, wearied of the lack of resolution. Now in the exhaustion of defeat, she wanted the struggle to be over too. Evan was "so good" in *other* ways, why debilitate their marriage by continual quarreling. Besides, she told me, "Women always adjust more, don't they?"

One day, when I asked Nancy to tell me who did which tasks from a long list of household chores, she interrupted me with a broad wave of her hand and said, "I do the upstairs, Evan does the downstairs." What does that mean? I asked. Matter-of-factly, she explained that the upstairs included the living room, the dining room, the kitchen, two bedrooms, and two baths. The downstairs meant the garage, a place for storage and hobbies—Evan's hobbies. She explained this as a "sharing" arrangement, without humor or irony—just as Evan did later. Both said they had agreed it was the best solution to their dispute. Evan would take care of the car, the garage, and Max, the family dog. As Nancy explained, "The dog is all Evan's problem. I don't have to deal with the dog." Nancy took care of the rest.

For purposes of accommodating the second shift, then, the Holts' garage was elevated to the full moral and practical equivalent of the rest of the house. For Nancy and Evan, "upstairs and downstairs," "inside and outside," was vaguely described like "half and half," a fair division of labor based on a natural division of their house.

The Holts presented their upstairs-downstairs agreement as a perfectly equitable solution to a problem they "once had." This belief is what we might call a "family myth," even a modest delusional system. Why did they believe it? I think they believed it because they needed to believe it, because it solved a terrible problem. It allowed Nancy to continue thinking of herself as the sort of woman whose husband didn't abuse her—a self-conception that mattered a great deal to her. And it avoided the hard truth that, in his stolid, passive way, Evan had refused to share. It avoided the truth, too, that in their showdown, Nancy was more afraid of divorce than Evan was. This outer cover to their family life, this family myth, was jointly devised. It was an attempt to agree that there was no conflict over the second shift, no tension between their versions of manhood and womanhood, and that the powerful crisis that had arisen was temporary and minor.

The wish to avoid such a conflict is natural enough. But their avoidance was tacitly supported by the surrounding culture, especially the image of the woman with the flying hair. After all, this admirable woman also proudly does the "upstairs" each day without a husband's help and without conflict.

After Nancy and Evan reached their upstairs-downstairs agreement, their confrontations ended. They were nearly forgotten. Yet, as she described their daily life months after the agreement, Nancy's resentment still seemed alive and well. For example, she said:

> Evan and I eventually divided the labor so that I do the upstairs and Evan does the downstairs and the dog. So the dog is my husband's problem. But when I was getting the dog outside and getting Joey ready for childcare, and cleaning up the mess of feeding the cat, and getting the lunches together, and having my son wipe his nose on my outfit so I would have to change—then I was pissed! I felt that I was doing *everything*. All Evan was doing was getting up, having coffee, reading the paper, and saying, "Well, I have to go now," and often forgetting the lunch I'd bothered to make.

She also mentioned that she had fallen into the habit of putting Joey to bed in a certain way: he asked to be swung around by the arms, dropped on the bed, nuzzled and hugged, whispered to in his ear. Joey waited for her attention. He didn't go to sleep without it. But, increasingly, when Nancy tried it at eight or nine, the ritual didn't put Joey to sleep. On the contrary, it woke him up. It was then that Joey began to say he could only go to sleep in his parents' bed, that he began to sleep in their bed and to encroach on their sexual life.

Near the end of my visits, it struck me that Nancy was putting Joey to bed in an "exciting" way, later and later at night, in order to tell Evan something important: "You win, I'll go on doing all the work at home, but I'm angry about it and I'll make you pay." Evan had won the battle but lost the war. According to the family myth, all was well: the struggle had been resolved by the upstairs-downstairs agreement. But suppressed in one area of their marriage, this struggle lived on in another—as Joey's Problem, and as theirs.

NANCY'S "PROGRAM" TO SUSTAIN THE MYTH

There was a moment, I believe, when Nancy seemed to *decide* to give up on this one. She decided to try not to resent Evan. Whether or not other women face a moment just like this, at the very least they face the need to deal with all the feelings that naturally arise from a clash between a treasured ideal and an incompatible reality. In the age of a stalled revolution, it is a problem a great many women face.

Emotionally, Nancy's compromise from time to time slipped; she would forget and grow resentful again. Her new resolve needed maintenance. Only half aware that she was doing so, Nancy went to extraordinary lengths to maintain it. She could tell me now, a year or so after her "decision," in a matter-of-fact and noncritical way: "Evan likes to come home to a hot meal. He doesn't like to clear the table. He doesn't like to do the dishes. He likes to go watch TV. He likes to play with his son when he feels like it and not feel like he should be with him more." She seemed resigned.

Everything was "fine." But it had taken an extraordinary amount of complex "emotion work"—the work of *trying* to feel the "right" feeling, the feeling she wanted to feel—to make and keep everything "fine." Across the nation at this particular time in history, this emotion work is often all that stands between the stalled revolution on the one hand, and broken marriages on the other.

HOW MANY HOLTS?

In one key way the Holts were typical of the vast majority of two-job couples: their family life had become the shock absorber for a stalled revolution whose origin lay far outside it—in economic and cultural trends that bear very differently on men and women. Nancy was reading books, newspaper articles, and watching TV programs on the changing role of women. Evan wasn't. Nancy felt benefited by these changes; Evan didn't. In her ideals and in reality, Nancy was more different from her mother than Evan was from his father, for the culture and economy were in general pressing change faster upon women like her than upon men like Evan. Nancy had gone to college; her mother hadn't. Nancy had a professional job; her mother never had. Nancy had the idea that she should be equal with her husband; her mother hadn't been much exposed to that idea in her day. Nancy felt she should share the job of earning money, and that Evan should share the work at home; her mother hadn't imagined that was possible. Evan went to college, his father (and the other boys in his family, though not the girls) had gone too. Work was important to Evan's identity as a man as it had been for his father before him. Indeed, Evan felt the same way about family roles as his father had felt in his day. The new job opportunities and the feminist movement of the 1960s and '70s had transformed Nancy but left Evan pretty much the same. And the friction created by this difference between them moved to the issue of second shift as metal to a magnet. By the end, Evan did less housework and childcare than most men married to working women—but not much less. Evan and Nancy were also typical of nearly 40 percent of the marriages I studied in their clash of gender ideologies and their corresponding difference in notion about what constituted a "sacrifice" and what did not. By far the most common form of mismatch was like that between Nancy, an egalitarian, and Evan, a transitional.

But for most couples, the tensions between strategies did not move so quickly and powerfully to issues of housework and childcare. Nancy pushed harder than most women to get her husband to share the work at home, and she also lost more overwhelmingly than the few other women who fought that hard. Evan pursued his strategy of passive resistance with more quiet tenacity than most men, and he allowed himself to become far more marginal to his son's life than most other fathers. The myth of the Holts' "equal" arrangement seemed slightly more odd than other family myths that encapsulated equally powerful conflicts.

Beyond their upstairs-downstairs myth, the Holts tell us a great deal about the subtle ways a couple can encapsulate the tension caused by a struggle over the second shift without resolving the problem or divorcing. Like Nancy Holt, many women struggle to avoid, suppress, obscure, or mystify a frightening conflict over the second shift. They do not struggle like this because they started off wanting to, or because such struggle is inevitable or because women inevitably lose, but because they are forced to choose between equality and marriage. And they choose marriage. When asked about "ideal" relations between men and women in general, about what they want for their daughters, about what "ideally" they'd like in their own marriage, most working mothers "wished" their men would share the work at home.

But many "wish" it instead of "want" it. Other goals—like keeping peace at home—come first. Nancy Holt did some extraordinary behind-the-scenes emotion work to prevent her ideals from clashing with her marriage. In the end, she had confined and miniaturized her ideas of equality successfully enough to do two things she badly wanted to do: feel like a feminist, and live at peace with a man who was not. Her program had "worked." Evan won on the reality of the situation, because Nancy did the second shift. Nancy won on the cover story; they would talk about it as if they shared.

Nancy wore the upstairs-downstairs myth as an ideological cloak to protect her from the contradictions in her marriage and from the cultural and economic forces that press upon it. Nancy and Evan Holt were caught on opposite sides of the gender revolution occurring all around them. Through the 1960s, 1970s, and 1980s masses of women entered the public world of work—but went only so far up the occupational ladder. They tried for "equal" marriages, but got only so far in achieving it. They married men who liked them to work at the office but who wouldn't share the extra month a year at home. When confusion about the identity of the working woman created a cultural vacuum in the 1970s and 1980s, the image of the supermom quietly glided in. She made the "stall" seem normal and happy. But beneath the happy image of the woman with the flying hair are modern marriages like the Holts', reflecting intricate webs of tension, and the huge, hidden emotional cost to women, men, and children of having to "manage" inequality. Yet on the surface, all we might see would be Nancy Holt bounding confidently out the door at 8:30 A.M., briefcase in one hand, Joey in the other. All we might hear would be Nancy's and Evan's talk about their marriage as happy, normal, even "equal"— because equality was so important to Nancy.

Chapter
10

Variations in Family Experience

Reading 32

Intergenerational Relationships Across Cultures

*Paulette Moore Hines,
Nydia Garcia-Preto,
Monica McGoldrick, Rhea Almeida,
and Susan Weltman*

The powerful influence of ethnicity on how individuals think, feel, and behave has only recently begun to be considered in family therapy training and practice as well as in the larger human services delivery system.

In our efforts to promote the melting-pot myth and the notion that all individuals are equal, we tend to perpetuate the notion that to be different is to be defi-

From Families in Society: *The Journal of Contemporary Human Services.* Copyright © 1992 Family Service America, Inc. 11700 West Lake Park Drive, Milwaukee, WI 53224.

cient or bad. Although similarities exist across individuals and groups in this country and the push for acculturation is strong, differences among groups need to be recognized, valued, and integrated into our thinking and practice of family therapy. Human behavior cannot be understood properly in isolation from the context in which an individual is embedded.

Ethnicity is a critical, but not sufficient, consideration for understanding personal development and family life throughout the life cycle. McGoldrick (1982) defined ethnicity as a sense of commonality transmitted over generations by the family and reinforced by the surrounding community. Our cultural values and assumptions, often unconscious, influence every aspect of our being, including what we label as a problem, how we communicate, beliefs about the cause of a problem, whom we prefer as a helper, and what kind of solutions we prefer.

The rules governing intergenerational relationships in families throughout the life cycle vary across cultures. For instance, considerable differences exist among ethnic groups as to the degree of intergenerational dependence and sharing expected between adult children and their aging parents. Whereas Italians or Greeks are likely to grow up with the expectation that eventually they will take care of their parents, white Anglo-Saxon Protestant (WASP) parents' worst nightmare might be that eventually they will have to depend on their child for support. Minimal interdependence is expected or fostered so that adult children feel relatively guilt free when they have to put their parents in a nursing home. Conversely, adult children avoid asking their parents for support beyond paying for their education.

Another significant difference among groups is the way in which cultures define responsibilities and obligations according to gender roles. Groups differ profoundly in their expectations of motherhood and fatherhood as well as in their treatment of sons and daughters. Families evolve through the life cycle and encounter conflicts at different developmental phases. Marriage, child rearing, leaving home, and caring for the elderly demand changes in relationships that are inherently stressful, especially when ascribed cultural rules for dealing with these stages are challenged or cease to be functional. When conflict erupts, families usually attempt resolution by drawing on the strengths and legacies passed from one generation to the next.

Needless to say, it is difficult to share personal and clinical observations about our respective ethnic groups without generalizing. Thus, readers should understand that, among other variables, the following portraits of ethnic groups are affected by gender, generation, residence, education, socioeconomic status, and migration as well as by the life experience of the authors. We acknowledge that significant variations exist within groups and that ethnic values and practices are constantly evolving.

Clinicians need to remain open to what families tell us about themselves and take care to enter the therapeutic process without predetermined conclusions about families based merely on ethnic generalizations. Equally important is the fact that clinicians neither formulate theories nor conduct interventions in a vacuum. Our cultural lenses dictate our world view and what we consider "normal." It is also useful to have a point of departure in one's work that is larger than one's own limited experiences; hypotheses are simply starting points from which one proceeds to look for data that support or contradict one's initial notions. In the interests of offering that starting point for practitioners, this article addresses rules for relationships, common conflicts, resources and/or legacies that promote or hinder conflict resolution, and implications for assessment and intervention with African American, Hispanic, Irish, Asian Indian, and Jewish families.

AFRICAN AMERICAN FAMILIES

African traditions, the experience of slavery, assimilation into the American mainstream, the psychological scars of past and current discrimination, age, education, religion, and geographic origins allow for great heterogeneity within African American culture. However, survival issues based on interdependence and oppression due to racism are commonalities that transcend individual and group differences.

Despite conscious and consistent efforts by members of the dominant culture to erase all remnants of African culture from the memories and practices of African slaves and their descendants, a sense of "oneness," as exemplified in the practice of greeting one another as "sister" or "brother," is critical to understanding the dynamics of relationships among African Americans. A general assumption exists among African Americans that regardless of the educational or economic advantages of individuals, the legacy of slavery, racism, and oppression is a common bond.

Family relationships, moreso than bank accounts, represent "wealth" and guarantee emotional and concrete support in the face of negative feedback from the larger society. The emotional significance of relationships is not determined solely by the immediacy of blood ties. In fact, "family" is an extended system of blood-related kin and persons informally adopted into this system (Hines & Boyd-Franklin, 1982; Boyd-Franklin, 1989). Extended-family systems tend to be large and constantly expanding as new individuals and their families are incorporated through marriage. Commonly, three or four generations live in proximity, sometimes residing in the same household.

Strong value is placed on loyalty and responsibility to others. This value is reinforced through the belief that everything one does in the public domain reflects on one's family and other African Americans. Similarly, African Americans often believe that one does not succeed just for oneself but for one's family and race as well. In essence, African Americans believe that "you are your brother's keeper."

Among African Americans, respect is shown to others because of their intrinsic worth and character, not for their status or what they have accumulated in material wealth. Personal accomplishments are considered the dual consequence of individual effort and, importantly, also due to the sacrifice of others. Success is to be acknowledged and celebrated but not overemphasized, as positive outcomes cannot be guaranteed despite one's efforts in a racist environment. Furthermore, even when success is achieved, it may be short lived. Intelligence and education without character and "common sense" have little value. Good character involves respect for those who helped one succeed and survive difficult circumstances.

Family members are expected to stay connected and to reach out and assist others who are in need (McGoldrick, Garcia-Preto, Hines, & Lee, 1989).

The elderly are held in reverence. Older women, more than men, are called upon to impart wisdom as well as to provide functional support to younger family members. Older adults are testimony to the fact that one not only can survive but can transcend difficult circumstances as well. They serve as models for self-sacrifice, personal strength, and integrity. By example, they show that although suffering is inevitable, one can grow from hardship and adversity. Children and adults are expected to show verbal and nonverbal "respect" to the elderly. Titles such as Mr., Mrs., Aunt, and Uncle are used to convey respect, deriving from the slavery and post-slavery eras during which African American men and women, irrespective of their age, were treated and referred to as objects or children.

Children and adolescents may express their feelings and opinions but are not allowed to argue with adults after a final decision has been made. Although adults have the liberty to voice dissenting opinions to those who are older, younger adults are expected to acknowledge respectfully the older adult's opinion and perspective. To fail to do so shows disrespect for the life experience of the older person. Use of profanity in an intergenerational context is generally not acceptable.

Young adulthood for African Americans is a critical period during which poor decisions and impulsive behavior can have life-long consequences (Hines, 1989). The usual stressors on intergenerational relationships during this phase of the family life cycle can be both eased and complicated by the numerous adults who may be intensely concerned about a young adult's well-being. Young adults with few employment possibilities and who find it difficult to achieve adult status while living at home may move in with relatives until they become economically self-sufficient. They remain subject, however, to older family members' collective efforts to protect them from life hardships that might be avoided.

Some young African American adults fear failure and disappointing significant others. Others fear success as a result of internalizing the older generation's concerns about losing one's cultural connectedness. Some young adults are ambivalent about personal success because they are materially comfortable while significant others, especially parental figures, are struggling for basic survival. Conflicts may arise when younger adults believe that the advice of older adults is not appropriate to the context in which the young adult operates. Sometimes older adults may minimize the concerns and distress of younger people because they feel that such concerns are trivial compared with their difficult life experiences. Consequently, some young adults find it difficult to seek help within their families for fear of being perceived as weak; others are afraid that they will overwhelm family members who are already burdened by other life stresses. Young adults may be reluctant to pursue help from appropriate professionals in the work setting for fear of being negatively labeled as well as adversely affecting opportunities for other African Americans. The consequence of these scenarios is over- or underfunctioning, which may result in or exacerbate internal and intergenerational conflicts.

Similar intergenerational issues may surface in families with young children and adolescents. The role flexibility (exchange of responsibilities) characteristic of African American families allows adults to help children thrive in environments with many "mine fields" (Hines, 1990). The proverb "It takes a village to raise a child" works well as long as roles are clearly defined, rules are consistent, and ultimate authority is clearly established. However, boundaries may not be clearly delineated, which creates confusion. Intergenerational conflicts are most likely to arise as a result of a child's "disrespectful" behavior at home or school, poor academic functioning, and behaviors that may put the youth at risk of compromising his or her personal freedom. The primary concerns are that male adolescents will get into trouble with legal authorities and that female adolescents will act out sexually or, worse, become pregnant. Parents may resort to overfunctioning (i.e., become inflexible) and turn to relatives for help. Male adolescents from female-headed households are particularly inclined to rebel against the power and influence of their mothers and other females in positions of authority (Hines, 1990).

Although African Americans have the capacity to be openly expressive of their feelings, such expression may be held in check in an effort to minimize intergenerational conflicts. Such conflicts threaten unity and diminish energy needed to deal with everyday life. Conflict often occurs when individuals are perceived to have lost hope, self-respect, and/or self-responsibility; when they are perceived to be wallowing in sorrow, engaging in self-destructive behaviors, or pursuing individual interests without concern for significant others, particularly children and older adults.

Intergenerational conflicts may revolve around whether children are being taught traditional values basic to the survival of African American people. Parents who invest in providing material things and opportunities to their children that were not available to them while growing up may be perceived by other family members as "spoiling" their children. Conflicts are likely to focus on how to teach children survival skills without depriving them of the fruits of the previous generation's labor. . . .

American clients are uncomfortable in groups in which, as the sole African American participant, their problems might seem to be "exceptional" or different from everyone else's. Clients should be offered the opportunity to discuss such concerns, and alternatives should be made available. Young adults should also be encouraged to develop and use natural support groups within their work and social environments if they are struggling under the weight of unrealistic family- or self-imposed expectations as well as challenged by the inherent stress of working in a bicultural setting.

HISPANIC FAMILIES

The web of relationships that extends across generations in Hispanic families provides a support network sustained by rules of mutual obligation. These rules are perpetuated by patterns of caretaking that fulfill expectations of emotional, physical, and economic support for those who need it from those capable of providing it. Rules of respect also play an important role in preserving this intergenerational network of close personal relationships. Children, for example, learn to relate to others according to their age, sex, and social class. When the system works, that is, if sacrifices do not border on martyrdom, the support and emotional acceptance provided can be very healthy and nurturing as well as reassuring and validating.

The sense of responsibility and mutual obligation can be so ingrained among Hispanics that individuals with few resources run the risk of self-sacrifice. Women, in particular, are expected to assume caretaking roles in the family and tend to experience more pressure than do men to devote their lives to the welfare of others. Becoming martyrs gives them special status, in that family members often seen their sacrifice as exemplary. However, the price they pay for "carrying this cross" is often too high (Garcia-Preto, 1990). This behavior is reinforced by the cultural concepts of *marianismo* and *hembrismo,* which contribute to the complexity of Hispanic gender roles.

Marianismo stems from the cult of the Virgin Mary, whereby women are considered morally superior to men and, therefore, capable of enduring the suffering inflicted by men (Stevens, 1973). *Hembrismo,* which literally means femaleness, has been described as a cultural revenge to *machismo* (Habach, 1972) and as a frustrated attempt to imitate a male. *Hembrismo,* within a historical context, shares common elements with the women's movement in the areas of social and political goals (Gomez, 1982). *Hembrismo,* according to Comas-Diaz (1989), connotes strength, perseverance, flexibility, and the ability to survive. However, she adds that it can also translate into a woman's attempt to fulfill her multiple-role expectations as a mother, wife, worker, daughter, and community member—in other words, the "superwoman" working a double shift at home and on the job. In therapy, many Hispanic women present symptoms related to *marianista* behavior at home and *hembrista* behavior at work (Comas-Diaz, 1989).

Men, on the other hand, are more likely to assume financial responsibility for elderly parents, younger siblings, and nephews and nieces. This behavior, too, is admired and respected. Grandparents and other elderly relatives, although not expected to contribute financially to the family, often do so indirectly by caring for grandchildren and thus enabling parents to work or go to school. In return for this assistance and by virtue of their being in need, it is expected that the elderly will be cared for by their adult children. If such expectations are not met, intergenerational conflicts are likely to occur throughout the family system.

A common source of intergenerational conflict in Hispanic families who enter therapy is the struggle between parents and children who have grown apart while trying to adapt to American culture. Traditionally, Hispanic children tend to have closer relationships with their mothers than with their fathers. Perhaps because women are responsible for holding the family together, they tend to develop very strong relationships with their children and other family members. This central position in the family system gives them a measure of power, which is reflected in their alliances with children against authoritarian fathers, who are perceived as lacking understanding with regard to emotional issues. Relationships between sons and mothers are close and dependent; it is not uncommon for a son to protect his mother against an abusive husband.

Mothers and daughters also have close relationships, but these are more reciprocal in nature. Mothers teach their daughters how to be good women who deserve the respect of others, especially males, and who will make good wives and mothers. Daughters usually care for their elderly parents, often taking them into their homes when they are widowed. Relationships between Hispanic women and their fathers vary according to family structure. In families in which fathers assume an authoritarian position, the father-daughter relationship may be marked by distance and conflict. While attempting to be protective, fathers may become unreasonable, unapproachable, and highly critical of their daughters' behavior and friends. On the other hand, in families in which men are more submissive and dependent on their wife to make decisions, fathers may develop special alliances with their daughters, who in turn may assume a nurturing role toward them.

When Hispanic families arrive in the United States, the children ususally find it easier to learn English and adapt to the new culture than do parents. The parents, on the other hand, may find English too difficult to learn and the new culture unwelcoming and dangerous. They may react by taking refuge in the old culture, expecting their children to do the same. When this occurs, children typically rebel against their parents' rigidity by rejecting parental customs, which are viewed as inferior to the American way of life.

Children may become emotionally distanced from their parents, who often feel they have lost control. Parents usually react by imposing stricter rules; corporal punishment may be used. Commonly, parents will demand respect and obedience, cultural values that are traditionally seen as a solution to misbehavior. Parents may become very strict and overprotective of adolescents, especially if the family lives in a high-crime community where drugs are prevalent. Daughters, especially, may be overprotected because they are viewed as being more vulnerable than males in a society with loose sexual mores. Such patterns of overprotection are more characteristic of families who are isolated or alienated from support systems in the community and when extended-family members are not available (Garcia-Preto, 1982).

Children who are caught in the conflict of cultures and loyalties may develop a negative self-image, which can inhibit their chances for growth and accomplishment. Parents, then, may feel thwarted at every turn and consequently give up on their children. In therapy, it may be useful to see adolescents alone if they are unable to speak freely in front of their parents. Issues of respect and fear about their parents' reactions may inhibit adolescents from speaking about sex, drugs, incest, problems at school, or cultural conflicts at home and in the community. In such instances, obvious goals include helping adolescents define and share with their parents personal issues that affect their relationship in an effort to find compromises. Discussing a family's migratory history and acculturation process may help clarify conflicts over cultural values. The therapist can also encourage parents to redefine privileges and responsibilities and to discuss their genuine concern for the child. By encouraging parents to express their love, concern, and fear to their children, therapists help parents and children relate in a more positive manner (Garcia-Preto, 1982). . . .

As stated earlier, intergenerational conflict is often caused by the inability of one generation to provide care for another. Adult children who are unable to care for their elderly parents, especially if the parents are ill, may experience stress and guilt. Conflicts with siblings and other family members may result. Practitioners need to encourage communication among family members in order to help them find ways to contribute to the care of elderly parents. Women who devote themselves to caring for elderly parents may express their stress and resentment through somatic complaints and/or depression. Therapists can help these women express their resentments openly as well as assist them in finding support from other family members or community resources.

Leaving the family system (e.g., through divorce or separation) is extremely risky for both men and women because it implies loss of control, support, and protection. For couples who are still adjusting to American culture, the loss of the family system can be devastating. For example, women usually depend on other women in the extended family for help with child-rearing and domestic tasks, because men are not expected to share these responsibilities. Without the help of their mother, mother-in-law, grandmothers, aunts, or sisters, Hispanic women may become overburdened and begin demanding assistance from their husband. The husband may, in turn, resent these demands and become argumentative and distant, perhaps turning to alcohol, gambling, or extramarital affairs. The extended family can provide a measure of control for aggression and violence by intervening in arguments and providing advice to couples. Helping couples make connections with relatives, friends, or community supports may be the therapist's most crucial task.

IRISH FAMILIES

Intergenerational relationships among the Irish are not generally characterized by intimacy. Unlike many other groups, such as African Americans, Italians, or Hispanics, who tend to view the extended family as a resource in times of trouble, the Irish tend to take the attitude that having a problem is bad enough, but if your family finds out, you have two problems: the problem and your embarrassment in front of your family. It is said of the Irish that they suffer alone. They do not like others to see them when they are in pain. It is not so much a fear of dependence, as with WASPs, but a sense of embarrassment and humiliation at not being able to keep up appearances. Intergenerational secrets are common. The Irish would often rather tell almost anything to a stranger than to a family member, but if they do share it with a family member it is usually told to someone of the same sex and generation as the teller. . . .

Within the family, intergenerational relationships throughout the life cycle are handled primarily by the mother. She cares for both the old and the young. She views caretaking as her responsibility, as does everyone else in the family. Her main supporters are her daughters, though she might also call on her sisters.

The Irish sense of duty is a wonderful resource. Parents want to "do the right thing" for their children; it is not a lack of care, but a lack of attention to detail that most often interferes with appropriate nurturing of their children. The Irish tend to focus more on their children's conformity to rules than on other aspects of their child's development, such as emotional expression, self-assertiveness, or creativity. Should a child be brought to the school principal for misbehavior, a traditional

Irish mother's reaction to the child might be: "I don't want to hear your explanations or excuses. Just never let it happen that the principal has to contact me again." Traditionally, the Irish have believed that children should be seen and not heard. They should not bring outside notoriety to the family, especially for bad behavior. Less emphasis is placed on being a star student than on not standing out from the group for misbehavior. Irish parents tend to have a superficial sense of child psychology, hoping that keeping their children clean, out of trouble, and teaching them right from wrong will get them through. When children develop psychological symptoms, Irish parents are often mystified. When children act out, parents tend to blame outside influences, although privately they blame themselves.

During the child-rearing phase, the biggest problem in Irish families occurs if a child gets in trouble with outside authorities such as the school system. When the adults have problems at home during this phase, for example, if the father is an alcoholic, Irish children can be remarkably inventive in developing strategies to obey family rules of denial while appearing to function well. However, they may later pay a high price emotionally for having learned at an early age to suppress unacceptable feelings.

During the adolescent phase and the launching years, heavy drinking may become a major, often unidentified, problem that the parents—primarily the mother—do not know how to handle. It therefore may be ignored, often with disastrous consequences.

Irish fathers play a peripheral role in intergenerational family relationships, whereas Irish mothers are at the center. They are indomitable. But the stereotype of the "sainted Irish mother" is not totally positive (McGoldrick, 1991; Rudd, 1984; McGoldrick, 1982; Diner, 1983; McKenna, 1979; Scheper-Hughes, 1979); she can also be critical, distant, and lacking in affection, less concerned about nurturing her children than about control and discipline. She may worry about their dirty underwear lest they be in an accident and she be called in to claim the body. She can be sanctimonious, preoccupied with categories of right and wrong and about what the neighbors think, consciously withholding praise of her children for fear it will give them "a swelled head." Such attitudes and behaviors make sense in a culture with such a long history of foreign domination, in which Irish mothers sought control over "something" through whatever means were available to them and felt a need to keep their family in line to minimize the risk of members being singled out for further oppression.

Sons and daughters rarely voice resentment toward their mothers. To do so is to risk guilt and to undermine their admiration for her stoic self-sacrifice. For generations, Irish women have held rule in their families, including control of the family money. Children tend to speak of "my mother's house," dismissing the role of the father (Diner, 1983). Irish mothers often fail to recognize their own strength or ability to intimidate their children, whether through teasing, ridicule, a disapproving glance, or a quick hand. One Irish mother in therapy described her son's arrest for a drunken escapade as follows:

> Joey's afraid of me. I know he is, because when he got arrested and I went down there to pick him up, the policeman expected when I walked in there that he'd see a big

witch of a woman coming through the door, because Joey had said to him, "Just promise me one thing, just protect me from my mother." But I didn't do anything. When I went in there, I just gave him a smack across the face, because I didn't need that nonsense.

Implicit in her comment are ridicule for her son's fear of her and a bold assertion of her own righteousness.

Perhaps because of their history of oppression, the Irish tend to communicate indirectly, often believing that putting feelings into words only makes things worse. They can also be uncomfortable with physical affection (Rudd, 1984; McGoldrick, 1982; Barrabe & von Mering, 1953) and tend to relate to their children through fixed labels: "Bold Kathleen," "Poor Paddy," and "That Joey." Children are loved, but not intimately known (Rudd, 1984).

As a result of her need for ambiguous communication and ambivalence with regard to self-assertion, a mother may indirectly belittle her child for "putting himself ahead" while in the same breath chide him for not being more aggressive and achievement oriented. Irish mothers tend to dote on their sons, overprotecting them and drawing them into powerful bonds more intense than their marital tie. Conversely, Irish parents tend to underprotect their daughters, treating them like sisters and often not allowing them much of a childhood by raising them to be overresponsible and self-sufficient, just like the mothers (Byrne & McCarthy, 1986). This failure to protect daughters teaches them to repress personal needs and contributes to an ongoing fatalism, emotional repression, and stoicism in the next generation of women.

Irish women have little expectation of or interest in being taken care of by a man. Their hopes are articulated less often in romamtic terms than in aspirations for self-sufficiency. They are often reluctant to give up their freedom and economic independence for marriage and family responsibilities.

What about Irish fathers and daughters? One pattern involves the "dutiful daughter," especially if the mother is absent, who becomes the caretaker for her father without much real intimacy in the relationship. In other families, the daughter may become "Daddy's girl," even his companion, who is sent to bring him home from the bar or chosen to work with him, especially if there is no son in the family. Generally, however, father-daughter relationships are distant, possibly because the father fears that closeness will be confused with trespass of sexual boundaries. Moreover, Irish families are not very good at differentiating among anger, sexuality, and intimacy. A father may maintain distance from his daughter, or perhaps be sarcastic and teasing, not because such behavior reflects his true feelings but because he is unsure how to approach her.

With sons a father may share sports, work, and jokes, although the teasing and ridicule that are so common in Irish parent-child relationships may be very painful to a son. Some Irish fathers remain silent, almost invisible, in the family. Another common pattern is the father who is jovial or silent, except when drinking, at which time he becomes a fearsome, intimidating, larger-than-life antagonist, who returns to his gentler self when sober with no acknowledgment of this transformation. Children are kept off guard in such relationships. They may be drawn to the humor and fun, yet terrified of the unpredictable and violent moods. In cultures with less dissociation of self from negative behaviors (such as among Italians or Puerto Ricans), children may fear a parent who drinks, but they will not be as mystified by parents' denial of an out-of-control situation.

Resentment over class differences may surface when Irish children marry. The Irish tend to measure others hierarchically as being "better than" or "inferior to" themselves. Thus, parents may criticize children for "marrying up" and putting on airs (which usually means marrying a WASP) or may criticize them for "marrying down." Both of these parental reactions are deeply rooted in tensions stemming from the Irish history of oppression by the British, which left the Irish with a deep sense of inferiority.

When Irish children reach their mid-20s or more, they may begin to resent the denial and emotional suppression of their childhood. Such resentments may be evident in their young-adult relationships with others. Irish communication patterns are generally characterized by a high degree of ambiguity and confusion. Because Irish parents often control their children via indirect communication, such as humor, teasing, sarcasm, and ridicule, outsiders may not understand why children become so frustrated dealing with their parents and feel a need to distance themselves from the family in order to feel "sane." The resentments that Irish children have buried since childhood often continue into adulthood without realization that resolution is possible.

Resentments and distancing may become more intense throughout the adults' life, especially if parents' subtle disapproval continues or if adult children assume caretaking responsibilities for their parents. Unlike other children—such as African American, Greek, Italian, or Jewish—who are freer to express their resentments, Irish children may be extremely sensitive to perceived slights, such as favors shown to siblings, or other imagined wrongs. They may never confront the parent or the sibling with their feelings, dutifully continuing their caretaking responsibilities while maintaining tense silence with regard to their emotional wounds.

As parents age, intimacy typically does not increase. The mother may maintain her matriarchal role within the family. She may be seen as intimidating and indomitable. She may be unaware of the hold she has on her family because inwardly she feels that hold slipping.

Although unmarried children may continue to be emotionally dependent on their parents (and outwardly deny this dependence), they have no strong sense of filial responsibility. For example, placing a parent in a nursing home when the time comes may be acceptable to both children and parents, who prefer to "suffer alone" and never become a burden to their children. . . .

ASIAN INDIAN FAMILIES

In the past 10 years, Asian Indian immigration to the United States has been opened to nonprofessional classes. Twenty years ago, families immigrating here were primarily of the professional class. Today, however, the influx of uneducated families settling into menial jobs has created many problems similar to those experienced by earlier groups of immigrants from other countries.

Despite the intersecting influences of caste, region, and religion, predictable intergenerational conflicts emerge among family members. Relationships within and across generations are influenced by beliefs in caste and karma. These beliefs are pervasive despite the diversity among Asian Indians in the "old country" and in the United States (Malyala, Kamaraju, & Ramana, 1984). However, the degree to which these beliefs affect adaptation to life in Western society is influenced by level of education and acculturation (Segal, 1991; Matsuoka, 1990). For example, an educated family living in this country for 10 to 20 years will adapt to Western values around education and socialization for their children. However, they frequently revert back to Indian values as the marriage of a child approaches.

The caste system is a stratified social system into which one is born as a result of one's fate or karma. Karma can be changed only through death and subsequent rebirth. It is believed that with each rebirth a person moves from a lower caste (pollution) to a higher caste (purity) until "nirvana" (eternal afterlife) is achieved. These beliefs perpetuate values of passivity and tolerance, suffering and sacrifice. The more accepting one is of one's karma (passivity), the greater assurance one has of achieving spirtual afterlife (tolerance).

Hindu culture portrays women in paradoxical positions. Women are sacred (pure) in the afterlife yet they are devalued (polluted) in present life (Bumiller, 1990; Almeida, 1990; Wadley, 1977). Although men share power with women in the scriptures, in present life the male-centered family system exerts enormous social and economic power over women and children. With its concepts of "purity" and "pollution," the caste system shapes both intragenerational and intergenerational relationships. Prejudices related to lighter vs. darker shades of skin color are deeply embedded within the culture, with light skin symbolizing "purity" and dark skin symbolizing "pollution." These "ideals" are carried into the acculturation process in that Asian Indian immigrants find it easier to connect with white Americans than with non-whites, including other Asians. Asian Indian experiences of racism are generally not talked about, as though acknowledgment of racism might connect them with others who are similarly discriminated against. Although work and educational opportunities are available to all, women and lower-caste men have fewer choices regarding marriage partners. Such contradictions are pervasive and are explained in terms of karma.

Karma focuses on past and future life space. Current life dilemmas are explained in terms of karma. For example, a wife who is mistreated by her in-laws might say, "I must deserve this for something bad I did in a past life. If I endure my current life, I know I will be taken care of by God in a future life." Making choices to alter current life struggles is possible within this belief system. Sacrificial actions may alter one's current life and thus are meaningful. Fasting, praying, somatic complaints, head shaving, and suicide alter "karma" and move one toward a better life. In working with Asian Indian clients, therapists might suggest culturally appropriate constructions of less destructive "solutions" such as limited fasting, praying, mediatating, or even haircutting.

Intergenerational patterns are embedded and negotiated within a collective consciousness. Relationships are other-directed rather than self-centered. Spirituality and simplicity are applauded, and family-centered decisions take priority over individual preferences. Within the family of origin, older men assume decision-making authority over all members of the family. Fathers are responsible for the education of their male children and for the care of their elderly parents. Emotional connectedness between sons and fathers, as well as among other extended family members, is not expected. However, intimacy between the son and mother is emphasized. Fathers are responsible for the dowry and marriage of their daughters; uncles or older male siblings take on this responsibility in the event of a father's death. Mothers expect their sons to control their wives with regard to money, work, and social activities. Older women gain status and power through the mother-in-law role. Younger women are socialized by their mothers and sisters to idealize the role of "mother-in-law." The cultural system (i.e., caste and karma with their values of tolerance and passivity) supported by the male-family lineage (endorsing tolerance and passivity) enables this process. In this system, women realize power by exerting control over women of lesser status. Caretaking of grandchildren and food preparation are used as "covert" means of gaining power in family relations. A mother-in-law, in charge of preparing food while the daughter-in-law works, might cook only according to her son's desires. Young children are generally overprotected by grandparents, while being taught to respect their elders. Children are taught to avoid direct eye contact with their elders and to avoid disagreeing with them. Older sisters-in-law assume a degree of power over younger women entering into the male-centered family system.

Education of male children is considered necessary for the economic needs of the entire family, whereas education for female children increases their marketability as brides. Aging parents are cared for within the family by adult married male children and, in rare instances, by female children who have families of their own.

Child rearing is a shared responsibility of the women in the male-extended-family system. These women can be aunts or friends of the family from India who visit for extended periods during the family's initial years of child rearing. When young mothers are forced to parent without this extended-kinship system, children are more at risk, because family conflicts tend to be expressed in the mother-child dyad rather than in the marital dyad.

Power in Western marriages is directly connected to the economic resources of each partner. This notion of power and relationships is less applicable to Asian Indian families, because a couple's economic resources are distributed across the extended male-oriented family system (Conklin, 1988). Unlike the white, American, middle-class nuclear family, in which marriage stands at the center of the family system, men and their mothers are at the center of the Asian Indian family system. The mother-son tie is prominent in both Hindu and Christian Asian Indian families (Almeida, 1990; de Souza, 1975). Sons provide their mothers and grandmothers with the ultimate pride and status afforded women in "this" life (Issmer, 1989). Young wives do not participate in this system of power, even when they contribute economically to the family unit (Chakrabortty, 1978). Marriage is complicated by overarching problems of caste, dowry, and expensive weddings.

Arranged marriages are the norm in the adopted country as well as in India. When the family chooses to emphasize college education over marriage, or if the child asserts his or her personal rights over the parents' choice of mates or chooses career and money over marriage, major conflicts within the family system arise. Parents expect daughters to be married between 18 and 22 years of age and sons between the ages of 22 and 26. When this does not occur, parents lack a clear role in their adult child's life. The process of differentiation of self from family, which has various implications for Asian Indians as a result of their cultural norms, is particularly problematic at this stage. Despite their efforts to create choices for their sons and daughters, cultural expectations for "arranged" marriages take precedence.

> An Asian Indian family entered therapy because of their 21-year-old daughter's difficulty completing her last semester of college. They expressed their helplessness in dealing with her launching. The mother said, "Shiva is very immature and irresponsible; it worries me that she does not know the meaning of money or getting a job, and yet she is about to graduate. I think of her as a selfish brat sometimes. She says she is not ready to think about marriage, and I believe it sometimes, but all of our friends and relatives think I am being neglectful in my responsibility to find her a nice man. If she waits until she is 30, then by the time she is 40, when she should be taking care of us, she and her husband will still have the responsibility of young children. I might be too old to be the kind of grandparent I have to be. Of course, I know that if Shiva gets married, then I will be pushing her to give me grandchildren, so I suppose I have to trust that my husband's and my choice to allow her to be independent will turn out OK.

An Asian Indian woman's status within the family is determined by the gender order of her children. First-born males are preferred. First-born females are vulnerable to conflict between the mother and her in-laws and are perceived as diminishing the father's status with the deities. However, a second-born male child helps normalize the situation. A second-born female child following a first-born female child is at risk for premature death through malnutrition and abuse, even in the United States, if the family does not have sufficient social and economic support. Male children offer the family greater economic support and thereby afford better marital opportunities for the female children in the family. A woman's relationship with her mother-in-law may become strained and the marriage may suffer if she is infertile and thus does not meet the family's role expectations. Sons who are unable to support the elderly family members, widowed mothers, or unmarried sisters extort large dowries from their brides as solutions to this intergenerational legacy (Ramy, 1987).

These intergenerational patterns often conflict with Asian Indian acculturation (Sluzki, 1979). Although most Asian Indians accommodate to the work ethic and value of education, they maintain strong cultural ties to Asian Indian concepts of marriage, child rearing, parenting, and the sharing and allocation of economic resources.

Western values of privacy and individualism conflict with Indian values of collectivity and family-centeredness. In the context of separation, less acculturated families view adolescents' and young adults' struggles with independence as disrespect. When Asian Indians speak of *respect,* they mean *obedience* to the family and culture. Similarly, it is difficult for these family members to understand that the

Western ideal of love includes separation and independence from the family of origin. Consequently, the Asian Indian concept of love includes control (Mukherjee, 1991). . . .

JEWISH FAMILIES

Judaism has the unusual distinction of being both a religion and an ethnic identity (Farbet, Mindel, & Lazerwitz, 1988). Jews, who have a long tradition of intellectual debate and dialogue, carry on a never-ending discussion about who is a Jew and what it means to be a Jew. This debate has been engendered in part by the Jewish history of exclusion, discrimination, and wandering, culminating in the Holocaust and the founding of Israel. As waves of Jewish immigrants entered the United States, including early settlers from Germany who were relatively wealthy, the poor and less assimilated Eastern Europeans before and after World War I, Holocaust survivors, and, most recently, Russian and Israeli Jews, the question of essential Jewishness has continued to be debated—a legacy that has led to sensitivity over issues of discrimination and a sense of being "other." Although "Jewishness" may not be apparent to the outsider, most Jews are sensitive to interactions that might be perceived as anti-Semitic and thus may adopt a defensive posture that seems inexplicable to non-Jews.

Jews in the United States have been both fearful of and fascinated by assimilation into the mainstream culture (Herz & Rosen, 1982). Many families are overwhelmingly concerned that family members marry within the faith, or, if members marry outside the faith, that they maintain their Jewish traditions. A primary concern for many parents who move to a new community is whether their children will have other Jewish children with whom to play and date. The issue is further complicated by the diversity of Jewish religious practice; acceptable "Jewishness" in one family may be considered "too assimilated" in another.

Families often enter treatment to deal with conflicting feelings with regard to intermarriage, which may be perceived as destroying the integrity of the family and the faith. Generally, the families' most immediate concerns revolve around who, if anyone, will be expected to convert, who will perform the wedding, and how the grandchildren will be raised. Intermarriage is often felt to be a failure on the part of the parents, who, somehow, should have prevented this from happening. Such feelings exist even in families that are "culturally" rather than religiously observant Jews and are not affiliated with a synagogue.

When intermarriage is an issue, it is important that therapists attempt to gather concerned family members together. The parent or grandparent who is most upset may be difficult to engage. Because Jews traditionally have had a high regard for discourse and the transmission of cultural tradition and history, it can be helpful to review family history and to engage the family in searching for other families for whom intermarriage did not result in leaving the faith. Jewish families respond well to information and the sharing of stories; thus, referrals to a support group and/or interfaith classes run by Reform synagogues can be effective.

Regardless of geographic distance among family members, maintaining close family ties is important to Jewish families. It is important that the therapist identify family members who are critical to the treatment process but who are not immediately available. Soliciting these persons' involvement as consultants (through inclusion in family sessions, a joint phone call, or a letter) can help promote change.

Jewish families' focus on children, particularly their education and nurturing, can be a mixed blessing. Children are expected to be a source of pride and pleasure for parents and grandparents. However, children may find it difficult to be the focus of so much attention, with so many people having an expressed point of view. Young people may find it difficult to operate independently in their own interests (Farber et al., 1988). Separation and individuation are difficult to achieve if the family has rigid definitions of acceptable and successful behaviors. Young Jewish men and women often enter treatment because they are having difficulty dealing with enmeshment issues. Parents may perceive themselves as being generous and supportive and feel hurt by their children's efforts to become more independent. Reframing and relabeling their adult children's need to separate as "successful" and productive behavior can be an effective treatment approach.

The changing mores of late 20th century American life have been stressful for Jewish families. Traditionally, Jewish women stayed home, complying with the dictum to "be fruitful and multiply." Jewish law has rigidly defined rules for men's and women's behavior, with women having a minor function in religious ritual. Such traditions are less rigidly observed in Reform and Conservative congregations, where women now can be ordained as rabbis and participate in religious ritual. Despite the fact that many Jewish laws concerning gender roles are neglected in all but Orthodox families, these laws still have a subtle influence on role definition and expectations.

In Jewish families, women have traditionally held power at home while the husband faced the work world. Jewish mothers have been responsible for maintaining traditions and culture. However, because many Jewish women were employed outside the home during the Great Depression in the 1930s, many families remember grandmothers or other female relatives who worked out of necessity. Their daughters were primarily homemakers, and their granddaughters now expect themselves to be "supermoms" (Hyman, 1991). The dilemma faced by all three generations has been how to reconcile social expectations with cultural expectations. Women who saw their mothers helping support the family during the Depression came to value their homemaker role. The granddaughters have aspired to raise their family while participating in the educational and professional world. Issues faced by American women in the 1980s and 1990s have been especially complicated for Jewish women due to the emphasis Jewish culture places on education, social consciousness, and tradition. In such situations, the grandmother may serve as a role model for both working and maintaining a family.

Significant shifts in the role of the Jewish husband/father have also occurred. Jewish men have experienced discrimination and violence in the community. Traditionally, their home has been the place where they achieve respect and authority. Because both spouses may work, the father may be called upon or may wish to be a more active parent. But when he does take an active role, he risks the scorn of his own parents, who see him in an unconventional role. The extended family may not be supportive of these changes.

Religion is another source of intergenerational conflict. The majority of Jews in the United States are affiliated with Reform congregations, which do not follow many of the commandments that Orthodox and Conservative Jews follow. Intergenerational conflict may arise over the perceived religious laxity or conservatism of family members. Parents may be disappointed if their child chooses not to be affiliated with a synagogue and not to have a bar mitzvah for their grandson or a bas mitzvah for their granddaughter.

Conversely, some young people have become more observant of the Jewish faith than their families, perhaps joining an Orthodox congregation and living a life-style that is foreign to their families (keeping a kosher home, not traveling on the Sabbath, not practicing birth control). Conflicts in some families may occur if younger family members emigrate to Israel, thus separating parents from their children and grandchildren. Families may enter treatment to deal with feelings of loss and may need help in understanding that their needs are acceptable even if they differ from those of their parents.

Jewish families tend to seek expert opinions and may ask a therapist many questions about professional degrees and competence. Although such inquiries may make practitioners feel uncomfortable and challenged, they may help clients feel more comfortable in therapy. Directing Jewish families to appropriate reading materials about their problems can be helpful, because many Jewish persons place value on being well-informed. Referrals to self-help groups can also be helpful.

Jews are avid consumers of psychotherapy, in part as a result of their comfort with discourse, their search for solutions, and expectation that family life should follow predefined rules (Herz & Rosen, 1982). However, extensive analysis does not always lead to resolution of problems. . . . Families may need to be reminded that the goal of therapy is not to tell a good story or to be "right" in the eyes of the therapist, but to resolve the conflict or assuage the pain that brought the family to therapy.

REFERENCES

Almeida, R. V. (1990). Asian Indian mothers. *Journal of Feminist Family Therapy*, 2(2), 33–39.

Barrabe, P., & von Mering, O. (1953). Ethnic variations in mental stress in families with psychotic children. *Social Problems*, 1, 48–53.

Boyd-Franklin, N. (1989). *Black families in therapy*. New York: Guilford.

Bumiller, E. (1990). *May you be the mother of a hundred sons: A journey among the women of India*. New York: Random House.

Byrne, N., & McCarthy, I. (1986, September 15). *Irish women*. Family Therapy Training Program Conference, Robert Wood Johnson Medical School, Piscataway, NJ.

Chakrabortty, K. (1978). *The conflicting worlds of working mothers*. Calcutta, India: Progressive Publishers.

Comas-Diaz, L. (1989). Culturally relevant issues for Hispanics. In V. R. Koslow & E. Salett (Eds.), *Crossing cultures in mental health.* Washington, DC: Society for International Education, Training and Research.

Conklin, G. H. (1988). The influence of economic development and patterns of conjugal power and extended family residence in India. *Journal of Comparative Family Studies, 19,* 187–205.

de Souza, A. (1975). *Women in contemporary India.* New Delhi, India: Manohar.

Diner, H. R. (1983). *Erin's daughters in America.* Baltimore, MD: Johns Hopkins University Press.

Farber, B., Mindel, C. H., & Lazerwitz, B. (1988). In C. H. Mindel & R. W. Habenstein (Eds.), *Ethnic families in America: Patterns and variations.* New York: Elsevier.

Garcia-Preto, N. (1982). Puerto Rican families. In M. McGoldrick, J. K. Pearce, & J. Giordano (Eds.), *Ethnicity and family therapy.* New York: Guilford.

Garcia-Preto, N. (1990). Hispanic mothers. *Journal of Feminist Family Therapy, 2*(2), 15–21.

Gomez, A. G. (1982). Puerto Rican Americans. In A. Gaw (Ed.), *Cross cultural psychiatry* (pp. 109–136). Boston: John Wright.

Habach, E. (1972). Ni machismo, ni hembriso. In *Coleccion: Protesta.* Caracas, Venezuela: Publicaciones EPLA.

Herz, F. M., & Rosen, E. J. (1982). Jewish families. In M. McGoldrick, J. K. Pearce, & J. Giordano (Eds.), *Ethnicity and family therapy.* New York: Guilford.

Hines, P. (1989). The family life cycle of poor black families. In B. Carter & M. McGoldrick (Eds.), *The changing family life cycle: A framework for family therapy* (2nd ed.). New York: Gardner Press.

Hines, P. (1990). African American mothers. *Journal of Feminist Family Therapy, 2*(2), 23–32.

Hines, P., & Boyd-Franklin, N. (1982). Black families. In M. McGoldrick, J. K. Pearce, & J. Giordano (Eds.), *Ethnicity and family therapy.* New York: Guilford.

Hyman, P. (1991). Gender and the immigrant Jewish experience. J. R. Baskin (Ed.), *Jewish women in historical perspective.* Detroit, MI: Wayne State University Press.

Issmer, S. D. (1989). The special function of out-of-home care in India. *Child Welfare, 68,* 228–232.

Malyala, S., Kamaraju, S., & Ramana, K. V. (1984). Untouchability—need for a new approach. *Indian Journal of Social Work, 45,* 361–369.

Matsuoka, J. K. (1990). Differential acculturation among Vietnamese refugees. *Social Work, 35,* 341–345.

McGoldrick, M. (1982). Irish Americans. In M. McGoldrick, J. K. Pearce, & J. Giordano (Eds.), *Ethnicity and family therapy.* New York: Guilford.

McGoldrick, M. (1991). Irish mothers. *Journal of Feminist Family Therapy, 2*(2), 3–8.

McGoldrick, M., Garcia-Preto, N., Hines, P., & Lee, E. (1989). Ethnicity and women. In M. McGoldrick, C. Anderson, & F. Walsh (Eds.), *Women in families.* New York: W. W. Norton.

McGoldrick, M., Garcia-Preto, N., Hines, P., & Lee, E. (1991). Ethnicity and family therapy. In A. Gurman & D. Kniskern (Eds.), *The handbook of family therapy* (2nd ed.) (pp. 546–582). New York: Guilford.

McKenna, A. (1979). Attitudes of Irish mothers to child rearing. *Journal of Comparative Family Studies, 10*, 227–251.

Mukherjee, B. (1991). *Jasmine.* New York: Fawcett Crest.

Ramu, G. N. (1987). Indian husbands: Their role perceptions and performance in single- and dual-earner families. *Journal of Marriage and the Family, 49*, 903–915.

Rudd, J. M. (1984). *Irish American families: The mother-child dyad.* Thesis, Smith College School of Social Work.

Scheper-Hughs, N. (1979). *Saints, scholars, and schizophrenics.* Berkeley, CA: University of California Press.

Segal, U. A. (1991). Cultural variables in Asian Indian families. *Families in Society, 72*, 233–241.

Sluzki, C. (1979). Migration and family conflict. *Family Process, 18*, 379–390.

Stevens, E. (1973). Machismo and marianismo. *Transaction Society, 10*(6), 57–63.

Wadley, S. (1977). Women and the Hindu tradition. *Journal of Women in Culture and Society, 3*(1), 113–128.

Reading 33

9/15/94

Developments in Research on Black Families: A Decade Review

Robert Joseph Taylor,
Linda M. Chatters,
M. Belinda Tucker,
and Edith Lewis

The literature on black families from the past decade is reviewed. An overview of topics and issues of importance to black families considers *(a)* black families in relation to their age, gender, and family roles, *(b)* substantive issues of relevance to black American families, including social support and psychological well-being, and *(c)* an examination of recent demographic trends in black family structure. The conclusion provides comments on research on black families and recommendations for future efforts.

The past ten years have witnessed a tremendous increase in the diversity and breadth of research on the family lives of black Americans. Despite this impressive growth, significant limitations persist in the dissemination of these efforts and their integration into the corpus of family life literature. It is frequently the case that books investigating black family issues are not well publicized and, as a consequence, remain relatively obscure. Other works that employ predominantly black samples fail to use the term *black* (or other racial designations) in their title (e.g., Furstenberg, Brooks-Gunn, and Morgan, 1987; Thompson and Ensminger, 1989), thus making it difficult to locate these materials. Similarly, it is not uncommon that research on black families is overlooked in major reviews of family life research.

Robert Joseph Taylor, Linda M. Chatters, M. Belinda Tucker, Edith Lewis from *The Journal of Marriage and the Family*, 52 (November, 1990), pp. 993–1014. Copyrighted 1990 by the National Council on Family Relations, 3989 Central Ave. N.E., Suite #550, Minneapolis, MN 55421. Reprinted by permission.

As with all social science, research and writing on black families transpires within a larger social and political context that influences the nature and direction of inquiry, as well as the interpretation and application of findings. The area of black family studies has been particularly sensitive to the impact of various competing paradigms or orientations that have served both to identify significant areas of inquiry and to frame the nature and scope of debate on issues of black family life (Allen, 1981; Farley and Allen, 1987). Although extant models of black family life emphasize their resilient-adaptive features (Farley and Allen, 1987), remnants of the pathological-disorganization or cultural deviant perspective on black families are evident in several current writings (e.g., Anderson, 1989; Schoen and Kluegel, 1988), as are frameworks that place inordinate emphasis on the social problems facing black Americans (e.g., Jaynes and Williams, 1989, chap. 10). These works stand in contrast to emerging research that (a) employs resilient-adaptive perspectives on black families, (b) examines a broad range of topics and their interrelationships, and (c) illuminates the diversity of family life among black Americans (Hill et al., 1990).

The scope of research and writing dictates a selective approach to reviewing literature on black families. In an attempt to address the breadth of concerns in a fairly comprehensive manner, several priorities have been adopted in providing an overview of topics and issues of importance to black families. First, this article almost exclusively relies on material that has been published since the last decade review (Staples and Mirande, 1980), and priority is given to more recent research. Second, topics such as family violence and family policy are not discussed here. The organizational structure of the review is as follows: the first section considers black families in relation to their age, gender, and family roles; the second focuses on substantive issues of relevance to black American families, including social support and psychological well-being; and the third section examines recent demographic trends in black family structure. The conclusion provides final comments on research on black families and recommendations for future efforts.

LIFE COURSE ISSUES

This section of the literature review addresses distinct family issues related to life course position. Research reviewed in this section examines black children and racial socialization, the period of adolescence, gender and role behavior among black couples, role strain among black women, the salience of the provider role among black men, and informal support networks of elderly black adults.

Black Children

One of the most researched areas addressing children in black families is that of racial socialization (Spencer, Brookins, and Allen, 1985). Black parents, like all parents, play a pivotal and crucial role in instructing their children on how to participate successfully as citizens in the wider society. The general goals of the socialization process are to provide children with an understanding of roles, statuses, and prescribed behaviors within society and an appreciation of their position within the social structure (Thornton, Chatters, Taylor, and Allen, 1990). For the most part, parental socialization values mirror those of the wider community and society, and in turn, societal agents (e.g., schools, religious institutions) reinforce the socialization themes that are expressed in the family context. However, for black parents, racial prejudice and discrimination are important intervening factors in this process. For black Americans, socialization occurs within a broader social environment that is frequently incompatible with realizing a positive self and group identity.

In the 1980s, there was much speculation about the manner in which parents and the family environment functioned as a buffer between the child and this hostile social climate (Jackson, McCullough, and Gurin, 1988; Peters and Massey, 1983). During this period, several studies examined family socialization techniques (Bowman and Howard, 1985; Peters, 1985; Spencer, 1983) as intermediaries between the child and the immediate context. The process of explicit racial socialization is clearly a distinctive childrearing activity that black parents engage in as an attempt to prepare their children for the realities of being black in America. However, recent studies suggest that close to a third of black parents do not report conveying racial socialization messages to their children (Bowman and Howard, 1985; Thornton et al., 1990). Among those who do, the family sometimes provides specific socialization messages stressing a proactive orientation toward existing social inequalities (Bowman and Howard, 1985; Peters, 1985). For some black parents, issues of race are a central concern in raising their children. Their efforts involve explicit preparation for their unique situation and experiences as black Americans (Peters, 1985) or an attempt to forewarn their children concerning the nature of the broader social environment (Harrison, 1985).

Bowman and Howard (1985) and Thornton et al. (1990) identified various structural factors that were significantly correlated with whether or not parents imparted racial socialization messages to their children. Differential patterns of socialization emerged, particularly with regard to sex of the child and of the parent. Black male adolescents were more likely to be cautioned about racial barriers, whereas young women were more likely to be socialized with reference to issues of racial pride (Bowman and Howard, 1985). Reflecting differences for men and women (Thornton et al., 1990), fathers who were older and who lived in the Northeast (versus the South) were more likely to impart race-related socialization strategies to their children, while being widowed or never married decreased the probability of this practice. Mothers who resided in neighborhoods in which the racial composition reflected roughly equal numbers of blacks and whites were more likely to socialize their children racially than were mothers who lived in all-black areas. Mothers who had never been married were less likely, while highly educated, older women were more likely to familiarize their children with racial realities. Among the many unexplored topics in the area of racial socialization, there remains scant information concerning the conflict between the socialization messages of the family and society and the manner in which these differences are resolved.

Adolescence

Historically, literature on the nature of adolescence has had as its primary focus the variety of challenges and problems that face this group, and the general depiction of adolescence is that it is a developmental period characterized by conflict and transition. What is unique to the study of black adolescents is the extent to which being black and adolescent has come to be viewed as synonymous with a variety of social problems. Even a cursory examination of the statistics on physical and mental health, educational attainment, teenage pregnancy and parenting, crime (as perpetrator and victim), substance abuse, and job and employment patterns attests to the fact that these problems are both numerous and significant.

What is not evident in the literature on this group is an appreciation for the diversity of black youth as individuals who come from different family, neighborhood, and community settings and socioeconomic backgrounds (Jones, 1989). Black youth are monolithically portrayed as urban, low-income, plagued by a multitude of problems, and lacking in the resources and/or motivation to effect change in their lives. Further, by restricting the scope of research on black adolescents to social problems and/or "problem youth," we have learned relatively little about issues of motivation, personality and psychological development, cognitive and moral development, identity and self-esteem, attitude formation, family relationships with parents and siblings, family socialization issues—in short, issues for which there exists an established and burgeoning literature regarding white youth.

Married Couples

A collection of research findings suggests that gender distinctions in the provider and homemaker roles are not as rigid in black families as they are in white families (Beckett and Smith, 1981; Ericksen, Yancey, and Ericksen, 1979). Black women have historically had higher levels of participation in the paid labor force than white women, and black men are more likely than white men to endorse the view that women should be employed (Huber and Spitze, 1981). The involvement of black women in the provider role may reflect a wider acceptance of women's labor force participation among blacks generally and/or reflect an economic necessity in relation to the precarious and uncertain conditions that characterize the employment and earning patterns of black men within particular segments of the labor market. With regard to the homemaker role, black husbands are more likely than their white counterparts to share housework and child care (Ericksen et al., 1979). Greater levels of egalitarianism in the division of household labor among black couples is maintained when the analysis controls for wife's employment status, relative earning power, and sex-role attitudes (Ross, 1987). Despite the fact that black households are more egalitarian, gender differences in contributions to household work indicate that black women still perform the majority of the traditional chores of cooking, cleaning, and laundry, and are more likely than black men to feel overworked (Broman, 1988a).

Black Women

As noted in other sections of this review, the status and position of black women in relation to general issues such as psychological well-being (Brown and Gary, 1985, 1987), informal support networks (H. McAdoo, 1980) and extended-family households (Beck and Beck, 1989) is well represented in the literature. One of the more interesting areas of research among this group addresses the correlates and consequences of role strain. Thompson and Ensminger (1989) argue that among poor, black women, long-term single parenting represents a chronic stressor. Two studies examined the correlates of role strain within the areas of parenting, economic concerns, and household maintenance among black mothers (Lewis, 1988, 1989). With regard to the parental role, black mothers who had a current partner, fewer children in the household, and extended kin who lived some distance away but not out of state were less likely to report strain in this area. Black mothers who indicated that they had someone to help with child care were less likely to report role strain in the area of household maintenance. Women who had a current partner, earned higher incomes, and were older were less likely to report experiencing economic role strain. An examination of the multiple roles of middle-aged and elderly black women found that traditional social roles of parent and spouse did not significantly affect their psychological and physical health (Coleman, Antonucci, Adelmann, and Crohan, 1987).

Black Men

In contrast to the volume of work focused on the position of black women, the role of black men in families is one of the most conspicuously neglected areas of family research. The absence of a reliable knowledge base on the role of black men in families has resulted in a portrayal of black men as peripheral to family and as performing poorly in the family roles of spouse and father (Allen, 1981; J. McAdoo, 1981). A few studies have investigated the saliency of the provider role and perceptions of role performance among black men. Cazenave found that the role of economic provider was a frequently cited familial role among both middle-income black fathers (1979) and blue-collar black men (1984). Among middle-income black fathers, the goal of exceeding the socioeconomic status of their own fathers (who had low incomes and irregular employment) was central to their self-perceptions of being better providers for their families (Cazenave, 1979). Other research (Taylor, Leashore, and Toliver, 1988) found that personal income and age were positively associated with the likelihood that black men perceived themselves as being good providers for their families. Provider role strain, however, was found to affect life happiness adversely among a sample of married black fathers (Bowman, 1985). The centrality and significance of the provider role for this group is supported by the findings that having a higher personal income is associated with the probability of being married among black men (Tucker and Taylor, 1989) and satisfaction with family life among black husbands (Ball and Robbins, 1986a).

Research efforts examining the affective roles and functions of men in black families are exceedingly rare. Limited work among lower-middle to middle-class families suggests that black men are highly involved in the parental and childrearing role (J. McAdoo, 1981) and are successful in that capacity, as evidenced by their producing children who are well adjusted and positively motivated on several indicators (Allen, 1981). In addition, research indicates that both black fathers and mothers are involved in the racial socialization of children (Thornton et al., 1990).

Black Elderly

A vast majority of research on the family life of elderly blacks has addressed their informal social support networks. An analysis of the correlates of support from extended family (Taylor, 1985) found that for those elderly persons with children, gender, income, education, region, and familial interaction were all significant predictors of the frequency of support. Among the childless elderly, however, having an available pool of relatives was of singular importance. Gibson and Jackson (1987) found that the support resources of older black adults were tailored to their individual needs, specifically in relation to age and physical and functional health status. Family members figured prominently in the support networks of the elderly. Adverse changes in the economic viability of black families are viewed as potentially jeopardizing these support resources.

Two sets of analyses found that sociodemographic and family factors influenced the size and composition of informal helper networks of elderly blacks (Chatters, Taylor, and Jackson, 1985, 1986). Marital status was particularly important, with married older blacks having larger helper networks consisting of immediate family. Unmarried elderly persons had smaller networks that comprised a wide variety of individuals. The significance of region for the size and composition of the helper network was particularly intriguing and suggested that Southern residents had larger networks that were more likely to include a diverse group of helpers (see Taylor, 1988a, for a review of this literature).

SUBSTANTIVE ISSUES

This section of the literature review examines research and writings on extended-family household arrangements, intergenerational relations, informal social support networks, social support and psychological well-being, and family therapy.

Extended-Family Households

Existing research has consistently documented that blacks are more likely to reside in extended-family households than are whites (Angel and Tienda, 1982; Beck and Beck, 1989; Farley and Allen, 1987; Hofferth, 1984; Tienda and Angel, 1982). A longitudinal analysis of the incidence of extended-family households among middle-aged women (Beck and Beck, 1989) revealed that 6 out of 10 black women experienced some form of household extension during the period from 1969 to 1984. Racial comparisons revealed that the higher proportion of extended households among black women was primarily due to the presence of grandchildren residing within their households (Beck and Beck, 1989).

Racial differences in household composition are sustained even in the presence of controls for socioeconomic status. Farley and Allen (1987) found that, when they controlled for income, extended living arrangements were twice as common among black compared to white households. In contrast, marital status emerges as an important predictor of household extension. Research suggests that both blacks and whites who are not married have a higher probability of residing in an extended household (Beck and Beck, 1989; Farley and Allen, 1987).

Extended-family arrangements are recognized to have important economic benefits and are viewed as an effective mechanism for pooling limited economic resources. The practice of "doubling up" in extended households has an important bearing on the economic welfare of the family and, in comparison to direct cash transfers, is generally a less expensive method of providing for needy relatives. Angel and Tienda's (1982) research on sources of household income suggests that among blacks, the relative contributions of a wife, adult children, and non-nuclear relatives constitute a greater portion of the total household income than is the case among whites. Because of the generally lower earnings of black heads of households, supplemental income from family members was required to achieve a desired standard of living or, in many cases, simply to meet daily needs.

Other supportive benefits have been examined in relation to extended-family household arrangements, and in particular, the presence of non-nuclear adults within the household has been associated with the reallocation of employment and domestic responsibilities. Research suggests that another adult in the household (who assists with child care and other household duties) may help alleviate the burden associated with caring for an impaired family member or provide the opportunity for a single parent with a young child to pursue educational goals and obtain employment outside the home (Hogan, Hao, and Parish, 1990).

Intergenerational Relations

The majority of recent research on intergenerational relationships within the black population has been concerned with the exchange of assistance across generations. In particular, several studies have examined the role that adult children play in the support networks of elderly black adults and the assistance that black grandmothers provide to children and grandchildren. Elderly black adults who had children had a greater likelihood of receiving support from extended-family members (Taylor, 1985, 1986) and church members (Taylor and Chatters, 1986a). Similarly, elderly black adults who were parents had a larger helper network (Chatters et al., 1985) and utilized more informal helpers in response to a serious personal problem (Chatters, Taylor, and Neighbors, 1989). Adult children, daughters in particular, were selected most frequently by older black adults as the person who would help them if they were sick (Chatters et al., 1986). In contrast, childless elderly persons were more likely to rely upon brothers, sisters, and friends (Chatters et al., 1986). Despite these substitutions, childless elderly adults were still at a distinct disadvantage with regard to the size of their informal helper networks. An investigation of the use of informal helpers during an emergency demonstrated that the parent-child bond is important across the life course. Younger adults tended to rely heavily on their parents, older adults relied on their adult children, and middle-aged black adults tended to depend on both their parents and children (Taylor, Chatters, and Mays, 1988).

Racial comparisons of the grandparent role reveal that, in comparison to whites, black grandparents take a more active part in the parenting of grandchildren (Cherlin and Furstenberg, 1986). The greater involvement of black grandparents may be due to several circumstances. First, the greater probability of blacks residing with grandchildren and in three-generation households (Beck and Beck, 1989) provides increased opportunities for involvement in active grandparenting (Hogan et al., 1990). Second, a higher incidence of marital (i.e., separation, divorce), employment (i.e., layoffs, unemployment) and health (i.e., morbidity and mortality) events among blacks (Cherlin and Furstenberg, 1986) may have important consequences for both household arrangements and family child-care responsibilities. Finally, it may be the case that there are explicit cultural norms in support of extended-family relations in operation among black Americans (Sudarkasa, 1981).

Research indicates that mothers of black teenage parents play a prominent role in the lives of their children and grandchildren. The assistance that adolescent mothers receive from their extended family generally and their own mothers in particular has a positive impact on their educational and economic achievement and parenting skills and their children's development (Brooks-Gunn and Furstenberg, 1986; Stevens, 1984, 1988; M. Wilson, 1989).

Recent and accelerating changes in family structure (e.g., increase in nonmarital childbearing, shortened length of time in marriage) among blacks may have important consequences for intergenerational relationships (Burton and Dilworth-Anderson, in press). Burton and Bengtson (1985) investigated the role perceptions and concerns of women who experienced, in a normative sense, early (median age 32 years) vs. on-time (median age 46 years) entry into the grandmother role. The pattern of early grandmotherhood tended to result from two generations of teenage pregnancy: their own and their daughter's. "Early" grandmothers expressed significant discomfort in their role as a result of the inordinate caretaker burdens and childrearing responsibilities for both their adolescent child and grandchild and the role incongruency arising from being young and a grandmother.

Informal Social Support

Extended Family Networks   During the past decade, one of the most significant areas of research in the black family literature has concerned the role and functioning of the extended family in informal support networks. Indeed, much of the research focusing on intergenerational relationships and the family lives of elderly black adults has addressed questions that pertain, either directly or indirectly, to informal support networks. Several recent literature reviews that are concerned with extended-family networks in relation to childhood development (M. Wilson, 1986, 1989) and aging black adults (Taylor, 1988a) attest to the significance of this substantive area.

Taylor (1986) found that both family and demographic factors were important predictors of receiving support from extended-family members among black Americans. With regard to family variables, having an available pool of relatives, frequent interaction with family members, and close familial relationships were predictors for receiving support from extended family. A recent study examined the level of familial involvement among two groups of black adults who reported that they did not receive assistance from their extended families (Taylor, 1990). Multivariate analyses contrasting individuals who had never received assistance (support-deficients) with those who reported that they had never needed assistance (self-reliants) indicated that self-reliants reported significantly higher levels of familial involvement. Dressler, Hoeppner, and Pitts's (1985) examination of household structure in a black community found evidence of diverse household forms that varied on the basis of gender of household head and level of integration in extended networks, and that were related to one another through mutual interaction and support exchange. Collectively, these findings underscore the importance and pervasiveness of extended-family members in the support networks of black Americans.

Two studies investigated the use of informal helpers specifically in relation to a serious personal problem that the respondent had experienced (Chatters et al., 1989; Neighbors and Jackson, 1984). Neighbors and Jackson's (1984) investigation of informal and professional help utilization revealed that 8 out of 10 respondents enlisted informal help solely or in conjunction with professional assistance. Chatters et al. (1989) found that being female, having higher income, and maintaining greater levels of contact with family were all predictive of larger informal helper networks. Significant differences by problem type indicated that respondents with interpersonal, economic, and emotional problems utilized smaller networks than persons who indicated that they had a physical health problem.

Friendship and Church Support Networks   Emergent research has investigated the role of friends and church members in the informal support networks of black Americans. Several studies have indicated that friends, neighbors, coworkers, and in-laws are important sources of assistance for black Americans (Brown and Gary, 1987; Chatters et al., 1986, 1989; Dressler, 1985; Ellison, 1990; Jackson and Berg-Cross, 1988; H. McAdoo, 1980; Malson, 1983; Oliver, 1988; Taylor, Chatters, and Mays, 1988; Ulbrich and Warheit, 1989). However, it is generally agreed that kin are more prevalent in informal networks than non-kin (Chatters et al., 1986, 1989). An analysis of the use of kin and non-kin during an emergency revealed that older blacks were more likely than younger blacks to use non-kin (Taylor, Chatters, and Mays, 1988). Among elderly black adults, those who indicated that they were not affectively close to their families, and the childless elderly, had a higher probability of having helper networks comprised of friends (Chatters et al., 1986).

Marital status has shown a significant predictive relationship with the composition of support networks. Unmarried elderly black adults apparently compensated for the absence of a spouse by using other relatives and non-kin in their informal helper networks (Chatters et al., 1985, 1986). In comparison to married respondents, divorced elderly blacks were more likely to use friends and neighbors as helpers, widowed persons were more likely to utilize friends, and the never-married were more likely to select neighbors (Chatters et al., 1986).

The past few years have witnessed an emergence of interest in the area of religion and families, and specifically, the role and functions of religious institutions as a surrogate for the family. The majority of this research has addressed these issues among black Americans. This area of work is particularly relevant for this racial group because blacks consistently display higher levels of religiosity than whites (see Taylor, 1988b), and religious participation has been found to buffer psychological distress among blacks (Brown and Gary, 1987). Church members have been found to be a critical source of support among blacks. Dressler (1985) found that church members were important sources of assistance in coping with stress associated with racism, marital difficulties, and psychological problems. In an investigation of church support networks, church attendance, church membership, and subjective religiosity were positively related to the receipt of support from church members, whereas being Catholic (as opposed to Baptist), divorced (as opposed to married), older, and female were negatively associated (Taylor and Chatters, 1988). Similarly, research among elderly blacks notes the importance of church attendance as a predictor of both the frequency and the amount of support received from church members (Taylor and Chatters, 1986a). Taylor and Chatters (1986b) examined concomitant support to elderly blacks from family, friends, and church members. Observed patterns of support revealed that if elderly blacks received help from church members, it was likely that family and friends were also part of the network. An examination of the types of support provided indicated that church members provided advice and encouragement, help during sickness, and prayer (Taylor and Chatters, 1986b).

Psychological Well-being

A long tradition of work has explored the nature and correlates (i.e., family and marital life influences) of subjective well-being (SWB) among the general population. However, relatively few investigations have explored SWB and its correlates among black adults (Chatters, 1988). Marital status was not significantly associated with psychological distress (i.e., reports of significant personal problems) among a national sample of black Americans (Neighbors, 1986) or an urban sample of black women (Brown and Gary, 1985). Among black women with school-age children, however, those who lived with a spouse or another adult had lower levels of psychological distress than those who were the only adult in the household (Thompson and Ensminger, 1989).

With regard to the impact of marital status on reports of life satisfaction, happiness, and other indicators of psychological well-being, married blacks generally express higher levels of well-being than their unmarried counterparts (Broman, 1988b; Jackson, Chatters, and Neighbors, 1986; Zollar and Williams, 1987). Broman (1988b) found that separated and divorced statuses were both negatively associated with life satisfaction, and further, being divorced was negatively related to family life satisfaction. Among black adults who were 55 years and older, persons who were widowed and separated had lower levels of happiness as compared to married individuals (Chatters, 1988). Marital status, however, was not significantly related to self-esteem or perceived control among middle-aged and older black women (Coleman et al., 1987). Further, Ball and Robbins (1986b) found that while marital status was not related to reports of life satisfaction among women, for men being married was associated with generally lower levels of satisfaction (see Chatters and Jackson, 1989, for a comprehensive review of subjective well-being research among black adults).

Although the diverse effects of parental status on psychological well-being have been routinely investigated among whites, these issues remain a neglected research area among blacks. Preliminary evidence suggests that while being a parent is associated with lower levels of happiness and satisfaction and higher levels of anxiety among whites (McLanahan and Adams, 1987), it is unrelated to SWB among blacks. Parental status was unrelated to *(a)* both life satisfaction and family life satisfaction (Broman, 1988b) and *(b)* self-esteem and perceived control among middle-aged and older black women (Coleman et al., 1987). In addition, black parents with children residing in the home had lower levels of psychological distress than their childless counterparts (Reskin and Coverman, 1985).

Social Support and Psychological Well-being

A growing collection of research findings suggests a connection between involvement in extended-family support networks and mental health and psychological well-being. Black adults with supportive family and friendship relations were found to have heightened self-esteem and personal efficacy (Hughes and Demo, 1989). Similarly, reported satisfaction with social support from family and friends significantly reduced psychological distress among both employed and unemployed black women (Brown and Gary, 1988). Among blacks who were experiencing an economic crisis (Neighbors and LaVeist, 1989), those who received financial assistance reported lower levels of psychological distress; the primary sources of financial aid were family and friends. The literature is somewhat equivocal concerning the effects of gender on social support and the relationship between structural characteristics of support networks and well-being. With regard to gender differences, Brown and Gary (1987) found that perceived support from family buffered psychological distress, but only among women. In contrast, Dressler (1985) found that this relationship existed solely among men. In several studies, structural aspects of supportive networks, such as frequency of contact between network members (Thomas, Milburn, Brown, and Gary, 1988), number of extended kin (Dressler, 1985), and proximity of relatives (Warheit, Vega, Shimizu, and Meinhardt, 1982) failed to influence psychological distress. Brown and Gary (1987), however, found that the number of proximate relatives reduced distress among black women. Antonucci and Jackson's work (1989) on older black adults suggests that the potential for feelings of dependency and exploitation in support relationships are diminished when social exchange are governed by normative rules and expectations regarding reciprocity. The notion of reciprocity is a useful framework for examining supportive behaviors across the life course as well as how involvement in supportive behaviors may be related to positive individual outcomes (e.g., personal competency, perceptions of control, successful adaptation to aging).

Family Therapy

The decade of the 1980s has focused specific attention on the role of ethnicity and race in family intervention. The family therapy literature among black Americans reflects the renewed interest in the impact of race and culture. An edited volume addressing social work practice among black Americans families (Logan, Freeman, and McRoy, 1990) critiques past perspectives on and orientations toward the family (particularly with regard to issues of diversity in family forms). Further, this work attempts to develop a framework for practice that is grounded in current literature on the black family and addresses the culturally specific needs of black families. Robinson's recent work (1989) suggests that race has a definite and significant impact on the clinical treatment of black families. She presents a framework and a specific treatment strategy for working with black clients, incorporating issues of (a) the racial identity congruence of the client, (b) the implications of race in the presenting problem, and (c) the racial awareness of the clinician. Wilson (1986) suggests that intervention approaches within black extended families should recognize the validity of extended-family forms, clarify the role relationships among family members and generational patterns of influence, and assess members' resources in developing and realizing the goals of family therapy. Barbarin's (1983) work proposes a model of coping among black families and elaborates classes of variables specific to black Americans that may affect the process of adaptation (i.e., appraisal, behavioral strategies, and access to coping resources and support). These and other recent efforts reflect an attempt to (a) acknowledge the cultural distinctiveness of black families, (b) make explicit the broader social context and its impact on the presentation of problems and the therapeutic relationship, and (c) propose specific therapy and intervention approaches that are appropriate for black clients and families. Finally, Boyd-Franklin's (1989) critique of various models of family therapy underscores the importance of identifying the historical, social, and political variables that have an impact on family process and outcome.

DEMOGRAPHIC TRENDS IN FAMILY STRUCTURE

In the past three decades, American families have experienced a number of substantial demographic changes. These demographic trends include declining rates of marriage, later ages at first marriage, higher divorce rates, an increase in female-headed households, a higher proportion of births to unmarried mothers, larger percentages of children living in female-headed families, and a higher percentage of children living in poverty (Jaynes and Williams, 1989; W. Wilson, 1987). Although these changes have been experienced by both blacks and whites, black families have disproportionately suffered their impact. This section of the review examines these demographic trends in black family structure. In particular, this section presents research investigating fertility patterns, well-being of black children, teenage pregnancy, adolescent mothers and fathers, single-parent families, demographic constraints on marriage among blacks, interracial marriage, and the black underclass.

Fertility

One of the major trends in fertility over the past few decades among both blacks and whites is the increase in the percentage of unmarried women who give birth (Farley and Allen, 1987; Garfinkel and McLanahan, 1986; Jaynes and Williams, 1989). In 1960, the proportion of out-of-wedlock births among blacks was 22%. By 1984, almost 6 to 10 black babies were born to unmarried mothers, whereas among whites, 1 birth in 8 occurred to an unmarried woman (Farley and Allen, 1987; Jaynes and Williams, 1989). This increase in the percentage of out-of-wedlock births among blacks was due to two demographic changes (Farley and Allen, 1987; Jaynes and Williams, 1989). First, the age at which black women marry has risen and the overall length of time they are married has shortened. Consequently, among black women the length of time in which a nonmarital pregnancy can occur has increased, while the period of marital childbearing has shortened. Second, there has been a greater decline in the fertility rate of married black women than of unmarried black women. This difference in fertility rates results in an increase in the percentage of total births to unmarried black women. Therefore, it is erroneous to interpret the increase in the percentage of births to unmarried black women as a rise in their birth rate. In reality, the birth rates of unmarried black women actually declined during the seventies and early eighties (Farley and Allen, 1987, Table 4.1).

Children's Well-being

Three aspects of black children's well-being are addressed: living arrangements, foster care, and childhood poverty.

Living Arrangements of Children   The increasing number of female-headed families has important implications for the living arrangements of black children. In 1985, half (51%) of all black children (persons under age 18) lived with their mothers but not with their fathers (Jaynes and Williams, 1989). The incidence of single-father families among blacks is very low; only 2% of black children lived in these households in 1980 (Sweet and Bumpass, 1987). In addition, it has been projected (Bumpass, 1984) that 86% of all black children are likely to spend some time in single-parent households.

Foster Care   In addition to the high proportion of children residing in female-headed households, black children are more likely than whites or Hispanics to reside with neither biological parent. Although the practice of informal adoption among black extended families absorbs many children, a disproportionate number of black children live in institutions, in group homes, and with foster families. Research on foster care is limited by a lack of high-quality national data and the failure of many states and communities to keep relatively current and reliable information. Available research, however, has noted several consistent findings (Jenkins and Diamond, 1985; Morisey, 1990). First, black children have a higher likelihood of being placed in foster care because of neglect (e.g., leaving children without adequate supervision, inadequate housing, nutrition). Second, it has been estimated that black children are three times more likely to be in foster care than white children. Last, black children remain in foster care for longer periods of time and, consequently, are more likely to undergo multiple placements. Because of the developmental risks associated with long-term residence in the foster care system, this is a high-risk group that deserves serious attention from both researchers and policymakers (see NBCDI, 1989, for a more detailed examination of black children in foster care).

Childhood Poverty   In the last two decades, the rate of poverty among black children has increased dramatically, and in 1986, close to half of all black children lived in poverty (Zill and Rogers, 1988). The high incidence of poverty among black children is partially due to the lower earnings of black men relative to white men, higher rates of female-headed households among blacks, and a decline in the real value of government cash transfers directed at children. Within the larger group of individuals and families in poverty, there are those for whom poverty status may be of a temporary nature. Consequently, researchers delineate between those individuals who have temporary "spells" of poverty in contrast to persons and families who are persistently poor (Bane and Ellwood, 1986).

Research on the duration of poverty status suggests that while long-term poverty is a rare occurrence for whites, it is much more common among the black population (Ellwood, 1988). Duncan and Rodgers (1988) investigated the length of childhood poverty during a 15-year period, using data from the Panel Study of Income Dynamics. Fewer than one in seven black children lived comfortably above the poverty line during the entire 15-year period. Further, almost a quarter of black children were poor for 10 of those 15 years. Blacks accounted for almost 90% of the children who were poor during at least 10 out of 15 years. Length of poverty was longer for black children who lived in families in which the household head was disabled and for those who resided with a single parent. Living in poverty places a large proportion of black children in jeopardy for serious health problems, low educational achievement, and minimal labor market participation (Jaynes and Williams, 1989).

Zill and Rogers (1988) argue that two recent changes in black American families are beneficial for children's well-being: a reduction in the proportion of families that have large numbers of children and an increase in the educational level of parents. Although a black child is presently more likely to live in a single-parent family than a comparable child was in the '60s and '70s, the child's mother has a higher probability of having completed high school or attended college.

Teenage Pregnancy

Although adolescent pregnancy affects every racial and income group, it has a disproportionate impact on black teenagers. Estimates for 1984 indicate that 41% of black females and 19% of white females became pregnant by the age of 18 (Furstenberg, Brooks-Gunn, and Chase-Lansdale, 1989). Two demographic patterns in the last 25 years help explain the rate of pregnancy and nonmarital births among black teenagers: relatively high rates of sexual activity among teenagers and a decreasing incidence of marriage among blacks generally and among younger blacks in particular.

With regard to sexual activity, data from the National Longitudinal Study of Youth (NLSY) reveal that young unmarried black females (ages 15 to 19) were more likely to have engaged in sexual intercourse than their white counterparts. In 1982, 53% of black females in this age group had engaged in sexual activity, as compared to 40% of white females (Hayes, 1987). It is important to note that although a higher percentage of young black females engage in sex, they have intercourse less frequently than their white counterparts (Zelnik, 1983). NLSY data also reveal large gender differences in the age of initiation of sexual activity among blacks. Among black males, 42.4% of those who were 15 and 85.6% of those who were 18 years of age indicated that they were sexually active. The corresponding percentages among black females were 9.7% and 59.4%, respectively (Hayes, 1987).

Because of the inconsistent use of contraceptives, a substantial number of sexually active black and white teenagers eventually become pregnant (Hayes, 1987). Black teenagers are less likely to use a contraceptive method than are white teens (Hayes, 1987; Moore, Simms, and Betsey, 1986; Zelnik and Shah, 1983), but these differences are substantially reduced when age of sexual initiation is controlled (Zelnik, Kantner, and Ford, 1981). Among teenagers who use some form of contraception, however, black females are more likely to use oral contraceptives and white females are more likely to use withdrawal (Moore et al., 1986).

A nonmarital pregnancy can result in one of several outcomes, including abortion, adoption, and childbearing outside of marriage. Black teenagers are less likely to terminate a pregnancy by abortion than are white teenagers (Farley and Allen, 1987; Hayes, 1987). Since black teenagers had a higher incidence of unintended pregnancy, however, their abortion rate in 1981 was twice as high as the rate for white girls aged 15 to 19: 68.9 per 1,000 women compared with 35.8 per 1,000 (Hayes, 1987). With regard to adoption, available data indicate that despite the high levels of unintended pregnancy, 9 out of 10 black and white teenagers kept and raised their children (Bachrach, 1986; Hayes, 1987).

Black adolescents are more likely to give birth outside of marriage than white adolescents. In 1984, the rate of nonmarital childbearing among persons 15–19 years old was 87 per 1,000 unmarried black women compared to 19 per 1,000 white women. Between 1970 and 1984, however, the rate of nonmarital childbearing decreased by 10% among blacks, whereas among whites it increased by 74% (Farley and Allen, 1987; Hayes, 1987). Consistent with the fertility data presented earlier, the declining rates of marriage among blacks have contributed to the high rate of nonmarital childbearing among black adolescents. In 1960, almost a third of black women 18–19 years old were married, whereas in 1984 less than 3% were married. Consequently, by the mid-1980s, almost all children born to adolescent mothers were out of wedlock (Furstenberg et al., 1987). For a more thorough examination of adolescent pregnancy and sexual behavior, refer to the work of Furstenberg et al. (1987), Furstenberg et al. (1989), Hayes (1987), Hofferth and Hayes (1987), and Moore et al. (1986).

Adolescent Mothers

In the past decade researchers have investigated several consequences of adolescent pregnancy for the mother. In particular, research has examined issues such as family structure, family size, educational achievement, and labor force participation. Early marriage is strongly associated with early childbearing and there is a high incidence of divorce among persons who marry at young ages (Hayes, 1987; Sweet and Bumpass, 1987). Furstenberg and colleagues' (1987) 17-year follow-up of a sample of adolescent mothers (mostly black) found that among those who had married early, approximately two of three of their marriages had been dissolved. With regard to family size, the adolescent mothers in this study tended not to have a large number of children. About a fifth never had a second child (20.8%), two-fifths had one additional birth (41.3%), and one-fourth had two more children (26.0%).

The interruption of school with a birth generally decreases the educational attainment of young girls. This decrease in educational attainment, however, is smaller for black adolescents than for their white counterparts. Furstenberg et al. (1987) found that many of the adolescent mothers in their sample resumed their education after the birth of the first child. Most of the educational attainment following the birth of a child took place 6 or more years later. The educational attainment of this group, however, was still significantly lower than that of comparably aged black women who postponed childbearing.

Early childbearing has important implications for eventual labor force participation and economic attainment. In comparison to mothers who have children later in life, early childbearers have a lower likelihood of finding stable employment and a greater tendency to go on welfare (Furstenberg et al., 1989). These differences are more notable at younger ages, but many early childbearers recover from these interruptions later in life (Furstenberg et al., 1989). For instance, the rate of welfare use among the respondents in the Furstenberg et al. (1987) sample decreased substantially as the women reached middle age. Racial variations in the labor force participation of black and white early childbearers indicate that black mothers accumulate more work experience than their white counterparts, and the difference in work experience between early and late childbearers is smaller among blacks (Hayes, 1987; Hofferth and Hayes, 1987).

Adolescent Fathers

Research on adolescent pregnancy and parenting demonstrates the relative scarcity of work examining the role of adolescent fathers (Hendricks and Montgomery,

1983). This absence of information hampers a comprehensive understanding of teenage pregnancy and parenting (Lerman, 1986; Marsiglio, 1989; Parke and Neville, 1987). Methodological critiques of this literature (Parke and Neville, 1987: 146) include issues of sampling (e.g., determining appropriate age ranges, use of volunteer samples, samples from clinic or service agency-based populations), method (e.g., reliance on self-report and proxy questionnaires vs. other methods), and design (e.g., inclusion of appropriate comparison groups, use of longitudinal data). Reservations in the use of volunteer samples reflect the concern that such samples are biased toward adolescent males who are more accepting of parental responsibilities. This concern is particularly crucial if attitudes about early childbearing vary for distinct subgroups of the population (i.e., higher acceptance of early childbearing and out-of-wedlock births among black Americans) (e.g., Marsiglio, 1987).

The emergent literature on black adolescent fathers suggests a greater appreciation for the diversity of this population group in relation to the developmental aspects of adolescence (Parke and Neville, 1987) and their individual enactment of the fatherhood role. Black adolescent fathers have distinctly different patterns of fatherhood experiences (i.e., age at paternity, timing of fatherhood in relation to work and educational experiences, number of children, length of fatherhood experience, relationship with child's mother, marital experience). A study of attitudes among unwed black adolescent fathers (Hendricks and Montgomery, 1983) suggests that parenthood was desirable, and in retrospect, fathers indicated being prepared for that role. In an earlier investigation (Hendricks, Howard, and Caesar, 1981), black adolescent fathers were less sanguine and reported problems in interpersonal relationships and in social and economic areas (i.e., educational and occupational).

Marsiglio's (1987) examination of initial living arrangements, marital experiences, and educational outcomes for adolescent fathers found that young black men were more likely than Hispanics or whites to have had a nonmarital first birth and were least likely to live with that child. However, in comparison to other adolescent fathers, blacks were more likely to complete high school. Adolescent fathers have a higher probability of living apart from their partner and/or child than do nonadolescent fathers (Danziger and Nichols-Casebolt, 1988), and this is particularly the case among black adolescent fathers (Lerman, 1986; Marsiglio, 1987). However, a recent report among a sample of teenage-mother families (Danziger and Radin, 1990) suggests that father's absence from the home does not necessarily reflect noninvolvement in parenting; minority fathers were more likely to be involved than were white fathers. Separate analyses for minority teen-mother families (predominantly black) indicated that fathers were more likely to be involved if they were younger (roughly 6 out of 10 minority fathers were under 21 years of age), if they had been employed in the last year, and if their child was younger.

Female-Headed Households

As compared to whites, black families are considerably less likely to be headed by a married couple and more likely to be headed by single females. In 1980, one in four black households was headed by a single female (27.2%). In the past 20 years there has been a significant increase in the proportion of female-headed households among both blacks and whites. Among blacks the increase in female-headed households is due primarily to a decreasing propensity to marry among young black men and women. This declining likelihood of marriage is strongly linked to the high levels of unemployment and low earnings of young black men (Wilson and Neckerman, 1986).

Black female-headed families are one of the most impoverished groups in America. Among black Americans, 53% of female-headed families were in poverty, as compared to 15% of male-headed families (Farley and Allen, 1987). Similarly, in 1985, black female-headed families were twice as likely to have incomes at the poverty level than were white female-headed families (Jaynes and Williams, 1989). Jaynes and Williams (1989: 525) and McLanahan and Booth (1989) have identified several mechanisms that explain the disproportionate degree of poverty of black female-headed families. First, many black families rely on the income of two employed adults to remain out of poverty. Simply because of its reliance on a sole wage earner, a single-parent family has a higher likelihood of being poor. Second, because black women have lower incomes than black men (Farley and Allen, 1987), among single-parent families, those with a female head are more likely to be poor than those with male head. Third, young black women who form single-parent households generally come from poor households and often lack the skills to generate high earnings. Fourth, because of the scarcity of inexpensive child care and lack of health insurance associated with lower-status occupations, many black single mothers of young children cannot earn enough from employment to justify working outside the home. Fifth, Aid to Families with Dependent Children (AFDC, or welfare) and food stamps accounted for 28% of the income for black female-headed households (Garfinkle and McLanahan, 1986, Table 2); AFDC benefits are recognized to be woefully inadequate. Sixth, child support and alimony payments to single mothers are meager, accounting for only 3.5% of the income of black single mothers (McLanahan and Booth, 1989). Finally, the birth of a child may disrupt the educational or job experiences of the mother and reduce future earning potential.

Several studies have suggested that there are important intergenerational consequences with regard to the subsequent socioeconomic and marital status of children who live with mother-only families as compared with two-parent families. These studies indicate that among black children, those who live with their mothers only generally do less well on several social indicators than those who live with two parents. There is some evidence to suggest that black children who reside with one parent are less likely to be in school at the age of 17 and less likely to graduate from high school (McLanahan, 1985). Daughters of black single mothers were found to be at a higher risk of establishing a female-headed household at the age of 16 than were daughters of two-parent black households (McLanahan, 1988). This risk was increased if the marital disruption of the parents occurred when the child was older (15–16) as opposed to younger (12 or less). Controlling for income reduced but did not eliminate the risk of a daughter establishing a single-parent household (McLanahan, 1988). In another analysis (McLanahan and Bumpass,

1988), black daughters who spent part of their childhood in a single-parent family because of marital disruption (i.e., divorce, separation) or because the parent never married were 36% more likely to have a teenage birth, 52% more likely to have a premarital birth, and 32% more likely to have a marital disruption. The effects of residing in a single-parent family on these various outcomes were much more pronounced among whites than blacks. In addition, Hogan and Kitagawa (1985) found that black adolescent girls from single-parent families were more likely to be sexually active and to have premarital births than adolescents from two-parent households. It is important to note that this collection of findings is not definitive (Jaynes and Williams, 1989), and it remains to be seen whether some other variables are more important than family structure in determining the future socioeconomic and marital status of black children.

Garfinkle and McLanahan (1986) argue that the negative intergenerational consequences of residing in single-parent families may be attributed to economic deprivation, maternal employment, and the absence of a residential father. Since black female-headed families have such a high incidence of poverty, it is not surprising that their offspring fare worse in adulthood than children from two-parent families. It is also important to note that extended-family involvement may help mitigate some of the differences between being raised in single versus two-parent households.

Constraints on Marriage

Rapidly changing marriage patterns among African Americans has spawned a renewed focus on the determinants of marriage behavior. The long-established pre-1950 pattern of blacks marrying earlier than whites has been replaced by an increasingly divergent pattern of blacks marrying later than whites (Cherlin, 1981). Between 1975 and 1985, the proportion of black women who had ever married declined sharply from nearly 80% to 65% (compared to an 89% to 82% drop among whites) (Norton and Moorman, 1987). Also, the percentage of black women who were divorced increased from 22% to 31% (compared to 18% to 27% among whites) (Norton and Moorman, 1987).

The decline in expectation of marriage for black women has been particularly striking. When Rodgers and Thornton (1985) used annual synthetic cohorts to estimate proportions of groups expected to marry by age 44, they found that between 1970 and 1979, the proportions had declined to approximately 90% for white men and women, as well as black men. However, the proportion of black women expected to marry declined from the already low figure of 86% to 76%, meaning that by 1980, one-quarter of the existing population of black women were not expected to have married by their 44th birthday. Projecting proportions of later cohorts likely to ever marry (by projecting cumulative marriage probabilities), Rodgers and Thornton (1985) estimated that close to 90% of white males and females and 86% of black males born in 1954 will have married by their 45th birthday; but only 70% of black females born in 1954 are expected to marry. In contrast, 94% of black women born in the 1930s eventually married.

Among the consequences of these trends are an increase in the number of female-headed households, an increased burden of childrearing for women, and an increase in the percentage of women and children living in households with incomes below the poverty level. Concerns about the societal consequences of having large numbers of young males unattached to the traditional socializing structures have also been raised (Rossi, 1984).

Theories of Causation   Significant changes in the distribution between the sexes have been posited as a possible factor in these shifts in marital patterns in the general population. Known as "marriage squeeze" among demographers, it is hypothesized that a decrease in the availability of marriage partners for female members of the "baby boom" has led to delays in marriage and lower marriage rates, particularly for women (Glick, 1981; Rodgers and Thornton, 1985; Schoen, 1983). This shortage of partners is the result of the ever-increasing cohort sizes that characterized the post–World War II baby-boom years, coupled with the tendency of women to marry men who are two to three years older. Baby-boom women were therefore seeking husbands from older and numerically smaller cohorts. Although the marriage squeeze phenomenon affected blacks as well as whites, it also served to exacerbate the impact of the long-standing black male shortage that is due primarily to differential mortality rates. The black sex ratio has been steadily decreasing since the 1920s, and some have suggested that this prolonged shortage of men has led to a broadening of mate selection standards among black women. Spanier and Glick (1980) found that black women compared to white women were more likely to marry men who were previously married, less educated, and older.

Guttentag and Secord (1983) have argued that imbalanced sex ratios (i.e., the number of men per 100 women) have had major societal consequences. Male shortages, in particular, have been accompanied by higher rates of singlehood, divorce, out-of-wedlock births, adultery, and transient relationships; less commitment among men to relationships; lower societal value on marriage and the family; and a rise in feminism. Guttentag and Secord (1983) have asserted that the extended male shortage in the black American population is a major contributor to marital decline among blacks and an increasing out-of-wedlock birth rate. There is some empirical support for these theories. Tucker's (1987) analysis of sex ratios for five ethnic groups (including blacks) found fairly substantial associations between sex ratio and percentage divorced and separated, percentage of single women aged 25–34 (peak marriage ages), and percentage of households with female heads and no husbands. Using international data, South (1986) found female shortage to be associated with lower female marriage and fertility rates, higher age at marriage among women, and higher female literacy, divorce, and crime involvement (South and Messner, 1987). U.S. sex ratio studies have typically relied on census data, which are biased by an undercount of black men. Even when corrected for coverage errors, the black ratio remains about five points below that of whites, and therefore, in the view of Guttentag and Secord (1983), still likely to have significant effects on social structure. Yet, Tucker and Mitchell-Kernan (in press) argue that sex ratio is only one component of the constraints on mate availability that have resulted in declining marriage among blacks. That is, numerical availability is further qualified by an individual's *potential* for relationship formation, which is shaped by willingness or ability to enter into relationships with the opposite sex (e.g., heterosexual, noninstitutionalization), attractiveness (how one measures up on the basis of specific sociocultural preferences—e.g., economic status, physical features); and eligibility (whether one fits the socioculturally prescribed definitions of eligibility—e.g., same race). Although there is little research that explores how these three factors might differentially affect black marriage behavior, sociologists and economists have been particularly concerned about the relationship between the economic condition of black males and black family structure. William Wilson (Wilson, 1987; Wilson and Neckerman, 1986) and Darity and Myers (1986–87) have argued that the increasing economic marginality of black males makes them less attractive as potential husbands, since they are constrained in the ability to perform the provider role in marriage. Views of the economic incentive associated with marriage may undergo change when the societal inclination for women to marry men of higher (or at least equal) socioeconomic status is coupled with the substantial joblessness, underemployment, and decreasing educational attainment that are disproportionately characteristic of major segments of the black male population. These factors reduce the likelihood that marriage will occur, as well as undermine the stability of existing partnerships. There is some support for these economic arguments. Testa, Astone, Krogh, and Neckerman (1989) found that employed fathers in inner-city Chicago were twice as likely as nonemployed fathers to marry the mother of their first child. Also, Tucker and Taylor (1989) found that, among men, personal income was positively associated with the probability of marriage but unrelated to the probability of being involved in a nonmarital romantic relationship.

Interracial Marriage

Overall, interracial marriage involving black Americans remains relatively rare. In 1988, only 4.6% of black males' marriages and 2.1% of black females' marriages included partners of other races. Yet these figures can overshadow significant geographic differences in outmarriage behavior (Tucker and Mitchell-Kernan, 1990). According to the 1980 Census, intermarriage rates among blacks ranged from a low of .6% among black females in the South to 12.3% among black males in the West (U.S. Bureau of the Census, 1985). Furthermore, as Tucker and Mitchell-Kernan (1990) point out, there is evidence of a rather dramatic rise in outmarriage in Western states. One out of every six black men in the West who married for the first time between 1970 and 1980 (i.e., more recent marriages) married women of another race.

Overall, as well as by region, intermarriage for black females remains about one-quarter the male level. Lieberson and Waters (1988) used 1980 Census data to calculate odds ratios representing the tendency to marry in one's ethnic group versus marrying out of one's ethnic group (i.e., percentage in/percentage out) and have determined that black women have the highest overall odds of any ethnic group in the United States of marrying another black when they marry for the first time: 32,998 (as compared to 3,468 for Puerto Rican women; 743 for Mexican women; and 16 for American Indian women). However, the odds of black women under 25 years of age marrying a black man drops to 8,602 (in contrast to a ratio of

115,660 for black women aged 55 to 64 years). Therefore, although blacks still remain relatively unlikely to marry persons of other races, the likelihood of inter-racial marriage among younger blacks had increased substantially by 1980. Inter-censal estimates from the Current Population Surveys indicate that the level of interracial marriage among blacks increased 1.1 percentage points for males as well as females between 1981 and 1988. It seems likely that interracial marriage rates will continue to rise for black Americans.

Tucker and Mitchell-Kernan (1990) examined the structural factors that are associated with black interracial marriage, using 1980 census data for Los Angeles County (where black interracial marriage rates are relatively high). They found that the predictors of interracial marriage were virtually identical for black men and black women: interracially married blacks compared to those who married within the race tended to be younger, were more likely to have been married pre-viously, and had greater spousal age differences (both younger and older). Addi-tionally, interracial marriage seemed to be associated with living away from your place of birth, coupled with having been raised in a more racially tolerant region of the country. These findings suggested that social control (from the community of origin) still strongly supports black marriage within the race. Schoen and Wool-dredge (1989), examining marriage choices in North Carolina and Virginia, found a greater likelihood of intermarriage among more highly educated black men.

The rate of interracial marriage has implications for mate availability, particu-larly in the West, where outmarriage among black men is relatively high and quite different from the black female outmarriage rate. Moreover, marriage squeeze in the general population may account for an increased tendency for white women to consider black men as mates (Guttentag and Secord, 1983). Further declines in the marital expectations for black women will occur should black men define their pool of eligible mates as including nonblacks, while black women limit their mate choices to those of the same race.

Black Underclass

During the past decade, a significant body of research has addressed the develop-ment of a black underclass. Much of this work, as it relates to family issues, inves-tigates topics that have been previously discussed in this review (e.g., the increase in female-headed households, poverty and family structure). However, a remain-ing issue germane to our review of research on black families is the increasing economic marginality of black men. Recent research efforts have examined the growing economic marginality of black men in relation to the underclass. Black men have a higher likelihood than white males of being unemployed and working part-time (Farley and Allen, 1987; Jaynes and Williams, 1989). Black men are dis-proportionately employed in low-wage jobs, unprotected by seniority, and work in industries that are particularly sensitive to business downturns (Jaynes and Williams, 1989).

As noted previously in this review, the declining economic status of black men has important ramifications for family structure. The precarious economic situa-tion of black men is a major predictor of the decreasing rates of black marriage (W.

Wilson, 1987; Wilson and Neckerman, 1986). Additionally, the decreasing rate of marriage among blacks is an important contributing factor in the substantial increases in both nonmarital births and female-headed households (Farley and Allen, 1987). Collectively, these findings reinforce the argument that black family structure and the economic situations of black men and women are inextricably linked (see Danziger and Weinberg, 1986; Ellwood, 1988; Glasgow, 1981; and W. Wilson, 1987, 1989, for detailed discussions of underclass issues).

CONCLUSION

Although the scope of this review makes it difficult to propose specific recommendations for research, it is useful to summarize four general trends in research on black families and to suggest how they might influence future research directions. First, there was phenomenal growth in this area, reflected in both the quantity and quality of efforts to examine the nature of black family life, as well as the manner in which black families were regarded in the social scientific community. The increase in volume of research encouraged replication, debate, synthesis, and the generation of new efforts. Further, black family researchers acknowledged the value orientations that framed their work, as well as the political ramifications of research (Dilworth-Anderson, Johnson, and Barton, in press; Fine, Schwebel, and James-Myers, 1987).

Second, investigations of black families during this decade demonstrated greater conceptual, methodological, and analytic sophistication. Conceptually, research displayed a greater appreciation for the relationships between macro-level and micro-level influences in relation to black family phenomena (e.g., Staples, 1985). With regard to sample selection, design, and analytic frameworks, important improvements were made, including the availability of nationally representative samples of black respondents, the development of adequate samples of blacks within comparative studies, the use of nonclinical groups of respondents, greater efforts to recruit and utilize groups that are difficult to locate, and the development of appropriate comparative frameworks (i.e., black to white and within-black contrasts).

Third, as a result of the first two trends, a more balanced depiction of black family life emerged. Research increasingly reflected an appreciation for variability in the status of black families overall, as well as within particular social strata. As a result, a more precise understanding emerged concerning the operation of relevant causative factors for particular family phenomena and the specific consequences for individual families. Finally, related to the recognition of diversity in black family status and form, the past decade saw the establishment of black families within the legitimate body of family research. It can be argued that with few exceptions, the raison d'etre of research on black families was not to explore basic questions of family functioning, but to explain black families in comparison to white, middle-class families.

The racial comparative rationale and framework that guided this research was increasingly called into question by numerous researchers (many of whom identified this problem prior to the 1980s). Central among their criticisms is that the exercise of simple racial comparisons in which white behaviors are designated as the standard or baseline invariably indicates the presence of deficiencies in blacks. Further, black behaviors have no inherent significance other than the extent to which they differ from that of whites. Rather than advancing the legitimate task of generating knowledge concerning commonalities across racial groups, the simple and routine application of comparative frameworks ultimately denies the significance of differences for informing the scientific enterprise and ignores the mechanisms through which observed disparities are manifested. A comprehensive understanding of the impact of race on any phenomena is fundamentally incompatible with such an orientation and framework for research.

At this point, we consider some implications of these general trends for the current state of research on black families. First, continuing research on black families must consider the impact and interrelationships among factors that operate at varying levels (i.e., micro- versus macro-level) and potentially manifest themselves through diverse behaviors and phenomena. For example, additional work is needed to examine the linkages between changes in family structure (e.g., nonmarital adolescent births) and alterations in family relationships and functioning (e.g., changes in the grandparent role) or household structure (e.g., multigeneration household arrangements). Second, it is clear that research on black families must occur within expanded disciplinary frameworks. The use of an interdisciplinary approach is an important corrective to viewing black family phenomena in isolation and separate from other perspectives. For example, in research on black adolescence, it may be productive to team a professional in the area of child welfare and social policy with a researcher whose areas of expertise include human development. The dual concentration on issue of both applied and basic research will bring a clearer and more comprehensive focus to the examination of black adolescence. This expanded perspective will provide important information about black adolescence as a developmental stage (i.e., by identifying commonalities across youth), the varied ways that being young and black relate to one's position within the social structure (i.e., by distinguishing experiences unique to black youth), and the relationship between social location and developmental phenomena.

Finally, the tendency to view black families as a collection of the problems and challenges they face has diverted attention from important and basic issues of family function, structure, and relationships and restricted the research focus to that of "problem black families." This caution is particularly relevant for current considerations of the black underclass, whose position and status in society are especially urgent and compelling. Among both lay and scientific communities, there exists a real concern for the serious difficulties and problems that face significant numbers of black families. Certainly, to deny the existence of these problems or to underestimate their impact would be both naive and irresponsible. Likewise, to permit their existence to dominate or restrict the research agenda and/or compromise the research process in relation to black families would be equally detrimental. As students of African American families we would do well to remember that our attempts to understand and address phenomena (including those identified as social problems) that are of relevance to black families requires the application of our best scientific efforts to specify their character and identify causes and consequences and the exercise of the scientific method in the most precise and scrupulous manner possible.

REFERENCES

Allen, Walter R. 1981. "Moms, dads, and boys: Race and sex differences in the socialization of male children." Pp. 99–114 in Lawrence E. Gary (ed.), Black Men. Beverly Hills, CA: Sage.

Anderson, Elijah. 1989. "Sex codes and family life among poor inner-city youths." Annals of the American Academy of Political and Social Science 501: 59–78.

Angel, Ronald, and Marta Tienda. 1982. "Determinants of extended household structure: Cultural pattern or economic model?" American Journal of Sociology 87: 1360–1383.

Antonucci, Toni, and James Jackson. 1989. "Successful aging and life course reciprocity." Pp. 83–95 in A. M. Warnes (ed.), Human Aging. London: Hoder and Stoughton.

Bachrach, Christine A. 1986. "Adoption plans, adopted children, and adoptive mothers." Journal of Marriage and the Family 48: 243–253.

Ball, Richard E., and Lynn Robbins. 1986a. "Black husbands' satisfaction with their family life." Journal of Marriage and the Family 48: 849–855.

Ball, Richard E., and Lynn Robbins. 1986b. "Marital status and life satisfaction among black Americans." Journal of Marriage and the Family 48: 389–394.

Bane, Mary Jo, and David T. Ellwood. 1986. "Slipping into and out of poverty: The dynamics of spells." Journal of Human Resources 21: 1–23.

Barbarin, Oscar A. 1983. "Coping with ecological transition by black families: A psychological model." Journal of Community Psychology 11: 308–322.

Beck, Ruby W., and Scott H. Beck. 1989. "The incidence of extended households among middle-aged black and white women: Estimates from a 5-year panel study." Journal of Family Issues 10: 147–168.

Beckett, Joyce O., and Audrey D. Smith. 1981. "Work and family roles: Egalitarian marriage in black and white families." Social Service Review 55: 314–326.

Bowman, Philip. 1985. "Black fathers and the provider role: Role strain, informal coping resources and life happiness." Pp. 9–19 in A. W. Boykin (ed.), Empirical Research in Black Psychology. Rockville, MD: NIMH.

Bowman, Philip, and Cleopatra Howard. 1985. "Race-related socialization, motivation, and academic achievement: A study of black youth in three-generation families." Journal of the American Academy of Child Psychiatry 24: 134–141.

Boyd-Franklin, Nancy. 1989. Black Families in Therapy: A Multisystem Approach. New York: Guilford.

Broman, Clifford L. 1988a. "Household work and family life satisfaction of blacks." Journal of Marriage and the Family 50: 743–748.

Broman, Clifford L. 1988b. "Satisfaction among blacks: The significance of marriage and parenthood." Journal of Marriage and the Family 50: 45–51.

Brooks-Gunn, Jeanne, and Frank F. Furstenberg. 1986. "The children of adolescent mothers: Physical, academic, and psychological outcomes." Developmental Review 6: 224–251.

Brown, Diane R., and Lawrence E. Gary. 1985. "Social support network differentials among married and non-married black females." Psychology of Women Quarterly 9: 229–241.

Brown, Diane R., and Lawrence E. Gary. 1987. "Stressful life events, social support networks, and physical and mental health of urban black adults." Journal of Human Stress 13: 165–174.

Brown, Diane R., and Lawrence E. Gary. 1988. "Unemployment and psychological distress among black American women." Sociological Focus 21: 209–220.

Bumpass, Larry L. 1984. "Children and marital disruption: A replication and update." Demography 21: 71–81.

Burton, Linda M., and Vern L. Bengtson. 1985. "Black grandmothers: Issues of timing and continuity of roles." Pp. 61–77 in Vern L. Bengtson and Joan F. Robertson (eds.), Grandparenthood. Beverly Hills, CA: Sage.

Burton, Linda M., and Peggye Dilworth-Anderson. In press. "The intergenerational family roles of aged black Americans." Marriage and Family Review.

Cazenave, Noel A. 1979. "Middle-income black fathers: An analysis of the provider role." Family Coordinator 28: 583–593.

Cazenave, Noel A. 1984. "Race, socioeconomic status, and age: The social context of American masculinity." Sex Roles 11: 639–656.

Chatters, Linda M. 1988. "Subjective well-being evaluations among older black Americans." Psychology and Aging 3: 184–190.

Chatters, Linda M., and James S. Jackson. 1989. "Quality of life and subjective well-being among black adults." Pp. 191–214 in R. L. Jones (ed.), Adult development and aging. Berkeley, CA: Cobb and Henry Publications.

Chatters, Linda M., Robert J. Taylor, and James S. Jackson. 1985. "Size and composition of the informal helper network of elderly blacks." Journal of Gerontology 40: 605–614.

Chatters, Linda M., Robert J. Taylor, and James S. Jackson. 1986. "Aged blacks' choices for an informal helper network." Journal of Gerontology 41: 94–100.

Chatters, Linda M., Robert J. Taylor, and Harold W. Neighbors. 1989. "Size of the informal helper network mobilized in response to serious personal problems." Journal of Marriage and the Family 51: 667–676.

Cherlin, Andrew J. 1981. Marriage, Divorce, Remarriage. Cambridge, MA: Harvard University Press.

Cherlin, Andrew J., and Frank F. Furstenberg, Jr. 1986. The New American Grandparent: A Place in the Family, a Life Apart. New York: Basic Books.

Coleman, Lerita M., Tony C. Antonucci, Pamela K. Adelman, and Susan E. Crohan. 1987. "Social roles in the lives of middle-aged and older black women." Journal of Marriage and the Family 49: 761–771.

Danziger, Sandra K., and Ann Nichols-Casebolt. 1988. "Teen parents and child support: Eligibility, participation, and payment." Journal of Social Service Research 11: 1–20.

Danziger, Sandra K., and Norma Radin. 1990. "Absent does not equal uninvolved: Predictors of fathering in teen mother families." Journal of Marriage and the Family 52: 636–642.

Danziger, Sheldon H., and Daniel H. Weinberg (eds.). 1986. Fighting Poverty: What Works and What Doesn't. Cambridge, MA: Harvard University Press.

Darity, William, and Samuel L. Myers. 1986–87. "Public policy trends and the fate of the black family." Humboldt Journal of Social Relations 14: 134–164.

Dilworth-Anderson, Peggye, Leanor Boulin Johnson, and Linda M. Burton. In press. "Reframing theories for understanding race, ethnicity, and families." In Pauline Boss, William Doherty, Ralph La Ross, Walter Schumm, and Suzanne Steinmetz (eds.), Sourcebook of Family Theories and Methods: A Contextual Approach. New York: Plenum Press.

Dressler, William W. 1985. "Extended family relationships, social support, and mental health in a Southern black community." Journal of Health and Social Behavior 26: 39–48.

Dressler, William, Susan Haworth Hoeppner, and Barbara J. Pitts. 1985. "Household structure in a Southern black community." American Anthropologist 87: 853–862.

Duncan, Greg J., and Willard L. Rodgers. 1988. "Longitudinal aspects of childhood poverty." Journal of Marriage and the Family 50: 1007–1021.

Ellison, Christopher G. 1990. "Family ties, friendships, and subjective well-being among black Americans." Journal of Marriage and the Family 52: 298–310.

Ellwood, David T. 1988. Poor Support. New York: Basic Books.

Ericksen, Julia A., William L. Yancey, and Eugene P. Ericksen. 1979. "The division of family roles." Journal of Marriage and the Family 41: 301–313.

Farley, Reynolds, and Walter R. Allen. 1987. The Color Line and the Quality of Life in America. New York: Russell Sage Foundation.

Fine, Mark, Andrew I. Schwebel, and Linda James-Myers. 1987. "Family stability in black families: Values underlying three different perspectives." Journal of Comparative Family Studies 18: 1–23.

Furstenberg, Frank F., Jr., Jeanne Brooks-Gunn, and Lindsay Chase-Lansdale. 1989. "Teenaged pregnancy and childbearing." American Psychologist 44: 313–320.

Furstenberg, Frank F., J. Brooks-Gunn, and S. Philip Morgan. 1987. Adolescent Mothers in Later Life. New York: Cambridge University Press.

Garfinkel, Irwin, and Sara S. McLanahan. 1986. Single Mothers and Their Children: A New American Dilemma. Washington, DC: Urban Institute Press.

Gibson, Rose C., and James S. Jackson. 1987. "The health, physical functioning, and informal supports of the black elderly." Milbank Quarterly 65: 421–454.

Glasgow, Douglas. 1981. The Black Underclass. New York: Vintage Books.

Glick, Paul C. 1981. "A demographic picture of black families." Pp. 106–126 in Harriette P. MacAdoo (ed.), Black Families. Beverly Hills, CA: Sage.

Guttentag, Marcia, and Paul F. Secord. 1983. Too Many Women: The Sex Ratio Question. Beverly Hills, CA: Sage.

Harrison, Algea. 1985. "The black family's socializing environment." Pp. 174–193 in Harriette P. McAdoo and John L. McAdoo (eds.), Black Children. Beverly Hills. CA: Sage.

Hayes, C. D. (ed.). 1987. Risking the Future: Adolescent Sexuality, Pregnancy, and Childbearing (Vol. 1). Washington, DC: National Academy Press.

Hendricks, Leo E., Cleopatra Howard, and Patricia Ceasar. 1981. "Help-seeking behavior among select populations of unmarried adolescent fathers: Implications for human service agencies." American Journal of Public Health 71: 733–735.

Hendricks, Leo E., and Teresa Montgomery. 1983. "A limited population of unmarried adolescent fathers: A preliminary report of their views on fatherhood and the relationship with the mothers of their children." Adolescence 18: 201–210.

Hill, Robert B., Andrew Billingsley, Eleanor Ingram, Michelene R. Malson, Roger H. Rubin, Carol B. Stack, James B. Stewart, and James E. Teele. 1989. Research on African-American Families: A Holistic Perspective. Boston: William Monroe Trotter Institute.

Hofferth, Sandra L. 1984. "Kin networks, race, and family structure." Journal of Marriage and the Family 46: 791–806.

Hofferth, Sandra L., and C. D. Hayes (eds.). 1987. Risking the Future: Adolescent Sexuality, Pregnancy, and Childbearing (Vol. 2). Working Papers and Statistical Reports. Washington, DC: National Academy Press.

Hogan, Dennis P., Ling-Xin Hao, and William L. Parish. 1990. "Race, kin networks, and assistance to mother-headed families." Social Forces 68: 797–812.

Hogan, Dennis P., and Evelyn M. Kitagawa. 1985. "The impact of social status, family structure, and neighborhood on the fertility of black adolescents." American Journal of Sociology 90: 825–855.

Huber, Joan, and Glenna Spitze. 1981. "Wives' employment, household behaviors, and sex-role attitudes." Social Forces 60: 150–169.

Hughes, Michael, and David H. Demo. 1989. "Self-perceptions of black Americans: Self-esteem and personal efficacy." American Journal of Sociology 95: 132–159.

Jackson, Jacqueline, and Linda Berg-Cross. 1988. "Extending the extended family: The mother-in-law and daughter-in-law relationship of black women." Family Relations 37: 293–297.

Jackson, James S., Linda M. Chatters, and Harold Neighbors. 1986. "The subjective life quality of black Americans." Pp. 193–213 in F. M. Andrews (ed.), Research on the Quality of Life. Ann Arbor: Institute for Social Research, University of Michigan.

Jackson, James, Wayne McCullough, and Gerald Gurin. 1988. "Family, socialization environment, and identity development in black Americans." Pp. 242–256 in H. McAdoo (ed.), Black Families (2nd ed.). Beverly Hills, CA: Sage.

Jaynes, Gerald David, and Robin M. Williams, Jr. (eds.). 1989. A Common Destiny: Blacks and American Society. Washington, DC: National Academy Press.

Jenkins, Shirley, and Beverly Diamond. 1985. "Ethnicity and foster care: Census data as predictors of placement variables." American Journal of Orthopsychiatry 55: 267–276.

Jones, Reginald L. (ed.). 1989. Black Adolescents. Berkeley, CA: Cobb and Henry Publishers.

Lerman, Robert I. 1986. "Who are the young absent fathers?" Youth and Society 18: 3–27.

Lewis, Edith A. 1988. "Role strengths and strains of African-American mothers." Journal of Primary Prevention 9: 77–91.

Lewis, Edith A. 1989. "Role strain in black women: The efficacy of support networks." Journal of Black Studies 20: 155–169.

Lieberson, Stanley, and Mary C. Waters. 1988. From Many Strands: Ethnic and Racial Groups in Contemporary America. New York: Russell Sage Foundation.

Logan, Sadye M. L., Edith M. Freeman, and Ruth G. McRoy. 1990. Social Work Practice with Black Families. White Plains, NY: Longman.

Malson, Michelene. 1983. "The social-support systems of black families." Marriage and Family Review 5: 37–57.

Marsiglio, William. 1987. "Adolescent fathers in the United States: Their initial living arrangements, marital experience, and educational outcomes." Family Planning Perspectives 19: 240–251.

Marsiglio, William. 1989. "Adolescent males' pregnancy resolution preferences and family formation intentions: Does family background make a difference for blacks and whites?" Journal of Adolescent Research 4: 214–237.

McAdoo, Harriette. 1980. "Black mothers and the extended family support networks." Pp. 125–144 in L. F. Rodgers-Rose (ed.), The Black Woman. Beverly Hills, CA: Sage.

McAdoo, John L. 1981. "Black father and child interactions." Pp. 115–130 in Lawrence E. Gary (ed.), Black Men. Beverly Hills, CA: Sage.

McLanahan, Sara S. 1985. "Family structure and the reproduction of poverty." American Journal of Sociology 90: 873–901.

McLanahan, Sara S. 1988. "Family structure and dependency: Early transitions to female household headship." Demography 25: 1–16.

McLanahan, Sara, and Julia Adams. 1987. "Parenthood and psychological well-being." Annual Review of Sociology 13: 237–257.

McLanahan, Sara S., and Karen Booth. 1989. "Mother-only families: Problems, prospects, and politics." Journal of Marriage and the Family 51: 557–580.

McLanahan, Sara S., and Larry Bumpass. 1988. "Intergenerational consequences of family disruption." American Journal of Sociology 94: 130–152.

Moore, Kristin A., Margaret C. Simms, and Charles L. Betsey. 1986. Choice and Circumstance: Racial Differences in Adolescent Sexuality and Fertility. New Brunswick, NJ: Transaction Books.

Morisey, Patricia G. 1990. "Black children in foster care." Pp. 133–147 in Sadye M. L. Logan, Edith M. Freeman, and Ruth G. McRoy (eds.), Social Work Practice with Black Families. New York: Longman.

National Black Child Development Institute. 1989. Who Will Care When Parents Can't? A Study of Black Children in Foster Care. Washington, DC: National Black Child Development Institute.

Neighbors, Harold W. 1986. "Socioeconomic status and psychologic distress in adult blacks." American Journal of Epidemiology 124: 779–793.

Neighbors, Harold W., and James S. Jackson. 1984. "The use of informal and formal help: Four patterns of illness behavior in the black community." American Journal of Community Psychology 12: 629–644.

Neighbors, Harold W., and Thomas A. LeVeist. 1989. "Socioeconomic status and psychological distress: The impact of financial aid on economic problem severity." Journal of Primary Prevention 10: 149–165.

Norton, Arthur J., and Jeanne E. Moorman. 1987. "Current trends in marriage and divorce among American women." Journal of Marriage and the Family 49: 3–14.

Oliver, Melvin L. 1988. "The urban black community as network: Towards a social network perspective." Sociological Quarterly 29: 623–645.

Parke, Ross D., and Brian Neville. 1987. "Teenage fatherhood." In Sandra L. Hofferth and C. D. Hayes (eds.), Risking the Future: Adolescent Sexuality, Pregnancy, and Childbearing (Vol. 2). Washington, DC: National Academy Press.

Peters, Marie. 1985. "Racial socialization of young black children." Pp. 159–173 in H. McAdoo and J. McAdoo (eds.), Black Children. Beverly Hills, CA: Sage.

Peters, Marie, and G. Massey. 1983. "Chronic vs. mundane stress in family stress theories: The case of black families in white America." Marriage and Family Review 6: 193–218.

Reskin, Barbara F., and Shelly Coverman. 1985. "Sex and race in the detriments of psychophysical distress: A reappraisal of the sex role hypothesis." Social Forces 63: 1038–1059.

Robinson, Jeanne B. 1989. "Clinical treatment of black families: Issues and strategies." Social Work 34: 323–329.

Rodgers, William L., and Arland Thornton. 1985. "Changing patterns of first marriage in the United States." Demography 22: 265–279.

Ross, Catherine E. 1987. "The division of labor at home." Social Forces 65: 816–833.

Rossi, Alice S. 1984. "Gender and parenthood." "American Sociological Review 49: 1–10.

Schoen, Robert. 1983. "Measuring the tightness of the marriage squeeze." Demography 20: 61–78.

Schoen, Robert, and James R. Kluegel. 1988. "The widening gap in black and white marriage rates: The impact of population composition and differential marriage propensities." American Sociological Review 53: 895–907.

Schoen, Robert, and John Wooldredge. 1989. "Marriage choices in North Carolina and Virginia, 1969–71 and 1979–81." Journal of Marriage and the Family 51: 465–481.

South, Scott J. 1986. "Sex ratios, economic power, and women's roles: A theoretical extension and empirical test." Journal of Marriage and the Family 50: 19–31.

South, Scott J., and S. F. Messner. 1987. "The sex ratio and women's involvement in crime: A cross-national analysis." Sociological Quarterly 28: 171–188.

Spanier, Graham B., and Paul C. Glick. 1980. "Mate selection differentials between whites and blacks in the United States." Social Forces 58: 707–725.

Spencer, Margaret. 1983. "Children's cultural values and parental child-rearing strategies." Developmental Reviews 3: 351–370.

Spencer, Margaret, Geraldine Kearse Brookins, and Walter Recharde Allen. 1985. Beginnings: The Social and Affective Development of Black Children. Hillsdale, NJ: Lawrence Erlbaum Associates.

Staples, Robert. 1985. "Changes in black family structure: The conflict between family ideology and structural conditions." Journal of Marriage and the Family 47: 1005–1014.

Staples, Robert, and Alfredo Mirande. 1980. "Racial and cultural variations among American families: A decennial review of the literature on minority families." Journal of Marriage and the Family 42: 157–173.

Stevens, Joseph H., Jr. 1984. "Black grandmothers' and black adolescent mothers' knowledge about parenting." Developmental Psychology 20: 1017–1025.

Stevens, Joseph H., Jr. 1988. "Social support, locus of control, and parenting in three low-income groups of mothers: Black teenagers, black adults, and white adults." Child Development 59: 635–642.

Sudarkasa, Niara. 1981. "Interpreting the African heritage in Afro-American family organizations." Pp. 37–53 in Harriette P. McAdoo (ed.), Black Families. Beverly Hills, CA: Sage.

Sweet, James A., and Larry L. Bumpass. 1987. American Families and Households. New York: Russell Sage Foundation.

Taylor, Robert J. 1985. "The extended family as a source of support for elderly blacks." Gerontologist 26: 630–636.

Taylor, Robert J. 1986. "Receipt of support from family among black Americans: Demographic and familial differences." Journal of Marriage and the Family 48: 67–77.

Taylor, Robert J. 1988a. "Aging and supportive relationships among black Americans." Pp. 259–281 in James Jackson (ed.), The Black American Elderly: Research on Physical Health. New York: Springer.

Taylor, Robert J. 1988b. "Structural determinants of religious participation among Black Americans." Review of Religious Research 30: 114–125.

Taylor, Robert J. 1990. "Need for support and family involvement among black Americans." Journal of Marriage and the Family 52: 584–590.

Taylor, Robert J., and Linda M. Chatters. 1986a. "Church-based informal support among elderly blacks." Gerontologist 26: 637–642.

Taylor, Robert J., and Linda M. Chatters. 1986b. "Patterns of informal support to elderly black adults: Family, friends, and church members." Social Work 31: 432–438.

Taylor, Robert J., and Linda M. Chatters. 1988. "Church members as a source of informal social support." Review of Religious Research 30: 193–203.

Taylor, Robert J., Linda M. Chatters, and Vickie Mays. 1988. "Parents, children, siblings, in-laws, and non-kin sources of emergency assistance to black Americans." Family Relations 37: 298–304.

Taylor, Robert J., Bogart Leashore, and Susan Toliver. 1988. "An assessment of the provider role as perceived by black males." Family Relations 37: 426–431.

Testa, Mark, N. M. Astone, Marilyn Krogh, and Kathryn Neckerman. 1989. "Employment and marriage among inner-city fathers." Annals of the American Academy of Political and Social Science 501: 79–91.

Thomas, Veronica, Norweeta G. Milburn, Diane R. Brown, and Lawrence E. Gary. 1988. "Social support and depressive symptoms among blacks." Journal of Black Psychology 14: 35–45.

Thompson, Maxine S., and Margaret E. Ensminger. 1989. "Psychological well-being among mothers with school-age children: Evolving family structures." Social Forces 67: 715–730.

Thornton, Michael, Linda M. Chatters, Robert J. Taylor, and Walter R. Allen. 1990. "Sociodemographic and environmental influences on racial socialization by black parents." Child Development 61: 401–409.

Tienda, Marta, and Ronald Angel. 1982. "Headship and household composition among blacks, Hispanics, and other whites." Social Forces 61: 508–531.

Tucker, M. Belinda. 1987. "The black male shortage in Los Angeles." Sociology and Social Research 71: 221–227.

Tucker, M. Belinda, and Claudia Mitchell-Kernan. In press. "Sex ratio imbalance and Afro-Americans: Conceptual and methodological issues." In Reginald Jones (ed.), Advances in Black Psychology. Berkeley, CA: Cobb and Henry.

Tucker, M. Belinda, and Claudia Mitchell-Kernan. 1990. "New trends in black American interracial marriage: The social structural context." Journal of Marriage and the Family 52: 209–218.

Tucker, Belinda, and Robert J. Taylor. 1989. "Demographic correlates of relationship status among black Americans." Journal of Marriage and the Family 51: 655–665.

U.S. Bureau of the Census. 1985. 1980 Census of the Population, Subject Reports: Marital Characteristics. Washington, DC: Government Printing Office.

Warheit, George, William Vega, D. Shimizu, and Kenneth Meinhardt. 1982. "Interpersonal coping networks and mental health problems among four race-ethnic groups." Journal of Community Psychology 10: 312–324.

Wilson, Melvin N. 1986. "The black extended family: An analytical consideration." Developmental Psychology 22: 246–259.

Wilson, Melvin N. 1989. "Child development in the context of the black extended family." American Psychologist 44: 380–385.

Wilson, William Julius. 1987. The Truly Disadvantaged. Chicago: University of Chicago Press.

Wilson, William Julius (ed.). 1989. "The ghetto underclass: Social science perspectives." Annals of the American Academy of Political and Social Science 501: 8–192.

Wilson, William Julius, and Kathryn J. Neckerman. 1986. "Poverty and family structure: The widening gap between evidence and public policy issues." Pp. 232–259 in Sheldon H. Danziger and Daniel H. Weinberg (eds.), Fighting Poverty: What Works and What Doesn't. Cambridge, MA: Harvard University Press.

Ulbrich, Patricia M., and George J. Warheit. 1989. "Social support, stress, and psychological distress among older black and white adults." Journal of Aging and Health 1: 286–305.

Zelnik, Melvin. 1983. "Sexual activity among adolescents: Perspectives of a decade." In Elizabeth McAnarney (ed.), Premature Adolescent Pregnancy and Parenthood. New York: Grune and Stratton.

Zelnik, Melvin, John Kantner, and Kathleen Ford. 1981. Sex and Pregnancy in Adolescence. Beverly Hills, CA: Sage.

Zelnik, Melvin, and Farida K. Shah. 1983. "First intercourse among young Americans." Family Planning Perspectives 15: 64–72.

Zill, Nicholas, and Carolyn C. Rogers. 1988. "Recent trends in the well-being of children in the United States and their implications for public policy." Pp. 31–98 in Andrew J. Cherlin (ed.), The Changing American Family and Public Policy. Washington, DC: Urban Institute Press.

Zollar, Ann Creighton, and J. Sherwood Williams. 1987. "The contribution of marriage to the life satisfaction of black adults." Journal of Marriage and the Family 49: 87–92.

Reading 34

9/15/94

Growing up in a Gay Home

Daniel Goleman

Michael McCandlish, 12 years old, spends five nights a week with his mother and two with his stepmother. And every now and then, he spends time with his Dad.

But even in this day of ever-mutating family ties, Michael's situation stands out as unusual. While his "Mom," Dr. Barbara McCandlish, is his biological mother, the woman he calls his "Step-Mom" was his mother's lesbian lover—and co-parent—until they separated when Michael was 5. Michael's "Dad" is his biological father, a gay man who was an anonymous sperm donor at the time Michael was conceived, but whom Michael has since gotten to know.

Michael, a sixth-grader in Santa Fe, N.M., is on his school's basketball team, plays in Little League baseball, and is a snowboarding enthusiast.

Does Michael feel uncomfortable with his unorthodox parents? "It's never been a problem," Michael said. "I've always been pretty open about it, and I don't worry about it."

STUDIES DISPUTE LONG-HELD VIEWS

And, according to a review of new studies in the current issue of the journal *Child Development,* children raised by gay parents are no more likely to have psychological problems than those raised in more conventional circumstances. While they may face teasing or even ridicule, especially in adolescence, the studies show that, over all, there are no psychological disadvantages for children like Michael in being raised by homosexuals.

That conclusion challenges a view long held by some mental health specialists. And the prevailing view has been reflected in court rulings in custody disputes around the country where judges, even more than psychotherapists, have assumed that being raised by gay or lesbian parents is damaging to a child's emotional and sexual development. As a result, homosexual parents have great difficulty winning custody of their children from a heterosexual partner in divorce proceedings.

In recent years, though, the scientific consensus has begun to change, as more and more experts conclude it is based on anecdotal reports and biased research rather than scientifically gathered evidence. New studies come to very different conclusions.

"What evidence there is suggests there are no particular developmental or emotional deficits for children raised by gay or lesbian parents," said Dr. Michael E. Lamb, chief of the Section on Social and Emotional Development at the National Institute of Child Health and Human Development. "The research is still relatively sparse, but it all suggests the same thing: these kids look O.K."

"INVISIBLE" GAY HOUSEHOLDS

Estimates of the number of children being raised by homosexual parents range from 6 million to 14 million, in at least 4 million households. While those estimates, from sources like the American Bar Association, may seem high, those who make them point out that the majority of such families are "invisible," in that few outsiders realize there is a homosexual parent. Sometimes the children themselves do not know until they are teen-agers.

"The great majority of gay and lesbian parents are not out in the open about it," said Tim Fisher, director of Communications for Gay and Lesbian Parents Coalition International in Washington, which has 40 chapters in the United States and Canada. There are at least 100 other informal support groups for homosexual parents in the country, Mr. Fisher said.

In the large majority of such households the children were conceived in heterosexual marriages that ended in divorce after one parent came out as homosexual. In recent years families in which children are conceived or adopted by gay couples are growing more common.

Mr. Fisher, for example, is raising a $2\frac{1}{2}$-year-old girl and a 6-month-old boy, both by surrogate mothers. His gay lover is employed outside the home, while Mr. Fisher works at home so he can care for the children.

Despite the large numbers of such families, the topic itself was largely ignored by researchers who were not themselves homosexual. Early research suggesting that homosexuals made bad parents were largely based on individual case studies of troubled children. "Early on, the studies were done by researchers with an ax to grind," Dr. Lamb said.

UNANIMITY OF STUDIES

By contrast, the new studies all point in the same direction. "There is no adverse effect on any psychological measure," said Dr. Julie Gottman, a clinical psychologist in Seattle, who has done one of the best-designed studies on the topic. Her study was published in 1990 in *Homosexuality and Family Relations* (Huntington Park Press).

Dr. Gottman compared two groups of 35 adult women with 35 who had been raised by lesbian mothers after a divorce from the father. The children were 25 years old on average when Dr. Gottman studied them.

As a group, the children of lesbians did not differ from children of heterosexual mothers in their social adjustment or their identity as a boy or a girl, Dr. Gottman found. The children of lesbians were no more likely to be homosexual than those of heterosexual mothers.

"What mattered most for their adjustment was whether the mother had a partner in the home, whether male or female," Dr. Gottman said. "If so, those children tended to do somewhat better than the others in self-confidence, self-acceptance and independence. But the sexual orientation of the lesbian mothers had no adverse effects."

That conclusion was confirmed by about three dozen studies reviewed in *Child Development* by Charlotte Patterson, a psychologist at the University of Virginia. When children raised by homosexuals were compared with those raised by heterosexuals, no differences emerged over all on any measure of social or emotional development used in the studies.

No study found any impact on a child's feelings about being a boy or girl or sexual preference from being raised by a homosexual parent. For example, a 1983 study of 9- and 10-year-old girls and boys who were raised by lesbian mothers found that none wished to be a member of the opposite sex.

ROOTS OF HOMOSEXUALITY

There is as yet no sure scientific consensus on the roots of homosexuality. Recent studies finding differences between the brains of homosexual and heterosexual men have strengthened the position of those who argue for a biological basis. Still, "most experts assume there are both biological and social causes of homosexuality," said Dr. Greg Herek, a psychologist at the University of California at Davis, who is an editor of *Contemporary Perspectives on Gay and Lesbian Psychology*.

Having homosexual parents "does not cause homosexuality or gender confusion in children," said Dr. John Money, a specialist in sexual disorders at Johns Hopkins University medical school.

For example, in a 1981 study of 6- to 9-year-old children of lesbian and heterosexual mothers, there were no differences in toy and play preferences. The strongest influence on the children was not their mothers, but their playmates.

Researchers say the definitive study, which would follow the adjustment of large numbers of children over several decades, has yet to be done. And data from a study by Dr. Patterson, to be published early next year, show that the children of lesbian mothers are more likely than others to report feelings of anger and fear, as well as more positive feelings like contentment. It is unclear whether the findings reflect greater stress among the children of lesbians or a greater openness about their feelings.

Dr. Patterson concluded, "Not a single study has found children of gay or lesbian parents to be disadvantaged in any significant respect."

Even so, courts have been slow to reconcile custody decisions with scientific findings. Although the data showing there are no psychological setbacks for children of homosexuals have been mounting for the last decade, "Lesbian and gay parents struggle in courts for custody and visitation rights," said Paula Ettelbrick, legal director of Lambda Legal Defense, a national legal gay and lesbian organization in New York City.

"But," Ms. Ettelbrick added, "a growing awareness of these studies is slowing down the number of outright denials. The situation is still mixed, but it's getting better."

Although there are no developmental disadvantages for children of homosexuals, Dr. Patterson acknowledged that there could be rocky times for some children of homosexual parents. "If problems occur at all, you see them in early adolescence, when kids want to be like everyone else," Dr. Patterson said.

That is the age that children of homosexual parents are likely to feel most stigmatized. "The anecdotal evidence is that if other kids know, children of gays and lesbians do meet with some ridicule, especially in the early teen years," Mr. Fisher said. "But gay and lesbian parents are often well equipped to help them through it, since they've dealt with such problems themselves."

While there may be no discernible developmental cost for children raised by homosexual parents, there are undeniable social pressures, if only from those who disapprove of homosexuality. For that reason, many homosexual parents are cautious about the arrangement in public.

"It's clear that you need to be honest and open within the family with the kids," said Dr. McCandlish, Michael's mother. A psychologist in Santa Fe, Dr. McCandlish said that unlike Michael's "stepmother," she no longer considered herself lesbian. Dr. McCandlish added: "There may be some situations when you can't be completely open with people on the outside. Michael does not announce the situation to people, but there were never any secrets with him."

School is perhaps the most difficult arena. Heterosexual teachers and homosexual parents may have different ideas about sex roles, said Dr. Virginia Casper, a developmental psychologist at the Bank Street College of Education in New York City, herself the lesbian mother of a 7-year-old girl.

CONVENTIONAL ROLE MODELS

In a study of 35 homosexual parents, their children and the children's teachers, Dr. Casper found that the teachers had far more conventional ideas about the best kind of sexual role models than did the parents. In a report of her research published in the current *Columbia Teacher's College Record*, Dr. Casper and her co-authors argue that teachers and administrators should acknowledge that there are children whose parents are homosexual to help remove the stigma.

Reading 35

The Family in an Aging Society: A Matrix of Latent Relationships

Matilda   White   Riley

I am going to talk about families and the revolution in longevity. This revolution has produced configurations in kinship structure and in the internal dynamics of family life at every age that have never existed before.

Over two-thirds of the total improvement in longevity from prehistoric times until the present has taken place in the brief period since 1900 (Preston, 1976). In the United States, life expectancy at birth has risen from less than 50 in 1900 to well over 70 today. Whereas at the start of the century most deaths occurred in infancy and young adulthood, today the vast majority of deaths are postponed to old age. Indeed we are approaching the "squared" mortality curve, in which relatively few die before the end of the full life span. For the first time in all history, we are living in a society in which most people live to be old.[1]

Though many facts of life extension are familiar, their meanings for the personal lives of family members are elusive. Just how is increasing longevity transforming the kinship structure? Most problematic of all, how is the impact of longevity affecting those sorely needed close relationships that provide emotional support and socialization for family members (see Parsons and Bales, 1955)? To answer such questions, I must agree with other scholars in the conclusion that we need a whole new way of looking at the family, researching it, living in it, and dealing with it in professional practice and public policy.

Indeed, an exciting new family literature is beginning to map and interpret these unparalleled changes; it is beginning to probe beneath the surface for the subjective implications of the protracted and intricate interplay of family relationships. As the kinship structure is transformed, many studies are beginning to ask new questions about how particular relationships and particular social conditions

From *Journal of Family Issues*, Vol. 4, No. 3, September 1983, pp. 439–454. Copyright © 1983 by Sage Publications, Inc. By permission of Sage Publications, Inc.

can foster or inhibit emotional support and socialization—that is, the willingness to learn from one another. They are asking how today's family can fill people's pressing need for close human relationships.

From this developing literature, four topics emerge as particularly thought-provoking: (1) the dramatic extension of the kinship structure; (2) the new opportunities this extension brings for close family relationships; (3) the special approaches needed for understanding these complex relationships; and (4) the still unknown family relationships of older people in the future. I shall touch briefly on each of these topics. From time to time I shall also suggest a few general propositions—principles from the sociology of age (see M. W. Riley, 1976; forthcoming) that seem clearly applicable to changing family relationships. Perhaps they will aid our understanding of increasing longevity and the concomitant changes about us. The propositions may guide us in applying our new understanding in research, policy, and practice.

THE CHANGING CONFIGURATIONS OF THE KINSHIP STRUCTURE

I shall begin with the kinship structure as influenced by longevity. The extent and configurations of this structure have been so altered that we must rethink our traditional view of kinship. As four (even five) generations of many families are now alive at the same time, we can no longer concentrate primary attention on nuclear families of young parents and their children who occasionally visit or provide material assistance to grandparents or other relatives. I have come to think of today's large and complex kinship structure as a matrix of latent relationships—father with son, child with great-grandparent, sister with sister-in-law, ex-husband with ex-wife, and so on—relationships that are latent because they might or might not become close and significant during a lifetime. Thus I am proposing a definition of the kinship structure as a latent web of continually shifting linkages that provide the *potential* for activating and intensifying close family relationships.

The family literature describes two kinds of transformations in this structure that result from increasing longevity: (1) The linkages among family members have been prolonged, and (2) the surviving generations in a family have increased in number and complexity.

Prolongation of Family Relationships

Consider how longevity has prolonged family relationships. For example, in married couples a century ago, one or both partners were likely to have died before the children were reared. Today, though it may seem surprising, couples marrying at the customary ages can anticipate surviving together (apart from divorce) as long as 40 or 50 years on the average (Uhlenberg, 1969, 1980). As Glick and Norton (1977:14) have shown, one out of every five married couples can expect to celebrate their fiftieth wedding anniversary. Because the current intricacy of kinship structures surpasses even the language available to describe it (our step-in-laws might not like to be called "outlaws"), it sometimes helps to do "thought experiments" from one's own life. As marital partners, my husband and I have survived together for over 50 years. What can be said about the form (as distinct from the content) of such a prolonged relationship?

For one thing, we share over half a century of experience. Because we are similar in age, we have shared the experience of aging—biologically, psychologically, and socially—from young adulthood to old age. Because we were born at approximately the same time (and thus belong to the same cohort), we have shared much the same historical experiences—the same fluctuations between economic prosperity and depression, between periods of pacifism and of war, between political liberalism and reactionism, and between low and high rates of fertility. We have also shared our own personal family experiences. We shared the bearing and raising of young children during our first-quarter century together; during our second quarter century we adjusted our couplehood to our added roles as parents-in-law and grandparents. The third quarter-century of our married life, by the laws of probability, should convert us additionally into grandparents-in-law and great-grandparents as well. In sum, prolonged marriages like ours afford extensive common experiences with aging, with historical change, and with changing family relationships.

Such marriages also provide a home—an abiding meeting place for two individuals whose separate lives are engrossed in varied extrafamilial roles. Just as longevity has prolonged the average duration of marriage, it has extended many other roles (such as continuing education, women's years of work outside the home, or retirement). For example, Barbara Torrey (1982) has estimated that people spend at least a quarter of their adult lives in retirement. Married couples, as they move through the role complexes of their individual lives, have many evening or weekend opportunities either to share their respective extrafamilial experiences, to escape from them, or (though certainly not in my own case) to vent their boredom or frustration on one another (see Kelley, 1981).

Thus two features of protracted marriages become apparent. First, these marriages provide increasing opportunity to accumulate shared experiences and meanings and perhaps to build from these a "crescive" relationship, as suggested by Ralph Turner (1970) and Gunhild Hagestad (1981). But second, they also present shifting exigencies and role conflicts that require continual mutual accommodation and reaccommodation. As Richard Lazarus (DeLongis, et al., 1982) has shown, "daily hassles" can be more destructive of well-being than traumatic family events. And Erving Goffman (1959:132) warns that the home can become a "backstage area" in which "it is safe to lapse into an asociable mood of sullen, silent irritability."

Many marriages, not ended by death, are ended by divorce. The very extension of marriage may increase the likelihood of divorce, as Samuel Preston (1976:176–177) has shown. Returning to my personal experience, I was the only one of four sisters who did not divorce and remarry. But as long as their ex-husbands were alive none of my sisters could ever entirely discount the remaining potential linkages between them. These were not only ceremonial or instrumental linkages, but also affective linkages that could be hostile and vindictive, or (as time passes and need arises) could renew concern for one another's well-being. Whatever the nature of the relationship, latent linkages to ex-spouses persist. Thus, a prolonged marriage (even an ex-marriage) provides a continuing potential for a close relationship that can be activated in manifold ways.

The traditional match-making question—"Will this marriage succeed or fail?"—must be replaced and oft-repeated as the couple grows older by a different question: "Regardless of our past, can we—do we want [to]—make the fresh effort to succeed, or shall we fail in this marriage?"

Here I will state as my first proposition: *Family relationships are never fixed:* they change as the self and the significant other family members grow older, and as the changing society influences their respective lives. Clearly, the longer the relationship endures (because of longevity) the greater the opportunity for relational changes.

If, as lives are prolonged, marital relationships extend far beyond the original nuclear household, parent-offspring relationships also take on entirely new forms. For example, my daughter and I have survived together so far for 45 years of which only 18 were in the traditional relationship of parent and child. Unlike our shorter-lived forebearers, my daughter and I have been able to share many common experiences although at different stages of our respective lives. She shares a major portion of the historical changes that I have experienced. She also shares my earlier experience of sending a daughter off to college, and will perhaps share my experience of having a daughter marry and raise children. Of course, she and I differ in age. (In Alice Rossi's study of biological age differences, 1980, the consequences for parent-offspring relationships of the reciprocal tensions between a pubescent daughter and her older mother who is looking ahead to the menopausal changes of midlife were explored.)[2] Although the relational age between me and my daughter—the 26 years that separate us—remains the same throughout our lives, the implications of this difference change drastically from infancy to my old age.

Number and Stability of Generations

I have dwelt at length on the prolongation of particular relationships to suggest the consequent dramatic changes in the family structure. Longevity has, in addition, increased the stability and the number of generations in a family. A poignant example of this instability (Imhof, n.d.) can be found in an eighteenth century parish where a father could spawn twenty-four offspring of whom only three survived to adulthood—a time in which "it took two babies to make one adult." With increased longevity each generation becomes more stable because more of its members survive. For the young nuclear family in the United States, for example, though the number of children born in each family has been declining over this century, increased longevity has produced a new stability in the family structure. In an important quantitative analysis, Peter Uhlenberg (1980) has shown how the probability of losing a parent or a sibling through death before a child reaches age 15 [has] decreased from .51 in 1900 to .09 in 1976. Compared with children born a century ago, children born today are almost entirely protected against death of close family members (except for elderly relatives). To be sure, while mortality has been declining, divorce rates have been increasing but less rapidly. Thus, perhaps surprisingly, Uhlenberg demonstrates that disruptions of marriage up through the completion of child rearing have been declining since 1900. In other words, many marriages have been broken by divorce, but overall more have remained intact because of fewer deaths! Thus the young family as well as each of the older generations becomes more stable through survival.

At the same time, the number of older generations has been increasing. Looking up the generational ladder, increasing numbers of a child's four grandparents survive. Among middle-aged couples, whereas back in 1900 more than half had no surviving elderly parents, today half have two or more parents still alive (Uhlenberg, 1980: 318). Conversely looking down the generational ladder, each set of elderly parents has adult children with spouses and children of their own. Meanwhile, the increase in divorce and remarriage (four out of five divorced people remarry) compounds the complexity of this elaborate structure, as Andrew Cherlin (1981) has shown. In my own family, for example, each of our two middle-aged children have their own children, and they also have us as two elderly parents; my daughter's husband also has two parents; and my son (who has married twice) has his ex-wife's parents and his current wife's mother, father, and step-mother in addition to us. A complex array!

Of course, as these surviving generations proliferate and overlap, each generation is continually growing older and moving up the generational ladder to replace its predecessor until ultimately the members of the oldest generation die. Because of longevity, every generation—the oldest as well as the youngest—is increasingly stable and more likely to include its full complement of surviving members.

CHANGING DYNAMICS OF CLOSE FAMILY RELATIONSHIPS

What, then, are the implications of this greatly expanded kinship structure for the dynamics of close family relationships? How does the matrix of latent kinship linkages provide for close ties between particular individual lives, as these lives weave in and out of the intricate and continually shifting kinship network? Under what conditions do some family members provide (or fail to provide) recognition, advice, esteem, love, and tension release for other family members?

The answer, it seems to me, lies in the enlarged kinship structure: It provides many new opportunities for people at different points in their lives to select and activate the relationships they deem most significant. That is, the options for close family bonds have multiplied. Over the century, increased longevity has given flexibility to the kinship structure, relaxing both the temporal and the spatial boundaries of optional relationships.

Temporally, new options have arisen over the course of people's lives because, as we have seen, particular relationships have become more enduring. Particular relationships (even following divorce) are bounded only by the birth and death of members. Now that the experience of losing family members by death is no longer a pervasive aspect of the full life course (and is in fact rare except in old age), people have greater opportunity to plan their family lives. They have time to make mutual adjustments to personal crises or to external threats such as unemployment or the fear of nuclear war. Here we are reminded of my first proposition: Family relationships are never fixed, but are continually in process and subject to change. As family members grow older, they move across time—across history and through their own lives—and they also move upward through the generations in their own families and the age strata of society.[3] As individual family members who each pursue a separate life course, thoughts and feelings for one another are developed; their lives weave together or apart so as to activate, intensify, disregard, or disrupt particular close relationships. Thus the relationship between a mother and daughter can, for example, become close in the daughter's early childhood, her first years of marriage, and again after her children have left home although there may be interim lapses. Or, as current norms permit, couples can try each other out through cohabitation, before deciding whether or not to embark upon marriage.

Just as such new options for close ties have emerged from the prolongation of family relationships, other options have arisen because the number and variety of latent linkages has multiplied across the entire kinship structure. Spatially, close relationships are not bounded by the nuclear households that family members share during their younger lives. Given the intricacy of current kin networks, a wide range of linkages can be activated—between grandchild and grandparent, between distantly related cousins, between the ex-husbands of sisters, or between a child and his or her new step-parent. (Only in Grimm's fairy tales, which reflected the earlier frequency of maternal deaths and successive remarriages, were step-mothers always "wicked.") Aided by modern communication and transportation, affection and interaction can persist even during long periods of separation. On occasion, long-separated relatives or those not closely related may arrange to live together or to join in congregate housing or communes.

Given these options, let me now state a second general proposition: As active agents in directing the course of their own lives, *individuals have a degree of control over their close family relationships.* This control, I submit, has been enhanced because longevity has widened the opportunities for selecting and activating relationships that can provide emotional support and advice when needed.

This part of my discussion suggests a new view of the family. Perhaps we need now to think of a family less as the members of one household with incidental linkages to kin in other households and more as a continuing interplay among intertwined lives within the entire changing kinship structure. The closeness of these intertwined lives and the mutual support they provide depend on many factors (including the predispositions of each individual and the continuing motivation to negotiate and renegotiate their joint lives) but the enlarged kinship structure provides the potential.

NEW APPROACHES TO FAMILY RESEARCH AND PRACTICE

Before considering how the oldest family members—those in the added generation—fit into these intertwined lives, let me pause to ask how we can approach these complex and changing family relationships. If the tidy concept of the nuclear family is no longer sufficient, how can we deal in research and in professional practice with the newly emerging concepts? Clearly, special approaches are required for mapping and understanding the centrifugal and centripetal processes of family relationships within the increasing complexity of the kinship matrix. Such approaches must not only take into account my first two propositions (that relationships continually change, and that family members themselves have some control over this change) but must also consider a third proposition: *The lives of family members are interdependent* such that each person's family life continually interacts with the lives of significant relatives. Though long-recognized by students of the family, this proposition takes on fresh significance in the matrix of prolonged relationships.

As case examples, I shall describe two or three studies that illustrate how we can deal with the family as a system of interdependent lives. These studies are also important as they add to our understanding of emotional support and socialization under current family conditions.

In one study of socialization outcomes, Mavis Hetherington et al. (1977) have shown how parental disruption through divorce has a complex impact on the still-intertwined lives of the spouses and on the socialization of their children. Over a two-year period, detailed investigations were made of nursery school boys and girls and their parents, half of whom were divorced and the other half married. Differences were detected: Divorced parents showed comparatively less affection for their children, had less control over them, and elicited more dependent, disobedient, and aggressive child behavior—particularly in mother-son interactions. But relations between the parents also made a difference in these parent-child relationships: If divorced couples kept conflict low and agreed about child rearing, their ineffectiveness in dealing with children could be somewhat offset. This two-year tracing of the three-way interrelationships among spouses and children in disrupted families yields many insights into the interdependence of life course processes.

As family relationships are prolonged, socialization is more frequently recognized as a reciprocal process that potentially extends throughout the lives of parents and children as well as of marital partners. How can socialization operate across generations that belong to differing periods of historical change? One key mechanism, as Marilyn Johnson (1976) has demonstrated, is normative expectations. Parents can influence offspring by expecting behavior that is appropriate to social change, and can in turn be guided by offspring in formulating these expectations. Such subtleties to intergenerational influence are illustrated in a small study which Johnson and I made of high school students in the early 1960s (see Riley, 1982). Just as women's careers were burgeoning, we found that most girls looked forward to combining a career with marriage, whereas most boys did not anticipate marrying wives who worked. How had these young people been socialized to such sharply conflicting norms? We questioned their mothers and fathers to find out. Indeed we learned that, on the whole, parents wanted self-fulfillment for their daughters both in marriage and in work outside the home, while for their sons they wanted wives who would devote themselves fully to home and children. These slight yet provocative findings did presage the future impact of the women's movement on family lives, but I note them here as another instance of research that fits together the differing perspectives of the several interdependent family members.

Analyzing such studies of close relationships impresses one with the problem of studying families from what is often called the "life course" or "lifespan perspective" (see Dannefer, forthcoming). We are indeed concerned with people moving through life. Yet we are concerned not with a single life or a statistical aggregate of lives, but with the dynamic family systems of interdependent lives. An example I often use in teaching comes from the early work of Cottrell and Burgess in predicting success or failure in marriage. Starting with a case study, Cottrell (1933) saw each partner in a marriage as reenacting his or her childhood roles. He showed how the outcome of the marriage depended upon the mesh between these two different sets of early-life experiences—that is, how nearly they would fit together so that each partner met the role expectations of the other. Unfortunately, however, these researchers subsequently departed from this admirable model by questioning large samples of men and women as individuals and then analyzing the data for separate aggregates of men and women rather than for male-female pairs. Each individual was given a score of likely success in marriage, but without considering the success of a marriage between a particular man and a particular woman! Because the interdependent lives were not examined jointly, the central objective of the project was lost.

This difficulty, which I now call "life-course reductionism," still persists. Although many studies purport to study families as systems, they in fact either aggregate individual lives (as Cottrell and Burgess did) or reason erroneously from the lives of single members about the lives of other family members significant to the relationship. The danger of not considering a key family member is highlighted, for example, in Frank Furstenberg's (1981) review of the literature on kinship relations after divorce. Some studies had suggested that divorce disrupts the relations with parents-in-law (that is, with the parents of the ex-spouse) but these studies failed to include the children of the broken marriage. Only after examining the children's generation was it learned that they, by retaining contact with both sets of their grandparents, could help to link divorced spouses to their former in-laws. Supporting this clue from a small study of his own, Furstenberg found that the ties between grandparents and grandchildren did continue to exist in most cases, even though for the divorced parents (the middle generation) the former in-law relationships were largely attenuated or broken. In reconstituted families, then, grandparents can perhaps serve as "kinkeepers."

Among the studies that pursue close relationships across three generations is a national survey of divorce and remarriage now being conducted by Frank Furstenberg, Andrew Cherlin, Nicholas Zill, and James Peterson. In this era of widespread divorce and remarriage, this study is examining the important hypothesis that new intergenerational ties created by remarriage will balance—or more than balance—

the losses incurred as a result of divorce. Step-relationships may replace disrupted natural relationships. The intricacy of interdependent lives within our proliferating kinship structure is dramatized by the design of this study. Starting with a sample of children aged 11 to 16 and their parents (who were originally interviewed five years earlier) the research team will now also question these children's grandparents; note that there can be two sets of grandparents where the parents are in intact first marriages or have been divorced, three sets if one parent has remarried after divorce, and four sets (no less than eight grandparents) if both have remarried. Thus, as surviving generations proliferate, their part in the family system will be explored in this study by questioning the many members of the grandparent generation. Surviving generations cannot be fully understood (as many studies of three generations have attempted) by examining a simple chain of single individuals from each of the generations.

These studies, as models for research, reflect the complex family relationships within which people of all ages today can seek or can give affection, encouragement, companionship, or advice.

OLDER GENERATIONS OF THE FUTURE

About the fourth generation (great-grandparents) that is being contributed by longevity, I want to make three final points.

First, it is too early to tell how an enlarged great-grandparent generation will fit into the kinship structure, or what close family relationships it may form. It is too early because the marked increase in longevity among the old began only in recent decades and are still continuing at a rate far exceeding earlier predictions (Preston, 1976; Manton, 1982; Brody and Brock, n.d.). Will this added generation be regarded as the more familiar generation of grandparents has been regarded—either as a threat to the young adult generation's independence, or as a "social problem" for family and community, requiring care from the mid-generation that is "squeezed" between caring for both young children and aging parents? Or will an added fourth generation mean new coalitions and new forms of personal relationships? And what of five-generation families in which a grandmother can be also a granddaughter (see Hagestad, 1981)? It is still too early to tell what new family norms will develop (see Riley, 1978).

Second, while we do not know how a fourth or even a fifth generation may fit in, we do know that most older family members are not dependent or disabled (some 5 percent of those 65 and over are in nursing homes). For those requiring care or instrumental support, families generally make extraordinary efforts to provide it (see Shanas, 1979). Yet most of the elderly, and especially those who are better educated and more active, are stronger, wiser, more competent, and more independent than is generally supposed. Public stereotypes of old people are far more negative than old people's assessments of themselves (National Council on the Aging, 1981). Healthy members of this generation, like their descendants, must earn their own places in the family and create their own personal ties. They cannot expect obligatory warmth or emotional support.

Third, at the close of their lives, however, old people will need advice and emotional support from kin. This need is not new in the annals of family history. What is new is the fact that terminal illness and death are no longer scattered across all generations but are concentrated in the oldest one. Today two-thirds of all deaths occur after age 65, and 30 percent after age 80 (Brody and Brock, n.d.). And, although most deaths occur outside the home, programs such as the hospice movement are being developed for care of the dying in the home where the family can take part (see J. W. Riley, forthcoming).

In conclusion, I have attempted to trace the impact of the unprecedented increases in longevity on the family and its relationships. In our own time the kinship structure has become more extensive and more complex, the temporal and spatial boundaries of the family have been altered, and the opportunities for close family relationships have proliferated. These relationships are no longer prescribed as strict obligations. They must rather be earned—created and recreated by family members throughout their long lives. Each of us is in continuing need of advice and emotional support from one another, as we contend with personal challenges and troubles, and with the compelling effects of societal changes in the economy, in technology, in culture, and in values. We all must agree with Mary Jo Bane (1976) that the family is here to stay, but in forms that we are beginning to comprehend only now. As members of families and students of the family—whether we are theorists, researchers, counselors, or policy makers—we must begin to realign our thinking and our practice to incorporate the new realities that are being engendered by increasing longevity.

NOTES

1. Note that increasing longevity in a society is not necessarily the same as increasing proportions of old people in the population, a proportion influenced in the long-term more by fertility than by mortality. Longevity affects individual lives and family structures, while population composition affects the total society.
2. Gunhild Hagestad (1982) talks even of menopausal grandmothers with pubescent granddaughters.
3. Of course, divisions between generations are only loosely coterminous with age divisions (see the discussion of the difference between "generations" and "cohorts" in the classic piece by Duncan, 1966, and a definitive formulation of this distinction in Kertzer, forthcoming). As Gunhild Hagestad (1981) puts it, "people do not file into generations by cohorts." There are wide ranges in the ages at which particular individuals marry and have children. In addition to the recognized differences by sex, there are important differences by social class. For example, Graham Spanier (Spanier and Glick, 1980) shows how the later marriage age in upper as compared with lower socioeconomic classes postpones many subsequent events in the lives of family members, thus slowing the proliferation in numbers of surviving generations.

REFERENCES

Bane, M. J. 1976. Here to Stay: American Families in the 20th Century. New York: Basic Books.

Brody, J. A., and D. B. Brock. n.d. "Epidemiologic and statistical characteristics of the United States elderly population." (unpublished)

Cherlin, A. J. 1981. Marriage, Divorce, Remarriage. Cambridge, MA: Harvard University Press.

Cottrell, L. S., Jr. 1933. "Roles and marital adjustment." American Sociological Society 27: 107–115.

Dannefer, D. Forthcoming. "The sociology of the life course." Annual Review of Sociology.

DeLongis, A., J. C. Coyne, G. Dakof, S. Folkman, and R. S. Lazarus. 1982. "Relationship of daily hassles, uplifts, and major life events to health status." Health Psychology 1: 119–136.

Duncan, O. D. 1966. "Methodological issues in the analysis of social mobility," pp. 51–97 in N. J. Smelser and S. M. Lipsett (eds.), Social Structure and Mobility in Economic Development. Chicago, IL: Aldine.

Furstenberg, F. F., Jr. 1981. "Remarriage and intergenerational relations," pp. 115–142 in R. W. Fogel et al. (eds.), Aging: Stability and Change in the Family. New York: Academic Press.

Glick, P. C., and A. J. Norton. 1977. "Marrying, divorcing, and living together in the U.S. today." Population Bulletin 32. Washington, D.C. Population Reference Bureau.

Goffman, E. 1959. The Presentation of Self in Everyday Life. Garden City, NY: Doubleday.

Hagestad, G. O. 1982. "Older women in intergenerational relations." Presented at the Physical and Mental Health of Aged Women Conference, October 21–22, Case Western University, Cleveland, OH.

——————. 1981. "Problems and promises in the social psychology of intergenerational relations," pp. 11–46 in R. W. Fogel et al. (eds.), Aging: Stability and Change in the Family. New York: Academic Press.

Hetherington, E. M., M. Cox, and R. Cox. 1977. "The aftermath of divorce," in J. H. Stevens, Jr. and M. Matthews (eds.), Mother-Child, Father-Child Relations, Washington, D.C.: National Association for the Education of Young Children.

Imhof, A. E. 1982. "Life course patterns of women and their husbands—16th to 20th century." Presented at the International Conference on Life Course Research on Human Development, September 17, Berlin, Germany.

Johnson, M. 1976. "The role of perceived parental models, expectations and socializing behaviors in the self-expectations of adolescents, from the U.S. and West Germany." Dissertation, Rutgers University.

Kelley, H. H. 1981. "Marriage relationships and aging," pp. 275–300 in R. W. Fogel et al. (eds.), Aging: Stability and Change in the Family. New York: Academic Press.

Kertzer, D. I. Forthcoming. "Generations as a sociological problem." Annual Review of Sociology.

Manton, K. G. 1982. "Changing concepts of morbidity and mortality in the elderly population." Milbank Memorial Fund Q. 60: 183–244.

National Council on the Aging. 1981. Aging in the Eighties: America in Transition. Washington, D.C.: Author.

Parsons, T., and R. F. Bales. 1955. Family, Socialization and Interaction Process. New York: Free Press.

Preston, S. H. 1976. Mortality Patterns in National Population: With Special References to Recorded Causes of Death. New York: Academic Press.

Riley, J. W., Jr. Forthcoming. "Dying and the meanings of death: sociological inquiries." Annual Review of Sociology.

Riley, M. W. 1976. "Age strata in social systems," pp. 189–217 in R. H. Binstock and E. Shanas (eds.), Handbook of Aging and the Social Sciences. New York: Van Nostrand Reinhold.

——————. 1978. "Aging, social change, and the power of ideas." Daedalus 107, 4: 39–52.

——————. 1982. "Implications for the middle and later years," pp. 399–405 in P. W. Berman and E. R. Ramey (eds.), Women: A Development Perspective NIH Publication No. 82-2298. Washington, DC: Dept. of Health and Human Services.

——————. Forthcoming. "Age strata in social systems," in R. H. Binstock and E. Shanas (eds.), The New Handbook of Aging and the Social Sciences.

Rossi, A. S. 1980. "Aging and parenthood in the middle years," in P. B. Baltes and O. G. Brim, Jr. (eds.), Life-Span Development and Behavior 3. New York: Academic Press.

Shanas, E. 1979. "Social myth as hypothesis: the case of the family relations of old people." The Gerontologist 19: 3–9.

Spanier, G. B., and P. C. Glick. 1980. "The life cycle of American families: an expanded analysis." J. of Family History: 97–111.

Torrey, B. B. 1982. "The lengthening of retirement," pp. 181–196 in M. W. Riley et al. (eds.), Aging from Birth to Death, vol. II: Sociotemporal Perspectives, Boulder, CO: Westview.

Turner, R. H. 1970. Family Interaction. New York: John Wiley.

Uhlenberg, P. R. 1969. "A study of cohort life cycles: cohorts of native born Massachusetts women. 1830–1920." Population Studies 23, 3: 407–420.

——————. 1980. "Death and the family." J. of Family History (Fall): 313–320.

Chapter
11

The Cultural Politics of Family Life

Reading 36

Motherhood and Morality in America

Kristin Luker

According to interested observers at the time, abortion in America was as frequent in the last century as it is in our own. And the last century, as we have seen, had its own "right-to-life" movement, composed primarily of physicians who pursued the issue in the service of their own professional goals. When abortion reemerged as an issue in the late 1950s, it still remained in large part a restricted debate among interested professionals. But abortion as we now know it has little in common with these earlier rounds of the debate. Instead of the civility and colleagueship that characterized the earlier phases of the debate, the present round of the abortion debate is marked by rancor and intransigence. Instead of the elite male professionals who commanded the issue until recently, ordinary people—and more to the point, ordinary women—have come to predominate in the ranks of those con-

From *Abortion and the Politics of Motherhood* by Kristin Luker, pp. 192–215. © 1984 The Regents of the University of California. Reprinted by permission of the University of California Press. Some text has been omitted.

cerned. From a quiet, restricted technical debate among concerned professionals, abortion has become a debate that seems at times capable of tearing the fabric of American life apart. How did this happen? What accounts for the remarkable transformation of the abortion debate?

The history of the debate, as examined in previous chapters in this book, provides some preliminary answers. Technological advances in obstetrics led to a decline in those abortions undertaken strictly to preserve the life of the woman, using the narrowly biological sense of the word *life*. These technological advances, in turn, permitted (and indeed forced) physicians over time to make more and more nuanced decisions about abortion and eventually brought to the fore the underlying philosophical issue that had been obscured by a century of medical control over abortion: is the embryo a person or only a potential person? . . . [O]nce this question is confronted directly, a unified world view—a set of assumptions about how the world is and ought to be organized—is called into play. . . . [W]orld views are usually the product of values so deeply held and dearly cherished that an assault upon them is a deeply disturbing assault indeed. Thus to summarize the argument of this book up to this point, the abortion debate has been transformed because it has "gone public" and in so doing has called into question individuals' most sacrosanct beliefs.

But this is only part of the story. This article will argue that all the previous rounds of the abortion debate in America were merely echoes of the issue as the nineteenth century defined it: a debate about the medical profession's right to make life-and-death decisions. In contrast, the most recent round of the debate is about something new. By bringing the issue of the moral status of the embryo to the fore, the new round focuses on the relative rights of women and embryos. Consequently, the abortion debate has become a debate about women's contrasting obligations to themselves and others. New technologies and the changing nature of work have opened up possibilities for women outside of the home undreamed of in the nineteenth century; together, these changes give women—for the first time in history—the option of deciding exactly how and when their family roles will fit into the larger context of their lives. In essence, therefore, this round of the abortion debate is so passionate and hard-fought *because it is a referendum on the place and meaning of motherhood.*

Motherhood is at issue because two opposing visions of motherhood are at war. Championed by "feminists" and "housewives," these two different views of motherhood represent in turn two very different kinds of social worlds. The abortion debate has become a debate among women, women with different values in the social world, different experiences of it, and different resources with which to cope with it. How the issue is framed, how people think about it, and, most importantly, where the passions come from are all related to the fact that the battlelines are increasingly drawn (and defended) by women. While on the surface it is the embryo's fate that seems to be at stake, the abortion debate is actually about the meanings of *women's* lives.

To be sure, both the pro-life and the pro-choice movements had earlier phases in which they were dominated by male professionals. Some of these men are still active in the debate, and it is certainly the case that some men continue to join the debate on both sides of the issue. But the data in this study suggest that by 1974 over 80 percent of the activists in both the pro-choice and the pro-life movements in California were women, and a national survey of abortion activists found similar results.

Moreover, in our interviews we routinely asked both male and female activists on both sides of the issue to supply information on several "social background variables," such as where they were born, the extent of their education, their income level, the number of children they had, and their occupations. When male activists on the two sides are compared on these variables, they are virtually indistinguishable from one another. But when female activists are compared, it is dramatically clear that for the women who have come to dominate the ranks of the movement, the abortion debate is a conflict between two different social worlds and the hopes and beliefs those worlds support.

WHO ARE THE ACTIVISTS?

On almost every social background variable we examined, pro-life and pro-choice women differed dramatically. For example, in terms of income, almost half of all pro-life women (44 percent) in this study reported an income of less than $20,000 a year, but only one-fourth of the pro-choice women reported an income that low, and a considerable portion of those were young women just starting their careers. On the upper end of the income scale, one-third of the pro-choice women reported an income of $50,000 a year or more compared with only one pro-life woman in every seven.

These simple figures on income, however, conceal a very complex social reality, and that social reality is in turn tied to feelings about abortion. The higher incomes of pro-choice women, for example, result from a number of interesting factors. Almost without exception pro-choice women work in the paid labor force, they earn good salaries when they work, and if they are married, they are likely to be married to men who also have good incomes. An astounding 94 percent of all pro-choice women work, and over half of them have incomes in the top 10 percent of all working women in this country. Moreover, one pro-choice woman in ten has an annual *personal* income (as opposed to a family income) of $30,000 or more, thus putting her in the rarified ranks of the top 2 percent of all employed women in America. Pro-life women, by contrast, are far less likely to work: 63 percent of them do not work in the paid labor force, and almost all of those who do are unmarried. Among pro-life married women, for example, only 14 percent report any personal income at all, and for most of them, this is earned not in a formal job but through activities such as selling cosmetics to groups of friends. Not surprisingly, the personal income of pro-life women who work outside the home, whether in a formal job or in one of these less-structured activities, is low. Half of all pro-life women who do work earn less than $5,000 a year, and half earn between $5,000 and $10,000. Only two pro-life women we contacted reported a personal income of more than $20,000. Thus pro-life women are less likely to work in the first place, they earn less money when they do work, and they are more likely to be married to a skilled worker or small businessman who earns only a moderate income.

These differences in income are in turn related to the different educational and occupational choices these women have made along the way. Among pro-choice women, almost four out of ten (37 percent) had undertaken some graduate work beyond the B.A. degree, and 18 percent had an M.D., a law degree, a Ph.D., or a similar postgraduate degree. Pro-life women, by comparison, had far less education: 10 percent of them had only a high school education or less; and another 30 percent never finished college (in contrast with only 8 percent of the pro-choice women). Only 6 percent of all pro-life women had a law degree, a Ph.D., or a medical degree.

These educational differences were in turn related to occupational differences among the women in this study. Because of their higher levels of education, pro-choice women tended to be employed in the major professions, as administrators, owners of small businesses, or executives in large businesses. The pro-life women tended to be housewives or, of the few who worked, to be in the traditional female jobs of teaching, social work, and nursing. (The choice of home life over public life held true for even the 6 percent of pro-life women with an advanced degree; of the married women who had such degrees, at the time of our interviews only one of them had not retired from her profession after marriage.)

These economic and social differences were also tied to choices that women on each side had made about marriage and family life. For example, 23 percent of pro-choice women had never married, compared with only 16 percent of pro-life women; 14 percent of pro-choice women had been divorced, compared with 5 percent of pro-life women. The size of the families these women had was also different. The average pro-choice family had between one and two children and was more likely to have one; pro-life families averaged between two and three children and were more likely to have three. (Among the pro-life women, 23 percent had five or more children; 16 percent had seven or more children.) Pro-life women also tended to marry at a slightly younger age and to have had their first child earlier.

Finally, the women on each side differed dramatically in their religious affiliation and in the role that religion played in their lives. Almost 80 percent of the women active in the pro-life movement at the present time are Catholics. The remainder are Protestants (9 percent), persons who claim no religion (5 percent), and Jews (1 percent). In sharp contrast, 63 percent of pro-choice women say that they have no religion, 22 percent think of themselves as vaguely Protestant, 3 percent are Jewish, and 9 percent have what they call a "personal" religion. We found no one in our sample of pro-choice activists who claimed to be a Catholic at the time of the interviews.

When we asked activists what religion they were raised in as a child, however, a different picture emerged. For example, 20 percent of the pro-choice activists were raised as Catholics, 42 percent were raised as Protestants, and 15 percent were raised in the Jewish faith. In this group that describes itself predominantly without religious affiliation, therefore, only 14 percent say they were not brought up in any formal religious faith. By the same token, although almost 80 percent of present pro-life activists are Catholic, only 58 percent were raised in that religion (15 percent were raised as Protestants and 3 percent as Jews). Thus, almost 20 percent of the pro-life activists in this study are converts to Catholicism, people who have actively chosen to follow a given religious faith, in striking contrast to pro-choice people, who have actively chosen not to follow any.

Perhaps the single most dramatic difference between the two groups, however, is in the role that religion plays in their lives. Almost three-quarters of the pro-choice people interviewed said that formal religion was either unimportant or completely irrelevant to them, and their attitudes are correlated with behavior: only 25 percent of the pro-choice women said they *ever* attend church, and most of these said they do so only occasionally. Among pro-life people, by contrast, 69 percent said religion was important in their lives, and an additional 22 percent said that it was very important. For pro-life women, too, these attitudes are correlated with behavior: half of those pro-life women interviewed said they attend church regularly once a week, and another 13 percent said they do so even more often. Whereas 80 percent of pro-choice people never attend church, only 2 percent of pro-life advocates never do so.

Keeping in mind that the statistical use of averages has inherent difficulties, we ask, who are the "average" pro-choice and pro-life advocates? When the social background data are looked at carefully, two profiles emerge. The average pro-choice activist is a forty-four-year-old married woman who grew up in a large metropolitan area and whose father was a college graduate. She was married at age twenty-two, has one or two children, and has had some graduate or professional training beyond the B.A. degree. She is married to a professional man, is herself employed in a regular job, and her family income is more than $50,000 a year. She is not religiously active, feels that religion is not important to her, and attends church very rarely if at all.

The average pro-life woman is also a forty-four-year-old married woman who grew up in a large metropolitan area. She married at age seventeen and has three children or more. Her father was a high school graduate, and she has some college education or may have a B.A. degree. She is not employed in the paid labor force and is married to a small businessman or a lower-level white-collar worker; her family income is $30,000 a year. She is Catholic (and may have converted), and her religion is one of the most important aspects of her life: she attends church at least once a week and occasionally more often.

INTERESTS AND PASSIONS

To the social scientist (and perhaps to most of us) these social background characteristics connote lifestyles as well. We intuitively clothe these bare statistics with assumptions about beliefs and values. When we do so, the pro-choice women emerge as educated, affluent, liberal professionals, whose lack of religious affiliation suggests a secular, "modern," or (as pro-life people would have it) "utilitarian" outlook on life. Similarly, the income, education, marital patterns, and religious devotion of pro-life women suggest that they are traditional, hard-working people ("polyester types" to their opponents), who hold conservative views of life. We may be entitled to assume that individuals' social backgrounds act to shape and mold their social attitudes, but it is important to realize that the relationship between social worlds and social values is a very complex one.

Perhaps one example will serve to illustrate the point. A number of pro-life women in this study emphatically rejected an expression that pro-choice women tend to use almost unthinkingly—the expression *unwanted pregnancy*. Pro-life women argued forcefully that a better term would be a *surprise* pregnancy, asserting that although a pregnancy may be momentarily unwanted, the child that results from the pregnancy almost never is. Even such a simple thing—what to call an unanticipated pregnancy—calls into play an individual's values and resources. Keeping in mind our profile of the average pro-life person, it is obvious that a woman who does not work in the paid labor force, who does not have a college degree, whose religion is important to her, and who has already committed herself wholeheartedly to marriage and a large family is well equipped to believe that an unanticipated pregnancy usually becomes a beloved child. Her life is arranged so that for her, this belief is true. This view is consistent not only with her values, which she has held from earliest childhood, but with her social resources as well. It should not be surprising, therefore, that her world view leads her to believe that everyone else can "make room for one more" as easily as she can and that therefore it supports her in her conviction that abortion is cruel, wicked, and self-indulgent.°

It is almost certainly the case that an unplanned pregnancy is never an easy thing for anyone. Keeping in mind the profile of the average pro-choice woman, however, it is evident that a woman who is employed full time, who has an affluent lifestyle that depends in part of her contribution to the family income, and who expects to give a child as good a life as she herself has had with respect to educational, social, and economic advantages will draw on a different reality when she finds herself being skeptical about the ability of the average person to transform unwanted pregnancies into well-loved (and well-cared-for) children.

The relationship between passions and interests is thus more dynamic than it might appear at first. It is true that at one level, pro-choice and pro-life attitudes on abortion are self-serving: activists on each side have different views of the morality of abortion because their chosen lifestyles leave them with different needs for abortion; and both sides have values that provide a moral basis for their abortion needs in particular and their lifestyles in general. But this is only half the story. The

---

°As might be imagined, it is not an easy task to ask people who are anti-abortion activists about their own experiences with a certain kind of unanticipated pregnancy, namely, a premarital pregnancy. Most pro-choice people were quite often open about having had such pregnancies; their pregnancies—and subsequent abortions—were central to their feelings about abortion. Pro-life women, by contrast, were deeply reluctant to discuss the topic. Several of them, after acknowledging premarital pregnancies, said that they did not want people to think that their attitudes on abortion were merely a product of their personal experiences. Thus we have no comparative figures about the extent to which the values represented here are the product of different experiences or just different opinions. We know only that unanticipated pregnancy was common among pro-choice women, and the interviews suggest that it was not uncommon among pro-life women. The difference in experience is, of course, that those in the first group sought abortions and those in the second group, with only a few exceptions, legitimized their pregnancies with a marriage.

values that lead pro-life and pro-choice women into different attitudes toward abortion are the same values that led them at an earlier time to adopt different lifestyles that supported a given view of abortion.

For example, pro-life women have *always* valued family roles very highly and have arranged their lives accordingly. They did not acquire high-level educational and occupational skills, for example, because they married, and they married because their values suggested that this would be the most satisfying life open to them. Similarly, pro-choice women postponed (or avoided) marriage and family roles because they chose to acquire the skills they needed to be successful in the larger world, having concluded that the role of wife and mother was too limited for them. Thus, activists on both sides of the issue are women who have a given set of values about what are the most satisfying and appropriate roles for women, and they have made *life commitments that now limit their ability to change their minds.* Women who have many children and little education, for example, are seriously handicapped in attempting to become doctors or lawyers; women who have reached their late forties with few children or none are limited in their ability to build (or rebuild) a family. For most of these activists, therefore, their position on abortion is the "tip of the iceberg," a shorthand way of supporting and proclaiming not only a complex set of values but a given set of social resources as well.

To put the matter differently, we might say that for pro-life women the traditional division of life into separate male roles and female roles still works, but for pro-choice women it does not. Having made a commitment to the traditional female roles of wife, mother, and homemaker, pro-life women are limited in those kinds of resources—education, class status, recent occupational experiences—they would need to compete in what has traditionally been the male sphere, namely, the paid labor force. The average pro-choice woman, in contrast, is comparatively well endowed with exactly these resources; she is highly educated, she already has a job, and she has recent (and continuous) experience in the job market.

In consequence, anything that supports a traditional division of labor into male and female worlds is, broadly speaking, in the interests of pro-life women because that is where their resources lie. Conversely, such a traditional division of labor, when strictly enforced, is against the interests of pro-choice women because it limits their abilities to use the valuable "male" resources that they have in relative abundance. It is therefore apparent that attitudes toward abortion, even though rooted in childhood experiences, are also intimately related to present-day interests. Women who oppose abortion and seek to make it officially unavailable are declaring, both practically and symbolically, that women's reproductive roles should be given social primacy. Once an embryo is defined as a child and an abortion as the death of a person, almost everything else in a woman's life must "go on hold" during the course of her pregnancy: any attempt to gain "male" resources such as a job, an education, or other skills must be subordinated to her uniquely female responsibility of serving the needs of this newly conceived person. Thus, when personhood is bestowed on the embryo, women's nonreproductive roles are made secondary to their reproductive roles. The act of conception therefore creates a pregnant woman rather than a woman who is pregnant; it creates a woman whose life, in cases where roles or values clash, is defined by the fact that she is—or may become—pregnant.

It is obvious that this view is supportive of women who have already decided that their familial and reproductive roles are the major ones in their lives. By the same token, the costs of defining women's reproductive roles as primary do not seem high to them because they have already chosen to make those roles primary anyway. For example, employers might choose to discriminate against women because they might require maternity leave and thus be unavailable at critical times, but women who have chosen not to work in the paid labor force in the first place can see such discrimination as irrelevant to them.

It is equally obvious that supporting abortion (and believing that the embryo is not a person) is in the vested interests of pro-choice women. Being so well equipped to compete in the male sphere, they perceive any situation that both practically and symbolically affirms the primacy of women's reproductive roles as a real loss to them. Practically, it devalues their social resources. If women are only secondarily in the labor market and must subordinate working to pregnancy, should it occur, then their education, occupation, income and work become potentially temporary and hence discounted. Working becomes, as it traditionally was perceived to be, a pastime or hobby pursued for "pin money" rather than a central part of their lives. Similarly, if the embryo is defined as a person and the ability to become pregnant is the central one for women, a woman must be prepared to sacrifice some of her own interests to the interests of this newly conceived person.

In short, in a world where men and women have traditionally had different roles to play and where male roles have traditionally been the more socially prestigious and financially rewarded, abortion has become a symbolic marker between those who wish to maintain this division of labor and those who wish to challenge it. Thus, on an intimate level, the pro-life movement is women's version of what was true of peasants in the Vendeé, the part of France that remained Royalist during the French Revolution. Charles Tilly has argued that in the Vendeé, traditional relationships between nobles and peasants were still mutually satisfying so that the "brave new world" of the French Revolution represented more loss than gain, and the peasants therefore resisted the changes the Revolution heralded. By the same logic, traditional relationships between men and women are still satisfying, rewarding, and meaningful for pro-life women, and they therefore resist the lure of "liberation." For pro-choice women, however, with their access to male resources, a division of labor into the public world of work and the private world of home and hearth seems to promise only restriction to "second-class" citizenship.

Thus, the sides are fundamentally opposed to each other not only on the issue of abortion but also on what abortion *means*. Women who have many "human capital" resources of the traditionally male variety want to see motherhood recognized as a private, discretionary choice. Women who have few of these resources and limited opportunities in the job market want to see motherhood recognized as the most important thing a woman can do. In order for pro-choice women to achieve their goals, therefore, they *must* argue that motherhood is not a primary, inevitable, or "natural" role for all women; for pro-life women to achieve their goals, they *must* argue that it is. In short, the debate rests on the question of whether women's fertility is to be socially recognized as a resource or as a handicap.

To the extent that women who have chosen the larger public world of work have been successful, both legally and in terms of public opinion and, furthermore, are rapidly becoming the numerical majority, pro-life women are put on the defensive. Several pro-life women offered poignant examples of how the world deals with housewives who do not have an official payroll title. Here is what one of them said:

> I was at a party, about two years ago—it still sticks in my mind, you see, because I'm a housewife and I don't work—and I met this girl from England and we got involved in a deep discussion about the English and the Americans and their philosophies and how one has influenced the other, and at the end of the conversation—she was a working gal herself. I forget what she did—and she says, "Where do you work?" and I said, "I don't." And she looked at me and said, "You don't work?" I said "No." She said, "You're just a housewife . . . and you can still think like that?" She couldn't believe it, and she sort of gave me a funny look and that was the end of the conversation for the evening. And I've met other people who've had similar experiences. [People seem to think that if] you're at home and you're involved with children all day, your intelligence quotient must be down with them on the floor someplace, and [that] you really don't do much thinking or get yourself involved.

Moreover, there are subtle indications that even the pro-life activists we interviewed had internalized their loss of status as housewives. Only a handful of married pro-life activists also worked at regular jobs outside the home; but fully half of those who were now fulltime homemakers, some for as long as thirty years, referred to themselves in terms of the work they had given up when they married or had their first child: "I'm a political scientist," "I'm a social worker," "I'm an accountant." It is noteworthy that no one used the past tense as in "I used to be a social worker"; every nonemployed married woman who used her former professional identification used it in the present tense. Since this pattern was not noticed during the interviewing, what the women themselves had in mind must remain speculative. But it does not seem unreasonable to imagine that this identification is an unconscious bow to the fact that "just plain" individuals, and in particular "just plain housewives," lack the status and credibility of professionals. Ironically, by calling on earlier identifications these women may have been expressing a pervasive cultural value that they oppose as a matter of ideology. They seemed to believe that when it comes to making public statements—or at least public statements to an interviewer who has come to ask you about your activities in the abortion debate—*what* you are counts more than *who* you are.

Because of their commitment to their own view of motherhood as a primary social role, pro-life women believe that other women are "casual" about abortions and have them "for convenience." There are no reliable data to confirm whether or not women are "casual" about abortions, but many pro-life people believe this to be the case and relate their activism to their perception of other people's casualness. For example:

> Every time I saw some article [on abortion] I read about it, and I had another friend who had her second abortion in 1977 . . . and both of her abortions were a matter of convenience, it was inconvenient for her to be pregnant at that time. When I talked to her I said, "O.K., you're married now, your husband has a good job, you want to have

children eventually, but if you became pregnant now, you'd have an abortion. Why?" "Because it's inconvenient, this is not when I want to have my child." And that bothered me a lot because she is also very intelligent, graduated magna cum laude, and knew nothing about fetal development.

The assertion that women are "casual" about abortion, one could argue, expresses in a short-hand way a set of beliefs about women and their roles. First, the more people value the personhood of the embryo, the more important must be the reasons for taking its life. Some pro-life people, for example, would accept an abortion when continuation of the pregnancy would cause the death of the mother; they believe that when two lives are in direct conflict, the embryo's life can be considered the more expendable. But not all pro-life people agree, and many say they would not accept abortion even to save the mother's life. (Still others say they accept the idea in principle but would not make that choice in their own lives if faced with it.) For people who accept the personhood of the embryo, any reason besides trading a "life for a life" (and sometimes even that) seems trivial, merely a matter of "convenience."

Second, people who accept the personhood of the embryo see the reasons that pro-abortion people give for ending pregnancy as simultaneously downgrading the value of the embryo and upgrading everything else but pregnancy. The argument that women need abortion to "control" their fertility means that they intend to subordinate pregnancy, with its inherent unpredictability, to something else. As the pro-choice activists . . . have told us, that something else is participation in the paid labor force. Abortion permits women to engage in paid work on an equal basis with men. With abortion, they may schedule pregnancy in order to take advantage of the kinds of benefits that come with a paid position in the labor force: a paycheck, a title, a social identity. The pro-life women in this study were often careful to point out that they did not object to "career women." But what they meant by "career women" were women whose *only* responsibilities were in the labor force. Once a woman became a wife and a mother, in their view her primary responsibility was to her home and family.

Third, the pro-life activists we interviewed, the overwhelming majority of whom are full-time homemakers, also felt that women who worked *and* had families could often do so only because women like themselves picked up the slack. Given their place in the social structure, it is not surprising that many of the pro-life women thought that married women who worked outside the home were "selfish"—that they got all the benefits while the homemakers carried the load for them in Boy and Girl Scouts, PTA, and after school, for which their reward was to be treated by the workers as less competent and less interesting persons.°

Abortion therefore strips the veil of sanctity from motherhood. When pregnancy is discretionary—when people are allowed to put anything else they value in

°In fact, pro-life women, especially those recruited after 1972, were *less* likely to be engaged in formal activities such as Scouts, church activities, and PTA than their pro-choice peers. Quite possibly they have in mind more informal kinds of activities, premised on the fact that since they do not work, they are home most of the time.

front of it—then motherhood has been demoted from a sacred calling to a job.° In effect, the legalization of abortion serves to make men and women more "unisex" by deemphasizing what makes them different—the ability of women to visibly and directly carry the next generation. Thus, pro-choice women are emphatic about their right to compete equally with men without the burden of an unplanned pregnancy, and pro-life women are equally emphatic about their belief that men and women have different roles in life and that pregnancy is a gift instead of a burden.

The pro-life activists we interviewed do not want equality with men in the sense of having exactly the same rights and responsibilities as men do, although they do want equality of status. In fact, to the extent that *all* women have been touched by the women's movement and have become aware of the fact that society often treats women as a class as less capable than men, quite a few said they appreciated the Equal Rights Amendment (ERA), except for its implied stand on abortion. The ERA, in their view, reminded them that women are as valuable *in their own sphere* as men are in theirs. However, to the extent that the ERA was seen as downplaying the differences between men and women, to devalue the female sphere of the home in the face of the male sphere of paid work, others saw it as both demeaning and oppressive to women like themselves. As one of the few married employed pro-life women argued:

> I oppose it [the ERA]. Because I've gotten where I am without it. I don't think I need it. I think a woman should be hired on her merits, not on her sex or race. I don't think we should be hiring on sex or on race. I think we should be taking the competent people that are capable of doing the job. . . . I don't think women should be taking jobs from the breadwinner, you know. I still think that our society should be male . . . the male should be the primary breadwinner. For example, my own husband cannot hope for promotion because he is white and Anglo, you know, I mean white male. He's not going to get a promotion. If he could get the promotion that others of different minorities have gotten over him, I probably wouldn't have to work at all. So from my own point of view, purely selfishly, I think we've got to consider it. On the other hand, if I'm doing the same job [as a man], I expect to get the same pay. But I've always gotten it. So I really don't think that's an issue. I see the ERA as causing us more problems than it's going to [solve]. . . . As I see it, we were on a pedestal, why should we go down to being equal? That's my feeling on the subject.

It is stating the obvious to point out that the more limited the educational credentials a woman has, the more limited the job opportunities are for her, and the more limited the job opportunities, the more attractive motherhood is as full-time occupation. In motherhood, one can control the content and pace of one's own work, and the job is *intrinsically meaningful.* Compared with a job clerking in a supermarket (a realistic alternative for women with limited educational credentials) where the work is poorly compensated and often demeaning, motherhood can have compensations that far transcend the monetary ones. As one woman de-

---

°The same might be said of all sacred callings—stripped of its layer of the sacred, for example, the job of the clergy is demanding, low status, and underpaid.

scribed mothering: "You have this little, rough uncut diamond, and you're the artist shaping and cutting that diamond, and bringing out the lights . . . that's a great challenge."

All the circumstances of her existence will therefore encourage a pro-life woman to highlight the kinds of values and experiences that support childbearing and childrearing and to discount the attraction (such as it is) of paid employment. Her circumstances encourage her to resent the pro-choice view that women's most meaningful and prestigious activities are in the "man's world."

Abortion also has a symbolic dimension that separates the needs and interests of homemakers and workers in the paid labor force. Insofar as abortion allows a woman to get a job, to get training for a job, or to advance in a job, it does more than provide social support for working women over homemakers; it also seems to support the value of economic considerations over moral ones. Many pro-life people interviewed said that although their commitment to traditional family roles meant very real material deprivations to themselves and their families, the more benefits of such a choice more than made up for it.

> My girls babysit and the boys garden and have paper routes and things like that. I say that if we had a lot of money that would still be my philosophy, though I don't know because we haven't been in that position. But it's a sacrifice to have a larger family. So when I hear these figures that it takes $65,000 from birth to [raise a child], I think that's ridiculous. That's a new bike every year. That's private colleges. That's a complete new outfit when school opens. Well, we've got seven daughters who wear hand-me downs, and we hope that sometime in their eighteen years at home each one has a new bike somewhere along the line, but otherwise it's hand-me-downs. Those figures are inflated to give those children everything, and I think that's not good for them.

For pro-life people, a world view that puts the economic before the noneconomic hopelessly confuses two different kinds of worlds. For them, the private world of family as traditionally experienced is the one place in human society where none of us has a price tag. Home, as Robert Frost pointed out, is where they have to take you in, whatever your social worth. Whether one is a surgeon or a rag picker, the family is, at least ideally, the place where love is unconditional.

Pro-life people and pro-life women in particular have very real reasons to fear such a state of affairs. Not only do they see an achievement-based world as harsh, superficial, and ultimately ruthless; they are relatively less well-equipped to operate in that world. A considerable amount of social science research has suggested, at least in the realm of medical treatment, that there is an increasing tendency to judge people by their official (achieved) worth. Pro-life people have relatively fewer official achievements in part because they have been doing what they see as a moral task, namely, raising children and making a home; and they see themselves as becoming handicapped in a world that discounts not only their social contributions but their personal lives as well.

It is relevant in this context to recall the grounds on which pro-life people argue that the embryo is a baby: that it is genetically human. To insist that the embryo is a baby because it is genetically human is to make a claim that it is both wrong and impossible to make distinctions between humans at all. Protecting the life of the embryo, which is by definition an entity whose social worth is all yet to come, means protecting others who feel that they may be defined as having low social worth; more broadly, it means protecting a legal view of personhood that emphatically rejects social worth criteria.

For the majority of pro-life people we interviewed, the abortions they found most offensive were those of "damaged" embryos. This is because this category so clearly highlights the aforementioned concerns about social worth. To defend a genetically or congenitally damaged embryo from abortion is, in their minds, defending the weakest of the weak, and most pro-life people we interviewed were least prepared to compromise on this category of abortion.

The genetic basis for the embryo's claim to personhood has another, more subtle implication for those on the pro-life side. If genetic humanness equals personhood, then biological facts of life must take precedence over social facts of life. One's destiny is therefore inborn and hence immutable. To give any ground on the embryo's biologically determined babyness, therefore, would by extension call into question the "innate," "natural," and biological basis of women's traditional roles as well.

Pro-choice people, of course, hold a very different view of the matter. For them, social considerations outweigh biological ones: the embryo becomes a baby when it is "viable," that is, capable of achieving a certain degree of social integration with others. This is a world view premised on achievement, but not in the way pro-life people experience the world. Pro-choice people, believing as they do in choice, planning, and human efficacy, believe that biology is simply a minor given to be transcended by human experience. Sex, like race and age, is not an appropriate criterion for sorting people into different rights and responsibilities. Pro-choice people downplay these "natural" ascriptive characteristics, believing that true equality means achievement based on talent, not being restricted to a "women's world," a "black world," or an "old people's world." Such a view, as the profile of pro-choice people has made clear, is entirely consistent with their own lives and achievements.

These differences in social circumstances that separate pro-life from pro-choice women on the core issue of abortion also lead them to have different values on topics that surround abortion, such as sexuality and the use of contraception. With respect to sexuality, for example, the two sides have diametrically opposed values; these values arise from a fundamentally different premise, which is, in turn, tied to the different realities of their social worlds. If pro-choice women have a vested interest in subordinating their reproductive capacities, and pro-life women have a vested interest in highlighting them, we should not be surprised to find that pro-life women believe that the purpose of sex is reproduction whereas pro-choice women believe that its purpose is to promote intimacy and mutual pleasure.

These two views about sex express the same value differences that lead the two sides to have such different views on abortion. If women plan to find their primary role in marriage and the family, then they face a need to create a "moral cartel" when it comes to sex. If sex is freely available outside of marriage, then why should men, as the old saw puts it, buy the cow when the milk is free? If many women are willing to sleep with men outside of marriage, then the regular sexual activity that comes with marriage is much less valuable an incentive to marry. And because pro-life women are traditional women, their primary resource for marriage is the promise of a stable home, with everything it implies: children, regular sex, a "haven in a heartless world."

But pro-life women, like all women, are facing a devaluation of these resources. As American society increasingly becomes a service economy, men can buy the services that a wife traditionally offers. Cooking, cleaning, decorating, and the like can easily be purchased on the open market in a cash transaction. And as sex becomes more open, more casual, and more "amative," it removes one more resource that could previously be obtained only through marriage.

Pro-life women, as we have seen, have both value orientations and social characteristics that make marriage very important. Their alternatives in the public world of work are, on the whole, less attractive. Furthermore, women who stay home full-time and keep house are becoming a financial luxury. Only very wealthy families *or families whose values allow them to place the nontangible benefits of a full-time wife over the tangible benefits of a working wife* can afford to keep one of its earners off the labor market. To pro-life people, the nontangible benefit of having children—and therefore the value of procreative sex—is very important. Thus, a social ethic that promotes more freely available sex undercuts pro-life women two ways: it limits their abilities to get into a marriage in the first place, and it undermines the social value placed on their presence once within a marriage.

For pro-choice women, the situation is reversed. Because they have access to "male" resources such as education and income, they have far less reason to believe that the basic reason for sexuality is to produce children. They plan to have small families anyway, and they and their husbands come from and have married into a social class in which small families are the norm. For a number of overlapping reasons, therefore, pro-choice women value the ability of sex to promote human intimacy more (or at least more frequently) than they value the ability of sex to produce babies. But they hold this view because they can afford to. When they bargain for marriage, they use the same resources that they use in the labor market: upper-class status, an education very similar to a man's, side-by-side participation in the man's world, and, not least, a salary that substantially increases a family's standard of living.

It is true, therefore, that pro-life people are "anti-sex." They value sex, of course, but they value it for its traditional benefits (babies) rather than for the benefits that pro-choice people associate with it (intimacy). Pro-life people really do want to see "less" sexuality—or at least less open and socially unregulated sexuality—because they think it is morally wrong, they think it distorts the meaning of sex, and they feel that it *threatens the basis on which their own marital bargains are built.*

These differences in social background also explain why the majority of pro-life people we interviewed were opposed to "artificial" contraception, and had chosen to use natural family planning (NFP), the modern-day version of the "rhythm method." To be sure, since NFP is a "morally licit" form of fertility control for Catholics, and many pro-life activists are very orthodox Catholics, NFP is attractive on those grounds alone. But as a group, Catholics are increasingly using contraception in patterns very similar to those of their non-Catholic peers. Furthermore, many non-Catholic pro-life activists told us they used NFP. Opposition to contraception, therefore, and its corollary, the use of NFP, needs to be explained as something other than simple obedience to church dogma.

Given their status as traditional women who do not work outside of the home, the choice of NFP as the preferred method of fertility control is a rational one because NFP enhances their power and status as women. The NFP users we talked with almost uniformly stated that men respect women more when they are using NFP and that the marriage relationship becomes more like a honeymoon. Certain social factors in the lives of pro-life women suggest why this may be so. Because NFP requires abstinence during the fertile period, one effect of using it is that *sex becomes a relatively scarce resource.* Rather than something that is simply there—and taken for granted—sex becomes something that disappears from the relationship for regular periods of time. Therefore, NFP creates incentives for husbands to be close and intimate with their wives. The more insecure a woman and the less support she feels from her husband, the more reasonable it is for her to want to lengthen the period of abstinence to be on the safe side.* The increase in power and status that NFP affords a woman in a traditional marriage was clearly recognized by the activists who use NFP, as these two quotations suggest:

> The rhythm [method] is the most freeing thing a woman can have, if you want me to tell you the honest-to-God truth. Because if she's married to someone that she loves, and she ought to be, then you know [when she abstains] she's got a romance time, she's got a time when she doesn't have to say she has a headache. He's just got to know, hey, either we're going to have another baby and you're going to pay for it or we're going to read our books tonight. And once in a while we're going to get to read our books, that's the way I look at it. I think it's wonderful, I really do, it might not sound too romantic to people, but it is, this is super romantic.

> You know, if you have filet mignon every day, it becomes kind of uninteresting. But if you have to plan around this, you do some things. You study, and you do other things during the fertile part of the cycle. And the husband and wife find out how much they can do in the line of expressing love for one another in other ways, other than genital. And some people can really express a lot of love and do a lot of touching and be very relaxed. Maybe others would find that they can only do a very little touching because they might be stimulated. And so they would have to find out where their level was. But they can have a beautiful relationship.

NFP also creates an opportunity for both husbands and wives to talk about the wife's fertility so that once again, something that is normally taken for granted can

---

*One NFP counselor described a case to me in which a woman found herself unavailable for sex an average of twenty-five days a month in what seemed a deliberate attempt to use sex to control a spouse's behavior. But the interpretation of oneself as fertile (and hence sexually unavailable unless the spouse wishes to risk the arrival of another child) need not be either calculating or conscious. The more insecure a woman is in her marriage the more insecure she may be about interpreting her fertility signs, both because the insecurity in her marriage translates into a more general insecurity and because she may wish to err "on the safe side" if she is worried about the effects of a pregnancy on a shaky relationship.

be focused on and valued. Folk wisdom has it that men and women use sexuality in different ways to express their feelings of caring and intimacy: men give love in order to get sex and women give sex in order to get love. If there is some truth to this stereotype (and both popular magazines and that rich source of sociological data, the Dear Abby column, suggest that there is), then it means that men and women often face confusion in their intimate dialogues with one another. Men wonder if their wives really want to have sex with them or are only giving it begrudgingly, out of a sense of "duty." Wives wonder if husbands really love them or merely want them for sexual relief. Natural Family Planning, by making sex periodically unavailable, puts some of these fears to rest. Some women said their husbands actually bring them flowers during the period of abstinence. Though husbands were much less forthcoming on this topic; it would seem reasonable that a woman who has been visibly reassured of her husband's caring for her might approach the renewal of sexual activity with the enthusiasm of someone who knows she is cared for as a whole person, to the husband's benefit and pleasure.

Furthermore, a few mutually discreet conversations during our interviews suggest that during abstinence at least some couples find ways of giving each other sexual pleasure that do not involve actual intercourse and hence the risk of pregnancy. Given traditional patterns of female socialization into sexuality and the fact that pro-life women are both traditional and devout women, these periods of mutual caressing may be as satisfying as intercourse for some women and even more satisfying than intercourse for others.°

The different life circumstances and experiences of pro-life and pro-choice people therefore intimately affect the ways they look at the moral and social dilemmas of contraception. The settings of their lives, for example, suggest that the psychological side benefits of NFP, which do so much to support pro-life values during the practice of contraception, are sought in other ways by pro-choice people. Pro-choice people are slightly older when they marry, and the interviews strongly suggest that they have a considerably more varied sexual experience than pro-life people on average; the use of NFP to discover other facets of sexual expression is therefore largely unnecessary for them. Moreover, what little we know about sexual practices in the United States (from the Kinsey Report) suggests that given the different average levels of education and religious devoutness in the two

---

°In short, these interviews were describing both "petting" and oral sex. Feminist literature has called to our attention the fact that traditional notions about sexuality are "male-centered"; it is assumed that there will be insertion and that there will be a male ejaculation. Ironically, NFP—the birth control method preferred by the devout, traditional women we interviewed—may come very close to achieving the feminist ideal. Under NFP, the "rules" of "regular" sex are suspended, and each couple must discover for themselves what feels good. For a generation of women who were raised when long periods of "necking" and "petting" occurred before—and often instead of—intercourse, NFP may provide a welcoming change from genitally centered, male-oriented sexual behavior to more diffuse, body-focused "female" forms of sexual expression.

groups, such sexual activities as "petting" and oral-genital stimulation may be more frequently encountered among pro-choice people to begin with.°

The life circumstances of the two sides suggest another reason why NFP is popular among pro-life people but not seriously considered by pro-choice people. Pro-choice men and women act on their belief that men and women are equal not only because they have (or should have) equal rights but also because they have substantially similar life experiences. The pro-choice women we met have approximately the same kinds of education as their husbands do, and many of them have the same kinds of jobs—they are lawyers, physicians, college professors, and the like. Even those who do not work in traditionally male occupations have jobs in the paid labor market and thus share common experiences. They and their husbands share many social resources in common: they both have some status outside the home, they both have a paycheck, and they both have a set of peers and friends located in the work world rather than in the family world. In terms of the traditional studies of family power, pro-choice husbands and wives use the same bargaining chips and have roughly equal amounts of them.

Pro-choice women, therefore, value (and can afford) an approach to sexuality that, by sidelining reproduction, diminishes the differences between men and women; they can do this *because they have other resources on which to build a marriage.* Since their value is intimacy and since the daily lives of men and women on the pro-choice side are substantially similar, intimacy in the bedroom is merely an extension of the intimacy of their larger world.

Pro-life women and men, by contrast, tend to live in "separate spheres." Because their lives are based on a social and emotional division of labor where each sex has its appropriate work, to accept contraception or abortion would devalue the one secure resource left to these women; the private world of home and hearth. This would be disastrous not only in terms of status but also in terms of meaning; if values about fertility and family are not essential to a marriage, what support does a traditional marriage have in times of stress? To accept highly effective contraception, which actually and symbolically subordinates the role of children in the family to other needs and goals, would be to cut the ground of meaning out from under at least one (and perhaps both) partners' lives. Therefore, contraception, which sidelines the reproductive capacities of men and women, is both useless and threatening to pro-life people.

° Kinsey's data suggest that for males the willingness to engage in oral-genital or manual-genital forms of sexual expression is related to education: the more educated an individual, the more likely he is to have "petted" or engaged in oral sex (Alfred Kinsey, *Sexual Behavior in the Human Male,* pp. 337–81, 535–37). For females, the patterns are more complicated. Educational differences among women disappear when age at marriage is taken into account. But as Kinsey notes: "Among the females in the sample, the chief restraint on petting . . . seems to have been the religious tradition against it." The more devout a woman, the less likely she is to have ever petted (Kinsey, *Sexual Behavior in the Human Female,* pp. 247–48).

THE CORE OF THE DEBATE

In summary, women come to be pro-life and pro-choice activists as the end result of lives that center around different definitions of motherhood. They grow up with a belief about the nature of the embryo, so events in their lives lead them to believe that the embryo is a unique person, or a fetus; that people are intimately tied to their biological roles, or that these roles are but a minor part of life; that motherhood is the most important and satisfying role open to a woman, or that motherhood is only one of several roles, a burden when defined as the only role. These beliefs and values are rooted in the concrete circumstances of women's lives—their educations, incomes, occupations, and the different marital and family choices they have made along the way—and they work simultaneously to shape those circumstances in turn. Values about the relative place of reason and faith, about the role of actively planning for life versus learning to accept gracefully life's unknowns, of the relative satisfactions inherent in work and family—all of these factors place activists in a specific relationship to the larger world and give them a specific set of resources with which to confront that world.

The simultaneous and on-going modification of both their lives and their values by each other finds these activists located in a specific place in the social world. They are financially successful, or they are not. They become highly educated, or they do not. They become married and have a large family, or they have a small one. And at each step of the way, both their values and their lives have undergone either ratification or revision.

Pro-choice and pro-life activists live in different worlds, and the scope of their lives, as both adults and children, fortifies them in their belief that their own views on abortion are the more correct, more moral, and more reasonable. When added to this is the fact that should "the other side" win, one group of women will see the very real devaluation of their lives and life resources, it is not surprising that the abortion debate has generated so much heat and so little light.

Reading 37

The Norplant Debate

Barbara Kantrowitz and Pat Wingert

The Paquin School is a simple brick box of a building in a working-class Baltimore neighborhood. It doesn't look like the setting for a social experiment, but it is. Paquin's 300 students are all pregnant teens or new mothers; last month they became the first students in America to be offered the implantable contraceptive Norplant at school. For these girls, many of whom have babies at 13 or 14, Norplant's promise—no pregnancies for five years—could mean a second chance. "Our dream is to prevent them from getting pregnant again until they're at least 21," says Gracie Dawkins, a Paquin counselor.

But Melvin Tuggle, a black Baltimore minister, thinks making Norplant available at Paquin is genocide. "One third of us are in jail and another third is killing us and now they're taking away the babies," he says. "If the community, the churches and our white brothers don't stand up for us, there won't be any of us left." This week Tuggle and other black leaders say they'll use a Baltimore city council hearing to protest plans to expand Norplant to schools throughout the city. "We won't let a 12-year-old have a drink," he says, "and in the Baltimore school system, a 12-year-old needs a letter from her parents to go to the zoo. She needs permission to get aspirin but she needs nothing to get Norplant."

Or get pregnant. Consuelo Laws's mother didn't like her boyfriend, so she insisted that Consuelo's little brother go with her everywhere. He wasn't much of a contraceptive device. Consuelo was 13 when the doctor told her she was pregnant, "and with that," she says, "my teenage years were over." Now 19 and the mother of two, Consuelo thinks girls should get Norplant as soon as they start menstruating. "My mother thought she could protect me," Consuelo says. When her mother asked how it happened, Consuelo told her: "My little brother would . . . play with my boyfriend's brothers and sisters, while we went in another room." A Paquin senior, Consuelo has had Norplant for a year. "Without it I'd probably have more children," she says. "I want to complete my education."

When it was approved by the Food and Drug Administration in 1990, Norplant was heralded as the first innovation in birth control since the pill and the IUD in the 1960s. It's turned out to be as controversial as it is revolutionary. Nor-

From *Newsweek*, February 15, 1993.

plant is being touted as a cure not only for teen pregnancy, but also for welfare dependency, child abuse and drug-addicted mothers.

It's a heavy burden for a half dozen little sticks to carry. The Norplant system, as it is called, consists of six matchstick-size capsules surgically implanted in the arm that slowly release a low dosage of levonorgestrel, the same synthetic hormone used in several versions of the birth-control pill. Norplant is as good as the pill in preventing pregnancy, and its long-lasting effectiveness—up to five years—makes it especially attractive to younger women who want to delay childbearing. It's teen-ager-proof; girls don't have to worry about remembering to take the pill or use a diaphragm. Its only serious medical drawback: couples still need to use latex condoms to prevent the spread of sexually transmitted diseases, including AIDS. A recent survey of 21,276 women who received Norplant through Planned Parenthood found that the vast majority, 89 percent, were under 30, and 22 percent were 19 or younger. "We need long-term methods like this because failure rates are high" for younger women using other forms of contraception, says Laurie Schwab Zabin of the Johns Hopkins School of Hygiene and Public Health.

But even Norplant's most ardent supporters are troubled by the way the contraceptive has become the focus of an emotional debate about the fertility of poor women and teenagers. The issues here stretch well beyond poverty to the power of the state to regulate—or coerce—the reproductive choices of women. Put simply, if the state is expected to pay to support the children of the poor, do taxpayers have a say in whether the children will be conceived?

"There are all sorts of reasons why policies that might achieve a good goal— like the reduction of welfare costs and fewer poor babies—give too much authority to the government," says Arthur Caplan, a bioethicist at the University of Minnesota. "I'm not saying the goal is bad, but the means to get there will come at a terrible price, a scary price." Caplan thinks Norplant could be just the beginning of a whole range of efforts to cut public costs through control of reproduction. "I can see us mandating the genetic testing of embryos and fetuses," he says. "If we're willing to put Norplant into a 16-year-old today to contain costs, then why couldn't there be a government official saying you can't be a parent because you're likely to create a kid whose needs will cost society too much?"

To some lawmakers, Norplant is more than a contraceptive; it's a panacea. Last month, in his state-of-the-state speech, Maryland Gov. Donald Schaefer suggested requiring mothers on welfare to get Norplant or get off the dole. "The simple truth is, we've run out of money," he says. "We may be forced to make mothers take care of themselves." He's not alone. In the past two years, according to The Alan Guttmacher Institute, legislators in 13 states have proposed nearly two dozen bills that aim to use Norplant as an instrument of social policy. In Tennessee, officials wanted to pay women on welfare $500 to get Norplant and $50 a year for each year they kept it. The bill was approved by the state House with amendments offering a $500 incentive to men on Medicaid who got vasectomies. The measure foundered in the Tennessee Senate, but the sponsor, state Rep. Steve McDaniel, plans to reintroduce it in the next two weeks. Legislators in other states have proposed requiring Norplant for mothers convicted of felony drug abuse and mothers who have given birth to drug-addicted infants.

Politicians say they've turned to Norplant out of desperation. Last year Walter Graham, a state senator in Mississippi, proposed that his state require the contraceptive for women with at least four children who wanted any kind of government support. His legislation didn't pass, he says, because it got combined with another bill. But a new session has just begun and Graham thinks it will eventually be approved. "The taxpayer is willing to support one child, maybe even two children," he says. "But there's a point where if people want to continue to receive assistance, they will have to have an implant . . . Everyone supports the idea of helping the person who *cannot*. They just don't support the concept of helping the person who *will* not."

Norplant isn't just a social issue; it's also an economic one. Because the contraceptive is so expensive—$365 plus $200 or more to have it implanted and then an additional $100 or so to have it taken out—many women can't afford to pay for it out of their own pockets. Medicaid, the health insurance for people on welfare, covers Norplant in all 50 states. That means that only two groups of American women can generally afford Norplant: rich women and very poor women. In the Planned Parenthood survey, 69 percent of women who received Norplant at the organization's clinics had the cost covered by Medicaid. There are no studies of overall Norplant use, but Dr. Michael Policar, Planned Parenthood's vice president of medical affairs, estimates that roughly half of the 500,000 women in this country who use Norplant are covered by Medicaid.

The U.S. distributor of Norplant, Wyeth-Ayerst Laboratories, set the price in this country when it obtained FDA approval at the end of 1990. In 13 other countries where Norplant is used, the cost is much less, as low as $23. All contraceptives are more expensive in the United States than in other countries where medicine is often supported by government and international aid. But Wyeth-Ayerst says its price is fair because it has had to pay the cost of training 26,000 medical practitioners to implant Norplant, at a cost of $1,000 each. There's also the potential cost of litigation—a concern for anyone in the contraceptive business after lawsuits by IUD users.

Given these numbers, Norplant is increasingly viewed as a contraceptive for women on public assistance. That has helped to revive a long-dormant debate over who should control the fertility of poor women. If taxpayers are paying for their health care and paying for the support of their children through welfare, isn't the government entitled to set limits? In the first half of this century, compulsory sterilization was legal in the majority of states. Dr. Allan Rosenfield, dean of Columbia University's School of Public Health, estimates that between 1907 and 1945, as many as 45,000 Americans—most poor or mentally incompetent—were compelled to be sterilized. Since then, more progressive social policies—combined with the introduction of the pill and the IUD—presented a host of voluntary contraceptive choices. In 1974, the federal government issued guidelines for federally funded sterilizations that mandated counseling, informed consent and a ban on the procedure for minors. Those guidelines became law four years later. Now, sterilization by choice—normally tubal ligation—is the second most popular form of birth control for American couples, after the pill.

Before the introduction of Norplant, most available forms of reversible birth control were by nature voluntary. There's no way to make a woman swallow a pill every day or to force a man to use a condom during intercourse. But Norplant is different. Once inserted, it remains in a woman's arm until a medical practitioner takes it out. "Because it's the closest thing to sterilization, folks have seized on this and tried to impose it on the women who have the least power in our society," says Julia Scott of the National Black Women's Health Project. "They see it as social control for those women who they believe are responsible for all of our social issues."

That certainly wasn't the intent of Norplant's developers, the Population Council, a nonprofit group based in New York that sponsors contraceptive research. Doctors supported by the council began work on an implantable contraceptive in 1966. After years of clinical trials involving 40,000 women in 43 countries around the world, Finland became the first country to approve Norplant in 1983. A Finnish pharmaceutical company, Leiras Oy, is the only manufacturer of Norplant. Over the next decade, Norplant was approved in 23 countries, including Indonesia, Thailand and Colombia.

The United States is the only country where coercion has emerged as a serious issue. Just after Norplant was approved by the FDA, an editorial writer for The Philadelphia Inquirer suggested linking Norplant use to welfare payments. Within a week, after protests inside and outside the newsroom, the paper published an apology. A few months later, a California judge tried to make Norplant a condition of probation for a mother of five convicted of child abuse. The woman appealed, but the case was dismissed last year when she violated another condition of her probabtion and was sent to jail. In Texas, a judge also ordered a convicted childabuser to use Norplant. She didn't appeal, but developed medical problems and eventually had a tubal ligation instead.

While policymakers debate coercive use of Norplant, the contraceptive has gained popularity with women. Rosetta Stitt, the principal of the Paquin School in Baltimore, says many students chose Norplant even before it became available at her school. Some Paquin students see Norplant as a way to break a cycle of early motherhood. "The girls we have in our school today have seen two decades of what their aunts and mothers went through because they were teenage mothers, all the things they couldn't do because they had a baby," says Stitt. "They do not want to go through that, too."

Monica Irving, a 15-year-old ninth grader with a 3-month-old son, asked for Norplant right after her baby was born. She lives at home with her mother, Michele, 33. Monica's grandmother looks after the baby while Monica is at school. "I always thought I would get married and then have a child," Monica says. "I never thought of it happening when I was this young. If somebody had talked to me about Norplant before, I would have used it." Michele Irving supports her daughter's choice. "It broke my heart when Monica got pregnant," she says, "but I tried not to let her know that. Some mothers throw their daughters out when this happens. But I didn't. I have tried to back her up. But I am very happy she's on Norplant now."

Most studies have shown that women who use Norplant like it better than their previous contraceptives—mostly because it's much more reliable and effortless once it's implanted. The Planned Parenthood survey of women who received Norplant at the organization's clinics in the last two years showed a very high degree of satisfaction. Only 3.5 percent of women asked to have it removed, a much lower rate than the 10 to 25 percent in earlier Norplant studies. The women who complained generally cited the most common side effects: irregular bleeding, headaches, mood changes and weight gain.

But another study, of Norplant users in Texas, indicated that Norplant's growing popularity could have some negative consequences. Nearly half of former condom users said they wouldn't use condoms now that they have Norplant, putting them at risk for sexually transmitted diseases, especially HIV, the virus that causes AIDS. "If I had my druthers with kids, I would put them in a head-to-toe condom until they were 21," says Columbia's Rosenfield. "The best of both worlds would be if they would use Norplant and a condom, but I know it's hard to get them to use one."

Norplant's supporters say both the coercion issue and the risk of STDs without condoms point to the need for increasing sex education and adequate counseling for women—especially teenagers—who are considering Norplant. "This is one of the most critical issues in the adolescent population," says Dr. David Kessler, the commissioner of the FDA. "I think the risk of people using Norplant and not a condom is very real."

Some of Norplant's critics worry that for teenagers, the implant is a license for promiscuity. "If a girl has Norplant in her arm, the boy is going to say he can screw her because she's protected, she's not going to have a baby," says Tuggle. But Norplant researchers disagree. Dr. Philip Darney, a professor of obstetrics and gynecology at the University of California, San Francisco, participated in the clinical trials of Norplant. He's now studying teens and Norplant. "Some of the girls we have on Norplant are no longer sexually active," he says. "Twenty-five percent of them say they have no current partner—and they would have quit using birth-control pills. They keep the Norplant because they want to be protected if they do find a partner . . . In that sense, Norplant makes it easier for them to be sexually responsible." In truth, these are all just tentative conclusions; hard facts remain elusive. One area ripe for study: a comparison of the sexual activity of girls who start on Norplant while still virgins with those who come to it later.

"We're still going to be saying: abstain, abstain, abstain," says Gracie Dawkins, the Paquin guidance counselor. "But if you're not going to abstain, Norplant is an option." For their part, the students say they need better sex education in the earlier grades, too. "My mom had talked to me about my period, but it was all Greek to me," says 21-year-old Kimberly Lucas, the mother of an 8-year-old and a 2-year-old. "I remember her giving me a book with body parts in it, but I didn't realize what the big deal was." Kimberly learned about sex from her boyfriend. "When you're in middle school, and you run into a boy who's 19 and cute, he can teach you about sex in a few minutes. You don't want him to be the one who teaches your kid about sex, but if you don't, he will."

After listening to these sad truths all day, Rosetta Stitt, Paquin's principal, gets angry when she hears people criticize Norplant—or any other method of birth control that can help get young mothers' lives back on track. "Morality is one thing, reality is another," she says. "We have to deal with reality here every day. "The reality is that there's no silver bullet to stop teen pregnancy. But Norplant can be an effective weapon in an arsenal that includes sex education, better health care and the possibility of a future worth waiting for.

Reading 38

9/29/94

What Is a Family? Nature, Culture, and the Law

David M. Rosen

Throughout the United States, courts are grappling with the problem of how to define family and kinship relationships. Until recently, this appeared to be a relatively straightforward issue. The only family relationships given legal or jural recognition were those based upon blood ties, marriage, or adoption. But the emergence of new forms of domestic relationships, especially domestic relationships between gay and lesbian partners, have forced courts to decide whether traditional legal concepts of family relations should be extended to include new relationships that otherwise have no basis in law. In this article, I argue that deeply-rooted concepts of kinship underlie legal decision-making in this area, and define the boundaries of judicial discretion to modify the basic concepts of family law.[1]

To demonstrate this I analyze three recent cases in which New York courts have adopted three distinct strategies for meeting the legal challenges of new families. These strategies are:

1. The outright application of traditional family law concepts to new family arrangements.
2. The rejection of family law concepts as applicable to new family arrangements.
3. The rejection of the application of family law concepts to new families, coupled with the substitution of non-family-law legal concepts so as to provide judicial relief to the parties involved.

FIRST LEGAL STRATEGY: APPLICATION OF FAMILY LAW TO NEW FAMILY ARRANGEMENTS

An example of the first strategy is found in the New York case of *Braschi* v. *Stahl Associates Co.* (1989) in which the New York State Court of Appeals ruled that the

From *Marriage and Family Review*, vol. 17, No. 112. © 1991 by The Haworth Press, Inc. All rights reserved.

term "family" applied to a gay couple who had lived together for ten years. The practical issue involved was whether under New York law the survivor of a long-term domestic relationship had the right to possession of a rent-controlled apartment which the couple shared. In New York, this is a significant property right. The court, in upholding the right of the surviving partner, declared that protection against eviction "should find its foundation in the reality of family life. In the context of eviction, a . . . realistic, and certainly valid, view of a family includes two adult life-time partners whose relationship is long-term and characterized by an emotional and financial commitment and interdependence."

This decision of the court prompted the New York Division of Housing and Renewal to redefine the concept of family to include long-term gay and lesbian relationships. Although lesbian and gay couples will benefit greatly by these actions, the greatest beneficiaries are expected to be a wide range of non-traditional families, especially families of the poor.

SECOND LEGAL STRATEGY: REJECTION OF FAMILY LAW CONCEPTS IN REFERENCE TO NEW FAMILY ARRANGEMENTS

The second strategy is exemplified by the case of *Alison D.* v. *Virginia M.* (1990) in which a New York Appellate Division ruled that the term "parent" applied solely to biological relationships, and denied a former lesbian partner visitation rights to a child she and the biological mother of the child had parented together. In this case, the two women began living with each other in 1978. In 1980, they decided to raise a family, and Virginia M. was artificially inseminated. A boy was born, and the two women shared in the care of the child and jointly assumed all parenting responsibilities. In 1983, the relationship between the women ended, and Alison D. moved out of their home. Initially, she enjoyed regular visitation, but her former partner cut off all visitation in 1987. The Court's decision of May 1990 left Alison D. without any legal rights to see the child.

THIRD LEGAL STRATEGY: DENIAL OF THE FAMILY-LAW MODEL, BUT APPLICATION OF OTHER LEGAL THEORIES TO PROVIDE RELIEF TO THE PARTIES

An example of the third strategy lies in the case titled *The Estate of Steven Szabo* (1990) decided in July 1990. Here a New York Surrogate's Court determined that the term "spouse" did not apply to a gay life-partner, and denied the partner any inheritance rights in his deceased partner's estate. In this case, the two men had lived together for eighteen years before Mr. Szabo died. After his death, a will was probated. The will predated the relationship between the parties, and made no mention of the surviving partner.

Under New York law, a spouse cannot be disinherited, and if the spouse is unnamed in a will, he or she can by law obtain up to one half of the deceased's estate. In this case, had the surviving partner been deemed a "spouse" he would have been able to obtain a large share of the estate. Of particular importance was the cooperative apartment in which the couple had lived, but to which the deceased partner held title. The Court rejected the plaintiff's claim that he was a spouse, but it was willing to entertain his claims to the estate based upon proof of the financial arrangements between the partners during their lifetime together.

These instances show that these three terms in American kinship and law—family, parent, and spouse—have been treated in markedly different ways by New York Courts. While the decisions in all these cases involve complex legal reasoning, underlying these decisions are key concepts of American kinship, especially the concepts of "nature" and "culture." In brief, I argue that when "new" family relationships are modeled on traditional relationships grounded in "nature," the law is less likely to recognize the "new" relationship. Conversely, the more a "new" family relationship is modeled on a traditional relationship grounded in culture, the more likely it is that the law will legally recognize the new relationship. Consequently, kin terms such as "parent," "mother" or "father," which in American kinship are understood as involving cultural and legal recognition of an existing biological fact, are not readily transferred to new family relationships. A term like "family," which incorporates multiple relationships grounded in both nature and culture, is more easily applied to new family relationships. Finally, terms such as "spouse," "husband" or "wife," straddle the boundaries between nature and culture, and evoke a hybrid response from the courts.

THE ORDER OF NATURE, THE ORDER OF CULTURE, AND THE ORDER OF LAW

Kinship terms are cultural constructs which derive their meaning from their relationships with other concepts. In American kinship, as Schneider (1980) has pointed out, the world of relatives is constructed out of deeply felt assumptions about nature and culture.[2] Schneider has termed the distinction between nature and culture as the "order of nature" and the "order of law." Both of these orders are culturally constructed; that is, what is considered "nature" is itself culturally defined. Schneider's usage of the order of nature refers to the belief that some persons are considered relatives because they share a common heredity or blood. They are biogenetically connected. Schneider uses the "order of law" to refer to the belief that other persons are relatives because they are bound together by law or custom. For the purpose of this article, I distinguish between the order of nature, the order of culture and the order of law. All of these orders are culturally constructed, but they refer to specific ways in which human experience is symbolized.[3]

By the "order of nature" I mean that system of symbols that tend to define certain human characteristics as inherent. The symbolism of nature may describe the make up of persons, relations, or even sentiments, to the extent that these are perceived as arising from "nature."

By the "order of culture," I mean a system of symbols that stand for the world of customary beliefs, codes of conduct, and traditions created and imposed by human beings to serve as guidelines for action. The "order of law" is defined as a symbolic subdomain of the order of culture, which refers specifically to those codes of conduct created by judges, courts, legislatures and other law-making bodies in society.

In American kinship, the primary use of natural symbolism is found in the belief that some relatives are natural relatives because they share in a common substance: blood or heredity. But it is also the case that social actions and social relationships can be symbolized as more or less natural. For example, former United States Supreme Court Justice Berger, in his concurring opinion in the case of *Bowers* v. *Hardwick* (1985), resurrected with approval the commentaries of the eighteenth century English jurist Blackstone, that sodomy is "a crime against nature . . . the very mention of which is a disgrace to human nature" (p. 197). With this rhetorical flourish, a Georgia statute criminalizing homosexual relations was upheld as constitutional, and homosexuality was banished from the world of nature to the world of deviant culture.

Though Supreme Court Justices may see the distinction between nature and culture as relatively fixed, anthropologists have usually been of the mind that these categories are far more elastic. Some time ago, Ortner (1974) pointed out that the dichotomy between nature and culture was frequently used to define the relationship between male and female. Similarly, Barnes (1977) has demonstrated that the kin category of "mother" is usually more closely identified with nature than is the category of "father," even though both father and mother are equal participants in the genetic make-up of the child. All this suggests that the symbolism of nature and culture enters into human experience in a variety of predictable and unpredictable ways.

The orders of nature, culture and law combine to create American ideas of kinship. The primary elements are the combination of the order of nature and the order of culture. The combination of these two creates the world of relatives as these are understood in American kinship. The order of law may or may not recognize these relatives. That is, the relationships as they exist in nature, culture, or some combination thereof may or may not have any legally defined rights or obligations. [Figure 38.1] illustrates how the world of kinship is created through the intersection of nature and culture.

At the far left side of the chart are relatives that exist primarily in the order of nature and may include so-called "illegitimate children," as well as the offspring of sperm donors. These are relatives to whom an individual may be related "by blood," but for whom no significant relationship in culture or in law exists.

At the far right of the chart are relatives who exist by virtue of culture alone. These include all the various fictive kin relationships that exist in American culture. Fictive aunts and uncles, brothers and sisters, and adopted children. These may exist only in culture, as in the case of fictive "brothers" and "sisters," or they may exist in both culture and in law, as in the case of adopted children.

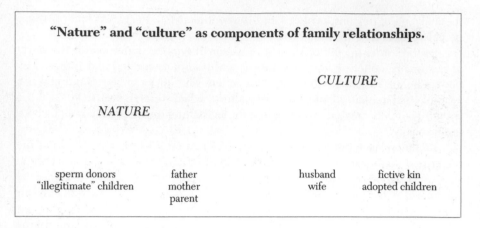

Figure 38.1

Finally, in the middle are two categories of relatives that exist in both nature and culture. These are relatives for whom the order of nature appears to be reified by the order of culture. Relatives such as father and mother exist both in nature and in culture because the code of conduct expressed in culture is understood as a symbolic reenactment or replication of inherent ties. Thus for Americans, much of what is called kinship is symbolized as a cultural recognition of biological or natural facts. Many of these relationships, (e.g., mother and father) also exist in the order of law, in that law-making bodies have created a special symbolic code for governing these relationships. Other relationships, such as the relationships between second or third cousins, do not necessarily exist in the order of law. These are relatives solely in nature and culture. In this paper, I place the husband and wife relationship in the orders of nature and culture. Obviously, husbands and wives are not usually "blood" relatives, but in American culture, the relationship is seen as arising out of the nature of male-female relationships and the natural desire of men and women to mate and reproduce. In addition, it is sometimes remarked that the husband-wife relationship involves an exchange of fluids (i.e., semen) which gives this relationship a natural quality mimicking that of blood. Moreover, one practically universal basis for the annulment of marriage in American law is the failure of this exchange of fluids to take place. An annulment is conceptually different from a divorce, in that while divorce terminates a marriage, an annulment decrees that a marriage never existed. Thus the essence of a marital relationship is a blend of nature and culture.

In addition, there is tension between nature and culture which pervades American thinking about kinship. For example, the literature on step-parenting indicates that stepmothers have far more difficulty in integrating themselves into reconstituted families than do stepfathers, because of the cultural perception that relationships between mothers and children are more deeply imbedded in nature than in culture. Stepfathers seem to more easily assume the more culturally defined father role (Johnson, Klee and Smith, 1988).

The tension between nature and culture is even more apparent in adoption. By law, adoption severs all the rights of the biological mother and father to the child. All these rights and duties are transferred to the adopting parents. Yet nature looms as an ever-present danger to the adopting parents, and a host of devices exist to keep nature at bay. In the not-so-distant past, the fact of adoption was kept a secret, to be withheld from a child until he or she was "old enough to know"; that is old enough so that the cultural definition of the parent could resist the "pull" of the biological parent. The fear that someday the biological mother might come to successfully reclaim the love and loyalty linked to blood is not far from the minds of many adoptive parents, even though this fearsome scenario rarely occurs in fact.

Adopting parents also use geographic and cultural distance as ways of keeping nature at bay. Children are frequently adopted from foreign countries or distant states. Language also plays a role in the process. In current adoption jargon, the biological mother is now called the "birth mother" while the adopting mother is now "the mother." Adoption literature is also careful to spell out that a child "was" adopted, rather than "is" adopted, so as to signify that adoption is a way of coming into a family rather than an eternal condition. And, a pregnant woman seeking to find an adoptive family for her baby is termed a "situation," a term that clearly distances the adopting parents from the compelling fact of biological kinship.

Finally, the innumerable personal and procedural barriers placed in the way of so-called "open" adoptions are clearly linked to the fears of adopting parents and the law of the powerful claim of the biological mother. At the root of these feelings lies the primordial fear that culture cannot triumph over nature.

The Law Grapples with Redefining Family Relationships

A more detailed look at the legal decisions described above will illustrate how the tensions between nature and culture manifest themselves in legal decision-making. It is important to note that in all these cases, none of the kin or family terms are defined by statute or regulation. It fell to the courts to provide the definitions.[4]

What Is a Family? In the case of *Braschi* v. *Stahl Associates Co.* (1989), the question was whether Miguel Braschi would be able to remain as a tenant in the apartment he had shared with his domestic partner Leslie Blanchard for more than ten years. At issue was the Court's interpretation of New York City Rent and Eviction regulations which provided that upon the death of a tenant in a rent controlled apartment, the landlord may not dispossess "either the surviving spouse of the deceased tenant or some other family member of the deceased tenant's *family* who has been living with the tenant" (p. 206). The Court of Appeals specifically focused upon the meaning of the term "family." It did not address the issue of the term "spouse."

The Court rejected the idea that the term "family member" should be construed consistently with New York's intestacy laws, which regulate the inheritance of property, to mean relationships of blood, consanguinity, or adoption (p. 209).

Instead, the Court argued that the non-eviction provisions are not designed to govern succession to property, but to protect certain occupants from the loss of their homes. In light of this, the Court argued that the term "family" should not be "rigidly restricted to those people who have formalized their relationship by obtaining, for instance, a marriage certificate or adoption order. The intended protection against sudden eviction should not rest on fictitious legal distinctions or genetic history, but instead should find its foundation in the reality of family life" (p. 211). The Court proceeded to provide a distinctly cultural view of family as "a group of people united by certain convictions or common affiliation" or as a "collective body of persons who live in one house under one head or management." Finally, the Court added that in using the term "family" the legislature had "intended to extend protection to those who reside in households having all of the normal familial characteristics" (p. 211). Indeed, the Court went on at length to describe how much the relationship between Braschi and Blanchard fit the facts of family life. As the Court put it:

> Appellant and Blanchard lived together as permanent life partners for more than 10 years. They regarded one another, and were regarded by friends and family, as spouses. The two men's families were aware of the nature of the relationship, and they regularly visited each other's families and attended family functions together, as a couple. Even today, appellant continues to maintain a relationship with Blanchard's niece, who considers him an uncle. (p. 213)

It is of considerable significance that the Court characterized the relationship between the parties as factually equivalent to a spousal relationship. Yet the issue of whether the parties were spouses to each other was apparently never raised or addressed. By resting his case on a cultural definition of family, Mr. Braschi obtained a favorable decision. Exactly how he would have fared had he relied on the idea that he was Blanchard's spouse cannot be ascertained from this case. However, the next case, *The Estate of Steven Szabo*, suggests that he would have had a more difficult time.

What Is a Spouse?   In the *Estate of Steven Szabo* (1990), the plaintiff presented a number of theories under which he should prevail. Each was predicated on the same set of facts, namely, that he and the deceased were gay life partners since 1970, and that they had agreed from the outset of their relationship to share living expenses and quarters, although they had signed no written agreement. According to the surviving partner, the financial arrangements between them were that he would give his entire monthly paycheck to Szabo, who then subtracted the cost of monthly household expenses, including the maintenance of the cooperative apartment that they shared. The balance of the money was placed in a savings account, and Szabo gave the plaintiff an allowance for weekly personal expenses. As seen earlier, when Szabo died, a will was probated, which predated the relationship and did not mention the plaintiff. In addition, there were no joint bank accounts, nor was the surviving partner the beneficiary of any life insurance policy. Title to the cooperative apartment in which they had lived together was also apparently held solely in the name of Szabo (p. 31).

It is easy to see, from the plaintiff's point of view, that this was a long-term relationship, like a marriage, in which the surviving partner was about to be evicted from the cooperative apartment he shared with the deceased without any of the money they had saved together for nearly twenty years. The plaintiff's most novel theory was that a gay life-partner is equivalent to a spouse. As previously stated, under New York law, a surviving spouse who is unnamed in a will is entitled to up to one-half of the net estate of the deceased partner. Therefore, if he were declared a spouse, he could obtain a substantial share of the estate solely by virtue of his spousal relationship and without having to prove any of the facts about their financial relationship.

However, the Court rejected this claim. Instead, the Court held that, by definition, a spouse means the person to whom one is legally married, and that the law made no provision for a marriage between persons of the same sex. "Marriage," the Court stated, "is and always has been a contract between a man and a woman" (p. 31). Here, of course the Court is emphasizing that marriage is a creation of both nature and culture. On the one hand, marriage is a contract, a cultural construction or transaction consisting of a series of mutual promises. On the other hand, it is grounded in nature, in that the only persons entitled to enter into such a contract are those persons who are heterosexual.

But the Court is able to separate the natural and cultural elements. For while nature and culture must come together in the creation of a marriage, and while the issue of inheritance flows from the natural side of the marriage, the financial relationships between the parties lie primarily in the world of culture. As a result, the Court allowed the plaintiff to proceed on two alternative theories; first on a claim for "money had and received," an old Common Law theory, which asserts that Szabo, and now his estate, received money that in equity and good conscience belong to the plaintiff; second, on the claim of "constructive trust," namely, that the estate has legal title to property in violation of some essential principal of equity. Under this theory the plaintiff would be permitted to show that the parties, by reason of their close relationship, were fiduciaries to each other, and that Szabo (and now, his estate) had a duty to act for his partner's benefit in connection with the money he had saved for him. These alternative theories find their bases in the world of business and commerce. They belong primarily to the world of culture. They derive from transactions into which all people, regardless of their natural connection to each other, can freely choose to enter.

What Is a Parent?   In *Alison D.* v. *Virginia M.* (1990) the Court was called upon to define the meaning of parent under New York's Domestic Relations law. At issue in this case was whether Alison D. had visitation rights to a child she and her former lesbian lover had parented together. Her basic claim was that she stood *in loco parentis* to the child, namely that the relationship the partners created gave her all the rights, duties, and responsibilities of a parent. As in the previous cases, the language of the law does not specifically define the term parent. Thus, the Court was asked to adopt the concept of parent as one standing *in loco parentis* (p. 23).

The Court saw no connection between the issues in *Braschi* v. *Stahl Associates Co.* and this case, but did not detail any reason why. The Court admitted that Alison D. and the child had a close and loving relationship, but it framed the entire dispute as one between a parent and a non-parent with respect to visitation of the child. Pronouncing Alison D. a "biological stranger," it chose to follow a line of cases which grants rights to non-parents only under extraordinary circumstances such as the unfitness of the biological parent.

Justice Kooper, who dissented in this case rejected the Court's reliance upon biology. She argued for a cultural definition of parenthood. In particular, she asserted that like the term "family," the term "parent" should be subject to a "frank inquiry into the realities of the relationship involved" (p. 24).

Interestingly, in this case the Court could have solved the problem by adopting the theory of equitable estoppel. Equitable estoppel is a vague legal concept which allows the Court to do justice by preventing a person from asserting a right he or she might otherwise have had. It is often used when the voluntary conduct of one party induces another to act in such a way that it is unjust for the party who does the misleading to assert his or her legal rights. Thus, in this case, the Court could have accepted the view that Virginia M. induced Alison D. into a long-term parental relationship and as a result, she should be barred from asserting the legal claim that Alison D. was not a parent. In this way, the Court would have done justice without actually having to redefine the concept of parent.

Significantly, this doctrine has sometimes been used to suppress biological claim to kinship. The classic example is where a woman becomes pregnant as a result of an adulterous relationship. Should she and her husband ultimately divorce, she will ordinarily be prevented from proving that the husband was not the biological father of their child. The doctrine of equitable estoppel creates the unrebuttable legal fiction that the child of a lawful marriage is the child of the husband and wife.

It might also be argued that adoption provides another model upon which the decision could have been based. After all, once adoption takes place, the issue of nature becomes legally irrelevant. Adoption could stand for the principle that a cultural-legal relationship can override a natural relationship even in parent-child relationships. A similar principle could be applied to lesbian and gay life-partner situations. This scenario is unlikely in the immediate future, since adoption was created through legislative action, rather than through judicial interpretation.

It is also clear that, adoption aside, parent-child relationships are one of the most difficult to redefine in the order of culture. Denmark, for example, allows for marriage-like unions for gay and lesbian couples which involve virtually all the rights and duties of marriage, but does not grant such couples the right to adopt or obtain joint custody of a child (Rule, 1989). The limited legal recognition of domestic partnerships in cities such as New York and San Francisco cannot deal with the issue of children.

The tension between the order of nature and the order of culture will continue to inform the domain of American family law. That the categories are undergoing constant revision is clear. In a recent surrogate mother case, a California Superior Court awarded full custody of the child to her genetic parents, and denied any rights to the surrogate mother, in whom a fertilized egg had been implanted after in-vitro fertilization. Whereas the New York Court dubbed Alison D. a "biological stranger," the California Court declared the surrogate mother a "genetic stranger." In making the decision, the Court was eventually forced to define the womb and the umbilical connection between the surrogate mother and the child as culture, analogizing it to a "fosterparent" relationship and a "home" for the embryo (Mydans, 1990).

CONCLUSION

Beginning in the 1930's, American law began to develop around the theory of legal realism. Legal realism was not as much a philosophical theory as it was an attitude. It called for an instrumental utilitarian use of law which rejected legal fictions. Law was a social tool (Friedman, 1985). In this light, it has sometimes been noted that family law has historically been the least amenable to legal realism and has been the most preoccupied with conscious creation of the symbolism of family life (Melton, 1987; Melton and Wilcox, 1989).

Certainly, the cases discussed in this article show some attempt to develop a more "realistic" view of family relationships. Nevertheless, it is clear that "realism," in the context of family law, requires a fundamental reordering of rather basic concepts of American kinship. This may be harder to accomplish than in other areas of law, where realism has triumphed. As this article has shown, the categories of nature and culture remain prime symbolic vehicles through which issues of family and kinship are addressed. "Adjudication," as Fiss puts it, "is interpretation . . . it is neither wholly discretionary nor . . . wholly mechanical" (Fiss, 1988). Judges will continue to bend and shape these categories, but they are not so easily abandoned. Judges will continue to make use of the cultural tools at hand to craft legal decisions.

NOTES

1. By family law, I mean the entire body of law which defines the rights and duties of kin. These laws may fall under the gloss of family law, domestic relations law, estate law, the law of wills, etc.
2. The following paragraphs constitute an extended dialogue with Schneider's text.
3. My use of the term symbol follows that of Clifford Geertz (1973). As to the specific issue of the symbolism of law, I take the view that law makes use of ideas and concepts that cut across all forms of social action, although in some societies law also makes use of a rather specialized vocabulary. For a fuller discussion of these issues see Geertz (1983) and Rosen (1989).
4. It is important to note that legal proceedings in the United States are shaped primarily by the parties to the issue and not the Court. Each side, plaintiff and defendant, comes to court with various theories as to why he or she should prevail. The theories must be offered by the parties themselves and the court will usually not substitute its own theories for those of the litigants. Moreover, litigants may present alternative and even incon-

sistent theories. The litigants usually try to present as many possible theories under which their side could prevail. The Court will normally have the opportunity to choose among a variety of legal justifications for its decision.

REFERENCES

Barnes, J. A. (1977). "Genetrix:genitor::nature:culture?", in J. Goody (Ed.), *The character of kinship,* Cambridge: Cambridge University Press.

Fiss, Owen (1988). "Objectivity and interpretation," in S. Levinson & S. Maillauz (Eds.), *Interpreting law and literature* (pp. 229–249) Evanston: Northwestern University Press.

Friedman, Lawrence (1985). *A history of American law* (pp. 688–89). New York: Simon and Schuster.

Geertz, Clifford (1973). *The interpretation of culture.* New York: Basic Books.

Geertz, Clifford (1983). Local knowledge: fact and law in comparative perspective, in his *Local Knowledge* (pp. 167–234). New York: Basic Books.

Johnson, C. E., Klee, L., and Schmidt, C. (1988). Conceptions of parenthood and kinship among children of divorce. *American Anthropologist,* 90: 136–144.

Melton, Gary B. (1987). The clashing of symbols: prelude to child and family policy, *American Psychologist,* 42:345–54.

Melton, Gary B. and Wilcox, Brian (1989). Changes in family law and family life, *American Psychologist* 44:1213–1216.

Mydans, Seth. Surrogate denied custody of child. (1990, October 23) *New York Times* p. A-14.

Ortner, Sherry (1974). Is female to male as nature is to culture?, in M. Rosaido and L. Lamphere (Eds.), *Women, culture and society,* Stanford: Stanford University Press.

Rosen, Lawrence (1989). *The anthropology of justice.* Cambridge: Cambridge University Press.

Rule, Sheila. Rights for gay couples in Denmark. (1989, October 2) *New York Times* p. A-19.

Schneider, David (1980). *American kinship: a cultural account.* Chicago: University of Chicago Press.

LIST OF CASES

In re Alison D. v. *Virginia M.,* (1990, March 9) *New York Law Journal,* p. 21

Bowers v. Hardwick, 478 U.S. 186, 197 (1985)

Braschi v. Stahl Associates Co., 74 N.Y.2d 201 (1989)

The Estate of Steven Szabo, (1990, July 16) *New York Law Journal,* p. 31

Reading 39

9/29/94

The Family and
The Culture War

James Davison Hunter

In many ways, the family is the most conspicuous field of conflict in the culture
war. Some would argue that it is the decisive battleground. The public debate over
the status and role of women, the moral legitimacy of abortion, the legal and social
status of homosexuals, the increase in family violence, the rise of illegitimacy particularly among black teenagers and young adults, the growing demand for adequate day care, and so on, prominently fill the headlines of the nation's newspapers, magazines, and intellectual journals. Marches and rallies, speeches and
pronouncements for or against any one of these issues mark the significant events
of our generation's political history. One might be tempted, then, to say that this
field of conflict is the beginning and end of the contemporary culture war, for the
issues contested in the area of family policy touch upon and may even spill over
into other fields of conflict—education, the arts, law, and politics. In the final analysis there may be much more to the contemporary culture war than the struggle for
the family, yet there is little doubt that the issues contested in the realm of family life
are central to the larger struggle and are perhaps fateful for other battles being waged.

Most who observe the contest over the family, however, tend to grasp the
controversy as a disagreement over the relative strength of this institution. One
observer, for example, has described the controversy as one between optimists and
pessimists. Both sides, he argued, agree that the family is changing yet they disagree sharply over the scope, meaning, and consequences of those changes. The
pessimists view rising trends in divorce, single-parent families, dual-income couples, couples living out of wedlock, secular day care, and the like, as symptoms of
the decline of a social institution. The optimists, on the other hand, regard the
changes as positive at best and benign at worst and, therefore, they believe that
social policy should reflect and accommodate the new realities. The American
family is not disintegrating, the optimists say, but is adapting to new social conditions.
The resilience of the family, therefore, signals that the family is "here to stay."

Observations such as these provide interesting perspective and insight on the matter, forcing us to consider the concrete social and economic circumstances of family life. But they miss what is really at stake. The contest over the family, in fact, reflects fundamental differences in the assumptions and world views of the antagonists. The issue, then, is not whether the family is failing or surviving. Rather, the contest is over *what constitutes the family* in the first place. If the symbolic significance of the family is that it is a microcosm of the larger society, . . . then the task of defining what the American family *is* becomes integral to the very task of defining America itself. For this reason it is also a task that is, on its own terms, intrinsically prone to intense political contention.

DEFINING THE FAMILY

But what is new in all of this? The family, as many have observed, has long been a social problem that has engendered heated political debate. One can observe, for example, profound anxiety about the well-being of the family in America and fears of its impending decline well into the nineteenth century. This was a time when industrialization was considered to threaten the cohesiveness of the family by severing its traditional ties to extended kinship, community, and church networks; when urbanization was viewed as threatening the moral development of the young and as brutalizing the integrity of family bonds. As a report to the National Congregational Council put it in 1892, "Much of the very mechanism of our modern life . . . is destructive of the family."

Yet, as tangible as these problems were, there was still a general cultural agreement about what exactly it was that was being threatened and, therefore, what it was that needed defending. The nature and contours of the family were never publicly in doubt. Not so anymore: as with so many other aspects of American life, the nineteenth-century consensus about the character and structure of family life has collapsed, leaving the very viability of the institution *as traditionally conceived* in question. The divisive issue now is in what form or forms contemporary families will remain viable.

Signs that the family would become an explicit public policy issue subject to polemical controversy appeared before the 1980s. The social science establishment began to raise the issue as a subject of national policy concern as early as the mid-1960s. Research and writing on the problem expanded through the 1970s. The abstract rhetoric of intellectual discourse, however, soon translated into the push and pull of real political debate. In 1973, for example, the United States Senate held hearings on "American Families: Trends and Pressures." "Family experts" offered their views of problems faced by the family and suggested how the government might deal with them. Then in 1977, the Carnegie Council on Children (founded in 1972) published a report recommending that "the nation develop a family policy as comprehensive as its defense policy." In the words of the report, "Our nation's professed belief in the importance of the family has not been matched by actions designed to protect the family's integrity and vitality. Although the sanctity of the family is a favorite subject for Fourth of July orators, legislators

rarely address the question of how best to support family life or child development." The call for concerted policy action would soon be answered.

Within the policy establishment itself, there were a wide range of perspectives
about what problems actually plagued the family as well as how they should best be
addressed. Among these "experts," a consensus was emerging that there was no
one family type to which a national policy would be oriented. Rather than viewing
families that were not nuclear, patriarchal, or self-sustaining as somehow deviant—families that were caught in what Daniel Patrick Moynihan called, in 1965, a
"tangle of pathology"—public policy would now have to recognize a diversity of
families. It was generally recognized that families differed in size, economic status,
national origin and custom, and, not least, structure and composition.

During the 1980 White House Conference on Families, the quandary over
how to define the American family was elevated to a permanent component of the
national family policy debate. Indeed, in the early stages of organization and preparation, the conference title itself was changed from the singular "family" to the
plural "families" because the organizers could not agree on what the American
family was supposed to be.

The conference, promised by President Carter during his 1976 presidential
campaign, pledged the power and prestige of the White House to explore the ways
in which public policy might strengthen U.S. families. Its outcome was mixed.
That the conference succeeded in becoming an event of national scope there is
little doubt. Statewide hearings and conferences took place in all fifty states, along
with five national hearings, culminating in three White House conferences—in
Baltimore, Minneapolis, and Los Angeles. But instead of generating a coherent set
of policy recommendations serving to strengthen American families, the primary
substantive accomplishment was to further crystallize and politicize, on a national
scale, differences of opinion over the nature, structure, and composition of the
family. . . .

THE FATE OF THE TRADITIONAL FAMILY

The White House Conference on Families was an important event in the history of
the family policy debate in its own right; however, its story is recounted here because it displays the level and intensity of discord over how Americans define the
family. Obviously, more is at stake than a dictionary definition of "the family." The
debate actually takes form as a political judgment about the fate of *one particular
conception of the family and family life.* The rhetoric of the activists, however,
misses the mark. Leaders within the orthodox alliance call it the "traditional" family, by which they mean persons living together who are related either by blood,
marriage, or adoption. But the family type they envision is "traditional" only in a
limited sense. What is in fact at stake is a certain *idealized* form of the nineteenth-
century middle-class family: a male-dominated nuclear family that both sentimen-
talized childhood and motherhood and, at the same time, celebrated domestic life
as a utopian retreat from the harsh realities of industrial society. Although such
bourgeois families were central in many ways to the flourishing of the early mod-

ern society, their fate is now in serious doubt. The political debate asks whether this family type should be preserved or abandoned. . . .

POLICY BRAWLS

The struggle to define the American family—whether public policy should embrace or reject the nineteenth-century middle-class family ideal—is practically enjoined not in its totality but in terms of its component parts. The clash, in other words, takes shape over specific concepts that underlie various policy proposals under debate—components that together make up a definition of the American family.

Authority

Families, however they are practically imagined, are a social unit that cooperates to carry out collective tasks—providing for the members' basic material and emotional needs, nurturing children to acceptable levels of social and moral responsibility, and so on. But who is responsible for these tasks and who will have the final say when difficult decisions need to be made? The issue here is one of *authority*. Should it rest with husband and father, as the orthodox and their culturally conservative allies prefer? Or should authority and responsibility be shared on egalitarian principles, as progressives and their liberal allies favor?

The issue of authority is implicit within several policy debates. Perhaps the most important, because it has been debated for the better part of the twentieth century, has been the Equal Rights Amendment (ERA). This amendment to the Constitution initially was introduced in Congress in 1923 through the efforts of the National Women's party. It finally was passed by Congress in 1972, yet it failed to be ratified by a sufficient number of state legislatures by a 1982 deadline. Reintroduced in 1983, the proposal lay largely dormant through the 1980s and early 1990s. Even so, the goal of the ERA has remained a central aspiration of the women's movement and of political progressives in general.

Advocates argue that the amendment guarantees equal protection under the law without regard for a person's gender. Conservatives claim that such protections are already guaranteed under the Constitution and that an amendment would be redundant. The deeper significance of the amendment, however, is symbolic. For progressivists, the Equal Rights Amendment symbolizes the formal recognition by the state (through the instrumentality of law) that women are autonomous from and therefore economically and politically equal to men. For those on the orthodox side, the amendment symbolizes a forsaking of the inherited structure of social relationships in the family and society as a whole. The ERA, claimed one conservative Illinois legislator, was "really an attack on the home. It [was] an attack on motherhood. It says that for a woman to have to be a mother and have to be a housewife is somehow degrading."

Moreover, many activists with orthodox commitments may also have mobilized against the ERA because it was viewed as way of "smuggling" legal protection of homosexual rights into a Constitutional amendment. One Fundamentalist opponent to the amendment put it this way: "If effective laws to help women are already on the books, who needs the ERA? Not women as a sex but lesbians and homosexuals need the ERA; and believe me, that's what it's really all about! Homosexuals and lesbians, who number perhaps 6 percent of the population, recognize their unpopular status. They decided early that the feminist movement and the ERA provided them with a handy vehicle to ride piggyback upon 'women's rights' and achieve homosexual rights. Fortunately, citizens who suddenly realized how close we were to the city limits of Sodom and Gomorrah successfully resisted the ERA." Other symbolic issues were at stake as well, such as the role of women in the military and the fate of single-sex institutions (such as Catholic seminaries and Orthodox Jewish schools) which discriminate according to gender for religious reasons. These issues remain key symbolic landmarks on both sides of the cultural divide.

The ERA is, of course, only one of the ways in which the issue of authority in family and society is played out in public policy. The identical arguments emerge in policy debates over such ideas as an "Equal Rights Act" and "comparable worth" or "pay equity." Though the latter issue technically deals with gender bias in wage setting, the symbolic meaning of the proposal is clear. Its advocates contend that the issue involves more than "just money," it involves "the esteem of half our population." Opponents insist that, among other things, pay equity "requires us to close our eyes to innate sexual differences which affect job preferences." The matter of authority is also contested in our very language. Language is not challenged at the level of federal law, although it is disputed at the level of organizational etiquette. This conflict focuses on the use of gender-specific language, as in the generic use of masculine pronouns (he, him, his) or the generic use of masculine titles (chairman, repairman, garbageman). What for traditionalists is the proper use of the English language is, for progressives, a pattern of speech that denigrates women and linguistically validates male domination. On both sides of the cultural divide, language itself—the ordering of symbols in our society—has become a politicized dimension of the culture war. This reality begins in the conflict over authority but it extends to the issue of abortion, homosexuality, euthanasia, and so on. The battle will be nearly over when the linguistic preferences of one side of the cultural divide become the conventions of society as a whole. . . .

Obligation

Another concept crucial to family life (however it is defined) is that of *obligation*. Of course, in a family there is a mutual obligation to care for and nurture each other. But to whom are we bound in this way? To what extent are we bound and for how long are we bound in this way? The answers to these questions reveal positions on matters of personal autonomy. No matter how tight the family is as a social unit, the family is made up of individuals who have needs and desires apart from the family. So, in addition to the questions surrounding obligation, a further question asks how the need for individual autonomy is to be balanced against the requirement of family obligation. Should the need for autonomy (the obligation to the self) take priority over the needs of the family (our obligation to others) or should personal needs be subordinated to the will and interests of the family?

Consider the matter of abortion. The sociologist Kristin Luker has argued cogently that the struggle over abortion is ultimately a struggle over the concept of motherhood. For pro-life activists, motherhood tends to be viewed as the most important and satisfying role open to a woman. Abortion, therefore, represents an attack on the very activity that gives life meaning. For pro-choice activists, motherhood is simply one role among many, and yet when defined as the only role, it is almost always a hardship. Abortion in this context is a means of liberating women from the burden of unplanned or unwanted childbearing and childrearing.

Luker's argument is certainly true as far as it goes, but beyond the concept of motherhood, abortion also raises issues of obligation and autonomy. Those holding to the orthodox vision tend to believe that family obligation extends not only to the born and living but to the unborn as well. Pro-life activists contend that the unborn have rights that must be protected by others, since they cannot defend those rights themselves. Because historically and religiously, the duty of motherhood is commonly viewed as the protection of children, legalized abortion represents an assault on the mother's principle obligation and her source of identity. Progressivists reject this idea and wonder how we can be obligated to what are, at best, "potential persons." The legal right to an abortion is seen as ensuring that women maintain their individual autonomy from men who might compete with them in the workplace or husbands who wish to restrict wives' freedom by keeping them in the realm of domestic travail. In this view, legislation that restricts access to abortion would, in the words of a statement from the National Abortion Rights Action League, "threaten the core of a woman's constitutionally valued autonomy . . . by violating the principle of bodily integrity that underlies much of the [Constitution's] promise of liberty . . . and by plac[ing] severe constraints on women's employment opportunities and . . . their ability to support themselves and their families."

The same issue of obligation underlies the policy debates over child care. With an increasing number of women in the work force and an increasing number of working women with young children, it is not surprising that child care would become politicized. The question is not really who has the obligation to care for young children. Everyone would agree that it is the parents or those acting as parents. The real question is, what are the legitimate ways that parents or guardians can meet those obligations? Two different understandings of parental responsibility have taken shape. Within the progressivist vision, parental responsibility is principally achieved in meeting the growing economic requirements of raising children at the end of the twentieth century. Besides meeting basic needs, this means making sure that children have the opportunities to develop their full potentials as human beings. As for moral and social development, progressivists tend to believe that the children of dual-career families do not necessarily suffer if some child care is given by someone other than a parent or family member. What matters is the *quality* of time spent with children. But the consensus among cultural conservatives is that children do suffer when others besides family members participate in child care. Parents, they claim, are the ones best suited to socializing the young, particularly when it comes to passing on a moral and religious heritage. "The education and upbringing of children is the primary responsibility of parents. Selfishly or ignorantly surrendering this role would be a grave disservice to our youth as well as our free society. The family must cling to its God-ordained roles or future generations will suffer the consequences."

These opposing views lead to predictable positions on public policy concerning child care. Policies promoting government-sponsored child care for dual-career families are seen as a way to give economic assistance to a growing number of women who have small children and must work, or as an abdication of the parental obligation to provide care and moral instruction to children. In the Act for Better Child Care, for example, we can see virtually all of the dimensions of the culture war. . . . [T]he act was supported by, among others, the National Organization for Women, *Ms.* Magazine, the Union of American Hebrew Congregations, and the United Methodist Board of Church and Society. The act was opposed by such orthodox groups as Concerned Women for America, the American Council of Christian Churches (and criticized by its Fundamentalist News Service), and James Dobson's Focus on the Family periodical *Citizen.* The bill assumed, according to its critics, that "the federal government is more capable than the parents to determine what is best for the child." Catholic constitutional lawyer William Bentley Ball said that the bill "reads flat out as a secularist prescription for the care of American children."

It is the sense that family obligations are being willfully abandoned that is behind the conservative complaint about the liberalization of divorce law (as in the idea and practice of "no fault divorce") and the concomitant rise in the rate of divorce as well. For many holding to a progressivist vision of moral life, the liberalization of divorce law is simply a means of guaranteeing individual autonomy when the obligations of marriage or of family life become burdensome and oppressive.

Sexuality: The Challenge of Homosexuality

Sexuality, of course, is also at the heart of family life. It is the family more than any other institution that establishes the rules for sexual intimacy—the codes that define the persons with whom, the time when, and the conditions under which sexual intimacy is acceptable. How the family enacts these rules also implies a judgment upon what "nature" will allow or should allow. But what is "natural" in matters of sexuality? The answer goes right to the heart of assumptions about the moral order: what is good, what is right, what is appropriate. Family life, however, is also a "school of virtue," for it bears the responsibility, as no other institution can, for socializing children—raising them as decent and moral people, passing on the morals of a community to the next generation. How parents view nature in matters of sexuality, therefore, is reflected in the ways they teach children about right and wrong. How the actors in the contemporary culture war view nature in matters of sexuality, in turn, will be reflected in their different ideals of how the moral order of a society will take shape in the future.

Perhaps with the exception of abortion, few issues in the contemporary culture war generate more raw emotion than the issue of homosexuality. The reason is plain: few other issues challenge the traditional assumptions of what nature will allow, the boundaries of the moral order, and finally the ideals of middle-class family life more radically. Homosexuality symbolizes either an absolute and fundamental perversion of nature, of the social order, and of American family life, or it is simply another way in which nature can evolve and be expressed, another way of ordering society, and an alternative way of conducting family life.

Both sides of the contemporary cultural divide understand the critical importance of homosexuality for the larger culture war. One apologist for gay and lesbian interests put it this way: "We should see anti-gay fear and hatred as part of a cultural offensive against liberal egalitarian social principles generally. Homophobia is a vehicle for the conservative ideology that links the defense of the patriarchal family with the maintenance of class, race, and gender hierarchy throughout society." To be gay, then, is to share the ordeal of other marginalized people in the nation; to be public about it places one in solidarity with the oppressed and their agenda of social change. Clearly, this is why major gay rights organizations participate in and often officially co-sponsor activism on behalf of abortion rights, women's rights, the homeless, and so on. As literature from the National Gay and Lesbian Task Force put it, they are "committed to ending systems of oppression in all forms."

The hostility to gay rights activism on the other side of the cultural divide follows much the same line as presented by Chuck McIlhenny or Rabbi Levin, for whom homosexuality represents an assault on biblical truths. Republican Congressman William Dannemeyer from California, for example, is quoted as saying that the homosexual movement represents "the most vicious attack on traditional family values that our society has seen in the history of our republic." Some in the orthodox alliance have argued that "the family is the fundamental unit of society, for it is the principle of permanence. For most persons it furnishes the primary experience of stability, continuity and fidelity. In this respect, and in many others, it is a school for citizenship. But it can maintain its function over the long run only if we accord it preferential status over alternative sexual arrangements and liaisons." The homosexual movement, therefore, is "destructive of the family and . . . a potent threat to society."

The rejoinder to this orthodox contention is an explicit affirmation of the aim to redefine the family—to proclaim "a new vision of family life." The response of the National Gay and Lesbian Task Force is that "lesbians and gay men are not a threat to families, but are an essential thread in the fabric of American family life." Ours, they contend, "is a vision of diverse family life that is directly opposed to the once-upon-a-time myth promoted by the right wing. Our vision is inclusive, not discriminatory. It is functional, rather than legalistic." Therefore, "threats to the American family do not come from the desire of gay men and lesbians to create loving relationships," but rather "from the right wing's manipulation of ignorance, bigotry and economic injustice. These threats to *our* families must be met with outrage . . . action . . . and resources."

And indeed the gay community has responded in this way within several areas of public policy. Perhaps the most important area over which the issue of the legitimacy of the "gay alternative" is concretely contested is the matter of marriage rights for homosexual couples. Let's be very clear about this: more is at stake here than the emotional rewards of formalizing a shared commitment in a relationship. The practical benefits of marriage are of tangible and often crucial importance to the lives of individuals: marriage partners may take part in the spouse's health plan and pension programs, share the rights of inheritance and community property, make a claim upon a spouse's rent-controlled apartment, and file joint tax returns. These legal and economic advantages were all designed to encourage the economic independence and interdependence of the traditional family unit and indeed, couples in traditional heterosexual marriages have long benefited from them. By the same token they have been denied to homosexual couples, heterosexual couples living out of wedlock, and living arrangements involving long-term platonic roommates—all of which may involve the same degree of economic and emotional dependence that occurs within a traditional family.

As the contemporary culture war has intensified, the general ambition of gay rights activists has been to push for the legal recognition of homosexual relationships as legitimate marriages or at least as "domestic partners" in order to ultimately secure these economic benefits. . . . While the fifty states have been reluctant to recognize the legality or legal rights of homosexual marriages, a handful of cities such as Los Angeles; New York; Madison, Wisconsin; and Takoma Park, Maryland, do provide bereavement leave for domestic partners who are municipal workers. A few others, such as Berkeley, Santa Cruz, and West Hollywood, offer health benefits for the same. This push has continued in still other cities around the country where laws prohibiting discrimination on the basis of marital status are being examined to see whether they extend to the living arrangements of homosexual couples.

Needless to say, such proposals pose a serious challenge to the traditional conception of marriage and family. The very idea is a "serious blow to our society's historic commitment to supporting marriage and family life," stated the archbishop of San Francisco in response to the domestic partners referendum in that city. Yet even in the gay community there is disagreement about this goal—not because it shares the archbishop's views, but because the legislation does not go far enough. The campaign for domestic partnership or gay marriage is misdirected, argued one lesbian activist, because it tries to adopt traditional heterosexual institutions for gays rather then encourage tolerance for divergent life-styles. "Marriage, as it exists today, is antithetical to my liberation as a lesbian and as a woman, because it mainstreams my life and voice."

The issues of bigotry and discrimination, in the view of homosexuals and of many activists for the progressivist vision, has gone beyond disputes over marriage rights or domestic partners to other areas of policy concern. For example, bigotry has been seen in the battles to either perpetuate or repeal "sodomy laws," as in the 1986 Supreme Court decision *Bowers* v. *Hardwick*, which upheld Georgia's sodomy law. Such laws (which still exist in twenty-four states), according to gay activists, "define our sexual lives as criminal, unnatural, perverse and repulsive." The perpetuation of these laws they feel, "gives the government's stamp of approval on individual people's homophobia, in much the same way that Jim Crow laws institutionalized racism and the segregation of black people in the American South." The struggle over the passage, in 1990, of the Hate Crime Statistics Act, requiring the federal government to collect statistics on crimes motivated by prejudice based on race, ethnicity, religion, or "sexual orientation" brought gay issues to the fore when Congress passed an amendment to this bill stating that "American family life is the foundation of American society" and "nothing in this act shall be construed" to "promote or encourage homosexuality." The symbolic significance of that amendment was not missed by the gay rights activists, even as they celebrated the bill's passage. Direct mail from the National Gay and Lesbian Task Force called the act "the most significant lesbian and gay rights victory in the history of the U.S. Congress!" Bigotry and discrimination in economic issues such as employment and housing have been sharply contested in policy debates over the Civil Rights Amendments Act. The original Civil Rights Act of 1964 prohibited discrimination on the basis of race, color, religion, or national origin; the new amendment (originally proposed in 1975) would extend the existing act to include the prohibition of discrimination relating to sexual orientation. In each of these policy areas, what is at stake is a tacit recognition on the part of the government that homosexuality is an authentic manner of life, social relationship, family, and community.

Interestingly, the stakes of recognition and legitimacy are raised to perhaps their highest symbolic level in those cases where the source of "discrimination and bigotry" is the military establishment itself. The military, of course, is an American institution that has long been defined by a rigid organizational hierarchy and by traditional notions of manliness: bravery, platonic bonding, emphatic heterosexuality, and the like. The contrast between U.S. military culture and a subculture that is defined by an intimacy among members of the same sex could not be more stark. The tensions are inevitable. A Naval cadet near the top of his class was expelled just two months before his graduation from the Annapolis Naval Academy after announcing to his friends that he was gay; fourteen lesbians at Parris Island boot camp were discharged from the Marine Corps in 1988; and twelve noncommissioned officers in the Air Force were discharged in 1989 for homosexual activity. These occurrences are not uncommon, for according to Department of Defense figures, an average of about 1,400 gay men and women are expelled from the armed forces every year. Legal challenges to incidents such as these, and to military policy that requires dismissal of gay officers in training from ROTC programs at universities (where the military often acquires more than half of its new officers) point to an intensification of the conflict that will be decisive for the larger controversy.

The other pivotal institutions in which the legitimacy of homosexuality has been contested are the churches. One might imagine that the deep and longstanding hostility of the Judeo-Christian faiths toward homosexuality would encourage homosexual men and lesbians to leave their faiths altogether. But for those who continue to identify with a particular religious tradition, there appears to be little desire to leave. . . . Said one priest, "My Catholicism is a deep part of my identity, as is my sexuality. I do not plan to give up either." Others have echoed this sentiment, "As members of Dignity we are a gay presence in the Church and a Christian presence within the gay community. We are proud that we can bring Christian values and beliefs to the gay community and equally proud that we can bring our gayness before the Church." One lesbian nun spoke for many others of every religious confession when she described herself as "very much of a prophet among my own sisters." The objective is not to be changed by the church but to change the church from the inside. The sense that they are succeeding in this was captured in the words of one layman who lamented, "What in 1963 was regarded as an offense against basic morality and a betrayal of solemn vows is today, alas, too often regarded as a legitimate 'sexual preference,' a 'human right,' and a 'progressive cause.' . . . [Today] those who still think that homosexual acts are sinful are accused of being 'homophobic,' while active homosexuals boldly proclaim their own moral superiority. . . .

As the strongest institutional bulwarks of traditionalist ideals of gender roles and sexuality, the military establishment and the churches are barometers of how the conflict over homosexuality fares in the larger social order. As the armed forces and the churches go on this issue, so may go the rest of American society.

What intensifies the struggle over the homosexuality issue is the AIDS crisis in the gay community. The quest for public recognition and legitimacy has become a matter of life and death because along with recognition and legitimacy comes the ability to credibly argue for and expect both public sympathy and increased public expenditure for medical research and health care. Cultural conservatives recognize this as well, many believing that "homosexuals and liberals are using the AIDS crisis to force our children to be taught their ultra-liberal views on sexuality and morality." A measure of the desperation that gays feel is seen in the practice of "outing"—intentional exposure of secret and usually prominent homosexuals (politicians, religious leaders, and the like) by other homosexuals. The rationale is that the gay rights movement needs all the support it can muster. These public figures could be helping the cause but either have chosen silence or have openly worked against the cause in order to protect their careers. They deserve "outing" for their "malicious hypocrisy on matters of life and death.

In Sum

The disputes over the nature and structure of authority, the moral obligations of parenting and marital commitment, the natural and legitimate boundaries of sexual experience, and so on, are all part of the struggle to define the family in its totality. In this struggle, it is important to point out that progressive activists have faced a difficult time shaking the image of being anti-family and anti-children. "Its enthusiasm for abortion and for day care," one observer remarked, "has strengthened this impression, suggesting that here are people who want to prevent children from being born . . . and failing this, to dump children so that mothers can pursue their selfish programs of self-realization." Progressive activists vehemently deny that their agenda is anti-family. They maintain that they desire a much more "inclusive vision of family life . . . of people who love and care for one another." Their insistence on this serves to confirm the argument made here, that each side of the cultural divide simply operates with a different conception of what the family is, how it behaves, and what its place and role should be. Which side is finally tarred with the label "anti-family" will depend on which model of the family finally prevails in public policy. . . .